Y0-BDF-110

MANUAL of Diagnosis and Professional Practice in MENTAL RETARDATION

MANUAL of Diagnosis and Professional Practice in MENTAL RETARDATION

Edited by
John W. Jacobson and
James A. Mulick

American Psychological Association
Washington, DC

First printing June 1996
Second printing February 1997
Third printing April 2000

Published by
American Psychological Association
750 First Street, NE
Washington, DC 20002

Copies may be ordered from
APA Order Department
P.O. Box 92984
Washington, DC 20090-2984

In the UK, Europe, Africa and the Middle East, copies may be ordered from
American Psychological Association
3 Henrietta Street
Covent Garden, London
WC2E 8LU England

Typeset in Century Schoolbook by EPS Group Inc., Easton, MD

Printer: United Book Press, Baltimore, MD
Cover Designer: Paul Perlow Design, New York, NY
Technical/Production Editor: Michele W. Kelliher

Library of Congress Cataloging-in-Publication Data
Manual of diagnosis and professional practice in mental retardation / editors, John W. Jacobson, James A. Mulick ; prepared by APA Division 33, Mental Retardation and Developmental Disabilities, for the American Psychological Association.
p. cm.
Includes bibliographical references and index.
ISBN 1-55798-341-0 (cloth : acid-free paper)
ISBN 1-55798-725-4 (pbk : acid-free paper)
1. Mental retardation—Handbooks, manuals, etc. I. Jacobson, John W. II. Mulick, James A. (James Anton), 1948– . III. American Psychological Association. Division of Mental Retardation and Developmental Disabilities.
RJ570.M36 1996
618.92′8588—dc20 95-53053
CIP

British Library Cataloguing-in-Publication Data
A CIP record is available from the British Library

Printed in the United States of America

Contents

Contributors

Editorial Board of the APA Division 33
Manual of Diagnosis and Professional Practice in Mental Retardation

Allan G. Barclay, St. Louis University
Dennis D. Drotar, Case Western Reserve University
Judith Favell, The AuClair Programs
Richard M. Foxx, Pennsylvania State University-Harrisburg
William I. Gardner, University of Wisconsin-Madison
Brian A. Iwata, University of Florida
John W. Jacobson, New York State Office of Mental Retardation and Developmental Disabilities
Johnny L. Matson, Louisiana State University
James A. Mulick, The Ohio State University
Sharon Landesman Ramey, University of Alabama at Birmingham
Donald K. Routh, University of Miami
Stephen R. Schroeder, University of Kansas
Robert L. Sprague, University of Illinois
Harvey N. Switzky, Northern Illinois University
Travis Thompson, Vanderbilt University

Michael G. Aman, The Nisonger Center UAP for Developmental Disabilities, The Ohio State University, Columbus, OH.

Margaret Atkins, State of Vermont Department of Mental Health and Mental Retardation, Waterbury, VT.

Bruce L. Baker, Department of Psychology, University of California-Los Angeles, Los Angeles, CA.

Allan G. Barclay, Department of Psychology, St. Louis University, St. Louis, MO.

George S. Baroff, Developmental Disabilities Training Institute, University of North Carolina at Chapel Hill, Chapel Hill, NC.

Alfred A. Baumeister, John F. Kennedy Center, George Peabody College, Vanderbilt University, Nashville, TN.

Sharon A. Borthwick-Duffy, School of Education, University of California-Riverside, Riverside, CA.

John D. Burchard, Department of Psychology, University of Vermont, Burlington, VT.

Sara N. Burchard, Department of Psychology, University of Vermont, Burlington, VT.

Deborah L. Coates, Department of Psychology, City University of New York, New York, NY.

Christine L. Cole, School Psychology Program, Lehigh University, Bethlehem, PA.

Catherine L. Costigan, Department of Psychology, Michigan State University, East Lansing, MI.

Daniel L. Coury, Department of Pediatrics, Children's Hospital, The Ohio State University, Columbus, OH.

J. P. Das, Centre for the Study of Mental Retardation, University of Alberta, Edmonton, Alberta, CN.

Robert Demerath, Our Lady of Victory Infant Home, Lackawanna, NY.

Ellen Dossett, Civitan International Research Center, University of Alabama at Birmingham, Birmingham, AL.

Dennis D. Drotar, Departments of Psychiatry, Pediatrics, and Psychology, School of Medicine, Case Western Reserve University, Cleveland, OH.

Jason R. Dura, Practical Programming Group, Bowling Green, OH.

Maureen S. Durkin, New York State Psychiatric Institute, G. H. Sergievksy Center, Columbia University, New York, NY.

Karen Echols, Civitan International Research Center, University of Alabama at Birmingham, Birmingham, AL.

Judith Favell, The Auclair Programs, Mount Dora, FL.

Frank J. Floyd, Department of Psychology, University of North Carolina at Chapel Hill, Chapel Hill, NC.

Richard M. Foxx, Behavioral Sciences Department, Pennsylvania State University-Harrisburg, Middletown, PA.

Kenneth D. Gadow, Department of Psychiatry, State University of New York at Stony Brook, Stony Brook, NY.

William I. Gardner, Rehabilitation Psychology Program, University of Wisconsin-Madison, Madison, WI.

Janice L. Graeber, Rehabilitation Psychology Program, University of Wisconsin-Madison, Madison, WI.

James M. Granfield, Department of Special Education, Southern Connecticut State University, New Haven, CT.

Stephen Greenspan, Department of Educational Psychology, University of Connecticut, Storrs, CT.

James Bradford Hale, Department of Psychology, Children's Hospital, Columbus, OH.

David Hammer, The Nisonger Center UAP for Developmental Disabilities, The Ohio State University, Columbus, OH.

Laird W. Heal, Departments of Special Education, Psychology, and Social Work, University of Illinois at Urbana-Champaign, Champaign, IL.

Nancy H. Huguenin, Applied Analysts, Inc., Groton, MA.

Anne DesNoyers Hurley, Department of Psychiatry, Tufts–New England Medical Center, Boston, MA.

Brian A. Iwata, Department of Psychology, University of Florida, Gainesville, FL.

John W. Jacobson, New York State Office of Mental Retardation and Developmental Disabilities and Independent Living in the Capital District, Albany, NY.

Richard J. Landau, Dykema Gossett, Ann Arbor, MI.

Mark H. Lewis, Department of Psychiatry, University of Florida, Gainesville, FL.

Thomas R. Linscheid, Departments of Pediatrics and Psychology, The Ohio State University, Columbus, OH.
Johnny L. Matson, Department of Psychology, Louisiana State University, Baton Rouge, LA.
Richard E. McClead, Jr., Department of Pediatrics, The Ohio State University, Columbus, OH.
Kevin S. McGrew, Department of Applied Psychology, St. Cloud State University, St. Cloud, MN.
James A. Menke, Department of Pediatrics, Children's Hospital, The Ohio State University, Columbus, OH.
James A. Mulick, Departments of Pediatrics and Psychology, The Ohio State University, Columbus, OH.
Beverly A. Mulvihill, Civitan International Research Center, University of Alabama at Birmingham, Birmingham, AL.
Dennis Munk, Department of Education, Carthage College, Kenosha, WI.
Jack A. Naglieri, The Nisonger Center UAP for Developmental Disabilities, The Ohio State University, Columbus, OH.
J. Grayson Osborne, Department of Psychology, Utah State University, Logan, UT.
Al Pfadt, New York State Institute for Basic Research in Developmental Disabilities, Staten Island, NY.
Laurie E. Powers, Dartmouth-Hitchcock Medical Center, Lebanon, NH.
Craig T. Ramey, Civitan International Research Center, University of Alabama at Birmingham, Birmingham, AL.
Sharon Landesman Ramey, Civitan International Research Center, University of Alabama at Birmingham, Birmingham, AL.
Dennis H. Reid, Western Carolina Center, Morganton, NC.
Alan C. Repp, Department of Educational Psychology, Counseling, and Special Education, Northern Illinois University and Educational Research and Services Center, DeKalb, IL.
Todd R. Risley, Department of Psychology, University of Alaska, Anchorage, AK.
Johannes Rojahn, The Nisonger Center UAP for Developmental Disabilities, The Ohio State University, Columbus, OH.
Donald K. Routh, Department of Psychology, University of Miami, Coral Gables, FL.
Richard R. Saunders, Schiefelbusch Institute for Lifespan Studies, University of Kansas, Lawrence, KS.
Mark Schachter, Private Practice, Buffalo, NY.
Stephen R. Schroeder, Schiefelbusch Institute for Lifespan Studies, University of Kansas, Lawrence, KS.
Rick J. Short, Department of School Psychology, University of Missouri, Columbia, MO.
Rune J. Simeonsson, School of Education, University of North Carolina at Chapel Hill, Chapel Hill, NC.
George H. S. Singer, Graduate School of Education, University of California-Santa Barbara, Santa Barbara, CA.

Nirbhay N. Singh, Departments of Psychiatry and Pediatrics, Medical College of Virginia, Virginia Commonwealth University, Richmond, VA.

Robert L. Sprague, Institute for Research on Human Development, University of Illinois, Champaign, IL.

Zena A. Stein, New York State Psychiatric Institute, G. H. Sergievsky Center, Columbia University, New York, NY.

Lynne A. Sturm, Riley Child Development Center, Riley Children's Hospital, Indianapolis, IN.

Harvey N. Switzky, Department of Educational Psychology, Northern Illinois University, DeKalb, IL.

Marc J. Tassé, The Nisonger Center UAP for Developmental Disabilities, The Ohio State University, Columbus, OH.

Travis Thompson, John F. Kennedy Center, George Peabody College, Vanderbilt University, Nashville, TN.

Dan Tomasulo, Holmdel, NJ.

Denise Valenti-Hein, University of Illinois at Chicago, Chicago, IL.

Peter M. Vietze, New York State Institute for Basic Research in Developmental Disabilities, Staten Island, NY.

Keith F. Widaman, Department of Psychology, University of California-Riverside, Riverside, CA.

Pamela Woodley-Zanthos, John F. Kennedy Center, George Peabody College, Vanderbilt University, Nashville, TN.

Preface

The field of mental retardation (MR) represents a particularly distinctive specialty within the clinical practice of psychology. Nationally, a significant amount of society's resources in the areas of maternal and infant health, public health, and human services are dedicated to support and intervention for this population.

The study of MR has a long history in psychology. From the time of the development of the early Binet test through its adaptation for use in the United States as the Stanford-Binet Test of Intelligence, the very concepts of human mental development and individual differences have evolved from an understanding of the evidence presented by MR and the special characteristics of people who display the condition (MacMillan, 1982). Mental tests, once used by psychologists to exclude individuals with MR from educational, vocational, and social options, became the tools for identifying individuals who would benefit from educational and preventive services and began to serve as important measures to ascertain the global effects of therapeutic intervention (Zigler & Seitz, 1982). Today the field of MR remains in the forefront of research concerned with how to improve early childhood intervention and education, basic learning processes, assistive technology, social and vocational integration, family intervention, and the study of brain-behavior and psychobiological processes in humans.

We feel there is no better arena for advancing human welfare and furthering psychological science than the field of MR and associated disorders of development. Progress has been steady in all areas of application. Assessment practices and technologies have become more refined and exact at every stage of the life span. Insights have been gained into early developmental processes, and the study of aging in people with MR has been established as a rapidly growing focus of scientific research (Wisniewski & Snider, 1986). In addition, from diagnostic classification problems in MR has emerged the concept of adaptive behavior, which has resulted in improving the practical description of human behavior in its social and cultural context.

With respect to intervention, MR has provided the behavioral sciences with an opportunity to test the limits of behavioral plasticity at many points along the developmental continuum (Grossman, 1977; 1983). It has helped to clarify the social significance of attribution and to indicate the boundaries between people that can hinder individual achievement. This has pointed the way toward new methods to reduce stigmatization and disadvantage (Seltzer & Seltzer, 1991). At the same time, MR has demonstrated the need for careful understanding of individual circumstances in planning intervention. The failure of individuals with MR to benefit as much as their typically developing peers from certain group formats of instruction and from certain social and mental health service delivery systems has revealed flaws in the assumptions made by human service professionals, social planners, and ideologically oriented visionaries over the years. In compensation, however, demonstrations of the modifiability of individual behavior when environmental and health variables are adequately controlled have shown that meaningful adaptive compensations for MR can be achieved (Berkson & Landesman–Dwyer, 1977). People with MR can change their behavior and can achieve more productive and rewarding participation in modern society when efforts are made jointly to normalize their behavior and to compensate in the environment for their physical, cognitive, and social limitations.

There has been an astonishing accumulation of psychological and biological knowledge as a direct result of work done in the field of MR. However, a comprehensive statement of what MR is, what it means for the individual and society, and how to serve the needs of affected individuals is specifically called for at the present juncture. Psychology is the discipline most focused on the individual and his or her interaction with the environment. As the most individualized perspective in which the whole person is the basic unit of analysis, responsibility for defining and conveying modern understanding of individual differences could not be relegated to any other discipline or committee of disciplines. We hope the result of these efforts proves to be useful to our colleagues, people with MR and their families, planners, and all interested groups. Above all, we hope that the student of psychology will be inspired to look deeper into the problems and issues raised in this book and that the standards and practices outlined herein will serve as a starting point for new advances in the field of MR and a more profound understanding of developmental and behavioral processes related to disorders of human development.

Acknowledgments

The editors are indebted to the members of the APA Division of Mental Retardation and Developmental Disabilities and the members of the Division's executive committee for their interest in this book and their mandate to produce it. We are grateful to the editorial board members for their timely participation in this project, their helpful guidance throughout, and their willingness to cooperate with the lengthy process of developing a consensus on the definition chapter. We are all indebted to the editorial staff of APA Books, who were always ready to help us through the production process. The support of the New York Office of Mental Retardation and Developmental Disabilities and The Children's Hospital of Columbus, Ohio, are gratefully acknowledged by the senior editors, although this does not imply specific agreement with the sentiments expressed herein by these organizations or their employees. J. A. Mulick was supported in part by the U.S. Department of Health and Human Services, Maternal and Child Health Bureau Special Project MCJ 009053.

Introduction

John W. Jacobson and James A. Mulick

Prior to the twentieth century, mental retardation (MR) was generally defined in terms of the development of social and vocational competence. However, in 1905 the intelligence test was developed. The availability of this test permitted prediction of childhood and adolescent success in education, because this was the criterion upon which it was founded. Because the economic viability of industrialized societies depends on the presence of an educated work force that can fulfill a wide range of productive functions, intelligence testing was widely and rapidly adopted as a social hygiene practice. Intelligence testing represented an important turning point in the history of psychology: It was the first applied, or clinical, service that could be provided by psychologists that was based on scientific methods and that was in high demand. Testing brought psychologists out of their laboratories and into schools and adult service settings.

History of the Study of MR

For the better part of this century, the pragmatic criterion of MR was a tested IQ below a criterion level (Trent, 1995), assessed during childhood or early adolescence. For a period following the middle of this century, this criterion was set at −1 *SD* from the mean IQ. Many educational systems continue to use cutoff scores at or near this level as one criterion for participation in special education services (Heber, 1961). By the early 1970s, there was recognition that although IQ scores in the range of −1 *SD* to −1.5 *SD* were more or less prognostic of general academic success, they (a) were far less prognostic of adult vocational achievement and (b) classified too large a portion of students with MR. Consequently, since the 1970s, in classification protocols, the IQ criterion was shifted to −2 *SD* to avoid overclassification, resulting in a large reduction in the number of people classified with MR (Grossman, 1977). However, it also became evident that although this shift resulted in improved prediction of academic attainment, adult outcomes for people scoring in the range of −2 *SD* to −3 *SD* remained highly idiosyncratic.

During the 1970s, there was also growing appreciation of the importance of the development of social, pragmatic, and vocationally salient skills in rendering predictions of adult functioning among people scoring below IQ criterion ranges. Thus, "adaptive behavior" deficits or limitations associated with intellectual impairments were also introduced into the definition of MR to validate the impact of intellectual impairment on pragmatic and social functioning and to enhance prediction of adult functioning. Specification and use of the adaptive behavior construct have evolved through a series of successive nomenclatures. A third change in classification criteria has involved modest extension of the definition of the developmental period (the period during which MR is defined to occur first) from 16 to 18 years of age (e.g., Grossman, 1983).

How MR has been defined since the middle of this century has largely reflected changing conceptions of the threshold at which MR may be clinically determined to be present in the individual case. The definition of MR used in this book corresponds generally with the definition set forth by the American Association on Mental Deficiency in the early 1980s.[1] It also corresponds generally with the definition set forth in the fourth edition of the American Psychiatric Association's *Diagnostic and Statistical Manual of Mental Disorders* (*DSM-IV*; American Psychiatric Association, 1994). A detailed discussion of this definition is presented in chapter 1 of this book.

Mental retardation has been a rapidly evolving field of service and research during the second half of the twentieth century. As a consequence of advances in psychological knowledge and changes in social policy, there have been consistent annual decreases in the extent to which people with MR, especially people with severe or profound MR, have been housed in institutions and steady increases in the extent to which supports and services involving community living have been made available in industrialized societies. In the United States these changes have occurred largely during the latter quarter of this century. They represent a return to a community orientation for people with severe disabilities and a retreat from the institutional orientation, which had been established in the late 1800s as the primary element of benevolent public policy.

Psychological activities in the field of MR encompass assessment, treatment, advocacy, research, and evaluation. Psychologists have made consistent and significant contributions in each of these realms, as well as in the formulation and accomplishment of communitization of services. Nevertheless, one especially important legacy of institutional practices has been the development of specialized services for people with MR and resultant difficulty in accessing other service sectors such as mental health, social welfare, and vocational services. Although, as in the mental health sector, broad aspects of social policy in MR have been driven by the civil and individual rights movements since the 1960s, this field also is marked

---

[1]Sources of definitions of MR have included the American Association on Mental Deficiency (later the American Association on Mental Retardation) in successive editions of its classification manual; the American Psychiatric Association in successive editions of its diagnostic and statistical manual; and the World Health Association in successive editions of the classification of diseases and, more recently, of handicaps and disabilities (Seltzer, 1983; Seltzer & Seltzer, 1991).

by a distinctive and enduring philosophical orientation, termed *normalization* (Wolfensberger, 1972). Normalization involves provision of services and supports to people with disabilities in the ways that they are most normally provided in society for people without disabilities. It has provided a touchstone for the context and structure of service delivery and doctrines of least restrictiveness in treatment.

In the 1980s the perspective of normalization was recast as social role valorization, which placed greater emphasis on the social–psychological dimensions (such as social acceptance, personal integration, and productivity) of the roles of people with MR in society (Wolfensberger, 1983). This philosophical shift toward a more social orientation has been reflected in aspirations to increase the individualization of services and supports for those with MR—for example, to replace group homes with individual living situations or, at the least, to provide living situations that are more like families in size and vocational situations in which people with disabilities are integrated with other workers. This shift has also fueled deprofessionalization in the field, which increases the difficulty of implementing prescriptive clinical treatments when they are needed on an individual basis, as well as resistance to use of treatment protocols that conflict with philosophical strictures. Although these difficulties are not new, they have increased during the past decade and present an immense challenge to the scientist–practitioner.

At the same time that these side effects of otherwise benign changes in MR policy have occurred, there has been a growth of antiscientific sentiment in society and within elements of academe that presents a severe challenge to behavioral science and the development of effective social technologies. The validity of the methods and findings of behavioral science has been rejected from the standpoint of an intellectual movement known as postmodernism, or constructionism, in which knowledge is specified to be socially constructed or socially derived (Gergen, 1994; Guerin, 1992; Sampson, 1993). In the field of MR, postmodern perspectives have become embodied in social role constructions of MR (Biklen & Duchan, 1994; Luckasson et al., 1992; Trent, 1995) in which the environmental component of Person × Environment interactions is the core construct, and elucidation of cognitive, affective, and behavioral functioning of people with MR, as well as other findings of behavioral science, is largely discarded. The majority of psychologists working in MR are not prepared to discard a specifically scientific and individually oriented approach and will continue to adopt a continuously interactionist perspective in dealing with problems of people with MR (e.g., Landesman & Ramey, 1989).

Social role formulations of MR are not novel. They have their origins in the social science literature of the 1960s and 1970s (Braginsky & Braginsky, 1971; Goffman, 1961; Gold, 1980; Szasz, 1961; Ullman & Krasner, 1975). Ironically, one of the earliest and most specific explications of social role development in mild MR was set forth by a behavioral scientist (Bijou, 1963). Moreover, respondents to postmodern criticism have noted that behavioral science may serve a purpose in identifying the utility of social policies (Kendler, 1993) and ascertaining matters of fact or of pragmatic import that transcend construction (Gergen, 1994; Guerin, 1992; Jacobson & Mulick, 1995; Whitehurst & Crone, 1994).

Organization of This Book

The organization and content of this book reasserts the validity of the scientist–practitioner, behavioral science perspective in the practice of psychology in MR. Although it has not been possible to address all subspecialization, contextual, and theoretical concerns in this volume, the principal areas of individual functioning and development and of clinical service by psychologists are encompassed here. As a professional text, this volume is intended to serve as a consolidated source of major findings from psychological science and practice presented in a form especially useful for psychologists in the field of MR. For psychologists in general community practice or in fields such as rehabilitation, pediatric, or child and family services, who are interested in serving people with MR, this volume may serve to introduce practitioners to the literature of greatest relevance to the field. Finally, use of this book as a resource to communicate the findings and practical implications of psychological science to practitioners in other professional and health disciplines is strongly encouraged.

The book is set forth in several parts. Part I, Foundations, includes what we view as the major contribution of this volume to professional practice, the collaboratively authored chapter, "Definition of Mental Retardation." This chapter provides guidelines for recognizing and classifying MR on the basis of psychological assessment. The responsibility for competence and independent practice in this important function should not be deferred or reassigned, and psychologists will find the present definition to be consistent with well-established standards of high-quality care, public policy, and relevant scientific research. Part I also includes chapters authored by leaders in the field of MR that address the key concepts needed to understand and use the definition of MR.

The definition of MR must be viewed in a social context (cf. MacMillan, Gresham, & Siperstein, 1993, 1995), albeit one consistent with current empirical findings and the requirements of definitional precision. Consequently, chapter 2 (by S. Ramey, Dossett, and Echols) on the social ecology of MR is provided to acquaint the reader with the most important implications of MR viewed from an interpersonal and societal perspective. The epidemiological approach to MR is discussed in chapter 3 (by Durkin and Stein) on the classification of MR. This material is most important in considering what is and can be accomplished by prevention and early intervention efforts and must be considered carefully when cross-cultural work on MR is contemplated. Chapter 4 (by Jacobson and Mulick) on psychometrics is included to address the basic issues in psychological measurement relevant to MR and its definition. Chapter 5 (by Routh) on intellectual development is intended to provide some theoretical and historical perspectives on the construct measured by the cognitive tests required in the definition of MR. Chapter 6 (by Widaman and McGrew) on the structure of adaptive behavior provides theoretical and historical perspective for the newer construct of adaptive behavior.

Part II, Assessment and Diagnosis, begins the detailed discussion of current content issues in the field of MR, both scientific and professional. Whereas part I offers much valuable information on the definition of MR and its application, it does not represent a finished body of research on professional activity. Part II, however, represents an in-depth review of the most salient issues involved in applying the definition of MR in today's practice and research environment.

As the reader will notice immediately, the issue of adaptive behavior is not settled at this point in the development of the field of MR. Rather, the measurement of adaptive behavior is still an active research area. Beyond issues of psychometrics alone, however, some thoughtful researchers continue to seek a better understanding of the underlying construct of adaptive behavior. Thus, two chapters of this book are concerned with adaptive behavior. Chapter 8 (by Greenspan, Switzky, and Granfield), which focuses on the recent work relating intelligence to adaptive behavior, represents a particularly salient challenge to practitioners and researchers to recognize the pragmatic implications of measurement practices and classification standards developed in the field of MR. Chapter 9 (by Simeonsson and Short) relates adaptive behavior to the concept of quality of life, a significant issue in evaluating services and supports for people with MR. When considered together with chapter 7 (by Das and Naglieri) on cognitive processes and MR, it is apparent that the present definition of MR, or at least the measures on which it will be based in individual assessment, will continue to be influenced by theoretical and measurement advances in coming years. Is this apparent spectrum of opinion a problem? Far from it. The vigor and intensity of ongoing research and thoughtful analysis of the core measures used in the assessment of MR suggest that the field is not stagnant or insulated from valid criticism. These chapters demonstrate that research on assessment is still quite active. Practitioners can expect to benefit from this research without loss of the basic tenets of measurement science or full appreciation of the reality of individual differences.

Chapter 10 (by Rojahn and Tassé) focuses on the assessment of psychopathology in MR. Most researchers believe that the issue of psychological disorder as separate from limitations associated with intellectual and adaptive behavior deficits has been neglected in the field of MR. Moreover, most have accepted that such limitation can easily mask psychological disorder in an individual with MR who presents with additional problems for treatment or habilitative services (e.g., Reiss, Levitan, & Szyszko, 1982). A comprehensive psychological evaluation should never fail to address possible psychopathology or behavior disorder or attribute the one to the presence of the other without compelling evidence. The most recent thinking is that psychological disorder is more likely today because of the psychological impact of MR on a person's ability to adapt to the demands of daily living and to display needed social skills (see chapter 11 on social skills by Matson and Hammer) and also that at least some physical conditions and illnesses that may result in developmental retardation may predispose the individual to neurophysiological syndromes associated with maladaptive behavior. Neuropsychological assessment thus attains great relevance to MR and is discussed in chapter 12 (by Schachter and Demerath).

The theme of developmental neuroscience is addressed again in chapter 13 (by McClead, Menke, and Coury) on advances in diagnostic technology. In this chapter, the most recent neurobiological technologies that improve understanding of the physical basis of developmental disabilities are explained and described. Few psychologists will be using these technologies outside the research laboratory in the near future, but the results of advanced imaging technology to view the living brain, functional imaging and other dynamic physiological measures, and genetic information will be available increasingly to psychologists in interdisciplinary settings. This information, when fully integrated into psychological science and practice, will lead to more sensitive and precise predictions about the feasibility and likely effectiveness of various intervention options for individuals.

Part II concludes with a discussion of behavioral assessment, probably the most important form of assessment in individual treatment and habilitation planning in MR, in chapter 14 (by Linscheid, Iwata, and Foxx), and then returns in chapter 15 (by Heal, Borthwick-Duffy, and Saunders) to issues concerning measurement of quality of life in MR. The measurement process used to assess learning and behavior problems in people with MR is much the same for problems encountered in measuring the acquisition of adaptive behavior such as toileting skills, production in vocational settings, or the acquisition of core prerequisites of cognitive advancement such as imitation and communication. Indeed, chapter 15 on assessing quality of life includes consideration of many behavioral components but serves to remind the practitioner that the individual meanings of behavior, production, and performance have broad motivational and emotional implications, in addition to their rate and topography.

Part III of this book addresses issues in professional practice related to the prevention and treatment of MR. Prevention of an emergent condition, such as MR, during human development is exceedingly complex. It can be caused by many factors, and the actual causes in an individual case will consist of only a subset of potential causes of MR. Biomedical intervention alone will never guarantee prevention of MR, although we often speak as though it can and does. For example, the toxic effects of phenylalanine in infants born with phenylketonuria (PKU) can be prevented by the early use of a special dietary intervention, but other biological and environmental factors will still influence brain function and learning. The PKU diet prevents only the one potential cause of MR, albeit a certain cause in affected children. The general issue of prevention of MR is addressed in chapter 16 (by C. Ramey, Mulvihill, and S. Ramey) on social and educational factors and in chapter 17 (by Baumeister and Woodley-Zanthos) on biological factors. The implementation of prevention, however, is always a social and environmental intervention, whether we focus on preschool educational services or on getting the needed diet to infants who test positive for PKU at birth. Further, conveying information about biological risk, such as the markedly increased risk of having a child with Down syndrome for mothers who are 40 years old, represents an educational intervention subject to psychological processes when it is successfully achieved.

Although this book is a product of a North American scientific and professional society (i.e., the APA) and focuses on cultural issues most relevant to the context of its sponsors and primary users, we are not insensitive to the issue of cross-cultural validity. We hope this book will be of use to psychologists in many other countries and to American psychologists who contemplate work that involves other cultures. Chapter 18 (by Coates and Vietze) on cultural considerations attempts to broaden the perspective of readers on the cultural aspects of using and understanding the construct of MR.

Subsequent chapters review significant treatment services. In chapter 19 (by Mulick and Hale) on communicating assessment results to caregivers, the impact of initial diagnosis is presented as an intervention designed to set the stage for using other indicated services. In chapter 20 (by Repp, Favell, and Munk) on teaching school-age children and adolescents, instructional intervention is described. Because the family remains important throughout the developmental period, we include two chapters on family intervention. Chapter 21 (by Floyd, Singer, Powers, and Costigan) discusses family therapy and family supports, and chapter 22 (by Baker) emphasizes the increasingly recognized role of the family in providing skilled instructional and behavioral treatment to the family member with MR.

Remaining chapters in part III focus on emerging intervention themes in psychological services in MR. Sexuality is addressed specifically in chapter 23 (by Valenti-Hein and Dura), which surveys major issues of the past and introduces more recent efforts to treat sexual dysfunction and to help people with MR better understand their own sexuality. Much work remains to be done in this socially sensitive area of practice. Chapter 24 (by Baroff) focuses on people with MR in the criminal justice system. This chapter also will be useful to general psychologists who work in forensic settings. Chapter 25 (by Lewis, Aman, Gadow, Schroeder, and Thompson) on psychopharmacology recognizes the essential role of the psychologist in research leading to effective psychopharmacological treatment and in measuring the behavioral effects of drugs in clinical practice in interdisciplinary MR service settings. Finally, chapter 26 (by Singh, Osborne, and Huguenin) on applied behavior analytic treatment, chapter 27 (by Gardner, Graeber, and Cole) on behavior therapies, and chapter 28 (by Hurley, Pfadt, Tomasulo, and Gardner) on psychotherapy issues are discussed as they apply to practice in the field of MR psychology.

Part IV, Service Delivery, includes chapters of considerable value to psychologists who are leaders, managers, and practitioners in the field of MR. Chapter 29 (by Risley and Reid) on management and chapter 30 (by Drotar and Sturm) on interdisciplinary collaboration provide more traditional conceptualizations of the delivery of services to people with MR. Chapter 31 (by Burchard, Atkins, and Burchard) on wraparound services emphasizes the need to move beyond established formats and institutional barriers to achieve a better fit between needs and interventions, a better utilization of personal and professional resources, and in the end a hoped for better quality of life for the person with MR. Finally, chapter 32 (by Landau) on advocacy and legal issues provides a crisp summary of the current status of legal issues that pertain to psychological practice in MR.

The editors and contributors are an optimistic group. We hope this optimism will be appreciated and shared. There has been much accomplished in scientific psychology and in the specialty area of MR, and we hope this book conveys the high standards of those who work and practice in the field of MR. It remains for the users of this book to extend the limits we document here. We look forward to the good work that is still to come.

Part I

Foundations

Introduction

Mental retardation (MR) is a concept based on systematic observation of human behavior during the developmental period and the recognition that significant failure to acquire knowledge, skills, and the ability to problem solve represents a genuine disability. Part I of this book provides a detailed definition of MR and discusses the fundamental concepts required to understand the definition, as well as the condition, in the context of society, causation, measurement principles, developmental phenomena, and notions about behavioral adaptation.

The formal principles to be considered in rendering a diagnosis of MR during individual assessment are presented in chapter 1, "Definition of Mental Retardation." This chapter represents the Editorial Board's consensus definition of MR. As a formal statement of the psychological understanding of what mental retardation is and how it should be discussed in a technical sense, it is offered to professionals and students for their use in clinical work and research. Part I of this book also addresses broad areas of inquiry and practical activity that underpin the conceptualization and understanding of MR. Hence, chapters are included here that present contemporary understandings of social ecology, the epidemiology of MR, the relevance of psychometrics, historical and individual aspects of intellectual development, and the nature and organization of adaptive behavior.

Chapter 2 on the social ecology of MR is concerned with how the social environment affects the behavior and development of people with MR and how individuals with MR influence their social environments. Studies of families and longitudinal adjustment of young children with developmental disabilities have detailed the social ecologies in which people with MR live. Chapter 3 focuses on epidemiological knowledge, which involves the causes and population features of MR as well as the classification of MR. Consistent classification organizes current knowledge of the heterogeneous conditions that comprise MR and facilitates communication between people of diverse backgrounds and interests in the field of MR on matters ranging from research to policy and practice. Psychometrics underlies the scientist–practitioner model in psychological practice within the field of MR and is discussed in chapter 4. Psychometrics has specific applicability in assaying the reliability and validity of clinical judgments and conclusions, in the development of practical measures with integrity and clinical utility, and in the review and evaluation of services.

The remaining two chapters in part I discuss further the core constructs underlying the classification of MR—intellectual or cognitive functioning and adaptive behavioral functioning. Chapter 5 on intellectual development explores some of the changes in concepts of intellect over the last several decades, with an emphasis on life span development and the relation between assessed intelligence and cognitive development. Chapter 6 on the structure of adaptive behavior addresses both theoretical and practical developments in the study and measurement of the typical performance of people with MR, that is, the level of skill a person typically displays when responding to challenges in his or her environment.

1

Definition of Mental Retardation

Editorial Board

Mental retardation (MR) refers to (a) significant limitations in general intellectual functioning; (b) significant limitations in adaptive functioning, which exist concurrently; and (c) onset of intellectual and adaptive limitations before the age of 22 years.

Significant limitations in intellectual functioning are determined from the findings of assessment by using a valid and comprehensive, individual measure of intelligence that is administered in a standardized format and interpreted by a qualified practitioner. The criterion of significance is an IQ or comparable normed score that is two or more standard deviations below the population mean for the measure.

Significant limitations in adaptive functioning are determined from the findings of assessment by using a comprehensive, individual measure of adaptive behavior. For adaptive behavior measures, the criterion of significance is a summary index score that is two or more standard deviations below the mean for the appropriate norming sample or that is within the range of adaptive behavior associated with the obtained IQ range sample in instrument norms. The latter would be used, for example, if the adaptive behavior instrument does not present information on the means and standard deviations of the norming sample. For adaptive behavior measures that provide factor or summary scores, the criterion of significance is multidimensional; that is, two or more of these scores lie two or more standard deviations below the mean for the appropriate norming sample or lie within the range of adaptive behavior associated with the intellectual level consistent with the obtained intelligence quotient, as indicated by the instrument norms. For adaptive behavior measures that permit assessment of both adaptive and maladaptive behavior, presence of clinically significant maladaptive behaviors in the absence of significant limitations in adaptive behavior, as defined here, does not meet the criterion of significant limitations in adaptive functioning.

The concurrent limitations in intellectual functioning and adaptive functioning must originate before the age of 22 years. For people first assessed after the age of 22 years, a classification of MR should be assigned only if their developmental and clinical history indicates a probability of onset prior to age 22. Onset may occur in infancy, childhood, or adolescence.

Classification requires that all three criteria must be met. Psychological diagnosis based exclusively on intellectual functioning and age of onset criteria is clinically inappropriate.

The etiology of concurrent limitations in intellectual and adaptive functioning, assuming a clinically appropriate and individualized assessment process, is not relevant to initial classification, although it may be of prognostic value and have implications for proper treatment. Furthermore, developmental prognosis is not a consideration in classification, because the definition is based upon functioning at the time of the assessment.

This chapter presents a foundation for classification of MR and addresses the following:

- implications of the various degrees of MR;
- distinctions between intellectual and adaptive performance;
- classification issues and assessment;
- relationship of genetic factors, basic cognition, and assessment to the dimension of intellectual performance;
- issues associated with distinctions between adaptive and maladaptive behavior, psychometrics, and research findings with respect to the dimension of adaptive performance; and
- concerns with regard to age of onset of delay or disability.

A series of appendixes to this chapter present succinct descriptions of adaptive performance of people with MR at four intellectual levels and five ages.

Degree of MR

MR is further classified within four distinctive ranges of severity, specified as mild, moderate, severe, and profound in degree. Severity is determined by concurrent presence of IQ scores within four ranges and adaptive functioning consistent with each range. In Table 1, for example, assume an intellectual measure with a mean of 100, *SD* of 15, and *SE* of 5.

Table 1. Degrees of MR

Degree of MR	IQ score range	IQ deviation	Extent of concurrent adaptive limitations
		Cutting point	
Mild	55–70	−2 *SD*	Two or more domains
Moderate	35–54	−3 *SD*	Two or more domains
Severe	20–34	−4 *SD*	All domains
Profound	Below 20	−5 *SD*	All domains

Note. IQ ranges are approximate due to *SE*. Limitations in adaptive functioning are relative to expected performance by chronological age and require scores at −2 *SD* or lower for significance. MR = mental retardation.

Using an intellectual measure with a *SE* of 5 provides the following ranges of cutting points: 70–75 (MR vs. not MR), 50–55 (mild MR vs. moderate MR), 30–35 (moderate MR vs. severe MR), and 15–20 (severe MR vs. profound MR). Differential classification, however, of the level of MR should be conducted regardless of whether the IQ score falls within these ranges in order to reconcile discrepancies between scores on intellectual and adaptive functioning measures. For normed individual intellectual measures, standard errors of measurement, which represent a normal distribution in which "true" scores are more likely to be closer to the "obtained" scores than to the limits of plus and minus one standard error, permit estimation of 95% confidence intervals for true scores. Adaptive functioning consistent with a milder degree of MR than indicated by an IQ score may justify classification at a less severe degree of MR. In general, substantial differences will be reconciled in this manner, although administration of an alternative intellectual measure also may be justified prior to classification. The alternative measure may provide additional support for a clinical decision to classify at one level or another. In instances when adaptive functioning is substantially delayed or depressed relative to findings of intellectual assessment, identification of possible contributing psychological, social, biological, or developmental factors is indicated. Interpretation of the entire clinical data set, the intellectual and adaptive behavior measures and observations, is understood to require a very important element of clinical and scientific judgment involving psychological knowledge and experience in addition to that information represented by the quantitative results of assessment. Diagnostic classification decisions are further understood to be based on an explicitly defensible rationale.

Implications of Degree of MR

Classification at each degree of MR is associated with differing patterns of practical and cognitive skill proficiency and development. This is demonstrated in both cross-sectional (Janicki & Jacobson, 1982, 1986) profiles of typical adaptive behavior and semilongitudinal (Eyman & Widaman, 1987) trends in the development of adaptive behavior. In cross-sectional data, people with mild and moderate MR are characterized by delays in development in instrumental activities of daily living, although attainments in these activities are superior for those with mild versus moderate MR. In contrast, individuals with severe or profound MR are distinguished by delays in motor-related or self-care–related activities of daily living and by more pronounced delays in instrumental activities of daily living, with performance in virtually all activities of daily living being superior for people with severe versus profound MR. These developmental attainments are exemplified by the population-level profiles presented by Janicki and Jacobson (1982) with respect to eight domains of adaptive functioning. Classification by degree of MR, especially when properly conducted during the primary school years, can be an effective predictor of adult cognitive functioning but is a less effective predictor of specific developmental adaptive behavior attainments. These attainments vary among individuals as a consequence of childhood enrichment, educational experiences, socialization considerations, adult habilitative and prevocational experiences, presence of physical disabilities or impairments, and socioeconomic background. Variations in adaptive behavior attainments are greater among people with mild or moderate MR than among people with severe or profound MR. Consequently, early classification of severe or profound MR is a better predictor of adult development than early classification of mild or moderate MR.

Semilongitudinal population data indicate clearly differing developmental trajectories in adaptive behavior for each degree of MR. The degree of MR is directly related to rate of adaptive development during childhood and adulthood, continued development of behavior into adulthood, and persistence of abilities through adulthood. People classified with more severe forms show more gradual skill development, whereas people classified with less severe MR show expected attainment of adaptive behavior relative to their childhood, adolescent, and adult-age peers (Eyman & Widaman, 1987). As noted by Eyman and Widaman (1987): "As levels of retardation were more severe, the growth curves for adaptive behavior flattened out and, in some instances, decreased. Hence, distinctly different life-span trends are evident for the different levels of retardation" (p. 567). Moreover, in population data, people are well differentiated across degrees of MR with regard to requirements for continuing treatment and training services by professionals; the extent of need for nonprofessional supports is more stable, varying principally in the combinations, rather than the intensity, of required supports across these groups (Jacobson & Janicki, 1987). Determination of individually needed professional services and nonprofessional supports (e.g., Luckasson et al., 1992) is an important element of the total process of service delivery and should be based on assessment findings that indicate that the classification is appropriate, as well as additional functional assessment information.

In addition to developmental trajectories, severe MR is differentiated from milder degrees of MR by three considerations: presence of biological anomalies, comprehensive versus restricted limitations in adaptive behavior, and persistence of adaptive behavior limitations (Patrick & Reschly, 1982; Reschly, 1988). Researchers generally agree that people with more severe degrees of MR are more likely to have a known, biologically determined (e.g., genetic, traumatic, or illness-related) etiology and related and unrelated neurological conditions or sensory and motor impairments. These people also are more likely to have more pervasive (in addition to more marked) adaptive limitations. Such factors indicate a more negative prognosis for development of sufficient adaptive behavior to permit independent living and competitive vocational productivity. However, people with mild MR do manifest concomitant conditions such as cerebral palsy and epilepsy (Jacobson & Janicki, 1983) at rates higher than those found in the general population. As Fryers (1987) noted: "Although they are generally perceived as handicapped on account of 'low intelligence' we know that most of those with intelligence levels over 50 IQ must exhibit other impairments, disabilities, behaviors, illnesses, or social problems to be included . . . as mildly mentally retarded" (p. 368). Significant cognitive and adaptive impairment (i.e., MR) is usually manifested as a result of numerous developmental influences, both biological and experiential, that render the concept of "sociocultural retardation" misleading.

The observation that people with mild MR may have more restricted or circumscribed limitations in adaptive behavior than other people with MR is implied by differences in cross-sectional and semilongitudinal population findings about adaptive behavior in the literature. However, some people with mild MR may demonstrate comprehensive limitations in adaptive behavior because of the presence of other conditions such as cerebral palsy, other motor or sensory dysfunction, or specific neurological factors. Researchers commonly observe that the prevalence of mild MR decreases after the school years; they infer that this shift reflects successful, more independent functioning and fulfillment of adult familial and vocational roles in environments that differ in their associated intellectual and pragmatic skill demands. In fact, few data are available to support such an interpretation. Generally, researchers have not followed entire cohorts of students after school departure for the period of time needed to assess social and vocational outcomes. More data, based on entire cohorts, are needed to better delineate successful and unsuccessful outcomes and the individual, situational, and social factors that are predictive of adult outcomes.

Confidence that successful adaptation typifies the adult experience for people with mild MR would require that such studies be undertaken (Richardson, 1989; Richardson, Koller, & Katz, 1986). The interpretation that prevalence decreases in adulthood (by virtue of successful adaptation) is unwarranted because "interpretations of such immense differences have tended to focus on bio-medical or IQ sub-groups, and largely failed to examine the administrative, legal, professional, attitudinal, social and cultural reasons for selection [of children and adults] as mildly mentally retarded" (Fryers, 1987, p. 375). Sociological findings and other available research (e.g., Edgerton, 1984; Zetlin & Murtaugh, 1990) indicate that both the course and extent of individual adaptation to adult role demands by people with mild MR are highly variable.

Mild MR

People classified with mild MR evidence small delays in the preschool years but often are not identified until after school entry, when assessment is undertaken following academic failure or emergence of behavior problems. Modest expressive language delays are evident during early primary school years, with the use of 2- to 3-word sentences common. During the later primary school years, these children develop considerable expressive speaking skills, engage with peers in spontaneous interactive play, and can be guided into play with larger groups. During middle school, they develop complex sentence structure, and their speech is clearly intelligible. The ability to use simple number concepts is also present, but practical understanding of the use of money may be limited. By adolescence, normal language fluency may be evident. Reading and number skills will range from 1st- to 6th-grade level, and social interests, community activities, and self-direction will be typical of peers, albeit as affected by pragmatic academic skill attainments. Baroff (1986) ascribed a mental age range of 8 to 11 years to adults in this group. This designation implies variation in academic skills, and for a large proportion of these adults, persistent low academic skill attainment limits their vocational opportunities. However, these people are generally able to fulfill all expected adult roles. Consequently, their involvement in adult services and participation in therapeutic activities following completion of educational preparation is relatively uncommon, is often time-limited or periodic, and may be associated with issues of adjustment or disability conditions not closely related to MR.

Moderate MR

People classified with moderate MR, because of more evident and consistent delays in their attainment of early developmental milestones, particularly in language facility and social play, are likely to be identified during the preschool years. At entry to primary school, these children may communicate through a combination of single words and gestures and evidence self-care and motor skills similar to those of average 2- to 3-year-olds. During primary school, they will develop the use of 2- and 3-word phrases to communicate and by age 12 may evidence useful, pragmatic communication skills. Skill development, both academically and adaptively, is delayed during middle school, compared to peers with mild MR. By age 14, they may develop basic self-care skills, undertake simple conversations, begin to read, and manifest cooperative social interaction skills. Baroff (1986) ascribed a mental age of 6 to 8 years to adults in this group. They generally have functional language, although their intelligibility may be poor, but reading and money, or number, skills are typically not functional, and some supervision of self-care may be necessary. Their vocational opportunities are limited by academic and adaptive deficits to unskilled work with direct supervision or assistance. Adult independence is typically not achieved. Lifestyle supports are usually required, including persistent residence with kin or movement to out-of-home care settings.

Severe MR

People classified with severe MR are typically identified during infancy (i.e., ages birth to 2 years) because of substantial delays in development and their increased tendency to display biological anomalies that can be readily detected (Reschly, 1988). Milestones such as standing, walking, and toilet training may be markedly delayed by several years. Compared to their peers, these children are at greatly increased risk for motor disorders (e.g., cerebral palsy) and the epilepsies. At school entry, basic self-care skills may not be evident, although between ages 6 to 9 years elements of self-feeding, self-dressing, and self-toileting typically are acquired. Primary school-age children may communicate with single words and gestures and will engage in parallel play. By age 12 years, some 2- to 3-word phrases may be used, and some children may engage in interactive play. Between the ages of 13 and 15 years, academic and adaptive performance similar to that of an average 4- to 6-year-old can be attained by many of these children. This is the mental age Baroff (1986) ascribed to adults classified in this range (i.e., 4 to 6 years). As adults, some self-care skills are attained, although assistance will be required. Receptive language is better developed than expressive language, and speech intelligibility is often poor; functional reading and number skills are essentially undeveloped. Although peer and friendship relationships may be formed, other expected adult role responsibilities will not be fulfilled. Vocational productivity is possible with continuing close supervision and assistance, given that substantial pragmatic skill limitations and difficulties in sustaining persistent performance will be encountered.

Profound MR

People classified with profound MR also are typically identified as infants because of marked delays in development and biological anomalies. The responsiveness of the older preschooler (i.e., 4 years) is similar to that of a 1-year-old, and the child may sit alone, imitate simple sounds, understand simple words (e.g., "No"), and recognize familiar people. These children have a markedly high early mortality rate compared to peers classified with severe MR (Switzky, Haywood, & Rotatori, 1982). Switzky et al. (1982) have identified two distinct subgroups: (a) people who totally lack all adaptive behavior skills and exist in a fragile medical state, and (b) older, less organically involved people with some ambulation, language, communication, and self-help skills. By age 10, some of these children will walk, acquire elements of basic self-care skills (but require supervision in performing self-care), communicate primarily through gesture, respond to selected requests, recognize familiar people, and engage in parallel play or activities. Baroff (1986) ascribed a mental age range of birth to 4 years for adults in this group, reflecting the considerable variation in development noted by Switzky et al. (1982) as well. The mobility of adults may be impaired by motor or sensory disabilities (e.g., vision or hearing impairments). Pragmatically, this group does not develop functional vocational, social, or community use skills, although simple vocational activities may be performed with continuous supervision and assistance. Social responsiveness varies markedly. Adults continue to benefit from individually structured stimulation through interaction with others to encourage development and use of basic skills.

Unspecified MR

People are classified with unspecified MR "when there is a strong presumption of mental retardation, but the individual is untestable by standardized intelligence tests" (American Psychiatric Association, 1980, p. 40). Infants may be too young to be tested with measures that yield an appropriate score, or older people may be too uncooperative to permit appropriate assessment. With infants it may still be possible to detect severe or profound MR because of diagnosed biological anomalies with known and predictable intellectual and developmental sequelae, but differential classification can remain difficult in many instances. Similarly, in exceptional cases, highly detailed histories for children, adolescents, and adults of academic, adaptive, and social development in combination with measures of current adaptive and social behavior may permit approximate classification.

Intellectual and Adaptive Performance

In considering the relative importance of intellectual and adaptive performance with respect to the construct of MR, it is useful to view conceptual intelligence (as measured by IQ and other norm-referenced, individually derived, ability measures; i.e., K-ABC score; Stanford-Binet score) as reflecting intellectual and academic ability and adaptive behavior measures as reflecting the application of practical intelligence (Bruininks & McGrew, 1987). This relationship also has been described as one of instrumental competence versus social competence (Greenspan & Granfield, 1992) or of optimal performance versus typical performance. Whitman (1990) has characterized MR as a disorder in which individuals have difficulty adapting to their environment and demonstrate difficulties in using what they have learned in nontraining situations. Zigler and Seitz (1982) have suggested that motivational factors are central to adaptation and social competence: "Although a motivational approach holds no promise of a dramatic cure for mental retardation, it can provide us with the means of helping retarded persons to use their intellectual capacities optimally" (p. 608; see also Haywood & Switzky, 1986; Switzky, in press). Clearly, poor generalization skills and motivational deficits are elements of the construct of MR, but the construct also refers to a condition of marked learning failure manifested by deficits in basic problem-solving process and in practical knowledge and skills.

The perspective of Zigler and Seitz (1982) and their colleagues places ultimate emphasis on intellectual performance (and on motivational influences that determine how this performance is realized in adaptation). Similarly, Scarr (1981) has suggested that intellectual competence is the result of a motivationally determined history of learning and that social competence is composed of physical health, formal cognitive ability, achievement in school, and motivational–emotional factors. However, historically, people were not classified as having MR when their adaptive functioning was within the socially required range of social competence. This use of combined standards of social and intellectual competence was the criterion for MR until the advent of the intelligence test. This perspective persists in contemporary culture (Greenspan & Granfield, 1992).

Historical practice has resulted in a situation where norms, basal referents, and implications of intelligence tests have generally continued to be stressed in practice over tests or measures of adaptive behavior in most service (as opposed to individual or clinical) settings, including educational settings. This is not surprising, considering the relative maturity of intellectual and adaptive behavior assessment in psychological research. However, during the past 15 years, a substantial body of research on both specific behavior measures and the measurement of adaptive behavior has emerged (almost certainly stimulated by the perspective on the importance of adaptive behavior set forth by Grossman, 1973, 1983). Thus, the literature on adaptive behavior can no longer be ignored. As previously noted, both intellectual and adaptive performance in early childhood have implications for development throughout childhood and adolescence (Bernheimer & Keogh, 1988; Eyman & Widaman, 1987; Schlottmann & Anderson, 1982; Zigler, Balla, & Hodapp, 1984).

Many studies have addressed the extent to which intellectual performance is associated with adaptive behavioral performance. Although it is clearly expected that people who score high on the first dimension will also score high on the second dimension, this relation may be attenuated by the insensitivity of measurement at the lower ranges of measured intelligence and at the higher ranges of adaptive behavior. (Intelligence tests typically used in such studies sample normative performance of the general population best, whereas adaptive behavior measures sample performance of people with MR best, making these tests less sensitive as generally constructed to extreme lower and higher ranges of performance; i.e., the reliability and validity of adaptive behavior measures are best at lower scores.) Physical disabilities may affect adaptive behavior differently (often more) than intellectual level, depending on when during the life span measures are taken and whether practical adaptive accommodations and environmental supports have been put in place. There also are manifold differences among studies in the extent to which (a) adaptive skills are assessed and (b) intellectively loaded or socially interactive sources of assessment information and methods of data collection are used (e.g., key adult informants, child or adult peers with disabilities, use of direct observation). Studies also differ in the composition of subject samples. Finally, use of measures that employ substantially different norming samples will affect estimates of the relationship between intellectual and adaptive functioning and have pragmatic ramifications in classification (Atkinson, 1990).

Kamphaus (1987) reported that correlations of intelligence to adaptive behavior are in the range of $r = .4$ to $r = .6$. Platt, Kamphaus, Cole, and Smith (1991) also have noted that the strength of the relationship between IQ and adaptive behavior varies among studies. Correlations for samples of more severely mentally retarded populations tend to be higher than those from less intellectually impaired or normal populations. In their research Platt et al. (1991) found that in a sample of 99 children and adolescents with mild or moderate MR, these values ranged from $r = .37$ to $r = .39$. Hull, Keats, and Thompson (1984) studied adults living in a variety of situations and found a correlation of $r = .48$ between IQ and a summary adaptive behavior score. In an evaluation study, Felce, deKock, Thomas, and Saxby (1986) found positive changes over time in both mental age and some areas of adaptive behavior favoring group-home residents over people living in congregate care settings; changes in mental age and adaptive behavior were correlated at $r = .31$.

It is clear that a relationship does exist between intellectual and adaptive performance. For example, Kahn (1983, 1992) found that initial measures of cognitive performance by young children with severe or profound MR successfully contributed to the explanation of their subsequent adaptive and language development. Salagaras and Nettelbeck (1983, 1984) demonstrated significant differences in profiles of adaptive behavior scale scores across intellectual-level groups of students and sheltered workers with MR. In summarizing prior research, Bruininks and McGrew (1987) and McGrew and Bruininks (1990) suggested that adaptive behavior is separate from, but moderately correlated with, measures of intelligence and school achievement (see also Cicchetti, Sparrow, & Rourke, 1991; Harrison, 1987; Sparrow & Cicchetti, 1987). Support for this conclusion is provided by Terrasi and Airasian (1989) who, in a factor analysis based on intellectual performance scores and adaptive behavior scores, found two distinct factors: one for intelligence and the other for adaptive behavior.

Classification Issues and Assessment

Although identification of MR during early adulthood, especially in the instance of concurrent MR and psychological disorder, has immediate ramifications for service eligibility and treatment planning, controversy has been focused on classification issues in the identification of children, particularly young, school-age children, with mild MR. In particular, during the past several decades there has been marked concern that children from diverse cultural or linguistic backgrounds will be at a disadvantage in intelligence testing (e.g., Mercer, 1973a, 1973b) and thereby might be inappropriately classified (Garcia, 1981). Specific reliance on intelligence tests as the principal method of assigning classification and variability among both states and localities in the use of cutoff scores for eligibility for educable mental retardation (EMR) services are important related issues (MacMillan, 1988; MacMillan, Meyers, & Morrison, 1980; Reschly, 1981a, 1981b; Zucker & Polloway, 1987). Furthermore, researchers have observed that "many students who are reasonably successful in relatively unstructured social or recreational activities have significant difficulty in the school setting in academic achievement, social skill development, and coping abilities" (Zucker & Polloway, 1987, p. 75; see also Terrasi & Airasian, 1989; Tombokan-Runtukahu & Nitko, 1992).

In a sample of children with EMR studied by Popoff-Walker (1982), 40% did not evidence adaptive behavior performance that fell below age expectations, indicating that there is considerable discrepancy between the educational classification of "educable MR" and the clinical classification of "mild MR," with the former including large numbers of children falling in the "borderline intellectual functioning" group (MacMillan, 1988; MacMillan et al., 1980).

A further consideration is parental socioeconomic status. The relationship between status (e.g., poverty) and intelligence is well documented (Popoff-Walker, 1982; Reschly, 1981b), and studies indicate that poor children are at greater risk of being classified as mentally retarded. However, "although the overwhelming majority of students with mild mental retardation come from poverty circumstances, an equally overwhelming majority of persons in *poverty* circumstances are never classified as mildly mentally retarded" (Reschly, 1988, p. 293). Moreover, although there is no significant disproportionality by race, social status, or gender in the classification of children as having more severe handicapping conditions, minority students are overrepresented in EMR services. Nevertheless, they represent only a very small proportion of minority students overall and represent only a slightly higher rate of identification than for White students (Reschly, 1981b). In summary, the extent to which socioeconomic status interacts with cultural factors to produce differences in the rates in which ethnic or cultural groups are classified as mentally handicapped during the school years is not well understood at this time.

Three strategies have been suggested for guarding against misclassification of children as mildly mentally retarded based on cultural or linguistic artifacts (aside from the obvious necessity of testing children in their preferred language and dialect). The first is to develop a scheme to compensate for cultural test bias. Although such schemes have been suggested, their use has been found to result in universal declassification of children in EMR services (Reschly, 1988; Zucker & Polloway, 1987). The second is to employ a more stringent cutoff score as an intellectual performance criterion. This approach produces more consistency in practices and reduces ethnic overrepresentation (Reschly & Jipson, 1976). The third strategy is to apply criteria that are sensitive to both intellectual and adaptive behavior performance instead of relying principally on IQ (E. Horn & Fuchs, 1987; Lambert, 1979, 1986; Reschly, 1981a, 1981b; Slate, 1983). Depending on the criterion used to define adaptive behavior deficits, this latter strategy also can result in extensive declassification (Harrison, 1987; Reschly, 1981a), which may be appropriate when the local criteria for EMR services differ from clinical criteria for mild MR.

Cutoffs for adaptive behavior criteria have been suggested at one standard deviation below the population mean (McCallum, Helm, & Sanderson, 1986), especially in areas of adaptive behavior that are educationally significant (Reschly & Ward, 1991). Limited research has suggested that adaptive behavior criteria are usefully applied in differential classification of the degree of MR (Cantrell, 1982; Roszkowski & Spreat, 1981). Reschly (1988) has suggested that particular attention be given in assessment of adaptive behavior to aspects that are sensitive to underlying cognitive or practical academics, in areas like independent functioning, social functioning, functional academic skills, and vocational or occupational skills. He further suggested that attention to such common concerns as severe and chronic achievement deficits across most achievement areas and the presence of learning problems that have not responded to regular educational interventions are relevant to classification (Reschly, 1988). Presently, in clinical practice, the most promising method to avoid inappropriate overrepresentation of specific population groups in the classification of mild MR is to apply combined intellectual and adaptive performance criteria.

McCarver and Campbell (1987) have argued that there are two reasons to include adaptive behavior in the definition of MR: The first is to control for potential cultural bias of intelligence tests when they are used with cultural minority or low-socioeconomic status groups, and the second is to avoid labeling people who had IQs in the range of MR in school but were absorbed in the general population after the school years. Although the dimensions of these issues are less clear when a more conservative IQ cutoff (i.e., lower, in the range of two standard deviations below the mean) is used, consistent application of criteria should occur across the life span.

The Dimension of Intellectual Performance

> There is much that is not known about human abilities, but there is much that is known. (Carroll & Horn, 1981, p. 1013)
>
> They remain the best—not perfect, but remarkably good—means of measuring underlying, generalized, permanent ability to learn, which has validity in its own right, as a means of classifying people by the degree to which they display a very important human characteristic. (Fryers, 1987, pp. 367–368)
>
> Although we acknowledge that intelligence tests are socially designed and socially administered, we further maintain that these tests are able to assess cognitive inefficiencies. (Hodapp & Zigler, 1986, p. 117)

The interpretation of results of intellectual assessments administered in a standardized manner requires consideration of cultural, situational, and psychological or emotional physical health and of sensory factors that may influence test performance. Situational factors that may partially explain performance levels or patterns include overt behaviors, emotionality, animation or lethargy, attentiveness or distractibility, mannerisms of speech, preferred language, tone and quality of voice, gait, posture, and atypical movements or movement dysfunction (Morgenstern & Klass, 1991). Biased results may stem from testing in a nonpreferred language, as well as in a preferred language, but in an inappropriate dialect (Scott, Swales, & Danhour, 1990).

Different intelligence tests may produce meaningfully different estimates of intelligence that may affect the proportion of people who fall below cutoff scores and the manner in which scores are appropriately interpreted in classification and reclassification decisions. Relevant findings have been presented by (a) Bloom et al. (1988) for K-ABC and Binet scores; (b) Flynn (1985) for different Wechsler Scale forms; (c) Goldman (1987) for the Wechsler Adult Intelligence Scale (WAIS) and the Wechsler Adult Intelligence Scale–Revised (WAIS-R) scores; (d) Naglieri (1985a) for the Wechsler Intelligence Scale for Children–Revised (WISC-R) and K-ABC scores and their relation to other measures; (e) Obrzut, Obrzut, and Shaw (1987) for K-ABC and WISC-R; and (e) Spitz (1986, 1988) for WAIS, WAIS-R, WISC, WISC-R, and Binet scores. Other cautions specific to cutoff scores and the calculation of IQ scores have been addressed by other researchers. For example, Atkinson and Cyr (1988) have indicated that the use of WAIS-R short forms may be inappropriate in lower IQ ranges.[1]

Genetic/Syndromic Relationships to Intelligence

Research suggests that genetic factors play a role in intellectual development (see Scarr & Carter-Saltzman, 1982) and that cognitive functioning varies as a consequence of different etiologies. Several examples are highlighted here. Using the K-ABC, Hodapp et al. (1992) identified differences in cognitive processes among children with fragile X and Down syndrome but found that sequential processing was lower than simultaneous processing or achievement in both groups.

Pueschel, Gallagher, Zartler, and Pezzullo (1987) identified patterns of cognitive development specific to people with Down syndrome. They presented research on Down syndrome–specific differences in the processing of some types of auditory information and difficulties in interpreting tactile–kinesthetic sensations, as well as superiority to other children with MR in visual–stereognostic and visual–tactile discrimination. In their study, which also used the K-ABC, children with Down syndrome had more difficulties in auditory–vocal and auditory–motor channels of communication, and sequential and simultaneous processing deficits relative to mental-age–matched controls and siblings.

In a study of 29 people with Down syndrome, phenylketonuria (PKU), or undifferentiated MR, Frank and Fiedler (1969) conducted a factor analysis of cognitive tasks, motor tasks, and adaptive behavior scale scores. Adaptive behavior loaded most strongly on factors related to performance, general intelligence, willingness and ability to follow directions, and physical development. Using factor scores, it was possible to discriminate effectively among the three etiological groups. Burack, Hodapp, and Zigler (1988) have concluded that there is evidence of differences between organ-

---

[1]Specific intelligence tests and measures will not be discussed in detail here. Readers are referred to the chapters on intellectual development and assessment of intelligence in part II of this book and to Cipani and Morrow (1991) and Morgenstern and Klass (1991) for information regarding selected popular measures.

ically retarded groups. They have further discussed differences among individuals in other etiological groups, including (a) a group in which etiology is unknown, (b) a group with familial MR in which there is at least one parent with MR, (c) a group of polygenic isolates with normal parents and nurturing environments, and (d) a sociocultural group with extremely poor rearing environments. As Burack et al. (1988) noted, although organic causes of MR include chromosomal abnormalities, metabolic imbalances, neurological insults, congenital defects, perinatal complications, and infections with highly variable developmental courses and outcomes, there are identifiable developmental courses that are associated with Down syndrome, cerebral palsy, and fragile X syndrome.

Intelligence, Basic Cognition, and Assessment

Research has demonstrated that when specific intellectual processes are studied with people with MR there "seems to be almost no mental process" that is unaffected (Detterman, 1987, p. 3). Both small samples and national standardization samples show greater intercorrelation at lower IQ ranges for subtasks on the WAIS-R and WISC-R (Detterman & Daniel, 1989). Measures of basic cognitive processes predict IQ better for people with MR than for college students (Detterman et al., 1992). However, these findings do not mean that all specific mental processes are impaired among these people or that all processes are impaired to a similar degree. Detterman (1987) theorized that eventually

> Mental retardation will be shown to be a deficit in one or more basic abilities and . . . these deficient abilities will have a moderate to high degree of centrality [i.e., tend to affect productive use of other abilities]. . . . Deficits may differ from person to person with respect to the abilities affected and the severity of the effect. . . . Some abilities will be intact and others will be impaired; mental retardation will not be a global depression of all abilities. (p. 8)

The relationship between cognition and MR is evident from studies involving reaction time, particularly a general slowing of information processing (Kail, 1992). Specifically, Campione, Brown, and Ferrara (1982) have referred to four general determinants of intellectual performance (i.e., "the ability to profit from incomplete instruction and of the intimately related ability to transfer old learning to new situations," p. 398). These determinants are "(a) the speed, or efficiency, with which elementary information processing operations are carried out; (b) the subject's knowledge base; (c) the role of various strategies in dealing with memory and problem-solving situations; and (d) metacognition and executive decision making" (p. 398).

A complementary perspective, based on neuropsychological and information-processing theory (Das, 1973; Naglieri, 1989; Naglieri & Das, 1990), identifies four interrelated and complementary processes: planning, attention, simultaneous processing, and sequential processing (or PASS; Naglieri, Das, Stevens, & Ledbetter, 1991). Naglieri (1989) observed that simultaneous and sequential task performance account for about 40% of variance in verbal and performance IQs: "Planning processes are involved when . . . an individual is required to analyze a task, develop a means of solving the problem, evaluate the effectiveness of the solution, modify the plan as needed, and demonstrate some effective and systematic approach to problem solving" (p. 198).

Assessment of intelligence, from this perspective, includes assessing the extent to which poor planning, deficient strategic behavior, and perseverative behavior are concerns in MR (Naglieri, Das, & Jarman, 1990). Research has suggested that there might be different uses of simultaneous and successive processing by people with and without MR and that people with MR score consistently lower than comparison subjects on tests such as Raven's Progressive Matrices (a culture-reduced test) and basic memory tasks (Das, 1973). Moreover, both children with learning disabilities and those with MR perform poorly on subtests with sequential aspects and academic content compared to peers who attend regular school classes, and distinctive subtest profiles are associated with these differences in performance on the K-ABC (Naglieri, 1985c). Linguistic and other basic mediational processes are implicated strongly in impaired cognition, and these impairments decrease learning accomplishment and problem solving progressively through the developmental period.

Each intelligence or cognitive measure will differ in the clarity with which its structure permits isolation of specific cognitive functions. In part, this will reflect the theoretical basis for each measure's content. Although classification should be based on standardized administration of measures, alternative methods of scoring or the use of subtests have utility for treatment planning. One example is ipsative scoring, in which the median age equivalent for subtest scores is substituted for chronological age in order to disclose greater score scatter (Hodapp et al., 1992; Reynolds & Clark, 1985). Testing of limits, rephrasing of questions, probing of problem-solving skills, and savings in learning and relearning may also prove valuable in treatment planning and can be employed in conjunction with standardized test administration (Morgenstern & Klass, 1991). Because people with MR may be unaware of specific problem-solving strategies (Foxx, Kyle, Faw, & Bittle, 1989), or may be aware of these but fail to apply them at the appropriate time, exploration of problem-solving skills can prove valuable when the examiner performs a metacognitive or executive function through hints, counterexamples, the reframing of statements and problem features, and similar supports (Campione et al., 1982). Modifications to standardization, of course, require acknowledgment during test interpretation and may preclude the use of norm tables.

The Dimension of Adaptive Performance

General Nature of Adaptive Behavior

Adaptive behavior can be defined in broad or specific terms, although most definitions stress the social embeddedness of behavior and the relationship of adaptive behavior performance to cultural expectations. Since 1975, major definitions of MR have included concepts such as social competence or social adaptation (E. Horn & Fuchs, 1987). Until recently, the prevailing foundational definition for adaptive behavior *deficits* was "significant limitations in an individual's effectiveness in meeting the standards of maturation, learning, personal independence, and/or social responsibility that are expected for his or her age level and cultural group" (Grossman, 1983, p. 11). Although maturation, learning, and personal independence relate directly to the person's skill development, reference to social responsibility broadens the sphere of adaptive behavior to include social expectations as a potential benchmark.

Nevertheless, adaptive behavior refers primarily to the performance of the individual as an end product at any point of person–environment interaction. Social competence is a higher order construct, albeit composed of adaptive behavior, social skills, and peer acceptance in combination (Gresham & Reschly, 1987). At the same time, items reflecting selected social skills often are incorporated in adaptive behavior measures, and development or limitation of adaptive behavior performance is recognized to be socially mediated, although conditioned by such factors as maturation, learning, and personal independence. As noted by Bruininks, Thurlow, and Gilman (1987), Kamphaus (1987), and Lambert and Hartsough (1981), the age-related nature of adaptive behavior means that the clinical significance of adaptive behavior deficits in different broad skills will vary at differing ages. Inclusion of socially relevant items indicates appreciation that "at developmentally earlier stages, self-help, grooming, and similar skills constitute social competence, whereas later phases focus on practical skills and social knowledge needed to function in social settings" (Simeonsson, 1978, p. 132) and that such items represent indirect measures of social cognition (e.g., those associated with role taking, empathy, and moral judgment). The importance of social cognition to a defining feature of MR that is, to adaptive behavior (Gresham & Elliott, 1987), is evident from the earlier discussion of performance in problem solving by people with MR. Problem solving is inherently pertinent to adaptive behavior in the realms of exhibiting initiative, adequate self-direction, responsible choice behavior, and contemplation of probable consequences of behavior that are necessary to normative social performance (Simeonsson, 1978).

To summarize, social standards are applied as a basis for stipulating normative or delayed adaptive behavior performance and are explicitly stated in most broad definitions of the adaptive behavior construct as:

1. the perceived fit between individual performance and societal expectations at any one point in time (H. G. Cohen, 1988);
2. the effectiveness with which an individual can cope with the social and personal demands of his or her environment (Bensberg & Irons, 1986);
3. the degree to which an individual performs those behaviors necessary for success in his or her environment (Terrasi & Airasian, 1989);

4. the ability to live independently and to abide by community standards of acceptable behavior (Greenspan & Granfield, 1992);
5. the ability to transfer learned skills to new situations and to function independently in the community, the school, and the general environment (Lambert, 1986);
6. the effectiveness with which an individual copes with the social demands of the environment and the perceptions of others regarding acceptable and unacceptable behavior (Mayfield, Forman, & Nagle, 1984);
7. the ability to meet standards of personal independence, social responsibility and the demands of the immediate environment and community (related to expectations of others and cultural and situational norms) (E. Horn & Fuchs, 1987);
8. the degree to which an individual evinces age-appropriate, independent functioning; assumes personal responsibility; and accepts social responsibilities in his or her environment (Slate, 1983);
9. the degree to which an individual engages in age-appropriate self-care, maintaining mutually rewarding relationships with others, working, or participating in other age-appropriate alternatives (Loveland & Kelley, 1988); and
10. the performance of daily activities in the community to meet personal needs, travel independently, get along with others, and be financially self-sufficient (H. G. Cohen, 1988; Harrison, 1987).

A functional definition of adaptive behavior, perhaps more general in its applicability, has been set forth by Cone (1987):

> Adaptive behavior is defined as those interactions of the individual with the environment that are functionally effective in that environment. Functionally effective interactions are those that are associated with the fewest restrictions, that is, the fewest constraints placed on the individual. From this definition, it can be seen that adaptive behavior is situationally defined or environmentally specific. What is functionally effective in one setting will not necessarily be so in another. (p. 128)

Cone's definition has applicability from educational, ecobehavioral, and differential classification perspectives, depending on the definition of environment or situation that is used. For the purposes of initial or later differential diagnosis and classification, the environment may be defined as the expectations or standards for normative development that are prevalent and accepted in the person's native culture. For the purposes of educational, behavioral, or psychosocial intervention, demands and expectations in the specific situations and circumstances in which the person functions on an everyday basis will constitute a special case of the culturally normative definition of environment.

Dimensions or Elements of Adaptive Behavior

Adaptive behavior. The dimensions of adaptive behavior differ dramatically, depending on whether they encompass both adaptive and maladaptive behavior or whether predetermined (e.g., scale) or factor structure is used to specify dimensions. Table 2, adapted from Halpern, Lehmann, Irvin, and Heiry (1982), indicates that there is a large sampling universe from which items may be selected for inclusion in comprehensive measures of adaptive behavior. Bruininks, Thurlow, and Gilman (1987) have suggested that there are 10 domains that are typically found in adaptive behavior measures, including self-help and personal appearance, physical development, communication, personal or social skills, cognitive

Table 2. Content Areas Within Adaptive Behavior Assessment

Content area	Examples
Basic developmental skills	Sensory development, motor development
Survival numerics	Basic mathematics, time management
Survival reading	Basic academics, functional reading
Communication	Expressive language, receptive language, writing and spelling skills
Knowledge of self	Self-awareness, self-concept
Emotional and personal adjustment	Coping, entering a new school or job, interpersonal conflict
Social and interpersonal skills	Basic interaction skills, group participation, play activities and skills
	Social amenities, sexual behavior, responsibility
Self-help skills	Dressing, eating, toileting, personal hygiene and grooming
Consumer skills	Money handling, banking, budgeting, purchasing
Domestic skills	Kitchen skills, household cleaning, household management, maintenance and repair, laundering and clothing care
Health care	Treatment for various health problems, preventive health measures, use of medications, corrective devices
Knowledge of community	Independent travel skills, community expectations, community awareness and use, telephone use
Job readiness	Job awareness, job application and interview skills, on-the-job information
Vocational behavior	Job performance and productivity, work habits and work attitudes, work-related skills, specific job skills, learning and transfer of job skills
Social behavior on the job	Interactions with supervisors, interactions with coworkers

Note. Data derived from Halpern, Lehmann, Irvin, & Heiry (1982).

functioning, health care and personal welfare, consumer skills, domestic skills, community orientation, and vocational skills. In a review of 51 adaptive behavior measures, Rinck (1987) found that the most common domains were, in descending frequency, social and interpersonal skills; communication and language skills; gross motor, vocational, and fine motor skills; and independent functioning, eating, and dressing. Most adaptive behavior scales do permit assessment of at least 3 skill domains: self-help, communication, and socialization (H. Cohen, 1988). Recent comprehensive or screening measures (Bruininks, Hill, Weatherman, & Woodcock, 1986; Bruininks, Woodcock, Hill, & Weatherman, 1985) may use a small number of domains but differentiate within these domains according to corresponding skills.

The application of factor analysis to data from comprehensive adaptive behavior measures dates from the 1960s. Earlier studies tended to identify two or three factors of adaptive behavior defining independence in functional autonomy, personal self-sufficiency, community self-sufficiency, or personal–social responsibility (Lambert & Nicoll, 1976; Nihira, 1976). Although more recent analyses can indicate the presence of three or more factors of adaptive behavior in some instruments (Eyman & Widaman, 1987; Harrison, 1987; Sparrow & Cicchetti, 1984; Widaman, Gibbs, & Geary, 1987), one- or two-factor solutions also are often identified (Janicki & Jacobson, 1986; Moss & Hogg, 1990; Silverstein, Wothke, & Slabaugh, 1988; Song et al., 1984; Thackrey, 1991; Widaman, Stacy, & Borthwick-Duffy, 1993). However, simpler structures are often conceptually compatible with more complex structures. Contrast, for example, Silverstein et al.'s (1988) structure of motoric or self-help and cognitive or social skills factors with Widaman et al.'s (1987) structure of motor skills, independent living skills, cognitive competence, and social competence factors. Current research finds few differences in the structure of adaptive behavior for study samples with and without MR (Bruininks & McGrew, 1987; Bruininks, McGrew, & Maruyama, 1988), and present conceptions of adaptive behavior have robust cross-cultural validity (Tombokan-Runtukahu & Nitko, 1992).

Several factors have led Widaman et al. (1987) to conclude that "the dimensional structure of adaptive behavior is currently open to question" (p. 348). These factors include the relatively short history of use of comprehensive adaptive behavior measures and the study of their structure, a lack of comparability of measures used across studies, failure to replicate findings of most studies (Widaman et al., 1987), and substantive differences among subject populations in most cases. Even with a highly restricted population, such as people with profound MR, very discrepant factors may be identified. Eyman and Widaman (1987) found a four-factor adaptive behavior structure for this population similar to that for less severely disabled people reported by Widaman et al. (1987), whereas Silverman, Silver, Lubin, and Sersen (1983) found a two-factor structure for such individuals that was characterized by more and less difficult items. Thus, the differing item content across instruments measuring adaptive behavior can be associated with strikingly different findings from analyses. Although these considerations do not permit absolute conclusions regarding the structure of adaptive behavior, it is possible, with some confidence, to draw preliminary conclusions (Bruininks, McGrew, & Maruyama, 1988; McGrew & Bruininks, 1989):

> The structure of adaptive behavior, as measured by available measurement scales, appears best represented by one to two dimensions. There is consistent evidence across scales and populations for the presence of a large general adaptive behavior factor. . . . A variety of secondary dimensions have been identified which include social responsibility and academic, physical developmental, and community-vocational functioning. (Bruininks & McGrew, 1987, p. 102)

Maladaptive behavior. Although the presence of psychosocial dysfunction does not constitute a sufficient basis for specifying deficits in self-direction (e.g., executive functioning or self-regulation) associated with MR, assessment or recording of maladaptive behavior is a common feature of comprehensive adaptive behavior measures. "Maladaptive behaviors are those that interfere with performance of adaptive tasks" (McGrew, Ittenbach, Bruininks, & Hill, 1991, p. 182). Using different samples and instruments, several studies have identified either one-factor (Eyman & Widaman, 1987; Nihira, 1969b) or two-factor structures of maladaptive behavior (Eyman & Widaman, 1987; Moss & Hogg, 1990; Nihira, 1969a; Widaman, Gibbs, & Geary, 1987). Bruininks and McGrew (1987) and McGrew et al. (1991) noted that two-factor solutions generally entail socially or externally directed behaviors and personally or internally directed behaviors, a dichotomy also observed in the literature on developmental psychopathology (i.e., Achenbach & Edelbrock, 1978). Although an internal factor can be identified across age- and intellectual-level samples, there is a broad external factor that may split into four other factors in selected age and ability groups (McGrew et al., 1991).

There is a moderate-to-small positive correlation between severity of MR and severity of maladaptive behavior as typically assessed by adaptive behavior measures (Jacobson, 1982; McGrew et al., 1991). However, these correlations may underestimate the magnitude of this relationship because of the difficulty in identifying some internally oriented forms of maladaptation among people with severe or profound MR. Furthermore, a serious undersampling of people with "simple, uncomplicated," mild MR in most population studies of both children and adults may have caused the severity of psychosocial dysfunction among people with mild MR to be overestimated in general.

Psychometric Concerns in Adaptive Behavior

During the past decade, adaptive behavior scales have exhibited generally adequate stability and interrater reliability (Harrison, 1987) and have been employed more frequently in the professional literature (Hawkins & Cooper, 1990). The literature is relatively unclear regarding how agreement should be assessed (e.g., by difference scores or correlation). Nonetheless, a range of findings regarding interrater reliability has been reported. In one study parents rated children as having greater ability than did teachers on several different behavior scales (Heath & Obrzut, 1984). In another study parent and teacher ratings on a comprehensive adaptive behavior measure were only moderately correlated but not significantly different (Bensberg & Irons, 1986). Finally, Foster-Gaitskell and Pratt (1989) found that parent and teacher ratings of children's adaptive behavior in terms of personal self-sufficiency and community self-sufficiency did not differ when the same informant procedure (e.g., interview) was used with one adaptive behavior measure.

The most commonly expected pattern is that parents will rate their children's adaptive behavior higher than will teachers (Gresham & Reschly, 1987). Yet, Mayfield et al. (1984) reported that special education teachers' ratings of students were higher than those of parents. Another study found differences between parent and teacher ratings on one behavior scale but not on the composite score of another (Ronka & Barnett, 1986). Soyster and Ehly (1987) have argued that there is limited agreement between parents and teachers on adaptive behavior measures but also suggested that parents' ratings of children's behavior may coincide with teachers' ratings under certain conditions (Soyster & Ehly, 1986).

The diversity of quantitative findings regarding interrater reliability indicates that there are a number of procedural and sampling artifacts in reliability studies. Although the manuals for more recent (1980s to present) comprehensive adaptive behavior scales present analytic findings signifying adequate reliability and validity, applied studies may be affected by differences in informants. These informant differences include familiarity with the assessment instrument, amount of observation time, experience with diverse reference groups, relationship with the child, perceptions of the significance of specific behaviors, variations in child behavior because of situational demands (Mayfield et al., 1984), and the history of the individual in each situation. In effect, the methods, settings, and content of specific assessment instruments will influence the type of information obtained and the possible levels of agreement (Gresham & Reschly, 1987).

A variety of instruments are needed to assess adaptive behavior for (a) people with very severe disabilities (especially if vision, auditory, or motor impairments are present); (b) highly capable people whose performance nevertheless warrants the diagnosis of MR; (c) infants and preschool children; (d) people exhibiting a range of intellectual performance who also have sensory deficits; (e) people who have concurrent developmental disability and psychosocial dysfunction; and (f) people referred for independent living services (Dunlap & Iceman, 1985; Rinck, Calkins, Neff, Griggs, & Brown, 1987). Few instruments are available that are suitable to address all these requirements. In fact, few comprehensive adaptive behavior measures are available that encompass the age range of preschool to old age and are suitable for people with possible mild to profound MR (Rinck, 1987).

As indicated by the need for different instruments to assess different subpopulations appropriately, there are real differences among adaptive behavior measures that reflect different norming groups. Relatively small norming groups that are geographically defined may necessitate the development of local norms (Scott, Mastenbrook, Fisher, & Gridley, 1982). Thus, the use of measures with more comprehensive norming may be preferred conceptually (especially because constrained norming groups may result in varying sequences of developmental ordering of items [Adams, 1985]). The norming groups for some scales, such as those developed initially for use with school-age groups, will limit their suitability with other populations (e.g., Vallecorsa & Tittle, 1985).

Aside from information presented in manuals for behavior scales, data have also been collected and analyzed regarding the interrater reliabilities (Cicchetti & Sparrow, 1981) of scales within single instruments (Roszkowski, Spreat, & Isett, 1983; Spreat, 1982b; Stack, 1984), of composite ratings (Lambert, 1986; Vandergriff, Hester, & Mandra, 1987), of the correspondence to global ratings of adaptive behavior (Roszkowski et al., 1983), as well as the effects of abbreviated scales or revised scoring methods for maladaptive behavior measurement (MacDonald & Barton, 1986; Roszkowski & Bean, 1981; Spreat, 1982c). Of particular interest is that adaptive behavior domains evidencing lower reliabilities are those involving social behavior and requiring informant social judgments that may not be based on discrete behaviors (Leva, 1976; Spreat, 1982b; Stack, 1984). Available analyses, however, indicate that the typical types of domains or scales contained in measures are coherent groups of activities (Bean & Roszkowski, 1982). Analyses of stability and reliability have generally confirmed the suitability of comprehensive adaptive behavior measures as assessment tools.

The differences in norming groups and domain or scale structures of comprehensive adaptive behavior measures and successive revisions of these measures may moderate correlations among developmental or standardized scores from these measures. Nonetheless, scores from a variety of measures have been found to be moderately to closely correlated (Heath & Obrzut, 1986; Middleton, Keene, & Brown, 1990; Pawlarczyk & Schumacher, 1983; Perry & Factor, 1989; Ronka & Barnett, 1986). Moreover, although adaptive behavior and cognitive measures may tend to converge (Pawlarczyk & Schumacher, 1983), standardized scoring may result in differing age equivalent and mental age scores (Bensberg & Irons, 1986). Successive revisions of comprehensive measures and different measures also may demonstrate contradictory classification implications at different ages (Britton & Eaves, 1986; Perry & Factor, 1989; Raggio & Massingale, 1990; Ronka & Barnett, 1986); however, it cannot be assumed that a revision of an instrument that classifies more individuals as disabled is more accurate or appropriate. Selection of adaptive measures should be based on practical considerations, characteristics of the person being assessed, and clinical purposes of the assessment (Carsrud, Carsrud, Dodd, Thompson, & Gray, 1981; Perry & Factor, 1989).

Although the use of informants as the source of clinical data for completion of adaptive behavior assessment measures can constitute a poorly controlled source of error or bias, there also are problems with primary reliance on observational data by the clinician in completing comprehensive assessments of adaptive behavior. Because intelligence tests are normed according to standardized testing procedures, and these procedures are intended, within expected motivational constraints that reflect skilled test administration, to elicit an approximation to optimal performance, there is no effective substitute for standardized one-to-one procedures in the assessment of intelligence. On the other hand, adaptive behavior measures are intended to provide an assessment of the degree to which intellectual and motivational factors (Leland, 1991) typically result in skilled and self-sufficient pragmatic and social performance. Except in cases where the person assessed is well known to the clinician, it often will be unfeasible to ensure adequate observational sampling of adaptive skills. A knowledgeable individual, usually a parent, immediate relative, or educator who is well acquainted with a child or adult, will often be the best source of information regarding the person's typical, cross-situational, and independent (i.e., unprompted) adaptive performance.

Research on adaptive behavior. A substantial number of studies have addressed issues related to the significance of adaptive behavior. Silverstein, Lozano, and White (1989) conducted a cluster analysis of three possible subgroups of adults with profound MR based on adaptive behavior measures. Futterman and Arndt (1983) found that psychometrically measured adaptive behavior was a better predictor of type of habilitative or vocational program participation than psychometric mental age, global adaptive behavior, or mental age estimates. Christian and Malone (1973) and Malone and Christian (1975) found that adaptive behavior performance discriminated among children in four levels of educational placement program; and Ilmer, Bruininks, and Hill (1988) predicted normally intelligent, trainable mentally retarded, and educable mentally retarded groups at above chance level using adaptive behavior, cognitive–intellectual, and social personality (social independence) measures.

Differences in adaptive behavior among classroom groupings of children also have been noted (Lambert & Hartsough, 1981; Richmond & Blagg, 1985), especially between children with autism and those with MR (Loveland & Kelley, 1991; Rodrigue, Morgan, & Geffken, 1991; Volkmar et al., 1987). Expectedly, these latter studies have shown that children with MR who have autism evidence less adept social and language skills than children with MR who do not have autism, although presence of psychosocial dysfunction, in general, may not be effectively detected in terms of adaptive behavior measures (Foster & Nihira, 1969). For example, Campbell, Smith, and Wool (1982) found that persons referred and never referred for institutionalization differed with respect to maladaptive behavior rather than adaptive behavior using a comprehensive measure of adaptive performance. A number of studies, including Conroy, Efthimiou, and Lemanowicz (1982), Kleinberg and Galligan (1983), Molony and Taplin (1990), and Sandford, Elzinga, and Grainger (1987), have verified the occurrence of changes in adaptive behavior following deinstitutionalization, movement to community settings, or provision of specialized treatment services.

Age of Onset

MR is a developmental disability. As such, MR may be diagnosed when onset or occurrence predates a person's 22nd birthday. This criterion reflects precedents established in federal legislation through the Developmental Disabilities Act of 1977 (Pub. L. No. 95–602, as subsequently amended) and educational acts (the Education for All Handicapped Children Act of 1975, Pub. L. No. 94–142 and the Individuals With Disabilities Education Act of 1985, Pub. L. No. 99–457). The intent of this legislation is to direct resources to assist people who become disabled before completion of the developmental period of life.

Grossman (1983) defined the developmental period as "the period of time between conception and the 18th birthday. Developmental deficits may be manifested by slow, arrested, or incomplete development resulting from brain damage, degenerative processes in the central nervous system, or regression from previously normal states due to psychosocial factors" (p. 11). Other previous definitions of MR have specified that the developmental period extends to either age 16 years (in 1959) or 18 years (in 1973).

Thus, the developmental period is not defined in terms of neurological maturation or attainment of formal operations cognitively, although development of reflective judgment continues after age 18 years (Brabeck, 1983; Kitchener, Lynch, Fischer, & Wood, 1993; Welfel, 1982; Welfel & Davison, 1986), as does development of other intellectual abilities (Ambuel & Rappaport, 1992; Hall & Tinzmann, 1989; Wilson & English, 1975). These markers would provide onset criteria that would typically occur during early adolescence. Recently, however, Luckasson et al. (1992) have suggested that "the cutoff age for the end of the developmental period and the beginning of adulthood may be relative to the social, cultural, and ethnic milieu. . . . The critical consideration would be whether the individual was functioning as an adult in . . . society prior to the onset of the observed cognitive and adaptive limitations" (p. 17). Previously, in Western society, graduation from secondary school (at age 18) or attainment of adult legal status (at age 16) served as one indicator of assignment of adult role status. However, in contemporary society, adolescent role status, as indicated by continuation of educational enrollment, nonparticipation in vocational involvements, financial dependence on family members, and deferred establishment of an independent household, is likely to persist through the 21st year. Achievement of skill consolidation and generalization requires experience and practice (Fischer, 1980; Fischer & Farrar, 1987), for example, in living and working independently.

The definition set forth in this book recognizes the changes that have occurred in Western society that affect attainment of adult status. It permits classification of MR during the ages of 18 through 21 years, when

Table 3. Sample for Behavioral Descriptions: Number of People

Intellectual level	Age group				
	4 Years	7 Years	10 Years	12 Years	16 Years
Mild MR	151	166	188	227	306
Moderate MR	157	166	176	244	375
Severe MR	53	163	165	179	232
Profound MR	24	76	114	200	244
Total	385	571	643	850	1,157

assessed intellectual and adaptive functioning are consistent with the criteria set forth and the person has not established an adult role status. In such instances, as at other adolescent ages, onset is likely to be a consequence of a traumatic event, including closed head injury, open head injury, anoxia or hypoxia, and toxic reactions, as well as infections, demyelinating or degenerative disorders, seizure disorders, toxic–metabolic disorders, malnutrition, and cumulative effects of environmental deprivation. However, onset within the range of 18 to 21 years permits assignment of an MR classification, or, if criteria for a specific neuropsychological syndrome are met, an appropriate alternative classification. Diagnosis in this age range remains a process entailing differential classification.

Behavioral Descriptions at Ages 4, 7, 10, 12, and 16 Years

In the appendixes to this chapter, behavioral descriptions are presented by intellectual level for children and adolescents with MR. The behavioral descriptors are drawn from the Minnesota Developmental Programming System Behavioral Scales–Alternate Form (MDPS-AF; Bock & Weatherman, 1977) using data from the New York Developmental Disabilities Information System (Janicki & Jacobson, 1982). The MDPS-AF is composed of eight domains (gross motor development, toileting skills, dress/grooming skills, eating skills, language skills, read/write skills, quantitative skills, and independent living skills) of 10 items each. To perform the behavior described, children and adolescents with MR may require physical, gestural, or verbal prompts. The sample that forms the basis for these appendixes is presented in Table 3. Because of the small numbers of children at the levels of severe and profound MR in the youngest age category, other sources, including descriptions provided by Grossman (1983), should be consulted for additional information.

Conclusion

MR refers to (a) significant limitations in general intellectual functioning, (b) significant limitations in adaptive functioning, which exist concurrently, and (c) onset of intellectual and adaptive limitations before the age of 22 years. MR is defined by the performance of an individual that reflects the cumulative effects of delayed or diminished development. Specifically, significant limitations in general intellectual functioning are determined by using a valid and comprehensive individual measure of intelligence, and significant limitations in adaptive functioning are determined by using a comprehensive individual measure of adaptive behavior. Psychological diagnosis based exclusively upon intellectual functioning and age of onset criteria is clinically inappropriate. MR may exist concurrently with other developmental disabilities or with neurological or mental disorders, and hence its classification should occur in the context of a comprehensive, differential assessment and diagnostic process. Thus, diagnosis or classification of MR should be conducted on an individual basis by an appropriately qualified clinical practitioner.

Appendix A: Adaptive Behavior Attainment Age 4 Years

Mild MR

50 percentile.
Runs.
Has bowel control.
Places a toothbrush in mouth and begins brushing motion.
Eats a complete meal with little or no spilling.
Says or indicates "Yes" or "No" in response to questions such as, "Do you want to go out?"
Turns pages in a book one at a time.
Separates one object from a group upon request (e.g., "Give me one block").
Participates in a single activity for 10 min if protected from interruption.

85 percentile.
Jumps up, both feet off floor at once.
Flushes toilet after use.
Puts shoes on correct feet.
Eats, supervised, in public without calling attention to eating behavior.
Names 10 common objects when asked, "What is this?"
Marks on a chalkboard or paper in circles and lines.
Sorts coins from other small metal objects.
Goes to public places in a group without calling unfavorable attention to behavior.

Moderate MR

50 percentile.
Runs.
Goes to bathroom with a reminder.
Removes slipover shirt.
Eats a complete meal with little or no spilling.
Stops an activity upon request such as, "No" or "Stop."
Turns pages in a book one at a time.
Separates one object from a group upon request (e.g., "Give me one block").
Participates in a single activity for 10 min if protected from interruption.

85 percentile.
Jumps up, both feet off floor at once.
Flushes toilet after use.
Puts shoes on correct feet.
Eats, supervised, in public without calling attention to eating behavior.
Names 10 common objects when asked, "What is this?"
Marks on a chalkboard or paper in circles and lines.
Separates one object from a group upon request (e.g., "Give me one block").

Goes to public places in a supervised group without calling unfavorable attention to behavior.

Severe MR

50 percentile.
Walks upstairs and downstairs, putting both feet on each step.
Eliminates when on toilet.
Extends and withdraws arms and legs while being dressed and undressed.
Uses spoon to pick up and eat food.
Follows a simple instruction such as, "Come here."
Scribbles with chalk, pencil, or crayon.
Does not separate one object from a group upon request (e.g., "Give me one block").
Does not participate in a single activity for 10 min if protected from interruption.

85 percentile.
Walks upstairs and downstairs using alternating feet.
Goes to bathroom with a reminder.
Places a toothbrush in mouth and begins brushing motion.
Eats, supervised, in public without calling attention to eating behavior.
Says or indicates "Yes" or "No" in response to questions such as, "Do you want to go out?"
Turns pages in a book one at a time.
Separates one object from a group upon request (e.g., "Give me one block").
Goes to public places in a supervised group without calling unfavorable attention to behavior.

Profound MR

50 percentile.
Does not sit without support.
Does not eliminate when on toilet.
Does not extend and withdraw arms and legs when being dressed and undressed.
Does not drink without spilling from a glass or cup with assistance.
Does not follow a simple instruction such as, "Come here."
Does not scribble with chalk, pencil, or crayon.
Does not separate one object from a group upon request (e.g., "Give me one block").
Does not participate in a single activity for 10 min if protected from interruption.

85 percentile.
Walks 5 ft.
Eliminates when on toilet.

Extends and withdraws arms and legs when being dressed and undressed.
Drinks without spilling from a glass or cup with assistance.
Follows a simple instruction such as, "Come here."
Scribbles with chalk, pencil, or crayon.
Does not separate one object from a group upon request (e.g., "Give me one block").
Participates in a single activity for 10 min if protected from interruption.

Appendix B: Adaptive Behavior Attainment Age 7 Years

Mild MR

50 percentile.
Stands on tiptoe for 10 s.
Asks location of bathroom in new situations.
Dries entire body with towel after bathing.
Eats a complete meal with little or no spilling, using all normal dishes and utensils.
Speaks in phrases or sentences clearly enough to be understood by someone not familiar with him or her.
Follows printed material left to right.
Chooses correct number of objects up to five upon request (e.g., "Give me one block, two blocks, etc.").
Attends to an assigned task or activity for one-half hour—may need to be encouraged.

85 percentile.
Stands on tiptoe for 10 s.
Chooses correct restroom in a public place.
Washes, rinses, and dries hair.
Serves self in family-style setting.
Says address of residence clearly when asked.
Reads aloud alphabet from A to Z—may look at letters.
Counts from 10 to 20.
Crosses residential street intersections, looking in both directions and waiting for traffic to clear before crossing.

Moderate MR

50 percentile.
Jumps up, both feet off floor at once.
Obtains help with any toileting problem.
Blows nose in tissue or handkerchief.
Eats, supervised, in public without calling attention to eating behavior.
Expresses feelings, desires, or problems in complete sentences—subject-verb.
Traces with pencil or crayon around the outside of a 6-in circular object in a continuous motion.
Answers correctly when asked, "Is it day or night?"
Attends to an assigned task or activity for one-half hour—may need to be encouraged.

85 percentile.
Stands on tiptoe for 10 s.
Asks location of bathroom in new situations.

Puts on outerwear without reminder in response to cold or rain.
Serves self in family-style setting.
Carries on a conversation with another person for 10 min.
Follows printed material left to right.
Chooses correct number of objects up to five upon request (e.g., "Give me one block, two blocks, etc.").
Sets a table with plates, cups, forks, spoons, and knives—need not be a formal setting.

Severe MR

50 percentile.
Walks upstairs and downstairs, alternating feet.
Has bowel and bladder control.
Places a toothbrush in mouth and begins brushing motion.
Uses a fork to pick up and eat food.
Says or indicates "Yes" or "No" in response to questions such as, "Do you want to go out?"
Turns pages of a book one at a time.
Separates one object from a group upon request (e.g., "Give me one block").
Goes to public places in a supervised group without calling unfavorable attention to behavior.

85 percentile.
Stands on tiptoe for 10 s.
Obtains help with any toileting problem.
Blows nose in tissue or handkerchief.
Eats a complete meal with little or no spilling, using all normal dishes and utensils.
Says first and last name when asked.
Draws a line connecting three dots on a piece of paper.
Answers correctly when asked, "Is it day or night?"
Attends to an assigned task or activity for one-half hour—may need to be encouraged.

Profound MR

50 percentile.
Walks 5 ft.
Eliminates when on toilet.
Extends and withdraws arms and legs while being dressed and undressed.
Picks up food with fingers and puts food in mouth.
Follows a simple instruction such as, "Come here."
Does not scribble with chalk, pencil, or crayon.
Does not separate one object from a group upon request (e.g., "Give me one block").

85 percentile.
Jumps up, both feet off floor at once.
Removes clothing, sits on toilet, eliminates, and replaces clothing.
Removes slipover shirt.
Eats a complete meal with little or no spilling—may use only fingers and spoon.
Stops an activity upon request (e.g., when told "No" or instructed to "Stop").
Scribbles with chalk, pencil, or crayon.
Separates one object from a group upon request (e.g., "Give me one block").

Appendix C: Adaptive Behavior Attainment Age 10 Years

Mild MR

50 percentile.
Stands on tiptoe for 10 s.
Asks location of bathroom in new situations.
Washes, rinses, and dries hair.
Serves self in a family-style setting.
Says address of residence clearly when asked.
Reads aloud sentences with five common words.
Tells or identifies birth date: month, day, and year.
Crosses residential street intersections, looking in both directions and waiting for traffic to clear before crossing.

85 percentile.
Stands on tiptoe for 10 s.
Chooses correct restroom in a public place.
Changes dirty clothing without reminder.
Orders and eats in public dining facility.
Invites others to participate in an activity such as going for a walk or going to a movie.
Reads for information and entertainment.
Exchanges the correct number of mixed coins for a quarter.
Initiates self-involvement in a hobby, not including reading or watching TV.

Moderate MR

50 percentile.
Stands on tiptoe for 10 s.
Asks location of bathroom in new situations.
Dries entire body with towel after bathing.
Eats a complete meal with little or no spilling, using all normal dishes and utensils.
Speaks in phrases or sentences clearly enough to be understood by someone not familiar with him or her.
Follows printed material left to right.
Chooses correct number of objects up to five upon request (e.g., "Give me one block, two blocks, etc.").
Sweeps a floor with a broom, picks up sweepings in a dustpan, and empties pan.

85 percentile.
Stands on tiptoe for 10 s.
Chooses correct restroom in a public place.

Washes, rinses, and dries hair.
Orders and eats in public dining facility.
Says address of residence clearly when asked.
Reads aloud sentences with five common words.
Tells or identifies birth date: month, day, and year.
Prepares a meal of a sandwich and cold beverage.

Severe MR

50 percentile.
Walks a straight line 10 ft.
Eliminates when on toilet.
Extends and withdraws arms and legs while being dressed and undressed.
Uses spoon to pick up and eat food.
Stops an activity upon request (e.g., when told "No" or instructed to "Stop").
Scribbles with chalk, pencil, or crayon.
Does not separate one object from a group upon request (e.g., "Give me one block").

85 percentile.
Jumps up, both feet off floor at once.
Has bowel control.
Puts shoes on correct feet.
Eats, supervised, in public without calling attention to eating behavior.
Says or indicates "Yes" or "No" in response to questions such as, "Do you want to go out?"
Marks on a chalkboard or paper in circles and lines.
Separates one object from a group upon request (e.g., "Give me one block").

Profound MR

50 percentile.
Does not sit without support.
Does not eliminate when on toilet.
Does not extend and withdraw arms and legs while being dressed and undressed.
Does not drink without spilling from a glass or cup with assistance.
Does not follow a simple instruction such as, "Come here."
Does not scribble with chalk, pencil, or crayon.
Does not separate one object from a group upon request (e.g., "Give me one block").
Does not participate in a single activity for 10 min if protected from interruption.

85 percentile.

Walks upstairs and downstairs, putting both feet on each step.
Goes to bathroom with a reminder.
Extends and withdraws arms and legs while being dressed and undressed.
Picks up food with finger and puts food in mouth.
Follows a simple instruction such as, "Come here."
Scribbles with chalk, pencil, or crayon.
Does not separate one object from a group upon request (e.g., "Give me one block").
Participates in a single activity for 10 min if protected from interruption.

Appendix D: Adaptive Behavior Attainment Age 12 Years

Mild MR

50 percentile.
Stands on tiptoe for 10 s.
Chooses correct restroom without reminder.
Changes dirty clothing without reminder.
Orders and eats in public dining facility.
Invites others to participate in an activity such as going for a walk or going to a movie.
Reads aloud sentences with five common words.
Exchanges the correct number of mixed coins for a quarter.
Obeys lights and "Walk," "Don't Walk" signals at a light-controlled intersection.

85 percentile.
Stands on tiptoe for 10 s.
Chooses correct restroom in a public place.
Changes dirty clothing without reminder.
Orders and eats in public dining facility.
Invites others to participate in an activity such as going for a walk or going to a movie.
Reads for information or entertainment.
Counts change from a purchase of one dollar or less.
Uses public transportation on one local route such as from residence to work and back.

Moderate MR

50 percentile.
Stands on tiptoe for 10 s.
Asks location of bathroom in new situations.
Puts on outerwear without reminder in response to cold or rain.
Serves self in family-style setting.
Carries on a conversation with another person for 10 min.
Writes or prints first and last names with no example to look at.
Answers what day of the week it is now.
Sets a table with plates, cups, forks, spoons, and knives—need not be a formal setting.

85 percentile.
Stands on tiptoe for 10 s.
Chooses correct restroom in a public place.
Changes dirty clothing without reminder.
Orders and eats in public dining facility.

Invites others to participate in an activity such as going for a walk or going to a movie.
Reads for information and entertainment.
Tells or identifies birth date: month, day, and year.
Obeys lights and "Walk," "Don't Walk" signals at a light-controlled intersection.

Severe MR

50 percentile.
Jumps up, both feet off floor at once.
Flushes toilet after use.
Blows nose in tissue or handkerchief.
Eats, supervised, in public without calling attention to eating behavior.
Names 10 common objects when asked, "What is this?"
Marks on a chalkboard or paper in circles and lines.
Sorts coins from other small metal objects.
Attends to an assigned task or activity for one-half hour—may need to be encouraged.

85 percentile.
Stands on tiptoe for 10 s.
Asks location of bathroom in new situations.
Puts on outerwear without reminder in response to cold or rain.
Serves self in a family-style setting.
Expresses feelings, desires, or problems in complete sentences—noun-verb.
Writes or prints first and last names with no example to look at.
Chooses correct number of blocks up to five upon request (e.g., "Give me one block, two blocks, etc.").
Sets a table with plates, cups, forks, spoons, and knives—need not be a formal setting.

Profound MR

50 percentile.
Runs.
Goes to bathroom with a reminder.
Removes slipover shirt.
Picks up a glass and drinks from it without spilling.
Follows a simple instruction such as, "Come here."
Scribbles with chalk, pencil, or crayon.
Does not separate one object from a group upon request (e.g., "Give me one block").
Participates in a single activity for 10 min if protected from interruption.

85 percentile.

Jumps up, both feet off floor at once.
Flushes toilet after use.
Soaps and rinses hands.
Dries entire body with towel after bathing.
Says or indicates "Yes" or "No" in response to such questions as, "Do you want to go out?"
Turns pages of a book one at a time.
Separates one object from a group upon request (e.g., "Give me one block").
Goes to public places without drawing unfavorable attention to behavior.

Appendix E: Adaptive Behavior Attainment
Age 16 Years

Mild MR

50 percentile.
Stands on tiptoe for 10 s.
Chooses correct restroom in a public place.
Changes dirty clothing without reminder.
Orders and eats in a public dining facility.
Invites others to participate in an activity such as going for a walk or going to a movie.
Reads for information and entertainment.
Counts change from a purchase of one dollar or less.
Initiates self-involvement in a hobby, not including reading or watching TV.

85 percentile.
Exceeds highest MDPS-AF item content.

Moderate MR

50 percentile.
Stands on tiptoe for 10 s.
Chooses correct restroom in a public place.
Washes, rinses, and dries hair.
Serves self in family-style setting.
Says address of residence clearly when asked.
Reads aloud alphabet from A to Z—may look at letters.
Tells or identifies birth date: month, day, and year.
Crosses residential street intersections, looking in both directions and waiting for traffic to clear before crossing.

85 percentile.
Stands on tiptoe for 10 s.
Chooses correct restroom in a public place.
Changes dirty clothing without reminder.
Orders and eats in public dining facility.
Invites others to participate in an activity such as going for a walk or going to a movie.
Reads for information or entertainment.
Exchanges correct number of mixed coins for a quarter.
Initiates self-involvement in a hobby, not including reading or watching TV.

Severe MR

50 percentile.
Jumps up, both feet off floor at once.
Obtains help with any toileting problem.
Blows nose in tissue or handkerchief.
Eats a complete meal with little or no spilling, using all normal dishes and utensils.
Names 10 common objects when asked, "What is this?"
Traces with pencil or crayon around the outside of a 6-in. circular object in a continuous motion.
Answers correctly when asked, "Is it day or night?"
Attends to an assigned task or activity for one-half hour—may need to be encouraged.

85 percentile.
Stands on tiptoe for 10 s.
Chooses correct restroom in new situations.
Washes, rinses, and dries hair.
Orders and eats in public dining facility.
Says address of residence clearly when asked.
Writes or prints first and last names with no example to look at.
Counts from 10 to 20.
Prepares a meal of a sandwich and cold beverage.

Profound MR

50 percentile.
Walks a straight line 10 ft.
Goes to bathroom with reminder.
Removes slipover shirt.
Picks up a glass and drinks from it without spilling.
Stops an activity upon request (e.g., when told "No" or instructed to "Stop").
Scribbles with chalk, pencil, or crayon.
Does not separate one object from a group upon request (e.g., "Give me one block").
Participates in a single activity for 10 min if protected from interruption.

85 percentile.
Jumps up, both feet off floor at once.
Flushes toilet after use.
Soaps and rinses hands.
Eats, supervised, in public without calling attention to eating behavior.

Says or indicates "Yes" or "No" in response to questions such as, "Do you want to go out?"
Turns pages of a book one at a time.
Separates one object from a group upon request (e.g., "Give me one block").
Goes to public places in a supervised group without calling unfavorable attention to behavior.

2

The Social Ecology of Mental Retardation

Sharon Landesman Ramey, Ellen Dossett, and Karen Echols

The social ecology of mental retardation (MR) represents a relatively new area of focused scientific inquiry (Berkson, 1978; Berkson & Landesman-Dwyer, 1977). Yet, recognition of the importance of the interactions between individuals and their social environments has long been a central concern to practitioners and investigators in the field of MR (Begab & Richardson, 1975; MacMillan, 1982; Robinson & Robinson, 1976; Windle, 1962). Indeed, the construct of MR itself is influenced by social ecology, as are the services and supports provided by a given society at a given period of time. In this chapter we provide an overview of social ecology as a field of inquiry and explore its application to the study of transactions between individuals with MR and their environments.

What Is Social Ecology?

The term *social ecology* has been used in two distinct ways. One way refers to the delineation of a specialty area within environmental psychology (Cronbach, 1975; Magnusson, 1981; Mischel, 1977; Moos, 1973; Pervin & Lewis, 1978; J. A. Russell & Ward, 1982). In this usage, social ecology is the study of the relationships and interactions between people and their environments. The social ecology of MR is thus concerned with how the social environment (e.g., family environment, peer groups, community acceptance) affects the behavior and development of people with MR, as well as how individuals with MR influence their social environments (e.g., school, family, work). When social ecology is expanded to a longitudinal framework, the mutuality or transactional nature of influences becomes an increasingly central feature of the scientific inquiry. Such transactions affirm that individuals directly influence and are influenced by their social environments.

Social ecology has helped reveal likely reasons why individuals with similar types or degrees of MR diverge significantly in their lifelong development. Similarly, social ecology has fostered a broader appreciation of the role of environmental factors in the etiology of MR (e.g., pervasive poverty, societal complexity, expectations) and the origins of many negative behavior patterns. MR often had been assumed to be the primary cause of aberrant behavior, such as stereotypies, self-injurious behavior, and socially maladaptive behavior, rather than being the result of environmental factors or the interactions between individuals and their environments.

Another frequent use of the term *social ecology* has been to describe the nature of the social environment of MR and families affected by MR. In this way, the term is used interchangeably with *social environment*, *social milieu*, or *social context*. In the past decade, articles on families and on the longitudinal adjustment of young children with developmental disabilities have detailed the social ecologies (e.g., family, school, work settings) in which children, adolescents, or adults with MR live, learn, work, and play. Sustained and valuable contributions have come from the Sociobehavioral Research Group (e.g., Edgerton, 1984, 1988; Edgerton & Bercovici, 1976). Edgerton's early pioneering work in the anthropological study of MR opened up new ways of viewing and interpreting the everyday behavior and environmental adjustment of individuals with MR. In *The Cloak of Competence*, Edgerton (1967) demonstrated that detailed knowledge (obtained through participant observation) about the behavior and self-knowledge of individuals who previously had lived in "institutions for the retarded" was invaluable in understanding the diverse ways that they adapted to new community environments. Other exemplary research on environments includes the work of Berkson, Blacher, Bristol, Crnic, Dunst, Gallimore, Glidden, Greenberg, Krauss, Landesman, Meyers, Mink, Nihira, Sackett, and Zetlin (see Crnic, Friedrich, & Greenberg, 1983; Dunst, Trivette, Hamby, & Pollock, 1990; Gallimore, Weisner, Bernheimer, Guthrie, & Nihira, 1993; Kavanaugh, 1988; Krauss, Simeonsson, & Ramey, 1989; Landesman & Vietze, 1987; Nihira, Weisner, & Bernheimer, 1994).

Why Is Social Ecology Relevant to MR?

Interest in the social ecology of MR increased as a result of both accumulating scientific evidence and altered social awareness. Scientifically, the findings that have fueled interest in the social environment have included those from behavior modification, epidemiology, family adjustment, and cross-institutional research. Scores of studies have demonstrated that to create lasting, positive behavioral change in an individual, what happens outside the therapeutic setting is as important (or maybe more so) than what occurrs during one-on-one intensive treatment (King, Raynes, & Tizard, 1971; Landesman-Dwyer & Butterfield, 1983; Schroeder & MacLean, 1987; Stokes & Baer, 1977). Research has demonstrated two important findings: (a) Almost all individuals can learn new behavior or decrease socially undesirable old behavior when they are given the opportunity to participate in carefully designed, highly structured programs or settings; and (b) these same individuals rarely maintain new or more desirable behavior unless their everyday social environments also value, reward, and support these altered behavior patterns.

The classic Mimosa study (Spradlin & Girardeau, 1966) in Kansas is a good example of these two findings. Under a highly controlled incentive and reward program, adults with significant intellectual limitations acquired positive new behavior to prepare them for community living. Eventually, the program's graduates were judged to be "ready" to go out into the community. As they left their familiar home and ventured out, they also dropped their new positive behaviors and returned to their former selves, behaving in ways that made them visibly deviant. No one had anticipated that they were learning only situation-specific behavior that would not generalize outside the setting in which such behavior was reinforced. From a practical perspective, those interested in designing effective behavior modification and learning programs have had to pay considerable attention to the social ecology of each person's life. Through careful observation of the conditions under which certain behaviors are more or less likely to occur, interventions can now be tailored for each individual. Information about social ecology thus helps to inform initial intervention strategies as well as to identify environmental influences that are likely to increase the maintenance and generalization of desired behavior.

From early on, studies of family adjustment provided some discrepant findings: The diagnosis of MR did not produce a crisis for all families (Keltner & Ramey, 1992, 1993; S. L. Ramey, 1991; S. L. Ramey, Krauss, & Simeonsson, 1989). Results indicated that families varied in ways that also could affect how well they accepted their son's or daughter's intellectual abilities, when and what types of support they sought to help advance their child's competencies, and the degree to which their child was integrated into the family's everyday routines.

A series of landmark studies about differences across institutions (King et al., 1971; Zigler, Balla, & Butterfield, 1968) revealed that the social and adaptive competencies of individuals varied as a function of characteristics of the institutions themselves. These studies raised fundamental questions about simple classification schemes for residential environments, given that considerable variation exists within a specific type of setting. Indeed, one of the most remarkable early findings—illustrating what is now considered a basic principle of social ecology, that of Person × Environment interaction—was that the same institutional environment could be stimulating or enhancing for one child (if the child had come from an extremely impoverished home environment) and depriving for another child (if the child had come from a more advantaged previous setting).

Social Ecology and the Construct of MR

For more than 30 years, MR has been defined by the American Association on Mental Retardation as a condition that reflects significant limitations in both adaptive behavior and tested intelligence (Grossman, 1977, 1983; Heber, 1961; Luckasson et al., 1992). The inclusion of a functional component, or "adaptive behavior," as an essential feature of MR, one that is measured relative to an individual's age and cultural context, has had profound implications for understanding what MR is and is not. Above all, MR is a social construct that ascribes an explicit value to patterns of everyday behavior and demonstrated cognitive ability within a developmental and ecological framework. Social ecology is directly relevant to assessing and understanding who will be classified as having MR and who will not. That is, rather than identify absolute levels of skills or performance as the diagnostic signs for determining whether MR exists, the clinical diagnosis is made within a specific ecological framework. MR is thus fundamentally a relativistic construct that is affected by multiple ecological dimensions. The ecological dimensions include the demands and expectations of a given culture for a given cohort and the degree to which the environment affords opportunities for learning and the expression of specific competencies. Identical performance of two individuals in different cultural or societal contexts may yield different conclusions about whether they do (or do not) have MR. Furthermore, a given individual could be judged to have MR in some settings or at some ages, but not necessarily in others. Above all, the construct of MR acknowledges the tremendous significance of an individual's functional relationship to his or her environment.

Adaptive behavior encompasses a wide range of functional abilities, from sensorimotor, self-help, communication, and social skills in infancy and early childhood to academic skills, reasoning, community survival skills, social judgment and responsibility, self-direction, and vocational aptitude in later years. Although adaptive behavior and measured intelligence are closely related, their observed correlation is not perfect. Accordingly, assessing intelligence and adaptive behavior independently can minimize the incorrect labeling of a child who scores poorly on an intelligence test for noncognitive reasons such as test anxiety, language difference, poor social compliance, and motivational problems or who lags in adaptive behavior skills because of physical, emotional, or environmental constraints rather than lack of basic intelligence. There are not yet any accurate, useful measures of adaptive behavior that are sensitive to the effects of both age and culture (Meyers, Nihira, & Zetlin, 1979; Sundberg, Snowden, & Reynolds, 1978). Ideally, an assessment of individual competence would be conducted in a manner that includes evaluation of the individual's environmental history (Landesman & Ramey, 1989).

Social Ecology and the Epidemiology of MR

As Landesman-Dwyer and Butterfield (1983) summarized, the epidemiological picture of MR is neither static nor sharply focused. The reasons for this include the changing definition of MR, the lack of consensus on how to measure MR in a general population, and the basic multidimensional and relativistic nature of the construct itself. An accurate historical review of who makes up the population with MR is exceptionally difficult. In addition to the varying definitions used (with IQ alone being the most widespread), obtaining an accurate picture of its incidence (the rate of new occurrence in a population) and its prevalence (the detected cases in a population) is extremely difficult. First, the prevalence of MR varies with age. Second, rates of mild MR, unlike the more severe forms, have markedly different prevalence rates across different cultures, countries, and time periods. Age-specific prevalence rates from communitywide surveys are extremely low during infancy, reach a dramatic peak among 10- to 15-year-olds, and then decline in the adult years (Gruenberg, 1964; Mercer, 1973b).

These age-related changes are consistent with the view that judgments of intellectual incompetence are relative to the demands of the environment. In school settings, where major demands are placed on children for task-oriented, academic, and socially compliant behavior, the likelihood of identifying poor performers is far greater than when the same children are younger or older and are in less structured and less supervised contexts. In the United States, most children with mild MR are identified after they enter school (Birch, Richardson, Baird, Horobin, & Illsley, 1970; Mercer, 1973b). Rates of mild MR drop by almost 50% when children leave school and enter young adulthood (Susser, 1968). The phenomenon of higher prevalence during the school years has been labeled "the six-hour retarded child" (President's Committee on Mental Retardation, 1970). Such children have been identified in both urban and rural areas and disproportionately are from economically impoverished and minority families. To what extent such children could have been identified as having MR during the preschool years is not fully known. Whether they continue to function in the mentally retarded range during adulthood also is unknown because investigators seldom have assessed adult adjustment of individuals who lose their MR label when they leave school (Henshel, 1972).

Estimates of the prevalence of mild MR differ by as much as 30-fold from country to country (Grunewald, 1979; Stein & Susser, 1975). By contrast, the prevalence rates for severe and profound MR are relatively constant (Abramowicz & Richardson, 1975). Many ecological factors influence how prevalence is judged in different societies. Among the influential variables are a society's degree of industrialization, urbanization, reliance on individual decision making, the use of extended family networks, and dependence on symbols and abstract concepts in everyday communication. In the People's Republic of China, for example, where the central government tries to match individuals to school and work settings and to provide such necessities as shelter, food, clothing, medical care, transportation, and social support, the opportunities for individual failure are minimized. Consequently, MR, at least mild MR, has been an unused and alien concept (Robinson, 1978). Presumably, children in such societies show the full range of cognitive abilities and individual differences, but they are not classified as having "more" or "less" of what intelligence tests measure. That is, the adaptive behavior skills associated with success in the People's

Republic of China seem to be less correlated with IQ scores than they are in Western, industrialized, and individually competitive societies.

Even within the United States, tremendous variation exists regarding standards for adaptive behavior within subgroups. A description of an isolated and impoverished setting in the hollows of the Appalachian mountains provides a dramatic illustration of the saliency of social ecology:

> The youngsters are not required to fulfill obligations consistent with their abilities and age. Under these relaxed conditions, they feel secure in a family setting where they are able to measure up to the low expectations of their clan. Parental and sibling approval is based on them as they are not on their behavior or their contributions. . . . Parents are not distressed over a child's failure to develop in physical size, increasing skills, and complexity of function, if indeed they assess his progress at all. If undersized upon attaining school age, his introduction into formal education is delayed until he has "growed more." Behavioral patterns are likewise ignored, with no thought given to the many factors responsible for deviation. The youngsters, particularly the infants, are strikingly inadequate in motor coordination such as grasping and manipulating objects; language and speech development closely parallels that of parents and siblings; responsiveness and power to concentrate are conspicuously absent. Deafness and poor vision go unnoticed. For the most part, the child must fend for himself as best as he can. (Gazaway, 1969, pp. 88–89)

By the standards of the outside world, most members of this Appalachian community did have MR. Inbreeding, malnutrition, primitive living conditions, widespread and untreated illnesses, and a virtually barren physical environment contributed to low performance in all aspects of adaptive behavior. Should external standards be applied to make judgments about MR in such a setting? If so, why?

Dimensionalizing the Environment and Levels of Influence

In 1978, Berkson wrote about the social ecology of MR as building on the naturalistic orientations of ecological psychology, anthropology, and ethology that explicitly value describing environments and the behavior of individuals within them. Berkson described the ideal for scientific inquiry in the field of MR as involving four processes:

> The first [process] is a qualitative description of major events occurring in natural environments. The approach involves seeing the situation from as many perspectives as possible. Sampling adequately across subjects and situations, use of informants, and participation observation are all features of this qualitative phase.
>
> Qualitative description permits one to identify major important behaviors and environmental variables. However, it lacks quantitative precision and is ambiguous with regard to causal relationships. The second step is a specification of the frequency, duration and order in

> which natural events occur. This involves a selection of behavioral events and characteristics of the environment to be recorded, followed by disciplined observation procedures with demonstrated observer and event reliability.
>
> From the second process emerges the possibility of a third step, causal analysis. Finding different distributions of events in different situations allows one to think about the possible environmental factors determining these differences. Predictability among events through patterns of association in time permits one to imagine that the events are connected by a unifying process. The results of these interaction analyses undoubtedly provide more important descriptions of events than do raw frequency and duration data derived in the second process. They are also important in the development of units of description for further study.
>
> The fourth process cannot be called the most important because it depends on the quality of accomplishment in the previous three. However, it is the culminating stage that ensures true understanding and verifies the significance of the research. In this process, a change agent manipulates one or a group of events and measures the consequence of that manipulation. (The term "change agent" is used rather than "experimenter" because this stage is not only done in the laboratory, but also occurs frequently in natural settings when, for instance, new training procedures or other institutional arrangements are imposed.) Here again, disciplined, multivariate, multisituational observational methods of the kind used in the third process are appropriate—and perhaps necessary—if one wishes to obtain a sophisticated understanding of the manifestations of causal events.
>
> These four processes are the components of a full analysis. Proceeding through them requires "common sense and hard work" and also a long term commitment to the solution of what inevitably is a complex problem. Constant revision of hypotheses and categories of observation, without loss of the sense of the central issue of the research, is necessary for full success. In this area of investigation, the single isolated study has little place. (pp. 406–407)

Concerning the conceptualization of levels of environmental or ecological influence, Bronfenbrenner (1977, 1979, 1989) has had a highly influential role. He wrote about how environmental influences, from proximal (micro) to distal (molar), theoretically may exert distinctive and simultaneous effects on the course of individual development. The empirical challenge has been how to target precisely which of the innumerable environmental variables to select and measure carefully. In many cases, investigators have relied on readily available and often global measures of environment, rather than more precise measures of the different levels of environmental influence.

The environmental tool used most often in both developmental research and MR research is the Home Observation for the Measurement of the Environment (HOME; Bradley, Caldwell, & Elardo, 1977; Bradley, Caldwell, et al., 1989), which assesses the quality of stimulation in the home environment. The HOME repeatedly has demonstrated good predictive validity for children's subsequent IQ. Through systematic measurement of discrete elements in young children's environments, reliable estimates of children's later cognitive performance can be made. These findings are provocative because they raise key theoretical issues about causality. Because parent IQ and education are correlated with HOME scores, it has not been possible to differentiate purely environmental levels of influence. On the other hand, trying to separate environmental effects (nurture) from biological ones (nature) may be misguided because intergenerational, individual, and ecological variables combine to influence intelligence (Moser, Ramey, & Leonard, 1983).

Findings about the saliency of children's home environments for their intellectual development are consistent with the social ecological principle of *environmental affordance*. This principle affirms that the degree to which the environment affords opportunities for the emergence and expression of certain behaviors (in this case, the collection of behaviors that yields higher vs. lower scores on standardized tests of intelligence) will be a significant determinant of the presence of these behaviors.

Efforts to develop full taxonomies of the environments relevant to MR have been limited. Landesman (1986), for example, proposed a detailed strategy for a taxonomy of home environments designed to permit informative comparisons across studies, settings, and time and to advance theory about the environment. This theory-guided topology combined structural and functional aspects of home environments and recognized that home settings are not static, do not exist apart from the people who live there, and must be evaluated from both objective and subjective perspectives to yield a maximally useful description. Furthermore, it was recognized that home environments are responded to as a whole, as well as in terms of discrete features that are separable from the whole.

Person × Environment Interactions Over the Life Span

Social ecology is based on the assumption that to understand the behavioral patterns of individuals, context must be taken into account. This is readily apparent in changes in treatment philosophy, social support services, and educational programs that have affected individuals with MR and their families in recent decades. Several decades ago, many infants born with central nervous system defects were relegated to institutional care, largely because professionals believed that these children had no significant learning potential. That belief changed dramatically with innovative applications of scientific principles of learning and social behavior (Berkson & Landesman-Dwyer, 1977; Bijou, 1963, 1966; Butterfield, 1983). Most children with MR now grow up in their family homes and receive education in public schools, increasingly in settings integrated with children who do not have MR. Accordingly, the "typical" behavioral profile of children with Down syndrome and other children with severe or profound MR in the 1950s and 1960s (Berkson, 1973; Farber, 1959, 1960) is markedly different from that of such children in the 1990s.

Two fundamental axioms in social ecology include the following: (a)

Behavior cannot be studied apart from the environment in which it occurs, and (b) substantial differences may occur in the behavior of the same individuals when they are in different milieus (Moos, 1973). The basic interdependency of people and environments appears to be an obstacle to separating out critical influences on development. However, the opportunity to view an individual's total ecological niche and to study the ways in which he or she adjusts to different settings constitutes the "natural experiment" (Parke, 1979) that is life.

An important aspect of social ecology is its explicit value orientation and its concern with promoting maximally effective human functioning (Insel & Moos, 1974). In essence, social ecology is a young, idealistic subdiscipline in psychology that seeks a merger of practical, philosophical, and theoretical perspectives; hoping to take everything important into account; and gleaning the best from the methodologies developed over the past century (cf. Stokols, 1981, 1982). As Moos (1973) proposed,

> essentially, every institution in our society is attempting to set up conditions that it hopes will maximize certain types of behavior and/or vectors of development. . . . In this sense, it may be cogently argued that the most important task for the behavioral and social sciences should be the systematic description and classification of environments and their differential cost and benefits to adaptation. (p. 662)

J. M. Hunt (1961) labeled this "the problem of the match." The concept of matching children to environments is based on an assumption that environments are not inherently good or bad. Rather, environments are best evaluated in terms of the degree to which they meet the needs of the individuals at specified stages of development. The factors that promote cognitive growth in some types of individuals, for example, may not do so for others, and what constitutes an ideal environment at one time is not likely to remain ideal as an individual changes. Because individuals and environments are multidimensional, it is likely that the environmental variables that contribute to positive developmental outcomes in one domain (e.g., cognitive abilities or independence) will not necessarily do so in other domains (e.g., maturity or creative expression).

Psychology is largely the study of Person × Environment effects (Cronbach, 1975; Pervin & Lewis, 1978). Research in the field of MR has often focused disproportionately on one of the two sides of the Person × Environment interaction. Many investigators have studied children's characteristics, many have evaluated the effects of environmental variables, but few have focused on Child × Environment interactions. This principle is one that can be helpful in explaining findings that at first appear contradictory.

An important conclusion is that the quality of environments cannot be judged without reference to the specific characteristics and needs of the people in those environments (Landesman, 1987; Landesman-Dwyer, 1981; Windle, 1962). For example, in 1939, Kuenzel studied "feebleminded" children in foster care settings. She concluded that homes with greater physical, social, and cognitive resources did not facilitate better adjustment, a surprising finding. Similarly, Rautman (1949) also noted that the match between environmental expectations and children's abilities was an important factor in the personal adjustment of children with MR. In family settings in which the importance of intellectual achievement was lower, children with low IQs often were observed to be better adjusted socially and to be more accepted. Theoretically, a mismatch between children and environments could increase the probability of negative social exchanges and decrease opportunities for a child to learn developmentally appropriate skills and strategies. If unreasonably high demands are placed on a child, the child is likely to experience repeated failure, which, in turn, may decrease his or her willingness to engage in challenging activities. An excessively demanding environment is less likely to provide information in ways that maximize its assimilation and use (Haywood & Wachs, 1981). Conversely, an environment that fails to demand increasingly mature and independent responses from a child may restrict development by not providing problems to solve and by not offering feedback about the child's developmental accomplishments (S. Ramey & Ramey, 1992).

The scientific or clinical evaluation of how well matched an environment is to the needs of individuals depends on the outcome measures selected as well as the values and goals of those involved in such assessments. Successful adaptation is not unidimensional, and an individual's progress in one domain, such as solving academic problems, is not always predictive of other behavior, such as forming and maintaining friendships.

In terms of long-term predictions of the cumulative effects of Person × Environment interactions, much remains to be learned. In a follow-up of previously institutionalized adults, Edgerton and Bercovici (1976) found that some of the (seemingly) least competent adults had made remarkable gains in their adaptive behavior. In other words, reliable predictions could not be made from early to late adulthood. Apparently, this predictive failure again underscores the principle of Person × Environment interaction. In certain environments, individuals may not show the full range of their abilities or may not have any reason to acquire new skills. To our knowledge, there have been no assessment or observational methods designed to predict an individual's future resourcefulness or potential for adaptive change in new settings or at later ages.

Conclusion

Social ecology represents a scientific and clinical orientation that is relevant to the field of MR. Because the construct of MR itself is one that relates individual behavior to environmental adaptation, careful study of the environment is likely to be informative for understanding the causes of MR and the factors that determine the developmental course of MR. Social ecology recognizes the basic interactive nature of human development within multiple environmental contexts. The opportunities to advance understanding of how individuals and families adapt to the challenges associated with MR are strengthened by the concepts and tools provided by social ecology.

3

Classification of Mental Retardation

Maureen S. Durkin and Zena A. Stein

Mental retardation (MR) involves altered human functioning presumed or known to exist on several levels. One level focuses on the underlying causes, or etiology, wherein alterations may occur in the genetic code, micronutrients, oxygen supply, or other factors, some of which are established and others hypothesized. Three additional levels of MR have been referred to as impairment, disability, and handicap (Susser, 1990; World Health Organization [WHO], 1980b). The term *impairment* in MR refers to the physiological level of brain structure and function; given current knowledge and technology, damage or alterations at this level are established in only a minority of MR subtypes. The term *disability* in MR refers to deficits in intellectual abilities and adaptive functioning (usually measured by intelligence tests and scales of adaptive behavior). It is in terms of disability that MR has traditionally been conceptualized, defined, and classified. A *handicap* occurs at the societal level and refers to altered social roles resulting from an interaction between cognitive disability and the demands and resources of a particular social environment. Provision of necessary supports and environmental modifications can reduce or eliminate handicap and perhaps disability associated with MR.

In theory, the wide diversity of phenomena within MR could be classified in terms of any one of the levels just specified. In practice, MR has been classified at the levels of etiology (by specific cause) and intellectual functioning or disability (by grade of intellectual disability). Both these approaches are incorporated into the widely used 1983 revision of the American Association on Mental Retardation's (AAMR's; formerly known as the American Association on Mental Deficiency) classification of MR (Grossman, 1983). The WHO's (1980a) ninth edition of the *International Classification of Diseases* (*ICD-9*) classifies MR primarily by grade of intellectual deficit, but also includes codes for selected causes. The fourth edition of the *Diagnostic and Statistical Manual of Mental Disorders* (*DSM–IV*); American Psychiatric Association, 1994) classifies MR exclusively by grade of intellectual deficit. In the most recent revision of the AAMR definition, a radically different approach is proposed, one that abandons classification of MR by grade (on the basis of IQ) and proposes distinguishing severity in terms of variations in the degree of support required for a given individual with MR to function in society (Luckasson et al., 1992).

In this chapter we provide an overview of the two widely used approaches to classifying MR (by etiology and by grade of intellectual deficit) and discuss uses, advantages, and disadvantages of each approach. We assume that classification in MR should serve two primary purposes: to organize current knowledge of the heterogeneous conditions that make up MR and to facilitate communication between people of diverse backgrounds and interests in the field of MR on matters such as service provision, assessment, education, research, program planning, prevention, and policy (Grossman, 1983). Zigler and Hodapp (1986) pointed out that a useful and well-specified system of classification in any field is one that (a) allows reliable placement of individuals into different classes (i.e., that allows classification with a high degree of agreement between different classifiers) and (b) conveys a large amount of information about an individual in a given class (i.e., that each class has a number of meaningful correlates). These principles guide our discussion of advantages and disadvantages of various approaches to classification in MR, as it has guided the discussion of MR and the levels of severity of MR in the definition presented in this book.

Etiological Classification

The major known causes of MR can be categorized as shown in Table 1. Within these general categories, many specific causes have been described; the largest number is in the single-gene category, in which more than 100 specific causes (many of them extremely rare) have been identified (Durkin, Schupf, Stein, & Susser, 1994; McKusick, 1992).

Classification of MR by specific cause is clearly optimal for at least

Table 1. Major Categories of Known Causes and Examples of MR

Causal category	Example
Chromosomal	Down syndrome, cri du chat
Single gene	Phenylketonuria, fragile X syndrome
Hormonal	Hypothyroidism
Specific nutritional deficiency (prenatal)	Iodine, folate
Infection	
Prenatal	Rubella, toxoplasmosis
Perinatal	HIV, syphilis
Postnatal	Measles encephalitis
Toxic exposure	
Prenatal	Ionizing radiation, fetal alcohol syndrome
Postnatal	Lead
Traumatic brain injury, anoxia, or both	
Perinatal	Prolonged, obstructed labor
Postnatal	Motor vehicle collision, fall, near-drowning

three purposes: planning primary prevention, understanding pathogenesis, and providing information to families and service providers.

Planning Primary Prevention

Phenylketonuria exemplifies the process by which classification of individuals by presumed cause or subtype of MR can lead to discovery of a specific cause that, in turn, has resulted in effective prevention. Maternal folate deficiency, an identified risk factor for neural tube defects, is another example. In the case of neural tube defects, effective prevention programs have been put in place even before the mechanisms by which maternal folate deficiency contribute to their occurrence are understood.

Understanding the Genesis and Nature of Intellectual Disability Associated With Specific Causes

As knowledge of specific causes of MR increases, opportunities arise to investigate correlations between specific causal characteristics and phenotypic expressions, including physical and psychological profiles. For example, cognitive and behavioral test results of individuals with Down syndrome and those with fragile X syndrome show distinct profiles associated with each cause (Hodapp et al., 1992). These findings provide insights into the genesis and nature of cognitive disability that would not be possible without classification of MR by specific cause. Even within a given causal category, specific attributes of etiology may be associated with a given profile of cognitive strengths and weaknesses. Thus, in fragile X syndrome, the severity of intellectual deficit has been shown to be associated with the size of the expanded gene as well as the mode of inheritance (maternal vs. paternal; Hinton et al., 1992).

Providing Information to Families, Clinicians, and Other Caregivers

Families of children with MR often want to know the cause of it. This knowledge can sometimes result in the prevention of MR in later-born children. Better classification of forms of MR by cause will allow more efficient dissemination of information. Classification by specific cause also would enrich epidemiological studies of the prevalence and distribution of MR in populations, as well as planning and evaluation of educational, medical, occupational, and residential services.

Despite these uses and advantages of classifying MR by specific cause, there are limitations, given the current state of knowledge. Fewer than half of the cases of MR in population-based studies are associated with known causes. Among individuals with severe MR (IQ < 50), known causes account for the majority of cases, but within the mildly affected (IQ = 50–69), which make up the majority of cases in the population, specific causes can be identified for only a small proportion of cases. Thus, classification by specific cause currently leaves the majority of cases of MR unclassified.

Zigler and colleagues (Burack et al., 1988; Zigler & Hodapp, 1986) advocated the use of a crude, two-group "causal" classification of MR: (a) organic (associated with organic or biological abnormalities) and (b) familial (associated with a family history of mild MR and not known to be associated with biological abnormalities). A third "unclassified" (not classified as organic or familial) group also is recognized. This broad approach has some validity in that there are several epidemiological correlates to the two groups—organic and familial—corresponding in part to the correlates of severe and mild MR. These are discussed next and are outlined in Table 2.

Nonetheless, there are serious problems with this approximation to an etiological classification. One is that it lumps many diverse causes and forms of MR into a single class (e.g., organic). Within each class, levels of intellectual disability, patterns of cognitive strengths and weaknesses, and needs for support vary widely. Thus, the classification of MR in an individual as "organic" conveys relatively little about that individual. A second problem is that as knowledge of specific causes of MR increases, many forms that might once have been called familial could be classified as organic. Thus, the organic–familial classification scheme represents an extremely crude state of knowledge. As the causes of MR become better understood, it should be possible to use a more refined causal classification system.

Another limitation of virtually all forms of etiological classification is that the costs of definitive diagnostic assessments are high and the outcome may not be relevant either to prevention or to care. Thus, classification by cause may not provide a guide for the appropriate care of individuals with cognitive disabilities. Resources might be better used for treatment, care, and rehabilitation programs. Nevertheless, in some cases the etiology will indicate possibilities for prevention within the family and will be associated with specific rehabilitation needs and prognoses in terms of a range of expected functions.

Classification by Grade of Intellectual Deficit

Following the development of intelligence testing at the turn of the twentieth century, people with MR in developed countries have been classified regularly and universally by grade of intellectual deficit. Four grades of intellectual deficit demarcated by IQ cutpoints are distinguished in the 1983 AAMR classification (Grossman, 1983), as well as in the *ICD-9* (WHO, 1980a) and the *DSM–IV* (American Psychiatric Association, 1994; see Table 3). A full discussion of these grades is provided in chapter 1 of this book.

Classification by grade has several important uses. It can provide a basis for current educational, residential, and occupational placements as well as for future planning. The grade of intellectual functioning often relates to prognosis and can therefore aid in informing expectations for independent living, educational achievement, and occupational roles. For these purposes, classification by grade of intelligence serves as a preliminary guide but should not dictate. Children classified as having mild MR often function in the normal range as adults. The course for individuals functioning in the severe and profound ranges is more stable.

The advantages of classifying MR by grade are that it is an approach that is widely used nationally and internationally to facilitate communication between diverse professionals and can be assigned regardless of whether the etiological diagnosis is known. To the extent that IQ testing produces reliable and valid results, classification by grade of intellectual

Table 2. Epidemiological Characteristics of Severe and Mild MR

Variable	Severe MR	Mild MR
Prevalence range in childhood (per 1,000)		
Countries with advanced medical care	2.5–5.0	2.5–40.0
Less developed countries	5.0–25.0	Estimates not available
Life expectancy	Less than general population; strong negative association with presence of congenital heart disease and with severity of MR and restricted mobility	Somewhat shorter than general population
% With other neurodevelopmental or sensory disorders	About 85%	Minority
% With other psychiatric disorders	Higher frequency than general population	Higher frequency than general population
% With known genetic cause	About 50%	Small percentage
% With unknown cause	Minority	Majority
Usual age at recognition	Infancy or preschool years	School age
Duration	Lifelong	May be restricted to school age
Male:female ratio	Male excess (1.1 to 1.4:1)	Male excess (1.1 to 1.8:1)
Major demographic risk factors	Maternal age a strong predictor of trisomies, which cause about 30% of severe MR	Low socioeconomic status
Association with social class	Prevalence relatively even across the social classes	Occurs predominantly in children of low-income parents

Note. Data derived from Durkin et al., 1994; Eyman, Grossman, Chaney, & Call, 1990; Kiely, 1987; Stein & Susser, 1984; and Susser & Stein, 1992.

deficiency also should be relatively reliable and valid. Imposing categories on a continuous measure does, however, result in an inevitable loss of information.

In epidemiological studies, moderate, severe, and profound grades of MR are typically combined into a single category of severe or serious MR. Serious MR is distinct from mild MR in most epidemiological characteristics (Durkin et al., 1994; Kiely, 1987; Stein & Susser, 1984; Susser & Stein, 1992; also see Table 2). The prevalence of severe MR in developed countries is relatively consistently found to be 2.5–5 per 1,000 people and to vary little across the social classes. Estimates of the prevalence of mild MR, on the other hand, range widely and show a strong social class gradient (with higher prevalence rates being associated with low socioeconomic status). People with severe MR are much more likely to experience a restricted life expectancy, neurological disorders, and lifelong disability than are people with mild MR.

Elevated rates of severe MR in less developed countries (5–25 per 1,000; see Table 2) may be attributable to an increased role of nongenetic causes such as infections, nutritional deficiencies, and trauma. The prevalence of mild MR is difficult to estimate in populations without universal schooling and with pastoral or other economies that may not demand high levels of intellectual functioning.

The major limitations associated with classifying MR by grade are the following: (a) It provides global ratings that emphasize individuals' deficits and mask profiles of cognitive strengths and weaknesses (a related concern is that the label can be difficult for an individual to shed when it is used to shape expectations on the part of family members and educators and other service providers); (b) it does not convey information about adaptive behavior (other than indicating that the criterion of at least some deficit in adaptive behavior was met); (c) it is not directly informative of the levels and types of support required; and (d) in its reliance on IQ testing, it may invite the possibility of cultural bias and inappropriate labeling of people as having MR (usually mild MR) due to their lack of familiarity with the dominant language and culture (Mercer, 1992).

Table 3. Classification of MR by Severity Based on IQ and *ICD-9* (WHO, 1980a)

Severity	*ICD-9* code	Approximate IQ range
Mild	317.00	50–70
Moderate	318.00	35–49
Severe	318.10	20–34
Profound	318.20	<20
Unspecified	319.00	

Note. Precise IQ cutpoints may vary to allow for differences between tests. Guidelines of the American Association on Mental Deficiency (Grossman, 1983) and the fourth *Diagnostic and Statistical Manual of Mental Disorders* (American Psychiatric Association, 1994) recommend the use of these or similar cutpoints as well as clinical judgment and assessment of adaptive skills in the diagnosis and classification of severity of mental retardation. *ICD-9* = *International Classification of Diseases* (9th ed.).

Conclusion

The multiaxial approach advocated in the 1983 revision of the AAMR classification allows classification by both etiology and grade, as well as the presence of associated disabilities. When this is done, there is often no one-to-one correspondence between etiology and grade of intellectual deficit. For example, in the case of the fragile X syndrome, most affected people appear to function in the moderate and mild ranges, but the full spectrum can range from profound MR to normal intellectual functioning. These and numerous other examples strongly support the retention of at least two axes for the classification of MR recommended by the AAMR: etiology and grade (Grossman, 1983) or etiology and "degree of support required" (Luckasson et al., 1992).

4

Psychometrics

John W. Jacobson and James A. Mulick

Psychometrics—psychological measurement—is the mathematical expression of the parameters of psychological activity involving the specification of behavior and response. This is true regardless of whether psychology is defined as the science of the predication and control of behavior or as the science of behavior, cognition, and affect. These mathematical expressions are founded on the inherently probabilistic characteristics of human activity. Responses requiring psychometric appraisal occur in the context of recording the behavior of others, verbalization elicited by standardized questions, or the reporting of private events, and they arise from the behavior of the observer and that of the observed. In this chapter we explore the intimate interrelationship of psychometrics with the key, foundational constructs of reliability and validity and the role of psychometrics in the development of credible assessment schema and in the review and evaluation of treatments, services, and supports.

Applying psychometric procedures is necessary to determine the confidence with which the information gathered and the conclusions drawn on the basis of human experience are valid and may be generalized beyond the time and place in which they occur. This is because inferential processes, including interpersonal processes that involve arriving at consensual inferences, are subject to "irreducible error" (Sagan, 1993). Such errors, for example, may be increased in observations entailing global behaviors of interest when raters code behavior (T. R. Cunningham & Tharp, 1981) or when observers have different access to information (i.e., different relevant histories) and render social comparisons (Ernst, Bornstein, & Weltzein, 1984).

Psychometrics is used to determine the extent of this error and as a metric to reduce error attributable to changes in the behavior of the observer or redefinition of a phenomenon. In some instances, it may be incorrectly assumed that the use of psychometrics is an artifact of the use of scientific models in psychology. This is not entirely so. Rather, it is the probabilistic nature of behavior itself (and cognition and affect) in human agency that dictates the application of psychometric procedures in the measurement and study of behavior. These procedures can be used readily within a scientific model, with a number of functional implications summarized by Scarr (1985):

> Science is an agreed-upon set of procedures, not constructs or theories. . . . Psychology has developed good techniques to avoid the personal biases of knowers through requirements for reliability and validity. The "facts" must be reproducible across some units of time and across similar populations and situations. . . . Observations that are shared among observers and that prove useful can be separated from those that are not useful, are idiosyncratic, and are based on limited experience. (pp. 500–501)

During the past two decades, scientific conceptualizations of human behavior and the natural world have been challenged by general philosophical perspectives, such as hermeneutics and social constructionism. Hermeneutics holds that scientific findings are "epistemologically embedded within a world of intersubjective cultural meanings that are constitutive of the conceptual categories within which the science operates" (Woolfolk & Richardson, 1984, p. 777). In other words, the generalizability of behavioral science is determined by cultural context and

> the truth of a proposition has to do not with its isomorphism with sense data, but with its revelation of reality . . . the truth of a proposition has to do with its being warranted or justified, rather than being related to sense data in some inscrutable way. (Woolfolk, 1992, p. 219)

By contrast, social constructionism holds that all knowledge, including that of the physical, life, behavioral sciences, and social consensus, are equivalently relative (Woolfolk, 1982). A strong interpretation of the social constructionist perspective would be to assert that all knowledge is arbitrary and that scientific procedures, among others, have no ultimate superiority.

A strong position of this form, however, also may require a social constructionist appraisal of the validity of social constructionism itself, vitiating the intellectual utility of a strong position, in that no standpoint might be asserted to be greater utility than another, including that of social constructionism. As a result, not surprisingly, psychologists who have discussed this perspective at length (e.g., Gergen, 1994; Guerin, 1992; Woolfolk, 1992; Woolfolk & Richardson, 1984) have adopted positions acknowledging that certain classes of behavioral findings, those with pragmatic importance, may have particular validity as generalizable phenomena with verifiable implications. For example, Woolfolk and Richardson (1984) distinguished between the goals of behavior therapy and the findings of behavior therapy research. Guerin (1992) noted that "we all turn doorknobs in similar ways, but this is not socially constructed knowledge because it is the same stimulus conditions and the same automatic consequences of opening doors that control the similar behaviors" (p. 1425). From this vantage point, phenomena differ in the extent to which their nature and function are socially constructed, whereas interpretation of their significance and meaning may be culturally constructed. Therefore, scientific procedures can be used profitably with phenomena having pragmatic implications, because the procedures will permit the estimate of error and the degree of generality that might otherwise further distort cultural practices. Stated more succinctly, social judgment informed by specific information regarding bias is more useful than social judgment that is not.

Error

When behavior or a response is characterized or measured, counts or scores are imperfect and are therefore affected by error. Mathematically, this is because "we measure latent continuous variables with error at the manifest level" (Borgatta & Bohrnstedt, 1981, p. 26). Psychometrics addresses nonsystematic (or random) error and bias. Bias involves "systematic error in the measurement process. . . . The term is . . . distinct from the concepts of fairness, equality, prejudice, or preference. . . . Bias . . . denotes nothing more or less than the consistent distortion of a statistic" (Osterlind, 1983, p. 10).

The probability that bias will affect counts or scores in applied or clinical research is relatively high, and confidence in the generality of findings may be highly restricted unless adequate and specific procedures are used to address threats to generality. These issues involve considerations such as the methods of constructing samples from a larger universe; possible preexisting differences between groups studied; problems with the inadequate specification or implementation of treatments; inadequate specification of measures; nonindependence of groups studied; and sequential effects when participants undergo more than one, or alternating, treatments. Sources of both random error and bias in applied contexts have been detailed by T. D. Cook and Campbell (1979) and discussed in the context of the goals of studies by Sulsky and Streiner (1991). An excellent example of errors threatening the generality of conclusions from clinical research was provided by Parker (1990), and threats to the generality of conclusions regarding psychotherapeutic outcomes were discussed by N. S. Jacobson and Revenstorf (1988).

Whether research is undertaken to predict or to explain and describe behavior (Sulsky & Streiner, 1991), the practical dimension addressed by psychometrics is generality: To what extent can the findings be generalized to other individuals in other settings at other times? Generality is an empirical issue to be addressed by successive demonstrations of the same effect. More fundamentally, in any research study, generality is based on two constructs that form the core of psychometrics: reliability and validity.

Reliability

Reliability is "the ability to obtain consistent results in successive measurements of the same phenomenon" (H. Jacob, 1984, p. 33), for measurements to be free from measurement error. Differences in obtained measurements are not considered errors of measurement if they are due to the nature of the phenomenon being measured or to the effects of meaningful events, such as intervention or developmental progression (American Psychological Association [APA], 1985). In practice, reliability is assessed as the extent to which (a) two independent observers produce the same score or counts from the same stimuli (interrater reliability), (b) two independent assessments of an individual produce the same score or counts (test–retest reliability), or (c) items on a scale or measure cohere (internal consistency). Each of these forms of reliability is usually assessed using an index of association (Suen, 1988; Suen, Ary, & Ary, 1986), although indexes that adjust raw levels of association for chance agreement (kappa and intraclass correlations) or that use variance ratios may be preferable in many applications (J. Cohen, 1960; Fleiss & Cohen, 1973).

Interrater agreement is occasionally, and weakly, tested in some behavior analytic and behavior therapy research by using an index of agreement [(agreements/total observations) × 100%], but both interrater and test–retest reliability are more appropriately assessed in most cases by using a Pearson correlation coefficient (*r*), the regression slope of one variable on the other, or an intraclass coefficient from an analysis of variance (ANOVA). Advantages of intraclass coefficients include simultaneous assessment of multiple components of error (Suen, 1988). Internal consistency is typically assessed with Cronbach's alpha (a variance ratio), item–total coefficients, simple (alternating items) and all-permutations split-half coefficients, and, in advanced applications, factor analysis (D. J. Jackson & Borgatta, 1981; Marradi, 1981). Test–retest reliability when different clinicians complete scales over time is often a pertinent issue in professional practice. As a result, published test–retest values for the same raters over time will often overstate the stability of scores to be expected in practice.

Test–retest reliability is affected by lasting general and specific characteristics of the person, temporary and specific characteristics of the person, systematic or chance factors affecting test administration or appraisal of performance, and unaccounted variance (E. B. Page, 1980). Systematic factors affecting appraisal of performance include observer drift (Suen, 1988). Cronbach (1970) enumerated temporary and specific individual factors such as changes in fatigue and motivation; fluctuations in attention, coordination, standards of judgment, or memory for particular facts; levels of practice on required skills or knowledge; temporary emotional states or elicitation of habits; and luck in guessing.

The constructs of reliability and validity are related in the sense that a less accurate (i.e., reliable) score is less valid (Cronbach, 1970). As Marradi (1981) noted, "the low reliability of an indicator is strong evidence against its validity, but the converse is not true" (p. 17). This is because measures can be consistently in error or consistently incorrect. However, in contrast to reliability, for which specific metrics are readily available for specific types of reliability, the assessment of validity can be more complex and require greater inference.

Validity

Validity is a unitary concept that refers to the degree to which specific evidence supports the inferences made from obtained measurements (APA, 1985). As noted by H. Jacob (1984), "an indicator is said to be valid when the fit between it and the underlying concept is close" (p. 16). The "indicator" in this context may be a single item, a unidimensional measure, or a multidimensional (e.g., multiple-domain, multiple-score) measure. In general, longer measures are both more reliable and more valid than shorter measures because they are less influenced by chance (Cronbach, 1970) and may more readily consist of constructs that initially may appear unidimensional but are actually multidimensional (D. J. Jackson & Borgatta, 1981). Single-term measures (including binary measures such as present vs. absent) may present special problems: "They tend to be less valid, less accurate, and less reliable than their multi-item equivalents. . . . Their degree of validity, accuracy, and reliability is often unknowable" (McIver & Carmines, 1981, p. 15). One way to improve both the reliability and validity of single and multiple-item measures is by increasing the specification (e.g., definition) of criteria for scoring (H. Jacob, 1984; Rinck & Brown, 1987).

Conventionally, several aspects of validity are usually distinguished (Cronbach, 1970): "Criterion Validity, or 'How do measures of some valued performance (criterion) relate to test scores?'; Content Validity, or 'Do the observations truly sample the universe of tasks they are claimed to represent?'; and Construct Validity, or 'How can scores on the test be explained psychologically? Does the test measure the attributes it is said to measure?' " (pp. 124–125).

Criterion validity is typically assessed by correlating scores or measures with well-established measures that are typically used as indexes of similar or closely related phenomena or that correspond to logically related phenomena (e.g., scores on a psychopathology measure differ for people who are or are not treated with major psychoactive medications; Sturmey & Bertman, 1994).

Content validity is a function of adequate specification of the domains of a measure, the use of representative sampling of those domains in developing a measure (both in terms of item or question content or scoring criteria and in terms of the nature of samples of people who are assessed), and specific methods to evaluate responses and combine them in scores (Linehan, 1980, p. 153). It has been suggested (Mathews, Whang, & Fawcett, 1980) that social validity is a special case of content validity involving the goals of measurement, the appropriateness or acceptability of the procedures, and the social implications of measuring a phenomenon.

Construct validity is a comparison of scores or measures with internal criteria (e.g., whether, in multidimensional measures, expected relationships are present among several scores) or to factorial criteria (e.g., M. C. Brown et al., 1988). Construct validity also may be demonstrated when developmental patterns are apparent in measures constructed for developmental applications or when different population subgroups or diagnostic groups are distinguished by scores in expected ways (Bruininks, Woodcock, Hill, & Weatherman, 1985).

Psychometrics: Developing Measures

In this section, the procedures underlying the development of two adaptive behavior measures—the Scales of Independent Behavior (SIB; Bruininks et al., 1985) and the Developmental Disabilities Profile (DDP; M. C. Brown et al., 1988)—are presented as examples of how psychometric issues may be addressed in an application of increasing concern in developmental disabilities.

Scales of Independent Behavior

Procedures for ascertaining the reliability and validity of the SIB, a comprehensive individual adaptive behavior measure, were reported by Bruininks et al. (1985). Because the scales were intended for eventual use with a wide age range and wide ability range of diverse people with developmental disabilities, the general sampling frame for people on whom the scales were normed (e.g., initially tested as a reference group) included young children, adolescents, and adults, some of whom had mild-to-profound disabilities and some of whom had no disabilities. Further sampling frames included classification based on sex, race, Spanish origin, occupational status, occupational level, geographical region, and type of community, which permitted generalization of measurement practices and scores across these groups as indicated to be warranted by statistical analysis. Use of a population-representative norming group is necessary to allow analysis of construct validity, to ensure that distributions of responses are reflective of population distributions to the extent possible, and to satisfy some requirements of social validity.

Content validity was addressed, in part, by a broad sampling strategy of adaptive behavior, which permitted use of the SIB as a comprehensive adaptive behavior measure. Reliability was addressed by use of a consistent item scoring format, statements involving observable behavior in items, procedures that minimized comprehension and memory requirements for raters, and more than 50 interviewers for the norming sample with education and training backgrounds similar to those of many informants and potential raters. Generally, subscale items were constructed to approximate equal interval scales based on item difficulty statistics. To enhance the usability (Klausmeier & Ripple, 1971) of the SIB, a variety of adjusted scoring methods were developed, which enabled assessors to make a variety of comparative analyses appropriate to different clinical assessment purposes.

To assess the reliability of the SIB scores, standard errors of measurement (an index of the imprecision of a measure, or the difference between observed and "true" scores; Bruininks et al., 1985), split-half indexes, corrected split-half indexes, and test–retest and interrater indexes were computed for scores derived at several structural levels of the measure. Score bias was assessed through regression models that predicted scale and subscale scores with demographics taken from the sampling frame for the norming group. These results indicated that chronological age was the primary predictor of scores, an expected and desirable finding.

Construct validity of the SIB was verified by analyses (as described) showing that SIB scores were distributed developmentally; through a comparison of the factor and domain structure of the SIB with those of other measures; by analyses of the comparability of scale performance among demographically structured subsamples (partitioned from the norming sample); by identification of expected variations in scale performance corresponding to differences among samples defined by diagnostic groups; and by subscale and cluster intercorrelation methods.

The criterion validity of the SIB was verified through correlations of subscale and cluster scores with those of other adaptive behavior and problem behavior scales administered to the same respondents and to those derived from a psychoeducational battery (i.e., convergent validity). The stability of scores that were based on using parents and teachers as informants was assessed, and discriminant classifications of respondents according to diagnostic ability groups and educational program types using SIB scores were conducted (i.e., discriminant validity). Finally, in addition to indications of content validity associated with norming procedures and selected analyses already noted, this form of validity also was demonstrated by the successful prediction of a community adjustment indicator using the SIB scores (Bruininks et al., 1985).

Developmental Disabilities Profile

Procedures for ascertaining the reliability and validity of the DDP, an individual summary of diagnostic characteristics and measure of functional characteristics of people with developmental disabilities, were reported by M. C. Brown et al. (1988). The instrument was developed for use with the range of individuals receiving developmental disabilities services in one state. The initial development and analysis sample was structured to be broadly representative of the service population with respect to demographics, overt disability characteristics, and forms of participation in services. Efficient sampling was enabled by preexisting uniform information on these salient features of people served.

Internal consistency reliability of additive indexes and scales in the DDP was assessed using Cronbach's alpha. Test–retest reliability of adaptive and behavior indexes (parcels or bundles of conceptually related items) was assessed using the Pearson correlation coefficient, the slope of the regression of Time 2 scores on Time 1 scores, and the intraclass coefficient derived from ANOVA. Interrater agreement of these scores was assessed by applying these statistics to scores derived for the same individuals. Further analyses entailed ascertaining the characteristics of raters and interrater agreement, including agreement between informants in residential and day service settings, interrater agreement at the item level, and comparison of the reliability of the DDP with published values for other instruments containing comparable scales or scores.

Content validity of the DDP during the development process was reinforced by continuous user and expert feedback on the adequacy of successive forms of the measure. This was done by convening advisory groups of experienced service providers and clinical expert advisors, by revisions based on characteristics of items involving important clinical needs of individuals identified in rate (payment level) appeals by providers of services, and by review of instruments with a similar focus or purpose.

Construct validity was verified through analyses indicating that, as expected, basic skill indexes are interrelated (adaptive skills are moderately positively correlated, as are two indexes of behavior problems), that behavior indexes are not related to primary skills indexes and are not related to self-care and daily living indexes, and that a broad independence factor and behavioral factor describe the instrument. The latter finding is consistent with the foundational structure of other adaptive behavior measures.

Criterion validity was established through the identification of significant and consistent differences in scores across residential settings differing in restrictiveness and day service settings differing in focus (e.g., developmental or vocational). Furthermore, through regression, DDP scores significantly predicted the scale scores of two other comprehensive adaptive behavior measures (one of which was the SIB) and an adaptive behavior measure developed for use with infants and toddlers with developmental disabilities or children and adults with profound mental retardation (M. C. Brown et al., 1988).

As suits the breadth and comprehensiveness of their applications, reliability and validity analyses of the SIB and DDP are extensive and intensive. In practice, such analyses often are more circumscribed for many measures. There are representative studies involving the establishment of the reliability and validity of instruments and observational methodologies pertinent to developmental disabilities issues by Farrell, Curran, Zwick, and Monti (1983), Feinstein, Kaminer, Barrett, and Tylenda (1988), Freeman and Schroth (1984), Heimberg, Mueller, Holt, and Liebowitz (1992), Nihira, Weisner, and Bernheimer (1994), Ramirez and Kratchowill (1990), Spense and Liddle (1990), Sturmey and Bertman (1994), and Widaman, Stacy, and Borthwick-Duffy (1993).

Beyond Testing: Psychometrics in General Research and Evaluation Methodology

Psychometric considerations have implications for the methodology of research and program evaluation, including the evaluation of the direct therapeutic or indirect social effects of interventions. As in research, the key issue is the extent to which the findings reported in a study can be generalized to other people with similar or related conditions who are living or participating in services in similar situations. The ability to generalize reliably and validly in program evaluation is the foundation for assertions that a professional therapy or technique has utility, because "the practice of adopting treatments for widespread use before they are subjected to rigorous comparative trials is very dangerous!" (W. A. Silverman, 1993, p. 7).

When, and perhaps because, conventional curative treatments are unavailable for most developmental disabilities, such as autism, family members and other devoted caregivers for people with disabilities are known to be vulnerable to seeking treatments of questionable reason and merit in an attempt to alleviate these disabilities (D. P. H. Jones, 1994). Although the psychometric underpinnings of adaptive behavior scales and other clinical measures have general and long-standing ramifications for diagnosing disabilities and disorders, methodological corollaries in treatment evaluation to psychometric requirements play an even more critical role in the prevention of the use of ineffective or harmful procedures (e.g., Biklen, 1993) or the misapplication and misrepresentation of procedures with highly circumscribed effects (Green, 1994; Starr, 1994).

Psychometric requirements for establishing reliability in treatment assessment include, minimally, clarity and specificity of precedent in established knowledge of human functioning, a clear definition of the phenomenon treated or targeted, a clear definition of the treatment or technique, and an unambiguous definition of standards for the recognition of benefit (e.g., Wheeler, Jacobson, Paglieri, & Schwartz, 1993). Validity in treatment assessment is a function of procedures established to prevent error and bias from other naturally occurring simultaneous, contemporary, and historical influences on measurement and treatment response, the content and criterion-referencing of outcome measures, and authentic and consistent implementation of treatment.

To the degree that these threats to the generality of findings are present, it becomes impossible to demonstrate the reliability or validity of findings (e.g., if a phenomenon is classified as ineffable or resistant to specification, outcome criteria are idiosyncratic and highly variable from case to case; Biklen, 1993). Mental retardation (MR) is characterized as one of the few mental disabilities for which the existing nomenclature provides objective intellectual and functional criteria for classification. Adequate reliability and validity of the measures used to ascertain whether these criteria are met are absolutely critical to consistent and responsible clinical practice because MR may persist on a lifelong basis. Furthermore, sufficient validity and reliability of measures of treatment effects, especially in the instance of severe or life-threatening maladaptive behavior, are equally crucial to prevent neglect of people who may not be able to indicate independently the ineffectiveness of specific treatments. In some instances, evidence of treatment effects may be set forth only through persuasive expression. Persuasion bolstered by logical inference provides a weak justification for professional selection of therapies to be provided, techniques to be taught to students, and advice to be given to caregivers. For these reasons, ethical standards for scientist–practitioners in health-related fields such as psychology, speech pathology, and medicine stipulate that demonstrated generality of supportive research should be the foundation of clinical practice in MR and other service sectors.

Conclusion

Measurement is a foundational process that is inherent in the field of scientific basic and applied psychology. Measurement that is (a) reliable, in that successive measurements of a phenomenon are consistent, and (b) valid, in that evidence exists to support the inferences that are rendered, operates to reduce error in the necessarily imperfect characterization of complex behavior and environmental events that is the subject matter of psychology. Measurement procedures are the foundation of evidentiary processes in research, permitting falsification of hypotheses about human development and functioning in the context of a broader experimental design to reduce confounding influences. Measurement is the basis in psychological science for the discernment and confirmation of individual differences, behavior changes, and commonalities in human learning and development. Finally, measurement is a fundamental characteristic of efforts in psychological science to place human development and behavior in context and to enhance social and therapeutic technologies.

5

Intellectual Development

Donald K. Routh

Intellectual development includes processes of growth, maintenance, and decline in people's higher mental abilities. Young infants neither speak nor appear to understand what is said to them. Their thought processes seem to be far simpler than those of older individuals. Yet, even within the first year of life, the beginnings of a remarkably rapid process of intellectual development are evident. The condition of mental retardation (MR) represents a fundamental disturbance of the average course of intellectual development. Thus, psychologists who work in the field of MR should have a clear understanding of intellectual development.

A brief summary of average intellectual development might be as follows: Young children soon acquire language and begin to learn the customs of their society, including feeding and dressing themselves and caring for their personal needs, symbolic play, and the elementary forms of social interaction. They begin to realize that other people also have thoughts and feelings like their own (Wellman, 1990). Not long afterward, children who attend school learn to read, write, do simple mathematical calculations, and understand the basic concepts within many areas of knowledge. Their appreciation of the subtleties of the mental processes of others and of social interaction grows as well. After puberty, the more able individuals, especially those who continue their education, can progress further in their ability to appreciate logic and mathematics and to understand more advanced concepts within various fields. Their social interaction also is increased in complexity.

Uneducated people and those in traditional cultures without elaborate educational systems can nevertheless engage in activities of considerable cognitive complexity, albeit not necessarily involving the Western European concepts of logic and mathematics. The kinds of rapid intellectual development observed in infants, children, and adolescents level off in adulthood, although some individuals may continue to advance within narrower domains of accomplishment. As adult age increases, well practiced intellectual skills are remarkably well buffered against deterioration, even in the face of sensory and motor impairment and declines in processing speed, short-term memory, and ability to reason about novel intellectual material.

The preceding description summarizes some of the current views of how intellectual development proceeds. Several of the statements may appear to represent common sense or the way psychologists have always understood this topic. Actually, some of these generalizations are notable departures from traditional ones. Therefore, in the remainder of this chapter, I explore some of the changes in the concepts over the past several decades.

Spearman's Concept of General Ability

In 1904, Spearman published some observations that provided the foundation of psychologists' current concept of general intellectual ability. He analyzed students' marks in different school subjects, the type of research that could no doubt be replicated today with any set of academic transcripts. Then, as now, students who got higher grades in one subject tended to get higher grades in the other subjects. In other words, the correlation matrix describing the relationships among grades in different subjects showed what is called a "positive manifold," or a propensity for all these variables to be positively intercorrelated. The same kind of positive manifold is found when the intercorrelations among academic achievement tests instead of grades are calculated and when the matrix includes performance on tests involving novel tasks. However, sensory and motor skills do not show a similar positive manifold.

Spearman (1904) hypothesized that a single underlying general dimension or factor (*g*) could account for the systematic common variance in students' marks. His work was the origin of the statistical technique known as factor analysis, later developed more extensively by Thurstone (1931) and others. It turned out that Spearman's hypothesis of a single factor was not correct (i.e., more than a single factor is required to explain the common variance among such variables), but it is generally accepted that there is no more than a relatively small set of such underlying factors. Most contemporary theorists prefer a hierarchical scheme, with several correlated factors and a second-order general factor. Note also that the various factors that have been identified do not necessarily encompass the whole domain of intellectual development.

Current definitions of MR (e.g., Luckasson et al., 1992) continue to use the concept of general intelligence that owes much to Spearman's work. The 1992 definition of MR by the American Association on Mental Retardation has been criticized (MacMillan, Gresham, & Siperstein, 1993), but not because of its continued use of the *g* concept. Zigler, Balla, and Hodapp (1984) argued that measured general ability should be used as the sole criterion for defining MR. Detterman and Daniel (1989) showed that the intercorrelations among different cognitive abilities, and hence the variance accounted for by *g*, was greater among children and adults in the lower range of distribution of intelligence.

The concept of general ability also underlies the use of many commonplace measures, such as secondary school or undergraduate grade point averages or total Scholastic Aptitude Test or Graduate Record Examination scores in college and graduate admissions, or assessment procedures, such as the Wonderlic Personnel Test (Wonderlic & Hovland, 1939) in employment settings. Critics such as Ceci (1990) argued that the estimated percentage of variance accounted for by *g* might have been overestimated by the use of tasks with unnecessarily similar (e.g., verbal) components and that the apparent importance of *g* also might have been influenced by the similar curricula of children in school systems influenced by Western European educational philosophies. Similarly, Sternberg (1985) posited that psychologists' concept of intelligence should be far more comprehensive than psychometric *g* and should include, for example, adaptation to new environments, selection of environments, and creating environmental changes. This more comprehensive view of intelligence incorporates features of individual functioning that are immediately relevant to the conceptualization of MR.

Binet's Test and Its Successors

As is well-known, Binet and Simon (1905) devised the first practical intelligence test. In contrast to their predecessors in the study of individual differences in human performance, Binet and Simon had their participants, who were school-age children, carry out relatively complex tasks rather than simple sensory or motor ones. Binet's concept of intelligence seemed to be inherently a developmental one, and he used only test items that showed an increase in the percentage of children passing them with increasing age. Binet also seemed at least implicitly to endorse Spearman's (1904) concept of a general factor (*g*) in that the only items retained were those that showed high internal consistency with the items already selected. Binet and Simon's test and its successors significantly distinguished children with MR from typically developing children and significantly predicted academic and vocational performance (Schmidt & Hunter, 1981).

Yerkes and colleagues demonstrated during World War I that a group adaptation of the Binet test (the Army Alpha examination) and an alternative procedure with less of a verbal emphasis intended for illiterate people (the Army Beta) could be successfully used for mass screening of military recruits (Yerkes, 1921). In the process of doing so, they learned inadvertently that "mental age" (i.e., the overall test score) does not increase consistently (or smoothly) year after year into adulthood. The work of Yerkes and colleagues led the way toward the widespread use of standardized group intelligence tests that is prevalent today, both in educational systems and industry.

At Stanford University in California, Terman (1916, 1925) and colleagues developed a standardized version of Binet's scale and collected extensive normative information with it. This new standardized measure, the Stanford-Binet Intelligence Scale, first introduced the ratio IQ, an intelligence quotient, based on Stern's (1914) concept, but later replaced it with a standard score in order to correct for the fact (which is actually of some interest developmentally) that the standard deviations of total test scores changed with age. The mental age concept, which had some importance as a measure of a child's overall level of intellectual development, became somewhat submerged by the use of standard scores in relation to each child's age peers. Terman also began a longitudinal study of "gifted" children (those with high Binet scores) that is still under way with those gifted older participants who are still alive. (This study did not attempt to control for the socioeconomic advantages of the families of most of the original participants.)

Wechsler (1939) was the person most responsible for developing intelligence tests for adults. After more than 50 years, the various Wechsler tests still dominate the scene in the area of individual intellectual assessment for both children and adults. Long before others, Wechsler realized that the concepts of mental age and the ratio IQ were not suitable for use in describing adult ability. He pioneered the redefinition of "IQ" as a standard score in relation to a normative group of adults the same age as the participant. From a developmental viewpoint, however, this type of standard score has the shortcoming of masking any longitudinal decline in adult intellectual performance during later life. From World War I military examiners, Wechsler adapted the idea of a separate test of "performance" or nonverbal abilities. Wechsler's Performance IQ measure and the Wechsler subtest cluster often referred to as a measure of "freedom from distractibility," in combination with the Verbal IQ measure, have long served important purposes in individual clinical assessment.

The Question of Separate Functional Modules in the Brain

In Lashley's (1929) well-known research involving ablation of different parts of rodents' brains in relation to their maze-learning performance, it proved practically impossible to show that separate parts of the brain performed different functions. Instead, Lashley described the different brain structures as having "equipotentiality" and noted that it was the amount of brain tissue removed, rather than its location, that seemed to determine the degree of neurological impairment. Nevertheless, clinicians and researchers from Broca (1861) to Fodor (1983) have developed abundant evidence that there are different "modular" systems in the brain that are involved with different aspects of higher mental processes.

Thus, in adults with inborn or acquired neurological impairments, it is possible to identify distinct syndromes of cognitive deficits, each producing its own "notches" in the profile of abilities, so to speak, without necessarily bringing the other parts of the profile down. Luria (1973) emphasized that these syndromes are often not so clearly selective; thus, this use of the term *notches* may be a good hedge. In addition, there is the problem that one almost never has premorbid measures. For example, in distinct contrast to Broca's (1861) aphasia (involving mainly expressive speech and language impairment), there is Wernicke's aphasia (i.e., fluent expression but with impaired comprehension). Specific impairment of recent memory produced by damage to the hippocampus has been well documented (Milner, 1970). Right-hemisphere damage can produce other syndromes, such as specific deficits in facial recognition (termed *prosopagnosia*).

H. Gardner (1983) argued, on the basis of such findings and other evidence, that psychologists should speak of several different kinds of "intelligences" rather than emphasizing general ability so much. After all, in the highest ranges of human achievement, it is more common to see individuals with peak performance in one particular domain (a Mozart, Shakespeare, or Newton) than a pattern that generalizes across the whole profile of possible accomplishments. Gardner's work has had greater influence on educators than on scholars in the field of intelligence. This perspective is consistent with the trend toward using more "authentic" measures of achievement, such as portfolios of successful student projects, as opposed to standardized achievement tests in education.

That there is considerable specificity as well as generality in any cognitive task was shown by Gettinger and White (1979). They gave schoolchildren multiple opportunities to learn particular lessons involving academic tasks such as spelling or arithmetic. Time to learn such material proved to be a far better predictor of future performance on each type of task than either general intelligence or a one-time academic achievement test in the same area.

Part of the "modularity" of cognitive functioning is simply the result of differences in what people have learned during their lives. To paraphrase Will Rogers, all people are ignorant, only on different subjects. Independent of age, various systematic differences have been found between "experts" and "novices." Consider a study carried out by Chi (cited in Canfield & Ceci, 1992, p. 278). Expert younger chess players, compared with adults who were only beginning players, were far better at remembering after a single glance the location of pieces on a chessboard photographed during a game.

Piaget's Theory and Related Research

The research of Jean Piaget during the 1930s through the 1950s brought a fresh perspective to the study of child cognition. Indeed, from the standpoint of philosophy and theory, Piaget (1950) can almost be considered the founder of the study of intellectual development (Flavell, 1963). It is sometimes not realized, however, how much Piaget owed to the prior work of Baldwin (1894), from whom he derived his concepts of "assimilation" and "accommodation." According to Piaget (1950), a child typically at first assimilates a new environment by carrying out familiar routines there, only accommodating or changing these routines when necessary in response to the novel demands of the setting. In this way, an equilibrium develops that uniquely combines the child's prior experience and the requirements of the setting in an adaptive way. Piaget thus explained how cognitive growth occurs. Unfortunately, Piaget seemed to spend much more of his efforts studying the nature of each developmental stage or substage than the processes of transition between one stage and another. The research of Case (1985), a neo-Piagetian, addressed more clearly how these transitions occur. According to Case, at first during problem solving and exploration, a child might advance to a more sophisticated form of reasoning on a particular type of task. Later, a consolidation or automization process could occur in which the new form of reasoning would gradually be generalized to other tasks. Thus, during developmental epochs marked by transitions, a child may use more advanced strategies (or schemas) to solve some problems and less advanced ones to solve others.

Some of Piaget's work has consisted of filling in some of the content of cognitive development and elaborating the nature of the sensorimotor, preoperational, concrete operational, and formal operational stages of development (Flavell, 1963). Much research, particularly within American developmental psychology, has been devoted to the detailed study of certain Piagetian tasks. The most popular tasks concerned the infant's concept of object permanence, the conservation of number or of liquid quantity, and the use of systematic cognitive strategies in more advanced problems of physics and chemistry. Information-processing researchers using a particular task have often been able to demonstrate Piagetian phenomena in children younger than those studied by Piaget himself (Case, 1985). Such research often involves simplifications of the classic Piagetian tasks, and in some other cases it represents social or cultural differences in children's task performance.

A colleague of Piaget's, Inhelder (1968), carried out research linking Piagetian theoretical concepts to the field of MR. Not surprisingly, it turned out that people with MR fail to reach the Piagetian stage of formal operations. Indeed, the development of people with more severe levels of MR may be arrested at a preoperational or even a sensorimotor stage. The sequence of cognitive development appears to be much the same in typically developing children and those with MR, but the rate is much slower in the latter. Neo-Piagetians also have extended the applicability of such developmental models from cognitive activities to the social and emotional realms, for example with respect to social play, person perception, and prosocial behavior (Damon, 1983). This is reflected in the literature on developmental differences in problem solving by people with MR (Campione, Brown, & Ferrara, 1982).

The Issue of Infant–Adult Continuity

It became apparent early after the appearance of intelligence tests that IQ scores were relatively stable over time, enough so to permit meaningful predictions in the individual case. For a time early in the twentieth century it was thought that the IQ was constant, but this proved to be an exaggerated view. The problem is not just that IQs are not completely constant. It also is likely that at least part of this "constancy" is accounted for by the stability of environmental factors over time. After all, children tend to move through life not alone but as a part of a "convoy" of family members and peers. For example, in one study IQ scores from age 4 to 13 correlated .72, and environmental risk scores over the same interval of time correlated .76 (Sameroff, Seifer, Baldwin, & Baldwin, 1993). Moreover, the IQs of children have been shown to be less stable than those of adults. For children below about age 5, one may generally make a better prediction of their academic performance by knowing the parents' educational and occupational levels than from the child's test score.

Naturally, the question has arisen as to whether an individual's intellectual status can be measured in infancy and, if so, whether this would be predictive of adult ability. Indeed, infant tests were devised, at first simply as downward extensions of the Binet. Bayley (1969) developed the most widely accepted standardized mental test for infants and collected extensive and representative normative data for it. Despite the adequate psychometric properties of this test over short intervals of time, however, the Bayley scores of infants did not prove to have significant long-term predictive validity. Yet, Piaget's theories, among others, were based on the assumption that the "sensorimotor" abilities that are characteristic of infants provide the foundation for the trajectory of later cognitive development.

Piaget's theory turned out to be correct on the issue of continuity, but new assessment techniques were necessary to demonstrate this. Fantz (1964) pioneered the study of a novel visual recognition memory procedure in which the infant was shown a pair of visual displays. Observation was then made of the infant's choice. As infants matured, they showed an increasing preference for novel over familiar displays and thus indicated their ability to remember familiar faces and other such visual configurations. Eimas, Siqueland, Jusczyk, and Vigorito (1971) developed a habituation procedure in which the infant sucked on a pacifier in order to produce a certain repeated "vocal" sound. After the infant's rate of sucking declined, the sound was changed in some subtle way (e.g., from "bababa" to "papapa"). An increase in the infant's rate of sucking following this change signified the infant's ability to detect the change. Bornstein and Sigman (1986), in an influential review, documented the significant predictive value of such laboratory measures of infant attention and memory, whether assessed using visual, auditory, or other sensory modalities. Their conclusions were confirmed by a subsequent meta-analysis based on a larger sample of studies (McCall & Carriger, 1993). The procedures used in assessing infants' attention and memory are far more elaborate and cumbersome than traditional test items and are less reliable over the short term. Nevertheless, these new procedures do have a significant predictive value, opening the way toward the ultimate development of practical procedures for assessing infant cognitive processes and screening for risk of intellectual disabilities (Columbo & Fagen, 1990).

Cattell's Concept of Fluid and Crystallized Ability and Related Research

There are many populations of individuals who might have perfectly adequate cognitive skills, but who are not able to demonstrate these on traditional intelligence tests. The development of nonverbal "performance" tests of intellectual ability has already been noted in relation to the evaluation of illiterate recruits for the U.S. Army during World War I. Other difficult-to-evaluate groups include those with sensory or motor handicaps (e.g., people with hearing impairments, visual impairments, or cerebral palsy).

It is particularly challenging to try to assess the abilities of people with linguistic and cultural backgrounds different from those of the original American normative populations. Because tests are made up of materials representing one particular culture, some kind of anthropological inventory of the contrasting "target" culture would seem to be necessary in order to devise a suitable translated version. Even that seems insufficient. It is clearly going to be necessary to go beyond "tests" and study complex cognitive activities in their natural context. Ceci (1990) pointed out the incorrectness of the belief that IQ has much to do with intelligent performances in many real-world settings. For example, IQ seems to be minimally correlated with some of the complex cognitive performances of natives of South Pacific islands (Lancy & Strathern, 1981; Rivers, 1926), people in the outlying regions of the former Soviet Union (Vygotsky, 1934/1962), Kung San hunters in Africa (Super, 1980), dairy workers (Scribner, 1984), or expert racetrack handicappers (Ceci & Liker, 1986).

Cattell (1949) used a different strategy, that of trying to devise or select novel cognitive tasks that would not be representative of any existing culture, in order to produce a "culture-free" or "culture-fair" intelligence test. Unfortunately, this effort did not succeed in eliminating differences in test scores among different cultural groups. However, this effort no doubt played a role in the development of the theory of crystallized and fluid abilities (Cattell, 1963; J. L. Horn & Cattell, 1966; J. L. Horn & Hofer, 1992). Crystallized abilities are those that are highly practiced as a result of the emphasis placed on them at school, on the job, or in the kinds of experiences that are typical of a culture. Examples from the Wechsler subtests include defining words and recalling familiar information. Fluid abilities are those manifested in tasks that are novel to the individual, such as (for most of us) the Kohs Block Designs (Wechsler, 1939), which require copying visual patterns using blocks with red and white painted surfaces. Crystallized abilities are not necessarily verbal, nor are fluid abilities necessarily nonverbal.

Obviously, at birth there is no such thing as a crystallized ability; all cognitive challenges represent the use of fluid ability. Some skills become more and more crystallized as development proceeds, perhaps by means of the kind of differentiation and hierarchical integration of which Werner (1957) spoke. By adulthood, the difference between fluid and crystallized abilities has become distinct, and the two increasingly begin to diverge.

Cattell's (1963) hypothesis was that as adult age increases, the individual continues to carry out familiar (crystallized) activities without loss of skill, perhaps even posting modest gains in performance, despite the various gradual sensory and motor changes characteristic of aging. However, after a peak at about 20 years of age, fluid ability appears to decline more steeply than crystallized ability. Perhaps second-language learning could be an example of a fluid ability (and of a certain modular system within the brain as well). Young children seem to learn new languages relatively effortlessly. However, this task is far more difficult for an adult or an elderly person, who will at best speak the new language with a foreign accent.

Early research on adult cognitive development (e.g., based on the original Wechsler adult normative samples) was cross-sectional. Such studies made it appear that there were relatively steep declines in all ability domains as adult age increased. However, these studies confounded age with educational levels. In fact, research has revealed a marked influence of education on the skills assessed by such tests. The direct effects of schooling on IQ tests have been confirmed by findings of small IQ decrements associated with the summer vacations of school-age children (e.g., Heyns, 1978). Subsequent longitudinal studies of the Wechsler adult test (e.g., the work of W. A. Owens, 1953) made it clear that, at least for verbal skills and other highly practiced domains, there was little decline as adults grew older.

J. L. Horn and Hofer (1992) presented some refinements within the research tradition of Cattell. They described some abilities (e.g., fluid reasoning, short-term memory, processing speed) as being "vulnerable" to the effects of aging. Other abilities (e.g., acculturation knowledge, long-term memory, quantitative knowledge) tend to be "maintained" as aging proceeds. Thus, the same conceptual distinction described by Cattell (1963) as "fluid versus crystallized" is still evident. Horn and Hofer's hypothesis about why some abilities are maintained so well with age is that they constitute a dense, highly integrated network. This network is thought to exist both in terms of cognitive or associative cross-linkages and actual neurons. Thus, if certain threads to a particular "node" are lost, many other connecting threads remain by which the item of information can be retrieved. Salthouse (1988) devised an elaborate theory of spreading activation and a computer simulation of such a network to explain cognitive aging.

Dementia and Other Pathological Aspects of Aging

Just as MR or "amentia" includes diverse pathologies affecting early intellectual development, so dementia is an umbrella label for diverse forms of pathology associated with general mental deterioration in adulthood or old age. There are a number of important differences between the two conditions. One is the important need for diagnosticians working with adults to rule out "pseudodementia" caused by depression or polypharmacy (there is no corresponding differential diagnostic issue in the cognitive assessment of children, although the concept of depression occurring in childhood is now accepted). Another is the much more prominent role of memory disorders in early dementia than in MR. Finally, although MR typically has a static course, dementia is usually progressive, ending in the person's death. There also are similarities between MR and dementia, perhaps even at a biological level. For example, Down syndrome, a genetic etiology of MR, apparently includes an increased risk for Alzheimer's disease in adulthood, at least in terms of findings of neuritic plaques and neurofibrillary tangles at autopsy. Plaques and tangles have been found to be common among young adults with Down syndrome who are asymptomatic for dementia (Wisniewski & Rabe, 1986). (It can be difficult at a behavioral level to diagnose dementia superimposed on MR.) As an additional complication, Down syndrome typically involves a gradual decrease in IQ even in childhood (Pueschel, 1984).

Dementia is associated with Alzheimer's disease (i.e., senile dementia of the Alzheimer's type), multiple strokes, multiple head injuries, and other causes. It typically involves a lowered IQ and the loss of many different cognitive skills (Folstein, Folstein, & McHugh, 1975), even well-practiced ones, although some isolated skills (e.g., playing familiar tunes on an organ) may be preserved. According to J. L. Horn and Hofer (1992), brain damage is likely to have a greater and a more lasting effect on "vulnerable" than on "maintained" abilities. Thus, brain damage would tend to magnify the effects of nonpathological aging.

Conclusion: Contemporary Cognitive Neuroscience

Even though hundreds of different biological syndromes have been identified that are associated with MR or dementia, there is still a fundamental lack of knowledge about what (if anything) these syndromes have in common that causes such generalized cognitive deficits. Similarly, the neurodevelopmental factors underlying the dramatic cognitive changes seen from infancy to adulthood and from adulthood to old age are largely unknown.

There is great hope that the "decade of the brain," as the 1990s have been labeled by the U.S. government, and surely the next century will bring great strides in cognitive neuroscience that will unlock some of the mysteries of intellectual development as well as many other puzzles (Plomin & McClearn, 1993). The Human Genome Project (T. F. Lee, 1991) will be productive in this respect because so many genetically based inborn errors of metabolism associated with MR already have been identified. The use of computed tomography scanning and magnetic resonance imaging will help elucidate many aspects of the neuropathology of MR and dementia, without the necessity of awaiting autopsy data. Positron emission tomographic scans, cerebral blood flow studies, and the study of cortical evoked potentials will no doubt help to uncover many of the brain structures and processes associated with different types of human performance on cognitive tasks such as those listed by J. L. Horn and Hofer (1992). It seems likely that the entire enterprise of studying human intellectual development will be revolutionized in ways that cannot now be anticipated in detail. Scientifically exciting times lie ahead, well beyond the present horizons.

6

The Structure of Adaptive Behavior

Keith F. Widaman and Kevin S. McGrew

For more than 30 years, the construct of adaptive behavior has been a core component in the diagnosis and classification of mental retardation (MR). To be identified as having MR, a person must exhibit both significantly subaverage intelligence and deficits in adaptive behavior during the developmental period. The dimensional structure of the adaptive behavior domain is an important concern because this structure provides the taxonomy of types of adaptive behaviors on which people may exhibit deficient levels of performance. In this chapter, we discuss a number of issues that affect any evaluation of adaptive behaviors and their dimensional structure. These issues include (a) the nature of adaptive behaviors, which enables the specification of behaviors included under the rubric "adaptive behaviors"; (b) the alternative theoretical structures proposed for this behavioral domain; (c) methodological considerations that might influence the outcomes of empirical studies of the structure of adaptive behaviors; and (d) the findings reported in empirical studies of the adaptive behavior domain, including both the structure of adaptive behaviors and life span developmental trends that support the distinctions among different dimensions of behavior.

The Nature of Adaptive Behaviors

Before discussing the structure of adaptive behavior, we first discuss the nature of adaptive behaviors. Adaptive behaviors are the behavioral skills that people typically exhibit when dealing with the environmental demands they confront. Because adaptive behaviors involve behavioral skills, the behaviors assessed using measures of adaptive behavior are related to behaviors encompassed by measures of physical and mental skills, abilities, or intelligence. Traditionally, measures of intellectual and

---

This work was supported in part by Grants HD-21056 and HD-22953 from the National Institute of Child Health and Human Development and an intramural grant from the Academic Senate, University of California, Riverside to Keith F. Widaman and a contract from the University of Minnesota's Rehabilitation Research and Training Center to Kevin S. McGrew. We thank John Jacobson for his suggestions for improving earlier versions of this chapter.

behavioral skills have been identified as measures of *maximal* performance. That is, measures of intellectual and behavioral skills attempt to determine the optimal level of performance of which a person is capable. To pass an item on a measure of intellectual skill, the person being assessed must show that she or he can perform the task presented by the item, regardless of whether she or he typically exhibits this level of performance.

The concept of "ability as maximal performance" contrasts in informative ways with measures of adaptive behavior. Measures of adaptive behavior are usually measures of *typical* performance, assessing the level of skill a person typically displays when responding to challenges in his or her environment. As a result, items measuring adaptive behavior often implicitly assess motivational components of behavior. Thus, to exhibit a form of behavior typically, the person must be motivated to perform the behavior in most situations that she or he confronts. This motivation may be a stable traitlike attribute of the person or may result from contingencies in the environment. Nonetheless, the behavioral capacities assessed as adaptive behaviors implicitly include motivation to perform the behaviors in typical life situations.

Theoretical Structures

Implicit Approaches

Virtually every instrument for assessing adaptive behaviors groups items into an implicit structure of adaptive behaviors. For example, the AAMR Adaptive Behavior Scale (ABS; Nihira, Foster, Shellhaas, & Leland, 1969, 1975) contains one major division of behaviors, between adaptive behaviors and maladaptive behaviors. Additional distinctions are drawn among 10 domains making up adaptive behaviors, including independent functioning, physical development, economic activity, and numbers and time. Some domains are further subdivided into subdomains (e.g., the language development domain is broken down into subdomains of expression, comprehension, and social language development), whereas other domains are not broken down into subdomains. Maladaptive behaviors assessed by the ABS are categorized into 14 domains, such as antisocial behavior and withdrawal, and none of these domains is further divided into subdomains.

This domain structure of the ABS is one attempt to characterize the structure of adaptive and maladaptive behaviors. However, to verify the validity of a conceptual structure, several patterns of convergent and discriminant validation should be evident in empirical data. First, items within a subdomain should be consistent, having high internal consistency and similar relations with other variables, to justify placement within a single subdomain. Second, subdomains within a given domain should obey somewhat different psychological laws to justify distinctions among the subdomains; however, subdomains also should still exhibit some "family resemblance" in their relations with other variables to justify their placement within a single domain. Finally, domain scores should exhibit differential relations with other measures of individual functioning, or follow different psychological laws, to justify the conceptual distinctions among the several domains. At this time, systematic investigations to demonstrate the patterns of empirical findings just proposed have not been undertaken with the ABS. As a result, the structure of adaptive behavior implicitly proposed has yet to be fully supported by empirical investigation.

Explicit Summaries

Contrasting with implicit approaches are attempts to provide explicit delineations of the structure of adaptive behaviors. These explicit approaches consist of summaries of the types, or domains, of adaptive behaviors and are informed by reviews of the item content of measures of adaptive behavior, as well as results of empirical studies, that reveal different results for subsets of adaptive behaviors.

Adaptive behaviors. In their authoritative review of adaptive behavior, Meyers, Nihira, and Zetlin (1979) summarized the types of behavioral domains included in existing measures of adaptive behavior. On the basis of this review, Meyers et al. suggested that seven domains of adaptive skills and competence are commonly represented in adaptive behavior scales. These domains are (a) self-help skills, including the abilities to satisfy personal needs such as feeding, dressing, toilet training, and grooming; (b) physical development, assessing development and coordination of basic perceptual–motor skills, which likely are antecedent to the acquisition of specific self-help skills; (c) communication skills, including articulation, expression, comprehension, social interaction, and negotiation with others; (d) cognitive functioning, involving, among other skills, reading, writing, and the ability to deal with numbers and time; (e) domestic and occupational activities, which include chores such as cleaning, cooking, and washing, and occupational activities such as assembly of parts, operation of machinery, and job search skills; (f) self-direction and responsibility, dealing with the originating and engaging in purposive activity based on the person's own volition, which relates to assessment of autonomy and motivation; and (g) socialization, assessing the degree of interaction and cooperation with others, consideration for and helping others, and participation in group activities.

More recently, Kamphaus (1987) offered a five-domain structure of the types of behavior assessed by major adaptive behavior inventories, a structure consisting of a slight rearrangement of the domains posited by Meyers et al. (1979). The five domains cited by Kamphaus, together with reference to similar domains from Meyers et al., are (a) motor/physical activities, essentially the physical development domain from Meyers et al.; (b) self-help/independence, similar to the self-help domain in Meyers et al.; (c) interpersonal/social, corresponding to the socialization domain of Meyers et al.; (d) responsibility/vocational, largely a combination of the domestic and occupational activities domains and the self-direction and responsibility domains from Meyers et al.; and (e) cognitive/communication, a combination of the communication and cognitive functioning domains proposed by Meyers et al.

Maladaptive behaviors. The structure of maladaptive behaviors was simpler for Meyers et al. (1979) to characterize. Across a number of studies, there appear to be two general types of maladaptive behavior: (a) social maladaption, covering primarily externally directed aggressive, destructive, and antisocial types of behavior in which other people or others' property were in danger of hurt or damage; and (b) personal maladaption, representing primarily internally directed self-aggressive and autisticlike behaviors.

Because of the comprehensive nature of their reviews, the five to seven domains that Kamphaus (1987) and Meyers et al. (1979) outlined merit consideration as a first cut at the "primary" dimensions for the adaptive behavior domain, as do the two dimensions characterizing the maladaptive behavior domain. The next, necessary step is to determine whether these conceptual distinctions are reflected in empirical data, a topic discussed later.

Methodological Considerations

Study Design

In the interpretation of results from studies of the structure of adaptive behavior, methodological aspects of these studies must be considered in detail. Two important aspects of study design involve the selection of participants and the selection of variables.

Subject sampling. Many statistical procedures invoke random sampling of participants from a specifiable population to ensure the accuracy of results, such as significance tests. However, many studies use subject samples of convenience, which may produce results that differ from those based on random samples. Future research should explore the impact of this issue.

Of perhaps greater importance, the aims of a study often lead to restrictions on the selection of participants. That is, participants may be selected only from restricted portions of the life span (e.g., children, adolescents) or from restricted ranges of ability (e.g., only people with mild MR). Restrictions of these types may influence patterns of results, leading to different outcomes from those based on less restricted samples of participants.

At present, only a small number of adaptive behavior scales have been normed or tested on large, unrestricted, representative samples of participants, and few studies of the structure or development of adaptive behaviors have been based on comprehensive samples. As a result, firm conclusions regarding the structure of adaptive behaviors may be premature; future research should supplement existing literature on these issues.

Variable sampling. Of comparable importance to the sampling of participants is the sampling of variables in investigations of the structure of adaptive behavior. The term *referent generality* refers to the notion that measures selected for a study should reflect the population of measures in the given domain (Heal, 1985; Heal & Fujiura, 1984). To ensure that a representative structure of the adaptive behavior domain is obtained, researchers should address the issue of referent generality, including items assessing all types of behaviors that fall under the rubric of adaptive behaviors, to the extent possible. If item samples differ in breadth of coverage, differences in the resulting structural representations are likely to occur.

Items on adaptive behavior scales assess behaviors that are observable and typically or often occur in everyday settings. Most item samples include content reflecting behaviors that are developmentally typical of children and range to behaviors typical of young adults. Thus, both breadth and developmental range are key dimensions for item sampling.

One additional issue arises in studies of the structure of adaptive behavior. To define a separate common factor, three variables must be present in the data set to identify the factor well. If only a single indicator variable for a particular type of behavior is included, then a factor representing this type of behavior cannot be adequately defined. As discussed next, differences across studies in the selection of variables for analysis have contributed to variation across studies in the structures of adaptive behavior identified.

Analytic Techniques

One set of problems that arise when evaluating studies of the structure of adaptive behavior is the analytic methods used in studies. A short review of analytic choices at various stages of the conduct of a factor analysis is offered here; more comprehensive treatments are available in books on factor analysis, such as Gorsuch (1983) and Comrey and Lee (1992).

Exploratory factor analysis. Exploratory factor methods are used in situations in which the researcher has no explicit hypotheses regarding the pattern of loadings of variables on factors. In effect, exploratory factor analysis is used to identify factor structures rather than to verify factor structures based on a priori hypotheses. Given a matrix of correlations among measures of adaptive behavior, three major decisions must be made to conduct the analysis. These three decisions involve the choice of a factor analytic model, the determination of the number of factors, and the choice of a rotation for the factors extracted. Most researchers have opted to use principal-components extraction of factors, selecting all components with eigenvalues greater than 1.0, and varimax orthogonal rotation of the components retained.

Unfortunately, these common analytic choices frequently lead to problems in the interpretation of results. Among others, Widaman (1990, 1993) showed that principal-components extraction of factors often leads to serious levels of positive bias in factor pattern loadings and negative bias in correlations among factors. Cliff (1988) noted several crucial problems with the "eigenvalues greater than or equal to 1.0" rule for the number of factors, and Monte Carlo studies (e.g., Zwick & Velicer, 1986) have shown that this rule is an inconsistent indicator of the correct number of factors. Finally, orthogonal rotations are seldom appropriate for behavioral domains, such as adaptive behavior, in which the resulting factors are likely to be moderately correlated.

As a result, researchers should use analytic techniques that are more adequate for the domain of adaptive behavior. Specifically, researchers should use (a) a common factor method of factor extraction (e.g., principal axes, maximum likelihood), which involves estimation of communalities; (b) one or more well-founded tests for the number of factors such as the scree test (Cattell, 1966) or the parallel analysis criterion (Montanelli & Humphreys, 1976; see Widaman, Gibbs, & Geary, 1987); and (c) an oblique analytic rotation to simple structure, such as the promax rotation or the Harris-Kaiser orthoblique rotation (see Gorsuch, 1983). These procedures have produced well-defined factor solutions in the mental ability domain for many years and also represent adaptive behavior factors well (Widaman et al., 1987).

Confirmatory factor analysis. In contrast to exploratory factor analysis, confirmatory factor methods are used in situations in which the researcher has clear, explicit hypotheses regarding the pattern of loadings of variables on factors. Thus, confirmatory factor analysis is used to verify whether data are consistent with proposed factor structures based on a priori hypotheses, which are derived from prior research and/or theory. During the past 15 years, confirmatory factor analysis has become more widely used in psychological research, although this method has been used only sparingly in studies of adaptive behavior to date. This is partly because of the small number of direct replication studies of adaptive behaviors. As this method becomes more widely used, greater attention to the details of analyses will be required. At present, optimal ways of performing confirmatory factor analysis are still in flux; details regarding these types of analyses can be found in Bollen (1989), Jöreskog and Sörbom (1989, 1993), and Loehlin (1992).

Empirical Findings

Research on adaptive behaviors may be informed by a historical consideration of research on mental abilities. The structure of the mental ability domain has undergone considerable revision and expansion since the early studies by Spearman (1927) on general intelligence and those by Thurstone (1938), and Thurstone and Thurstone (1941) on the primary mental abilities, which usually had seven to nine dimensions. Considerable consensus is now emerging that as many as 60–70 first-stratum, narrow dimensions and 8–10 second-stratum, broader dimensions may be needed to span the primary ability domain (Carroll, 1989, 1993) and that the intellectual ability domain is a hierarchically structured set of abilities of varying breadth, ranging from narrow to broad (Gustafsson, 1984; J. L. Horn, 1986, 1988; J. L. Horn & Hofer, 1992). Findings of differential life span aging trends for different ability dimensions (J. L. Horn, 1988) attest further to the validity of the factor analytically derived factors of mental ability.

The relative utility of the empirically based, factor analytic approach continues to be demonstrated for the intelligence domain, and the implications for the adaptive behavior domain are no less significant. Factor analytic research on adaptive behavior, pursued in earnest for about 20 or 30 years, is in its infancy relative to research on mental abilities. Although much work remains to be done, some areas of agreement on the structure of adaptive behavior are discernible.

Factor Analyses of the Adaptive Behavior Domain

Exploratory factor analyses. At present, two major positions on the structure of adaptive behaviors may be discerned: a unifactorial position and a multifactorial one. These parallel the distinction in the intellectual ability domain between the two-factor theory of Spearman (1927), in which a single factor termed *g* was hypothesized to be the single source of common variance among tests of ability, and multifactorial positions proposed by several researchers, such as the primary mental abilities of Thurstone (1938) and the theory of fluid (*Gf*) and crystallized (*Gc*) intelligence of Cattell (1963, 1971) and J. L. Horn (1986, 1988; J. L. Horn & Hofer, 1992).

Nihira (1969a, 1969b) was perhaps the first to propose a single-factor conception for the adaptive behavior domain. In these two studies, Nihira analyzed the 10 adaptive and 12 maladaptive domain scores from the Adaptive Behavior Checklist, an early version of the ABS. Data were obtained for three samples of children and adolescents (with sample sizes ranging from 102 to 107) and one sample of adults ($n = 919$). For each of the four samples, Nihira reported that a single factor, Personal Independence, represented the relations among the 10 adaptive behavior domain scores, although two factors, Social Maladaption and Personal Maladaption, were required to represent the 12 maladaptive domain scores.

More recently, Bruininks, McGrew, and Maruyama (1988) analyzed data from seven samples of participants, including several samples of people without MR. The five age-graded samples of people with MR spanned the range from preschool through adulthood; sample sizes were fairly large (median sample size = 460). The two samples of individuals with MR were children (mean age = 10.0 years, n = 110) and adolescents or adults (mean age = 25.9 years, n = 178). The variables analyzed were the 14 subscales of the Scales of Independent Behavior (SIB; Bruininks, Woodcock, Weatherman, & Hill, 1984). The general outcome of these analyses was that the single-factor hypothesis received the strongest support, as Bruininks et al. reported that only a single factor was found in four of the seven samples. Across all seven samples, even in those samples for which more than a single factor was extracted, Bruininks et al. suggested that a General Development factor or a Personal Independence factor was a dominant feature, supporting a single major dimension of adaptive behavior across the multiple samples.

At least three additional studies have indicated that a single factor represented the relations among the subscales of one or another adaptive behavior measure (Hug, Barclay, Collins, & Lamp, 1978; Katz-Garris, Hadley, Garris, & Barnhill, 1980; Millsap, Thackrey, & Cook, 1987). These researchers tended to analyze a small number of variables, failing to provide multiple indicators of domains hypothesized by Meyers et al. (1979) and Kamphaus (1987) and thereby limiting the factorial structures that could be found.

On the other hand, a number of studies have provided fairly strong support for a multiple-factor conception of the domain of adaptive behavior. For example, Nihira (1976) analyzed the 25 subdomain scores from the AAMR Adaptive Behavior Scale obtained on eight samples of people with MR. The participants in the eight samples were 4–69 years of age (median sample size = 400, N = 3,354). Three comparable factors represented the subdomain scores across the eight samples of participants, although a fourth factor was required at the youngest age levels. The three factors were Personal Self-Sufficiency, Community Self-Sufficiency, and Personal–Social Responsibility. Although these three factors appear to be replicable and interpretable, they bear no simple relation to the domains posited by Meyers et al. (1979) or Kamphaus (1987).

Widaman et al. (1987) reported analyses of data from 14 samples of people who had mild, moderate, or severe MR; they analyzed scores from the Client Development Evaluation Report, a 66-item instrument developed by the California State Department of Developmental Services (1978). A two-step analytic strategy was used. The first step involved item-based factor analyses of data from two samples of more than 3,000 people, which led to a six-factor structure. The second step commenced with the formation of 3 parcels of items for each factor, in which each item parcel was the sum of a subset of items for a given factor. The resulting 18 parcels—3 parcels for each of six factors—were then factor analyzed for each of the 14 samples.

The 14 samples were drawn from a statewide sample of 68,000 people cross-classified on the basis of residence, age, and level of MR. The 14 samples ranged in size from 200 to 1,000 people, resulting in a total of 9,464 participants. Six factors were obtained for each sample, and factors were simple across all samples. Four of the factors represented dimensions defined by adaptive behavior items; these factors were characterized as

(a) Motor Development, measuring gross and fine motor skills, ambulation, and basic eating and toileting skills; (b) Independent Living Skills, assessing skills in completing household chores, dressing, bathing, making food, and washing dishes; (c) Cognitive Competence, assessing receptive and expressive language, reading and writing skills, handling money, and other cognitive skills; and (d) Social Competence, measuring the formation and maintenance of friendships, interaction with others, and participation in group activities. These four factors correspond well to four of the five domains discussed by Kamphaus (1987) as well as to domains described recently by Greenspan and Granfield (1992).

The remaining two factors were defined by parcels of items assessing maladaptive behaviors. These factors were termed Social Maladaption, which assesses aggressive behaviors, resistiveness, destruction of others' property, temper tantrums, and negative reactions to frustration, and Personal Maladaption, which includes the frequency and severity of self-injurious behavior, hyperactivity, and presence of repetitive body movements. These two factors correspond well to the two dimensions discussed by Meyers et al. (1979) as spanning the maladaptive behavior domain and reflect the emotional competence domain described by Greenspan and Granfield (1992).

Several additional multifactor studies also have been published. At least six studies were based on item-level analyses (Levine & Elzey, 1968; Nihira, 1978; W. M. Reynolds, 1981; Silverman, Silver, Lubin, & Sersen, 1983; Sparrow & Cicchetti, 1978, 1984), and at least five additional studies were based on subscale-level factor analyses (Guarnaccia, 1976; Lambert & Nicoll, 1976; Owens & Bowling, 1970; Song et al., 1984; Walsh & McConkey, 1989). The factor structures from these studies varied somewhat from study to study, primarily because of the differential selection of item content. However, each of the four adaptive behavior factors from Widaman et al. (1987)—Motor Competence, Independent Living Skills, Cognitive Competence, and Social Competence—received support from several of the studies cited.

An interesting study by McGrew, Ittenbach, Bruininks, and Hill (1991) focused on the maladaptive part of the adaptive behavior domain. Analyses were performed on 16 scale scores from the maladaptive section of the SIB (Bruininks et al., 1984); analyses were performed on 12 samples of participants (N = 8,255), who represented the life span and all levels of MR (mild through profound). Although two- to four-factor solutions appeared across samples, all factors appeared to reflect the two primary dimensions of Personal Maladaption and Social Maladaption.

In reviews of exploratory factor analytic studies of the structure of adaptive behaviors, McGrew and Bruininks (1989) emphasized findings with regard to a single Personal Competence dimension, whereas Widaman, Borthwick-Duffy, and Little (1991) stressed the need for multiple factors to represent the domain. However, both McGrew and Bruininks (1989) and Widaman et al. (1991) argued that differences in the breadth of variables factored may have led to important differences across studies in the number of factors identified. For example, McGrew and Bruininks found that item-based studies reported the largest number of factors (8–10 factors), followed by item parcel (3–6 factors) and subscale studies (1–2 factors). This suggests that, depending on the breadth of the adaptive behavior variables analyzed (i.e., items, item parcels, and subscales), different studies may identify adaptive behavior factors at different strata in an adaptive behavior hierarchy. Such an interpretation would parallel the synthesis by Carroll (1993) of factor analytic research on human intellectual abilities, in which he identified three levels of cognitive factors varying in breadth or generality (i.e., many narrow first-stratum factors, a small number of broad second-stratum factors, and a single broad third-stratum factor).

Confirmatory factor analyses. Only a small number of confirmatory factor analytic studies have been published. In one study, McGrew and Bruininks (1990) analyzed 11 scale scores: 8 scales from the SIB and 3 scales from the Woodcock-Johnson Tests of Cognitive Ability. Analyses were performed on data from three samples consisting primarily of people without disabilities: early childhood, childhood, and adolescent or adult (sample sizes varied from 100 to 192). The hypothesized four-factor structure was confirmed in each sample; the four factors were labeled Physical Competence (i.e., Motor), Practical Intelligence (similar to Independent Living Skills), Conceptual Intelligence (i.e., Cognitive Competence), and Emotional Competence (a combination of Personal and Social Maladaption). The only variation across samples occurred for the early childhood sample, in which the Physical Competence and Practical Intelligence factors collapsed onto a single dimension.

In a second study, Ittenbach, Spiegel, McGrew, and Bruininks (1992) analyzed 10 scale scores from the Early Screening Profiles (Harrison et al., 1990), based on a sample of 183 young children with and without disabilities. Three latent variables were specified and confirmed; these factors were labeled Physical Competence, Practical Intelligence, and Conceptual Intelligence. These factors appear to be similar to three of the factors reported by McGrew and Bruininks (1990) and to three of the factors found by Widaman et al. (1987).

McGrew, Bruininks, and Johnson (in press) described analyses of 17 variables: 10 scale scores from the Inventory for Client and Agency Planning (Bruininks, Hill, Weatherman, & Woodcock, 1986), 4 scale scores from the Woodcock-Johnson Psycho-Educational Battery–Revised (Woodcock & Johnson, 1989), and 3 experimental social scale scores adapted from items on the Checklist of Adaptive Living Skills (Morreau & Bruininks, 1989). Analyses were performed for samples of students with mild (n = 180) and moderate-to-severe (n = 143) MR. After deleting three SIB scales because of insufficient variability, the remaining 14 scale scores were specified to represent four latent variables. With minor amounts of model respecification, the four-factor structure held well; these four factors were labeled Practical Intelligence, Conceptual Intelligence, Social Intelligence, and Emotional Competence (a merger of Personal and Social Maladaption).

Recently, Widaman, Reise, and Clatfelter (1994) performed a series of six item-level confirmatory factor analyses, one analysis on each of the six factors reported by Widaman et al. (1987). That is, one analysis was based on the 12 items making up the Motor Competence factor of the Client Development Evaluation Report, a second analysis used the 9 items making up the Independent Living Skills factor, and so on. All analyses were based on a sample of 4,000 people with MR, 1,000 at each of the levels of mild, moderate, severe, and profound. Each of the six analyses revealed that item content could be subdivided further. For example, four more narrow factors were found for the Cognitive Competence domain, factors reflecting Money Handling, Functional Academics, Language, and Nonverbal Communication. However, a higher order Cognitive Competence represented well the relations among these four more narrow dimensions, explaining the majority of the variance of each of these more narrow factors. The Widaman et al. (1994) results confirmed the six-factor structure of adaptive and maladaptive behaviors of Widaman et al. (1987), although these six factors emerged as second-order factors in the Widaman et al. (1994) study.

Finally, Widaman, Stacy, and Borthwick-Duffy (1993) reported the results of a multitrait–multimethod evaluation of four dimensions from the Client Development Evaluation Report: Cognitive Competence, Social Competence, Personal Maladaption, and Social Maladaption. The sample consisted of 157 people with moderate, severe, or profound MR who were residing in a large state residential facility. One indicator for each dimension was developed from the Comprehensive Development Evaluation Report; two additional indicators for each dimension were obtained from semantic differential ratings completed by day-shift and evening-shift personnel who knew the target participants well. A series of structural equation models were fit to the data, following suggestions by Widaman (1985). In short, the four dimensions of adaptive and maladaptive behavior were well confirmed, with moderate to high levels of convergent validity, clear discriminant validity among the factors, and modest levels of method variance. The multitrait–multimethod approach is frequently offered as a particularly demanding form of construct validation; the findings from the Widaman et al. (1993) study provide strong support for the validity of the factors studied, and future research should seek to extend this approach to validation.

Life Span Developmental Changes

Given the consistent factor analytic structures for adaptive and maladaptive behaviors, issues related to life span change in levels of adaptive behavior naturally arise. Only a brief overview of relevant results can be given here; fuller accounts are available elsewhere (Widaman et al., 1991).

In a large cross-sectional study, Janicki and Jacobson (1986) presented data on more than 10,500 people with MR who ranged in age from 45 to 90+ years. The data were obtained from the New York Developmental Disabilities Information System, which includes eight scales derived from the Minnesota Developmental Programming System. The most prominent findings varied as a function of the level of MR. For the mild and moderate levels, people aged 50–54 years and older appeared to decline on gross motor and independent living skills, but they maintained levels of functioning on the remaining six scales through 70–74 years of age, on which some aging losses were shown. By contrast, people with severe or profound MR exhibited early losses only for gross motor skills, with aging losses evident only late in life (e.g., after 70 years of age or later) on each of the remaining seven scales. Although these findings could be the result of cross-sectional measurement if, for example, older cohorts had different experiences than younger cohorts, the results are consistent with the findings of a related study by Eyman and Widaman (1987).

Eyman and Widaman (1987) analyzed data on more than 30,000 people with MR assessed using the Client Development Evaluation Report. The participants had been assessed once each year for 4 consecutive years so that both cross-sectional and semilongitudinal approaches to estimating life span aging trends could be used (see Eyman & Widaman, 1987; Widaman et al., 1991). The most notable findings were that the comparability of cross-sectional and semilongitudinal aging trends varied as a function of type of ability and level of MR and the different dimensions of adaptive behavior showed different life span aging trends.

Differential aging as a function of type of adaptive behavior also has been shown in other related studies. For example, Zigman, Schupf, Lubin, and Silverman (1987) contrasted the aging trends for 2,144 adults with Down syndrome against trends for a comparison sample of 4,172 people without Down syndrome. Data were obtained on the same eight behavioral scales from the Minnesota Developmental Programming System as used by Janicki and Jacobson (1986). Zigman et al. formed two composite scales, one was termed *Daily Living Skills* (a combination of five motor and independent living scales) and the other was labeled *Cognitive Skills* (a combination of three cognitive scales). Differential aging declines were found between the people with Down syndrome and those without Down syndrome. Interestingly, the relative declines in performance by the people with Down syndrome were much more pronounced for the Daily Living Skills composite than for the Cognitive Skills composite.

These findings are only a sampling of results on life span aging of adaptive behaviors by people with MR. As noted earlier, summaries of these and additional studies are available elsewhere (e.g., Widaman et al., 1991). However, we note that the documenting of differential aging across the multiple dimensions of adaptive behavior supports the notion of a multifactorial structure of adaptive behaviors. If all adaptive behaviors exhibited similar life span aging trends, then a single, general dimension of adaptive behavior might be sufficient to encompass the entire domain of adaptive behavior. However, as the preceding studies have shown, life span aging trends vary across dimensions of adaptive behavior, supporting the need for multiple factors of adaptive behavior in order to characterize well aging trends for adaptive behavior.

Conclusion

The results of both exploratory and confirmatory factor analyses of indexes of adaptive behavior support strongly the presence of multiple factors for the domain. Specifically, across a number of studies, four of the five adaptive behavior domains posited by Kamphaus (1987) were confirmed. The four dimensions may be characterized, variously, as (a) motor or physical competence (or development); (b) independent living skills, daily living skills, or practical intelligence; (c) cognitive competence, communication, or conceptual intelligence; and (d) social competence or social intelligence. As McGrew et al. (in press) noted, these four dimensions also correspond well to four components of personal competence posited by Greenspan and Granfield (1992). Of the adaptive behavior domains discussed by Kamphaus (1987), only the responsibility/vocational domain has not been widely supported. The failure to identify a Responsibility/Vocational factor likely has at least two bases: (a) few adaptive behavior scales assess specific behaviors that are clearly vocationally relevant to any great extent and (b) responsibility/motivation is an implicit component of many adaptive behavior items, as noted earlier. Thus, rather than identifying a separate Responsibility factor, all factors of adaptive behavior contain an implicit loading with personal responsibility or motivation.

In addition to adaptive behavior factors, the Personal Maladaption and Social Maladaption factors have frequently been found in studies that included several indicators of each type of maladaptive behavior. These two factors for maladaptive behavior tend to be correlated at low levels with factors of adaptive behavior and demonstrate the robustness of the factors for the maladaptive domain posited by Meyers et al. (1979).

Additional research is clearly warranted on the structure of adaptive behaviors, but the future trends appear clear. As with the domain of human abilities, a hierarchically organized, multifactorial approach appears to hold the most promise. Although a number of studies have isolated only a single, general personal independence dimension, many studies have replicated several broad dimensions of personal competence. Importantly, a hierarchical model can accommodate such findings. Thus, a structure of adaptive behaviors that is hierarchical in nature will contain broader or more general factors at higher levels in the hierarchy and narrower or more specific factors at lower levels. Indeed, the resolution of the unifactorial and multifactorial positions may reside in concluding that both are correct to a certain extent. The factorial structure obtained depends on the level of the structure at which a study is undertaken, and the level at which a study is conducted is dictated by the breadth of the variables measured. Analyzing large numbers of items is likely to lead to numerous, narrow, lower stratum factors, whereas basing analyses on subscales results in a smaller number of broader, higher stratum factors that subsume the item-based factors. Such a view enables one to resolve the seemingly contradictory results reported across studies. Replicating and extending the hierarchical structure of adaptive behaviors will be an important goal for future investigation.

One final important issue involves the need for clear and consistent distinctions among theoretical terms. Currently, one person's definition of adaptive behavior is indistinguishable from another's notion of personal competence and from a third researcher's construct of social competence. For example, Widaman et al. (1987) identified six factors of behavior, interpreting the six-factor structure as making up the adaptive behavior domain. In a later study, McGrew et al. (in press) isolated a number of factors that appeared to match factors from the Widaman et al. study. However, McGrew et al. (in press) interpreted their results differently, reserving the term *adaptive behavior* for only a single dimension (i.e., practical intelligence) and considering the set of factors as representing the domain of personal competence. These differences in interpretation point to a crucial problem: The consistencies that emerge from factor analytic research often may be lost in differences in terminology. Thus, researchers should attend to the terms or labels attached to their factors as they attempt to place these factors within the hierarchical structure of adaptive behaviors. The end result will be an increasingly comprehensive and adequate understanding of the nature of adaptive behaviors, their structure, and their development.

Part II

Assessment and Diagnosis

Introduction

The assessment and diagnosis of mental retardation (MR) differ from those of most other disabilities in that classification is based primarily on normed, criterion performance in the realms of intellectual and adaptive behavioral functioning. Unlike the diagnosis of other disabilities, in which classification involves the presence of characteristic behaviors in combination and with an inferred or known common etiology, or the presence of identifiable organic impairments, MR is defined by the performance of an individual that reflects the cumulative effects of delayed or diminished development. The efficiency of classification depends entirely on the accuracy, with regard to false-positives and misses, of the combination of diagnostic measures used.

In this context, it is important to understand the history of the construct of intelligence, as embodied in intelligence tests, and the status of definition and measurement of the construct of adaptive behavior. However, diagnostic issues and concerns in the field of MR are not confined to the process and accuracy of initial classification, reclassification, or adaptive development. Assessment remains a prominent activity of practitioners involved in all phases of treatment and habilitation of people with MR. Indeed, accurately discerning the presence of psychopathology among people with MR has become an issue that has generated both research interest and focused clinical activity in recent years as the importance of interpersonal and social skills to successful participation in society has become evident in both the field of MR and other clinical specializations in psychology. Similarly, the measurement of social skills; identification of neuropsychological factors that influence development; genetic, biological, and neurological factors that affect development and behavior; behavioral changes associated with treatment; and lifestyle outcomes are especially prominent functions of assessment activity in contemporary service settings and community psychological practice with people with MR. The shared purpose of these diverse assessment activities is to achieve improved predication and influence on individual growth and development, providing a foundation for clinical service.

7

Mental Retardation and Assessment of Cognitive Processes

J. P. Das and Jack A. Naglieri

The 1992 American Association on Mental Retardation's (AAMR's) definition of mental retardation (MR) illuminates a fundamental difference between the interests of service providers and those of researchers. We suggest that it is not necessary to make a distinction between the task of the scientist and that of the practitioner inasmuch as many scientific discoveries are first suggested through practice; however, without knowledge to apply, the practitioner would be operating in ignorance. Thus, one definition of MR for the service provider and the researcher should suffice. Assuming that this is the case, we propose a unified model and method for cognitive assessment of people with MR that has both a scientific formulation and demonstrated clinical utility.

Our approach to diagnosis and professional practice is being written for those who are interested in the cognitive processes and behavior of individuals with MR. Developmental psychologists are interested in the growth and development of those with MR, and cognitive psychologists are interested in the manner in which they process information. Neuropsychologists want to relate brain functions to behavior, and practicing psychologists are interested in applying knowledge from any of these fields for beneficial purposes. Psychologists attempt to translate research findings into practice, much like an engineer who uses facts from physics and mathematics in engineering. In fact, engineering is a good analogy for the field of MR. For example, consider a contractor who has assembled technicians and material resources to build a bridge and a consultant whose function is to provide the design and specifications for the bridge. Without the consultant, the contractor cannot build the bridge. The role of the research psychologist is that of the consultant, and the role of the service provider is that of the contractor. The consultant and the contractor have different objectives, and they would view the bridge according to their own perspectives. It is unproductive to provide a definition of the bridge that does not incorporate specifications from either side if acceptable functioning of the bridge is the general aim of the project. Similarly, separate definitions of MR for the scientist and the service provider are unnecessary. To show how these two perspectives can be unified, we discuss the following topics in the remainder of this chapter: (a) a model of cognitive processes, (b) measures of these processes and their comparison with existing standardized tests of intelligence, (c) the utility of the model in understanding both intelligence and adaptive skills, and (d) application of the model to study individuals with and without Down syndrome.

A New Look at Intelligence

Dissatisfaction with both the concept and the measurement of intelligence was one of the reasons why the 1992 AAMR definition did not emphasize intelligence. Researchers had been similarly disappointed with the existing definition of intelligence, which was often quoted as being what intelligence tests measure, and with the stagnant character of the popular standardized tests that continue to dominate the assessment of intellectual functions. Some researchers, such as Green, Mackay, McIlvane, Saunders, and Sraci (1990) and Whitman (1990), attempted to redefine MR without using an IQ criterion, but these alternatives have not been widely accepted.

An examination of the conceptualization of intelligence outside the field of MR reveals that there have been several significant developments stemming from information-processing theories and neuropsychological data on intellectual functioning. The cognitive revolution begun by Miller, Galanter, and Pribram (1960) and by Broadbent, Estes, Simon, and Sperry (cited in Lachman, Lachman, & Butterfield, 1979) influenced the measurement of individual differences in intellectual abilities (E. Hunt, 1987). The few commonly used standardized tests of IQ, however, remained unchanged, impervious to developments in the field of intelligence (Naglieri & Das, 1990). Newer models of intelligence have begun to successfully challenge a monolithic view of general ability, a scale of merit on which all human beings, irrespective of their diverse talents, could be measured (Das, 1992).

In the field of MR, serious attempts to reconceptualize MR in terms of cognitive abilities and processes have been made as exemplified by Das (1973) and Sternberg (1984). The model of intellectual processes favored here was presented by Das, Kirby, and Jarman (1979) and by Das, Naglieri, and Kirby (1994) and is discussed in the next section. However, before discussing that, we provide a definition of intelligence as follows: Intelligence is composed of three components. The first is attentional processes, which provide focused cognitive activity; the second is information processes of two types (simultaneous and successive); and the third is planning processes, which provide (a) the control of attention; (b) the use of information processes, internal and external knowledge, and cognitive tools; and (c) overall self-regulation to achieve a desired goal.

The PASS Theory

Summaries of the Planning, Attention, Simultaneous, Successive (PASS) theory and related research have been presented in detail elsewhere (Das et al., 1979, 1994; Naglieri, 1989; Naglieri & Das, 1990; Naglieri, Das, & Jarman, 1990); therefore, only a brief review is provided here. The focus in this chapter is on the basic aspects of the theory of intelligence rather than on the supporting experimental evidence.

The PASS theory is based on the following assumptions: (a) a modern theory of intelligence should include the basic neuropsychological components of human cognitive activity; (b) the use of cognitive processes is influenced by the neurological system as well as the individual's habitual mode of processing and the demands of the task; (c) knowledge available and obtained from the cultural and social background of the individual has substantial influence on the form of mental activity; (d) PASS cognitive processes require cultural interaction for development and cultural tools, especially language; and (e) planning processes provide the means to organize and direct all cognitive activity to achieve desired goals.

Relationships among the PASS processes. The PASS processes are dynamic in nature, respond to the cultural experiences of the individual, are subject to developmental changes, and form an interrelated interdependent system. Effective functioning is accomplished through the integration of cultural knowledge with planning, attentional, simultaneous, and successive processes as demanded by the particular task. Although each type of process is an independent component with distinct functions, they are joined into a complex functional system consisting of cognitive processes and biological and sociocultural subsystems. Simultaneous and successive processes and planning interact to facilitate acquisition of knowledge, and at the same time these higher functions depend on a proper state of arousal to provide the opportunity for learning. The information to be processed can arrive through any of the receptors (e.g., eyes, ears, skin, muscle movements) in a serial (e.g., over time) or synchronous (i.e., concurrent) manner; several stimuli may be presented to the individual at one time or one at a time (e.g., hearing two different words at the same time or two words in a series). Auditory information is often presented serially while visual information is frequently presented as a synchronous array. Despite the type of presentation, information is processed according to the requirements of the task and is not dictated by the method (serial or concurrent) of presentation.

Because the PASS processes are viewed as interactive, they act in concert to provide specific functions to virtually all tasks performed in everyday life. (See Figure 1.) This is not to say, however, that all of the processes are equally involved in all tasks; one or two processes may be especially demanded in a particular task. Because planning requires an adequate state of arousal so that attention can be focused, an appropriate level of activation, attention, and arousal is needed so that plans of action can be generated and used. Effective planning requires an appropriately aroused state as well as the inhibition of an inappropriate level of arousal. Selectively inhibiting or facilitating arousal and attention is one of the important functions of the third functional unit that is associated with planning. Because real-life tasks often can be cognitively processed in dif-

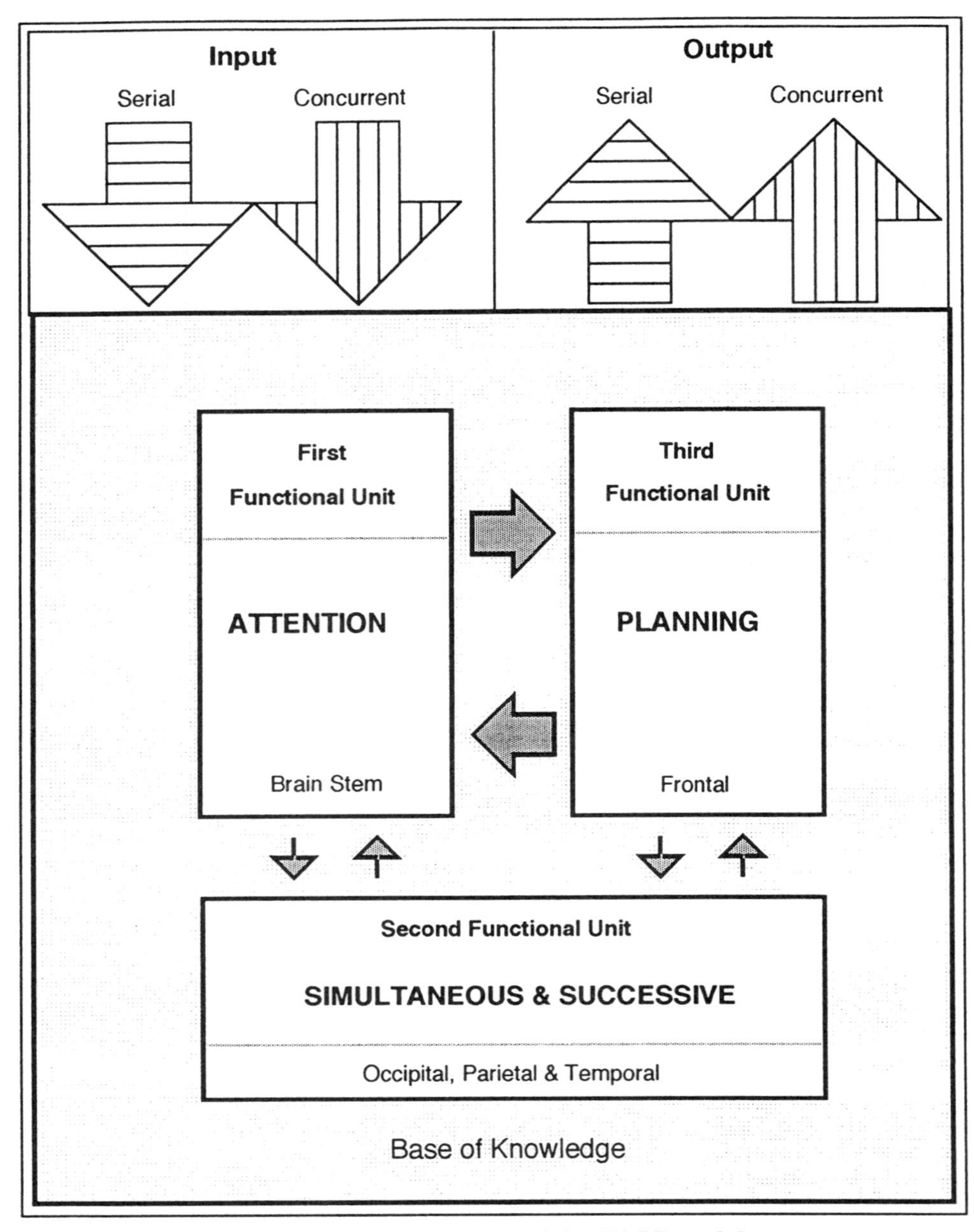

Figure 1. A diagram of the PASS model

ferent ways, how one manages the information is a planning function that influences the cognitive process used. The application of simultaneous and successive processes will be influenced by the executive function of planning. This has been illustrated by E. B. Hunt (1974), who described how Raven's matrices could be solved using a gestalt or analytic approach and by Lawson and Kirby (1981), J. R. Kirby and Das (1978), and J. R. Kirby and Lawson (1983), who found that the application of these processes to solving matrix items can be influenced by training.

The output dimension of the PASS theory is a complex function in itself. Following processing activities that are a result of the demands of the task, cognitive tools, and knowledge base, output may require additional processes. For example, simultaneous processes may predominate in the solution of a task, but motor programming may be required if the response is a written one. An individual may have competence in processing but fail to initiate the motor program required to respond.

Planning. Planning processes provide for the control of attention and use of simultaneous and successive processes, as well as the base of knowledge, to achieve a goal. Planning allows the individual to determine and use an efficient way to solve a problem through the application of attentional, simultaneous, and successive processes in conjunction with the base of knowledge. This includes, in addition to the development of plans of action, evaluation of the effectiveness of these plans and needed modifications as well as impulse control, regulation of voluntary actions, and linguistic functions such as spontaneous speech. Planning involves a series of executive actions that includes the components shown in Figure 2 and provides an individual with the means to solve problems. It may be a complex or simple task, and it may involve attentional, simultaneous, and successive processes, but the main requirement is to determine how to solve the problem. Once the need for a plan is apparent, the individual may search his or her base of knowledge for an approach. If an approach is not within the present knowledge base, an initial plan of action is developed and the plan is examined to determine whether it is reasonable. If it is acceptable, the plan is implemented, but if not, a new plan is devised. If the plan is put into action, decisions are made to modify the effectiveness of the approach, continue applying the plan, modify it to achieve the most efficient approach to problem solving, or generate another one. This last step is iterated until the task is completed.

Attention. Attentional processes allow the individual to voluntarily respond to a particular stimulus and to inhibit responding to competing stimuli. Measurement of attention within the PASS model involves tasks that require the participant to respond to target stimuli and not respond to nontarget stimuli. Attention becomes increasingly difficult when the nontarget stimuli are more salient than the target stimuli. The functional architecture of attention, presented in Figure 3, shows that attention tasks require the individual to direct his or her cognitive activity to a particular stimulus and suppress reacting to competing stimuli. This process is defined by the requirement that a number of stimuli are presented and the individual intends to respond to one stimulus and ignore the others.

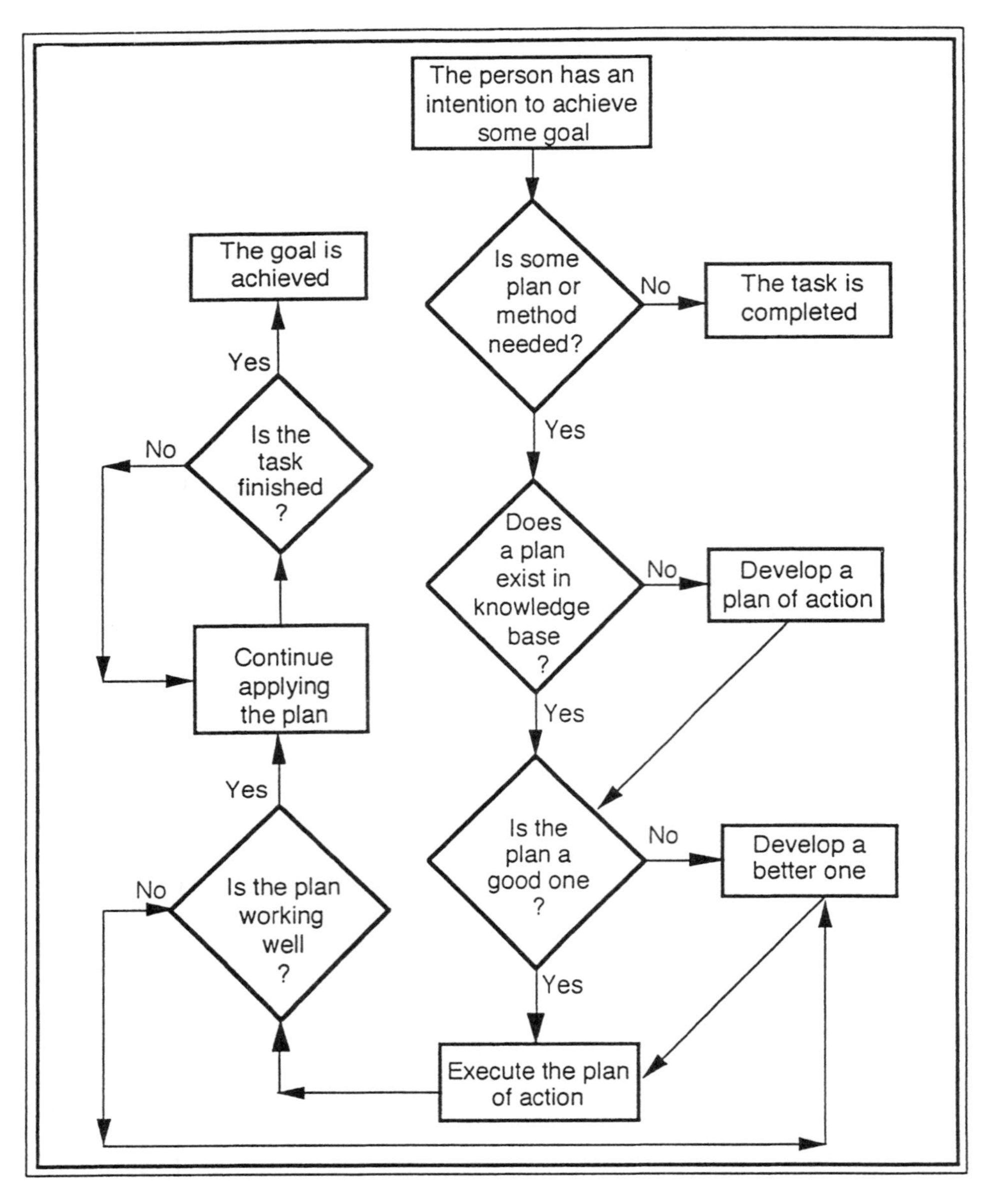

Figure 2. A flowchart for planning

Simultaneous. Simultaneous processes allow the individual to integrate stimuli into groups in which each component of the stimulus array must be interrelated with every other. Simultaneous processing may take place when stimuli are perceived (e.g., when a child copies a design such as a cube), remembered (e.g., when the design is drawn from memory), or conceptualized (e.g., when the child reasons about a design, as in Raven's, 1956, or Naglieri's, 1985a, figural matrices). Simultaneously processed information is said to be surveyable because the elements are interrelated

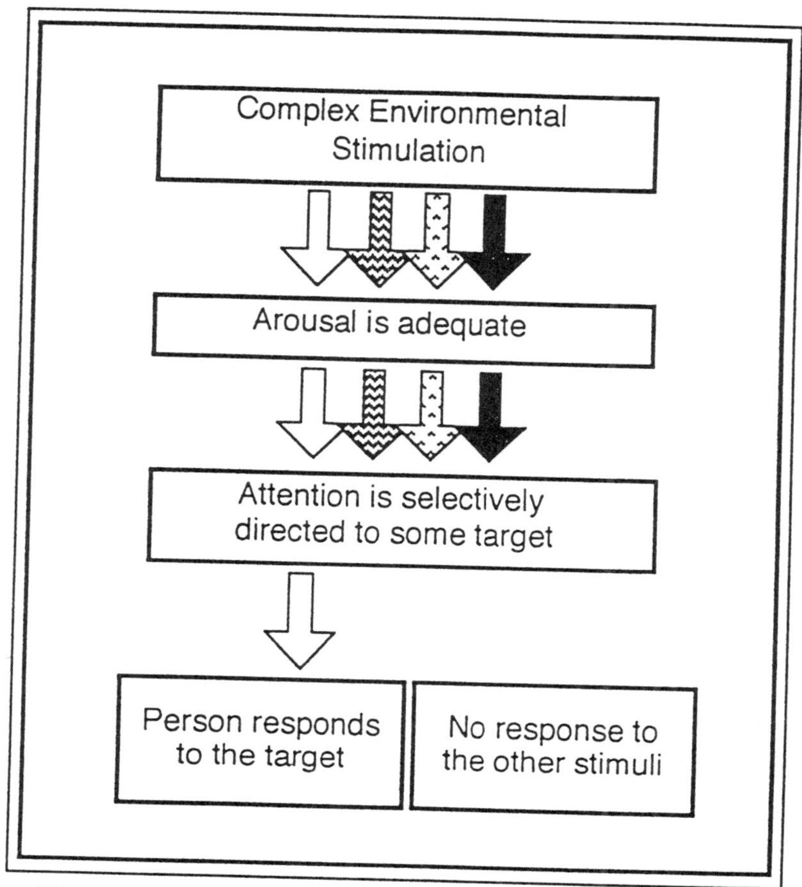

Figure 3. A diagram of the arousal–attention relationship

and accessible to inspection either through examination of the actual stimuli during the activity (as in the case of design copying) or through memory of the stimuli (as in the case of reproduction of a design from memory). Simultaneous processing aspects of language involve logical grammatical relations (e.g., in comprehension of a statement such as "My mother's father was his oldest son"). The distinguishing characteristic of this type of processing is that the component parts need to be interrelated.

Successive. Successive processes provide the integration of stimuli into a serial order in which the elements form a chainlike progression. The distinguishing quality of successive processing is that the elements are related only linearly and that each stimulus is related only to the one it follows. For example, successive coding is needed for skilled movements (e.g., writing) because this activity requires "a series of movements which follow each other in a strictly defined order . . . without surveyability" (Luria, 1966, p. 78). In the early stages of the formation of the skilled movement, each successive link exists as a separate unit and may be taught as a specific step in a larger behavior. Only when each aspect becomes automatic can the initial stimulus in the chain become the signal that leads to the automatic execution of the complete successive action. Linguistic tasks involving successive processing require appreciation of the linearity of stimuli with no requirement for interrelating of the parts. For example, to answer the question, "The girl hit the boy, who got hurt?" the ordering of the words within the sentence must be appreciated.

PASS and MR

The major dimensions of the PASS model are input, processing, knowledge base (which includes cognitive tools), and output. Each of these has relevance for the assessment and understanding of the cognitive functions of individuals with MR.

Input

Because input can occur through any of the receptors, the two primary forms of input—visual and auditory—are considered here. Research on eye movement is one of the instances in which visual input plays an important part in determining cognitive processing. Ross and Ross (1984) reviewed eye movement functions of individuals with MR and found that people with MR experienced unusual difficulties in oculomotor processing. The more severe the MR, the greater the problem with oculomotor function. Similarly, input through the auditory channel may have a restrictive effect on cognitive processing. For example, it has been suspected that people with Down syndrome may have special difficulties with auditory processing. However, that has not been found to be true in recent research (Marcell & Cohen, 1992). In any case, because vision and hearing are important ways of receiving information, it is necessary to know if people with a mental impairment have specific problems associated with visual and auditory input. Correcting the input problem alone can improve cognitive functions, a point that should be considered carefully during assessment and treatment planning.

Processing

Of the four pass processes, attention and arousal have been studied for a long time. Visually and auditorially transmitted information is known to invoke elementary forms of attention, such as the orienting response. Given a warning signal and then a target to respond ("Press when you hear *man* preceded by the word *box*"), individuals with MR give a greater orienting response to *man*, whereas people with no disability give a greater response to *box* (Das & Bower, 1971). Arousal and attention are disturbed in children with hyperactivity, some of whom also may have MR. Higher forms of attention, as revealed in discrimination learning, have featured prominently in the literature on MR (Krupski, 1977; Zeaman & House, 1963). In studies of simultaneous and successive information coding, we have found strength or weakness of an individual in only one of these processes but not the other (Das, 1984). For instance, in comparing three categories—people with brain damage, those with Down syndrome, and those who have mental impairments of no known organic causes—it was observed that participants with Down syndrome were particularly poor in successive processing. Those with brain damage who also were classified as having MR were superior to those with Down syndrome and to the individuals with nonorganic MR in all three processes of planning, simultaneous, and successive (Snart, O'Grady, & Das, 1982).

In another study, Das and Mishra (1995) examined individuals with Down syndrome and individuals of comparable mental impairment without Down syndrome to determine whether PASS cognitive processes would decline with age. Participants with and without Down syndrome were divided into age groups of 26–40 and 41–60 years. Results show that articulation was declining faster in the sample with Down syndrome at and above 40 years of age. Specifically, the tests that showed significant effects were Number Finding (planning), Expressive Attention (attention), and Speech Rate (successive). These tests may hold promise for diagnosing early signs of dementia of Alzheimer type.

Planning, or planful behavior, is probably unique to human beings. Its development is closely associated with the development of language or other symbolic systems such as sign language and is represented in the frontal lobes. It is one of the most active areas of research in cognitive and neuropsychological functions. Individuals with MR often are thought to be completely unable to plan or to use strategies. In fact, they are specifically poor in transferring strategies learned in one situation to another. However, a closer scrutiny of problem-solving behavior of people with MR reveals that some amount of planning can be observed in their behavior (Ferretti & Cavalier, 1991). Ferretti and Cavalier suggested that to facilitate the transfer of strategies, specific strategy training must be practiced. This suggestion is consistent with other observations (Ashman, 1978, 1982, 1985), in that training individuals with MR for transfer should not follow metacognitive training but that specific strategy training of an intensive nature would be able to exploit their limited capacity in problem solving and planning.

Two cognitive activities, working memory and speed of processing, have often been related to the general cognitive functions of people with MR. For example, Ferretti and Cavalier (1991) suggested that the slow speed of information processing may be the most critical determinant of poor working memory and that this could be the locus of the diminished mental ability of individuals with MR. How does speed, or working memory, fit in with the PASS model?

Briefly, speed is common to a number of tasks in the PASS model that are timed measures of efficiency (Das & Dash, 1983; Das et al., 1994). For example, the time scores of our planning tests do not correlate with the speed of reading words or saying the name of colors. Similarly, memory is widely distributed among the various tests of PASS and is involved in simultaneous verbal and nonverbal tests, and in successive tasks. Moreover, confirmatory factor analytic studies have shown that planning and speed do not load on the same factor (Das & Dash, 1983; Naglieri, Prewett, & Bardos, 1989). Thus, it is more economical to study the PASS components involved in information processing than to study global components such as speed, working memory, and thinking. In other words, speed and working memory deficits can be specifically located in one or more of the PASS tasks.

Knowledge Base and Cognitive Tools

Knowledge base, of course, is to be assessed before or along with any assessment of cognitive functions. All cognitive processes are based on the knowledge that the person has acquired either formally through instruction and apprenticeship or informally through experience. The latter, informal or experiential knowledge is frequently identified with practical intelligence (Sternberg, 1984). Practical intelligence, which is not much different from social intelligence, determines to a great extent the adaptive skills of an individual with MR. Adaptive behavior, apart from simple living skills, is essentially the judgment that the individual displays in social situations (Das, 1984a, 1984b). Judgment itself depends equally on cognitive processes as represented by PASS, but especially planning because of its self-regulatory and self-evaluative dimensions, and personality factors that also include motivation.

Cognitive tools are the outgrowth of processes and external knowledge, which makes human functioning a complex and distinctive activity. These tools include physical entities, such as inventions provided by the culture (e.g., computers) as well as the human body itself (e.g., the hands and tongue), and the less tangible tools such as speech and language, which arise out of a child's social interactions. Cognitive tools also include procedural methods of how to solve problems in general (e.g., self-regulation used to approach problems that, for example, require careful completion) as well as formally transmitted knowledge of how to complete a task (e.g., instructional facts about how to manually do long division or write a sentence). It is through the combination of both physical and intellectual tools that higher cognitive activity results (Vygotsky, 1978).

Language is an important tool used for thinking. It is used for planning and mediated learning and, more important, plays a vital role in the regulation of behavior. In all of these functions, individuals with MR have significant difficulties. They also experience difficulties using external tools such as the computer. Consequently, their cultural learning will be adversely affected as new demands on these cognitive tools are made, and their adaptive behavior will suffer unless compensatory measures are instituted.

Output

The last component of PASS that has great relevance for the assessment of MR is output. Many research articles and books have been written on the motor development and deficits in motor development of individuals with MR (e.g., H. P. A. Whiting & Wade, 1986). Simply by providing alternative methods of output, one could enable a person with MR to respond competently. Motor processing strategies can be trained and their development can be recorded reliably, as discussed by Whiting and Wade.

We offer PASS as a much more useful model for the assessment of cognitive capabilities, including motor development and motor control of individuals with MR. The model has obvious advantages over assessment of a general intelligence level, as obtained from existing standardized IQ tests. It has the additional advantage of unifying both adaptive and intellectual skills within one theoretical concept.

Current IQ Tests and PASS

The description of PASS provided here allows one to consider which of these processes may or may not be measured by current IQ tests. This topic was discussed by Das et al. (1994) in some detail on the basis of a content analysis and an examination of the empirical studies of the Binet, Wechsler, and Kaufman Assessment Battery for Children (K-ABC). They concluded that, from the PASS perspective, these tests mainly measure only two of the four processes. Simultaneous processes are involved in tests that appear on the Wechsler Intelligence Scale for Children–III Performance subscale, the Stanford-Binet Intelligence Scale: Four Abstract Visual subscale, and the K-ABC Simultaneous scales. Successive processes are involved in tests such as the Wechsler Intelligence Scale for Children–Revised Digit Span Forward, Binet: Four Memory for Digits, and most of the K-ABC Sequential scale subtests (excluding Hand Movements above age 8 years). The verbal subtests of these three IQ tests can best be described as verbal–achievement measures that are related to general academic achievement–knowledge base and varying amounts of any of the PASS processes. This analysis of current tests leads to the conclusion that the field of intellectual assessment as represented by the Binet, Wechsler, and K-ABC essentially represents a limited view of intelligence. Moreover, it suggests that the general intelligence model used by Wechsler and Binet, and the constrained approach adopted by Kaufman, lacks the sensitivity to planning and attentional processes. This is an important omission, especially when a comprehensive evaluation of individuals with MR is required.

Using PASS to Identify Individuals with MR

Using the PASS theory as a perspective from which to evaluate when a person may have MR provides the advantage of measuring a broader spectrum of human functioning than is available with current IQ technology and one that is not laden with achievement (e.g., Verbal scale subtests such as Arithmetic or Information). This could provide important information when diagnosis and treatment planning decisions are made. For example, an individual with Wechsler IQs in the upper 60s on the Verbal subscale, as a result of poor verbal–achievement (knowledge base), and Performance (simultaneous processing) scale could have relatively higher scores on planning, attention, or both. In such a scenario, this person would likely perform better than the IQ scores would predict on measures of adaptive functioning. Adequate functioning of this person in planning, attention, or both would suggest that (a) adaptive functioning is related to an undetected cognitive strength in planning and (b) the diagnosis of MR may be reconsidered. Only when each of the four processes is significantly subaverage (below the 70–75 standard score criterion included in the AAMR definition) would there be adequate evidence of impaired intellectual functioning. However, even then, as the studies of individuals with MR who have and do not have Down syndrome have illustrated, this approach would provide a more valid evaluation of individuals suspected of having MR.

Conclusion

In this chapter we have suggested that any definition of MR must include both a theoretical and operational definition of intelligence to serve as a bridge between practitioners and researchers. The most recent AAMR definition appears to be designed for practitioners and consumers. We see the PASS approach as one that provides a sound theory of human abilities and one that can serve as a more effective tool than traditional IQ tests. For example, because PASS is both theoretically and practically informative about the problems of individuals with MR, it allows, for example, for greater differentiation of those with and without Down syndrome. This, in turn, leads to the selection of particular remedial plans (e.g., those individuals with Down syndrome who have poor planning and attention would be selectively reminded about the relevant aspects of the working environment, efforts would be made to keep them alert, and planning of daily routines at home would be provided for them to the greatest extent possible). Therefore, the PASS approach would provide a more relevant method for the practitioner and a more theoretically sound perspective for the researcher.

8

Everyday Intelligence and Adaptive Behavior: A Theoretical Framework

Stephen Greenspan, Harvey N. Switzky, and James M. Granfield

The construct of adaptive behavior is central to any effort to revise the definition of mental retardation (MR; Reschly, 1985). Invention and use of this construct must be understood within the historical context of efforts to return the definition and classification of MR to something more intuitive and more based on how people behave in their everyday lives. These efforts are driven by the concern that the tendency to base the diagnosis so heavily on an individual's IQ score is somehow wrong. The key to devising an adequate constitutive (i.e., theoretical) definition of MR is to base it on a broader model of intelligence, one that relies heavily on measures of everyday (i.e., social and practical) intelligence and not so exclusively on a measure of academic intelligence (i.e., IQ; Greenspan, 1979, 1981; Greenspan & Granfield, 1992).

The authors of the recent American Association on Mental Retardation's (AAMR's) definition and classification manual (Luckasson et al., 1992) cited this framework as a partial rationale for shifting the basis for a definition of MR from adaptive behavior to adaptive skills. However, their operational model of adaptive skills does not maintain a clear focus on intelligence and puts little emphasis on social intelligence. This is a critical problem with both the former and current AAMR definitions because the notion of "everyday intelligence" provides a key to devising a useful and acceptable definition of MR.

MR, like other disability categories, is a "class" that is used to determine whether an individual is eligible for certain forms of assistance or treatment. As M. C. Reynolds (1991) pointed out, a class differs from a "taxon" in that a class is politically or administratively constructed, whereas a taxon exists in a natural form. Ideally (as is often true in medicine), classes and taxa—as in the case, for example, of Down syndrome—should be identical. In MR, as in other areas of psychiatry, education, and human services, classes are invented constructs using criteria that are functional, often indirect, and to some extent arbitrary. This poses difficulties because criteria cannot efficiently delimit the boundaries of the disorder, especially (in the case of MR) at the upper limit, where the extent of disability may not be as intuitively apparent. The key to devising an adequate definition of the class of MR that is closely aligned with what its taxon is therefore to substitute natural for artificial criteria.

One way to do this is to essentially eliminate the category of mild MR (Zigler, Balla, & Hodapp, 1984) by reducing the IQ cutoff score to 50. Such an approach would include only those cases of MR with organic etiology and would align the class with the taxon of MR in two ways: (a) most diagnosed individuals also would have medical (etiological) diagnoses, and (b) most individuals would likely manifest global incompetence, thus substituting intuitive judgments of adaptive behavior deficit for an adaptive behavior score and thus eliminating need for an adaptive behavior criterion. However, the majority of individuals currently eligible for MR services, including many people needing significant supports, would be in danger of being denied these services. Some new category would be required for use with people who have mild intellectual impairments, perhaps a variation on learning disabilities (MacMillan, 1993). The problem of defining the upper limits of MR would be shifted over into some other arena, but without necessarily solving the problem of devising an adequate definition of the class.

The key to redefining the class of MR to attain closer congruence with the underlying taxon of MR is to base it on the intuitive template that experienced professionals and laypeople possess for determining the presence of MR. A central aspect of that template, an aspect not centrally featured in existing definitions, is that people with MR have demonstrated deficits in everyday intelligence. In this chapter we explore this idea, discuss relevant theoretical and empirical literatures, and point out implications for resolving current classification and measurement controversies.

Historical Overview

The inclusiveness or exclusiveness of the definition of MR has risen and fallen cyclically over the years in order to accommodate two largely incompatible objectives: (a) to ensure that all who should qualify for the class (and related services) are included and (b) to ensure that those who are truly "normal" are not harmed by inappropriate inclusion. The initial expansion of inclusiveness came in the early part of the twentieth century with the "discovery of the moron" and invention of feeblemindedness by Howe, Kerlin, Goddard, and others (Gelb, 1987; Trent, 1994). A period of contraction of inclusiveness was initiated in the 1960s and 1970s with the incorporation of the "adaptive behavior" criterion (Heber, 1961) and the dropping of the borderline category (Grossman, 1973).

The recent AAMR definition (Luckasson et al., 1992) represents an effort to make eligibility easier to obtain by raising the IQ cutoff score by 5 points and substituting the minimal screen of 2 out of 10 adaptive skills deficits for the more stringent—even if often ignored—requirement of general adaptive behavior deficit. This shift appears to be related to concerns that some people were disenfranchised by the elimination of the borderline category in the 1970s and are denied services that they need.

A basic dilemma in any effort to redefine MR on the basis of IQ cutoff score was noted 20 years ago: "An upper borderline for subnormality is impossible to define with any degree of precision in IQ terms (A. M. Clarke & Clarke, 1974, p. 22). Even with formal legitimation of a 5-point increase in the IQ cutoff, which would increase eligibility by more than 100%, there will still be people above that line who fit an intuitive template for MR (i.e., they lack everyday intelligence and have a real need for everyday supports). The same is obviously true in reverse: Except for a dramatic lowering of the IQ cutoff, there will always be many people below it who do not fit an intuitive template for MR.

The concept of adaptive behavior was apparently intended to address this difficulty in discriminating people believed to either "have" MR in spite of an IQ above the cutoff score or who were believed to "not have" MR in spite of an IQ below the cutoff score. However, adaptive behavior has been used only to establish "normality" in cases of low IQ, not to establish "abnormality" in cases of too-high IQ. Adaptive behavior has been used only as a corrective against possible abuse of IQ (i.e., false-positives).

Although the construct of adaptive behavior was intended to ground the class of MR more in the natural taxon of MR, it has not succeeded in doing so. Several critics (e.g., Clausen, 1972) have pointed out that the construct as operationalized in 1961, and as represented in various measures, does not succeed in capturing the essence of MR and does not contribute to a clarification of the class of MR. The lack of an adequate operational definition of adaptive behavior has meant that, although it is difficult to develop an adequate definition of MR without an adequate definition of adaptive behavior, it is impossible to develop an adequate definition of adaptive behavior without specifying what experienced people understand to be the essence of MR.

A problem with the manner in which adaptive behavior was operationally defined was the mixing of an intellective component (e.g., Part 1 of the Vineland Adaptive Behavior Scale and other instruments, which taps what has been termed *practical intelligence*) and a psychopathological component (Part 2 of many measures; "maladaptive behavior"), with the latter not clearly grounded in the notion of broadened intelligence. Where the 1961 (and subsequent) AAMR manuals erred was in not retaining a conception of MR that was entirely grounded in a notion of intelligence, albeit one broader than just IQ (i.e., conceptual or academic intelligence). Instead, Greenspan and colleagues have argued for substituting the construct of adaptive intelligence, referred to here as everyday (i.e., social and practical) intelligence, in the place of adaptive behavior (Greenspan, 1979, 1981; Greenspan & Granfield, 1992). Adaptive behavior refers to everyday functioning and is affected by a mix of cognitive and noncognitive abilities. Everyday (formerly, adaptive) intelligence, on the other hand, refers only to those cognitive abilities that contribute to adaptive behavioral outcomes. One could make a plausible case that people with a demonstrated absence of everyday intelligence should qualify for MR services, even in the presence of an IQ above any particular IQ cutoff. The notion of everyday intelligence fits the natural and historical template for the taxon of MR, but the construct of adaptive behavior–adaptive skills (and even to some extent IQ) does not.

The 1992 AAMR manual is a step in the direction of recapturing the "intellectual" basis for the class, but it substituted the construct of "adaptive skills," a construct that emphasizes relative competence. The operational list of 10 skill domains were derived from a largely atheoretical community skills curriculum (Ford et al., 1989). Of these 10 adaptive skill domains (Luckasson et al., 1992, pp. 40–41), 8 are more or less measures of practical intelligence (although some, such as leisure, have elements of social intelligence embedded within them); one (functional academics) is essentially a measure of conceptual intelligence; and only one ("social skill") clearly involves social intelligence, although even here it is defined in a manner linked to emotional competence (i.e., absence of internalizing or externalizing psychopathology) as much as to social intelligence. Thus, although a tripartite model of intelligence is cited as providing theoretical justification for the notion of adaptive skills, the 1992 AAMR manual still gives primary emphasis to academic intelligence (IQ) as a necessary condition for the diagnosis, secondary emphasis to practical intelligence (reflected in most of the 10 adaptive skills), and virtually no emphasis to social intelligence. This is unfortunate because one can argue plausibly that a social intelligence deficit lies at the heart of the taxon of MR and may, in fact, provide a more justifiable basis for making the diagnosis than IQ.

The Role of Social Intelligence

Current arguments about the need to deemphasize IQ and recapture the natural basis of MR were made in much the same form at the outset of the field. Efforts by A. F. Tredgold (1922) and Doll (1936) to promote a definition of MR that was grounded in demonstrated social incompetence were based on a belief that failure to function normally in everyday social settings lay at the heart of the disorder. Preceding the advent of formal intelligence testing, people were identified as "intellectually subnormal" on the basis of the immaturity of their behavior in public (Sarason & Doris, 1969). Identification of people as having MR on the basis of their social behavior changed, however, with the invention and widespread adoption of the Binet-Simon Intelligence Scale and its successor tests. Gelb (1987) provided an account of the efforts of Goddard to use the Binet in the early part of this century to provide a scientific basis for describing and "uncovering" (and erecting defenses against) the phenomenon of mild MR. Goddard (1914) coined the term *moron* to refer to those relatively capable people (sometimes also referred to as *moral imbeciles*) whom he claimed (J. D. Smith, 1985), through dubious scholarship regarding the Kallikak family, to be a threat to society. Thus, as Gelb pointed out, the use of IQ tests (originally developed for the purpose of educational screening) as a means for the identification and social exclusion of people now likely to be labeled as having mild MR was an attempt to provide a "scientific" basis for a classification system that had its origins in the realm of social functioning.

Dissatisfaction with the substitution of low IQ for judgment of social immaturity led Doll (1936) to argue that it was possible for someone to be considered to have MR even with an IQ above a particular cutoff score, just as it was possible for someone to be considered normal, even with an IQ below a particular cutoff score. The critical factor in deciding whether an individual should be put in one diagnostic category or another, according to Doll (1936), was the quality of the individual's interpersonal judgment and wisdom. An even more forceful case for grounding the definition of MR in perceived deficits in social competence (i.e., in need for supports in fulfilling age-appropriate social roles) was made by the British physician A. F. Tredgold (1922), who argued that social incompetence (by which he appeared to mean the relative lack of social and practical intelligence) should, alone, be the defining criterion.

The solution of the definition of MR is intricately tied in with the equally intractable problem of the solution of the definition of intelligence. R. F. Tredgold and Soddy (1963) noted this problem more than 30 years ago in stating that the lack of an adequate definition of intelligence lay at the heart of the problem of adequately defining MR. Numerous conceptions of intelligence abound, and there is still much debate on the subject (see Sternberg & Detterman, 1986). One formulation that may be particularly germane is Hebb's (1949) "Intelligence A" (pure intelligence, or *g*) and "Intelligence B" (intelligence as manifested in everyday behavior). To these, Vernon (1956) added "Intelligence C" (intelligence as expressed in the IQ measure). A problem with most efforts to define and diagnose MR in this century is that Intelligence C (IQ) was used as the main criterion for determining incompetence, although what really counts is Intelligence B (application of intellect in real-world situations).

An attempt to ground the definition of MR in Hebb's (1949) Intelligence B was proposed in a series of articles pointing out the implications of a model of personal competence (Greenspan, 1979, 1981; Greenspan & Granfield, 1992). A tripartite model of intelligence (E. Thorndike, 1920), which contains the elements of social intelligence, practical intelligence, and conceptual intelligence, is central to understanding personal competence. Use of the tripartite model of intelligence as the basis for defining MR would substitute deficits in social intelligence—defined by E. H. Taylor and Cadet (1989, p. 424) as "the ability to act wisely in human relations"—for maladaptive behavior, with practical intelligence being more or less isomorphic with the daily living competencies tapped in most measures of adaptive behavior. An advantage of this formulation is that it lessens the role of IQ (still retained as a measure of conceptual intelligence) but maintains the historical grounding of MR in the notion of intelligence.

The perspective that intelligence has multiple content aspects has been explored in recent years (e.g., Carroll, 1986; H. Gardner, 1983; Guilford, 1967). The work of Sternberg is particularly relevant to definitional controversy regarding MR. In writing about "some proposed loci of mental retardation," Sternberg (1984) made a distinction between "academic intelligence" (relevant to performance in school settings) and "practical intelligence," which he defined as "people's ability to adapt successfully to the real-world environments in which they find themselves, and to exercise at least some significant degree of mastery over this environment [*sic*]" (p. 93). In describing what he meant by practical intelligence, Sternberg gave primary emphasis to cognitive competence applied to interpersonal situations, or what psychologists (and occasionally Sternberg himself) refer to as "social intelligence" (e.g., Sternberg & Wagner, 1986). Sternberg (1984) noted that psychometric support for the construct is weak but suggested that this reflects "a narrow interpretation of what practical intelligence is" (p. 93). In other words, relevant measures parallel closely what is tapped in IQ tests and thus correlate highly with IQ, as was noted by R. Thorndike (1936) 60 years ago. Sternberg argued that there is strong support in the social psychology literature for the everyday significance of social intelligence and that practical intelligence, by which he meant some combination of what Greenspan (1979, 1981) termed *practical* and *social intelligence*, provides a more important basis for diagnosing MR than IQ because someone can be (and often is) deficient in academic intelligence (i.e., has low IQ) but relatively normal in the practical and social domains of functioning.

Support for use of a tripartite model of intelligence for defining MR was provided by McGrew, Bruininks, and Johnson (in press), in which structural equation modeling techniques were used in two samples: one with mild MR and one with moderate-to-severe MR. The model proposed by Greenspan and Granfield (1992)—which McGrew et al. referred to as "Greenspan 4"—was strongly supported, although an earlier version of that model ("Greenspan 3") did not differ appreciably. Both received considerably greater support than the 1992 AAMR "adaptive skills" model and a similar model proposed by Mathias and Nettelback (1992). Mathias and Nettelbeck used exploratory factor analysis to test the Greenspan 3 model. As noted by Greenspan and McGrew (1993), confirmatory factor analysis performed on Mathias's correlation matrix provided considerably greater support for the Greenspan 3 model than was found using exploratory methods. Also, as noted by McGrew et al. (in press), Mathias and Nettelbeck used only one measure of practical intelligence and thus did not satisfy statistical assumptions necessary to demonstrate a lack of differentiation between practical and social intelligence.

The main issue in this controversy concerns the extent to which social intelligence should be dealt with as a separate component of "adaptive behavior" or should be combined with practical intelligence in an undifferentiated way, as in the 1992 AAMR manual's listing of adaptive skills. McGrew and colleagues (McGrew & Bruininks, 1990; McGrew et al., in press) provided strong empirical support for separating social intelligence and practical intelligence (especially in the sample with mild MR) and for viewing both as definitive features of MR.

Although factor analytic procedures can indicate methods to specify the structure of intelligence in people with MR, they cannot establish what the definition should be. Support for the proposition that social and practical intelligence should be cornerstones of a definition of MR can be found in several places. One is the finding from various studies (Chadsey-Rusch, 1992; Greenspan & Shoultz, 1981; Greenspan, Shoultz, & Weir, 1981) that social intelligence deficits account for many of the problems of work maladjustment in people with MR. Another is the finding (Greenspan & Delaney, 1983) that people with Down syndrome, when matched on IQ with same-age MR people without Down syndrome, are equally incompetent on social and practical intelligence, even when better adjusted in other aspects of personal competence (i.e., temperament and character). Another is the finding (e.g., Gresham, Elliot, & Black, 1987; Leffert & Siperstein, 1994) that interpersonal skill deficit is a critical problem for the social acceptance of children and youth with mild MR mainstreamed into general classrooms.

Conclusion: Measurement Issues and Proposed Definition

An obvious obstacle to the use of social intelligence as a defining characteristic of MR has been lack of psychometrically sound measures. This problem has been cited by most investigators, including advocates for its use such as Sternberg (1984) and McGrew et al. (in press). Although there has been a tremendous recent growth of interest in social intelligence in social and personality psychology (Cantor & Kihlstrom, 1987) and by psychologists interested in intelligence (Sternberg & Wagner, 1986), child development (Bennett, 1993; Frye & Moore, 1991), and other disabilities such as autism and learning disabilities (Baron-Cohen, Tager-Flusberg & Cohen, 1993; Bryan, 1991; Greenspan & Love, in press), measures have tended to be experimental and narrow in focus. The absence of adequate measures of social intelligence may have been a factor in the decision not to incorporate the tripartite model of intelligence into the 1992 AAMR manual's definition (personal communication, S. R. Reiss, April 12, 1993).

Although this issue presents difficulties, the notion that a construct should not be considered as a core component of a disorder unless it can be measured precisely represents a continuation of the Goddardian tradition that a test score is the best basis for determining that someone has MR. Reliance on test scores (as opposed to judgments of professionals and laypeople) in determining whether a person has MR is a reflection of what Goodnow (1986) described as the tendency to view intelligence as "a quality residing in the individual" (p. 85) rather than as something that other people attribute to the individual based on the way that person behaves in the real world. Goodnow noted that psychologists do not use tests to determine whether someone is attractive or ugly, gregarious or reserved and wondered why the same approach might not be equally appropriate in determining whether someone is smart. Such a point would appear particularly pertinent in responding to the implicit assertion that intelligence in the social domain cannot be used in a clinical diagnostic process until measures meet psychometric standards. However adequate one's test of social or practical intelligence, the most valid indication that someone manifests "social retardation" is likely to be the manner in which that person presents himself or herself to other people.

According to this view, the essence of MR may be found in the tendency to behave in ways that cause people in one's own cultural setting to view one as having MR. Given that such a phenomenon occurs at all ages and in all cultures—including cultures in which educational achievement and literacy receive little or no emphasis—it is clear that everyday (i.e., social and practical) intelligence is probably the central, and perhaps only, basis for concluding that someone has MR. In line with this argument, we propose the following definition of MR: MR is a term used to describe people who habitually act in everyday social settings (e.g., school, residence, work, and recreation) in a manner that causes them to be viewed—relative to same-age peers of similar socioeconomic, linguistic, and cultural background—as having impairments in intellectual processes needed to understand and solve interpersonal, practical, or academic problems that typically arise in those settings, with the resultant need for special supports or services in order to have a greater likelihood of succeeding in those settings.

In this proposed definition, information about the precise level of IQ deficit, although of potential interest, should not be the primary basis for determining whether a particular child or adult has MR. An individual who consistently demonstrates serious impairment in everyday intelligence, manifested, for example, in being viewed by peers and older people in one's social ecology as needing special supports or protection and who possesses some plausible explanation for such difficulties (e.g., a congenital brain malformation), could qualify as having MR even if his or her IQ were well above the IQ criterion prevailing at a particular time. This proposed definition is based on the position that competence to engage successfully in interpersonal and practical activities forms the basis of the natural taxon of MR. Reliance on a particular IQ cutoff results in an artificial class that, although correlated with the natural taxon, is often discrepant from it.

The key question in terms of assessing everyday intelligence is whether it is necessary to measure underlying intellectual processes (e.g., egocentrism or perspective taking) directly or whether it is sufficient to obtain information (either quantitatively or clinically) of behavioral tendencies—such as peer rejection, failure in work settings, or examples of social and practical ineptness—that are strong indirect indicators of significant impairments. Some combination of these two approaches is most likely to result in a true understanding of any particular individual, although clinical and historical information about actual functioning should be given greater weight until more adequate direct measures are developed and refined. Given the parallelism, initial efforts by Binet and Simon (1905/1976) to measure academic intelligence involved just such use of these qualitative and descriptive methods.

A key consideration in developing more adequate direct measures of everyday intelligence or adaptive behavior is that measures should incorporate the dynamic and interactive nature of intelligence and social adaptation, as reflected in Anastasi's (1986) statement that "intelligent behavior is essentially adaptive, insofar as it represents ways of meeting the demands of a changing environment" (pp. 19–20). According to Leland (1992), the original AAMR formulation of adaptive behavior (Heber, 1961) was based on what might now be termed the *Vygotskyian historical–contextualist worldview* (Rogoff, 1990; Vygotsky, 1978), but this dynamic, contextualist dimension was not emphasized in later operationalizations of the construct.

Implicit in the historical–contextualist perspective are two important and related assumptions: (a) Humans are embedded in a social context, and human behavior is effective or sophisticated in relation to goals, values, and resources operative within that context (Rogoff, 1990); and (b) one's actual developmental level can be understood only by looking directly at the process of learning and change and at the ability to benefit from mediating interactions, not just by looking at the products of learning. If incorporated into efforts to measure everyday intelligence (whether under the rubric of adaptive behavior, adaptive skills, or some other term), these assumptions would be reflected in greater attention to the sociocultural and family context (Switzky & Utley, 1991) and related issues of motivation (Switzky, in press), and use of dynamic and interactive assessment methods (cf. Feuerstein, Klein, & Tannenbaum, 1991; Haywood & Switzky, 1986) and related cognitive education methods (Resnick & Klopfer, 1989) for assessing and enhancing everyday skills.

The 1992 AAMR manual is congruent with a historical–contextualist perspective in many ways, especially in its emphases on the possibility of growing out of the condition and on direct measurement of needed supports, although the definition reflects a more static and IQ-dominated paradigm (Greenspan, 1994). In a sense, the view of MR proposed here as a condition marked by deficits in everyday intelligence in socially relevant and important contexts, and that persists in spite of skilled interventions, is a return to the early twentieth century notion of MR as reflecting "stupidity" rather than "ignorance" (A. F. Tredgold, 1922). Critics of the approach outlined in this chapter might argue that the greatest remaining conceptual problem for incorporating ideas about everyday intelligence into the conceptualization of MR remains the differentiation of MR from other conditions affecting adaptation, such as degenerative neurological disorders and severe mental illness, to the extent that this is necessary or desirable in particular areas of clinical usage. Nevertheless, by recapturing the historical and phenomenological basis of MR, it will be possible to define the class in a manner that will be congruent with the natural taxon, win wider professional acceptance and use, and provide a legitimate basis for making correct decisions about service eligibility for people who may need help in adapting to everyday life.

9

Adaptive Development, Survival Roles, and Quality of Life

Rune J. Simeonsson and Rick J. Short

Although the concept of adaptive behavior has been central to the definition of mental retardation (MR), operationalizing the concept has constituted a significant challenge for assessment, diagnosis, eligibility, and service considerations. The extent of this challenge is evident in the array of terms used to define the concept, including *social maturity*, *social intelligence*, *adaptive functioning*, and *adaptive development*. In this chapter, we use the terms *adaptive behavior* and *adaptive development* to refer to this domain of development.

The nature and role of adaptive behavior were formalized in a 1983 classification manual in which the concept was defined as "significant limitations in an individual's effectiveness in meeting the standards of maturation, learning, personal independence, and/or social responsibility that are expected for his or her age level and cultural group" (Grossman, 1983, p. 11). This formalization stimulated the development of a variety of standardized measures designed to assess the dimension of adaptive functioning in persons identified with MR and persons demonstrating significant intellectual limitations on standardized intelligence tests. The last decade has witnessed a substantial body of research using such measures devoted to documenting the nature of adaptive behavior and its correlates. Findings, although extensive, have not contributed to a coherent and consensual view of what adaptive behavior is or how it should be assessed.

The field is thus faced with the new challenge of operationalizing the most recent iteration of the concept in the 1992 American Association on Mental Retardation (AAMR) definition of MR, which requires the co-occurrence of two or more limitations in the "following applicable adaptive skill areas: communication, self care, home living, social skills, community use, self-direction, health and safety, functional academics, leisure and work" (Luckasson et al., 1992, p. 1). The nature of this definition and its implications for the identification of individuals with MR have become the subjects of considerable applied research and social policy concerns and have elicited a substantial amount of critique. A comprehensive review by MacMillan, Gresham, and Siperstein (1993) is representative of such critiques, focusing on a range of difficult issues including those germane to the assessment of adaptive behavior.

The array of terms for adaptive behavior, the associated variable definitions, and the inclusive nature of domains encompassed by the terms reflect continuing problems in operationalizing the concept in practical contexts. The purpose of this chapter is to examine the concept of adaptive behavior and its development by (a) reviewing current issues as they relate to this concept, (b) advancing the need for organizing conceptual models, and (c) proposing a framework for the specification of adaptive behavior and development, building on complementary contributions of policy goals, survival roles, and quality-of-life conceptions.

Conceptual Issues

Adaptive behavior, including its development and role in defining MR, has received frequent attention in the literature. The significance of the concept to the field of MR is widely endorsed; however, its measurement and application have been the focus of persistent debate. At least three major problems may account for this state of affairs: definitional variability, inclusive and overlapping domains, and lack of conceptual frameworks or models.

The problem of variable terms and definitions is evident in references to adaptive behavior, adaptive functioning, social maturity, and social competence. One of the key conceptual dilemmas precipitated by these models is whether adaptive behavior should be conceptualized in its own right, as adaptive skills, or as social or social–developmental maturity and sophistication. On the basis of various terms employed to represent essentially the same concern, a variety of measures, tests, and inventories have been developed to assess the extent to which an individual's functioning meets established criteria for typical or atypical personal and social performance.

A second, related problem with regard to use of the adaptive behavior concept in services for persons with MR has been the overlapping nature of domains of many of the measures. Under the rubric of adaptive behavior, it is not uncommon to find a long list of skills, abilities, and behaviors. The 1992 definition of adaptive skill areas provides a good illustration of this point. This range may include intellectual, academic, and vocational skills, as well as measures of social maturity and personal competence. Additional domains are likely to encompass motor skills, communicative behaviors, and items often defined in terms of activities of daily living. Furthermore, maladaptive or problem behaviors have often been included as essential components. The overly inclusive nature of the concept in operationalization on specific scales has precipitated much of the debate that has occurred about the structure of adaptive behavior.

Adaptive behavior has variously been defined as unidimensional, two-dimensional, or multidimensional in nature. As Bruininks, McGrew, and Maruyama (1988) have noted, variability is likely attributable to differences in methodology, items, and samples. In a well-designed study using the Scales of Independent Behavior, these investigators sought to address these methodological problems. The findings revealed that a single general factor accounted for much of the variance across samples of different age and mental ability levels. Additional factors were found for some subsamples, but their contribution to explained variance was modest, leading Bruininks and colleagues to conclude that these results reinforced other findings of a general dimension of adaptive behavior. In the general population, it is quite likely that there are obvious developmental components to this construct. Thus, even though adaptive behavior measures may encompass a substantial number of subscales, in practice what is measured involves overlapping aspects of a common derived factor of Personal Independence. The fact that adaptive behavior indexes are often correlated with measures of intelligence and achievement continues to raise questions about the uniqueness of the concept as currently measured. At the same time, since these correlations between intelligence and adaptive behavior measures are only moderate in size, there is a value to assessing both aspects of individual functioning.

Problems in determining the dimensional structure of adaptive behavior may also involve the way in which the measures were developed. A methodological concern noted in an earlier review of this topic (Simeonsson, 1978) still obtains: Instruments are largely developed on a pragmatic basis, defined by an aggregation of items that are often derived from clinical consensus of models that are validated empirically using factor analysis. To advance the construct of adaptive behavior and its measurement, there is a need for conceptual frameworks to guide the development and empirical validation of instruments. The fact that important aspects of personal competence such as motivation and social inference are typically not included in measures of adaptive behavior (Bruininks et al., 1988) reflects the lack of underlying conceptual frames for the construct. This problem could be addressed by incorporating items from the domains of interpersonal competence that are based on contributions from social cognitive theory and research. Simeonsson (1978) suggested that social cognitions defined by such skills as role taking, person perception, and referential communication should be a central feature of a broad adaptive behavior construct that is sensitive to a person's social context and his or her ability to influence this context. Along a similar line, but in a more detailed manner, Greenspan (1979) advanced a comprehensive model of social intelligence. In addition to expanding the construct of adaptive behavior, these conceptual frameworks draw on major perspectives in social cognitive theory and can thus address problems of sensitivity to developmental issues in current adaptive behavior assessment.

Organizing Frameworks

Continuing changes in the philosophy and nature of programs for persons with MR require changes in conceptualizations of adaptive development that can advance more situationally sensitive assessment and intervention practices. Of fundamental importance is the identification of organizing frameworks reflecting ideological changes and providing consistent approaches to the concept of disability. To this end, three frameworks are presented here with reference to the concept of adaptive development and behavior for persons with MR. These provide a means to expand usefulness of these concepts rather than specific recommendations to challenge contemporary definitions of MR. As noted earlier in this chapter, MacMillan and colleagues (1993) extensively reviewed the problems raised by the most recent definition, with particular respect to the issue of how to reliably measure dimensions of adaptive skills and needed supports. Rather than repeating that critique, the following material offers an alternative framework for how most usefully to operationalize adaptive development.

In the search for ways to expand the concept of adaptive behavior, there are at least three organizing frameworks of potential usefulness. In general terms, these frameworks derive from theory, from broad policy principles, and from the concept of disablement (Wood & Badley, 1978). Although they differ in derivation and content, these notions are advanced as having potential complementarity for specification of the construct of adaptive behavior in that they focus on dimensions of the individual's interpersonal competence, goals for societal adaptation, and the nature and extent of such adaptation, respectively. Drawing on contributions from cognitive constructivist theory, Greenspan (1979) proposed a comprehensive model of social intelligence that encompasses hierarchical dimensions of social reasoning, comprehension, and inference, the latter including rational, logical, and social inference. In particular, Greenspan emphasized the importance of differentiating instrumental from social competence (Greenspan & Granfield, 1992). In other words, these terms emphasize a distinction between effectiveness in getting things done oneself and in getting others to do the thing with which one needs help. The latter remains an important and relatively poorly assessed dimension, especially of social functioning. As such, the model of social intelligence provides a framework in which aspects of personal adaptation not typically assessed in adaptive behavior scales can be differentiated and assessed. Although this model is underresearched, it may have significant potential as an important component of clinical decision making for the community practitioner.

A second organizing framework for specification of adaptive development can be drawn from major ideological principles defined in the Americans With Disabilities Act (ADA). These policy principles—equality of opportunity, full participation, independent living, and economic self-sufficiency—can be seen as societal standards whereby communal, social, personal, and economic adaptation are defined. They constitute, in effect, environmentally relevant domains of adaptive behavior. These categories define both the conditions under which and the extent to which an individual adapts to the environment. Although these principles are defined in terms of adults, they parallel principles of least restrictive environments and inclusion for children and students with disabilities and the competencies that are pertinent to these guiding perspectives.

A third organizing framework is the conceptual model of the dimensions of disablement originally presented in the *International Classifica-*

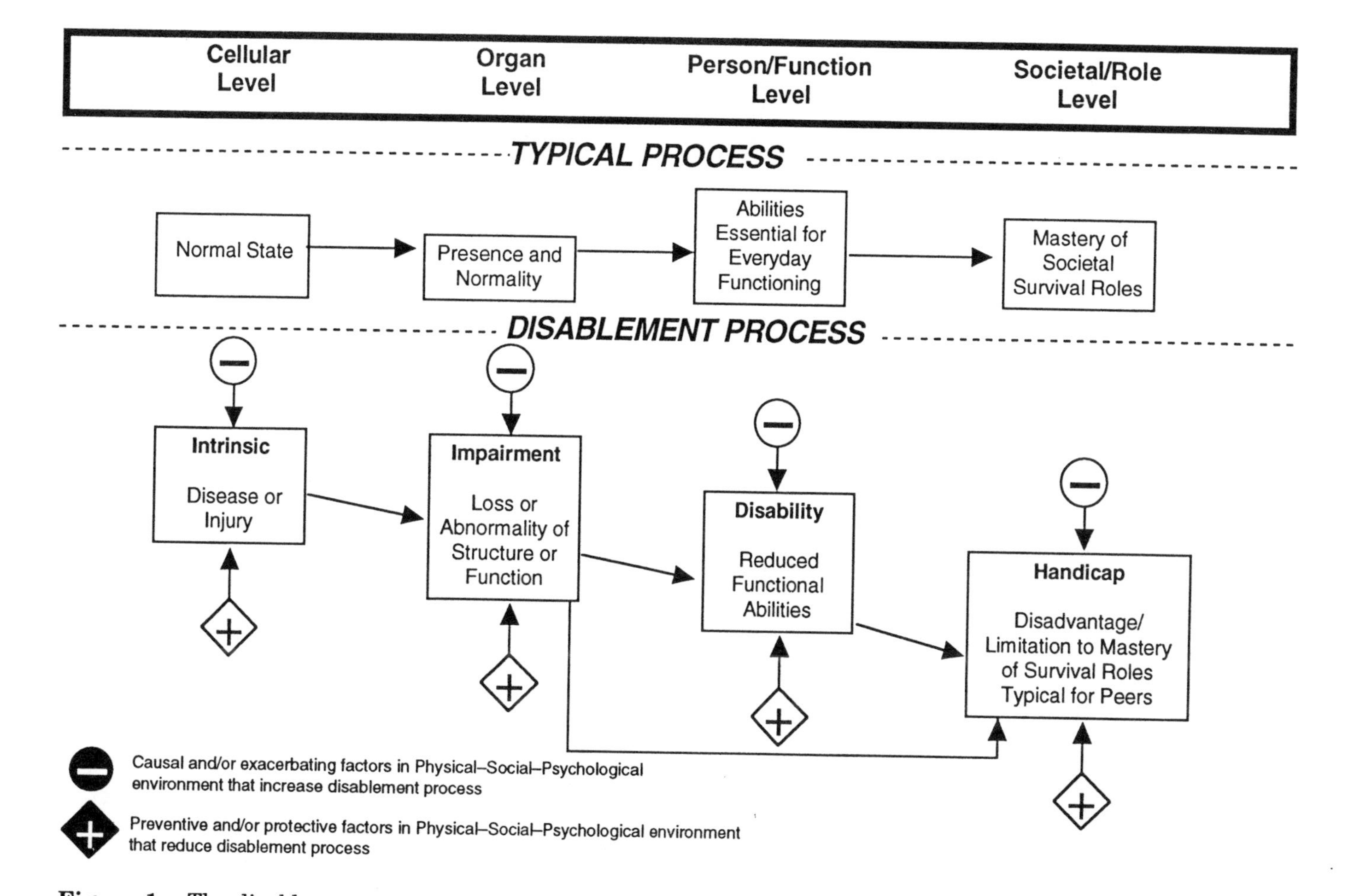

Figure 1. The disablement process and the role of the environment: A conceptual model of the *ICIDH* (WHO, 1980)

tion of Impairments, Disabilities and Handicaps (*ICIDH*; World Health Organization [WHO], 1980b) and currently in the process of revision to enhance its usefulness in clinical and research applications. The value of this framework, as illustrated in Figure 1, is that it provides a logical and semantically consistent approach to the consequences of an intrinsic condition attributable to a congenital or acquired cause. Although a sequential relationship is posited for impairments, disabilities, and handicaps, the sequence is not necessarily linear nor obligate. Thus, an impairment does not necessarily result in a disability, which, in turn, does not necessarily result in the experience of handicap. However, in practice, particularly in Western societies, general intellectual impairments typically result in the attribution of disability as well as handicap. Of particular relevance for this discussion is the distinction the model makes among impairment, disability, and handicap. Furthermore, given its international use, consideration of the *ICIDH* has important implications for promoting comparative policy and research. With reference to the condition of MR, the model would distinguish between impairment of intellectual structures and the possible consequences of such impairment in terms of disability and handicap. As such, it provides a way to differentiate limited intellectual capacity and associated disabilities from the experience of handicap or disadvantage.

In the context of this chapter, this distinction is posited to parallel the differentiation between intellectual and adaptive behavior deficits in the definition of MR. The term *handicap* in the *ICIDH* model differs from its typical use in North America and refers to

> a disadvantage for a given individual . . . that prevents or limits the fulfillment of a role that is normal for that individual. Disadvantage arises from failure or inability to conform to the expectations or norms of the individual's universe. Handicap thus occurs when there is interference with the ability to sustain what might be designated as "survival roles." (WHO, 1980b, p. 183)

These survival roles are identified as disadvantage or handicap relative to situational orientation, physical independence, mobility, occupation, social integration, and economic self-sufficiency. An examination of these survival roles suggests a correspondence with dimensions common to most adaptive behavior scales.

Functional Assessment

A research focus and clinical practice sensitivity to three different, but complementary frameworks to expand consideration of the construct of adaptive development and its application in services for individuals with MR have been recommended here. The conceptual usefulness of two of these frameworks, ADA goals and the *ICIDH* model, has been advanced in an article by S. C. Brown (1993) in the related area of defining indicators for research on disability programs. Given the fact that these frameworks are not well or fully represented in most existing measures of adaptive development and behavior, it would be useful to examine their applicability in assessment and intervention planning efforts in the field of MR. This task may be facilitated by two converging trends in the field of rehabilitation. Both of these trends pertain to the search for assessment approaches appropriate for documenting functional changes in individual ability.

One approach that has potential clinical value has been process-oriented, focusing on assessment of functional status. Although functional assessment has been defined in a number of ways, the typical format has been to document an individual's functioning across selected domains of physical and social skills and activities of daily living (Frattali, 1993; Granger, Cotter, Hamilton, & Fiedler, 1993). As such, the focus is usually on broad (molar) dimensions of functioning rather than specific features. Furthermore, functional assessment differs from standardized measures in a number of ways. These include a reliance on clinical judgment, the use of criterion-referenced items, and the ordinal scaling of items. There is a growing number of functional assessment measures across a variety of domains; most are adult-oriented and use some form of ordinal rating scale to yield a profile of individual functioning. Representative measures encompass domains among adults such as medical status (e.g., Patient Severity Index; S. D. Horn & Horn, 1986), activities of daily living (e.g., Barthel ADL Index; Wade & Collin, 1988), rehabilitation outcomes (e.g., Functional Independence Measure; Bonwich & Reid, 1991), and functional abilities of children (e.g., ABILITIES Index; Simeonsson, Bailey, Smith, & Buysse, in press).

A second approach has focused on a specific content area of functioning, termed *quality of life* (QOL; see chap. 15, this volume, for additional discussion of QOL measurement). Although *quality of life* has been an accepted scientific term for more than 15 years, there is no consensus on a definition and no single index recognized as the standard measure of QOL (Bech, 1992). Given this situation, a frequent approach to measurement of QOL is to use several measures covering overlapping functional domains of personal and social activity (Warshaw, Lavori, & Leon, 1992). Building on a functional assessment format, QOL scales typically call for judgments by significant others in the form of ordinal ratings of adaptation to individual life situations in areas such as safety, physical health, living conditions, and emotional well-being (Cummins, 1991). Commenting on the diversity of QOL measures, Bech (1992) emphasized the distinction between components involving health status and components involving subjective experience of the individual.

Along a similar line, Cummins (1991) proposed that QOL measures differ as a function of whether they are objective or subjective indicators. The distinction between an objective and a subjective indicator can be illustrated with respect to documented health status and perceived health. A specific example of an objective indicator is the QUALCARE Scale, a scale designed to rate the quality of caregiving for elderly individuals living at home using dimensions like physical hygiene, medical maintenance, and human rights (Phillips, Morrison, & Chao, 1990). The focus of a subjective indicator, on the other hand, is to capture the "manner in which individuals perceive and evaluate their personal QOL" (Thunedborg, Allerup, Bech, & Joyce, 1993, p. 45). Among protocols used to accomplish this task has been the repertory grid technique, in which a semistructured interview is administered to assess perceived QOL (Thunedborg et al., 1993). A comprehensive assessment of QOL, therefore, should encompass both objective and subjective features.

A consideration of adaptive development and behavior in the context of the domain coverage of QOL measures suggests significant commonality of such areas as self-help skills, socialization, and daily life activities in the home and community. The distinction between objective and subjective indicators further suggests that adaptation should be considered not only in terms of characteristics and attributes of the person in context but, of equal importance, in terms of an assessment of the person's subjective perceptions. The disproportionate emphasis on assessing objective, relative to subjective, indicators in QOL studies seems parallel to concerns about the potential role of personal dimensions relative to social dimensions in investigations of adaptive behavior (Bruininks et al., 1988). Similarly, the differentiation between practical and social intelligence described by Greenspan and Granfield (1992) seems consistent with the importance Bech (1992) and others have attached to documenting both objective and subjective aspects of QOL.

It is useful to note that two fields addressing the parallel problems of MR and clinical disability, respectively, have developed two separate traditions to measure adaptation of the individual to environmental demands. In the former tradition, the construct of adaptive behavior has been approached in a normative way. In the latter tradition, the approach has relied on clinical ratings of QOL. However, there is substantial overlap of the domains investigated, with growing interest in applying the QOL concept to MR and developmental disabilities (Goode, 1994; Schalock, 1994). Furthermore, there appear to be similar concerns in both traditions about the disproportionate focus placed on objective dimensions of adaptation relative to personal, subjective aspects. A major factor contributing to this state of affairs may well be the lack of conceptual frameworks to define the domains in a logical and comprehensive manner. The importance of conceptual bases, however, has been recognized with regard to adaptive behavior (Greenspan & Granfield, 1992) and QOL (Bech, 1992; Thunedborg et al., 1993), with recommendations made for assessment of each area, respectively.

Given the impetus for continued societal integration of children, adolescents, and adults with disabilities embodied in recent federal legislation and social policy, more inclusive models of the individual's adaptation to and perceptions of the demands of physical, social, and psychological environments are indicated. Thus, it would seem useful to synthesize complementary contributions from the two orientations toward QOL. This synthesis could provide an expanded framework within which future assess-

ADA Policy Goals	ICIDH Survival Roles Quality of Life Dimensions	
	Objective Opportunity	*Subjective Experience*
Equal Opportunity	OCCUPATION*	(Satisfaction)†
Full Participation	(Access)†	SOCIAL INTEGRATION*
Independent Living	MOBILITY* PHYSICAL INDEPENDENCE* (Action/Interaction)†	(Control)† (Freedom)† ORIENTATION*
Economic Self-Sufficiency	ECONOMIC SELF-SUFFICIENCY*	(Dignity)†

*Survival Roles (ICIDH / WHO)
†Reciprocal Dimensions

Figure 2. Adaptive development and quality of life: A juxtaposition of policy goals (ADA) and survival roles (*ICIDH*; WHO, 1980).

ment strategies and measures could be approached. Central to such a consideration are the four policy themes of the ADA. As summarized in Figure 2, these four policy goals define broad societal goals as well as the context for individual adaptation.

Adequacy of adaptation and QOL are thus defined by the extent to which survival roles are mastered or fulfilled (WHO, 1980b). Working within the survival role framework, reduced QOL is consistent with the definition of *handicap* or *disadvantage* that "arises from failure or inability to conform to the expectations or norms of the individual's universe" (WHO, 1980b, p. 183). Furthermore, as Cummins (1991) proposed, the nature of disadvantage may be expressed in both objective and subjective dimensions of QOL.

The importance of recognizing this difference is paralleled by the importance of the distinction between practical and social intelligence in the Greenspan and Granfield (1992) model of social competence. It is also recognized in the *ICIDH* description of disadvantage as "characterized by a discordance between the individual's performance or status and the expectations of the individual himself or the particular group of which he is a member" (WHO, 1980b, p. 183). The distinction between the objective and subjective experience of handicap has been illustrated in an interesting application of the *ICIDH* with individuals with muscular dystrophy (Ville, Ravaud, Marchal, Paicheler, & Fardeau, 1992). Recognition of the complementary nature of objective and subjective dimensions of adaptation is reflected in the differential assignment of survival roles relative to the four policy goals. Although the relevance of these survival roles to the dimensions and goals cannot be assumed to be mutually exclusive, the model should have heuristic value in identifying the focus of assessment. Furthermore, it is important to recognize that each survival role is likely to have a reciprocal dimension defined in terms of objective opportunity or subjective experience. Building on the literature in this review and extant studies, a variety of functional measures can be identified within the model to advance practice and research pertaining to assessment of adaptive development among persons with MR.

Conclusion

Although adaptive behavior and its development have been studied extensively, the construct remains debated and relatively elusive in the field of MR. There are a number of reasons that the debate continues, with the central issues being methodological variability and limited conceptual bases, particularly pertaining to the experience of adaptation as perceived by the individual. In this chapter we have advocated for an expanded and more focused approach to adaptive development by drawing on the framework of disablement and complementary contributions from investigations of functional assessment and QOL. Adaptive development can then be conceptualized as the extent to which survival roles are mastered and QOL is realized relative to major policy goals for the societal integration of persons with disabilities.

10

Psychopathology in Mental Retardation

Johannes Rojahn and Marc J. Tassé

The term *psychopathology* as used in this chapter encompasses two distinct clinical phenomena. On the one hand, it refers to classic psychiatric disorders, such as schizophrenia or affective disorders, which are also present in the population at large. Yet it may also refer to a variety of perplexing behavior disorders that are particularly prevalent in people with mental retardation (MR). The most common types of these behavior disorders are aggressive behavior directed against other people, destructive behavior, self-injurious behavior, and stereotyped behavior. This chapter discusses the prevalence of documented psychiatric diagnoses and behavior problems in two large populations receiving state-funded services for individuals with developmental disabilities. In addition, it points to some diagnostic issues specific to this population and reviews a selection of currently available screening and assessment techniques.

Since the 1970s, population surveys have repeatedly revealed that people with MR are particularly vulnerable to psychopathology—more so than nonhandicapped persons (Jacobson, 1990; Lewis & MacLean, 1982; Nezu, Nezu, & Gill-Weiss, 1992; S. Reiss, 1994; Rutter, Tizard, Yule, Graham, & Whitmore, 1976). In the meantime, psychopathology has become recognized as the most serious predicament for psychologists, schoolteachers, rehabilitation counselors, and other service agency workers in dealing with people with MR. Psychopathology becomes a special challenge when the goal is to advance personal independence (Eaton & Menolascino, 1982) and is frequently the cause of institutionalization (Hill & Bruininks, 1984).

Although there are currently no well-substantiated explanations for this enhanced emotional vulnerability, it comes as no surprise that individuals with deficits in intellectual abilities and social competence may have greater coping difficulties in a complex environment (Menolascino & Stark, 1984). Subaverage intellectual abilities and limitations in adaptive skills, which are inextricably associated with MR (Grossman, 1983; Luckasson et al., 1992), most likely contribute to recurring experiences of stress, fear, and lack of control and to a profound sense of uncertainty. Nezu et al. (1992) proposed Seligman's (1975) model of "learned helplessness" to explain the greater vulnerability of people with MR to psychopathology, whereas Baumeister's "new morbidity" model of MR suggests that inadequacies of cognitive skills and adaptive behavior repertoires in combination with biomedical, social, and environmental factors predispose these individuals to chronic emotional disturbances (Baumeister, Dokecki, & Kupstas, 1988).

Prevalence

People with MR do experience the full spectrum of psychiatric disorders (Nezu et al. 1992; S. Reiss, 1994). The reported prevalence of psychopathology in people with MR varies from 10%–40%. Table 1 presents prevalence studies reported on US populations published since 1980. For a more complete inventory of existing prevalence studies, the reader is referred to Jacobson (1990), Nezu et al. (1992), and S. Reiss (1994).

The variability in reported prevalence may be explainable by numerous factors:

1. *The population sampled.* Several studies have documented a strong relationship between the rate of occurrence of psychopathology and the level of MR (Borthwick-Duffy & Eyman, 1990; Jacobson, 1982). People with mild MR are more likely to be diagnosed with a psychiatric disorder, whereas behavior disorders such as self-injurious behavior are clearly more prevalent as the IQ level drops (Maurice & Trudel, 1982; Rojahn, 1994). A prevalence study should include a clear identification of the sample according to levels of MR.
2. *The definition of MR.* The diagnostic criteria used to define MR impacts the number of individuals identified with MR (A. T. Russell, 1988). If a prevalence study operationally defines MR with only an IQ cutoff criterion, the sample will be larger than if a second criterion of concurrent deficits in adaptive behavior is also included.
3. *Completeness of the list of psychiatric disorders surveyed.* S. Reiss, in an exhaustive review of published studies to date, identified obsessive–compulsive disorder, panic disorder, and possibly post-traumatic disorder as being less prevalent in individuals with MR than in the general population and reported that maladaptive personality traits and maladaptive behaviors may be more prevalent in individuals with MR than in the general population (S. Reiss, 1990, 1994). Reiss stated that if personality disorders and maladaptive behaviors are excluded from prevalence studies, the rate of psychopathology in individuals with MR is similar to that reported in the general population.
4. *The method employed for establishing the presence of psychopathology.* A lower prevalence rate is generally reported in studies examining case files rather than directly assessing individuals for psychopathology (S. Reiss, 1990). S. Reiss (1994) proposed three plausible explanations for the underreporting of psychiatric dis-

Table 1. Prevalence Studies Reported on US Populations Published After 1980

Study	Sample	N	Ages (years)	Identification method	Prevalence (%)
Borthwick-Duffy & Eyman (1990)	Individuals in California's MR/DD service database	78,603	All	Client Development Evaluation Report	10
Eaton & Menolascino (1982)	Participants in a community-based MR/DD program	798	6–76	Service referrals and individual psychiatric interviews	14
Hill & Bruininks (1984)	Survey of individuals in public and community facilities	2,271	All	Interviews with direct-care staff	Public 36 Commun. 30
Jacobson (1982)	Individuals in New York's MR/DD service database	30,578	All	Developmental Disabilities Information System	12
S. Reiss (1985)	Surveyed children with MR in public schools in Illinois	5,637	5–21	Review of IEP evaluations	10
S. Reiss (1990)	Individuals participating in community-based MR/DD programs	205	>12	Reiss Screen and psychological evaluation to confirm diagnosis	39

Note. MR/DD = mental retardation/developmental disabilities; IEP = individualized education plan.

Table 2. Prevalence (1:100) of Behavior Problems in Different Age Groups From the California and New York State Service Databases

	Age range and population size			
	0–10 n_{NY} = 2,724 n_{CA} = 26,841	11–20 n_{NY} = 8,837 n_{CA} = 16,897	21–45 n_{NY} = 34,122 n_{CA} = 45,681	0–45 n_{NY} = 45,683 n_{CA} = 89,419
Aggression	2.3	7.4	13.1	11.3
	7.6	13.8	14.9	12.5
Self-injurious	1.7	5.3	7.9	7.9
behavior	7.6	10.0	9.0	8.0
Destruction	0.5	2.6	4.3	4.3
	4.1	7.7	8.1	6.8
Stereotypies[a]	1.7	6.0	7.0	6.5
	4.1	6.9	7.9	6.5

Note. Top figure within a cell = prevalence from New York database; bottom figure within a cell = prevalence from California database. From "The Association Between Psychiatric Diagnoses and Severe Behavior Problems in Mental Retardation," by J. Rojahn, S. A. Borthwick-Duffy, and J. W. Jacobson, 1993, *Annals of Clinical Psychiatry, 5,* p. 166. Copyright 1993 by Plenum. Reprinted with permission.
[a]Stereotyped behaviors are conspicuous to the average person and appear unusual, strange, or inappropriate. They are voluntary, idiosyncratic actions that repeat or recur.

orders in case files: misunderstanding of vulnerability of people with MR to psychiatric disorders, absence of trained psychiatrists in the field of MR able to provide psychiatric evaluations of people with MR, and a tendency to attribute mental health symptomatology to consequences of MR rather than a psychiatric disorder. Reiss, Levitan, and Szyszko (1982) coined the term *diagnostic overshadowing* to depict the latter phenomenon. Epidemiologically sound studies of psychopathology in people with MR in the United States remain to be published. For a more thorough review of the existing limitations of current epidemiological studies, the reader should consult Jacobson (1990) and Stark, Menolascino, Albarelli, and Gray (1988).

Prevalence estimates of behavior disorders are presented in Table 2. Four types of behavior disorders are shown broken down into broad age cohorts. Figures for this table originated from the databases of two public developmental disabilities service agencies, one from California and the other from New York. The sample populations in both states were restricted to people from birth to 45 years of age who had a diagnosis of MR. All levels of MR were represented. In the age range of 0–45 years, these agencies combined served more than 130,000 people with disabilities (Rojahn, Borthwick-Duffy, & Jacobson, 1993).

Aggression was consistently the most frequent behavior disorder, ranging from 11.3% of the population who received public developmental disabilities support in California to 12.5% of this population in New York. The next most prevalent behavior disorder was self-injurious behavior.

The California database showed consistently higher prevalence estimates than the New York database across all four behaviors and age ranges. It must be cautioned that absolute prevalence estimates of behavior disorders are often unreliable from a scientific perspective. They are known to vary widely across different surveys, depending on a multitude of methodological discrepancies (Rojahn, 1994). Yet relative prevalence estimates of the various behavior disorders are more robust.

Diagnostic Issues

Current data suggest that the prevalence of diagnosed psychiatric disorders *drops* with declining levels of intellectual functioning, whereas the opposite trend has been noted with most behavior disorders (Jacobson, 1982). These epidemiological findings should be viewed with caution, however, particularly those concerning psychiatric diagnoses. Although the data may indeed reflect true prevalence of psychiatric disorders, it is more likely that they are strongly confounded by the fact that documented psychiatric *diagnoses* become increasingly scarce as intellectual level declines. The likelihood of a psychiatric diagnosis diminishes as the client's intellectual and verbal language capabilities decline because of the growing difficulty in obtaining a reliable diagnosis. This is particularly true for internalizing disorders. Declining levels of functioning are clearly much less of a concern for the identification of observable behavior disorders.

Since the publication of the early epidemiological studies of psychopathology in MR, researchers have sought to establish the existence of a relationship between psychiatric disorders and severe behavior disorders. Empirical support for such an intuitive relation remains elusive. Data presented in Table 3, taken from Rojahn et al. (1993), address this issue. Consistent across the two databases was the absence of a compelling linear relationship between any of the behavior disorders and the psychiatric disorders. None of these correlations exceeded a level of $r = .20$, and the majority were $r \leq .01$. This means that the presence of aggression, self-injurious behavior, destruction, or stereotypies does not determine whether a person receives a psychiatric diagnosis. Conversely, the absence of these behavior disorders should not rule out the presence of a psychiatric disorder (Rojahn et al., 1993). Substantial positive relationships did exist between the behavior disorders. For instance, aggression was strongly associated with destructive behavior and self-injurious behavior. Data on the relationship between self-injurious behavior and stereotyped behavior and between self-injurious behavior and destructive behavior were inconsistent across the two databases.

It remains difficult to specify the relationship between psychiatric disorders and behavior disorders definitively from the previously presented data. The apparent lack of relationship is true only as far as linear pairwise relationships are concerned. Univariate correlation analysis is certainly not the most powerful tool for exploring such interrelationships. Perhaps more sophisticated theory-driven analytic methods, such as struc-

Table 3. Correlations Between Major Psychiatric Diagnoses and Behavior Problems From the California and New York State Service Databases

Diagnosis	Aggression	Destruction	Self-injurious behavior	Stereotypies
Attention-deficit hyperac-	.03	.03	.02	−.00
tivity disorder	−.01	.00	−.00	.01
Conduct disorder	.06	.05	.02	.01
	−.02	−.01	−.02	−.02
Pervasive developmental	.01	.00	.01	.02
disorder	.02	.01	.03	.11
Adjustment disorder	.01	.01	−.00	−.01
	.00	.00	−.02	−.01
Anxiety disorder	.01	.01	.01	.00
	−.01	−.01	−.01	−.00
Organic brain syndrome	.01	.00	−.01	.00
	−.01	−.01	−.01	.02
Schizophrenic disorder	.18	.11	.04	.03
	.00	−.00	−.01	.01
Affective disorder	.05	.03	.01	−.00
	−.00	.01	−.00	−.01
Personality disorders	.01	.01	−.01	−.01
	−.01	−.01	−.01	−.01
Aggression	—	.40	.28	.16
		.23	.16	−.00
Destruction	—	—	.27	.17
			.08	−.01
Self-injurious behavior	—	—	—	.27
				.08

Note. Top figure within a cell is a φ coefficient from the California database (n = 89,419); bottom figure is a Pearson correlation coefficient from the New York database (n = 45,683). From "The Association Between Psychiatric Diagnoses and Severe Behavior Problems in Mental Retardation," by J. Rojahn, S. A. Borthwick-Duffy, and J. W. Jacobson, 1993, *Annals of Clinical Psychiatry, 5*, p. 176. Copyright 1993 by Plenum. Reprinted with permission.

tural equation modeling, would be more revealing. What these correlations do show, however, is that no simple relationships were found between behavior disorders and psychiatric disorders in these two databases.

Assessment

Interviews

Informal clinical interviews with the client (when possible) and informants who know the client well, such as parents, teachers, or day program supervisors, typically initiate the diagnostic process and precede structured assessment procedures. Standardized research interview protocols such as the Diagnostic Interview for Children and Adolescents (Reich & Welner, 1988) or the Structured Clinical Interview for DSM-III-R (Spitzer, Williams, Gibbon, & First, 1990) are available and have been used clinically in patients with MR. Unfortunately, there exists a paucity of psychometric data to ascertain the applicability of these interview protocols to individuals with MR. It can be assumed that they are much more suitable for people in the mild and high-moderate range of MR than for individuals in the severe-to-profound range of MR.

Rating Scales

The quality of standardized assessment instruments for psychopathology in MR is still rather modest. Psychometric properties for many of the available rating scales are often less than desirable. Nevertheless, several promising instruments have become available in recent years that can at least serve as useful screening tools for psychopathology in this population. Two types of rating scales are distinguishable: comprehensive scales that are intended to capture a broad range of conditions and more focused instruments with a narrow scope of measurements.

As far as comprehensive instruments go, there are two groupings of rating scales. The first group of instruments is based on mainstream psychiatric taxonomies such as the *Diagnostic and Statistical Manual of Mental Disorders* (*DSM-III-R*; APA, 1987) or the *International Classification of Diseases* (*ICD-9*; WHO, 1995). Thus, the development of such instruments was driven by a theoretical, a priori taxonomic model, and the scales are closely related to the diagnostic criteria listed in the *DSM* or *ICD* diagnostic systems. Items consist of rephrased statements that describe the diagnostic criteria to fit the population with MR. Examples of the theoretical approach are the Reiss Screen for Maladaptive Behavior (RSMB; S. Reiss, 1988), the Psychopathology Instrument for Mentally Retarded Adults (PIMRA; Matson, Kazdin, & Senatore, 1985), and the Diagnostic Assessment for the Severely Handicapped (DASH; Matson, Gardner, Coe, & Sovner, 1990). The RSMB is a screening instrument for psychiatric and behavior disorders in MR. It is completed by direct-care staff or other informants familiar with the client. The PIMRA is an assessment instrument intended to assist in the development of psychiatric diagnoses in adults with MR and the development and evaluation of treatment interventions. The PIMRA is available in an informant version and a self-report version. The DASH was designed to provide a comprehensive structured survey of psychiatric disorders, particularly in individuals with severe and profound MR. Of course, taxonomically driven scales may require periodic revision when the underlying taxonomy changes, such as revisions required by changes in diagnostic criteria between *DSM-III-R* (APA, 1987) and *DSM-IV* (APA, 1994), although this point is minimally relevant in the case of the scales discussed here.

The second type of instrument is based on an empirical, or a posteriori, taxonometric model. Rather than assuming the validity of psychopathology taxonomies, which are derived from nonhandicapped populations, these instruments consist only of salient behavioral items that were actually observed by clinicians. The subscales are derived in an inductive fashion through exploratory and confirmatory factor analytic procedures. Two popular examples of these instruments include the Aberrant Behavior Checklist (ABC; Aman, Singh, Stewart, & Field, 1985a) and the Strohmer–Prout Behavior Rating Scale (BRS; Strohmer & Prout, 1989). The BRS was intended to identify problem behaviors and personality characteristics in people with mild MR. The ABC, on the other hand, was originally developed primarily on the basis of data from institutionalized individuals in the lower ranges of cognitive abilities, but it has subsequently been shown to have a robust factor structure that validated its use with populations at all levels of MR (Marshburn & Aman, 1992).

In addition to these comprehensive, broad-spectrum instruments that cover a wide array of symptoms, there are other rating scales that focus either on specific psychiatric disorders or on specific behavior disorders. For example, the Self-Report Depression Questionnaire (SRDQ; W. M. Reynolds & Baker, 1988) is an instrument intended to assess the depth of the depressive symptomatology reported by adolescents and adults with mild-to-severe MR. Most of the SRDQ items correspond to one of the nine *DSM-III-R* symptoms for major depression, and each of the nine symptoms is represented by at least one SRDQ item. Internal consistency and test–retest reliability were reported to range from acceptable to very good. W. M. Reynolds and Baker (1988) also reported a solid correlation between the SRDQ and the Hamilton Scale, which they took as evidence of good criterion validity. The Behavior Problem Inventory (BPI; Rojahn, 1992) is a 32-item rating scale used to assess the frequency of behavior problems in people with MR. Items are rated on a 7-point scale, ranging from *never* to *more than hourly*. The BPI is an empirically developed assessment instrument that was originally designed for self-injurious behavior (SIB) and stereotyped behavior surveys (Rojahn, 1986) and was later expanded to include aggressive behavior (Rojahn, Polster, Mulick, & Wisniewski, 1989). The BPI is an instrument that is completed by an informant who knows the client well.

A critical and exhaustive review of available assessment instruments for psychopathology in MR was published by Aman (1991a). The interested reader is encouraged to consult this source directly for more details on these and other assessment instruments.

Direct Behavior Observation

Direct behavior observation relies exclusively on a trained observer, which makes it a particularly well-suited strategy for collecting reliable information on individuals with MR. During data collection, the observer classifies in an ongoing fashion targeted behavior into predefined, typically client-customized behavior categories. Standardized observation systems do exist (see, e.g., Schroeder, Rojahn, & Mulick, 1978). However, because this population is heterogeneous in etiology and presenting problems, the behaviors are highly idiosyncratic, making standardized observation systems less useful than with other clinical populations (e.g., patients who have conduct disorders or attention-deficit hyperactivity disorder [ADHD]).

Behavior is coded either in a discontinuous fashion, during certain time intervals (time sampling), or continuously. Continuous recording of behavioral events can consist of a simple count of the frequency of certain behaviors, or it can be highly complex, including ongoing real-time recording of exact times of onset and recording of duration of several concurrent behaviors of more than one individual (e.g., the client's behavior, the teacher's behavior, and peer behavior).

One of the advantages of observational techniques is their intuitive plausibility. Unlike tests and rating scales, their theoretical underpinnings and psychometric assumptions are relatively simple and straightforward, with results that are easily understood. Systematic observation techniques are often employed in addition and subsequent to interviews with parents or teachers. A more comprehensive account of observational methodologies as they relate to MR can be found in a chapter by Rojahn and Schroeder (1991).

Functional analysis refers to the procedure of identifying the factors maintaining a target behavior and is an important step in the process of planning any behavioral intervention (Konarski, Favell, & Favell, 1993; O'Neill, Horner, Albin, Storey, & Sprague, 1990). Ideally, functional analyses are based on the actual experimental testing of specific hypotheses concerning the maintaining conditions of the target behavior. These hypotheses are derived from unstructured behavior observations and interviews with people familiar with the client's behavior. Behavior motivation rating scales would be a more economical approach than actual clinical experimentation in which the client is repeatedly exposed to specific motivational conditions. Unfortunately, rating scales for motivational variables have proved to be unreliable.

Conclusion

People with MR experience the full spectrum of psychiatric disorders and clearly present more behavior disorders than are found in the general population. People with MR seem to be more vulnerable to emotional and behavioral disorders, and psychopathology in those with MR is reportedly more prevalent than in the general population. Psychiatric diagnoses become increasingly difficult to establish reliably as verbal communication skills, necessary to report emotional experiences or thoughts, and cognitive abilities decrease. Factors such as the level of MR of the population sampled, the definition of MR used to identify the sample, the completeness of the list of psychiatric disorders screened, and the method employed for establishing the presence of psychopathology may affect the reported prevalence of psychopathology in MR. Several assessment instruments have been developed to assist in screening for psychopathology in individuals with MR, but their general acceptance will require further refinement of the instruments and, quite possibly, of the diagnostic schema on which they are based as applied to MR.

11

Assessment of Social Functioning

Johnny L. Matson and David Hammer

Social behavior contributes to a range of human problems that can vary from mild adjustment difficulties to severe psychopathology. Nowhere is this issue more apparent than concerning people with mental retardation (MR), for whom skills and aptitudes for adjusting to day-to-day social events are often absent. This group has been shown to experience deficiencies in communication, self-control, anger management, correct recognition and labeling of affect in others, social problem solving, and a host of other areas at higher and more severe levels than the general population (Matson & Mulick, 1991a; also see chapter 10, this volume). Despite these difficulties, the mode of dealing with such problems for many years has been to isolate these people from society through institutionalization and special school programs, which has allowed for no interaction with the general population. This model of service provision further exacerbated the problem because little or no effort was made to help these people develop meaningful social, interpersonal, or psychological skills (Jacobson & Schwartz, 1991). Even at present, the philosophy of care that exists in many institutions and group homes is custodial. The treatment that is employed is largely reactive, with the major emphasis of programming on redirection, control, and confinement. Alternatively, passive learning is emphasized in the form of normalization. With this model, the notion is that the handicapped person will learn the requisite skills by observing normal behavior in others. Rarely have people with MR been taught to cope with their social deficiencies. Unfortunately, the limited research conducted to date suggests the need for active interventions to correct many of the social problems found in this group.

Because of this history of institutional inertia and misdirected, inefficient treatment, the recognition of social skills problems and means of remediation have gained slow acceptance in the field (Marchetti & Campbell, 1990). However, with the development of active interventions that proved effective through the efforts of behaviorally trained researchers and clinicians, parents and many mentally retarded people quickly recognized the value of a psychosocial approach as one means of reaching the goal of normal behavior. Social skills are essential in helping handicapped people adjust in the most normal fashion. Because effective interventions have been developed, social skills assessment and training should be considered an important priority in the assessment and treatment of people with MR.

Social Functioning Defined

The definition of social functioning used here follows the accepted social learning theory approach for social skills. Thus, *social skills* are defined as specific measurable interpersonal behaviors. This definition corresponds to the experimental literature in terms of the reference to skills that can be reliably assessed and of the terminology used, and it is reflected in the measures of social skills that are reviewed later in this chapter. Items that refer to internal mental events or psychic conflict as opposed to observable, definable behaviors are excluded because, in general, they are difficult to measure reliably. Additionally, many of the items identified as social skills in prominent adaptive behavior measures, such as eating and dressing skills, are not included in our definition because these are not social in an interactive sense. This interpersonal skills approach follows the general literature on social behavior.

Given that social skills should be defined as interpersonal in nature, many commonly used assessment techniques are inappropriate. Therefore, it is best not to rely on common measures of adaptive behavior such as the Vineland Social Maturity Scale or the American Association on Mental Retardation Adaptive Behavior Scale. These scales have subscales that are purported to measure social behavior, when in actuality the skills assessed are self-help skills or measures of disruptive behavior. Later in this chapter, we discuss social skills measures. However, these assessment tools are specific to discrete socialization behaviors such as establishing eye contact, making socially appropriate compliments, using appropriate social affect, and making helpful comments.

Value of Social Skills

Social skills permeate all aspects of a person's life (Matson & Ollendick, 1988). Deficiencies or excesses in these behaviors determine how well individuals are accepted by others, the number and quality of friends they have, and a host of other adaptive outcomes. Indeed, social skills have been a defining aspect of MR in the past (Grossman, 1983). Additionally, social skills problems have been linked to many other societal problems such as juvenile delinquency (Roff, Sell, & Golden, 1972) and mental health problems including schizophrenia (Hersen & Bellack, 1976), substance abuse (Monti, Abrams, Binkoff, & Zuick, 1986), and depression (Libet & Lewinsohn, 1973). Aggression and conduct problems, which are serious and common among people with MR, are also frequently influenced by social skills problems (Gardner & Cole, 1986). For example, children with conduct disorders are the patients most commonly referred to behavior therapists among all children (Abikoff & Klein, 1992), and childhood aggression is known to persist into adulthood (Olweus, 1979; Shechtman, 1970). Often, people aggress or act disruptively because they do not know how to deal with stressful situations in socially appropriate ways (a skills deficit). In other cases, the person may have learned the appropriate social skills, but the environment fails to reward their use (a performance deficit). Thus, social skills are important to consider for persons with MR. Furthermore, as many of the studies previously cited have shown, social skills problems can be remediated to a large extent. Although social problems are not considered to be criteria for making a diagnosis of MR, this area is of considerable importance for overall individual adjustment and happiness. In terms of helping people with MR live the most normal life possible, this area is undoubtedly one of the most critical. A brief review of methods for identifying social skills problems, a first step in remediating these deficiencies, follows.

Purpose of Assessment

The principal reasons for conducting assessments are threefold: diagnosis, treatment prescription, and evaluation of treatment effect. Much of this book focuses on the diagnosis of MR; however, the significance of assessment of social skills is not so much for diagnosis as it is for determining which behaviors to treat and for evaluating treatment effectiveness. A diagnosis is a global characteristic of an individual and does not describe all that needs to be assessed and targeted for treatment to promote normalized living. Thus, prescriptive social skills assessment is viewed as extremely important but augmentative to the diagnosis. However, such assessment is not optional; it represents, in fact, a necessary aspect of the comprehensive psychological assessment process for the person with a developmental disability. Diagnosis fulfills an important aspect of assessment, but so do evaluations that assist the professional in establishing the most effective treatment plan. Finally, treatment plans are always evaluated in terms of the practical outcome for the client; because social skills are frequently the focus of treatment, reassessment of social skills stands as a central feature of outcome evaluation.

Assessment Methods

Two methods of assessment have evolved as the dominant methods for evaluating social skills in people with MR. These techniques include direct observation and behaviorally oriented brief checklists (40–70 items).

Direct Observation

Direct observation typically involves counting the occurrences of discrete behaviors during predetermined, standard social situations (B. A. Taylor

& Harris, 1995) or in defined naturalistic situations (Sigafoos, 1995). Behaviors typically assessed include eye contact, content of the target person's response during an interaction, latency of speech (amount of time from the point that one person stops speaking until the target person starts speaking), social affect, and tone of voice (Bornstein, Bach, McFall, Friman, & Lyons, 1980; C. Hughes, Harmer, Killian, & Niarhos, 1995). Interrater reliability data are typically obtained by having two professionals independently evaluate the discrete target behaviors. Behaviors are typically rated as *occur* or *does not occur*. A second method is to rate the target behaviors on a Likert scale, typically of 5 points (Bates, 1980). The points are generally defined to give the rater some guidelines on how to assess each target behavior. For example, the points might be as follows: 1 (*not at all*), 2 (*infrequently*), 3 (*some), 4 (frequently*), and 5 (*all the time*). Typically 5–10 different social situations are presented, and the client is rated for each situation. Responses for all the scenarios are rated for each target behavior.

There are advantages and disadvantages to the assessment of discrete behaviors in this manner. Perhaps the greatest value of this approach is its usefulness in assessing treatment. Many measures have items that are too broad to reflect treatment gains or not similar enough to the behaviors being treated or learned. Conversely, a major disadvantage of this approach is that a fairly narrow band of change is measured. Thus, some have argued that the change may not be clinically relevant or significant (Gettinger & Kratochwill, 1987). Second, although reliability readily can be established empirically, the issue of validity must be considered. It could be argued that sufficient research has not been conducted to affirm that the targeted behaviors are useful measures of interaction or, if they are social in nature, that they are the most critical social skills. Although use of specific target behaviors in assessing social skills merits endorsement, the two criticisms noted should be taken into account. The best way to address the issue of a narrow measure is to ensure that it is not the only measure of social skills used. Specific target behaviors such as eye contact, speech content, and speech latency should be used together with a checklist of more global measures of social skills. This approach provides for more sensitive measurement, tailored to the specific person and situation (direct observation), as well as the collection of data on a more expansive instrument, the checklist. Furthermore, although validity research is needed on specific target behaviors, the massive use of this assessment approach in the social skills literature has provided a great deal of confirmatory data. The second form of assessment, the social skills checklist, is reviewed in the following section.

Checklists

Checklists can be divided into two categories: those for children or adults, and those for people with mild, moderate, severe, or profound MR. Support for these divisions can be obtained from a comparison of particular scales to empirically established development and adaptive skill levels. As a result, the technology of checklist development to date has focused on scales normed on adults with mild and moderate MR, child social skills measures, and more recently, scales for people with severe and profound MR. Examples of each of these checklist measures are reviewed in this section.

The Social Performance Survey Schedule (SPSS) was developed originally for adults of normal intelligence by Lowe and Cautela (1978). The scale consists of 99 items specific to social skills and has been commercially available for some time. It has some rudimentary reliability data. This measure was also normed on adults with mild and moderate MR (Matson, Helsel, Bellack, & Senatore, 1983). Interrater reliability data were obtained for each item, and the scale was shortened to 57 items; the items with the highest reliability were retained. Roughly equal numbers of positive and negative items were kept. Items included in the resulting scale were for the most part observable, which reduced the amount of inference needed concerning the possible motivations for the social behaviors. Typical items in the SPSS–Revised are (a) has eye contact while speaking, (b) asks questions when talking to others, (c) asks if she or he can be of help, (d) interrupts others, and (e) gives unsolicited advice. Despite the fact that the article by Matson et al. was published more than 10 years ago, no other studies on this scale have been published, and no other measures of social behavior of adults with mild and moderate MR have been developed. Social problems scale development for people with MR is an area that requires much greater attention, particularly because hundreds of treatment studies have been conducted in the last few years related to this topic.

Child social skills measures have received more attention. Two scales with fairly well-developed norms have emerged. These are the Matson Evaluation of Social Skills in Youths (MESSY; Matson, Rotatori, & Helsel, 1983) and the Social Skills Questionnaire (Gresham & Elliot, 1990). Both of these scales have extensive norms for people in the normal range of intelligence.

The MESSY was originally normed on 744 children from 4 to 18 years of age (Matson, Rotatori, & Helsel, 1983). Some people with mild intellectual handicaps have also been evaluated using this instrument. It has 62 items in the self-report version and 64 items in the teacher–parent report forms. An effort was made to assess a wide range of verbal and nonverbal social skills. Typical items are as follows: (a) joins in games with other children, (b) slaps or hits when angry, (c) is bossy, and (d) is friendly to new people he or she meets.

The Social Skills Questionnaire (Gresham & Elliot, 1990) has items comparable to specific social items on more general scales, items that are based on target behaviors from specific scales, and social behaviors that typically have been shown to predict peer acceptance and popularity in social skills research. The scale consists of 52 items that are filled out by a teacher or another adult informant familiar with the person being assessed. Typical items are as follows: (a) completes classroom assignments within required time, (b) praises peers, (c) displays sense of humor, (d) invites peers to play, and (e) uses free time in an acceptable manner. This scale, more so than the MESSY, is geared toward performance in the classroom. Both of these scales are primarily useful with adolescents and children with mild and moderate MR. For those identified on the basis of IQ tests and adaptive behavior scales to function in the severe and profound range of MR, clinicians are likely to find the Matson Evaluation of Social Skills for Individuals with Severe Retardation (MESSIER) a more appropriate alternative.

The MESSIER is specifically designed for use with children and adults with severe and profound MR (Matson, 1994). The items were designed after obtaining information from several sources that were deemed to be relevant. These sources included interviews with direct-care staff who worked with this population, interviews with parents, review of social behaviors targeted for intervention in the literature, and review of adaptive behavior scales used with this population. This scale, which uses a 4-point Likert rating method, has 98 items. Typical questions are as follows: (a) turns head in direction of caregiver, (b) extends hand toward familiar person, (c) distinguishes between people, (d) imitates phrases heard previously, (e) has a friend, (f) imitates sounds, (g) orients to noise, (h) stares, (i) disturbs others, and (j) cries at inappropriate times. As the reader readily can tell, this measure is much different from other social skills checklists in the content of the items. The reader easily can see the emphasis on nonverbal social behaviors and on items that can be scored in the affirmative with even very inactive or withdrawn clients who, pragmatically, evidence few skills. At present, the MESSIER is a unique instrument in this regard.

The critical role that social skills play in enabling social activity, engagement, and experience suggests that all people with MR can benefit from social skills training. One of the primary developmental learning tasks of all young children is to achieve social competence, first in the family and then in the community and society. Presence of remediable social skills, rather than the opportunity for integration, may be the most critical aspect in differentiating socially successful from unsuccessful young children (Ehrmann, Aeschleman, & Svanum, 1995). These checklists and direct observation methods can be beneficial for establishing training goals for individual habilitation plans (IHPs) and individual education plans (IEPs) and can be used periodically to assess individual progress. Using measures of discrete target behaviors, along with one of the checklists noted previously, can be of great value in enhancing the scope, reliability, and validity of social skills assessment. It is essential that assessments specific to interpersonal skills be used. However, it is also true that these assessments should not be seen as a major piece of the differential diagnostic battery, but rather as an aid in treatment planning. Social skills assessment, along with evaluations of performance at work or school and of adaptive skills, should provide the needed comprehensive evaluation for an overall treatment plan.

Conclusion

Social skills, although not considered in the diagnosis of MR, are a critical component in the development of treatment plans that promote normalized development. Research appears to support this view, and in fact, the prominence of social behavior in treatment plans appears to be increasing. The scales developed to date provide a satisfactory global means of evaluating social skills excesses and deficits. Existing scales may prove to have shortcomings in some areas of application, as do all psychological measures. Thus, the development of additional assessment methods to be used in conjunction with or in lieu of the measures that have been presented here is strongly encouraged. In the interim, these measures should provide a reasonable start in this area of assessment and should be used in conjunction with measures of other types of adaptive and communication behaviors to promote a well-rounded quality of life for people with MR.

12

Neuropsychology and Mental Retardation

Mark Schachter and Robert Demerath

This chapter presents findings related to the neuropsychological study of various mental retardation (MR) syndromes. Aspects of neuropsychological evaluation, theory, and experimentation are reviewed as they apply to the study and treatment of persons with MR. One might view the neuropsychological study of people with MR as a marriage of two fields with a natural affinity for each other: *Neuropsychology* is defined as "the study of the relation between brain function and behavior" (Kolb & Whishaw, 1990), and MR may be viewed as being caused by disruptions in brain anatomy and development. Neuropsychological testing can provide a fine-grained analysis of cognitive, perceptual, and sensory–motor skills of people with MR, and its results can form the basis for devising treatment plans and for measuring changes over time (Schachter, 1983).

In the course of neuropsychological research and evaluations with this population, difficulties may arise in administering neuropsychological tests to people with multiple impairments such as concurrent language and motor disabilities (Schachter, 1983). Persons with severe MR may be unable to comprehend or attend to tasks, thereby reducing performance in areas the test may not have been presumed to evaluate because it was developed for other populations (Lezak, 1995; Luria, 1980). Benton (1970) noted the difficulties inherent in administering tests to people with MR and in identifying brain–behavior relationships caused by malformations versus other forms of brain damage. Despite these difficulties, specific patterns of strength and deficit can be discerned in groups with MR of various etiologies (Benton, 1974).

Hooper, Boyd, Hynd, and Rubin (1993) commented that most neuropsychological research with exceptional children has focused on learning disabilities. The greater ease of evaluating these children compared to children with MR has contributed to this trend. The same can be said for studies of children with attention deficits. Neurobiological factors in MR have been reviewed by Hooper et al. (1993). These authors reviewed studies indicating that 83%–97% of individuals with retardation examined by postmortem autopsy showed brain abnormalities ranging from mild to severe. EEG abnormalities seem to increase with severity of retardation, except in Down syndrome, but this group has a high proportion of people with Alzheimer's dementia neurological changes.

Hooper et al. (1993) considered knowledge regarding neuropsychology and MR to be in its infancy. One means of addressing the issue is to develop normative data on the basis of samples with MR, work begun by Matthews (1974) for select measures from the Halstead–Reitan Neuropsychological Test Battery. Many measures were correlated with WISC Full Scale IQ. Unfortunately, the significance and usefulness of IQ-referenced norms is debatable: Lower than average IQ is a frequent sequel to brain insult. Therefore, referencing neuropsychological test scores to IQ level may serve to hide brain–behavior relationships. Additionally, deficits in attention and comprehension may be the cause of low scores. Thus, controlling for IQ may obfuscate rather than educate when test data are interpreted. Nonetheless, the normative data collected by Matthews (1974) may assist in interpreting assessment data in some cases.

Two questions arise regarding neuropsychology and MR. The first is, What can neuropsychology offer for the understanding and treating of MR syndromes? Research has sought to establish profiles of various MR and neurodevelopmental disorders. The second question is, What can MR syndromes contribute to the understanding of brain–behavior relationships? This line of inquiry is leading to the development of new techniques for assessing very young or very handicapped individuals.

Neuropsychological Profiles of MR Syndromes

Autism With or Without MR

Autism is a syndrome involving disturbance of social relatedness, communication, language, and modulation of sensory inputs. The incidence rate is 0.5% for the general population (Schopler, 1994). Symptoms may include abnormal ways of relating to people, objects, and events; language and speech impairments; and abnormal responses to sensation (Hooper et al., 1993). Some authors have proposed two types of autism, bilateral and left-hemispheric dysfunction subtypes (Delong, 1978). Although Ornitz (1985) proposed that autism involves brain stem–diencephalic dysfunction, a promising neuroanatomical hypothesis has been developed by Courchesne et al. (1994). This theory, bolstered by magnetic resonance imaging (MRI) morphometry, electrophysiological findings, and neuropsychological measures, proposes that hypo- or hyperplasia of the cerebellum impairs the autistic person's ability to shift attention rapidly. Furthermore, it is proposed that early maldevelopment of neocerebellar structures impairs the ability to follow the rapid changes that occur during reciprocal social interactions.

Courchesne et al. (1994) cited neuroanatomical evidence of loss of Purkinje cells, which are a primary component of the cerebellum. The cerebellar connections to various cortical areas include prefrontal and posterior parietal cortex and subcortical areas such as the reticular activating system. These authors argued for a rethinking of the role of the cerebellum, ascribing to it the task of coordinating attention as well as motoric acts. Impaired coordination of attention could impair joint social attention, the process whereby parent and infant direct attention to the same objects or events. Failure to develop joint social attention would disrupt normal social interchanges, thereby disrupting the development of communication and affect. Courchesne et al. (1994) cited autopsy data as well as neuroimaging by computed tomography (CT) and quantitative MRI to support the claim that dysplasia of the cerebellum is a central etiological agent in autism.

Courchesne et al. (1994) studied attentional shifting, the other component of their theory, in nonautistic children with neocerebellar astrocytomas, in normal children, and in children with autism. They required participants to shift attention rapidly between visual and auditory stimuli. Performance on a shift attention task was compared to performance on a focus attention task; children with autism had significantly more false alarms than the other participants in the shift attention task, but not in the focus attention task. Among the children with cerebellar astrocytoma, the ones with bilateral lesions of output pathways also had elevated false alarm rates. Patients with autism and those with cerebellar lesions also showed large decrements in initial performance when they changed from the focus to the shift attention task. Once sufficient time was given, however, they were able to detect successive targets, but they required five times longer to do so.

Courchesne's research gives strong evidence of neocerebellar damage as a central cause of autism. This work is noteworthy for its incorporation of psychological (joint social attention), anatomical (MRI studies), and cognitive factors. The authors (Courchesne et al., 1994) suggested that autistic children's preference for sameness is predicated on their difficulty in shifting attention. Joint social attention would be disrupted by cerebellar dysfunction such that parent and infant could not coordinate their focus of attention on one another or objects. This lack would lead to disruption of the temporal continuity required to develop knowledge of the social milieu; thus, disruption of social interaction and understanding would occur. Sigman (1994) proposed that social interaction and social understanding are core deficits in autism.

Ozonoff, Pennington, and Rogers (1990) proposed that deficits in emotion perception, theory of mind (i.e., the ability to infer others' intentions or beliefs; see Baron-Cohen, 1989), and executive functions are promising as the core deficits in autism; they suggested that deficits in theory of mind and in executive functions would be correlated and presumably are caused by the same brain insult. They employed tasks measuring emotion perception and theory of mind, as well as executive functions. Significant differences between controls and autistic persons were found in the domains of executive function, theory of mind, emotion perception, and verbal memory. The deficit found in verbal memory in autism was unexpected, but the authors noted that executive functions help on such tasks by enabling participants to group words using a strategy (e.g., rhyming words). The two most widespread deficits in autistic persons, compared to controls, were in executive functions and theory-of-mind composite variables.

Ozonoff, Rogers, and Pennington (1991), however, failed to replicate studies showing persons with autism to have poorer performance in discerning the intentions of others. Only executive function deficits were found in both persons with classic high-functioning autism and those with Asperger syndrome. The authors discussed various brain–behavior relationships in autism but did not compare their participants to children with known lesions in the implicated brain regions (e.g., prefrontal cortex), and quantitative MRI findings were not available. Thus, the work of Courchesne et al. (1994) seems more firmly grounded.

D. A. Hill and Leary (1994) proposed that there are overlapping symptoms between autism and neurological disorders such as Parkinson's disease and Tourette syndrome. Rather than directly assessing participants, they applied a rating scale to textbook descriptions of disorders. Many features of autism were noted to overlap with those of movement disorders, including abnormalities of posture and muscle tone, movements of head and face, grimacing, rigidity of facial expression, and abnormal trunk and limb movement. These shared features, however, appear to be based more on shared descriptive language than on behavioral similarity. Hill and Leary made little reference to cognitive or neuropsychological findings supporting the hypothesis of common etiological pathways for autism and movement disorders. There may indeed be an overlap between autism and movement disorders if autism is caused by cerebellar dysphasia, but combined neurophysiological, topological, and functional evidence has not been presented.

Down Syndrome

Down syndrome (DS) occurs every 600–900 live births (Wisniewski, Wisniewski, & Yen, 1985). Adults with Down syndrome almost always develop neurochemical and neuropathological changes consistent with Alzheimer dementia (Wisniewski et al., 1985). Despite these changes, only a minority of adults with DS show dementia (Schapiro, Haxby, & Grady, 1992). Neuropsychological evaluations in the search for a DS profile of abilities could identify early markers of dementia, provide impetus for intervention, and, in children, provide guidance in devising education and rehabilitation plans.

Neuropsychological research in DS has documented age-related declines in language (Young & Kramer, 1991) and senile dementia, Alzheimer-type, (SDAT) in adults with the syndrome. Young and Kramer identified declines with age on the receptive language measures but found no relationship between age and expressive language.

Haxby (1989) administered a neuropsychological test battery to 10 adults with DS who were older than age 35 and 19 who were younger than that age. Only 4 of the 10 older participants were judged to be demented.

Nondemented older participants had a pattern of selective neuropsychological deficit relative to younger participants: New long-term memory and visuoconstruction skills were diminished, but immediate memory and language were not. Haxby (1989; Haxby & Schapiro, 1992) demonstrated that the ability to commit new information to long-term memory is deficient even in nondemented older people with DS (a deficit demonstrated in early stages of SDAT as well). A pattern of impaired visuospatial skills with sparing of language is consistent in Haxby's DS group but is not a consistent finding in early- or intermediate-stage SDAT. Haxby noted that in younger persons with DS, language tends to be selectively weaker than other abilities. Thus, neuropsychological studies showed both similarities and differences between DS and SDAT participants.

Schapiro et al. (1992) suggested that studying patients with DS and SDAT can assist in the study of SDAT because of the single cause of dementia in these cases: Down syndrome. Their positron emission tomography (PET) and CT scan study revealed Alzheimer-type cellular changes in older demented participants with DS. Schapiro et al. (1992) further proposed that cognitive decline in DS occurs in two stages. The early stage coincides with accumulation of senile plaques before neurofibrillary tangles and cell loss are evident. The early stage is characterized by decline in new long-term memory and other measures but not in language. The second stage of decline coincides with development of neurofibrillary tangles and cell loss. There is decline and loss of overlearned behaviors, social behaviors, occupational skills, and adaptive (e.g., self-care) behaviors. This study showed progressive brain atrophy and decreased metabolism in the neocortex during this stage.

Williams Syndrome

Williams syndrome (WS) is a genetic disorder involving peculiar facies, frequently supravalvular aortic stenosis, peripheral pulmonic stenosis, and other features including physical abnormalities and MR (Wang et al., 1992). The incidence is estimated to be 1 in 25,000 live births (Wang et al., 1992). Quantitative MRI studies have shown persons with WS to have neocerebellar tonsils larger than those found in DS but equal to those of controls. The neocerebellar tonsils found in persons with WS were larger than those of controls if assessed as a proportion of cerebral volume.

Bellugi and colleagues (Bellugi, Wang, & Jernigan, 1994) have studied WS extensively and conclude it represents an unusual cognitive profile, including unusual awareness of some sounds before they are detected by others, unusual aversion to some sounds not considered aversive by others, MR in 95%, similarity of IQs to those found in DS, and spared language skills. The comparison of WS and DS has been a central feature in Bellugi's attempt to define the neuropsychological profile in Williams syndrome, especially concerning the mental impairment. Syntax is spared;

persons with WS show comprehension of passive sentences, ability to detect faulty syntax and correct it, and use of complex sentences and unusual words in conversation. Persons with WS have preserved narrative and discourse skills and use of affective prosody in speech compared to matched persons with DS.

In contrast to language skills, spatial cognition is impaired in WS. Although persons with DS usually do as poorly as those with WS, the former adhere to the overall configurations of a design in paper-and-pencil copying or in Block Design subtests of the WISC-III. Persons with WS reliably draw local features of a design, sometimes scattered about the page much like the drawings of patients with right-parietal-lobe damage. On Block Design, patients with WS show a fragmented approach, correctly reproducing internal fragments but not the gestalt.

Facial recognition is a spared ability in WS (Bellugi et al., 1994). These participants performed better than matched controls with DS and performed well on a task requiring identification of objects from unusual perspectives. WS and DS participants showed differing profiles in memory skills: WS participants showed superior forward and backward digit spans. On a verbal learning test, WS participants showed better performance than DS participants and used semantic clustering strategies more often.

WS seems to provide a natural experiment concerning dissociation of specific mental abilities from one another (Bellugi et al., 1994). Despite the fact that WS participants often do not have mastery of the Piagetian concept of conservation, they do understand passive sentences, a skill that accompanies conservation in normal children. Children with WS can comprehend semantically reversible sentences (e.g., The boy is followed by the girl) yet cannot conserve and do not demonstrate the ideas of reversibility and transitivity.

Because MRI studies do not show focal lesions in WS, Bellugi et al. (1994) proposed that the profile of abilities is the result of aberrant neural development, different from that shown in other populations using other experimental paradigms. WS is also dramatically opposed in neurobehavioral profile to autism. Persons with autism are deficient in language and social skills but may be strong in visual–constructional skills, whereas those with WS are socially engaging and verbally talented but do poorly on many visual–spatial tasks. The divergence in neocerebellar morphology shown by the two groups may account for some of these differences.

Turner Syndrome

Turner syndrome (TS) occurs in 1 in 2,000–5,000 live female births (B. J. White, 1994). It is a disorder associated with monosomy of the X chromosome. Classic features include short stature, webbed neck, and failure of gonadal development. There is a range of genetic subtypes including 45X, 45X mosaic karyotypes, and abnormal X chromosomes. The variation in karyotype correlates with different phenotypic abnormalities.

The study of TS offers a means to explore the effects of X chromosome absence abnormality and subsequent alteration of pre- and perinatal sex hormone status on patterns of cognitive functioning. Research has focused on electrophysiological and neuropsychological indices of cognitive processes in TS (Shucard, Shucard, Clopper, & Schachter, 1992). A common finding in studies of TS has been a relative deficit in Wechsler Performance IQ (PIQ) relative to Verbal IQ (VIQ) (Bender, Linden, & Robinson, 1994; Waber, 1979).

B. J. White (1994) reviewed the extant literature on neurocognitive profiles in TS. Her review identified deficits in visual–spatial functioning as the most frequently encountered problem in TS. Finer grained analysis of this deficit into components has shown that girls with TS tend to be inferior to controls on tasks of mental rotation. Rovet (1990) suggested that the left hemisphere may be compensating for right-hemisphere underdevelopment in TS.

B. J. White (1994) suggested that a neurodevelopmental model must be applied to provide an understanding of how phenotype and genotype interact to produce neurocognitive profiles. Different expressions of spatial processing deficits or no deficit may be found in individuals, depending on the type of genetic abnormality (pure XO or mosaicism; TS or fragile X) and on environmental influences.

Some of the variability in results, both across studies and across individuals, may reflect karyotypic variations. In specific studies, participants exhibiting the expected deficit composed only 9%–58% of samples. Persons with TS might have more than one type of cognitive deficit (Shucard et al., 1992), although Rovet (1990) indicated that right-parietal development is consistently affected in TS regardless of other, additional abnormalities.

Shucard et al. (1992) analyzed electrophysiological and neuropsychological measures in TS. An auditory evoked potential probe technique was used whereby irrelevant auditory stimuli were presented to participants while they performed visual–spatial tasks; resultant auditory evoked potentials (AEPs) provided data regarding the relative degree of activation and involvement of different brain areas. A neuropsychological test battery was also administered as were psychosocial questionnaires. Eight girls with TS and 8 female and 8 male controls were studied. Psychosocial data were within the normal range. There was a tendency for TS girls to have lower Arithmetic subtest scores than the controls and a lower PIQ. Block Design and Object Assembly also showed significantly lower scores for the TS group. Only half of the girls with TS showed the predicted inferiority of PIQ to VIQ.

On the Categories Test and tests of visual–motor integration and tactual performance, those with TS performed more poorly than controls. When right-minus left-hemisphere amplitudes on AEPs were compared to VIQ–PIQ difference scores, there was a significant correlation of AEP amplitude asymmetry and VIQ–PIQ differences. This finding indicated that the lower the PIQ relative to the VIQ, the higher the right-temporal AEP relative to the left during spatial tasks in TS girls. Generally, the lower the PIQ, the greater the right-hemisphere amplitude relative to the left. Results were interpreted to confirm the presence of specific spatial deficits in girls with TS.

Fragile X Syndrome

The fragile X disorder is a prominent cause of MR (Simensen & Fisch, 1993). The incidence of carriers and affected persons may be up to 1 in 833 in males and 1 in 500 in females (Simensen & Fisch, 1993). Features include excessive prenatal growth in males, narrow face, prominent forehead, midface hypoplasia, large ears, and macroorchidism. Physical features are variable, may not be prominent in young or Black people, and do not serve as diagnostic aids (Simensen & Fisch, 1993). The abnormality may be found in affected males or females and normal male carriers.

Genetically, the fragile X is characterized by a nonstaining gap on the long arm of the X chromosome. There is an expansion of the gene caused by random repeat of nucleotides; affected males have more than 200 repeats and show MR. Those with fewer repeats (50–200) have permutations of fragile X. Regression in IQ has been seen with increasing age (R. C. Rogers & Simensen, 1987). Difficulties among females appear more variable. These may include frontal lobe dysfunction (Mazzocco, Hagerman, Cronister-Silverman, & Pennington, 1992), general intellectual impairment, learning disabilities, Gerstmann's syndrome (Grigsby, Kemper, Hagerman, & Myers, 1990), and inferior VIQ relative to PIQ.

Mazzocco et al. (1992) indicated that 80% of males with fragile X are mildly to severely retarded, and 20% are unaffected carriers. In their research, this team found no deficits in verbal, nonverbal, or memory measures in heterozygous females. They did find that tasks sensitive to frontal lobe function were impaired. Unlike male fragile X heterozygotes, most females are not retarded; however, females with expressed fragile X were lower in IQ than control females. Carriers did not differ from controls in IQ. Expressing women did relatively poorly on all frontal lobe measures: They showed perseverative thinking, limited abstraction, and difficulty maintaining response set (Mazzocco et al., 1992).

A. L. Reiss, Freund, Abrams, Boehm, and Kazazian (1993) studied 34 women with fragile X permutation (500 repeats nucleotide insertion segment, $\mu = 208$). Their neuropsychological battery was more limited than that of Mazzocco et al. (1992) and showed no meaningful differences between women with fragile X permutation and controls. Grigsby et al. (1990) demonstrated deficits in praxis and math, suggesting parietal dysfunction in fragile X syndrome. Crowe and Hay (1990) also contended that males with fragile X have visual–spatial problems. Ciancetti et al. (1991) examined 149 members from 18 families with fragile X. Males with fragile X had IQ scores ranging from below 20 to 61, and heterozygotes had an IQ range of 20–80 in 22 cases and 81–99 in 14 cases. The higher IQ group showed poorer performances on the Raven Progressive Matrices, the Bender–Gestalt, and a test of digit memory. The authors suggested that heterozygous fragile X males have a deficit in spatial processing.

Hypoxia

The central nervous system is easily compromised under any form of oxygen deprivation. Lack of oxygen to the brain results from cardiac or vascular diseases, cerebral circulation difficulties, or airway obstruction, or as a result of genetic diseases or diseases of the kidney or lungs. Environmental exposures to lead and other substances such as alcohol are also a form of oxygen deprivation (histotoxic hypoxia). During periods of development and under other circumstances, the brain is more sensitive to differing forms of oxygen deprivation (Aschkenasy, 1957; Bogolepov, 1983; A. J. Lewis, 1976).

Bogolepov (1983) cited Charny's (1961) classification of differing forms of oxygen deprivation. Circulatory hypoxia (ischemia) is most commonly seen in clinical practice (Bogolepov, 1983). Researchers at times distinguish hypoxemia (i.e., decreased oxygen tension in arterial blood) from hypoxia. Hypoxia can simply mean an inadequacy in the amount of available oxygen relative to demand for it (Bogolepov, 1983; Charny, 1961; A. J. Lewis, 1976).

The results of similar degrees of oxygen deprivation vary among people. The structure of the brain cell can ultimately recover from some forms of oxygen deprivation under particular circumstances (Bogolepov, 1983). However, the same type of hypoxic episode in a physiologically less tolerant person, for example, during a sensitive developmental period of growth or change, may result in forms of paralysis or other long-term disabilities. The degree, duration, and type of oxygen deprivation are important determinants of outcome (Bogolepov, 1983; A. J. Lewis, 1976).

Oxygen deprivation or insult (such as in stroke) has obvious consequences for a child's intellectual development and adaptive functioning (Flick & Duncan, 1973; Fox, 1978; Powars & Imbus, 1980; Sander, 1985; L. Wright, Schaefer, & Solomons, 1979). Aphasia, ataxia, lethargy, general weakness, drowsiness, fatigue, paresis, perceptual–motor dysfunction, and auditory or visual problems resulting from oxygen deprivation have been shown to be related to, but not caused by, different types of genetic disorders and medical states such as liver problems or cardiac illness (Bosselman & Kraines, 1937; Gualtieri, 1987; Schroeder, 1987; Virmani, Robinowitz, & McAllister, 1985; L. Wright et al., 1979).

In sickle cell disease, a prevalent disorder in the United States, most permanent intellectual problems result from strokes and are not directly related to the disease. Strokes in this population contribute about 5% of all strokes in children (Haruda, Friedman, Ganti, Hoffman, & Chutorian, 1981). The disease is of substantial importance for the understanding of oxygen deprivation during growth and development, however. Oxygen deprivation from sickle cell disease includes exposure during gestation of a fetus without sickle cell disease from the mother with the disease, cases of adults with the disease who show no effects of oxygen deprivation during development, and just about every degree of deprivation-induced effect in between (Anaesthesia Advisory Committee, 1987; Demerath, 1988; Flick & Duncan, 1973; Fox, 1978; G. J. Gilbert, 1987; Grotta, Manner,

Pettigrew, & Yatsym, 1986; Harel & Anastasiow, 1985; J. G. Hughes, Diggs, & Gillespie, 1940; Kark, Posey, Schumacher, & Ruehle, 1987; Neel, 1977; C. H. Sander, 1985; Sullivan, 1987; Virmani et al., 1985; Wright et al., 1979).

In general, oxygen deprivation at different developmental levels has an effect on intellectual and adaptive function. Although specific areas of the brain are more sensitive to particular forms of oxygen deprivation, the scope of the influence of hypoxia on human behavior and development has been well identified (Cavaletti, Moroni, Garavaglia, & Tredici, 1987; Cormick, Olson, Hensley, & Saunders, 1986; Demerath, 1988; G. J. Gilbert, 1987; Gore, Weinberg, Anandappa, Shkolnick, & White, 1981; McQueen, Spence, Winsor, Garner, & Pereira, 1986; Milledge, 1985; Mountain, 1987; Prigatano, Parsons, Wright, Levin, & Hawayluk, 1983; Prigatano, Wright, & Levin, 1984; Ruth, Virkola, Petau, & Raivio, 1988; West, 1986).

Phenylketonuria

Phenylketonuria (PKU) is a genetic cause of MR affecting 1 in 10,000–20,000 live births (Welsh, Pennington, Rouse, & McCabe, 1990). Mutation of the gene that codes for the enzyme phenylalanine hydroxylase leads to an inability to convert dietary phenylalanine to tyrosine. Normal intake of phenylalanine in children with PKU results in MR. Fine-grained analysis of children with PKU who are treated using dietary restriction of phenylalanine or who suffer from hyperphenylalanemia, a milder form of the disorder, suggests a distinct neurocognitive profile. Welsh et al. (1990) proposed that even with early treatment it is possible that subtle dysfunctions could be evidenced by children with PKU. A prefrontal dysfunction hypothesis has been advanced by McKean (1972), suggesting that PKU contributes to low brain tyrosine levels. This deficiency would, in turn, lead to depressed levels of dopamine and norepinephrine in the brain (dopaminergic projections are found in the frontal lobes); therefore, PKU could lead to frontal or prefrontal dysfunction.

Although early studies of PKU with dietary intervention focused on IQ effects, later work has investigated specific neurocognitive functions. IQ scores of early treated patients are in the normal range, but lower than those of unaffected siblings (Koch, Azen, Friedman, & Williamson, 1984). There are suggestions that serum phenylalanine (Phe) levels correlate with cognitive testing results, but the finding is not consistent, and the possibility that elevated Phe levels have differential effects at different ages remains. Welsh et al. (1990) compared early treated children with PKU and normal IQ with unaffected controls on measures of executive functions. The PKU group performed significantly below the controls on a composite executive function measure. Concurrent Phe levels correlated inversely with executive function test composite scores.

A study of preschoolers was conducted by A. Diamond, Hurwitz, Lee, Grover, & Minarcik, (in press) comparing children with PKU, those with hyperphenylalanemia (the milder form), and normal controls; the authors found deficits in frontal-lobe–sensitive tasks even in infants. These tasks included the A not B paradigm, which requires participants to look for an object in a new hiding place after two successful trials of finding the object in a prior hiding place. Increasing delays between the act of hiding the object and allowing the infant to reach for it are imposed.

No significant differences were found between PKU and hyperphenylalanemia groups, controlling for plasma Phe level. There were notable differences on frontal tasks predicted by plasma Phe level regardless of group. Children with higher levels were impaired on all nine measures compared to normative data and on eight of nine tasks compared to matched controls. On 9 of 10 control tasks, the higher Phe level group did not differ from controls. Diamond et al. (in press) suggest that stricter restrictions of dietary Phe should be considered to prevent deficits.

In summary, some promising work on establishing neurocognitive profiles in people with specific MR syndromes is emerging. Often, the research involves persons who do not have expressed MR but whose genetic disorder might lead to retardation if left untreated, as in PKU, or if the genetic insertion were longer, as in fragile X. Other work has involved persons with MR and has led to comparison of neurocognitive abilities across etiologically distinct syndromes.

New Methods for Neuropsychological Assessment in MR

Neuropsychologists face a considerable challenge in assessing people with MR. Many tests are confounded by IQ (Matthews, 1974) or require levels of cognitive performance not yet attained by very young or severely intellectually impaired people. However, new methods that may aid neuropsychological evaluation are being developed.

A Not B Paradigm

A. Diamond and colleagues developed a paradigm for evaluating frontal lobe functioning in very young children (A. Diamond, 1985; A. Diamond & Doar, 1989). The A not B paradigm requires an infant to uncover an object hidden in one of two locations. The examiner hides an object in one hiding well. Once the infant reaches for the object correctly, it is hidden in an alternate location. The time delay between hiding and allowing the infant to retrieve the object increases with age between 7.5 and 12 months, and the delay needed to produce errors increases from under 2 sec to more than 10 sec. A. Diamond and Goldman-Rakic (1989) demonstrated that unoperated and parietally lesioned rhesus monkeys performed this task as well as 12-month-old human infants, but monkeys with bilateral dorsolateral prefrontal ablation performed only as well as 7.5- to 9-month-old human infants.

A. Diamond (1985) demonstrated large performance differences among children of the same age. An increase of approximately 2 sec per month of age in delay required to produce the error was also demonstrated. Reaching became random or perseverative with delays exceeding that required to produce initial errors by 2–3 sec. A. Diamond and Doar (1989) showed that the Delayed Response Task has an almost identical progression to that of the A not B paradigm. As previously noted, the A not B task has been used with infants with PKU and hyperphenylalanemia in research (A. Diamond et al., in press). These procedures show promise as exploratory tasks to study the relationship between IQ, age, and A not B errors at long delay intervals with persons with MR.

Quantitative MRI

The use of morphometric MRI has been discussed previously in this chapter in conjunction with Courchesne et al.'s (1994) work on autism. Quantitative MRI relies on indirect scanning of brain structure, converted to measures of the size of specific structures. In Courchesne's work, this technique gave supportive evidence for the theory that Purkinje cell loss is an anatomical basis for autism.

Although the technique holds much promise as a measure of anatomical features, the cost and complexity of quantitative MRI currently precludes widespread use in research or clinical practice. Additionally, identification of morphological differences alone cannot replace the fine-grained analysis of the neuropsychological evaluation in treatment and educational planning. Quantitative MRI is most useful in conjunction with neuropsychological assessments, when the two can be combined to ascertain brain–behavior relationships. These procedures can help clinicians to provide anatomical explanations for disability to parents of children with MR.

PASS Model of Cognitive Processing

Naglieri and Das (Hurt & Naglieri, 1992; Naglieri & Das, 1990; Naglieri & Reardon, 1993; Reardon & Naglieri, 1992; also see chap. 7, this volume) have proposed a model of intelligence and cognitive processing that is based on Luria's (1973) theories. The four types of processing posited are attention and arousal, simultaneous processing, successive processing, and planning.

Attention and arousal are carried out by Luria's first functional unit, the brain stem and subcortex. The Naglieri–Das system includes an expressive attention task, much like a Stroop task. Color names or colored shapes are printed on the first two pages of a booklet. On the third page, color names are printed in colors different from their name, and the participant must say the color of the ink. Another attention task is number finding, wherein the participant circles numbers printed in boldface, inhibiting responses to nonbold print.

Simultaneous processing is carried out by parts of Luria's second functional unit, the posterior cortex. This unit carries out reception, analysis, and synthesis of information. Simultaneous processing is done in the manner of a gestalt, interrelating stimuli with other elements. Sequential processing, in which information is formed into a series, linearly, is also carried out by the second functional unit. Simultaneous processing tasks include Figure Memory (similar to the Benton Visual Retention Test), Matrices (similar to the Raven), and simultaneous verbal tests. The latter requires the participant to identify the one of six illustrations that correctly matches a complex logical statement such as "a ball in a basket on the table" (Naglieri & Das, 1990, p. 323). Sequential tasks include sentence repetition, word recall, and sentence questions. The latter repeats the sentences in the sentence repetition task, but here the participant must answer questions regarding the material.

Planning is carried out by Luria's fourth functional unit of the brain, the frontal lobes. Das–Naglieri tasks for assessing this process include planned codes (similar to WISC-III Coding), planned connections (similar to the Trail Making Tests), and visual search. The fourth unit is composed of the frontal and prefrontal areas. The PASS model can be useful in reconceptualizing intelligence tests (see chap. 7, this volume) and in guiding the interpretation of neuropsychological assessments of people with MR.

Conclusion

The field of neuropsychology faces new prospects and old problems in research and clinical activity involving people with MR. Obstacles such as limited cognitive abilities may be overcome using the A not B paradigm to assess basic cognitive skills. Expanded knowledge of brain–behavior relationships through research can assist in treatment planning. Quantitative MRI can assist in identifying anatomical brain dysplasias. Coupled with neuropsychological analysis of cognitive functioning, it can provide new insights into atypical brain–behavior relationships. Better understanding of basic deficits in developmental disabilities can lead to more effective treatment plans. Identifying the specific deficits in conditions such as autism, Turner syndrome, and PKU may also improve differential selection of critical functions for assessment and suggest new strategies for remediation.

13

Major Technological Breakthroughs in the Diagnosis of Mental Retardation

Richard E. McClead, Jr., James A. Menke, and Daniel L. Coury

The etiology of mental retardation (MR) is known in approximately 60%–70% of cases (McLaren & Bryson, 1987). Many cases have a genetic basis such as Down syndrome (trisomy of chromosome 21), which is a major cause of moderate-to-severe MR. Structural or biochemical abnormalities in 30%–40% of cases without an identifiable cause suggest a prenatal origin of the condition leading to MR (Warkany, Lemire, & Cohen, 1981). Recent technological advances in neurodiagnostic imaging, neurometabolic spectroscopy, cytogenetic analysis, and molecular genetics have enhanced the ability to identify the neurophysiological cause of a child's MR. This chapter examines these technologies as they relate to the diagnosis of MR.

Advances in Neurodiagnostic Technologies

Neurodiagnostic imaging and neurometabolic spectroscopic techniques are of great value in defining the cause and pathogenesis of heretofore undiagnosed causes of severe MR (Doyle et al., 1983). These new diagnostic tools include magnetic resonance imaging (MRI), positron emission tomography (PET), single photon emission computed tomography (SPECT), magnetic resonance spectroscopy (MRS), and near-infrared spectroscopy (NIRS). We review here the basis and various uses of each of these technologies.

Magnetic Resonance Imaging

MRI is a new technique that produces superior anatomical detail when compared with ultrasonography (US) and computed tomography (CT). MRI can clarify brain development through better resolution of the gray–white matter differentiation and the progression of myelinization (Goplerud & Delivoria-Papadopoulos, 1993). It can help in the diagnosis of met-

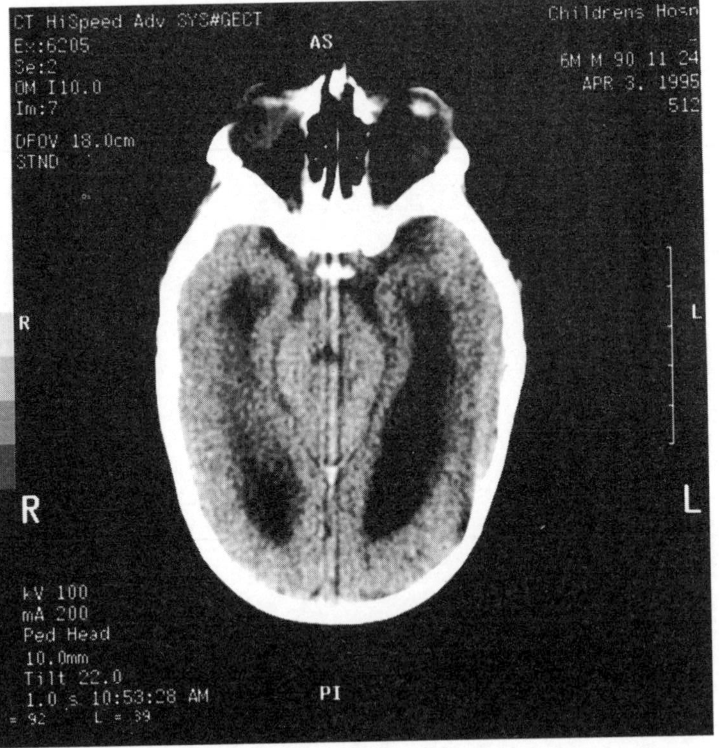

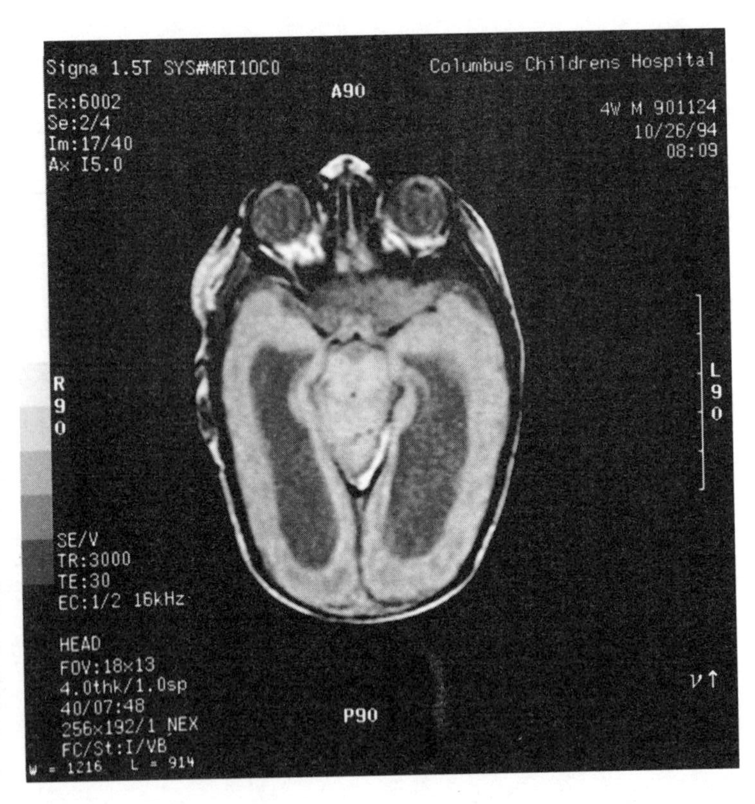

Figure 1. Similar views obtained by computed tomography (CT; left view) and magnetic resonance imaging (MRI; right view) of the brain of an infant with severe encephalomalacia. Note the difference in brain detail in the MRI compared to the CT scan. For example, the image on the right provides enough detail to appreciate the lens of the eye, seen as a darker area at the apex and midline of the image of each eyeball. The infant had received extracorporeal membrane oxygenation therapy (ECMO) for respiratory distress and persistent pulmonary hypertension of the newborn. He sustained a cerebellar hemorrhage and a left occipital–parietal infarct.

abolic and neurodegenerative disorders (Valk & van der Knapp, 1989; see chap. 12, this volume). Most important, it does not expose the patient to potentially damaging radiation. A comparison of the CT scan (left panel) and MRI scan (right panel), taken at two different points in time, of the brain of an infant who sustained a cerebellar hemorrhage and left occipital–parietal infarct is shown in Figure 1.

Magnetic resonance is a phenomenon exhibited by atomic nuclei with an odd number of protons and neutrons. When placed in a strong magnetic field, these nuclei, which are randomly arranged in their normal state, align themselves like small bar magnets. If they are then bombarded by a pulse of radiofrequency energy, they absorb energy and their alignment is disturbed. Discontinuation of the radiofrequency pulsation results in the release of the absorbed energy and the emission of a magnetic resonance signal by the nuclei. A receiver detects the magnetic resonance signal. A computer processes the information, calculates the position of the resonating nuclei, and generates an image. In biological tissues such as brain, the image is based primarily on the spatial distribution of hydrogen nuclei in water and lipid molecules (Goplerud & Delivoria-Papadopoulos, 1993).

Some conditions associated with MR for which MRI may be of diagnostic help are tuberous sclerosis, leukodystrophies, congenital infections, periventricular leukomalacia, posterior fossa tumors, and Hurler's disease (Dubowitz & Bydder, 1990). MRI may also be of help in the evaluation of neonatal asphyxia. Byrne, Welch, Johnson, Darrah, and Piper (1990) performed MRI on 15 asphyxiated term neonates at 4 and 8 months of age. In the 9 infants who developed cerebral palsy, the MRIs were abnormal at 8 months. Eight of these 9 infants had abnormal brain myelinization, and 1 infant had ventricular dilatation.

Although the lack of ionizing radiation permits frequent repeated MRIs on the same patient, the procedure does have technical limitations. MRI is not portable, and it requires a facility with special magnetic shielding; therefore, patients must be brought to the MRI facility. MRI usually requires sedation of infants to prevent movement during the 30-min examination. For obvious reasons, all ferromagnetic materials must be removed from the area of the patient. Thermoregulation is always a concern in the newborn. Precautions to prevent hypothermia and hyperthermia during the examination must be taken. MRI generates a lot of noise (80 dB for 30–60 min); this level of noise exposure is a potential hazard for developing ears. Fortunately, the magnetic fields generated during MRI do not appear to have any long-term adverse effects (Laptook, 1990).

Positron Emission Tomography

PET is a technique for imaging the distribution of a positron-emitting radionuclide. The technique is useful for measuring cerebral blood flow (Volpe, Herscovitch, & Perlman, 1985; Volpe, Herscovitch, Perlman, & Raichle, 1983), cerebral glucose metabolism (Doyle et al., 1983; Thorp et al., 1988), cerebral oxygen metabolism and cerebral blood volume

(Altman, Perlman, Volpe, & Powers, 1993), acid–base balance, receptor pharmacology, and neurotransmitter metabolism (Altman & Volpe, 1991).

Isotopes such as ^{15}O, ^{11}C, ^{13}N, or ^{18}F decay by emitting a positively charged particle called a *positron*. For PET scanning, radiotracers like $H_2^{15}O$ that incorporate these isotopes are infused intravenously or inhaled into a patient. When the ^{15}O decays, the emitted positron travels a few millimeters in a tissue before colliding with a negatively charged electron, producing an annihilation event. The annihilation event results in the release of two high-energy gamma photons. These photons are then detected by radiation detectors arranged circumferentially in multiple rings that allow simultaneous measurement of radioactivity of multiple transverse slices. An image of each slice (a tomograph) is reconstructed from the regional distribution of tissue radioactivity (Raichle, 1983).

Volpe et al. (1983) used PET to study premature infants who developed intraventricular hemorrhages (IVH) and hemorrhagic parenchymal infarction. Not only did these investigators find decreased blood flow in the area of the IVH, they also found areas of decreased brain blood flow in the affected hemisphere distant to the site of the IVH. This finding suggests that the original parenchymal infarct is part of a larger ischemic lesion, the etiology of which is not completely clear (Altman & Volpe, 1991). Understanding the mechanism that produces this larger ischemic lesion may be important to an understanding of the mechanism of brain damage and later MR caused by perinatal events such as IVH.

In another study, Volpe et al. (1985) performed PET scans and qualitatively measured the cerebral blood flow of 17 asphyxiated newborns during the acute phase of their illness. They noted a pattern of decreased flow to the parasagittal area, posteriorly more than anteriorly. The ratio of parasagittal blood flow to the highest flow recorded in the sylvian region correlated with neurodevelopmental outcome. Infants whose ratio was at least 0.78 developed normally; infants whose ratio was 0.6 or less suffered permanent neurological deficits. Although the biological significance of these findings remains to be determined, the clinical potential of PET for cerebral blood flow determination is promising.

PET may clarify the pathophysiology of perinatal events that result in MR. Before it is widely used, however, a number of technological and practical problems must be overcome (Altman & Volpe, 1991). First, spatial resolution of regional areas in the brain must improve. Separation of pure gray matter or subcortical white matter from surrounding tissues is not possible because the areas are just too small. Second, not all the photons generated by the annihilation events reach the external detectors because of attenuation (i.e., absorption of photons by surrounding tissues). A correction for photon attenuation must be performed for each infant, or the amount of radioactivity present in a tissue will be underestimated. Third, the positron-emitting isotopes have short half-lives. This offers some technical advantages; however, the isotopes must be produced on site or very nearby. Most hospitals are not affiliated with a facility containing a cyclotron or linear accelerator capable of producing these isotopes. Finally, determinations of cerebral blood flow, blood volume, and glucose and oxygen metabolism by PET are based on mathematical models that must be developed, tested, and standardized. Like all models, they have associated assumptions that may not always be valid.

Single Photon Emission Computed Tomography

SPECT is an old technology that has only recently become clinically relevant with the development of suitable radiopharmaceuticals and improved instrumentation (Holman & Tumeh, 1990). SPECT is a method of reconstructing cross-sectional images of the distribution of a radiotracer in a tissue. It provides a direct measure of regional organ function. It has the image quality of PET scanning but is far less expensive, and it is readily available in almost all clinical nuclear medicine facilities.

Most radionuclides emit many particles as they decay. SPECT involves the intravenous injection of nuclides that emit a single photon with each nuclear decay (e.g., iodine 123 and technetium 99m). These nuclides distribute to organs according to their regional blood flow. For studies of the brain, iodine 123 iofetamine and technetium 99m hexamethyl propyleneamine oxime are currently approved for use. These single-photon–emitting nuclides cross the blood–brain barrier, distribute in the brain according to regional blood flow, and remain fixed to brain tissues for sufficient time that a cross-sectional image can be generated by a rotating gamma camera or special-purpose ring-type imaging system. Following an insult to the brain, scans from imaging techniques such as CT and MRI that detect changes in the anatomy or morphology of an organ are normal for a few days. SPECT, however, documents the changes in blood flow and metabolism present at the onset of the injury (Hill et al., 1982, 1984). SPECT better defines the extent of the insult because it detects alterations in perfusion that are not identified by other imaging techniques (R. G. Lee, Hill, Holman, & Clouse, 1982).

In adults with neurological insults, SPECT is a useful tool to predict outcome, evaluate the effect of potential therapies, and plan rehabilitative therapy (Shankaran, Kottamasu, & Kuhns, 1993). In pediatric patients with a variety of brain disorders, SPECT is more sensitive than EEG, CT, or MRI at identifying brain abnormalities, but it is not very specific (Iivanainen, Launes, Pinko, Nikkinen, & Lindroth, 1990). Denays et al. (1989) studied 22 neonates at risk for neurodevelopmental deficits and found SPECT to be superior to sonography at detecting brain injury. In all the premature infants with either lateral ventricular dilatation or periventricular hyperechogenicity, SPECT confirmed cortical periventricular hypoperfusion. In premature infants with periventricular hemorrhage, SPECT demonstrated a more extensive area of hypoperfusion in surrounding brain tissue than suspected by sonography. Although additional studies with long-term developmental outcome measures need to be completed, SPECT appears to be of potential clinical value in predicting neurodevelopmental outcome in a high-risk population. Shankaran et al. (1993) reported the results of a study of 36 term infants at risk for hypoxic ischemic encephalopathy. SPECT data were correlated with US, CT, and physical and neurological assessments. Of 25 neonates treated for persistent pulmonary hypertension with extracorporeal membrane oxygenation, 22 were neurologically normal on follow-up examination at 2 years. US, SPECT, and CT each were 100% sensitive for predicting poor neurological outcome. Specificity, however, differed as follows: SPECT 50%, US 77%, and CT 64%. The poorer specificity of SPECT may relate to the inherent plasticity of the human infant brain. Thus, subtle areas of ischemia detected acutely by SPECT may resolve over time (Shankaran et al., 1993).

Magnetic Resonance Spectroscopy

MRS is another relatively old technology (Bloch, Hansen, & Packard, 1946; Purcell, Torrey, & Pound, 1946) that preceded the development of MRI but came onto the clinical research scene only in the last decade. This technology has potential for the noninvasive assessment of metabolism in vivo (Hope & Moorcraft, 1991). MRS has greatly facilitated the recognition of "energy failure" in the brain following perinatal asphyxia. Its forte may be the ability to identify injured brain tissues before they undergo irreversible changes such that neuroprotective interventions can be instituted (Goplerud & Delivoria-Papadopoulos, 1993).

MRS is based on the same principles as MRI. Instead of analyzing the positional information of the magnetic resonance signal, the computer analyzes the spectral data. These spectral data are derived from the very small variations in the magnetic resonance signal (known as chemical shifts) that occur depending on the molecular environment of the stimulated nucleus. Thus, the signal frequency of phosphorous and other nuclei will vary depending on the biochemical compounds in which they reside (e.g., adenosine triphosphate vs. adenosine diphosphate vs. phospholipids). When these nuclei reside in a variety of biochemical compounds (e.g., brain tissue), the magnetic resonance of individual compounds can be separated in a frequency spectrum. The amplitude of the magnetic resonance signal from specific nuclei will correspond to the total number of nuclei that resonate at that precise chemical shift. Therefore, MRS is a noninvasive technique for measuring the relative amount of different compounds containing the specific nuclei in a given tissue. These spectra may ultimately be used to assess developmental changes in the brain (Hamilton et al., 1986), brain catabolic activity (Younkin et al., 1988), and brain synthetic activity (Hope & Moorcraft, 1991); however, reproducibility among MRS centers is currently a problem. This problem will resolve with standardization of methodology for spectral processing and data handling and the establishment of normative data (Hope & Moorcraft, 1991).

The spectral data for ^{31}P in the human newborn brain contains seven peaks: phosphomonoesters (PME); inorganic phosphorus (Pi); phosphodiesters (PDI); phosphocreatine (PCr); and the gamma, alpha, and beta phosphorous nuclei of adenosine triphosphate (ATP; Goplerud & Delivoria-

Papadopoulos, 1993). Alteration in phosphorous MRS is noted following asphyxia (Hope et al., 1984). PCr falls and Pi increases relative to other phosphorus-containing compounds such as ATP. ATP falls only in the most severely asphyxiated infants and is a marker for impending death (Azzopardi et al., 1989). If MRS is performed sequentially in asphyxiated infants, a relatively normal pattern is seen during the first 12–24 hr followed by a deterioration of the MRS pattern suggestive of severe energy failure. These infants then either die or develop cerebral atrophy (Hope et al., 1984). Hope and Moorcraft (1991) speculated that this "secondary deterioration" may be due to damage by neurotransmitters, calcium entry into cells, or free radical injury.

To determine the ability of MRS to predict neurodevelopmental outcome at 1 year of age, Azzopardi et al. (1989) examined the parameters of validity in 61 infants (27–42 weeks' gestation) with documented cerebral hypoxia–ischemia and 30 healthy control infants. The phosphocreatine: inorganic phosphorous ratio (PCr:Pi) was the most predictive MRS parameter for death or multiple impairment (93% positive predictive value); however, sensitivity was only 74%. Four of five surviving infants with normal PCr:Pi ratios had major motor disorders.

MRS is currently limited in its ability to specify precisely the tissue to be studied (spatial localization of MRS). This problem may be overcome by future modifications of MRS (Blackledge et al., 1987; Moorcraft et al., 1989). Other limitations of MRS are its inability to study tissues other than brain and liver and the practical use of nuclei other than phosphorous. The latter problem may be resolved in the future with high-resolution proton (^1H) spectroscopy (Hope & Moorcraft, 1991; Peden et al., 1990).

Near-Infrared Spectroscopy

NIRS is a research tool that permits the noninvasive monitoring of tissue oxygenation, cerebral blood volume, and cerebral blood flow (Brazy, 1991). The status of an ill patient's oxygenation is an important parameter to be monitored. If inadequately oxygenated, a patient may suffer brain injury; if oxygen is used excessively, toxic, oxygen free radicals may accumulate. Either way, the patient suffers. The absorbance of light energy of specific wavelengths can be used to indicate oxygenation status. NIRS uses light in the near-infrared end of the spectrum (720–900 nm) to detect the differential absorbance of this light by the oxidized and reduced states of two blood proteins: hemoglobin and cytochrome a, a3. The former is key to tissue oxygen delivery; the latter, an enzyme, is key to intracellular oxygen utilization and energy conservation in mitochondria (Brazy, 1991).

The longer wavelengths of near-infrared light penetrate and traverse skin and bone, especially in premature infants. Hence, the cerebral tissues of premature infants can be studied noninvasively by placing the NIRS light source and receiver on opposite temples. If oxygen delivery is adequate, most of the hemoglobin and cytochrome a, a3 will be oxidized; conversely, if oxygenation is inadequate, these proteins will exist mostly in the reduced state. NIRS determines the relative amounts of the oxidized and reduced states of hemoglobin and cytochrome a, a3, thereby establishing an early and sensitive indicator of decreased cellular oxygen availability and potential for tissue injury (Brazy, 1991).

NIRS offers many advantages for monitoring cerebral blood flow and oxygenation in neonates. It is relatively noninvasive for the patient, nonintrusive to intensive care nursing, and noninjurious to underlying tissues. Premature infants are prone to cerebral circulatory problems that impair tissue oxygenation despite adequate systemic oxygenation. NIRS permits direct monitoring of brain oxygenation despite these circulatory problems. Moreover, NIRS is a technology that gives real-time information at the infant's bedside (Brazy, 1991). It can tell when either brain tissue oxygenation or blood perfusion is inadequate and how long it takes for these tissues to recover from a hypoxic or ischemic event. Delay in recovery may be an indicator of potential brain damage. NIRS may also detect adverse effects on cerebral oxygenation, blood flow, or blood volume induced by medical and nursing procedures (e.g., reflex bradycardia caused by airway suctioning), cardiovascular drugs (e.g., effects of dopamine and dobutamine), and other clinical conditions (e.g., hypoglycemia, patent ductus arteriosus, hypertension, and pneumothorax).

Advances in Diagnostic Genetics

Genetic disorders account for the majority of identifiable causes of MR. Advances in cytogenetic techniques, especially high-resolution banding and tissue culturing, and in molecular biology have led to improved genetic diagnosis of MR, improved detection of carrier states, and facilitated prenatal counseling (Bregman & Hodapp, 1991).

High-Resolution Chromosome Banding

Chromosomes are the threadlike structures that reside in the nucleus of cells. They are composed of protein and deoxyribonucleic acid (DNA). DNA is a double-stranded helix; it looks like a twisted rope ladder in which the two ropes are alternating deoxyribose (a sugar) and phosphate units, and the rungs are purine (adenine and guanine) and pyrimidine (cytosine and thymine) bases held together by hydrogen bonds (Nora & Fraser, 1994). The structural unit of DNA is the nucleotide (i.e., a unit of deoxyribose, phosphate, and either a purine or pyrimidine base). The structures of each of the bases dictate that a guanine on one strand of DNA can bind only with a cytosine on the other, complementary strand. The same is true for adenine and thymine. It is the sequence of the purine and pyrimidine bases that specifies a gene, the functional unit of DNA, and defines the genetic code. The code for each gene determines the sequence of amino acids of polypeptides and the structure and properties of proteins (Nora & Fraser, 1994). The code for each amino acid is specified by a sequence of three nucleotides, called a *trinucleotide*, or *codon*. For example, a trinucleotide composed of cytosine–thymine–thymine (CTT) codes for the amino acid glutamic acid. Because there are more combinations of nucleotides possible than there are different amino acids, several trinucleotide combinations may code for the same amino acid.

Alterations in the DNA sequence of nucleotides can lead to a decrease in the amount of the final protein product produced or can result in an abnormally functioning protein. These alterations in DNA are the basis for evolutionary advances as well as lethal genetic defects. More than 120 specific genetic lesions have been linked to clinically recognizable MR syndromes (Fryns, 1987).

Chromosomes exist in pairs, with each member of a pair coding for the same genetic information. There are 22 pairs of somatic chromosomes (numbered 1–22) and 1 pair of sex chromosomes (XX for females and XY for males). Each parent provides one of each pair of chromosomes. Human chromosomes contain approximately 3 billion nucleotides (Nora & Fraser, 1994). The largest chromosome contains approximately 300 million nucleotides; the smallest, only 50 million. This amount of DNA is sufficient to code for millions of average-size human genes, but in reality, only about 5% of this genetic material is active (Nora & Fraser, 1994). Of the approximately 100,000 genes, only 5,000 have been categorized (Cutting & Antonarakis, 1992). The "inactive" DNA is mostly composed of repetitive sequences of nucleotides, the role of which is largely unknown.

Chromosomes can be distinguished from each other only during cell division. Some of the 23 human chromosome pairs can be separated from one another on the basis of their size and shape. The others require special banding studies to be identified. Caspersson and Zech reported in 1972 that certain fluorescent dyes produced alternating bands of light and dark areas on the chromosomes. The patterns of the bands were chromosome-specific and reproducible from cell to cell, tissue to tissue, and person to person (Nora & Fraser, 1994).

Chromosome-banding techniques facilitated the development of cytogenetics analysis, a process by which chromosome aberrations and structural rearrangements are identified and characterized. Banding techniques also permit the precise localization of genes to specific chromosomal bands. In standard banding techniques, approximately 400 separate bands can be identified on each haploid set of chromosomes. The more bands identified, the greater the resolution of the chromosomal material and the greater the likelihood of identifying small changes in the chromosomal material. High-resolution banding techniques can identify more than 1,000 bands. Although this is a marked improvement over standard banding techniques, even a single high-resolution chromosome band contains more than 3 million nucleotide base pairs and hundreds of genes (Nora & Fraser, 1994).

Genetic Diseases Associated With MR

An example of a genetic defect associated with MR for which high-resolution chromosome-banding techniques have made a difference is the defect associated with the Prader–Willi and Angelman syndromes. Prader–Willi syndrome and Angelman syndrome are two phenotypically different syndromes associated with MR that share an abnormal chromosome-banding site. Patients with Prader–Willi syndrome suffer from severe MR, short stature, small hands and feet, hypotonia, obesity, and hypogonadism (K. L. Jones, 1988). Patients with Angelman syndrome have MR associated with an abnormal puppetlike gait, postnatal growth retardation, craniofacial abnormalities (microbrachycephaly, ocular hypopigmentation, maxillary hypoplasia, and prognathia), and EEG abnormalities (Clayton-Smith & Pembrey, 1992). Both syndromes are the result of a deletion on the long arm of chromosome 15 in region 1 from bands 1–3 (designated 15q11-13). The difference in the genetic defects in patients with these syndromes is the origin of the chromosome 15 that contains the deletion. In patients with Prader–Willi syndrome, the chromosome is derived from the father; in patients with Angelman syndrome, it is derived from the mother (Clayton-Smith & Pembrey, 1992).

To study chromosomes, cells must be cultured and induced to divide so that the chromosomes can be readily identified, separated, and counted. The development of new tissue culture techniques has resulted in the identification of nutrient-sensitive fragile sites on chromosomes. Breaks in the chromosomal material occur when these fragile sites are exposed to media lacking specific nutrients. The fragile sites are inherited by Mendelian genetics. One such site, the folate-sensitive fragile X site, is the second most common inherited cause of MR (Schaefer & Bodensteiner, 1992).

A sex-linked form of MR was first described by Martin and Bell in 1943 (as cited in K. L. Jones, 1988). An association of MR with a fragile site on the long arm of the X chromosome was noted by Lubs (1969). The nature of the fragile X mental retardation syndrome, however, did not become clear until Sutherland (1977) noted that expression of fragile sites on human chromosomes was dependent on the cell culture medium. This syndrome occurs 80% of the time in males and is characterized clinically by a long face, prominent ears, large testicles, and MR. Behaviorally, these patients exhibit autistic tendencies, hyperactivity, delayed language development, low motor tone, and learning disabilities (K. L. Jones, 1988).

This disorder is due to a lack of a protein (FMRP) that is normally produced by the fragile X mental retardation-1 (FMR-1) gene. The discovery of this gene was the result of an international effort in three laboratories in the United States and the Netherlands (Verkerk et al., 1991). The failure of the production of FMRP is the result of an amplification of a trinucleotide repeat, CGG_n, in the FMR-1 gene on the X chromosome at the Xq27.3 location. Normal individuals have 5–50 repeats of this trinucleotide. In other words, the normal gene repeats the trinucleotide sequence cytosine–guanine–guanine (CGG) 5–50 times. Carriers of the disorder have 51–200 repeats but are clinically unaffected provided the gene is appropriately methylated. In general, affected individuals have more than 200 CGG trinucleotide repeats, and their gene is always abnormally methylated (Devys, Lutz, Rouyer, Bellocq, & Mandel, 1993; Pieretti et al., 1991). Of course, the failure of the production of the FMRP can also occur if the FMR-1 gene is deleted (Gedeon et al., 1992) or if it contains an abnormal nucleotide that renders the gene nonfunctional (De Boulle et al., 1993). The function of FMRP is unknown; because of structural characteristics, it is thought to be involved in the synthesis of other proteins (Ashley, Wilkinson, Reines, & Warren, 1993; Gibson, Rice, Thompson, & Heringa, 1993).

Advances in Molecular Genetic Techniques

Advances in molecular genetic techniques have led to identification of many genetic abnormalities, some of which are associated with MR. Abnormalities that can be detected by these molecular genetic techniques include gross abnormalities (deletions, insertions, and rearrangements of DNA) involving thousands of nucleotides and small abnormalities of a few nucleotides (point mutations; Bregman & Hodapp, 1991). Some of these molecular genetic techniques involve amplifying small amounts of DNA into larger quantities. This is done by first cutting double-stranded DNA into specific fragments with enzymes and multiplying the amount of each DNA fragment either biologically, by inserting the fragment into bacteria that replicate the DNA fragment as part of normal cell division, or enzymatically, by the polymerase chain reaction (PCR).

PCR has revolutionized genetic diagnosis because it can generate large quantities of the defective DNA such that it can be studied directly. To use the PCR, the nucleotide sequence of the fragment of DNA to be studied must be known. A primer containing a few nucleotides is generated that contains the genetic defect and that recognizes its complement in the genomic DNA. Through a process of repeatedly unwinding genomic DNA, binding complementary DNA, and replicating the DNA with the DNA polymerase enzyme, large quantities of the DNA of interest can be generated in a short period of time (Cutting & Antonarakis, 1992).

Fragments of single-stranded DNA can be labeled with either radioactive nucleotides or with fluorescent dyes. These labeled DNA fragments can then be used to probe chromosomes for the specific location of complementary fragments of DNA. One such technique, fluorescent in situ hybridization (FISH), is being used in genomic mapping, that is, finding the location of genes on chromosomes (Nora & Fraser, 1994). With this technique, cytogenetic analysis is maturing from a relatively crude examination of chromosomes on a glass slide to a sophisticated system for analyzing DNA organization.

FISH is currently used in the rapid diagnosis of several genetic disorders, including some associated with MR. In addition to the Prader–Willi and Angelman syndromes, DNA probes for cri du chat syndrome, Miller–Dieker syndrome, and Wolf–Hirschhorn syndrome are available. Patients with cri du chat syndrome are characterized by an unusual catlike cry, microcephaly, other craniofacial abnormalities, and severe MR (K. L. Jones, 1988). The disorder is caused by a partial deletion of the short arm of chromosome 5. A balanced translocation, which carries a significant recurrence risk, can be seen in 10%–15% of parents of these children. The DNA probe facilitates diagnosis of affected infants and identification of parents with balanced translocations.

Miller–Dieker syndrome is associated with an incomplete development of the brain that results in lissencephaly (smooth brain). These patients are microcephalic, have craniofacial abnormalities, and are profoundly retarded. The disorder is due to a deficiency on chromosome 17 at the p13.3 band (K. L. Jones, 1988). Wolf–Hirschhorn syndrome, or 4p− syndrome, is associated with severe MR, ocular hypertelorism, microcephaly, cranial asymmetry, and low-set ears. The syndrome is the result of a deletion of all or part of the short arm of chromosome 4 (K. L. Jones, 1988).

In the next 15 years, the entire human genome, all 100,000 genes, will likely be known (Nora & Fraser, 1994). Eventually, scientists will know where the genes are located, what they do, and what happens when they do not do what they are supposed to do. This knowledge will lead to clearer understanding of the nature of all genetic diseases, including many instances of MR for which the etiology is currently unknown. In some cases, people will know about genes before they have an opportunity to be expressed. This powerful knowledge will present moral, social, and ethical dilemmas in the diagnosis and treatment of patients, the likes of which humanity has never experienced (Nora & Fraser, 1994).

Conclusion

Technological advances in recent years have significantly improved understanding of the etiology of MR. Neurodiagnostic imaging techniques such as MRI, PET, and SPECT allow examination of the fine structure of the brain in vivo. Neurometabolic studies with MRS and NIRS allow examination of the function of brain tissue in vivo. Advances in cytogenetic analysis and molecular genetics have greatly increased understanding of the genetic origins of many cases of MR. In the future, when the human genome is mapped, the genetic basis for all inherited causes of MR will be understood as well. These new technologies will continue to shed light on the biological processes underlying developmental disabilities, point to new medical treatments for at least some of the disorders, clarify the etiology of additional cases of MR, and reveal functional brain–behavior relations that will most likely have implications for individual education and long-term planning.

14

Behavioral Assessment

Thomas R. Linscheid, Brian A. Iwata, and Richard M. Foxx

Behavioral assessment differs from other forms of psychological assessment in that the objective measurement of performance is the subject of greatest interest rather than the measurement of psychological constructs such as intelligence or attitudes. Behavioral assessment (or behavior analysis) has been most useful in two areas: evaluating the effects of various treatment strategies (behavioral or other) and identifying functional relationships between behavior and the environment. Specific treatment effects, as well as more general environment–behavior interactions, are examined by assessing differential rates of behavior under varying antecedent and consequent conditions. This approach has a firm tradition in the field of mental retardation (MR) as a major approach to treatment, education, and the modification of behavior problems (Luiselli, 1989; Matson & Mulick, 1991a) and has more recently been prominent in elucidating the problems with fad treatments such as facilitated communication (Montee, Miltenberger, & Wittrock, 1995) and clarifying the effects of the social and cultural context on treatment in MR services (Mulick & Meinhold, 1992, 1994). This chapter provides a review of basic behavioral assessment procedures. In addition, it describes how behavioral assessment procedures are used to determine the function or cause of behavior and how they can be used in the ongoing monitoring of treatment effects.

Basic Behavioral Assessment Procedures

Although measurement of behavior change can focus on varying response characteristics, all assessment strategies use quantification of the overt aspects of behavior. Use of operationally defined behaviors promotes objectivity, reliability of measurement, and agreement as to which behaviors are important for measurement or modification.

Behavioral Assessment Techniques

Several basic behavior measurement procedures have been used singly or in combination to assess behavior changes and functional relationships as summarized briefly in the following discussion. For a more extensive review of behavior measurement techniques, see Linscheid, Rasnake, Tarnowski, and Mulick (1989).

Frequency recording. This is the easiest form of behavioral assessment, requiring an observer only to count the number of responses that occur. Although the method is simple, it should not be used with behaviors that may vary substantially in duration because frequency recording is insensitive to changes in response duration.

Duration recording. This technique measures the amount of time that a behavior lasts and provides an accurate assessment of the "amount" of behavior. It requires a timing device and can be cumbersome in attempts to measure high-frequency, short-duration behaviors.

Interval recording. With this method, observers simply note the occurrence or nonoccurrence of the behavior during consecutive and preset time intervals. Typically, short intervals such as 10 sec are used. Two variations consist of partial- and whole-interval recording: In partial-interval recording, a behavior is scored regardless of its duration, whereas in whole-interval recording, behavior must occur for the entire duration of the interval to be scored. The ease of observational measurement under this system allows for the assessment of multiple behaviors simultaneously, because the observer does not have to count instances of the behavior or measure its duration. The validity of the method is dependent on selection of the proper interval length. If the interval length is too long, the procedure may be insensitive to small changes in the behavior.

Time sampling. This method does not require constant observation of the behavior being assessed and is, therefore, sometimes selected for its ease of application. The occurrence or nonoccurrence of a behavior is recorded at the end of preset time intervals that either are selected on a random basis or are fixed, such as once every 5 min. As with interval recording, accurate measurement with time sampling is dependent on the nature of the behavior and the selection of time sample intervals.

Measurement by products. In this method, behavior is assessed indirectly by measuring, usually through frequency counts, products of that behavior. For example, arithmetic homework behavior could be assessed by counting the number of arithmetic problems completed correctly.

Reliability

A number of methods have been developed both to assess and to calculate the reliability of direct observation techniques. In behavioral assessment, reliability is generally expressed as a percentage agreement score between two independent observers, and different formulas may be used to account for extremely high or low base rates, chance agreement, or other sources of bias. When behavior is assessed over long periods, reliability must be periodically reassessed to ensure that observed behavior changes are not merely artifacts of "drifting" definitions. For a detailed description of reliability assessment procedures, see the work of T. J. Page and Iwata (1986).

Using Behavioral Assessment to Identify the Function of Behavior

In the most general sense, a functional analysis of behavior "requires a believable demonstration of the events that can be responsible for the occurrence or nonoccurrence of that behavior" (Baer, Wolf, & Risley, 1968, pp. 93–94). The most pressing question to be answered when attempting to identify the "current" functions of behavior is, What, if anything, in the environment maintains this particular behavior as it now exists in this individual? Over the past 10 years in the field of applied behavior analysis, methods for identifying both the structural and functional characteristics of behavior have been incorporated into the process of treatment development. These methods attempt to isolate the maintaining conditions or current "causes" of behavior using indirect, descriptive, and controlled methodologies (Iwata, Vollmer, & Zarcone, 1990).

Indirect Methods

Assessment procedures that do not require the collection of firsthand data are considered indirect or anecdotal methods, through which information about behavior is usually obtained from parents, teachers, caregivers, or other relevant people. These individuals usually are asked to recall previous observations or to draw conclusions about the causes of an individual's behavior on the basis of their observations. Questions may be open-ended and exploratory or may be structured according to a variety of formats and are designed to produce a clear description of the behavior itself, the situations in which it does or does not occur, antecedent events that may precipitate the behavior, and the typical reactions of others to the behavior.

An example of a structured rating scale is the Motivation Assessment Scale (MAS), a questionnaire designed to identify environmental contingencies that may be responsible for the occurrence of self-injurious behavior in individuals with developmental disabilities (Durand & Crimmons, 1988). The MAS uses a Likert-type scale in which respondents (e.g., teachers, parents, caregivers) indicate the extent to which an individual's self-injurious behavior seems to be correlated with access to attention or materials, escape from task demands, and so forth. Although questionnaires such as the MAS may provide quick answers with regard to which factors may be responsible for maintaining any given behavior, information gained by such methods may be highly unreliable (Newton & Sturmey,

1991; Zarcone, Rodgers, Iwata, Rourke, & Dorsey, 1991). In addition to reliability problems, questionnaires and rating scales may not yield results consistent with those obtained from direct observation of behavior. For example, C. W. Green et al. (1988) found that stimuli identified as reinforcers by staff members often differed from those identified by individuals allowed to exhibit reinforcer preferences.

Although data gathered through interviews, questionnaires, rating scales, and checklists can provide preliminary information about the severity and scope of the problem and can help form a basis for further inquiry, limitations with respect to reliability and validity indicate that these instruments should not be considered adequate in themselves as behavioral assessment tools. Prior to development of an intervention plan, direct observation should be conducted to verify the accuracy of information obtained from indirect methods.

Descriptive Analysis Through Direct and Naturalistic Observation

A descriptive analysis delineates observed relationships between the physical, social, and biological variables and the behavior of interest. The rate of occurrence of behaviors is assessed in relationship to environmental factors such as time of day, presence or absence of specific individuals, and task demands (Schroeder et al., 1982). In addition, biological states such as ear infections or seizures can be documented and their relationship to changes in rates of behavior recorded. Descriptive analyses usually do not involve the manipulation of environmental events and are used primarily to form hypotheses regarding the functional relationships between behavior and consequences.

Although more time-consuming than indirect methods of assessment, descriptive analyses, based on direct observation, possess a number of advantages. First, they are inherently more objective than verbal reports, because they are based on precisely defined and observed behaviors. Second, they provide quantitative rather than global estimates, a feature that permits greater confidence in conclusions regarding the degree of correspondence between behavior and other environmental events. Third, because behavior is observed in the natural environment, a broader range of potential behaviors and both antecedent and contingent events is subject to direct assessment.

One easily administered descriptive technique is the *scatter plot* (Touchette, MacDonald, & Langer, 1985), which allows assessment of differential rates of behavior across time and activities. The procedure involves specifying several levels of target behavior (e.g., none vs. one or two instances vs. three or more instances) and coding a data sheet according to the level of the observed behavior within set time intervals (e.g., a half hour) throughout the day. The scatter plot is a simple method compared to those requiring continuous recording, and the data record provides a visual distribution of behavior across time. Knowing an individual's schedule of activities, location, and companions throughout the day allows a comparison of the relative behavior rates by time of day, activity, and location. The scatter plot is a rather molar measure, however, and does not provide detailed information on relationships between behaviors and their relevant antecedents and consequences.

More recent refinements of descriptive analysis methods have focused on the use of continuous recording procedures across time or setting and data reduction techniques that are based on correlations or conditional probabilities (Mace & Lalli, 1991; Mulick & Meinhold, 1992; Schroeder, 1990; Vyse & Mulick, 1990). For example, with a detailed record of ongoing behavior and its context, it is possible to determine the extent to which a behavior problem is more likely to occur in a particular situation (e.g., when the individual is alone or when given task demands) by calculating conditional probabilities of behavior given an antecedent or consequent event of interest. Although still correlational in nature, these methods allow precise identification of environmental events associated with either high or low rates of behavior.

Functional Analysis Through Direct Controlled Observation

Functional analysis identifies the effects of behavior contingencies through direct manipulation. Iwata, Dorsey, Slifer, Bauman, and Richman (1982) developed a method for experimentally assessing variables that may be responsible for maintaining self-injurious behavior, and their approach has been applied subsequently to a wide range of behavior problems, including aggression (Mace, Page, Ivancic, & O'Brien, 1986), bizarre speech (Mace & Lalli, 1991), stereotypy (Durand & Carr, 1987; Wacker et al., 1990), destructive behavior (Slifer, Ivancic, Parrish, Page, & Burgio, 1986), and feeding problems (Munk & Repp, 1994).

The basic method of a functional analysis involves the generation of hypotheses regarding the environmental contingencies that maintain a problem behavior. Conditions are then developed to examine the effects of these variables on observed rates of behavior. In the case of self-injurious behavior, for example, contingencies such as positive reinforcement, negative reinforcement, and "self-stimulation" have been proposed as variables that may maintain self-injury (E. G. Carr, 1977). Iwata et al. (1982) developed test conditions for each of these factors, all of which could be manipulated independently. Higher rates of behavior under one condition relative to the other conditions can suggest which factors (contingencies) may be responsible for maintaining behavior outside of the experimental setting.

This information can be valuable in developing treatment plans. For example, a variety of extinction procedures have been described (Cooper, Heron, & Heward, 1987), but their effective use requires identification of the source of the reinforcement to be discontinued (Iwata, Pace, Cowdrey, & Miltonbeger, 1994). Likewise, approaches to treatment that are based on strengthening alternative behaviors are more likely to be effective if they provide access to the specific reinforcer that currently maintains the behavior problem (E. G. Carr & Durand, 1985a).

Iwata et al. (1994) recently published a summary of results obtained from 152 single-subject functional analyses conducted on individuals with self-injurious behavior. Differential rates of responding in the various experimental conditions were obtained in 95% of the cases. The most commonly identified "cause" of self-injury in their sample was social negative reinforcement (e.g., escape from demands; 38%), followed by social positive reinforcement (26.3%), automatic (sensory) reinforcement (25.7%), and a combination of these factors (5.3%). Nearly 5% of the cases showed either cyclical or inconsistent patterns. On the basis of these data, the authors concluded that functional analysis was extremely effective in identifying environmental contingencies that maintain self-injurious behavior.

In addition to examining the generality of functional analysis methods across behavior disorders, recent research has produced a variety of procedural variations for use in different settings, such as schools (Sasso et al., 1992) and outpatient clinics (Northrup et al., 1991). The latter extension is noteworthy because it involves an abbreviated assessment technique applicable to situations in which observations cannot be conducted for extended periods of time.

In spite of their many strengths, functional analysis methods have two potential limitations. First, because the assessment itself can be time-consuming, only a limited range of variables may be investigated. For example, escape from task demands has generally been used to evaluate the role of negative reinforcement in the maintenance of self-injurious behavior. However, E. G. Carr (1994) noted that social avoidance in general may reinforce some individuals' behavior and that an analysis that investigated the role of negative reinforcement using only task avoidance might not reveal the influence of social avoidance. Second, it is possible that although the behavior of the individual undergoing assessment may come under the control of the contingencies manipulated, it might not be maintained by these contingencies in the natural environment. Keeping the analysis itself as brief as possible serves to decrease this concern.

Behavioral Assessment of Treatment and Long-Term Effects

Perhaps the best known application of behavioral assessment techniques is in establishing causal relationships between treatment contingencies and behavior change. A variety of single-subject research methods have been developed that are capable of demonstrating the functional relationships between treatment and behavior change in individual cases. These generally involve the systematic introduction and removal of treatment contingencies (reversal designs) or the sequential introduction of treatment contingencies across behaviors, settings, or individuals (multiple baseline designs). Differential rates of the behavior under conditions in which the treatment is present or absent provide simple yet powerful demonstrations of treatment effectiveness. A thorough description and discussion of single-subject designs for assessing treatment effectiveness is beyond the scope of this chapter, but can be found in the work of Herson and Barlow (1976).

Most published reports of behavioral interventions have not included long-term follow-up assessments. A comprehensive in-depth evaluation of treatment and training requires that lengthy follow-up be conducted (e.g., see Foxx, 1990; Foxx, Bittle, & Faw, 1989; Foxx & Faw, 1990; Foxx & Livesay, 1984; Linscheid, Haertel, & Cooley, 1993). Long-term follow-up provides an evaluation of generalization and maintenance and reveals the "staying power" of interventions. Just as behavioral assessment strategies play an integral part in identifying the function of behavior and assessing treatment effects, they also play a central role in the examination of treatment durability. Maintenance refers to treatment effects or improvements that remain stable even after the explicit intervention is removed. Generalization occurs when treatment effects are apparent in settings or situations that are not involved in an obvious or explicit way in the original treatment (Foxx, 1982a), although stimulus commonalities are presumed to mediate such an outcome.

Follow-up assessment reveals useful and important information needed to ensure treatment success. For example, in one of the most comprehensive follow-up studies, Foxx and Livesay (1984) conducted a 10-year follow-up study of individuals with MR treated with overcorrection (Foxx & Bechtel, 1983) and reported the following:

1. Maintenance programs were likely to be discontinued after the primary researcher or therapist left.
2. The passage of time and changes in setting increased the likelihood of the individual being treated by a method that required less staff time and effort than the original program. The longer the period of time between the treatment program and the return of the misbehavior, the less likely that the original, successful program would be reinstated.
3. Higher functioning individuals showed longer term and better suppression of seriously maladaptive behavior than lower functioning individuals. This finding suggests that more direct programming of competing reinforcers and activities may be required in maintenance programs for persons with severe behavior problems.
4. The more serious the misbehavior, the greater the need for maintenance and generalization programming.

The information provided by Foxx and Livesay identified several factors that may be crucial to the success of treatment and has immediate implications for the design and evaluation of intervention programs. In addition, follow-up assessment should include repeated observations conducted over an extended period and should evaluate not only behavioral rates, but also treatment integrity (i.e., consistency of implementation) and the clinical significance of behavior change (Kazdin, 1977; Wolf, 1976). Generalization and maintenance should be assessed separately to prevent confounding of the two (R. L. Koegel & Rincover, 1977). Addressing generalization and maintenance also will promote ongoing evaluation of the individual's personal treatment goals and determination of what constitutes functional and relevant behaviors in the person's social environment (Monroe, 1988). Measurement systems must be developed that are capable not only of tracking behavior over time, but also of providing information concerning the nature of treatment implementation, social setting, and environmental changes as well as redefined functional goals. Favell and McGimsey (1993) suggested that this goal may require the addition of different recording methods (e.g., reliable and valid rating scales) that are cost-efficient and accurate in reflecting behavior and contextual change.

Conclusion

Behavioral assessment is a direct method to determine the relation between any definable behavior of educational or therapeutic interest and environmental events and conditions that account for it. The measurement and analytic technology this approach has spawned has made effective habilitation and treatment a reality for countless children and adults with MR over the past several decades. Furthermore, behavioral assessment has increasingly been useful in understanding how effective treatments work, determining the most effective component of multicomponent treatment packages, and studying the broad effects of the environmental context on the behavior of people with MR.

15

Assessment of Quality of Life

Laird W. Heal, Sharon A. Borthwick-Duffy, and Richard R. Saunders

In recent years, human service professionals have begun to examine the consequences of decisions made on behalf of people with mental retardation (MR) in the context of the multifaceted construct referred to as *quality of life* (QOL). Although the research and ideological traditions relating to QOL have developed separately for the population at large (e.g., Andrews & Withey, 1976; A. Campbell, 1981; Diener, 1984; Flanagan, 1978, 1982) and for people with disabilities (e.g., Borthwick-Duffy, 1986, 1992; Goode, 1994; Halpern, 1993; Jamieson, 1993; Parent, 1992; Schalock, 1990; Schalock, Keith, Hoffman, & Karan, 1989; Simon & Rosen, 1993), the two groups of authors have come to similar conclusions, with understandable adjustments for disabilities. It is commonly believed that QOL should be conceptualized similarly for individuals with or without disabilities (e.g., Goode, 1988, 1994). Indeed, it seems axiomatic that if QOL is to have status as a measurable construct in psychological research and treatment, it must have similar meaning for the entire range of mental (and physical) ability. Nevertheless, Flanagan (1982) proposed that QOL for people with disabilities should be evaluated within the context of individual physical, mental, or emotional disabilities. With regard to MR, it is important to recognize that discussions of QOL must address the wide range of intellectual ability included in this classification. Accordingly, this chapter should be applicable to individuals whose degree of disability ranges from the barely perceptible to the profound—from people who barely meet the definitional criteria of MR to people who are dependent on others to meet nearly all of their needs.

The objectives of this chapter are (a) to identify features of the definitions, conceptual models, and empirical findings regarding QOL that are

---

This report was supported in part by the Office of Special Education and Rehabilitative Services, U.S. Department of Education, under a contract (300-85-0160) to the Transition Research Institute at the University of Illinois, by Research Grants HD-22953 and HD-21056 from the National Institute of Child Health and Human Development to the University of California at Riverside and by Grant 90DD0322 awarded to the Schiefelbusch Institute for Lifespan Studies at the University of Kansas. We gratefully acknowledge the critical reviews of the editorial board of this volume.

likely to be universal and enduring for people with MR; (b) to provide information on available measures of QOL; and (c) to describe an integrated, universally applicable orientation for practitioners to use to promote QOL by maximizing a client's control in the pursuit of a satisfying life.

Quality of Life in the General Population

If QOL is to be minimally reduced by limitations associated with MR, it is important to consider the QOL literature for the general population. Maslow's (1954) enduring "hierarchy of needs," composed of the ordered levels of (a) *physiological needs*, (b) *safety*, (c) *affiliation and affection*, (d) *esteem*, and (e) *self-actualization*, contributes to an understanding of QOL by identifying domains relevant to QOL and by suggesting that the importance assigned to these dimensions may vary across individuals and across time. Using an empirical approach to evaluate, refine, and extend Maslow's classification, Flanagan (1978) asked a broad cross-section of nearly 3,000 people to identify experiences and behaviors that they found to be particularly important or satisfying in their lives. Flanagan then classified the approximately 6,500 "critical incidents" into 15 QOL components (i.e., sources of satisfaction), which he listed under five general headings: (a) *physical and material well-being*, including material well-being, financial security, health, and personal safety; (b) *relations with other people*, including relations with spouse; having and raising children; relations with parents, siblings, or other relatives; and relations with friends; (c) *social, community, and civic activities*, including helping or encouraging other people and participating in public and governmental affairs; (d) *personal development and fulfillment*, including intellectual development, personal planning and self-understanding, occupational role, and creativity and personal expression; and (e) *recreation*, including socializing, passive recreation, and active recreation. Similarities between Maslow's levels and Flanagan's components are apparent.

Notwithstanding the conceptual subdivisions of QOL, other investigators (e.g., Andrews & Withey, 1976; A. Campbell, 1981) found that the claim of a satisfying life by individuals in the general population is a single unidimensional trait, "subjective well-being," which correlates highly with each of Flanagan's sources of satisfaction. Furthermore, Zautra and Reich's (1983) meta-analysis confirmed that positive subjective well-being (lifestyle satisfaction) and negative psychological distress (lifestyle misery) are uncorrelated personal traits and represent different dimensions of well-being. Their findings suggested that positive, critical life events enhance subjective well-being but do not affect global distress; negative critical events appeared to have the opposite effect, elevating distress but not affecting lifestyle satisfaction. Diener's (1984) definitive summary and analysis of this literature documented the traitlike stability of subjective well-being through life's vicissitudes, which affect it only temporarily.

Scholars and practitioners concerned with the QOL of individuals with disabilities should probably assume that most of these general findings apply across the full range of human intelligence. It is also reasonable to expect that people with MR, like those without this diagnosis, will define their QOL in terms of Maslow's hierarchy and, especially, Flanagan's (1978) categories of important and satisfying life experiences. Furthermore, global life satisfaction is expected to be a relatively stable trait that is unassociated with occasional stressful events and temporary states of distress. Unfortunately, the primary implication of this stability for practice is the difficulty of improving one's subjective (psychological) well-being through interventions that improve objective QOL indicators, an implication that will surprise few readers. Nevertheless, the research reviewed by Zautra and Reich (1983) and Diener (1984) indicates that self-perceptions of well-being and distress are influenced, however gradually, by critical events. Thus, modest improvements would be expected from carefully selected therapies, environmental changes, increased client self-direction, or other interventions.

Quality of Life for Individuals with Mental Retardation

The status that QOL has attained in influencing recommendations for improved MR services might imply that professionals have arrived at consensus regarding its meaning and have developed a portfolio of widely accepted QOL measures. Recent reviews of the literature on QOL and developmental disabilities have indicated that this consensus is still emerging (Borthwick-Duffy, 1986, 1992; R. I. Brown, 1988; Copher, 1988; Dennis, Williams, Giangreco, & Cloninger, 1993; Emerson, 1985; Goode, 1988, 1994; Halpern, 1993; C. Hughes, Hwang, Kim, Eisenman, & Killian, 1995; Jamieson, 1993; Mittler, 1984; Parent, 1992; Parmenter, 1992; Schalock, 1990; Schalock & Heal, 1988; Schalock, Keith, Hoffman, & Karan, 1989; Trivedi, 1988; Willer & Intagliata, 1980; Wolfensberger, 1972, 1992). The differences observed appear to reflect the relative infancy of the QOL construct in the field of MR and appear to relate to confusion in terminology and minor variations in dimensional frameworks rather than to conflicting conceptual models.

Measurement of Quality of Life of People with Mental Retardation

Measurement of QOL has been approached through objective and subjective indicators of an individual's life conditions (Heal & Sigelman, 1990). A third approach, recently proposed, addresses the degree of congruence between needs and their satisfaction (Jamieson, 1993) or of congruence between environmental demands and individuals' competent control of resources to meet those demands (R. R. Saunders & Spradlin, 1991; Schalock & Jensen, 1986). Objective indicators, also described as social indicators,

Table 1. Measures Used to Assess the Quality of Life of Individuals With MR by Focus and Perceiver

Focus	Perceiver	Citation	Format	Description or Title
Individual	Self	Chadsey-Rusch, 1987	Q	Worker Loneliness Scale
		Halpern, 1993	Q	Choices, satisfaction, self-esteem
		Heal & Chadsey-Rusch, 1985; Heal, Harner, Amado, & Chadsey-Rusch, 1993	I	Satisfaction with home, work, friends, and community
		Simons, 1986b	I	Broad-ranging interview concerning conditions
	Intimate acquaintance	Conroy & Feinstein Associates, 1986	Q	Choice Making Scale
		Cummins, 1992	Q	Comprehensive Quality-of-Life Scale
		Newton et al., 1988	Q	Behavioral indices of integration and control
		Prudhoe Unit, 1987	Q	Residential Environmental Standards
		Raynes, Sumpton, & Pettipher, 1986	Q	Index of Adult Autonomy
		Schalock, Keith, & Hoffman, 1990	Q	Independence, integration, and satisfaction concerning home, work, community
		M. M. Seltzer & Seltzer, 1976	I	Independence, integration, and satisfaction concerning home, work, community
	Agent of society	—	P	Level of education
		—	P	Personal income
Environment	Self	Heal & Chadsey-Rusch, 1985; Heal et al., 1993	I	Satisfaction with home, work, friends, community
		Moos, 1975	Q	Physical, social, and organizational climate
	Intimate acquaintance	Cummins, 1992	Q	Comprehensive Quality-of-Life Scale
		McLain et al., 1979	Q	Staff vs. client management orientation
		Moos, 1975	Q	Physical, social, and organizational climate

		Pratt, Luszez, & Brown, 1979	Q	Management orientation: staff vs. client
		R. R. Saunders, Saunders, & Hull, 1991	Q	Congruence of client control and client needs
		Schalock & Jensen, 1986	Q	Fit of abilities to environmental challenges
		Schalock et al., 1990	Q	Independence, integration, and satisfaction concerning home, work, community
		Simons, 1986a	I	The Relative Schedule
		Wing, Holmes, & Shah, 1985	Q	Relatives' opinions of client's QOL
		—	Q	Sociometric scales concerning a targeted personal quality
	Agent of society	Berkson & Romer, 1980	O	Observation codes for types of friendships
Culture	Self	Hampson, Judge, & Renshaw, 1984	O	Environmental Checklist
		Halpern, 1993	Q	Choices, satisfaction, self-esteem
		Simons, 1986b	I	Broad-ranging interview concerning conditions
	Intimate acquaintance	Raynes, Pratt, & Roses, 1979	Q	Index of Community Involvement
		Schalock et al., 1990	Q	Independence, integration, and satisfaction concerning home, work, community
	Agent of society	Feinstein, 1985	Q	Life Safety Code Instrument
		Flynn & Heal, 1981	O	Culturally normative features of human services
		Joint Commission on Accreditation of Healthcare Organizations, 1994	O	Standards for congregate care facilities
		Thompson, Robinson, Graff, & Ingemey, 1990	O	Homelike features of residences
		Wolfensberger & Thomas, 1983	O	Culturally normative features of human services

Q = questionnaire; I = interview; O = observation; P = public record; QOL = quality of life.

might include material possessions, entertainment, social contacts, privacy, family support, generic health and protective services used, and control of one's environment. The individual's subjective impressions of these and other life features have been referred to as *psychological indicators* (Parmenter, 1992; Schalock, 1990). The scaled discrepancy between needs and their satisfaction can be operationalized as a goodness-of-fit index (Jamieson, 1993).

One way to classify measures of QOL is with a 3 (perceiver) × 3 (perspective) matrix. The perceiver can be the individual herself, an intimate acquaintance of the individual, or an agent of society (a third party). Similarly, the perspective, or focus, can be on the individual herself, on intimate social relationships, or on society at large. For example, a competitively employed dishwasher might be happy from her own perception but considered underemployed by her parent (intimate) or case manager (agent of society). On the other hand, the focus might be on relationships with coworkers or supervisors, or it might be on the value attributed to the client's contribution to the functioning of a large fast-food chain, a community, or a national economy.

Table 1 shows an incomplete list of measures organized by these nine perceiver–perspective combinations. The first column designates the focus, or perspective; the second indicates the perceiver; the third gives citations to the measure; the fourth tells the format of the measure (questionnaire, interview, observation, or public record); and the fifth gives a brief description of the measured characteristic or a descriptive title. Variations among QOL taxonomies or models proposed in the MR literature imply that the assessment of QOL depends substantially on the way the QOL concept is defined and the characteristics of the person being evaluated. Furthermore, although it is generally agreed that QOL is, at least in part, a subjective construct, the degree to which objective indicators are believed to be central to the definition of QOL will dictate the format and focus of assessment. Objective measures of life conditions, which Halpern (1993) described as *normative*, and subjective reactions to those conditions, which Halpern called *idiosyncratic*, have each been used singly or concurrently to index QOL, depending on the viewpoint of the writer (Borthwick-Duffy, 1992; Keith, 1990).

Some QOL assessments have been published and are easily available, but most need further psychometric development. None have the scale qualities that characterize the tools that have been used in assessment and evaluation of such well-defined constructs as intelligence or motor performance. Because quantifying QOL by checklists or other objective measures provides only part of the evaluation required to fully understand an individual's life conditions, improved measurement should be given high priority. The reader is directed to the thorough compendium by Raynes (1988) for descriptions of more than 60 instruments developed to assess QOL from a variety of perspectives and to the comprehensive review of QOL indicators in the community psychology literature by Zautra and Goodhart (1979).

Matching Abilities and Task Demands

Schalock and his associates (Schalock & Jensen, 1986; Schalock, Keith, Hoffman, & Karan, 1989) have asserted that the better the fit, or congruence, between the abilities of individuals and the requirements of their environments for success or survival, the higher the measured QOL. To operationalize this goodness-of-fit conceptualization, Schalock and Jensen (1986) inventoried clients' environments to determine the skills and supported skills that their tasks demanded and assessed the clients to determine the supports required, if any, to enable them to complete each task. Schalock and Jensen's goodness-of-fit index (GOFI) was computed by weighting the level of independence in performance by the percentage of required tasks that the client "could do."

Quality of Life as the Competent Reduction of Unmet Needs

In addition to being defined in terms of objective indicators or subjective claims of satisfaction, QOL has been defined as the goodness of fit between one's needs and one's satisfaction of those needs (Emerson, 1985; Jamieson, 1993; R. R. Saunders & Spradlin, 1991; Schalock & Jensen, 1986). It should not be controversial to suggest that QOL is related to the proportion of one's perceived needs that are being met. What might be controversial to practitioners, however, is the weight given to one's participation in satisfying one's own needs.

Competence, Choice, and Control

R. R. Saunders and Spradlin (1991) suggested that the most notable similarity between people with even the most profound retardation and those of normal ability is that "doing something for themselves feels good" (p. 35). They suggested, for example, that knowing that one can obtain food in response to hunger "feels good, diminishes frustration, and minimizes unproductive aberrant responses" (p. 35). Not limited to MR, competence has been identified as a key drive in human performance management and increased QOL in the workplace (Deming, 1982, 1986; T. F. Gilbert, 1978). Self-actualization is, after all, at the top of Maslow's (1954) hierarchy of needs. Indeed, the motivation to satisfy one's own needs has a rich tradition in the conventional psychology of motivation. R. W. White's (1959) seminal article documented the internal, apparently autonomous, evolutionarily adaptive drive for all organisms to develop mastery over the forces around them. Harter (1977, 1978), among others, provided data and analyses to suggest that this drive is modifiable through one's history of interacting with and being socialized by one's environment. Thus, some children, especially those with low intelligence, are socialized to depend on others to make the choices required for their security and comfort

(Harter, 1977; Haywood & Switzky, 1986). Nevertheless, reinstatement of the motivation for adolescents and adults with MR to make their own choices can be occasioned by surprisingly minimal interventions (Agran & Moore, 1994; Switzky & Haywood, 1991; Switzky & Heal, 1990), and this fact alone argues strongly for routine consideration of this aspect. In sum, the disposition to control outcomes through competent performances appears to be ingrained in human nature and is, accordingly, a crucial consideration in assessing QOL of people with MR (Jenkinson, 1993).

Control and Barriers to Control

Although Schalock and Jensen's (1986) goodness-of-fit index has an elegant simplicity, it neglects the element of choice. It reflects one aspect of self-actualization, competence, but neglects another, control. The right to choose, the right to *be* in control, and indeed the right to competence itself, which have been taken for granted in the QOL in the general population, have been nominated as major considerations in the QOL of individuals with and without limited mental ability (Goode, 1994; Jamieson, 1993; R. R. Saunders & Spradlin, 1991). Although increased competence should increase one's control over need satisfaction, an assessment of QOL should reflect both competence and control. According to this view, QOL is high by definition when the disparity between one's needs and one's achievements is moderate to low *and* when one is in control of initiating and competently using the responses, routines, activities, and assistance available from others to reduce the disparity. Competence in this sense is indicated by a relatively smooth, efficient performance, leading to positive (i.e., pleasurable or satisfying) consequences. Performances that are observed to be initiated often and performed the most fluently and enthusiastically are presumably the most functional for the performer in closing (or maintaining) the disparity between desire (need) and outcome.

Barriers to control (i.e., to independent initiation and completion) include many variables, but important among them are social and environmental conditions that cause dependence on others for access to the locations and resources necessary for initiation and completion of important performances or dependence on others to deliver the consequences for the performances. Barriers to competence include physical, cognitive, communicative, and other behavioral deficits. QOL is promoted by addressing these barriers through particular habilitation techniques: (a) teaching adaptive skills, (b) providing human assistance as needs arise, or (c) creating prostheses or adaptations for functioning in the environment (e.g., R. R. Saunders, Saunders, & Hull, 1991; Saunders & Spradlin, 1991; Schalock & Jensen, 1986).

Teaching adaptive skills. The literature is replete with examples of applied educational programs to increase the adaptive skills of individuals with MR. J. E. Martin (1988) reviewed this literature. On another plane, considerable effort has been made to teach individuals with MR to instruct themselves when they confront a novel problem (e.g., Agran & Moore, 1994).

Providing human assistance. Individuals who cannot create alternative performances to arrive at desired outcomes are dependent to some degree on others to initiate and complete performances. Because this dependency reduces control, it is also considered to reduce QOL. Fortunately, few individuals are dependent on others for every outcome or, at least, for all parts of the performance necessary to achieve every outcome. Permitting people with disabilities to have partial participation (Baumgart et al., 1982; Ferguson & Baumgart, 1991), to institute supported routines (R. R. Saunders & Spradlin, 1991), and to maximize opportunities for making choices can help people with even the most severe disabilities to enjoy a higher QOL. Shifting the focus from one's level of disability to one's use of support (cf. Luckasson et al., 1992) implies that QOL will increase as the client comes to control various types of support. Supported individuals come the closest to meeting the requirements for high QOL, in terms of minimized need–achievement discrepancy, when they can independently activate their own support systems, that is, when they can communicate what they want to do, when they want to be supported, and how much support they want provided.

Creating prostheses and environmental adaptations. For some individuals with physical disabilities, environmental engineering and prosthetic devices promote adaptation and QOL by creating an external bridge to the desired outcome and placing the performance under the more direct or immediate control of the disabled person. Eyeglasses, game-improvement golf clubs, big-headed tennis rackets, hand-control automobiles, calculators, and language boards are prostheses; ramped buildings and curbs, rebus-character signs, hydraulic wheelchair lifts, and elevators are examples of environmental engineering. Both prostheses and environmental adaptations are designed to circumvent or neutralize the handicapping effect of a disability and thereby increase the efficiency of achieving goals and elevate control of social and other environmental events.

Determining Needs and Aspirations

Providing choices can create problems in meeting service objectives for individuals with limited mental ability. In most cases, the assignment of a formal MR diagnosis brings with it involvement of professionals in decisions related to the client's education, supervision, or provision of care. The client is presumed or even declared legally to be incompetent to specify his own needs. Furthermore, some aspirations may be so unrealistic, self-defeating, or bizarre that they violate cultural norms and/or practitioner sensibilities. Thus, one of the practitioner's challenges is to balance the client's "dignity of risk" in making his own choices with societal or environmental realities in establishing realistic, culturally normative, QOL priorities.

Operationalizing Discrepancy Analysis

The comprehensive assessment and program planning system (CAPPS; R. R. Saunders, Saunders, & Hull, 1991), a recently developed system of evaluation, operationalizes the concept of goodness of fit with enhanced client control. In Phase 1, the practitioner assesses the degree to which the service network (environment, daily schedule, supporters, teachers, and co-workers) currently supports a partially independent individual in the everyday routines or situations commonly found in personal care, domestic activities, travel, work, and leisure pursuits. This phase is parallel to Schalock and Jensen's (1986) environmental inventories of situation-specific performance requirements. In contrast to Schalock and Jensen's approach, CAPPS also provides an estimate of the degree to which the supported individual is encouraged or permitted to be independent by her relatives, friends, case manager, or service providers. For example, the assessor may note that in the early morning, one person turns on the light in the bedroom of the individual, another person awakens him, and a third assists him into his wheelchair: supports that appear not to promote the individual's independence.

In the second phase of the assessment, the evaluator uses information compiled from more traditional assessment reports about the individual's preferences and personal characteristics: physical, health, sensorimotor, emotional, communication-related, and learning (similar to Schalock & Jensen's [1986] assessment of what the individual can do). The compiled information is used to identify the routines or situations in which the supports provided do not correspond to or are discrepant from the preferences and capabilities of the individual. In other words, an assessment is made of the discrepancy between the individual's current participation in a routine or situation and the individual's participation that would fully challenge her abilities, characteristics, and preferences. The presence of unnecessary supports that preempt the individual's consenting, independent performance indicates a need for (a) instructional programs to build new skills, (b) opportunities for greater participation, or (c) better adaptations or prostheses. Teaching the individual safer bed-to-wheelchair transfer sequences, providing the individual with an alarm clock, and creating a remote-controlled light switch are, respectively, examples of these types of changes.

Scaling QOL along the dimension of the discrepancy between one's needs and the competent fulfillment of those needs has appeal as a parsimonious, universal strategy QOL assessment. Under this conceptualization, QOL is maximized when the control one has over the resources to satisfy one's needs is maximized. This definition is particularly appealing because it can be applied to any setting and any level of ability; it is a definition that is culture-free, episode-free, and location-free. It is a definition that can be applied in schools, work settings, homes in any neighborhood, hospitals, or prisons. Given this definition, QOL can be measured with an instrument that objectively compares the disparity, or discrepancy, between an individual's needs and the degree and frequency with which their satisfaction is under the individual's control.

Conclusion

QOL is a construct that should be useful to scholars, ideologues, and practitioners as they contemplate the proper goals, opportunities, education and training, prostheses, and environmental modifications for individuals who have MR. Pragmatically, QOL must be defined in terms of two interrelated and sometimes reciprocating constructs: global satisfaction with one's lifestyle and control over the human and environmental resources that produce satisfactions. In this society, the democratic traditions are conspicuously directed toward pleasure. Although individual histories ensure that people seek different comforts and have different thresholds of comfort that would be relinquished to preserve or expand control over environments, all people seek a balance of these two constructs. Western cultures encourage their citizens in this enterprise. It should be no different for any person embraced as human. Service resources should always enhance an individual's comfort, control, or both, preferably at the individual's discretion.

Part III

Prevention and Treatment

Introduction

Clinical practice in the field of mental retardation (MR) draws on the clinical, community, social, educational, school, developmental, consulting, behavior analytic, health, rehabilitation, organizational, physiological, and psychopharmacological specialties in psychology. This breadth is perhaps inherent in a field defined by a condition that has associated diverse and distinctive etiological characteristics and effects on human development, rather than by a context (e.g., school, organization) or a segment of the life cycle (e.g., early development, adult development and aging). However, the breadth of clinical application in the field of MR also means that it has been possible to include only the most prominent and most salient issues and applications in this book. Informed readers will be able to identify many additional areas of activity that may have warranted inclusion.

Although in any clinical specialty the ideal intervention is one that prevents a disability from occurring to begin with (e.g., primary prevention), in pragmatic terms the primary focus of clinical activity most commonly involves early intervention to prevent the increase of, or to reverse, developmental or social adaptive delays (e.g., secondary prevention) or treatment to ameliorate the impact of the disability during the school years and adult life (e.g., tertiary intervention). Because primary prevention is so important, however, chapters on both social and biological prevention initiatives have been included. As these chapters indicate, although it is possible to prevent or substantially ameliorate the occurrence of MR, in practice the causes of a substantial proportion of cases of MR are unknown and thus not essentially amenable to prevention or, in some cases, early identification. Furthermore, some causes of MR involve lifestyle behaviors that are prevalent in society and multiple individual disposing social and biological factors, which when identified predict the occurrence of MR in only some cases (e.g., not all poor children have MR) and thus resist modification through service, education, and statute. Thus, it is evident that secondary and tertiary prevention services will represent the primary focus of clinical practice for the foreseeable future.

Treatment concerns addressed in this section include cultural and cross-cultural considerations, communicating assessment results to caregivers, instructional intervention in educational settings, family therapy and family supports, parent training, sexuality and sexual development, forensic practice, psychopharmacological activities, applied behavior analytic treatment, behavior therapy, and psychotherapy. Over the past decade, practices in interdisciplinary service settings have placed ever-increasing emphasis on the achievement of valued lifestyle outcomes by people with MR while deemphasizing the importance of interpersonal and social skills functioning to the realization of increased influence over one's life under such improved circumstances for people with MR. By contrast, from a psychological practice standpoint, the opportunity to participate in community life and to develop the skills and abilities required to influence the course of one's lifestyle are both important from a social and ecological validity standpoint. This commonality of intervention goals binds together the diverse content of the treatment chapters in this book.

16

Prevention: Social and Educational Factors and Early Intervention

Craig T. Ramey, Beverly A. Mulvihill, and Sharon Landesman Ramey

Mental retardation (MR) is the leading cause of major activity limitation among people of all ages (La Plante, 1989). Most cases of severe MR are recognized prior to the age of 6 years; however, identification of milder cases often does not occur until the school years. Mild MR and related disabilities have been linked to combined environmental and biological risk factors. Particular combinations of risk indicators may adversely influence developmental outcomes.

The New Morbidity

Public health initiatives, such as increased emphasis on universal immunizations and screenings for genetic and other disorders, have greatly decreased the incidence of many organic diseases. Sizable reduction has been achieved in forms of MR that have discrete biomedical etiologies, such as phenylketonuria (PKU), congenital hypothyroidism, measles encephalitis, congenital rubella, Tay-Sachs disease, and extreme premature birth (Crocker, 1992). A new phenomenon has been emerging, however, that profoundly affects the health and welfare of children. The term *new morbidity* has been used to describe a constellation of psychological and biological health risks. The *new morbidity* is the interaction of adverse environmental, behavioral, and biological factors that can place an individual at risk for a myriad of health and developmental problems. The framework of this model is based on the premise that the prevention of disability depends not only on the characteristics of the child but equally on the broader context of social and physical environments (Baumeister, Kupstas, & Woodley-Zanthos, 1993). Thus, being born into an adverse environment increases risk of poor developmental outcome and poor health, but such disadvantage does not affect all children equally owing to uniqueness of biological makeup and mitigating environmental factors.

Disadvantage is a relative term that has usually been indexed by family circumstances, child characteristics, or a combination of child and family factors. The term *disadvantage* typically is used interchangeably with the concept of *high risk*, with both denoting a significantly elevated probability that a child will not meet minimal expectations for successful performance. The primary empirical criterion for family disadvantage or high risk is family income. Inadequate family income is a powerful marker for a number of other negative life circumstances such as unemployment, insufficient health care, poor housing, limited parental education, and violent neighborhoods. Many children from low-income homes, however, show positive adaptation to school and exhibit average to superior intellectual performance. In contrast to the environmental definitions of disadvantage, child-focused definitions of disadvantage emphasize individual characteristics. Combined definitions of disadvantage, often presented as risk indices, take into account the simultaneous presence of low family and parental resources along with children's biological and experiential vulnerabilities (Coie et al., 1991; Escalona, 1982; C. T. Ramey & MacPhee, 1985; Sameroff, Seifer, Barocas, Zax, & Greenspan, 1987).

Effects of Early Intervention

Early educational intervention refers to systematic endeavors to provide supplemental educational experiences to children before they enter the formal educational system. Many forms of high-quality child care include beneficial early educational experiences; however, child care is often considered a single entity regardless of quality. Thus, early educational intervention should be distinguished from all other forms of nonparental child care. Early educational intervention represents one form of early intervention; other forms have a primary health or social support function

Table 1. Adolescent Mean Intellectual or Academic Test Scores for Three Early Education Programs

Program	Treated group	Control group
	Mean IQ score	
Abecedarian[a]	94.98	90.34
Perry Preschool[b]	81.02	80.71
Milwaukee[b]	101.06	91.13
	California Achievement Test (Range of percentile scores)	
Abecedarian	38–41	28–30
Perry Preschool	15–17	<10

[a]Based on the Wechsler Intelligence Scale for Children–Revised (WISC-R).
[b]Based on the Wechsler Intelligence Scale for Children (WISC).

(Olds, Henderson, Tatelbaum, & Chamberlain, 1986). Early educational intervention frequently includes other family and child services.

Three studies form the core of the longitudinal research on the long-lasting effects of early educational intervention. These studies provide evidence for the contention that intervening with children considered to be at risk for MR and developmental delay can have significant and enduring effects. Table 1 shows the mean midadolescent IQ scores reported by the three intervention studies.

The Abecedarian Project

This study constitutes one of the most intensive experimental early childhood programs ever provided for children of poor families (C. T. Ramey & Campbell, 1992). The intervention started in infancy, and the latest reported assessment of the children's intellectual and academic outcomes occurred at age 15 ($N = 92$). Four primary areas were addressed, with the following results (F. A. Campbell & Ramey, 1993):

1. There were different patterns of intellectual development from infancy through midadolescence for children who had early educational intervention compared with a control group. At age 15, members of the treated group were less likely to score in the mentally retarded or low-normal ranges of cognitive functioning.
2. There were detectable effects of early intervention in the academic test scores of treated individuals at age 15, 7 years after all treatment ended. A significant difference in academic test performance was maintained through 10 years in school for both reading and mathematics.
3. Across 10 years in school, there were differences in school progress (indexed by retention in grade or use of special education) as a function of early intervention. There were fewer instances of assignment to special education classes and retention in grade for those who participated in the preschool program.
4. The more optimal timing for intervention was during the preschool years.

The Perry Preschool Project

This project enrolled children age 3 or older with IQs at age 3 between 70 and 85 ($N = 128$; Schweinhart & Weikart, 1981). By age 7, the experimental group no longer showed a significant IQ advantage over controls, and by age 14 the groups differed by only 1 IQ point. In spite of the lack of IQ differences, significant academic benefits of the preschool program were maintained into adolescence, long after the intervention ended.

The Milwaukee Project

The researchers in this study limited their sample of economically disadvantaged families ($N = 35$) to children born to mothers with very low IQ (below 75; H. L. Garber, 1988). The treatment group consistently outscored the control group in IQ through age 14, the last time period for which scores are available. At age 14, there was a 10-point mean IQ difference. After 7 years in school, however, there were no group differences in academic performance.

Principles of Early Intervention

Despite some unresolved controversies, there are remarkable consistencies in major findings about early educational intervention characterized by the provision of intensive high-quality stimulation to children, the reliance on developmental theory to specify the content of the interventions, and the use of rigorous scientific designs with adequate controls (C. T. Ramey & Ramey, 1992b). Further review of the literature, on the basis of studies of children from economically impoverished families, children with combined environmental and biological risks, and children with disabilities identified in infancy, provides evidence to support six principles relevant to early intervention.

Principle 1: Timing

Generally, interventions that begin earlier and continue longer afford greater benefits to the participants than those that begin later and do not last as long. The age when children begin receiving early intervention services ranges from birth through 5 years. Most of the children served in Head Start, for example, are 3 and 4 years old, and a much smaller number of programs serves infants and toddlers. A number of the experimental and demonstration programs, however, initiate intervention when the children are infants or toddlers. These experimental programs, including the Abecedarian Project (C. T. Ramey, Bryant, Campbell, Sparling, & Wasik, 1988; C. T. Ramey, Yeates, & Short, 1984), the Brookline Early Education Project (Hauser-Kram, Pierson, Walker, & Tivnan, 1991), the Milwaukee Project (H. L. Garber, 1988), Project CARE (Wasik, Ramey, Bryant, & Sparling, 1990), and the Infant Health and Development Program (1990), have demonstrated some of the largest beneficial effects on children's cognitive and preacademic performance. Positive outcomes also were reported earlier from intensive programs that began when the children were 3 or 4 years old (Gray, Ramsey, & Klaus, 1982; Schweinhart & Weikart, 1981). High-quality programs for younger children that continue until kindergarten usually result in the greatest gains (C. T. Ramey & Ramey, 1992a). There is no compelling evidence, however, to support the notion that intervention that begins at a later age will not produce some beneficial effect. This is a principle of relative timing effects.

Principle 2: Intensity

More intensive programs, as indexed by the number of hours per day, days per week, and weeks per year, produce larger positive effects than less intensive interventions. Children who participate more show the greatest overall benefit. A common characteristic of early intervention programs that did not significantly change children's intellectual, academic, or social performance is their lack of intensity. For example, none of the 16 randomized trials of early interventions for children with disabilities conducted by the Utah State Early Intervention Research Institute (Casto & White, 1993) provided full-day, 5-day-per-week programs, and none demonstrated significant effects on children's developmental competencies. Scarr and McCartney (1988) provided intervention one time per week to economically impoverished families in Bermuda and also failed to find any positive cognitive effects for the children.

Additional empirical support for the intensity principle is provided in two other reports. Powell and Grantham-McGregor (1989) reported significant intellectual benefits from a home visit program at an intensity level of three visits per week, although no significant cognitive benefits were detected with interventions of less intensity. Similarly, the Brookline Early Education Project reported that only the most intensive services benefited the children from the least educated families, with low and medium intensities (frequencies) having no measurable consequences (Hauser-Kram et al., 1991).

At the individual level, C. T. Ramey et al. (1992) reported that the amount (intensity) of intervention each child and family received, which included daily, weekly, and monthly monitoring over 3 years, had a strong, positive linear relationship to the child's intellectual and behavioral development at 36 months. When expressed in terms of prevention of MR, the highest participation group had nearly a 9-fold reduction in the number of children participating in the intervention who were mentally retarded, compared to a group of children who did not receive the intervention. For the immediate participation group, retardation was reduced by a 4.9-fold factor, and for the low participation group, the reduction was only 1.3-fold. Especially noteworthy was that the amount of participation was not systematically related to parental education, family income, the child's birth weight, or ethnicity. These findings were recently extended to infants with low birth weight and prematurity, for whom there was a positive relationship at 24 and 36 months between the level of participation in early intervention and intellectual development, which was not related to program modality, maternal education, or infant birth weight (Blair, Ramey, & Hardin, 1995). Despite this evidence, the outcome cannot be ascribed solely to intensity, because other factors such as parental enthusiasm and commitment also may have affected outcomes.

Principle 3: Direct Provision of Learning Experiences

Interventions that directly alter children's daily learning experiences produce more positive and lasting results than those that rely primarily on indirect routes to change children's competencies. Examples of indirect routes include home-based visitations, parent training, and health and nutrition services.

Early interventions may be categorized in terms of reliance on direct educational services for the child versus use of an intermediary (usually the parent) to provide educational experiences. The findings clearly demonstrate that intermediary means are far less effective than direct means in improving children's intellectual performance (Casto & Lewis, 1984; Madden, Levenstein, & Levenstein, 1976; Scarr & McCartney, 1988; Wasik et al., 1990).

Wasik et al. (1990) conducted the first systematic comparison of direct versus intermediary forms of early educational intervention. They examined the results from a randomized controlled trial with economically disadvantaged, high-risk children from birth through 5 years of age. Cognitive gains were detected for children receiving direct learning experiences through an all-day center-based intervention (5 days per week, year-round) combined with weekly home visits. In contrast, intermediary experiences consisting of weekly home visits designed to support parents and to encourage parents to provide developmentally paced learning activities (parallel to those offered in the center-based intervention) had no discernible effects on children's performance, parents' attitudes or behavior, or the home environment. Children in the intermediary treatment group were comparable to those in the control group, who received only nutritional supplements and medical surveillance.

Principle 4: Breadth

Interventions that provide more comprehensive services and use multiple routes to enhance children's development tend to have stronger effects than interventions that are narrower in focus. Interventions that combine direct and indirect routes simultaneously to improve children's learning and school adjustment produce the most robust results.

The early educational efforts that have yielded larger effects, such as the Abecedarian Project (C. T. Ramey et al., 1988), Project CARE (Wasik et al., 1990), the Milwaukee Project (H. L. Garber, 1988), and the Infant Health and Development Program (1990), all have provided a multipronged approach. The approaches have included the provision of high-quality, regularly timed health-related and social services to families, transportation, assistance with crisis management and meeting immediate needs, and parent supports. In addition, these programs provided a strong child educational component, beginning before the age of 3, in specially created child development centers.

Principle 5: Individual Differences

Some children show greater benefits from participation in educational interventions than others. Thus far, the differences appear to be related to aspects of the children's initial risk status and the degree to which the program matches the children's learning style. Different individuals respond differently to the same program, and different programs may be needed to realize the desired benefits. The clinical and educational literatures have endorsed this principle for several decades, yet only recently have there been empirical studies related to this concept in the field of early intervention.

In providing broad-based early educational intervention for premature, low birth weight infants, the Infant Health and Development Program (1990) reported that children at greater biological risk (indexed by very low birth weight) did not benefit as much from the program as did vulnerable children, although both groups showed significant gains.

In examining the effects of early educational intervention for children with disabilities, K. N. Cole, Dale, Mills, and Jenkins (1993) found an interaction between the degree of the child's impairment and the form of the intervention provided. Feuerstein (1977) described mediated learning experience (MLE) as "the interaction between human environment–child, marked by the intention of the experienced adult to mediate the world to the child and transmit to him HIS culture, values, and cognitive skills" (p. 116). MLE is believed to enhance a child's capacity to use subsequent direct exposure to stimuli, and, in comparing MLE and more traditional direct instruction, an unexpected result was found. Students who scored higher on a pretest battery of cognitive, language, and motor tests gained more from direct instruction, whereas students with lower performance on the pretests showed greater benefits from the mediated learning situation.

Finally, an analysis of findings from the Abecedarian study showed that participating children who had the largest cognitive gains compared to control group children were those whose mothers had IQ scores below 70 (S. L. Martin, Ramey, & Ramey, 1990). Children who received the intervention and whose mothers had IQs below 70 scored at least 20 points higher (M = 32 points) than their mothers (Landesman & Ramey, 1989). These findings are comparable to the large benefits reported in the Milwaukee Project (H. L. Garber, 1988), which enrolled only economically disadvantaged mothers with IQs below 70, suggesting that children whose mothers are intellectually limited are likely to benefit more from intensive early intervention than children whose mothers are more intellectually competent.

Principle 6: Environmental Maintenance of Development

Over time, the initial positive effects of early intervention will diminish to the extent that there are inadequate environmental supports to maintain children's positive attitudes and behavior and to encourage continued learning relevant to the children's lives. For many programs, long-lasting and substantial effects on school achievement, grade retention, and special education placement have been detected. As well, there is ample evidence that many early childhood "gains" are not sustained throughout middle childhood and adolescence (Kagan, 1991). In some studies (H. L. Garber, 1988), the beneficial effects of early intervention on IQ scores diminish over time. Two important issues are relevant. First, it is not sufficient for poor or "at-risk" children to simply maintain the advantages realized from intervention in the preschool years. Rather, children must be supported to continue to develop at normative rates in multiple domains if they are to succeed in school settings. Second, poor school environments, suboptimal health, a seriously disrupted home environment, and many other conditions influence the performance of children at all ages. Inquiry about the long-term effects of early intervention must take into account the environments children encounter after the initial intervention.

A Systems Approach

Principles derived from the current body of early intervention research literature provide clues to effective intervention with children and families. The child and the child's family are elements of a larger developmental system including the household, neighborhood, and society, however. The experiences the child has in the presence of adult caregivers provide the child with MLE, which forms the young child's primary knowledge acquisition device (Feuerstein, 1977). Early childhood educators concerned with enhancing the development of high-risk children or preventing retarded development among mildly damaged or environmentally high-risk children have focused on either the child, the parent, or the parent–child relationship as the target for developmental change. Researchers and educators have delivered these interventions in children's own homes or within educational or developmental centers. Programs have differed considerably in the extent to which they have explicitly treated the family as a system embedded within a larger network.

Contemporary theories of development emphasize that cognitive and social development is influenced by multiple factors that interact as parts of larger ecosystems. These include the child's genotype, prenatal environment, health status, and familial and cultural environments, which influence both the child and the caregivers. Interactive experiences between children and caregivers that occur in the "zone of proximal development," in which the child is appropriately challenged to higher cognitive levels, are hypothesized to be particularly important for intellectual development (Vygotsky, 1978). Maximal cognitive development is assumed to occur only when the child has "varied programs of encounters with the environment which are appropriately matched to the intellectual structures developing within the child" (J. M. Hunt, 1961, p. 346).

A useful paradigm for describing how multiple systems interact to influence a child's development was first presented by C. T. Ramey,

MacPhee, and Yeates (1982) and adapted at a later date by K. R. White (1993). The representation is known as the biosocial systems model. Figure 1 presents a graphic adaptation of the original transactional model, in which multiple historical and current sources of influence contribute to the interacting child and caregiver system.

Cultural Competence

In addition to grounding early intervention programs in a strong theoretical base and using data to justify such programming, one must give careful consideration to ensuring that programs are derived from and sensitive to the cultural milieu of the community. P. P. Anderson and Fenichel (1989) emphasized that cultural sensitivity in early intervention involves being aware of the cultures represented in the locale, acquiring information about some of the general parameters of the cultures, and realizing that cultural diversity will affect the family's participation in intervention.

The Individuals with Disabilities Education Act of 1990, Public Law 101-476 (1990), emphasizes a partnership between families and professionals in providing early intervention services for children who have or are at risk for disabilities. Services provided to eligible infants and toddlers must be closely related to family values, beliefs, and traditions. If these values and beliefs are unheeded, the partnership may be seriously jeopardized. Basic issues of infant care, such as sleeping, eating, and exploring the environment, which typically are controlled by the family with little or no outside influence, become subject to multiple outside influences and provider involvements (Lynch & Hanson, 1992).

Challenges to Effective Early Intervention

Timely identification and treatment of children at risk for mild MR is a critical goal for preventing the deleterious effects of identified risk factors. In 1986, Public Law 99-457, the Education of the Handicapped Act Amendments, was passed, with additional amendments added in 1990. In 1990, the act became known as the Individuals with Disabilities Education Act (1990). Part H of this act has provided the guidelines for the determination of eligibility for services to infants and toddlers from birth to 3 years and their families. Full implementation of the legislation requires states to serve children who have developmental delays and those who have a physical or mental condition that is likely to result in a delay. States, at their own discretion, may also serve children who are at risk of having substantial developmental delay if early intervention is not provided. Early in the planning stage, a number of states indicated they would serve the at-risk population, but this number has decreased as concerns about cost have increased. Two years later, only 11 states are currently serving the at-risk population (Shackelford, 1992).

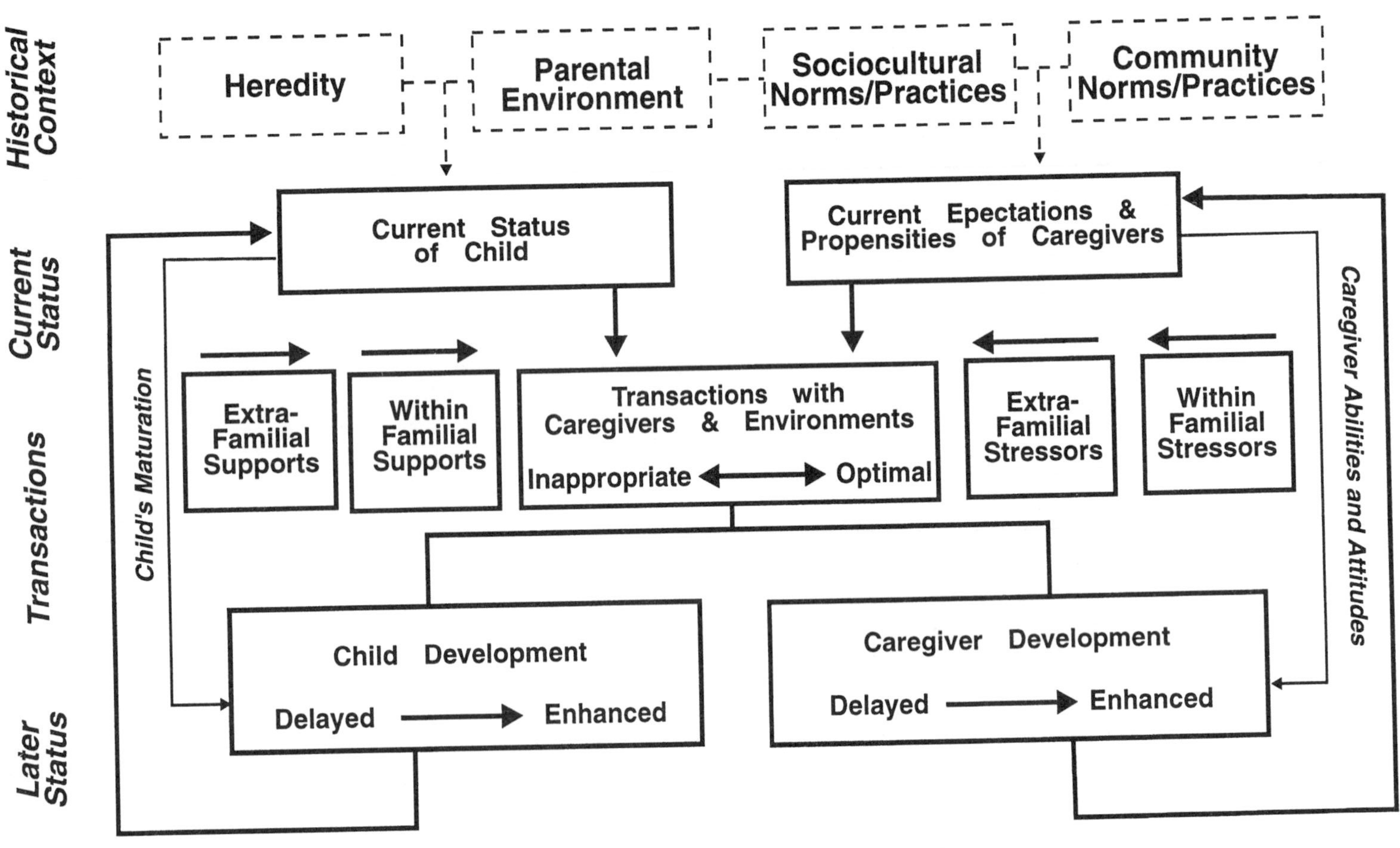

Figure 1. Biosocial systems model for early development.

The passage of Public Law 99-457, with its emphasis on providing services to infants and toddlers and their families, has dramatically changed the field of early intervention and early intervention research. The studies conducted at the Early Intervention Research Institute at Utah State University (K. R. White & Boyce, 1993) were analyzed to compare alternative types of early intervention programs and the implications of the findings for future practice and research. This massive undertaking was intended to provide data for second-generation researchers and program planners; because of methodological problems with the overall approach (Telzrow, 1993), however, the research may have raised more questions than it answered. Questions still remain regarding the types of interventions that are most effective for various populations and the point in time at which the intervention should begin; in other words, Who should be served, and when should they be served?

In addition to the unanswered questions surrounding early intervention services, recent paradigm shifts in the basic concepts of the field of MR are presenting further challenges. Earlier models identified the etiology of MR as being within the individual. The American Association on Mental Retardation now views MR as a description of an individual's functioning, which reflects the impact of intellectual and adaptive limitations on coping with the demands of the environment in which the individual lives, learns, works, and socializes (Luckasson et al., 1992). The developmental–behavioral model that emerged from the individual view of MR has failed to allow individuals with MR to become integrated and active members of the community. Fewer individuals are in large institutions, but few have been provided with the array of services that might assist their transition to more independent living situations. Coulter (1992) called for a comprehensive, coordinated, and integrated intervention and prevention strategy that reflects the ecology of prevention and will improve the lives of individuals at risk for MR.

Applications and Recommendations

The field of early educational intervention has developed from many independent lines of theory and practice involving many disciplines. No single conceptual framework has been widely used, although many explicit assumptions about children's and families' behavior appear to be shared by those engaged in early educational interventions. C. T. Ramey and Ramey (1992b) condensed the empirical early intervention findings into a set of practical recommendations that can inform early interventionists, parents, and educators about how to enhance children's lives.

1. *Encouragement of exploration.* Children are encouraged by adults to explore and gather information about their environments.
2. *Mentoring in basic skills.* Children are mentored, especially by trusted adults, in basic cognitive skills such as labeling, sorting, sequencing, and comparing.

3. *Celebration of developmental advances.* Children's accomplishments are celebrated and reinforced by those with whom they spend a great of deal of time.
4. *Guided rehearsal and extension of new skills.* Children are assisted by responsible others in rehearsing and extending newly acquired skills.
5. *Protection from harmful displays of disapproval, teasing, or punishment.* Constructive criticism and negative consequences for socially unacceptable behaviors appropriate to the child's ability to understand can be used to modify behavior, as opposed to adult disapproval, teasing, or punishment for behavior resulting from normal trial-and-error learning experiences (e.g., mistakes in attempting a new skill or unintended consequences of exploration or information seeking).
6. *A rich and responsive language environment.* Children are provided by adults with a predictable and understandable environment for communication. Spoken and written language is used to convey information, provide social rewards, and encourage the learning of new materials and skills.

The focus of these six recommendations is on activities that appear to be the most critical for learning and intellectual development and can be enhanced through the behavior of responsible, caring adults in children's lives. These suggestions are based on the assumption that these "essential daily ingredients" operate in a mutually supportive fashion.

Conclusion

From a programmatic point of view, more than 25 years of experience and research indicate that early educational intervention can be effective in improving developmental outcomes for at-risk children and their families. In 1988, the American Psychological Association launched a major search for effective model prevention programs (Price, Cowen, Lorion, & Ramos-McKay, 1988). The question was raised then and still remains regarding whether a model program should be followed as closely to the original form as possible or whether local modification and adaptation should be allowed and encouraged. It is now accepted that early educational interventions can prevent certain types of developmental difficulties. The precise developmental pathways or mediating mechanisms that constitute successful early educational interventions are less well understood. More programs must be taken from model, pristine, and controlled settings out into community-based settings. Core program elements that constitute the effective program characteristics and other elements that might be adapted to suit local circumstances without affecting program fidelity could be identified in these field-based settings. The effectiveness of the models under these less controlled settings can then be assessed and evaluated. This necessary step will provide the type of information that can convince leaders at the national, state, and local levels of the short- and long-term practical benefits of prevention efforts on social and educational outcomes for children and families.

17

Prevention: Biological Factors

Alfred A. Baumeister and Pamela Woodley-Zanthos

Among all the disabilities that beset the human condition, mental retardation (MR) represents the most complex constellation of circumstances with respect to prevention, etiology, manifestation, treatment, and prognosis. Although MR derives from numerous risk factors, both biomedical and social, generally speaking, the more severe the retardation, the more likely specific biological causes are implicated. In fact, at least one half of the people with MR whose IQs are below 50 have a genetically related condition.

Retardation of physical and intellectual development, stemming from biological causes, is often so severe that the child would be impaired in any environmental or cultural context. This is "absolute" MR. When one speaks of "relative" MR, one implicitly accepts the premise that different environments define competence differently. Nevertheless, even in those conditions in which a distinctly biological cause can be identified, the outcome is always conditioned, for better or worse, by behavioral, social, and other environmental factors. Any system of classification that aims to prevent or ameliorate MR due to biomedical causes must then take into account the constellation of risk factors that impinge on the outcome (Sameroff, Seifer, Barocas, Zax, & Greenspan, 1987).

More than 4,000 health disorders already have been attributed to genetic causes, although most are not directly associated with MR. Known biomedical causes of MR, many of which are cytogenetic (i.e., the study of heredity and variation dealing with cells and genes) or genetic, number in the hundreds, with new conditions, both endogenous and exogenous, being reported regularly (Baumeister, Kupstas, & Woodley-Zanthos, 1993). There are three major categories of genetic disorders: (a) single gene, including X-linked; (b) multifactorial, in which several genes interact with environmental conditions; and (c) chromosomal disorders.

More than 300 human single-gene disorders, the majority of which are phenotypically identified as MR, have been tracked to the point where the specific biochemical perturbation has been identified. These genes recently have been mapped on each chromosome (McKusick, Francomano, Antonarakis, & Pearson, 1994). As sequencing of the estimated 100,000 genes in the genome proceeds, along with analyses of specific mutations and alleles, more genetic disorders associated with MR and developmental disabilities certainly will be discovered.

The implications of these rapidly expanding technologies for screening the genome and manipulating genetic material for diagnosis, identification of carriers, prevention, and treatment are remarkable. There has been a dramatic increase in the ability to identify biochemical defects and to understand and alter the course of developmental processes. For example, gene cloning already has been accomplished for phenylketonuria (PKU), galactosemia, fragile X, and other diseases. Complete catalogues of known and suspected single-gene disorders are updated periodically (McKusick, Francomano, & Antonarakis, 1993).

This chapter focuses on (a) genetically determined conditions resulting in MR and (b) environmental factors, present either prenatally or during early development, that have biological consequences. The following list of conditions does not represent a comprehensive classification system. Only selected categories of conditions that produce serious outcomes and for which preventive interventions are possible are illustrated here.

Genetically Determined Conditions

Chromosomal Anomalies

Two chromosomal disorders, Down syndrome and fragile X syndrome, account for the vast majority of known genetically caused MR. Down syndrome, a disorder in humans marked by the presence of an extra chromosome 21, occurs at the rate of about every 1 in 1,000 live births in the United States (Baumeister, Kupstas, et al., 1993). In every child with Down syndrome, there is diminished brain development, with most cases being in the moderate-to-severe range of MR. Down syndrome, like most other conditions arising from biomedical factors, often presents with serious physical abnormalities, including heart defects, blockage of the upper intestinal tract, gross malfunctioning of the lower large bowel, and sensory impairments. At autopsy, 100% of individuals with Down syndrome over 40 years of age had Alzheimer-type morphological changes within the brain.

Three distinct chromosomal abnormalities have been associated with Down syndrome. The most common is trisomy 21, the presence of an extra, or third, chromosome 21 resulting from nondisjunction during meiosis. A narrow band at the long arm of the third chromosome contains the critical genes. As mapping of genes in that band continues, there is the real possibility that gene therapy may be able to prevent Down syndrome in the future.

Although the rate of infants born with Down syndrome rises to more than 10 per 1,000 live births in mothers over the age of 40, and advanced maternal, and probably paternal, age is the greatest known risk factor, most children with Down syndrome are not born to mothers over age 40 (Baumeister, Kupstas, & Klindworth, 1991; Baumeister, Kupstas, et al., 1993). Because age is a risk factor, however, diagnostic interventions, such as amniocentesis and chorionic villus sampling (CVS), are often used routinely with older pregnant women.

Fragile X syndrome is a sex-linked chromosomal abnormality. Current prevalence estimates of fragile X indicate 1 per 1,000 male births, and 1 per 750 females are affected. Because of underascertainment, these estimates may be misleading. The incidence of fragile X surpasses Down syndrome as the most common form of inherited MR.

The syndrome is variable in expression, most often resulting in moderate-to-severe MR, although 20% of affected males exhibit no clinical manifestation (Baumeister, Kupstas, et al., 1993). In addition, 30%–50% of carrier females are mildly affected, often exhibiting learning disabilities, speech and language delays, school failure, and mild MR (Dykens, Hodapp, & Leckman, 1994).

Until recently, the diagnosis of the fragile X syndrome was accomplished through a difficult and imperfect cytogenetic analysis that was particularly unreliable for identifying carriers. Recently, the fragile X gene has been isolated. Now direct and rapid diagnosis by DNA analysis is possible prenatally and postnatally and can be used to identify carriers.

Neural Tube Defects

Neural tube defects are defects in the spinal canal caused by abnormal fetal development. Such defects can occur at various points in the neural groove, with the most serious being a defect in closure at the anterior portion, resulting in anencephaly (literally, "without brain"). With some neural tube defects, failure of the spinal cord to close causes an outpouching of the spinal cord, the meninges, or the coverings of the spinal cord through the back of the absent bony vertebral column. Paralysis below the level of the bulge, with concomitant complications, is common. Hydrocephalus, or an increased level of cerebrospinal fluid within the skull, is often secondary to a neural tube defect. Depending on the nature of the defect and precise complications, clinical manifestations range from seizures, paralysis, or death to relatively mild intellectual impairment.

About 4,000 babies are born annually in the United States with neural tube defects, although the incidence varies year to year and geographically. In most instances, neural tube defects are thought to arise from complex Gene × Environment interactions. A recent large-scale study involving almost 24,000 women indicated that the relative risk for neural tube defects increased 2.2 times when pregnant women experienced fever during early pregnancy or when they were exposed to heat in the form of hot tubs or saunas (Milunsky et al., 1992).

A family history of this condition warrants antenatal diagnostic and prevention measures. Screening and diagnosis are usually accomplished through a combination of alpha-fetoprotein (AFP) screening and sonography. Recent large-scale studies indicate that, for women who have previously given birth to a baby with a neural tube defect, treatment with folic acid dietary supplementation provides significant protection against a recurrence (I. H. Rosenberg, 1992). Whether this trace element supplementation has a protective effect for initial pregnancies is less certain, although one large study showed that it did (Czeizel & Dudás, 1992). The U.S. Public Health Service recently advised that all pregnant women receive 0.4 mg of folic acid daily, either through diet or low-dose supplementation (Centers for Disease Control, 1992).

Inborn Errors of Metabolism

Between 6% and 8% of referrals to specialized pediatric centers are due to inborn metabolic errors (Baumeister, Kupstas, et al., 1993). Although prognosis for many children with these inherited diseases is not promising, for about one third a metabolic or genetic preventive intervention is possible.

PKU is a recessive single-gene disorder arising from a metabolic error that results in the inability to oxidize phenylalanine to tyrosine. Few people with untreated PKU have an IQ above 50. Some of the more salient characteristics of untreated patients with PKU are hyperactivity, irritability, and uncontrollable temper tantrums (Brunner, Brown, & Berry, 1987). The disorder is detectable through routine neonatal screening (mandatory in every state) using a simple assay. Early dietary treatment with a low-phenylalanine diet is effective in averting severe MR. Since the 1960s, when universal infant screening and treatment were introduced, about 6,000 cases of PKU have been identified and successfully treated (Baumeister et al., 1991; Baumeister, Kupstas, et al., 1993). Unfortunately, the restricted diet is unpleasant and difficult to follow, so many affected people terminate the diet during or after childhood. Thus, many adults with PKU have given birth to children with maternal PKU resulting from high levels of phenylalanine and other metabolic by-products in the pregnant woman that are toxic to the developing fetus. Because these children do not have PKU and will not respond to the phenylalanine-restricted diet, it is crucial that women with typical or atypical PKU reinstate the special diet prior to conception or as soon as possible during pregnancy.

Congenital hypothyroidism, a disease with heterogeneous etiology, is the most common condition detected by newborn screening, with a frequency of about 1 in 3,600 live births (Baumeister, Kupstas, et al., 1993). The disorder is most often the result of lack of development of the thyroid gland. Untreated congenital hypothyroidism or cases that are not treated early enough in the developmental period result in retardation of mental development and growth. Aggressiveness and other behavior problems also are common (Rovet, Ehrlich, & Sorbara, 1989).

Many infants at risk for severe retardation can be treated with thyroid hormone. Follow-up studies have shown that hormone treatment is cost-efficient and cost-effective, although treated children may later exhibit learning disabilities and behavior problems that may be mitigated through behavioral or pharmacological interventions (Rovet et al., 1989).

Blood Type Incompatibilities

The Rh factor is a relatively well understood form of fetal neurotoxicity. Problems arise when an Rh-positive mother delivers a baby who is Rh-negative. With mixing of maternal and fetal blood, the mother produces antibodies that destroy Rh-incompatible cells in subsequent pregnancies (the first child is not affected). Bile pigments are deposited in the brain and spinal cord, causing overt kernicterus or degeneration of nerve cells with severe damage to the brain. Blood transfusion was the treatment of choice for affected infants until the introduction of phototherapy to reduce and stabilize bilirubin levels. A recently developed treatment inhibits the enzyme that removes hemoglobin from red blood cells (Alexander, 1991). This enzyme inhibitor, tin protoporphyrin, appears to provide protection until the natural enzymes mature. Rh-incompatibility disease can be effectively prevented by treating Rh-negative mothers with Rh-immunoglobin shortly after their first delivery. Because Rh-incompatibility is no longer a frequent occurrence, overt kernicterus is much less likely to be observed in full-term babies who are otherwise well.

Prenatal Screening for Genetically Determined Conditions

Three general prenatal screening procedures are highly useful in the prenatal diagnosis of the conditions just listed, as well as of a number of other conditions. These include cytogenetic and genetic screening procedures (e.g., amniocentesis and CVS), maternal serum analyses (e.g., AFP analysis), and imaging (e.g., sonography). Those for whom these procedures are indicated include women at both ends of the reproductive age spectrum, women with a clear hereditary risk factor, women who are exposed to agents known to have adverse developmental effects, women whose own health is compromised or who engage in high-risk behavior, and women who appear to have pregnancy complications.

The best known and most widely used of these screening procedures is amniocentesis, the transabdominal withdrawal of amniotic fluid, which is usually performed around the 16th week of pregnancy. Various cytogenetic disorders, such as Down and fragile X syndromes, can be prenatally diagnosed through amniocentesis, as can neural tube defects, many inborn errors of metabolism, and intrauterine infections.

A more recent screening technique is CVS. This procedure is performed either transabdominally or transcervically, usually between the 9th and 11th weeks of pregnancy. Successful cytogenetic diagnoses were obtained in 99.7% of 11,000 cases obtained from nine centers in the United States (Ledbetter et al., 1992). Although there has been controversy surrounding the use of CVS, especially around the issue of fetal loss and elevated rates of limb reduction defects (Olney et al., 1995), large-scale prospective studies conducted by the National Institute of Child Health and Human Development in the United States, as well as similar studies in Europe, show no elevated risk associated with CVS in comparison with amniocentesis (Baumeister, Kupstas, et al., 1993).

Maternal serum AFP screening is important for all pregnant women. The AFP level in maternal blood is a prime biochemical indicator of fetal morbidity. Although used primarily for detecting open neural tube defects, elevated maternal serum AFP levels may indicate the presence of other congenital disorders. Low AFP values, combined with other maternal serum markers, may indicate autosomal trisomies, particularly Down syndrome (Baumeister, Kupstas, et al., 1993).

Cytogenetic and maternal serum analyses are complemented by other diagnostic and screening procedures, most notably sonography. This is a noninvasive, relatively inexpensive procedure that permits screening for many anomalies, including overall fetal condition, brain pathology, growth retardation, neural tube defects, intraventricular hemorrhages, hydrocephalus, and fetal organ status.

Recombinant DNA—genetic engineering—is a highly sophisticated technology that now can be used to identify many genetic diseases in amniotic cells, detecting certain DNA mutations and characteristics, called *polymorphisms*, that are linked to a specific gene. Although seldom used at present, with the rapid growth of recombinant DNA technology, it will become possible to routinely screen for perhaps hundreds of genetic disorders.

Combined with other procedures, prenatal screening can be used to avert many cases of potential mortality and morbidity. However, detecting fetal abnormalities through any of the prenatal screening procedures cannot be considered primary prevention because, when results are positive, the fetus is already affected.

Environmental Factors With Biological Consequences

Numerous clinical disorders and diseases are the immediate cause of MR and other developmental disabilities. Even when the putative cause of MR is distinctly biological, the environmental context in which biological perturbation occurs can have a significant effect on outcome. Conversely, underlying mechanisms that initiate the disease process are often environmental risk factors that give rise to biological consequences. Examples include premature birth; low birth weight; maternal substance abuse; infections, including sexually transmitted diseases; and prenatal and postnatal exposure to toxins, such as lead. These factors pose direct threats to the health of the child. In addition, they are often markers for other adverse conditions that will compromise development—in general, a dysfunctional rearing environment.

Infections

One group of common major infections is collectively known by the acronym TORCH: toxoplasmosis, other, rubella, cytomegalovirus, and herpes. The course of these diseases may vary widely among exposed children.

A leading occult infectious cause of MR is congenital cytomegalovirus, a virus belonging to the Herpesviridae family that occurs in 0.2%–2.2% of all live births (Baumeister, Kupstas, et al., 1993). The mortality rate among symptomatic newborns is about 30%, and more than 90% of survivors have neurological impairments, including microcephaly, seizures, MR, hearing problems, and visual disturbances.

The pathway of transmission of congenital cytomegalic inclusion disease is from mother to fetus through body fluids, usually placental blood. Risk to the developing fetus is greatest when the mother's primary exposure to the virus occurs during the first half of the pregnancy. Some newborns are at risk when exposed to infected breast milk, cervical secretions, or blood products. Most full-term infants exposed in this manner will be protected from symptoms by maternal antibodies; however, preterm infants can develop serious illness (Baumeister, Kupstas, et al., 1993).

There are few known behavioral risk factors for maternal infection, although the virus is believed to be transmitted sexually; congenital infection also may be related to maternal weight gains (Berge, Russo, & Utermohlen, 1991). Therefore, preventive efforts should focus on controlling the exposure of young women to primary infections through educational interventions. Because the incidence is higher among pregnant women who work with or are frequently exposed to increased numbers of young children, these women should be advised to wash their hands thoroughly after contact.

Toxoplasmosis is a disease caused by a protozoan that can be acquired either pre- or postnatally. The central nervous system is particularly vulnerable when the infection occurs congenitally, and the risk of transmission to the fetus is greatest during the third trimester. Depending on a number of factors, the child may present with microcephaly, hydrocephalus, cerebral palsy, epilepsy, or MR.

A primary maternal infection during pregnancy is almost always the cause of congenital toxoplasmosis. Generally, the earlier in pregnancy the infection occurs, if untreated, the more severe the consequences (Baumeister, Kupstas, et al., 1993). If detected early enough, treatment of the mother with spiramycin may prevent serious consequences to the infant. Later in gestation, the fetus may respond favorably to treatment with pyrimethamine and sulfadiazine.

Pregnant women are advised to avoid cat litterboxes because cats are the main hosts of the protozoa that multiply in infected cats and are excreted in feces. Raw or undercooked meat and unwashed produce also may harbor the protozoa. Pregnant women at elevated risk of primary exposure should be screened and, if the disease is detected, counseled about available treatments and options.

Rubella, a virus-caused disease confined to humans, has frequently occurring sequelae, including visual, auditory, cardiac, and neurological damage. Neurological manifestations often present as microcephaly, MR, and meningoencephalitis as well as softer signs revealed in long-term follow-up (Scola, 1991).

Development of the rubella vaccine following a 1964 epidemic, and subsequent widespread vaccination programs, resulted in a steady decrease in incidence until 1989. A resurgence of outbreaks during 1989–1991 was found to be related to less vigilant administration of the vaccine. Follow-up of women who contracted rubella indicated that the majority were women who were members of a minority group, poor, and medically underserved. Vigorous implementation of vaccination programs since 1990 has again led to a significant decline in incidence (Centers for Disease Control, 1993a).

Hemophilus influenzae type b (Hib), an invasive bacterium that can cause meningitis, is the most significant infectious cause of MR in the United States. About 18,000 children are infected annually, leading to about 5,000 new cases of MR each year. Hib is also the leading bacterial killer of children.

For several years, there has been a vaccine that is highly effective for children over 18 months of age, but it is ineffective for younger children, who represent three fourths of the cases. Conjugate vaccines have now been developed that protect infants as young as 2 months of age. Universal use of these vaccines will prevent MR and deafness caused by Hib (Alexander, 1991). In 1993, only about 55% of children in the United States had received the vaccine (Centers for Disease Control, 1994a). Another method, the vaccination of mothers late in pregnancy, recently has been tested and has been found to temporarily protect newborn babies from Hib until they can be vaccinated themselves. Through maternal vaccination antibodies are produced by the mother and transmitted to the fetus.

Low Birth Weight, Other Infections, and Pediatric HIV and AIDS

Low birth weight (<2,500 g) is the leading indicator for infant mortality and morbidity (Baumeister et al., 1991; Baumeister, Kupstas, et al., 1993). Compared with normal birth weight infants, low birth weight (LBW) babies are 40 times more likely to die during the neonatal period, and risk of death is elevated 5 times through the first year of life. Neonatal intensive care technology has now made it possible to save the lives of many low, very low (<1,500 g), and extremely low (<1,000 g) birth weight infants. However, LBW survivors present with neurodevelopmental impairments at three times the rate of normal birth weight babies. These impairments include long-term disabilities such as cerebral palsy, autism, MR, developmental delays, sensory impairments, and mental disorders, with risk increasing as birth weight decreases. About 25% of extremely LBW survivors experience severe impairments, whereas another 40%–65% present with learning disabilities, hyperactivity, attention deficits, and other problems (Baumeister, Kupstas, et al., 1993).

Despite numerous efforts to reduce the rate of LBW, the incidence in the United States has remained at about 7% for the past two decades. However, beginning in the mid-1980s, the percentage of LBW babies began to show a steady increase, particularly among Blacks. Rate of LBW among Black newborns is about double that among Whites. The United States ranks well behind other developed countries on this critical measure (Baumeister, Kupstas, et al., 1993).

Another important consideration is that teenagers contribute differentially to the number of LBW babies, especially among Blacks, those in poverty, and the unmarried. In 1990, about 835,000 (10%) teenagers (15–19 years of age) became pregnant (Centers for Disease Control, 1995a). The United States leads all developed countries in rates of teenage pregnancy and childbearing, although there may be a small decline in rates for the past 2 years. Even so, the adverse health, social, and economic consequences are enormous. Although there are different causes for LBW, the leading indicator by far is premature birth. Immediate antecedents of premature birth include (a) medical complications such as eclampsia, diabetes, and gestational hypertension; (b) preterm, premature rupture of the membranes (PROM); and (c) idiopathic premature labor (IPL). The most common and least understood are PROM and IPL.

For several decades, the medical community has been debating whether the incidence of PROM and IPL can be significantly reduced without an understanding of the underlying biophysiological mechanisms. There is widespread agreement that any level of prenatal care is better than no prenatal care and that provision of adequate and timely prenatal care to all women is the best intervention to date in decreasing rates of premature birth, LBW, and infant mortality (Baumeister et al., 1991). However, even among women who receive prenatal care, the incidence of these outcomes remains frustratingly stable. Rates are particularly high among impoverished women, Blacks, teenagers, unmarried mothers, and women with less than a high school education.

In the absence of an understanding of the mechanisms causing preterm labor and delivery, applied research has focused on the effects of enhanced or augmented prenatal care for women at high risk. Enhanced prenatal care usually involves standard care plus additional social supports such as those offered by multidisciplinary teams of nurse practitioners, nutritionists, social workers, and others who provide pregnant women with information on self-care and healthy behaviors during pregnancy. Unfortunately, the birth outcomes of the treatment group have not differed significantly from those of the control groups in any of the randomized, controlled studies comparing high-risk pregnant women who received enhanced care with those who received standard care.

Medical researchers are now concentrating on a multifactorial theory of prematurity that places infection, or bacterial growth, in the central role. Multiple microorganisms, many of which can be sexually transmitted, have been implicated. Currently, bacterial infections that are receiving special attention are gonorrhea, infection with group B streptococcus, *Chlamydia trachomatis*, or *Trichomonas vaginalis*, bacterial vaginosis, and herpes simplex infection. Because infection is commonly present in cases of PROM, it is suspected that even subclinical levels of a primary infectious process at the cervical portion of the fetal membranes may weaken the membranes, causing them to rupture prematurely. Thus, PROM would be a symptom of an existing infectious process (Iams, Johnson, & Creasy,

1988). Prenatal examinations and treatment with antibiotics are certainly indicated.

In the case of PROM, in which the fetal membranes no longer have a protective effect for the developing fetus, the risk is twofold. The baby is exposed to the same bacterial infection present in the mother plus any additional harmful bacteria that may present themselves following PROM. Outcomes can range from relatively mild to devastatingly severe. For example, transmission of group B streptococcus from mothers with nonimmunity to the bacteria and who are heavily colonized can result in severe sepsis in the infant (Iams et al., 1988). Brain and lung damage, blindness, cerebral palsy, or death may occur in such cases.

Although ongoing research on the role played by infections in preterm delivery is promising, unanswered questions limit clinical application at this time. However, a number of the harmful microorganisms are sexually transmittable; therefore, contraceptive education programs should include the potential obstetrical, as well as gynecological, consequences of unprotected sex prior to and during pregnancy. Because intrauterine or perinatally sexually transmitted diseases can seriously compromise pre- and postnatal development, the Centers for Disease Control and Prevention has recommended that all pregnant women be screened for syphilis, gonorrhea, *Chlamydia trachomatis*, and HIV-1 infection (Centers for Disease Control, 1993b).

Pediatric HIV and AIDS represent the most serious and long-range threats to our children's health. Expert predictions indicate that during the 1990s, the disease will become the fifth leading cause of pediatric mortality and a major acquired biological cause of MR. Infants who may not have the disease may test positive for HIV because of maternal antibodies. It is not known why some babies are infected through the mother and others are not. Estimates vary, but studies indicate that about 20%–40% of HIV-positive babies are directly infected and will develop AIDS (Dokecki, Baumeister, & Kupstas, 1989). Mortality among infected babies is relatively rapid, and the disease processes are devastating. Treatments with drugs such as azidothymidine and antibacterial agents have extended life for some children. However, 78%–93% of outcomes involved prominent central nervous system damage (G. W. Diamond & Cohen, 1987). The most common neurological abnormalities include developmental delays, chronic encephalopathy, seizure disorders, motor dysfunctions, microencephaly, and cortical atrophy, along with numerous other physiological and psychological symptoms (Dokecki et al., 1989).

Because HIV and AIDS are due almost solely to social, behavioral, and environmental factors, they are, in theory, entirely preventable. History has shown, however, that lifestyle habits, particularly when sex and addictive drugs are involved, do not change easily or rapidly (Klindworth, Dokecki, Kupstas, & Baumeister, 1989). Until a successful vaccine or cure has been developed, HIV and AIDS and pediatric HIV and AIDS will remain devastating and costly drains on human and economic resources.

An important study has demonstrated that risk of HIV transmission from mildly symptomatic pregnant women to their babies can be substantially reduced (up to two thirds) by antepartum and intrapartum administration of zidovudine to the mother and to the newborn for 6 weeks (Connor et al., 1994). This finding raises serious and troubling questions as to whether prenatal screening for HIV should be more universally undertaken, perhaps even required, especially for those who are in high-risk groups.

Such issues become all the more salient in view of the most recent and precise estimates of the extent of the epidemic. P. S. Rosenberg (1995) has found that infection rates are about 1 per 1,700, 100, and 200 among White, Black, and Hispanic women, respectively, in their late 20s and early 30s. These are conservative figures, given that the older Centers for Disease Control case definition of AIDS was used in Rosenberg's calculations and that there is known to be underreporting for certain groups. HIV prevalence among men in this age group is higher, but the difference is rapidly narrowing as more women become infected. Given that the disease produces no symptom for an average of 9 to 10 years, it is likely that infected women were exposed to the disease much earlier—within the prime childbearing age range.

Exposure to Toxins

Aside from the more exotic compounds synthesized in laboratories, four common toxins known to have adverse effects on the developing fetus are alcohol, drugs, tobacco, and lead.

Fetal alcohol syndrome (FAS) affected approximately 6.7 per 10,000 live births in the United States in 1993 (Centers for Disease Control, 1995b), with higher prevalence rates among Blacks and particularly Native Americans (2.7 per 1,000 live births). Nationally, about 1,500 newborns per year display dysmorphia associated with FAS, including growth deficiencies, specific facial abnormalities, and possible brain and heart malformations. Associated behavioral and cognitive impairments, including mild MR, also are often present (Baumeister, Kupstas, et al., 1993). For every child with the complete syndrome, there are others who do not exhibit the full clinical constellation of FAS, but are nevertheless affected. This is called fetal alcohol effects (FAE). The rate of FAS for 1993 was more than sixfold higher than for 1979 (Centers for Disease Control, 1995b).

FAS is a major cause of preventable MR (E. L. Abel & Sokol, 1991). There is no known level of alcohol exposure that is universally safe, although clearly there are wide variations in susceptibility. The most prudent approach is for the pregnant woman to avoid alcohol entirely, although the effectiveness of abstinence as a prevention initiative, especially among those already at risk, is questionable. Particularly significant is the increasing rates of drinking among teenagers. In 1992, among 14- to 17-year-olds, 65.6% used alcohol, and of these, 21% engaged in episodic heavy drinking (Centers for Disease Control, 1995b). Great sensitivity to cultural patterns of and attitudes toward alcohol use will be necessary to influence positively the drinking behavior of those most in need of this information (Baumeister et al., 1991). Undoubtedly, prenatal alcohol consumption is underreported.

There is abundant evidence in the scientific and clinical literature demonstrating that smoking during pregnancy impairs fetal growth, doubles the chance of LBW, and elevates the rate of stillbirth. Medical risks associated with maternal smoking include abruptio placenta, PROM, intrauterine growth retardation, MR, and heart defects (Baumeister et al., 1991). Women who smoke during pregnancy are also more likely to engage in other high-risk behaviors, such as drinking alcohol, making poor nutritional choices, and engaging in unsafe sexual practices. For this reason, cause-and-effect relationships are difficult to disentangle (Baumeister, Kupstas, et al., 1993). Cigarette use among female teenagers was 31.2% in 1993 and was significantly higher among Whites (Centers for Disease Control, 1995c).

There is no doubt that increased use of illicit drugs in the United States, particularly among women of childbearing age, has contributed to an alarming increase in the number of drug-exposed newborns. A 1988 survey indicated that approximately 375,000 such infants are born annually. This problem accelerated greatly with the increased use of the "crack" variant of cocaine (Baumeister, 1991).

As with alcohol consumption and smoking, it is difficult to isolate the effects of cocaine on the developing fetus because mothers who use drugs during pregnancy are far more likely to engage in a number of other high-risk behaviors. The current literature on the specific effects of crack on newborns does not reveal any particular patterns of symptoms or dysmorphia, but a number of effects have been observed. Among them are premature rupture of the placental membrane; intrauterine growth retardation; small head circumference; shortened gestational periods; LBW; and short-term tremulousness, irritability, and muscular rigidity (Baumeister, Kupstas, et al., 1993). Although some of these neuropsychological and developmental problems may be permanent and serious, there has been little conclusive evidence that prenatal exposure to crack is, in itself, seriously teratogenic. Drug exposure in newborns is more likely an indicator or marker for other environmental risks that may be far more detrimental to healthy growth and development than the drug itself, such as child neglect or abuse and a dysfunctional rearing environment (Baumeister, Kupstas, et al., 1993).

Adverse biophysiological effects of drugs, alcohol, and smoking on newborns are entirely preventable, but they will probably never be entirely prevented. Prevention efforts should focus on timely and adequate prenatal care for all women and intense educational and treatment programs targeted at women at high risk for engaging in these behaviors during pregnancy. Teenagers are particularly vulnerable. Nationally, 2.6% used crack, or free base forms, in 1993. Rates are highest among Hispanic students (Centers for Disease Control, 1995c).

Exposure to lead is one of the most commonly known chronic environmental pediatric health problems in the United States. The primary sources of lead exposure are lead-based paints, often sloughed off as dust; leaded gasolines; and ground that is contaminated with lead. Older homes may have plumbing systems with lead solder that can contaminate the water supply (Baumeister, Kupstas, et al., 1993).

Studies of both humans and animals have indicated that lead directly affects the central nervous system and can lead to decreases in intellectual functioning. By some estimates, currently about 1.7 million children aged 1–5 years have lead exposure sufficient to adversely affect intellectual development. Behavioral impediments and learning disorders also are frequently observed with lead exposure (Centers for Disease Control, 1994b). The developing nervous system is particularly sensitive to lead toxicity.

Even in moderate amounts, the effects of lead can be pervasive and enduring; however, if the damage is not too severe, the effects are sometimes reversible by flushing the metal from the bloodstream using chelation. Because a number of studies have indicated that even low levels of lead have subtle but enduring effects on children's neurological and cognitive development, the Centers for Disease Control reduced the maximum acceptable blood level in children from 25 to 10 μg/dl.

Socioeconomic and racial variables play major roles in understanding the epidemiology of lead poisoning and in suggesting effective prevention initiatives. For example, only about 7% of young children from medium- and high-income families are exposed to excessive lead levels, but the rate accelerates to 25% for poor White children and 55% for poor Black children. In addition, poor or racially segregated children are less likely to be evaluated for exposure. Rates are highest for all poor children living in urban areas, but particularly for Blacks (Baumeister, Kupstas, et al., 1993). Prevention measures include screening, treatment, and removal of contamination from various environmental sources. Although screening techniques are reliable, screening is severely limited, mostly because of the lack of public health resources. Removal of contamination from the environment also is costly, reaching about $10 billion over the past decade. On the other hand, progress has been made in that mean blood levels for all age groups have dropped almost fourfold over the past 20 years. This decline is due to a number of factors, most notably regulations that prohibited lead additives to gasoline (Centers for Disease Control, 1994b).

Implications for Prevention Initiatives

MR involves many syndromes with highly varied clinical features arising from numerous causes that are conditioned by environmental circumstances. It is essential to understand and address these complexities when designing prevention and intervention strategies, even in cases in which the putative cause is distinctly biomedical. For example, there are broad classes of social variables known to predispose a child to biomedical risks. The most salient of these is poverty, which, in itself, represents a complex accumulation of risk factors.

Impoverished women are more likely to receive no or inadequate prenatal care; to engage in less healthful preconceptual and pregnancy behaviors, including poor nutritional choices; to be exposed to more infections; and to deliver more often premature and LBW infants (Baumeister, Kupstas, et al., 1993). The child exposed to biomedical risk factors arising from adverse social conditions is often returned to a dysfunctional rearing environment in which the family is less likely to have access to medical and social support systems that could avert or ameliorate subsequent problems. It is illusory, then, to suppose that isolation of singular biological factors can ever be the foundation on which to construct a complete system for prevention of MR. Similarly, it is equally illusory to presume that isolated early behavioral or educational interventions can have a significant compensatory effect on children with MR and other disabilities arising from several metabolic, teratogenic, and biological risk factors.

An effective prevention program targets certain groups according to risk indicators. Some general initiatives—such as the provision of prenatal care and adequate nutrition—should apply to everyone. Other interventions should be applied more selectively to subgroups known to be at elevated risk, such as intravenous drug users, families in severe poverty, and pregnant teenagers. Individuals who are themselves at high risk include those having blood type incompatibilities, the gene for PKU, or a family history of neural tube defects.

Two concepts that are critical for assessing risks are sensitivity and specificity. In epidemiological studies, these indexes are typically determined by comparing a group of people who have a particular condition or disease with those who do not. Those who test positive on some measure and display the condition are called “true positives.” Sensitivity is the ratio of true positives to all those who have the condition. Specificity is a measure of those who are found to be “true negatives” relative to all those without the condition. Errors of ascertainment can occur in either measure. In the case of sensitivity, these errors are referred to as “false negatives”; for specificity, “false positives.” Sensitivity refers to correct identification of those who are in need of a particular service and who will benefit. Specificity refers to those who are not in need of a particular service or who will not benefit from that service. Identification procedures should be high on both indexes, but this ideal is not always achieved, particularly when dealing with global risk factors such as poverty.

Social, political, and health care systems have lagged behind the scientific enterprise in implementing prevention knowledge into practice within public health services based on epidemiological principles. Most programs and support systems are delivered within a model of medical intervention that is disease oriented, with little attention given to broader population-based social, demographic, and economic indicators and conditions that influence outcomes. Prevention of MR caused by biological factors inevitably rests in great measure on comprehensive public health initiatives that not only address an array of interrelated problems directly, but also ensure universal access to basic health, social, and educational services.

18

Cultural Considerations in Assessment, Diagnosis, and Intervention

Deborah L. Coates and Peter M. Vietze

In this chapter, we briefly review the significance of cultural experiences and contexts for assessment, diagnosis, and treatment of mental retardation (MR) in clinical settings. We discuss the concept of culture, its expression, and its significance for understanding development and developmental disability. We also review the ways that culture influences definitions of MR and the relationship of these embedded definitions on adaptation and psychosocial functioning of people with MR. We describe strategies to ensure that prevention and intervention efforts are culturally competent. Finally, we review some directions for future research in this area.

The Definition of Culture

The current zeitgeist of academics and clinicians in psychology makes use of the term *culture* frequently, and it is assumed to be understood. Psychologists think they know what culture is, and they certainly respond to it. The concept of culture, however, is difficult to understand and even more difficult to apply systematically and analytically because it is an abstract term that refers to the total life of a society. This difficulty is further complicated in that "societies," or cultural groups, particularly in contemporary urban areas, merge and interact with each other. Cultural influence also is difficult to disentangle because it often involves a series of processes that can occur at the individual, group, institutional, and societal levels (Turnbull, 1983).

Culture is a result of a group's history and expresses that group's particular adaptation to its environment as a psychological reality (Murphy & Leighton, 1965). The term *culture* was first used in 1871 by British anthropologist E. B. Tylor to define the complex whole that includes knowledge, beliefs, art, morals, law, and capabilities and habits acquired by an individual as a member of a society (Birrin, Kinney, Schaie, & Woodruff, 1981). This classic definition is still acceptable, but it also is assumed that the shared patterns of knowledge, basic values, and assumptions are internalized by members of the group and used to guide their conduct. Culture, for practical purposes, is considered to be the social, psychological, and physical environment milieu, including the material resources available to a group. This provides a context for a given individual that is composed of other individuals who share similar or reciprocal sociocultural experiences.

There are a number of important characteristics of culture that have implications for the development of human beings. The term *culture* is often used in the biomedical prevention literature to underscore that groups of people exist in particular circumstances of climate, resources, institutions, and conditions that might produce disease. More broadly, culture also involves acquired or learned capabilities. Although some significant capabilities are universal (e.g., walking, talking, and developmental change), the meaning of these behaviors in context also constitutes culture. Another important characteristic of culture is that it is not haphazard. It is a systematic expression of a particular society as a whole. Culture is made up of many interrelated parts, and it is difficult to understand one unique part without an appreciation of the other parts (Birrin et al., 1981). Individuals do not always choose to follow a cultural norm and may not be capable of responding appropriately to one. However, cultural norms are used by individuals and groups to try to shape the behavior of others. These cultural norms also are used to provide developing individuals with the information they may need to cope with their environmental circumstances.

The Developmental Significance of Culture and Its Expression

In considering the developmental significance of culture, M. Cole (1992) suggested that the intuitive notion underlying the word as used in English and Latin is useful. The linguistic definition of culture suggests the tending of something, usually in an agricultural context, and includes the notion of how best to promote development. Culture helps the nurturer to create a protected or controlled environment that supports the growth of young organisms so that they thrive. This "culturing" uses highly specialized tasks and tools that have been developed over generations.

M. Cole (1992) suggested that the gardening metaphor emphasizes that nurturers must attend not only to the specialized form of the environment, but also to ecological circumstances. These two classes of cultural phenomena occur independently but are interdependent. In considering the influence of culture on development, it is important to consider culture within and without the immediate circumstances of development. Several important developmental questions arise in this regard, including whether it is possible to always create the right conditions for optimal development. Obviously not, but one must be concerned with the conditions that maintain or enhance the necessary features of the immediate and artificial environment that promote development. Ecological or ecocultural approaches to the study of culture and development proposed by Bronfenbrenner (1979) and by B. Whiting and Edwards (1988) focus on understanding these conditions. These approaches examine the interdependence of physical ecology, economic activities, institutions, and the organization of a child's experiences as they influence development.

Among developmental scientists, despite the appreciation of culture's influence on development, few developmental texts devote significant attention to it, and often discussions of cultural influence focus on cultural difference. M. Cole (1992) argued that this focus on "difference" precludes appreciation of the universal mechanism of culture and the specific cultural forms that can be identified in any particular historical circumstance. M. Cole alternatively suggested a cultural–contextual model that incorporates three previously accepted theoretical frameworks for understanding human development through the prism of culture. These three perspectives are the biological–maturational, environmental learning, and the interactional frameworks. M. Cole's cultural–contextual perspective, unlike the other three approaches, presumes that biology and maturation and environment cojointly and equally influence development. The environment is conceptualized as consisting of universal characteristics and unique characteristics that are specific to historical situations. Both must be understood to fully appreciate cultural influence. In M. Cole's conceptual framework, major classes of variables, the biological–maturational and the environmental–contextual, interact indirectly through the medium of culture to influence development.

Investigations of the role of culture in development have benefited from the impressive variations in human behavior and conditions of human life that exist around the world. These lessons have advanced the understanding of how capable human beings are of adapting to a variety of situations. An important contribution of research with an emphasis on cross-cultural comparisons is that it has aided the realization that human functioning cannot be understood separately from the context in which it occurs (Rogoff, 1990; Rogoff & Morelli, 1989; Wozniack & Fischer, 1973). Development varies and depends on the cultural and immediate social context. Rogoff (1990) described work by developmental researchers who have conducted cross-cultural studies and observed that skills and behavior that did not appear in some contrived laboratory situations often occurred in the same individuals in everyday situations. Research participants who did not show a particular type of reasoning in a laboratory task were found to express these same skills or perhaps more complex skills outside of the laboratory.

In her book on the social context of cognitive development, Rogoff (1990) summarized the literature demonstrating the cultural contexts of cognitive activity. She argued that children's cognitive development is inseparable from the social milieu in which it occurs. As Rogoff (1990) pointed out, from the first days of their lives, children learn to use the perspectives of their society to learn, and this learning takes place with the assistance of other people. She referred to this type of learning as "guided participation." Rogoff defined cognitive development as "coming to find, understand, and handle particular problems, building on the intellectual tools inherited from previous generations and the social resources provided by other people" (1990, p. 190). She also suggested that this development is guided by certain sociocultural activities rather than occurring spontaneously. Rogoff also discussed sensitivity and challenge in guiding cognitive development. She speculated that the value of sensitivity may be curvilinear in that it is possible to have too little and perhaps too much sensitivity in this regard. In some cases, children may be left entirely on their own to discover the world, almost like children abandoned in the woods. Others may be kept by their parents from fully experiencing the world and thus not learn how to handle difficult situations. Children who are protected too thoroughly from error, for example, can have difficulty understanding how to solve problems on their own when particular events occur. Other examples of the critical importance of social context are found in the work of Forman and Minick (1993) and D. Harris (1992).

How Culture Is Expressed

Culture influences behavioral expression and socialization patterns. Being a member of a particular social or cultural group may influence how parents transmit the importance of schooling, how parents handle children's transgressions or requests for help, and what parents tell children about getting along in their community. Social class and socioeconomic status may mediate the effects of culture and in some cases override cultural influence. Cultures also differ in the roles they prescribe to men and women, and these gender-based cultural mores influence parental socialization. Finally, cultures may have specific norm expectations about children with disabilities or MR.

The beliefs mothers have about their role in socializing children influence the kinds of interactions they have with them from infancy throughout adolescence. These expectations will affect children directly and indirectly because parents will place children in specific social settings (e.g., with others who have certain kinship or sex or age relationships) that will create a preponderance of certain social interactions (Chisholm, 1989). These social experiences may determine which types of behavioral expressions are related to child developmental outcomes. In-depth studies of competence within cultural groups also have helped to shed light on culture's role in the expression of competence.

Mother–child interactions: An example of pervasive cultural variation. In considering a particular behavior across several cultures or even across different national groups, one is faced with the difficult question of whether the behavior has the same meaning in the different cultures. A comparative approach can be helpful in such circumstances. In studying mother–child interactions in different cultures, for example, one can escape from this dilemma of interpretation if one observes the actual interactions. For example, Sostek et al. (1981) sought to understand mother–

child interactions in a Micronesian culture in the South Pacific on the island of Fais. They selected instances from a filmed ethnographic record in which an infant was present and then observed the adults with the infant. To understand the meaning of the behaviors and the contexts of interaction, they then sampled similar situations in the United States and compared the two cultures. Similarly, if one is to understand the cultural context of any behavior, the meaning of the behavior, context, label, or performance must be explained. It might be discovered that a broader or narrower range of meanings can be attributed to particular behavioral phenomena in cross-cultural studies. Zaslow and Rogoff (1981) discussed this issue extensively in their article on the cross-cultural study of cognition and of early parent–child interaction. The use of observational methods is the predominant approach in understanding such interactions and affords relatively fewer inferential interpretations than other methods of the way in which adults in different cultural groups relate to their children. Such studies also reduce the potential for bias in measurement.

Social context and maternal style interact to create a social environment that influences behavior. Landry, Garner, Pirie, and Swank (1994) discussed the way in which parents of children with developmental disabilities make demands and impose restrictions on their children's behavior after the second year of life. They suggested that the type of scaffolding mothers provide in early social interactions may be particularly important for children with developmental problems. Landry et al. reviewed literature showing how children with Down syndrome have difficulty requesting objects from mothers and use fewer strategies to monitor their own behavior than do peers matched for mental age. Landry et al. demonstrated that mothers of children with Down syndrome are both similar to and different from mothers of children without developmental delays. Differences are a function of social context, risk group, and children's expressive language skills.

Families and schools. Culture is most often acted out within families (Laosa & Sigel, 1982; Sigel & Laosa, 1983; Super, 1987). Children's behavior must be analyzed and assessed as something that occurs within a rich matrix of emotions, beliefs, values, and physical influences. How families relate to other broad social contexts also must be used to interpret how culture influences behavior. Manifold social processes link families to work settings, schools, other families, churches, and other cultural institutions within a community. For example, researchers have recently explored the relationships between boys' experiences within families, as mediated by maternal attributes for children's behavior, and parental discipline and peer acceptance (Dishion, 1990; MacKinnon-Lewis et al., 1994; C. J. Patterson, Vaden, & Kupersmidt, 1991). Culture, in order to be understood, may need to be interpreted in the context of social status and its relationship to specific kinds of social expectations for children's behavior and specific social interactions that occur. A certain cultural group, because of its social position, may engage in particular social interactions and have particular social attributes that influence child behavior. Research scientists have not identified many of the key relationships among cultural experience, social attributes, social interactions and developmental sequence, timing, and skill attainment. Cultural experience also may be influenced by racism and the resulting social bias that creates particular social interactions.

Much of what is known about how culture is expressed and its impact on development has been learned from cross-cultural comparisons of children with MR and their families. Nihira, Webster, Tomiyasu, and Oshio (1988) offered an example of this approach. They conducted a study of 90 Japanese families and 93 American families who had a child who was educably mentally retarded. The American families, who lived in suburban areas of Southern California, were 67% White, 14% Hispanic, and 12% Black. The Japanese families lived in suburban areas of five large cities. Families in both cultures were middle-income and predominantly two-parent families; the mean age for children in both samples ranged from 9 to 10 years. About 56% of each sample were male. Nihira et al. used several standardized scales that measured the learning environment of the home and the socioemotional quality of the family dynamic present in the home relative to the child's social competency. They found that the relation between cognitive opportunities at home and the child's social competency was similar in the two cultures. Relationships between the affective aspects of the home environment and the child's psychosocial adjustment appeared to be different in the two cultures. Specifically, American families seemed to be more involved in encouraging children to learn school-related skills and more involved in various community activities. Japanese parents tended to depend more on teachers and other specialists to train their children who were educably mentally retarded.

The two sets of families had similar scores on the Family Environment Scale (FES; Moos, 1974), but their scores were strikingly different from the normative sample of American families on whom the FES was developed. Both groups of families in the Nihira et al. (1988) study tended to see themselves as being more cohesive, expressive, and organized and as having a more religious–moral emphasis than did the normative families in America. They also saw themselves as having less conflict, less emphasis on independence, and less emphasis on recreational and cultural orientations. The Japanese families had significantly higher self-ratings of cohesion, expressiveness, and organization than the American families, and the American families rated themselves higher on conflict and control. In general, the FES tended to predict child competency for American but not for Japanese children, as measured by the type and strength of correlations between environment and child variables. The absence of a cross-culturally consistent pattern of relationships between environment and child competence variables may indicate, according to Nihira et al., some qualitative differences between these two cultures in the purposes and goals of socializing children with MR. These data provide some strong evidence of the importance of accounting for cultural diversity in socialization processes among families with children with MR.

Cultural values and orientation play a strong role in motivating or inhibiting the learner in school (Gallagher, 1994; Ogbu, 1985, 1992). Some developmentalists have indicated that the development of children classified as ethnic minorities is influenced by their ancestral societies and culture. Greenfield and Cocking (1994) suggested that the development of minority children occurs as a continuous process in connection with their ancestral cultures. They suggested, for example, that the development of children of African origin can be viewed as continuously expressive of culture in African communities but that this developmental trajectory is modified by the cultural and political conditions in the country in which they live (e.g., France, Canada, United States). However, they did not take into account the diversity among cultural groups of African or Hispanic origin. Nonetheless, to understand the socialization and development of African American children, it is important to consider both the culture of origin and the culture of their societal context.

Ogbu (1992) observed an interesting social phenomenon about the minority status of children and their demonstration of competence in school situations. Minority children, according to Ogbu, will do well educationally in cultures where they are voluntary as opposed to involuntary immigrants (e.g., African Americans whose ancestors were brought to the United States as slaves). Ogbu observed Korean children in Japan and in the United States as an example of this phenomenon. These minority children did poorly in Japan, where they were involuntary minorities, and did well in the United States, where they were willing immigrants. Ogbu suggested that there seems to be a collective orientation among voluntary minorities toward making good grades in school and an overall striving for school success. Being unsuccessful in school is met with criticism and isolation. For involuntary minorities, although achievement is thought to be desirable, rarely is there a stigma associated with being a poor achiever. In addition, there are social pressures to reject the dominant culture that act to suppress involuntary minorities from adopting behaviors that might be viewed as part of a dominant and unsupportive culture.

Language. Snow and Pan (1993) suggested that language consists of a series of domains or set of skills that develop independently. This componential structure of language has implications for how the language of children with MR is assessed and how interventions are developed and applied. The domains that Snow and Pan identified included syntax, morphology, lexicon, phonology, speech acts, conversation, and discourse. They identified theoretical and empirical support for the notion that these domains are distinct aspects of language functioning. Their empirical work is based on research on individual differences in language development in normally developing children and in various populations of children with developmental disabilities. Snow and Pan proposed that some domains of language may be more sensitive to cultural and other environmental influences than others. Specifically, speech acts, conversation, and discourse might be heavily influenced by cultural perspectives. It is difficult to understand the nature of this potential influence because much of the research on children with Down syndrome or mild MR has been cross-sectional and not focused on the course of development of children's communicative skills. The research on language development in children with mild MR or Down syndrome, according to Snow and Pan's analysis, suggests that these children would be relatively good at lexical, speech act, and conversational skills but considerably delayed in morphology and syntax and even more extremely delayed in discourse skills. Some children may show a high proficiency in language skills, in contrast to cognitive skill. A componential view of language development is helpful in assessing how culture influences social functioning in groups of people with MR. Concept formation also is influenced by language production and whether a language is a first or second language. Collison (1974) compared the conceptual level that normal 12- to 14-year-old Ghanaian children expressed in their native language and in their school language of English. Collison reported that these children produced a higher conceptual language level in their native language than in English.

MR in Cultural Context

The definition of MR includes reference to the statistical distribution of intelligence, impaired adaptation, and manifestation during childhood. Only the first concept is difficult to convey to a person without any Western training. Serpell, Mariga, and Harvey (1993) reviewed relevant research on MR in Africa and suggested that the concept of MR only has social validity in rural African subsistence economies when the degree of MR is sufficiently severe to become conspicuous. In some cultures, MR may be especially difficult to detect, given Western standards, because age sets are more loosely defined and multiage groups of children are often seen doing things together. There also is much more flexibility in rural African communities than there is in Western school systems about the particular biological age at which a child is given a certain measure of social responsibility. With Western conceptualizations of MR, then, it would be expected that mild degrees of MR would not be a cause of parental anxiety or of stigma for the child in a traditional rural African setting. The child whose locally valued aptitudes lag a little behind those of other children born in the same month will effortlessly become integrated over the years with an appropriate set of peers whose social competencies match the child's. Western theories of socialization place great emphasis on autonomy; African parents tend to focus on the cultivation of social responsibility and nurturance. Therefore, social participation plays a greater role in defining maladaptation than does intellectual functioning, according to statistical criteria in African societies.

In Africa, debates over the terminology most appropriate for designating people with various types of learning difficulties have taken place at several meetings of experts on the continent. The term *mental retardation* is thought by some to be too global because it refers to all aspects of the mind. On the other hand, the disability to which it refers is only intellectual and is often narrowly focused in childhood. Another term used to describe children, *developmental delay*, has little meaning when referring to the adult period of the life span. Furthermore, the existence of many indigenous languages on the African continent makes precise definition for these difficult constructs even more problematic (Mittler & Serpell, 1985). Serpell (1990) argued that although it appears theoretically appropriate to objectively determine the nature and degree of a person's mental handicap (the term popular in African countries) or of the person's intellectual disability as a basis for subsequent decisions regarding intervention, in practice it is essential to recognize that the current range of service possibilities in African countries is limited. Generally, the primary goal of psychological assessment is to guide intervention efforts. If none are possible, or if they are limited, classification may not be necessary.

Treatment of MR in Primitive Societies

As stated in the introduction, one way in which psychologists can understand human development is to examine the human behavior cross-culturally. Robert Edgerton, a cultural anthropologist, has extended understanding of MR by considering its place in several dozen non-Western cultures. Part of the impetus for this analysis was the observation by Gladwin (1959) and Edgerton (1968, 1970) that little was known about MR as it exists in non-Western cultures. Using a variety of standard (Human Relations Area Files) and nonstandard (his own ethnographic studies and personal communication with other anthropologists) sources, Edgerton (1968, 1970) tested a number of common assumptions regarding MR in so-called primitive societies. The first assumption was that, to the extent possible in primitive societies, infants and children with severe MR are killed or left to die. A second assumption was that individuals with MR are cared for and tolerated as long as they do not interfere with or harm anyone. Examples were cited in Kenya, India, Manus, Borneo, and Sikkim. Edgerton (1970) concluded that given evidence of both kinds of treatment, neither generalization is wholly true. Rather, what seems to happen in primitive cultures is varied across and perhaps even within societies. Some were killed as custom dictated, and others were kept and cared for like other children whose parents loved them.

Another assumption Edgerton (1968, 1970) examined was that mild MR was not noticed or viewed as problematic in primitive societies. Edgerton concluded that the data are insufficient to support this assumption. Because there is no standard that can be used across cultures to measure mild MR, it is difficult to draw any conclusions. He pointed to evidence among many cultures that intelligence is prized and stupidity eschewed. However, it was difficult to come to any firm conclusion on this issue 25 years ago, and it is still unanswerable. A related hypothesis is that in most non-Western societies, individuals with mild MR are not stigmatized. Another way to think about this issue is to determine whether people with mild MR are victims of discrimination. Edgerton concluded that in the majority of cultures he examined, there is clear evidence that people with mild MR are stigmatized. There are noteworthy exceptions, however, in which people with MR take on religious significance and are considered and treated as "saints" (such as the Siwans of the Libyan desert). Nevertheless, this does not occur in the majority of the societies examined.

Finally, Edgerton (1968, 1970) considered the degree to which people with MR are a problem to society, their family, or themselves. Once more, there is no simple answer to this question. As in Western societies, there are customs and techniques that have been adopted to deal with problems presented by people with MR; primitive societies also have devised ways to manage such individuals. Thus, in some primitive societies, Edgerton found that people with MR were no problem at all, whereas in some societies they presented serious problems (e.g., the Nootka of northwest Canada, the Lepchas of Sikkim and in Manus).

Assessment and Culture

There is some evidence to suggest that cultural values and orientation can create barriers to learning and test performance in school settings, resulting in some children's behavior being considered incompetent or their being misclassified as having MR. During 1963 and 1964, data were collected for a comprehensive study of the rate of MR in Riverside, California. The purpose of this epidemiological survey was to study the distribution of MR in a medium-sized American city from both clinical and sociocultural perspectives. Mercer (1973a, 1973b, 1974a) documented an important finding about the influence of cultural status on the assessment of clinical MR. She found in both a field study and in a social system survey of community agencies that people from ethnic minorities, particularly Mexican Americans and African Americans, and lower socioeconomic levels were overrepresented among those identified as having MR. Using full-scale scores on the Wechsler Intelligence Scale for Children (Wechsler, 1974) and additional sociological data on the children's background, Mercer found that children whose social background was similar to that of the larger community had test scores that were statistically the same as test norms. Children who were least like the sociocultural model of the Riverside community, on the other hand, scored almost 1 *SD* below the norm on the Wechsler Intelligence Scale for Children (Wechsler, 1974) and thus would probably be labeled clinically retarded using traditional public school standards. Mercer argued that using only IQ tests to assess mental functioning might be ill-advised. She demonstrated that pluralistic assessment procedures that include a consideration of the sociocultural characteristics of the child's background in evaluating adaptation produce more accurate assessments of children's performance and avoids disproportionate representation of ethnic minorities in the population of those with MR. Mercer and others have developed culture-specific tests to incorporate this perspective in the diagnosis of mental functioning and adaptation (Mercer, 1974a, 1979; Mercer, Gomez-Palacio, & Padillo, 1986; R. L. Williams, 1972, 1974). However, the procedures recommended by

Mercer and Williams have not been widely accepted or adopted in general clinical practice. Consequently, the risk of possible misdiagnosis remains.

The Concept of Cultural Disadvantage

The terms *cultural disadvantage* and *cultural deprivation* were popular in the 1960s (see McNeil, 1969). They were often used as explanations for children's school failure or as reasons for poor performance on tests of intelligence. Today, it seems difficult to imagine that a person does not have a culture or that one culture is disadvantaged compared with another. What did this term mean in the 1960s? It meant generally that one did not have middle-class, Western European values; that one did not have White skin; or that one spoke no English or spoke it with an accent that indicated it was not one's native tongue. Ethnic children growing up in the United States were often described as "culturally disadvantaged." It was asserted that a culturally disadvantaged child would not learn adequately about the world and about the environment and thus would be rejected by the so-called "dominant" culture. It also was asserted that this disadvantage meant not having experiences that led to future opportunities; security in life; and a safe, uncomplicated career. Being a member of a minority group meant that there was a greater likelihood of economic disadvantage. This economic disadvantage was often assumed to cause cultural disadvantage, which limited what one learned about the world because economic circumstances precluded participation in many enriching activities. Culturally disadvantaged children also were presumed to be differently motivated than culturally advantaged children because of their perception that the opportunity structure would not reward school achievement.

Culturally Related Biological Factors

There are a variety of conditions leading to MR that are biological but are correlated with cultural factors. Among these are recessive hereditary disorders that occur in cultural groups who reproduce only within the group. For example, Tay-Sachs disease, a terminal disorder that causes MR, is a hereditary condition generally found among Eastern European Jews. Such culturally related examples are relatively rare. However, developmental disabilities that are associated with the continuum of reproductive casualty, as described by Lilienfeld and Pasamanick (1956), may be mediated by cultural variables and may be associated with being a member of a particular cultural group. Thus, because certain cultural groups may be overrepresented among families living in poverty, the relationship between group membership and the outcomes of reproductive casualty may be high; poverty predisposes a woman to a greater risk of reproductive problems and hence of developmentally impaired offspring.

Chisholm and Heath (1987) illustrated how particular cultural groups might transmit the effects of a stressful environment to their offspring. There are possible mechanisms whereby negative developmental outcomes mediated by complications of pregnancy and birth may originate in the way in which a cultural group behaves or is treated. Many years ago, Tarjan (1970) pointed out that the largest proportion of individuals with MR were either of the "cultural–familial" type or of the "environmental deprivation" type. This is still true today. Tarjan suggested that in instances of MR in which there is either no certain cause identified or in which the cause is attributed to cultural–familial origins or environmental deprivation, these latter two etiological classes also may be highly correlated with other circumstances leading to MR. These circumstances might include environmental toxins, substance abuse, nutritional deprivation, and as yet unidentified biological factors. This is not to say that psychogenic environmental conditions alone cannot cause MR, but that perhaps the incidence of MR attributable to environmental deprivation, especially when associated with cultural group membership, may be far smaller than is usually assumed. In summary, then, it is likely that there is a large overlap among individuals who are identified as having MR caused by biological factors, as yet undiscovered, and those who have MR caused by psychogenic deprivation. In both cases, cultural group membership, which may be associated with both types of causes, also may be mistakenly taken to pose an etiological explanation.

Cultural Competence in Services for Diverse Cultural Groups

The concepts of race and ethnicity, as markers for cultural expression, have had major salience for American culture, particularly in the 1990s. Recently, factors such as shifting population demographics, an increased focus on the global economy, and shifting social integration and interactions, which suggest multicultural rather than assimilative goals, have contributed to the salience of culture for all realms of human services (Isaacs & Benjamin, 1991). Because of this trend, the concept of cultural competence has begun to be used in many areas of social, public health, and educational services to refer to practices that sensitively and appropriately incorporate a consideration of the cultural background of service recipients (several related terms are *cultural diversity*, *cultural sensitivity*, *cultural relevance*, and *cultural awareness*). Many service professionals consider the term *cultural competence* to imply a more significant consideration than the related terms. Competence implies more than sensitivity, awareness, and tolerance, although it does include them. Competence implies skills that help to translate sensitivities and awareness and a cultural orientation into actions, policies, procedures, and the behavior of professionals in their interactions with individuals and families from a particular culture (see Roberts, 1989). A culturally competent system of services or practices would consider issues such as (a) determining how assessment and evaluation may be influenced by values, beliefs, and specialized knowledge; (b) identifying any underserved groups and barriers to the provision of services that culture might impose; (c) facilitating policy planning, staff training, and community participation in developing and maintaining culturally comprehensive services; (d) defining location, demand, type, number, and ethnography of culturally diverse populations within a service area; (e) building cross-cultural communication skills; and (f) helping communities organize to better offer and use services. In a culturally competent social system, the family, as defined by each culture, becomes the principal system of support and the preferred intervention agent. Furthermore, in this framework, it is understood that a family functions at least biculturally and perhaps multiculturally. It also is important to consider that families and individuals make choices on the basis of cultural influences and services; if services are to be helpful, these influences must be considered as well. Services, therefore, will be driven by cultural choices and will not be culture-free or blind interventions. Cultural competence also involves working with natural and informal support and helping networks such as religious institutions, community or spiritual leaders and healers, and community organizations in ways that extend self-determination to the community.

Isaacs and Benjamin (1991) identified five essential content areas that would contribute to a service system's or institution's ability to be culturally competent: (a) express an appreciation for diversity, (b) have the capacity for cultural self-assessment, (c) be aware of the dynamics that occur when cultures interact, (d) have institutionalized cultural knowledge, and (e) have developed adaptations to service delivery that show an understanding of cultural diversity. These program elements would exist at every level of a competent system, such as in policymaking, administration, service delivery, and service structures. The application of culturally competent practices is extremely complex; however, useful guidelines exist for implementing such practices (Bernard, 1991; Cross, Bazron, Dennis, & Isaacs, 1989; Isaacs, 1986; Isaacs & Benjamin, 1991; Mason, 1989; Orlandi, 1992; Rider & Mason, 1990; Roberts, 1989).

Suggestions for Future Research

In this chapter, we have briefly reviewed some of the concepts and issues concerning the way in which culture influences developmental disability. We emphasized the importance of cultural group membership in understanding MR and the need for continued research in this area.

Future research should focus on achieving a better understanding of how culture is expressed and the key relationships that exist among cultural experiences, social interactions and attributes, and the sequence and timing in the acquisition of developmental skills. Within this context, it also would be helpful to know more about the way in which social bias, like racism, may create particular developmental disadvantages. This is particularly critical in the recently revived climate of skin color and cultural stereotypes. In addition, we might learn more about culture and developmental disability if we expanded our cross-cultural framework to include multicultural comparisons within the American cultural context and across the international context. The work described by Nihira et al. (1988) and Edgerton (1968) provides excellent examples of how to approach this much needed research. In particular, although Edgerton's cross-cultural comparisons of social stigma were instructive, they reached no firm conclusions about cultural definitions of MR. Thus, we could use an update of this descriptive work that expresses the current experiences of persons with MR. Likewise, Mercer's (1974a) findings need to be updated. Because the assessment procedures that she recommended have not been widely accepted, should we expect a similar level of misdiagnosis 20 years later?

We also need research that better describes the developmental course of developmentally delayed children's communicative skills. Comparative studies with this particular focus that extends our understanding beyond the language behavior children with Down syndrome or mild MR are necessary to expand our knowledge base. Furthermore, it is important to explore the influence of learning a first language that is not the language used in later schooling on the assessment and functional aspects of developmental delay.

Finally, we need more research that explores the efficacy of particular treatments and interventions for specific MR populations and is based on sound principles and robust evaluation methodology. This research should include an assessment of the cultural competence of various services and treatments and the impact of cultural competence on service efficacy.

19

Communicating Assessment Results in Mental Retardation

James A. Mulick and James Bradford Hale

Psychological assessment is a professional activity intended to yield high-quality information about the current performance, cognitive functioning, emotional status, behavior, and differential characteristics of the person being examined. Sound assessment methodology, knowledge of the limitations of the techniques used, and thorough understanding of relevant scientific principles can result in valid and reliable information. Such information can have great practical value. It can lead to differential predictions about future behavior, the probable response of a person to changing circumstances, or a more realistic appraisal of a person's present status. Obtaining valid and reliable psychological assessments and then correctly interpreting them requires lengthy and rigorous advanced training. The psychologist is rightly viewed as a highly skilled professional when performing assessments.

The most likely ultimate beneficiaries of assessment information will, however, usually include nonpsychologists. Assessment is carried out in contexts such as clinical planning, placement, education, and medical care. Others involved in care and planning often lack the background to appreciate the details of the assessment process or the limitations of current practice. Therefore, interpretation of the results of psychological assessment is a major responsibility that requires forethought and an appreciation of the roles of others in the life of the person being evaluated.

In this chapter, we provide general and cautionary advice to professional psychologists who must interpret assessment findings and provide useful recommendations to nonprofessional caregivers. We emphasize communication and collaboration with parents and affectively committed caregivers who will maintain enduring or decision-making involvement with the child or adult with mental retardation (MR) who is the focus of assessment. It is rare to begin any sort of psychological evaluation without the involvement of caregivers, especially for children with suspected MR, and wise to involve parents and caregivers from the outset. The detailed analysis of critical aspects of collaborative communication with parents and caregivers will require the reader to delve much more deeply into the issues raised in this chapter. We think the reference citations included here are excellent places to start.

Initial Diagnosis

In the case of parents, the initial assessment leading to a diagnosis or classification of the child with MR is an anxiety-laden and stressful experience. The psychological evaluation will have been requested to confirm observations by teachers or caregivers of performance deficits suggesting developmental delays, to explain an apparent poor fit of a child with behavioral or academic standards in a service or educational setting, or to be a part of a multidisciplinary workup relating to a known or suspected syndrome, illness, or handicapping condition. There will have been an indication to parents that something is wrong. This reality is the first one that must be acknowledged in order to initiate a cooperative and informative relationship with the family during assessment.

Studies of referral for special education services in the schools suggest a strong association between referral and difficult-to-manage or disruptive behavior in children (Forehand & Baumeister, 1976; A. T. Russell & Forness, 1985). Behavior problems have served as the first noticeable indication that a child lacked prerequisite cognitive skills for engagement in and benefit from the ongoing school program or curriculum. This marker during the school years has declined somewhat in significance as a result of early health monitoring in pediatric primary care (Dworkin, 1989) and preschool child-find programs (Blackman, Healy, & Ruppert, 1992; Katz, 1989). Nevertheless, many children are missed during routine "well child" primary care (Glascoe & Dworkin, 1993) and continue to be "discovered" through observations of day-care providers, grandparents, preschool teachers, and primary school personnel roughly in negative correlation of age with severity of developmental delay.

The most likely initial referral questions in children revolve around hyperactivity, disruptive behavior problems, delayed speech and language acquisition, and delayed motor milestones because these are salient child characteristics (Demb, 1995). The evaluation setting, however, also contributes to the relative incidence of initial referral problems. Pediatric medical centers tend to attract referrals associated with delayed milestones and recognizable congenital health problems in the youngest children. School settings can be expected to attract referrals when behavior and learning problems predominate. Psychologists in these settings may find themselves asked to respond relatively more often to the diagnostic questions with which their institutional settings are most concerned and best equipped to serve. Therefore, there may be a tendency to focus more on such setting-specific issues during assessment than on those of greatest importance to the family or to the child's overall best interests and long-term needs.

For young children, the mandates of Public Law 99-457 serve to expand the scope of assessment beyond those narrowly associated with particular professional settings (Katz, 1989; Short, Simeonsson, & Huntington, 1990). Assessment guidelines in this preschool extension of the special education law establish the benchmark of focusing on the family, determining its unique strengths, and generating an intervention agenda termed an *individual family service plan* (IFSP). This is in contrast to the *individualized education program* (IEP) for primary- and secondary-age schoolchildren in which parent input is merely included, which was the previous benchmark under Public Law 94-142, the Education for All Handicapped Children Act (which, as revised, is now referred to as the Individuals with Disabilities Education Act). Clearly, learning and adaptation occur in all settings. The needs of caregivers will substantially influence the outcomes of all professional interventions at some, if not all, stages.

The wisdom of family empowerment and inclusion in the education and habilitation process has long been recognized, despite the frequent failure of the process in practice (R. L. Simpson, 1988; R. L. Simpson & Fiedler, 1989; A. P. Turnbull, 1983). In fact, parental perceptions of child development status tend to overestimate but to be highly correlated with psychometric assessment results (Sexton, Thompson, Perez, & Rheams, 1990), and they can be very useful as an additional source of relational developmental data. Successful inclusion of caregivers in the planning and implementation of education and habilitation services requires advanced planning and flexibility by the psychologist.

Family assessment is an additional dimension in which to view assessment of the child, supplementing and clarifying that of the direct measurement of child characteristics and abilities against normative standards (Katz, 1989; Konstantareas & Homatidis, 1989). Planning is required to permit allocating additional time to meet with the caregivers and to select appropriate assessment strategies that will reflect parental perceptions and directly assess parents' strengths and characteristics as they pertain to the child. Family issues and mental health concerns about caregivers are relevant to child assessment in this paradigm. Thus, interventions designed to benefit the child but initially focus on other family members may be considered to be legitimate (Gallagher, Beckman, & Cross, 1983; Kobe, Mulick, Rash, & Martin, 1994). In some cases, rational interpretation of a child's needs will indicate recommendations for parent training, individual therapy, or a residential intervention with a 24-hr habilitation or education plan (Birnbrauer & Leach, 1993; S. L. Harris, 1983). Psychological assessment can therefore legitimately include parental emotional variables, role perception, parenting skills, certain forms of knowledge or information, and belief or value systems related to parenting and family resources. True assessment with valid instruments and procedures will avoid the unfortunate possibility of simply stereotyping parents (S. D. Klein, 1993). Flexibility is always required to accommodate caregiver obligations and their emotional needs during the assessment process, and to reflect realistic variation in parental involvement during assessment and subsequently as indicated by the findings.

A strong case can be made that the initial assessment leading to the diagnosis of MR, or other significant disability, is the single most important diagnostic intervention during the entire course of providing services to the individual and family. Certainly, poignant recollections of parents reveal its lasting emotional significance, despite the many strains and shattered intimacies that the necessary intrusion of professional services subsequently will produce in the affairs of the whole family (Featherstone, 1980; Weyhing, 1983).

The emotional impact on parents and caregivers of receiving such a diagnosis is well described and documented (Fortier & Wanlass, 1984; S. D. Klein, 1993; Moses, 1983; Seligman & Darling, 1989). Psychologists must be aware of these emotional processes so that steps can be taken at the outset to lessen their negative impact. Conceptually, the entire assessment process should be regarded seriously as a potentially disabling or, as it should be framed, an enabling experience for the family in terms of their later willingness to seek and use services needed to optimize outcomes for the child. The most important outcome of assessment and its interpretation, interventions in their own right, is the movement of the child and family toward effective ameliorative and preventive interventions and professional services.

Process Guidelines

Sattler (1988) provided a standard, highly regarded text on clinical assessment, interpretation, and communication of assessment findings and a rich resource of clinical process advice. In this portion of the chapter, however, we summarize guidelines particularly relevant for the initial diagnosis of MR and build on such basic clinical premises. Reevaluation raises many of the same emotional and communication issues and requires similar professional management, but it tends to be more specifically problem oriented.

The first professional responsibility is the selection of appropriate assessment tools. This responsibility is not transferable under ethical and legal standards. These tools, such as norm- and criterion-referenced tests and inventories, interview and observation protocols, checklists, and behavior analytic schemes, should address the main referral questions and those related to deciding among likely alternative action plans. A rationale for assessment will emerge from available intake information and other historical sources. The rationale for assessment is the first interactive element in the professional relationship with the client and family. Modifications of standardized formats may be anticipated in many situations involving MR and the medical disorders associated with MR. These departures from standardization require judicious weighing of the implications of individual differences on assessment results and the uses of derived information (Eyde et al., 1993) and must be carefully documented. The data and the conclusions drawn from them will set the agenda for the important follow-up meeting or meetings with caregivers.

The planning, testing, observation, and interview sessions will have established an initial professional relationship with parents (S. D. Klein, 1993). Discussion should outline the tools to be used and the demands they will place on the client and family so that general expectations will reflect the amount of time and effort required. This is an opportunity to solicit reactions to the assessment rationale and to request information about caregiver expectations, thereby demonstrating sensitivity to family priorities and allaying anxieties connected with the professional assessment role and activities to follow.

Once planned data collection is completed, preliminary evaluation may reveal the need for additional data to answer questions arising during assessment. If no further information is required to complete the planned evaluation, full consideration of the findings and their implications should precede actually meeting with caregivers to discuss the results. It is often helpful to prepare the written report in advance, with the proviso that alterations or addenda may be required later for clarification or elaboration of points raised during the information-sharing session. Although not usually included in the written report of evaluation, the psychologist should be familiar enough with the specific tools used and general standards for psychological and educational testing (American Psychological Association, 1985) to be able to discuss and explain them frankly, including their practical value and limitations, in everyday language.

Candor and truthfulness are essential in presenting results and recommendations (Quine & Pahl, 1986). Anything less will set the stage for mistrust of professionals and tend to discourage future consultation. Such considerations are not unique to communicating psychological information, but they are typical of communicating most forms of technical information having implications involving risk or negative outcomes (Rowan, 1994). Intended meaning cannot be taken for granted; rather, it must be explored through the use of requests for caregiver reaction or exchange of interpretative views. Technical and diagnostic terms should be introduced and used appropriately, with explanation and qualification insofar as the degree of certainty requires (S. D. Klein, 1993). Predictions that can be supported should be provided, but generally in terms of their likelihood if certain interventions are made available or services provided. Realistic grounding of documented individual differences in various supportive or instructional contexts should be discussed to make predictions relevant to real-world settings.

The technical report also should be regarded as an intervention of sorts. The written documentation of psychological evaluation should be viewed as sensitive material but appraised as something that will only have meaning if it is read and acted on (Cornwall, 1990). Parents have an enduring relationship with children and will need to refer to the report in order to recall important points made by the psychologist or to obtain needed services. Other professionals who provide services to the client or family will need concise information about the client to better provide or modify services. Only relevant material should be included in the report, but this most often includes technical summary data as well, and conclusions or practical recommendations should be consistent with and derived from reported findings. Technical data are frequently necessary for service or program eligibility determination by other agencies, and the report serving as an archival document may be useful at a later date as a quantitative baseline to assess change. Thus, most reports will include an explanation of technical data in plain language, acknowledgment of expected measurement error, and an indication of the level of confidence to be placed in apparent quantitative differences among scores. A logical, well-written report is much more likely to be read and to be persuasive. Positive statements are always appropriate, even in the context of severe impairment. The meaningful relationships between the client and those who provide support should be recognized in the history and recommendations.

Environmental conditions during the information-sharing session are important. Care should be taken to create a setting conducive to the exchange of complex and emotionally laden ideas. This requires freedom from distractions and interruptions, readily accessible materials, good seating, and expressions indicating respect and concern for the comfort of participants. Perhaps the single most important element is time. Evidence that the psychologist is busy or preoccupied will not be conducive to understanding and comfort. Discourse is often facilitated by opening the discussion with concrete recollections of memorable events that occurred during the evaluation. Soliciting reactions to the evaluation process or restating the caregivers' primary concerns solicits their active participation, indicates caring, and conveys the impression that the purpose of the evaluation is to help (Sharp, Strauss, & Lorch, 1992).

Time, however, is limited, so guiding the discussion away from repetition and following a planned format toward a natural summary and a request for feedback from participants can create a natural breakpoint. Because of the potential emotional impact of the material and the complexity of the content, the option for future discussions, in person or by telephone, should be offered. Scheduling follow-up sessions obviously may sometimes be necessary as a result of apparent discomfort or clearly unresolved issues. Separate sessions with older clients with MR to review the important findings and recommendations, with or without their caregivers present, may require special efforts to present the information in a comprehensible manner appropriate to the client's ability to understand, but should be considered an ethical responsibility.

Even the most sensitive and well planned informative conference will leave the family with many unanswered questions and new concerns. Many families become defensive and may fail to ask about very intensely disturbing ideas or foreign concepts. It is useful to offer alternative sources of information, such as support and advocacy groups, information agencies, newsletters, and books. Videotapes devoted to intervention approaches, specific disabilities, and specialized programs are becoming available in many agencies for use with families. Pueschel, Scola, Weidenman, and Bernier (1995) have provided an affordable sourcebook for families of children with developmental disabilities, which includes explanations of technical terms, specialized evaluation procedures and therapies, medical procedures, social services, developmental concepts, and the training and typical responsibilities of professionals who commonly work in disability services, as well as lists of advocacy and professional groups and additional readings. Comprehensive reference works, such as this book or specialized readings, can clarify some issues better than follow-up appointments and are generally more cost-effective for the family.

Conclusion

The psychologist who performs evaluation services acts as an educator and facilitator. The psychological evaluation is of value only if it results in beneficial subsequent actions. Technical and theoretical expertise is of use only if tempered with sensitivity, compassion, and skill in communication. The client and family are the main parties to the evaluation process who can both actualize the recommendations and obtain the expected benefits. Immediate agreement with the conclusions of the evaluation should not be emphasized because time is often required to assimilate the new information and to decide on a course of action. The psychologist must be prepared to adjust the format and content of the information-sharing process to maximize its practical value to the client and family.

20

Cognitive and Vocational Interventions for School-Age Children and Adolescents With Mental Retardation

Alan C. Repp, Judith Favell, and Dennis Munk

Debate regarding appropriate means and criteria for diagnosing mental retardation (MR) has existed for decades, and it continues to influence perceptions of individuals with MR (Luckasson et al., 1992). Disagreement about the need for and purpose of MR definitions stems partly from the realization that definitions may obscure and minimize important individual differences and fail to provide clear direction for treatment. Recognition that affected people have difficulty learning is constant across all perspectives and definitions of MR (Repp, 1983). From this perspective, an important element of treatment becomes apparent: to provide instructional methods that facilitate the pace, course, and outcome of learning.

Interest in effective methods for teaching school-age children and adolescents (hereafter called *students*) has been driven by legal and political movements as well as by increased knowledge of the learning potential of students with MR. Decisions in cases such as *Brown v. Board of Education* (1954) and *Mills v. Board of Education of the District of Columbia* (1972) established the right of children with disabilities to educational services in a public school. These and other supporting cases influenced the scope of the Education for All Handicapped Children Act (EHA; Public Law 94-142), which was enacted in 1975. (In 1990, the EHA was renamed the Individuals with Disabilities Education Act [IDEA].) The EHA exceeded previous legal mandates in asserting the right of every child to receive an individualized and appropriate education in the least restrictive appropriate educational placement. Instructional goals and methods for evaluating learning were required, and interest in developing effective instructional procedures was influenced by the accountability required by the EHA. (See the discussion of legal and legislative forces affecting services and standards in chapter 32 in this book.)

Although there has been considerable legal and legislative activity in the rights movement, there also has been considerable scientific interest in the study of people with MR in various settings. Researchers have shown that specific procedures, when applied systematically, can produce greater than expected learning by individuals with MR (e.g., see portions of Matson & Mulick, 1991b; Thompson & Gabrowski, 1972). Research demonstrating that they are more capable of learning than previously thought stimulated legal and political advocates to emphasize that people with MR should be taught the skills necessary to live relatively normal lives and to benefit from supportive services in culturally typical environments.

One product of the interaction between the legal and political and scientific movements has been the substantial writing and research on effective instructional procedures. Instruction is the indicated treatment for all levels of MR, and the goal of instruction remains the same regardless of learner characteristics. Instruction is intended to teach a student to respond in a specific way to the presence of a defined stimulus or arrangement of complex stimuli. The goal of instruction is the development and sharpening of stimulus control for targeted responses ranging in complexity from touching a picture to calculating a math problem.

Although the goal of instruction remains the same regardless of the learner's level of retardation, the procedures for facilitating stimulus control do vary across levels. In this chapter, we refer to two groups: students with severe-to-moderate MR and students with moderate-to-mild MR. The moderate level is included in both groups because of variation in cognitive abilities exhibited by students with this classification. Some students with moderate MR learn new responses of a complexity and at a rate more similar to that of students with severe MR; others may learn more complex skills (e.g., reading) at a rate similar to that of students with mild MR.

In this chapter, we present an overview of both widely accepted and research-based teaching procedures. For each of the groups just mentioned, we describe what is being taught, how new responses are taught, and where teaching occurs.

Instructing Students With Severe-to-Moderate MR

What Is Taught

Awareness of the potential for these students to learn new skills and to gain independence has grown progressively. There also has been a realization that skills that are functional for a student are more likely to be learned and maintained because they correspond to the demands of the student's environment (L. B. Brown et al., 1979).

Functional skills are identified by conducting an ecological inventory of the student's environment. In general, an inventory identifies global environments or domains (e.g., home, school) and subenvironments or subdomains (e.g., bathroom, cafeteria) that call for certain skills or responses or that provide opportunities for certain responses to be reinforced. Functional skills are then targeted for each domain or subdomain.

Similarities in the domains of many students have led to construction of curricula of functional skills. One such curriculum, The Syracuse Community-Referenced Curriculum Guide (Ford et al., 1989), lists community-living domains for self-management and home living, vocation, recreation and leisure, and general community functioning. Goal areas are identified for each domain. For example, eating and food preparation are goal areas for home living, and community-based employment is a goal area for the vocational domain. Goal areas contain many specific skills that are targeted for instruction. Most curricula are useful for identifying functional tasks for a variety of domains and subdomains; however, instructional content should always be based on an ecological inventory of a student's environment.

Some skills are important in several environments. Motor skills, communication skills, and social skills affect student functioning across environments. Motor skills such as reaching for an object, grasping an object, or walking are prerequisites for many adaptive skills (Tawney, Knapp, O'Reilly, & Pratt, 1979). Communication deficits are common among students with severe-to-moderate retardation, and instruction in augmentative and alternative communications should be provided (Reichle, York, & Sigafoos, 1991). Augmentative or alternative communication devices include graphic symbols or tangible stimuli to which the student responds, which would be selected after conducting an ecological inventory of the demands and opportunities for communication within a student's environment (Sigafoos & York, 1991). For example, a generic symbol for "help" may meet the student's needs for assistance in several environments, but a specific symbol for "lift me" may be necessary in the bathroom.

Social skills may benefit a student in many environments, including integrated settings with nondisabled peers. Among the many responses considered, three are particularly important for improving social relationships: initiating interaction, responding to initiations, and continuing interactions (Brady & McEvoy, 1989; Haring, 1993). Curriculum models for social skills typically include peer interaction skills because they promote integration with other students (Haring, 1993).

The vocational domain has received increased attention by researchers and practitioners because services to promote transitions from school to work were initiated in 1983 (Rusch, Destefano, Chadsey-Rusch, Phelps, & Szymanski, 1992). Many skills (e.g., money handling) necessary for transitioning are subsumed in a curriculum of community-referenced functional skills. The selection of specific vocational and social skills should be functional within the student's vocational community (Rusch, Chadsey-Rusch, & Lagomarcino, 1987). Rusch, Schutz, and Agran (1982) reported that employers identified skills such as reciting one's full name on request, following one-step directions, and communicating basic needs as critical requisites to employment. For students with severe MR, such skills can be shaped in a school setting, but must also be taught in the vocational setting to ensure maintenance and generalization.

How New Responses Are Taught

Students learn more efficiently when instruction is systematic, defined, and replicable (Snell & Zirpoli, 1987). Models of systematic instruction generally include three phases: preinstruction planning, delivery of instruction, and evaluation of instruction (Kameenui & Simmons, 1990; Snell & Zirpoli, 1987). During preinstruction, the teacher plans procedures for reinforcement, error correction, prompting and fading, and selection of materials. One of these instructional components, prompting and fading, has received extensive research attention because of the impact of prompts on establishment of stimulus control by naturally occurring rather than artificial discriminative stimuli. Ideally, students will respond to naturally occurring cues; however, additional antecedent prompts or cues may be necessary to facilitate initial responding. The extent to which control of a response transfers to a naturally occurring stimulus determines the degree of independent responding and response maintenance exhibited by a student (Stokes & Baer, 1977; Stokes & Osnes, 1988).

Stimulus manipulation procedures have been used to teach a variety of functional skills. Within-stimulus and extrastimulus prompting involve manipulation of a stimulus in a way that facilitates correct responding (Lancioni & Smeets, 1986). Within-stimulus manipulations of fading and stimulus shaping and extrastimulus manipulations of superimposition and fading, superimposition and shaping, and delayed prompting have been described as errorless training procedures because they produce relatively low rates of errors during discrimination training. Stimulus fading involves the manipulation of one or more noncritical dimensions (e.g., color, shape, size) of two stimuli to be discriminated. Features of either the target stimulus (S+) or a distractor stimulus (S−) are gradually altered until they vary only in the critical feature. Stimulus fading has been used to teach students with MR to discriminate sizes and numbers (Zawlocki & Walls, 1983), spatial relations (Mosk & Butcher, 1984), letters (Wolfe & Cuvo, 1978), shapes (Schreibman & Charlop, 1981), and sounds (Schreibman, 1975). A package combining errorless procedures with a group teaching procedure (the task demonstration model) has proved superior to extrastimulus prompts for teaching a variety of discrimination tasks (Karsh & Repp, 1992; Karsh, Repp, & Lenz, 1990; Repp & Karsh, 1991; Repp, Karsh, & Lenz, 1990). Psychologists should be familiar with these instructional procedures and be prepared to provide appropriate guidance when learning difficulty occurs.

Stimulus shaping involves manipulating the topography or form of the stimuli to be discriminated. The initial level of the stimuli often do not resemble their final levels. Gradually, the form of the stimuli becomes more similar to the final stimuli to be discriminated. Stimulus shaping has been used to teach students to discriminate letters (Guralnick, 1975), words (Smeets, Lancioni, & Hoogeveen, 1984a), and body positions (Lancioni, 1983).

Superimpositions with fading or with shaping involve superimposing known stimuli (e.g., colors, objects) within the stimuli to be discriminated.

Fading includes pairing the stimuli (or S+ only) with known stimuli, which are then faded out as the student learns the discrimination. Guralnick (1975) superimposed color cues on the distinctive features of alphabet letters used in a discrimination task. The colors were eventually faded out as the discriminations were learned. Superimposition with shaping involves embedding known stimuli into the stimuli to be discriminated (e.g., the picture of a house behind the word *house*). Smeets, Lancioni, and Hoogeveen (1984b) taught students with severe-to-moderate MR to discriminate groups of three words by superimposing words and pictures corresponding to the stimuli. The superimposed words and pictures were reduced in size and shape into a distinctive feature of the related words, and many participants learned the discriminations with few or no errors.

Delayed prompting includes the presentation of a controlling prompt (e.g., the teacher's pointing finger) simultaneously with the S+ in a discrimination task. After several trials, the prompt is delayed so that the student comes to respond to the S+ prior to presentation of the prompt. Delayed prompting procedures have been used to teach students with MR to exhibit manual signs (Browder, Morris, & Snell, 1981), operate vending machines (Browder, Snell, & Wildonger, 1988), and read community survival signs (Ault, Gast, & Wolery, 1988).

The advantages of stimulus manipulation procedures are rapid acquisition, low error rates, and elimination of need for staff prompting. The disadvantages of these procedures are that they are not appropriate for tasks in which the stimuli cannot be controlled by the teacher and that they can be time-consuming (Etzel & LeBlanc, 1979).

Another type of extrastimulus prompting involves prompts or cues delivered pictorially or by another person (Wolery & Gast, 1984). Verbal instructions are the most common extrastimulus prompt. To maximize transfer of control to naturally occurring stimuli, the teacher should state the desired response (e.g., "Put on your shoes after your socks") during the acquisition of the response, but the teacher should prompt the student to attend to the naturally occurring cue (e.g., "What do you do next?") when the response is not maintained.

Prompting hierarchies are often used as a systematic approach to reducing prompt-dependent responding. Hierarchies include levels of prompts (e.g., verbal, model, physical) arranged in order of intrusiveness to the student and delivered in a least-to-most or most-to-least format. A least-to-most prompting hierarchy consisting of (a) verbal instruction, (b) verbal plus modeling, and (c) verbal plus physical guidance. This hierarchy has been used to teach students to put on hearing aids (D. K. Tucker & Berry, 1980), to cook (Johnson & Cuvo, 1981), and to reach and grasp (Correa, Paulson, & Salzberg, 1984). By contrast, some researchers have expressed concern that a least-to-most prompting system promotes prompt dependence, possibly because of a delay in the delivery of physical guidance (Glendenning, Adams, & Sternberg, 1983).

Graduated guidance is a system of most-to-least prompting in which the degree of physical guidance is gradually reduced as the student learns and begins responding correctly to less intrusive cues (verbal instruction) or to naturally occurring stimuli. Foxx (1981) described a graduated guidance procedure in which the teacher (a) uses full graduated guidance during initial instruction, (b) fades to partial graduated guidance by placing only a finger on the student's hand, and (c) shadows the student's movement without actually touching the student's hand. Most-to-least prompting hierarchies have been used to teach students to eat independently (Richman, Sonderby, & Kahn, 1980), dress themselves (Foxx, 1981), perform toileting skills (Azrin & Foxx, 1971), and perform vocational task assembly (Zane, Walls, & Thvedt, 1981).

Extrastimulus prompting procedures are problematic because they often lead to prompt dependence. Practitioners using prompting hierarchies can minimize the risk of dependence by (a) identifying naturally occurring stimuli for the targeted response, (b) using verbal instructions or questions to prompt students to observe the naturally occurring stimuli, and (c) providing more reinforcement for responses to the naturally occurring stimuli than to prompts (Wolery & Gast, 1984).

During instruction, the teacher is concerned with arranging natural reinforcers, arranging materials, and facilitating generalization (Snell & Zirpoli, 1987). Generalization is a critical consideration when teaching students with severe retardation. Exposure to positive and negative examples of the concept being taught has been used to facilitate generalization. This procedure, called *general case programming* (Albin & Horner, 1988; Horner, Sprague, & Wilcox, 1982), teaches students the full range of conditions under which the targeted response should occur by presenting multiple positive examples (S+) to demonstrate the range of the S+, along with negative examples (S−) that differ only in the noncritical dimension of the S+. General case programming procedures have been used to facilitate generalization of skills such as crossing streets (Horner, Jones, & Williams, 1985), using vending machines (J. R. Sprague & Horner, 1984), and dressing (Day & Horner, 1986). Other methods for promoting maintenance and generalization of skills include teaching relevant behaviors, recruiting natural communities of reinforcement, testing a range of appropriate responses, training loosely, using indiscriminable contingencies, and using common stimuli (Stokes & Osnes, 1988).

Where Teaching Occurs

Contrary to the widely held notion that one-to-one instruction is always superior, researchers have shown that students can be instructed in small groups and may as a class learn faster in groups of 2–6 than during one-to-one instruction (Favell, Favell, & McGimsey, 1978; Oliver, 1983; Repp & Karsh, 1991; Westling, Ferrell, & Swenson, 1982). Also, group instruction may provide important peer social interactions and modeling opportunities (R. Brown, Holvoet, Guess, & Mulligan, 1980).

Studies demonstrating the effectiveness of both in vivo and classroom-based (simulated) instruction have been reported. In vivo instruction has been used to teach street crossing (Horner et al., 1985), soap dispenser use (Pansofer & Bates, 1985), and vending machine use (J. R. Sprague & Horner, 1984). Simulated instruction has been used to teach videogame skills (Sedlack, Doyle, & Schloss, 1982), bank-depositing skills (Shafer, Ingle, & Hill, 1986), and fast-food restaurant skills (VanDenPol et al., 1981). In a study involving simulated and in vivo instruction combined with general case programming, Neef, Lensbower, Hackersmith, DePalma, and Gray (1990) found that the use of general case programming, rather than in vivo or simulated instruction, facilitated generalization of new laundry skills.

There has been considerable debate about appropriate instructional settings for students with severe-to-moderate MR (Fuchs & Fuchs, 1994). Arguments have been made for instructing these students (a) full time in special education classrooms, (b) part time in special education and regular education classrooms, or (c) full time in regular education classrooms (Lloyd, Singh, & Repp, 1991). Research suggests that student success may rest less on the type of classroom than on the type of instruction.

Instructing Students With Mild MR

What Is Taught

Curricula for students with moderate or mild MR also should focus on increasing competence in the natural environment. Interestingly, individualized education plans (IEPs) for these students have been reported to include primarily academic goals (Epstein, Polloway, Patton, & Foley, 1989), although academics are recognized as only one area of important skill development. Curricula for students with mild MR should prepare the student for life in the criterion environment, which, for younger students, must be anticipated by professionals and parents constructing an IEP. This need for planning emphasizes the necessity for a well defined curriculum designed to meet the demands of adult life. Traditional curricula have been characterized as focusing on (a) remediation, with an emphasis on basic skills and social competence; (b) maintenance of acquired skills, with tutorial assistance and instruction on learning strategies designed to help the student succeed with the regular classroom curriculum; or (c) development of functional skills, such as vocational and life skills (Patton, Cronin, Polloway, Hutchinson, & Robinson, 1989).

Although each emphasis has benefits, each also presents problems that limit the student's preparation for life. A remedial approach may focus on deficits without identifying strengths, ignore generalization of skills to postschool environments, or emphasize academic skills to the exclusion of practical skills. Curricula centered around skill maintenance may focus only on short-term objectives at the expense of long-term goals and neglect the more diverse skills needed for later transition to adult life. A functional skills approach includes an inherent risk that students will become locked into a basic vocational or life skills curriculum with minimal exposure to academic curricula (Polloway, Patton, Epstein, & Smith, 1989). Patton et al. (1989) proposed a "life skills" approach to curriculum development. This approach to curriculum development includes typical demands of adulthood separated into six adult outcome domains of (a) home and family, (b) recreational leisure, (c) personal development, (d) emotional and physical health, (e) community involvement, and (f) vocational education. School-based curricula should be designed to meet demands within each domain. Patton et al. cited the Adult Performance Level Curriculum (APLC; Adult Performance Level Project, 1975; LaQuey, 1981) as a curriculum based on functional skills for each of the life domains. Traditional academic areas such as reading and writing are addressed through functional tasks. For example, a junior high school student can practice functional reading by reading a job description, thereby increasing occupational knowledge as well as reading skills. The APLC is an example of a curriculum in which traditional academic skills (e.g., reading, computation) are acquired and practiced on functional tasks.

Academic curriculum tasks for students with mild disabilities may be identical to those of nondisabled peers. More commonly, adaptations are made to existing curricula to increase the student's success and to prepare the student for future demands. For example, a reading curriculum should be both functional and interesting to the student. In describing best practices in reading instruction, Mandlebaum (1989) recommended instruction on survival words (e.g., walk) and on functional reading materials (e.g., menus, labels, cooking directions, grocery lists, and vending machines). Instruction for elementary students should use interesting books with limited, repetitive vocabulary. Secondary students may enjoy and learn from reading newspapers, magazines, high-interest and low-vocabulary books, and biographies. Reading materials should be matched to the reader's abilities, experiences, and interests. Curricula and adaptations for academic areas such as arithmetic (Cawley, Miller, & Carr, 1989), written language (Decker & Polloway, 1989), social studies (Marshall, Lussie, & Stradley, 1989), and science (Serna & Patton, 1989) also have been described.

The need for a curriculum to improve social competence also has been recommended for students with mild MR (Balla & Zigler, 1979). Social skills instruction may not only facilitate school interaction, but also prove beneficial in adult life (Polloway & Smith, 1983). Social skills deficits vary among students, and instruction should target the specific interactional skills needed to function successfully (Korinek & Polloway, 1993) and to interact successfully with nondisabled peers (C. M. Nelson, 1988). Examples of such behavior include sharing, smiling, asking for help, attending, taking turns, following directions, and solving problems (McEvoy, Shores, Wehlby, Johnson, & Fox, 1990). Adolescents may benefit from instruction in skills such as giving and accepting feedback, resisting peer pressure, and following instructions (Hazel, Schumaker, Sherman, & Sheldon-Wildgen, 1981).

How Responses Are Taught

Students with moderate-to-mild MR must be able to demonstrate rudimentary knowledge forms such as simple facts, verbal chains, and discriminations, as well as more complex knowledge forms such as concepts, rule relationships, and cognitive strategies (Kameenui & Simmons, 1990). Thus, instructional procedures for facilitating stimulus control of individual responses (e.g., say a word when written word is presented) or of multiple step operations (e.g., adding three-digit numbers) are needed. Students with more developed cognitive abilities are likely to benefit from instruction involving modeling, imitating, and questioning. Thus, although techniques prescribed for students with severe-to-moderate MR (e.g., within- and extrastimulus prompting) also are effective with students with mild MR, less intensive techniques that increase exposure to materials and increase rates of student responding are more prevalent.

Hendrickson and Frank (1993) summarized research on effective teaching methods of students with mild disabilities and concluded that effective teaching practices involve high levels of successfully engaged time and effective use of performance feedback. Effective instruction is generally teacher directed (Engelmann & Carnine, 1982) and is delivered in a systematic, controlled manner. Instruction for students in regular or special classrooms is generally delivered to a group; therefore, procedures have been developed for use during teacher-directed group instruction.

Teachers should use lesson formats for introductory and practice lessons (Carnine, Silbert, & Kameenui, 1990; Kameenui & Simmons, 1990). During acquisition lessons, the teacher presents material in a model–lead–test format, in which the teacher models the response, then prompts, and finally tests by asking the student to respond independently (Kameenui & Simmons, 1990). Tasks are sequenced from easy to difficult to minimize student errors. During the test format, antecedent prompts or cues are faded as the student's response becomes controlled by the instructional stimulus (e.g., the test, problem, or teacher question). A practice lesson format should follow completion of acquisition lessons, and in these sessions the student should practice new skills with teacher supervision and feedback (Carnine et al., 1990). Lesson formats and the model–lead–test format are integral parts of the research-based direct instruction (DI) curriculum and instructional programs (Carnine et al., 1990). Additional features of DI include (a) systematic sequencing of materials to facilitate correct responding, (b) mastery criteria for each level of instruction, (c) systematic feedback and error correction, (d) unison responding, and (e) practice of previously mastered skills. DI has been shown to be effective for teaching language skills to students with severe or mild MR (Gersten, 1985; W. A. T. White, 1988), and it is widely used in classrooms for students with mild disabilities.

Teachers of students with moderate or mild MR use questions as either instructional stimuli or as cues to facilitate responses to instructional stimuli. Questions are used in much the same manner as prompting hierarchies; they can range in the degree of explicitness and can be manipulated to require more or less effort by the student.

Questioning strategies can serve diagnostic, instructional, and feedback purposes (Stowitschek, Stowitschek, Hendrickson, & Day, 1984). Hendrickson and Frank (1993) provided the following general guidelines for questioning students: (a) Have an objective for each question, (b) ask one question at a time, (c) state questions clearly and concisely, (d) wait for a student to formulate a response, (e) praise the correct response, (f) avoid random questioning, (g) avoid rephrasing questions unless facilitating generalization, (h) avoid using only yes or no questions, (i) include questions testing problem solving and higher order thinking, (j) use age-appropriate language, (k) make the objective of a question clear, (l) use relevant and specific questions, and (m) evaluate effectiveness of questions by student responses.

Because questions are the primary cues provided to students with mild MR, instructors should select a type of question appropriate for the desired student response. Basic questions (who, what, where, and when) are used to solicit a predetermined response. Lead questions are used to focus attention on a new topic and to set the stage for more difficult questions (Hendrickson & Frank, 1993). Response-dependent questions are used in response to student errors. Questions are arranged in a sequence that limits alternative student responses until the correct response is given (Hendrickson & Frank, 1993) and facilitates student responding to naturally occurring stimuli such as worksheets or teacher questions. Questions are the cue and feedback mode most often used by teachers of students with mild MR.

Students with mild MR have been taught to perform cognitive–behavioral strategies that reduce dependence on external prompting or cuing. Self-instruction, self-recording, or a combination of both have been used to improve academic (e.g., reading) and academic-related (e.g., remaining in one's seat) behaviors (Lloyd, Talbott, Tankersley, & Trent, 1993). Self-instruction is taught through the following steps: (a) The model performs the task while describing the steps aloud; (b) the student performs the task under the direction of the model; (c) the student performs the task while describing the steps aloud; (d) the student performs the task while whispering the steps; and (e) the student performs the task without verbalizing the steps (Meichenbaum, 1977). Students using self-recording are taught to periodically record the occurrence or nonoccurrence of a specified behavior. Self-recording is taught in the same fashion as self-instruction. Students also may be taught to self-reinforce, in which students learn to determine the occurrence of desired behaviors and then to reinforce themselves if the goal has been reached.

Self-instruction has been used to improve performance in attending to instruction (Burgio, Whitman, & Johnson, 1980), paraphrasing groups of sentences (Borkowski & Vanhagan, 1984), and developing math skills (Albion & Salzberg, 1982; Leon & Pepe, 1983; Whitman & Johnston, 1983). Self-recording has been used to increase on-task responding (Blick & Test, 1987), time spent in one's seat (Sugai & Rowe, 1984), appropriate vocalization (R. O. Nelson, Lipinski, & Boykin, 1978), reading (Chiron & Gerken, 1983), and writing (Anderson-Inman, Paine, & Deutchman, 1984). Lloyd et al. (1993) reviewed the use of cognitive–behavioral procedures, including self-instruction and self-recording, and concluded that both of these techniques have been proved effective and that more research is warranted on their use with students with mild MR.

In conclusion, instruction for students with mild MR include techniques effective for students with more severe disabilities (e.g., stimulus fading) as well as those used in regular classrooms (e.g., lesson formats). For students with mild MR, the focus of instruction is to maximize overt responding during instruction, minimize student errors by sequencing materials and providing immediate feedback, and use questions as cues and feedback effectively.

Where Teaching Occurs

Students are typically instructed in large or small groups. Choral responding (Heward, Courson, & Narayan, 1989) may be used to maximize opportunities to respond during group instruction. Small-group instruction is more effective when the student members are equally skilled (Hendrickson & Frank, 1993). Although most small-group instruction is teacher directed, alternatives have been described for students with mild disabilities. Peer tutoring (Delquadri, Greenwood, Whorton, Carta, & Hall, 1986) involves facilitation of instruction or practice by an older student or same-age peer. Classwide peer tutoring (Delquadri et al., 1986) involves training all students in the classroom to serve as tutor and tutee. Teachers train the tutors, prepare materials, and provide general supervision. Peer tutoring has been shown to produce gains in academic and cognitive skills as well as in self-esteem and social skills (Hendrickson & Frank, 1993).

Students with mild MR are generally instructed in regular education classrooms, special class-based programs, or part-time in both (Patton, Beirne-Smith, & Payne, 1990). Students may be instructed by itinerant staff in a resource room or diagnostic–prescriptive teaching center (Patton et al., 1990). Vocational training is delivered in both mainstreamed classes and separate classes. Cooperative placements in part-time paid employment also may be appropriate for some students with mild MR (Morley, 1989).

Conclusion

Instruction is the indicated treatment for students with MR of all levels, and considerable research on effective instructional methods has been conducted. We have described the status of effective instruction in terms of functional curricula, instructional techniques, and settings for two groups of students: those with severe-to-moderate MR and those with moderate-to-mild MR.

Identification of skill domains relevant to the student's environment and lifestyle should be recommended for all students with MR. Ecological inventories should be used to identify functional skills for students with severe-to-moderate MR. For students with milder disabilities, an adult outcomes emphasis should prevail. In this strategy, life domains (e.g., vocation and education, home and family, recreation and leisure, and community involvement) are incorporated into support domains (e.g., emotional and physical health, personal development) into a curriculum addressing skills needed for successful transition to postschool settings.

Effective instructional procedures facilitate student responding to targeted stimuli such as environmental events, instructional materials, or questions. Stimulus manipulation procedures of within- or extrastimulus prompting have been used to facilitate correct responding. Responding by students with mild MR also has been facilitated through teacher-directed questioning and by teaching students to self-regulate their responses.

Students with mild MR generally receive all or most instruction in regular education classrooms or in the community. The issue of appropriate setting for students with more severe MR is more controversial and appears to be linked to philosophical or political beliefs in the case of placement in regular education classrooms or to concern over generalization of skills in arguments for community-based, in vivo instruction. Empirical investigations of the effects of instructional setting have addressed only the effects of in vivo versus simulated training on skill generalization.

A significant body of research on effective instruction has accumulated. However, areas in need of further attention are evident. For example, learning strategies instruction has been recommended for students with mild mental disabilities (Alley & Deshler, 1979; Deshler & Schumaker, 1986). During such instruction, the student learns to follow a multistep strategy with each step serving as a discriminative stimulus for a desired response. At this time, data on the effectiveness of learning strategy instructions for students with mild MR have not been forthcoming.

Recent emphasis on the inclusion of students with severe-to-moderate MR in regular education classrooms has brought into question the effectiveness or social validity of instructional procedures tested in special settings. Instructional methods that have been found to be effective in special settings should be validated in the regular classroom, where staff-to-student ratios may be greater and the skill levels of students may be diverse.

Although research has shown how students with MR should be taught, the impact and dissemination is maximized only when school-based or consulting psychologists are familiar with effective practices. Indeed, psychologists can provide technical support, including procedures for systematically implementing instructional strategies, to educators in classroom- and community-based settings.

21

Families Coping With Mental Retardation: Assessment and Therapy

Frank J. Floyd, George H. S. Singer, Laurie E. Powers, and Catherine L. Costigan

The families of children with mental retardation (MR) undergo a lifelong process of adaptation in which, after a crisis period at the time of the initial diagnosis, they begin an atypical developmental course that may set them apart from friends, neighbors, and extended family. Clinicians have long recognized that the parents may experience chronic sorrow manifested as recurrent episodes of depression, frustration, and remorse when their child fails to master an expected developmental task (Olshansky, 1962; Wikler, 1981). However, adaptation also may engender growth for the entire family in the form of enhanced sensitivity and flexibility, increased cohesiveness, and greater involvement with supportive networks through advocacy groups (A. P. Turnbull & Turnbull, 1990). Currently, the national policy of inclusion, which asserts that people with MR have a fundamental right to live and grow within their local communities (S. J. Taylor, Knoll, Lehr, & Walker, 1989), has spawned an expanded system of family support services to enhance families' abilities to meet the special needs of a child with MR (S. Cohen, Agosta, Cohen, & Warren, 1989). The goals of this service system are to help families actively cope with disability, provide supports for managing difficulties, reduce the need to place children out of the home, and improve functioning of family systems.

Despite shared experiences, families of children with MR are highly diverse. Like all families, they are complex systems comprised of multiple components and subsystems that are densely interconnected and interdependent. Changing demands and stressors produce flux as families strive to achieve homeostasis and maintain a stable identity as a unit. The goals of most families are to remain intact while adapting to change and to foster the development and well-being of all members. Having a child with MR is only one of the many challenges that each family faces. Nevertheless, it is usually a pervasive influence on family identity, structure, roles, and relationships.

Clinicians working with these families face the challenge of disentangling the complex system of family processes typical for families in general from those unique to the situation in which one family member has special needs that may supersede the needs of others. A growing body of research and theory is available on adaptation, assessment, and interventions with families of children with MR. In this chapter, we summarize major developments in this literature to provide direction for clinicians.

Challenges to Familial Well-Being

Although the presence of MR in the family does not represent an insurmountable challenge to successful family life, it can pose a variety of difficulties. These difficulties constitute additive strains on the normal developmental tasks that families face. In the following discussion, we emphasize those aspects of living with a family member with MR that can lead to an accumulation of stressors beyond those normally encountered in family life. Management of these challenges is possible given the right kinds of information and supports.

Families of people with MR are normal families living in abnormal circumstances (Seligman & Darling, 1989). They are capable of achieving all of the desirable accomplishments of any family and are vulnerable to the full range of commonplace family stresses and conflicts. It is possible, even probable, that families can adapt successfully to the challenge of raising a child with MR. Research suggests that the majority of parents of children with MR come to see their child as a positive contributor to their family and quality of life (Behr & Murphy, 1993). Adjustment to the reality of MR in the family can be difficult at times, but it is commonly achieved. Comparative meta-analyses of studies of the mental health of families with and without children with disabilities suggest that a majority of parents and siblings in affected families do not experience abnormal levels of distress, although they do experience a higher than average incidence of family stress and parental depressive symptoms (Singer & Irvin, 1990).

Family Services and Family Needs

It is essential that therapists not assume that the presence of a family member with MR is the primary reason that a family seeks or requires therapy. If the family's primary complaint concerns the person with MR, the therapist should neither assume that the family does not have other, more common concerns nor infer that the difficulty is indicative of family maladjustment. Ironically, although family support services were intended to be broad in scope, families receiving these services may find it difficult to recognize and seek treatment for problems not directly linked to MR. Many provider agencies are not equipped to detect and respond to family needs not related to disability, and referrals for family therapy may be delayed. Service providers may presume that their roles as partners in helping the family cope with disability eclipses their responsibility to identify or address other family problems (Krauss & Jacobs, 1990). Families may fail to recognize problems not associated with MR, or they may attribute tensions to the stress of coping with the child's special needs. A first step for a family clinician may involve encouraging the family to adopt a broader view of the needs and functioning of the family system. Clinical experience has suggested that families are as likely to need help with problems such as marital discord, job-related stress, relationships with a teenage sibling, and behavior management of young siblings as they are to request help that centers specifically on the person with a disability. Also, families who do focus their concerns on this person may actually be struggling with many external stressors associated with lack of needed supports and resources (Singer et al., 1993).

Long-term positive outcomes for people with MR and their families are achievable. Therapists who assist these families should be familiar with contemporary model practices such as inclusionary schooling, naturally and professionally supported employment and living options, strategies to promote self-determination and self-advocacy, inclusive leisure practices, and assistive technologies. Without such knowledge, practitioners may rely on outdated assumptions about the life patterns of people with MR.

Families of people with disabilities have many changing needs, so supports must be provided from a variety of sources. Emerging model service systems attempt to mobilize a flexible array of specialized and generic supports for families (V. J. Bradley, Knoll, & Agosta, 1992; Dunst, Trivette, Starnes, Hamby, & Gordon, 1993; Singer & Powers, 1993a, 1993b). A critical component of family support involves contact with other families through self-help organizations. Practitioners who seek to assist such families should develop working alliances with parent-to-parent organizations (Santelli, Turnbull, Lerner, & Marquis, 1993).

Models of Families and MR

Researchers have attempted to characterize families along dimensions that would lead to stable group differences, and these attempts have led to some success in modeling important aspects of family functioning over time. When models of the family are successful, they can be helpful in understanding the kinds of choices families will make (e.g., regarding their use of resources, their use of training and instruction, and their interest in various intervention goals and practices).

Family Environment

Mink and her colleagues (Mink, Blacher, & Nihira, 1988; Mink, Meyers, & Nihira, 1984; Mink, Nihira, & Meyers, 1983) developed a typology of family environments that describes the psychosocial climate of homes with school-age children with MR. On the basis of self-reports and systematic observations of families, they identified three types of families across groups of children with mild, moderate, or severe MR: cohesive families, control-oriented families, and families who are highly responsive to the child. Other, less common clusters identified families on the basis of moral–religious emphasis, socioeconomic advantage, disclosiveness among family members, and achievement orientation. Widaman (1991) cautioned that the distinctive features of specific subtypes are sometimes ambiguous or seem inconsistent across different samples. Nevertheless, cluster membership is related to patterns of mutual influence between children and their families over time (Mink & Nihira, 1987; Nihira, Mink, & Meyers, 1985), and the typology illustrates a range of family functioning and adaptation.

Another framework for family environment (Landesman, Jaccard, & Gunderson, 1991) is based in developmental psychology, and, although not subjected to direct empirical evaluation, synthesizes research on family processes that influence child development. The model proposes that individuals and subsystems within the family each have goals that include development in the physical, emotional, social, cognitive, moral, and cultural domains. The family environment is made up of these goals, along with strategies, resources, and individual life experiences that members draw on to achieve goals. This framework is useful for alerting family clinicians to strivings that propel adaptation from within the family. Identifying family goals and devising means to achieve them may be a practical way to organize therapeutic interventions with families.

Family Life Cycle

The family life cycle is the series of normative developmental stages that families pass through over time, marked either by changes in the composition of the family unit, such as couplehood to parenthood, or by changes brought on by children's development, such as entering school (Carter & McGoldrick, 1988). Using normative transitions as a guideline, A. P. Turnbull, Summers, and Brotherson (1986) described the unique stressors and demands that families of children with MR face during each life cycle stage. These include altering expectations for the child in early childhood and confronting fears about the future, developing advocacy skills during the school-age years, confronting puberty without the child having normative peer networks, and coping with continued dependency in adulthood.

Focusing on the later years, M. M. Seltzer and Ryff (1994) argued that the long-term parenting of a child with MR creates a nonnormative life course for parents because usual family transitions are disrupted, off schedule, or completely foregone. This nonnormative life course may not be inevitably experienced as negative. The adult child with MR may enhance the parents' lives by providing companionship and other supports for aging parents and by offering mothers a fulfilling role as a caregiver (Krauss & Seltzer, 1993). On the other hand, prolonged caregiving and restriction of their postparental years may have negative effects on well-being for some women (Ryff & Seltzer, 1995).

Stress and Coping

Models of stress and coping by Lazarus and Folkman (1984) and by McCubbin and Patterson (1983) have been widely used to conceptualize the initial crisis period when a child is diagnosed with MR and ongoing adjustments required in living with a child with special needs (Bristol, 1987; Farran, Metzger, & Sparling, 1986). Adjustment problems can be viewed in terms of the stressors acting on the family and the coping resources that are available or lacking. Stress reactions are idiosyncratic and occur when people appraise events as threats that exceed coping abilities. Families may manage stress directly by accessing tangible assets such as wealth, skills, and social supports. J. D. Brown (1993) argued that a less direct coping style of cognitively recasting negative events in optimistic terms, even when the formulation is "unrealistic," may help families ward off despair that could impede effective functioning. Crnic, Friedrich, and Greenberg (1983) expanded on this framework to describe long-term adaptation and the ecological forces impinging on families.

Disability and Familial Depression

The parents of children with MR are at risk of experiencing unusual levels of depressive symptoms (Singer & Irvin, 1990). Comparative studies have consistently shown small-to-moderate effect sizes for self-reported symptoms of depression among caregiving parents when compared with parents of children without disabilities. In a large-scale study of mothers of children with developmental disabilities, Breslau and Davis (1986) found that 30% of these mothers had scores over the clinical cutoff score on the Center for Epidemiological Studies Depression Scale, twice the incidence in a comparison population of mothers of nondisabled children. Follow-up psychiatric interviews did not reveal a higher incidence of major depressive disorder among these parents. Thus, rather than indicating that these families are more likely to experience functional debilitation, these findings seem to suggest that up to one third of mothers of children with MR are struggling with feelings of sadness, fatigue, or hopelessness. It is important to note that some studies did not indicate higher levels of depressive symptoms in mothers of children with MR compared with mothers of healthy children (Walker, Ortiz-Valdes, & Newbrough, 1989). Moreover, Glidden, Kiphart, Willoughby, and Bush (1993) reported that adoptive mothers of children with MR did not show elevations in depression, suggesting that depression in birth mothers may be caused by dashed hopes for a typical child rather than burdens associated with the child's disability. There is little research regarding depressive symptoms in fathers. Our clinical experience suggests that fathers also ought to be assessed; some of these men also are struggling with demoralization.

Depressive symptoms may or may not require treatment. Depression may be a prime target for treatment via psychotherapy, and pharmacological interventions or depressive symptoms may be secondary to other problems such as lack of disability-related supports, marital discord, role strain, or coercive familial interactions. Several studies have shown significant correlates of depressive symptoms in practical daily problems associated with the care of children with disabilities (Bristol, Gallagher, & Schopler, 1988; Gowen, Johnson-Martin, Goldman, & Applebaum, 1989). Depressive feelings may emerge from these stressors and abate when the stressors are reduced. Parents should be assessed carefully; the resulting treatment may involve condition-specific psychotherapies and pharmacological interventions for depression, or it may focus on addressing other underlying problems that are giving rise to feelings of demoralization. Such issues highlight the importance of thorough and careful assessment.

Family Assessment

Structured Family Assessment

Family assessment using structured instruments and procedures, although frequently neglected in clinical practice, may be beneficial for initially evaluating families and monitoring their progress during the course of therapy (Floyd, Weinand, & Cimmarusti, 1989). Initial assessments help to pinpoint problems, isolate causal and maintaining variables, identify resources, and place problems in the larger context of family system dynamics. Assessment should be sufficiently broad to provide a comprehensive, ideographic picture of family life and current difficulties from the perspective of all family members. Comprehensiveness may be especially important for families with a member who has a disability so that difficulties associated with the disability do not overshadow other family needs or concerns. The process of discovery during assessment may be an important initial intervention with families, helping them to refocus attention and understand problems in new, more useful ways.

Family Assessment Framework

A comprehensive family assessment should use a variety of assessment methods, including interviews, questionnaires, and observations, and should assess multiple domains of family functioning. Most clinicians rely only on unstructured interviews. Available structured tools, many of which were developed for research purposes, have not yet gained regular use in clinical settings. Incorporating these measures into clinical assessments will improve accuracy and comprehensiveness. Ideally, a variety of instruments should be selected to evaluate insiders' and outsiders' perspectives, analyze micro- and macroevents to detect immediate functional relationships as well as global functioning (Floyd, 1989), and assess individuals as well as larger subsystems of the family.

Content Areas for Family Assessment

The content assessed with each family will depend on the specific concerns that led the family to seek therapy. We list several domains that research and clinical theory suggest are relevant to most families, along with measures that have documented usefulness with families of children with disability. More complete listings of measures for these and other domains can be found in Filsinger and Lewis (1981), Grotevant and Carlson (1989), and T. Jacob and Tennenbaum (1988). However, assessment instruments that are sensitive to the developmental stage of children may not be easily adaptable or interpretable with families of children with disabilities.

Family relationships and environment. Self-report instruments include the Family Adaptability and Cohesion Evaluation Scales by Olson, Portner, and Lavee (1985), as used by Floyd and Saitzyk (1992), M. M. Seltzer and Krauss (1989), and Shonkoff, Hauser-Cram, Krauss, and Upshur (1992), and the Family Environment Scale (Moos & Moos, 1986), which is a primary measure for Mink's classification system (Mink et al., 1983, 1984, 1988).

Observational measures include the Home Observation for Measurement of the Environment inventory (R. H. Bradley, Rock, Caldwell, & Brisby, 1989), which involves ratings of the physical and psychosocial characteristics of the home, and the Beavers-Timberlawn system for rating family competence and family styles (Beavers, Hampson, Hulgus, & Beavers, 1986; Hampson, Hulgus, Beavers, & Beavers, 1988). Microanalytic observational measures of behavior management practices, skills training, and patterns of rewarding and aversive parent–child exchanges also are available (Baker, 1989; Floyd & Phillippe, 1993).

Sibling relationships. Siblings' reports about their relationships with a brother or sister with MR have been assessed with the Sibling Relationship Questionnaire (Furman & Buhrmester, 1985; McHale & Pawletko, 1992) and with a briefer set of rating scales that can be administered in an interview format to younger children (Gamble & McHale, 1989). Stoneman and Brody (1993) described observational procedures for evaluating the quality of interactions between siblings that occur at home.

Stress, coping, and problem solving. The Questionnaire on Resources and Stress (Holroyd, 1974) is the most comprehensive self-report measure of stressors and strains specifically associated with caring for a child with a disability. The strengths and limitations of the scale and several short-form versions have been reviewed by Glidden (1993). Research with the Ways of Coping Scale (Folkman & Lazarus, 1980) suggests that the coping styles it describes are related to adaptation for parents of children with

MR (M. M. Seltzer, 1992). Assessment of attributional style and locus of control may identify general approaches to problem solving that can lead to successful and unsuccessful coping (Frey, Greenberg, & Fewell, 1989). Family problem-solving strategies can be observed during discussions of actual family problems or during unrevealed-differences tasks (Ammerman, VanHasselt, & Hersen, 1991; Beavers et al., 1986).

Marital quality. Marital quality is one of the most important predictors of adjustment to raising a child with MR (Friedrich, 1979), yet families of children with MR rarely identify marital therapy as a need, and this domain may be ignored by clinicians working with the family. The Dyadic Adjustment Scale (Spanier, 1976), along with observations of marital problem-solving discussions, can identify both strengths and difficulties in marital relationships (Bristol et al., 1988; Floyd & Zmich, 1991). Satisfaction with shared child care (e.g., Cowan & Cowan, 1988) and the quality of the parenting alliance (S. J. Frank et al., 1991) may be important issues for some couples.

Social support and family resources. Dunst, Trivette, and Deal (1988) wrote a helpful manual for practitioners that describes several methods to assess social support and other family resources and to empower families with disabled members to use resources effectively.

Individual well-being and child adjustment. Distress, well-being, and the individual adjustment of family members also should be evaluated to identify individual needs. Relevant domains for parents include depression (Glidden et al., 1993), self-esteem (Saitzyk & Floyd, 1992), and general psychological distress (Crnic et al., 1983). Emotional distress in children with MR and their siblings may be identified using parent-report or teacher-report rating scales of behavior problems (Achenbach, 1991a, 1991b) or with self-report measures of self-esteem (Harter, 1982).

Integration of Assessment Data

The primary challenge of clinical family assessment is to combine information about individuals and subsystems into a coherent picture of the family and to identify and prioritize intervention goals. From the outset, this task is best accomplished by sharing assessment data with the family and working together to determine immediate and long-term intervention needs. The process of setting and altering priorities continues throughout the course of intervention as various problems are solved, needs are met, and new issues come to the forefront.

Treatment Considerations

Responses to Disability

Parents commonly face two major categories of challenges in adapting to a child with MR: (a) problems of meaning and acceptance, and (b) practical day-to-day adaptations to disability. Clinicians often encounter these issues only after they have become crises. When these two categories of challenge are experienced as crises, they can be categorized as an existential crisis and a reality crisis, respectively (Glidden, 1986).

Existential Crisis

The discovery that a child has MR, at birth or in early childhood, often precipitates a crisis. Unwanted news transforms normal life events such as birth or beginning school into something more dire. Some parents experience these events as traumatic and undergo sequelae of trauma similar to reactions that people have to a sudden death in the family, victimization, or other major unexpected and undesirable life events (Singer & Nixon, 1996). In their study of almost 300 mothers of children with disabilities, Breslau and Davis (1986) found that mothers with major depressive disorder reported that the first onset of depression happened at the time of birth of their child with a disability (although only a small percentage of the mothers had such a severe reaction). Glidden et al. (1993) found that initial elevations in depression for birth mothers at the time of diagnosis had decreased to levels equal to adoptive mothers 5 years later, suggesting that the initial crisis reaction had abated.

Recent work on cognitive and emotional sequelae of traumatic events indicates that victims often experience disruption of basic beliefs about life: that the world is benign, others can be trusted, and the self is valuable (Janoff-Bulman, 1992). Therapists who work with parents should take a history of the child's condition and inquire about residual cognitive and emotional responses to events surrounding the identification of the child's MR. Most parents weather this period successfully, and the therapist should not assume maladaptation, but should nonetheless invite parents to explore any unresolved feelings and threatened beliefs.

Cognitive–behavioral intervention strategies. Parents may need assistance in acknowledging and understanding feelings of grief, learning ways to modulate their responses, and developing new cognitive assumptions that take into account diagnostic information about their child (Powers, 1993). Cognitive–behavioral counseling can be effective in assisting parents to resolve cognitive and emotional turmoil associated with the perceived trauma. For example, Nixon and Singer (1993) conducted a clinical trial of cognitive–behavioral therapy for a group of parents of children with severe disabilities. They identified a group of parents who experienced unusual levels of self-blame and guilt regarding their child. Group therapy identified and challenged common assumptions about their children and their roles as parents. Treatment led to significant reductions in depressive symptoms in men and women, as well as reductions in situational guilt and negative automatic thoughts. A treatment manual is available from Nixon (1992).

Similarly, clinicians have reported the successful use of cognitive–behavioral therapies to treat mothers of children with disabilities who experienced clinical depression (Biglan, 1989; N. E. Hawkins, Singer, & Nixon, 1993; Nixon & Singer, 1993; Singer, 1993). Although there were considerable differences in their approaches, treatment consisted of a combination of cognitive reframing to promote acceptance and coping skills training to increase parents' access to enjoyable activities and social connections. Biglan's work drew on recent developments in radical behavior therapy (Hayes, 1987) that emphasized teaching counselees to assume an accepting stance toward their difficult thoughts and feelings. In this approach, the therapist assists parents' acceptance by altering the stimulus value of troubling thoughts and feelings.

N. E. Hawkins et al. (1993) reported on the use of short-term, problem-focused behavior therapy for parents. Although much of their treatment was aimed at practical problems of daily living, they also addressed clients' thoughts and feelings. Nixon and Singer (1993) used a more purely cognitive approach that focused on parents' beliefs and involved challenging irrational beliefs and encouraging group discussion and venting of emotion. Singer, Irvin, and Hawkins (1988) demonstrated that a psychoeducational group intervention that taught stress management skills to parents of children with severe MR led to significant reduction in parental depressive symptoms and anxiety. Skills included long and short forms of progressive muscle relaxation, identification of negative automatic thoughts, self-monitoring of stress-related symptoms, and use of social support to alleviate stress. A treatment manual is available from N. Hawkins and Powers (1990).

The vast majority of parents learn to accept their child's MR, often over a period of several years (Behr & Murphy, 1993). Cognitive adaptation to the child's condition may be facilitated by contacts with other parents who have been through similar experiences. Some parent-to-parent networks have staff members who specialize in the task of making appropriate matches between newer parents and more experienced helping parents (Santelli et al., 1993).

Reality Crisis

Reality crises consist of practical difficulties that some parents of children with MR encounter. Chief among these are extensive caregiving tasks, behavior problems, sleep disruption, marital discord, and restricted leisure and social opportunities (Pahl & Quine, 1987; Slater & Wikler, 1984). These problems have more to do with daily hassles and practical time constraints than with cognitive adaptation. Therapeutic intervention for these issues should focus on problem solving, skill acquisition, and mobilization of formal and informal supports.

N. E. Hawkins et al. (1993) reported on the successful use of short-term, problem-focused behavior therapy for parents of children with MR. Their intervention consisted of a thorough assessment of family problems and resources followed by a joint negotiation of goals for therapy. Counseling focused on generating practical solutions to targeted problems. Sometimes solutions involved learning new approaches, such as assertiveness skills or behavior management techniques. In other instances, the solutions involved obtaining new resources from case managers and special education teachers or from informal sources such as neighbors and extended family.

Respite care is an essential resource for many families (Salisbury & Intagliata, 1986). In a randomized treatment trial, Rimmerman (1989) found that the use of respite care was associated with reductions in parental stress for a sample of parents of children with MR. In our clinical experience, we have found that some parents need counseling before they are willing to use respite care; leaving their child with another caregiver can cause anxiety. Counseling may focus on helping parents to identify strategies to manage anxiety and to clarify needs and expectations for safe and helpful respite. Some parents may require social skills coaching to assert their needs, recruit and orient respite providers, and negotiate needed services. As with all realistic adaptations, the problem may be lack of community resources, for which parents should be encouraged to link up with other families to advocate for change.

Families often benefit from group interventions that provide support to manage existential and reality-based disability-related distress. To address these varied needs, Singer et al. (1993) implemented multiple-component family support interventions with families of children with severe disabilities. Experimental families ($N = 67$) participated in stress management classes and behavioral parent skill–building classes. They also received respite care aimed at including their children in typical community activities. This intervention was associated with significant reductions in parental depression and anxiety, as well as increased community activities for the children. In a 1-year follow-up, improvements in levels of depression and anxiety were maintained.

Shank and Turnbull (1993) reported on a group problem-solving intervention for the single parents of young children with developmental disabilities. Intervention consisted of guided discussions through the stages of interpersonal problem solving (S. L. Foster, Prinz, & O'Leary, 1983). Participation in class sessions was associated with reduction in self-reported stress and parental distress. Neither this study nor the Singer studies used a control group, so findings must be considered suggestive. However, the focus on problem-solving coaching as a methodology for assisting parents with practical problems of daily living appears worthwhile. Taken as a whole, the literature on group psychoeducational interventions suggests that some parents can benefit from practical skills training in a context that encourages parents to share experiences and coping strategies. Therapists would be well advised to become familiar with stress management and problem-solving skills training procedures in working with this population.

Group counseling is not sufficient for addressing the wide variety of concerns that individual families may present. In many cases, intensive individual and family therapy can provide important support (Marsh, 1992). Common presenting problems that may warrant more intensive intervention include marital discord, severe child behavior management problems, serious concerns about siblings and extended family relationships, and complicated conflicts with the community service system. As we noted at the outset, therapists must be receptive to identifying these concerns, and they must acquaint themselves with information regarding the impact of disability on these factors and with current methodologies for supporting families who face these problems in the context of acclimating to disability and caregiving.

Conclusion

In conclusion, in this chapter we have summarized the research on families of greatest relevance to psychologists studying or working with families who have one or more members with MR. Families differ along many dimensions, with or without the presence of MR, and this results in different service needs and different responses to the daily challenges of living in modern society. MR affects family systems in some predictable ways, the most salient of which is the participation of the family in the MR services and educational systems. The use of family assessment clarifies the most proximal supports that can be marshaled to address the interaction of MR with other variables. The effects of treatment of the individual with MR often will be mediated by the family, and the family itself will sometimes be the focus of treatment for reasons that may or may not be directly related to MR.

22

Parent Training

Bruce L. Baker

Families are central to the early development of any child, but when a child has mental retardation (MR), parenting involves an expanded commitment of time, energy, and skills. Parents of children with MR often have lifelong needs for assistance, and an array of family support services is becoming available (Singer & Powers, 1993a). These include information, diagnostic and referral services, financial supports, respite care, parent self-help groups, self-instructional books, counseling, family therapy, and parent training (Dunst, Trivette, Starnes, Hamby, & Gordon, 1993). The focus of this chapter is on parent training, although it is not always distinct from these other services.

The term *parent training* refers in general to interventions with parents that are designed to influence their children (Callias, 1987). Typically in these programs, there is a planned curriculum, service providers collaborate with parents, parents actively teach their child, child change is the primary intervention goal, and child gains are assessed. Many support, counseling, and therapy programs for parents will share some of these characteristics with parent training.

Parent training programs have been popular during the past 25 years or so as a way to expand therapeutic effectiveness and to promote generalization from clinic or school settings to the home. Programs have evolved through several stages from (a) a narrow focus on parents carrying out specific behavior change programs, to (b) a broadening of training to include education in behavior change principles (Baker, 1989), to (c) a further broadening with a family systems emphasis to address parent and family variables as mediators of outcome or as outcomes themselves (Egel & Powers, 1989; N. E. Hawkins, Singer, & Nixon, 1993).

Most of the professional literature concerns families with intellectually normal children who present behavior or conduct problems (Barkley, 1987; Forehand & McMahon, 1981; G. R. Patterson, 1982). Although these studies have informed parent training in developmental disabilities, there are important differences. One is that when a child has MR, the primary behavior change focus is skill acquisition rather than behavior problem reduction. Another is that teaching requirements continue well past the normal childhood years so that parent training must prepare the family to tackle new challenges after training has ended. Parent training will, of necessity, be different, less focused on target problem behaviors, and more concerned with assessment, understanding teaching principles, and skill building.

In this brief chapter, I primarily consider parent training for families with a child with MR. There have been a number of reviews indicating that parents can successfully intervene with a child who has MR or other developmental disabilities (e.g., Baker, 1984; Breiner & Beck, 1984; Callias, 1987; Dangel & Polster, 1984; Egel & Powers, 1989; Graziano & Diament, 1992; S. L. Harris, Alessandri, & Gill, 1991; McConachie, 1986). Although noting positive outcomes, these reviews enumerated a number of shortcomings in this literature: inadequate description of participants; lack of specificity about training and trainers; limited assessment of treatment integrity; lack of appropriate controls against which to assess outcomes; overly narrow outcome measures; inadequate assessment of maintenance; failure to program for or measure generalization; and limited attention to parent and family characteristics that affect outcome. Although there is much room for improvement and many questions are still unanswered, studies of parent training have set a promising direction for child intervention.

Programs and Outcomes

There is much diversity in parent training programs, although most have been behaviorally oriented. Training sites, foci, and demands differ. Programs meet with parents in clinics, schools, or homes. Some focus narrowly on carrying out specific skill-teaching or behavior management programs, whereas others teach general principles of behavior change that should apply in a variety of situations. Program requirements range from attending one or a few training sessions to teaching at home for hours each day over years.

Parent training is sometimes the primary service for the child and family. One illustrative program is the Portage Project, begun in rural Wisconsin and widely replicated in the United Kingdom, South America, and elsewhere (D. E. Shearer & Loftin, 1984; M. Shearer & Shearer, 1972). The child with MR is taught at home by parents, from infancy through age 6 years or so. Home visitors, at first in weekly appointments, observe teaching, give feedback, evaluate progress, plan new programs, and model teaching. The Portage Guide includes a checklist of sequenced behaviors in five skill areas (i.e., cognition, language, self-help, motor, and socialization) as well as a card file with teaching suggestions for each of the 580 behaviors included on the checklist. This curriculum guide has greatly enhanced the exportability of the program.

Parent training is sometimes integrated with therapy for the child. In the highly successful Young Autism Project at the University of California, Los Angeles (Lovass, 1987; McEachin, Smith, & Lovaas, 1993), children below the age of 3 are taught at home for 40 hr/week by student volunteers; parents observe and teach some. In one variation of this program (S. R. Anderson, 1989), a home-based teacher is present for 15 hr/week, and parents agree to teach an additional 10 hr. These programs for children with autism typically involve parents intensively for a year or more. By contrast, most programs supplement other services and make much less extensive demands on parents. Baker's (1989) Project for Developmental Disabilities group training curriculum is typical, involving parents in 10 weekly 2-hr group sessions at a center; home teaching averages about 15 min/day. Although parent training programs differ in many ways, the following five components are common.

Selecting Families

For many programs, there is an active phase of publicity and recruitment (Callias, 1987). The response will depend on whether the program is accessible to families and addresses critical family needs. Baker (1989), for example, reported high enrollment rates in lower socioeconomic Spanish-speaking families when the program was made easily accessible (e.g., bilingual staff, child care, reimbursement for transportation). Compared with mothers who did not enroll, participants perceived higher burden from the child's skill deficits, bother from behavior problems, and frustration from handling behavior problems. To the extent, though, that a program recruits and enrolls only a small proportion of eligible families, it may be less effective in garnering participation of high-risk families, and its findings may not generalize to other families.

Assessing Progress and Setting Goals

A diagnosis of the child's MR, by any definition, is not particularly relevant for program planning. What is required is a comprehensive behavioral assessment of the child's present abilities across important skill domains, as well as an assessment of conditions under which the child learns and performs best. A thorough assessment of adaptive behavior is required to establish baselines for present functioning and to suggest behaviors for intervention. Regardless of the level of cognitive functioning, the setting of goals for intervention will be based on the child's skill repertoire, opportunities to use skills in his or her everyday environment, and developmental readiness. Goals also will be determined in collaboration with the child's parents, after assessing the parents' own strengths, resources, and priorities (N. E. Hawkins et al., 1993).

Conducting Training Sessions

Parents are taught skills necessary to implement behavior change. These may include a general set of behavioral teaching skills, including applications of reinforcement, punishment, shaping, prompting, fading, chaining, and related procedures. If training does not take place at home, the program also will need to include procedures for generalization of parent teaching and child behavior to the home. Training sessions involve active learning and use a combination of techniques to teach parents: individual consultation, lectures to groups, discussions, videotape modeling, live demonstrations, role playing, and supervised teaching.

The most common training format is individual consultation, which usually involves having the child present. A professional counsels, instructs, and models; parents teach and receive feedback. There may be a general curriculum, but it is flexible and the number of sessions varies within some broad limits. Less common, primarily because of logistics, are parent training groups. In contrast to more open-ended support groups, these training groups generally follow a specified curriculum. Most typically, groups enroll from 5 to 10 families, with one or two leaders. Most group programs meet weekly for six to ten 2-hr sessions, long enough to provide basic instruction and help parents get teaching programs under way, but not so long as to end by attrition. Most group training also includes some follow-up (Baker, 1989). Individual consultation would seem to have the advantage of most directly addressing each family's needs (M. R. Reese & Serna, 1986). Yet, group training holds the promise of greater cost-effectiveness for agencies and social support benefits for parents. Despite these speculations, studies contrasting the two approaches typically have found them to be equally effective (Brightman, Baker, Clark, & Ambrose, 1982; Christensen, Johnson, Phillips, & Glasgow, 1980; Kovitz, 1976; Salzinger, Feldman, & Portnoy, 1970).

There have been numerous comparisons of training content. Although some of these studies have indicated that the writer's own variant or addition to training is more effective, there have been virtually no reports of replication. Several that seem reasonable are demonstrations of enhanced child outcome when parents were formally taught social learning principles as well as specific behavioral techniques (McMahon, Forehand, & Griest, 1981) or when adjunctive treatment focused on parents' personal and marital adjustment (Griest et al., 1982).

Assigning Homework

Because parent training programs are aimed at modifying child behavior, parents are asked to implement assessment and teaching at home between sessions. Parents are involved in setting homework goals, which vary considerably across programs and families; these should be tailored to what the particular parents want to do and can do. Homework (e.g., results of carrying out a teaching program) is reviewed during the next session. Many programs also ask parents to read handouts prepared by the program leaders or a self-instructional book (Baker & Brightman, 1989; J. Carr, 1980; Hanson, 1987; Lovaas et al., 1980; G. R. Patterson, 1977; G. R. Patterson & Gullion, 1976).

Evaluating Outcome

Is parent training effective? Staff in every program address this inescapable question somehow, if only through informal discussions with one an-

Table 1. Did the Program Work? Some Criteria for Evaluating a Parent Training Program

1. Social validity: Do parents find the goals and the methods of the program worthwhile?
2. Enrollment: Do parents enroll in the program?
3. Completion: Do parents maintain good attendance?
4. Participation: Do parents become engaged in the program and carry out homework?
5. Consumer satisfaction: Do parents express satisfaction with the program?
6. Proficiency: Do parents learn what the program aims to teach?
7. Child gains: Do children show demonstrable gains?
8. Generalization of child gains: Do child gains generalize across settings? To nontargeted behaviors?
9. Maintenance of child gains: Do child gains last?
10. Maintenance of teaching: Do parents continue to put what they learned into practice at home months or years later?
11. Family benefits: Are there beneficial changes in the parents' well-being or in the family system?
12. Advocacy: Do parents become better advocates for their child's education?

Note. From *Parent training and developmental disabilities* (p. 12), by B. L. Baker, 1989, Washington, DC: American Association on Mental Retardation. Copyright 1989 by the American Association on Mental Retardation. Reprinted with permission.

other. Many programs, however, take a more formal look, and no single measure or perspective on the question suffices. Table 1 shows some of the ways that this question can be addressed. One issue for service providers is the utility of outcome assessment, or how this can be done with minimum investment of staff and parent time. Measures with high utility include paper-and-pencil measures of parents' satisfaction with the program (Baker, 1989; Forehand & McMahon, 1981), parents' knowledge of program content (Baker, 1989; O'Dell, Tarler-Benlolo, & Flynn, 1979), and children's behavior change.

One limitation is that outcome criteria are typically not chosen in collaboration with parents. Hence, for example, a family classified as a "failure" by a researcher's criterion of carrying out long-term teaching might actually classify themselves as a "success" by their own primary criterion of feeling more competent to handle problems that arise. In current practice, parents are becoming more involved in the determination of program outcome goals for themselves (Singer & Powers, 1993a); however, in program evaluations, measures continue to be uniform across families.

Who Benefits From Parent Training?

Parent training formats rarely produce different group outcomes. Yet, within any program, some families show gratifying gains, whereas others improve slightly or not at all. These two findings, of small variability between formats and large variability within them, suggest that the critical question is, Which participants benefit? However, even when predictive studies reveal group differences, they are not yet a firm basis for making clinical decisions about the value of parent training for a given family.

Although clinical experience suggests that highly dysfunctional families with children with MR are less likely to be successful in parent training (Petronko, Harris, & Kormann, 1994), there has been little study of how parent and family adjustment relate to outcome. One study assessed families a year after group parent training ended (Baker, Landen, & Kashima, 1991). Parents doing more teaching at follow-up had entered training with generally better adjustment, as evidenced by lower stress, higher marital adjustment, and greater satisfaction with family functioning. Studies of parent training with children with conduct disorders have shown parental depression (Webster-Stratton & Hammond, 1990), and single-parent status or marital conflict (Dumas, 1984; Webster-Stratton & Hammond, 1990) is predictive of poorer outcome.

More commonly, studies have related child characteristics and family socioeconomic status (SES) to outcome. Children with more severe retardation have, not unexpectedly, shown fewer gains on standardized measures (Barna, Bidder, Gray, Clements, & Gardner, 1980; Brassell, 1977). This may be due to reduced parental teaching efforts, but it is more logically due to the child's lower learning rate or ability. If child targets and outcome criteria are individualized, however, gains can be demonstrated regardless of extent of disability. Moreover, parent outcomes (e.g., behavioral skills, follow-through) have not related to the child characteristics of age, sex, diagnosis, or level of MR (Baker et al., 1991; Clark & Baker, 1983).

Much of the literature on parent training is based on middle-class families. Families designated as lower SES have been less likely to join (Hargis & Blechman, 1979) and complete (McMahon, Forehand, Griest, & Wells, 1981; Sadler, Seyden, Howe, & Kaminsky, 1976) parent training programs, as well as less likely to fulfill programming objectives, such as carrying out programs (Rinn, Vernon, & Wise, 1975) or producing child change (Brassell, 1977; Sadler et al., 1976). They have also been less likely to achieve competency levels at posttraining (Clark & Baker, 1983), which helps to explain other findings of less successful programming. Some parent trainers have increased program accessibility to lower SES and minority families by reducing class, culture, and language barriers (Prieto-Bayard & Baker, 1986; Rueda & Martinez, 1992). Others have minimized SES as an outcome predictor by adaptations in program content, such as following a competency-based program in which parents can proceed at their own pace (T. R. Rogers, Forehand, Griest, Wells, & McMahon, 1981) or emphasizing modeling and supervised teaching (Hudson, 1982; Prieto-Bayard & Baker, 1986).

Issues in Parent Training: Looking to the Future

The challenge for professionals who work with families is to adapt parent training to changing times while still maintaining what has proved effective. As a life span perspective is realized in a genuine continuum of services, parent training must find its best place.

Critical Period for Parent Training?

Is there an ideal time in the family life cycle (Carter & McGoldrick, 1989) for parents of a child with a developmental disability to enroll in a parenting program? Stated differently, where in the continuum of services does parent training most comfortably sit? There appear to be three critical, but not exclusive, periods, each with a different objective. During the child's infancy, parents are coming to terms with their child's disability (Blacher, 1984). Early intervention parent programs usually have a strong component of support, often from a group format. The demands on parents are typically few and flexible, emphasizing activities that facilitate developmental progress (Hayden & Haring, 1976).

During the preschool and school years, many parents want guidance in how best to teach their child. Parent training is legally mandated in federally funded preschool programs (under the Individuals with Disabilities Education Act, Pub. L. No. 101–476). Most programs are skill oriented, focusing on early development in self-help, speech and language, cognitive, or social skills. On the basis of clinical experience, it appears that most parents will do active systematic teaching on a daily basis only for a year or so (if for that long). This argues for an emphasis on more incidental teaching, on components to encourage parental persistence more explicitly, and on timing.

When is the best time for an intensive program? In most cases, this will be during the preschool years. With problem behaviors, Dishion and Patterson (1992) found that parent training was equally effective with preschool- or kindergarten-age children as with school-age ones but that fewer families of the younger children dropped out of training. The preschool years are a normative time in the life cycle of families to focus on child skill development. Following a period of intensive training, an integrated school–home program may strike the best balance of efforts while promoting maximum generalization and maintenance of parental instruction (C. E. Cunningham, Bremner, & Secord-Gilbert, 1993; Evans, Okifuji, Engler, Bromley, & Tishelman, 1993; Sandler & Coren, 1981). Better research is needed on critical periods for intensive training and best practices for school and parents to work together at this time.

During late adolescence and the transition to adulthood, parental concerns become more future oriented. As the child "ages out" of funded schooling, issues of long-term housing, employment, social relationships, and financial planning can weigh heavily. Services for parents at this stage are not so much oriented toward imparting skills as providing information and guidance. Many parents seek support in helping their son or daughter to develop social relationships, understand sexuality, resolve conflicts, and cope with the myriad demands of more independent living. Some who wish to keep their child in the family home seek behavior management skills to alleviate pressures for placement, whereas others who are moving toward placement seek guidance on how to remain meaningfully involved. There is a priority need here for innovative program development and evaluation.

Father Involvement

Parent training programs and research have almost exclusively focused on mothers. Although fathers are welcome in most programs, little is known about their participation in training and the benefits of training to them and to the family (Coplin & Houts, 1991). Researchers who have examined the "new father" of the late 20th century find that he is more involved in child rearing, but still primarily limited to the domains of engagement (e.g., playing with the child) and accessibility (e.g., being nearby to watch the child; Lamb, 1985). Attending parent training sessions and systematic home teaching seems to fall more under responsibility (making primary arrangements for child care and well-being), a domain that remains almost exclusively the mother's, even in families in which she is working full time (Lamb, 1985).

Meyer (1985) argued that increasing paternal involvement means attending to staff attitudes, treatment accessibility, and program content. Staff members must acknowledge fathers as important—sending them information, expecting them to be involved, and including male staff with whom they can relate. There must be scheduling flexibility to accommodate both working fathers and mothers, as their involvement is greater in evening programs. Most programs deal with issues of greater relevance and interest to mothers. They also should explore fathers' needs because there is evidence that these differ from those expressed by mothers (D. B. Bailey, Blasco, & Simeonsson, 1992).

However, is involving fathers beneficial? In studies in which researchers assigned some families to mother-only and some to mother-and-father conditions, father involvement made no difference in measured outcomes (Adesso & Lipson, 1981; Firestone, Kelly, & Fike, 1980; J. P. Martin, 1977). All these studies involved children of normal intelligence, however. It is possible that paternal involvement may be more crucial in families in which a child has MR, although this has not been demonstrated (Baker, 1989).

There may, however, be benefits to fathers themselves from participation, especially if the program is designed to meet their needs. McBride (1991a, 1991b) described a group program specifically designed for fathers and their preschool children. Relative to waiting-list controls, participating fathers reported decreased stress, increased parenting competence, and greater involvement with the child on three dimensions: interaction, accessibility, and responsibility.

Maintenance and Generalization

For parent training to have a truly meaningful impact, outcomes should generalize over time (maintenance), across settings (e.g., from the clinic to home or school), and perhaps beyond the specific child behaviors addressed in the program. In a classic article, Stokes and Baer (1977) outlined a technology for generalization, urging behavior therapists to abandon the unsuccessful "train and hope" strategy and actively promote generalization (e.g., train sufficient exemplars, train loosely, introduce to natural maintaining contingencies). That same year, Forehand and Atkeson (1977) noted how little generalization was planned for or assessed in parent training.

Since then, there has been considerable emphasis on evaluating long-term maintenance, with follow-ups of at least several months being almost mandatory. One year following training, parents of children with MR had maintained and were still using their behavioral skills (Baker, Heifetz, & Murphy, 1980) and 4–7 years after training most parents of children with autism were still using behavioral techniques (S. L. Harris, 1986). In both of these follow-ups, however, parents were more likely to be doing incidental teaching than conducting formal behavior modification procedures with data recording.

There also has been attention given to generalization of parental use of behavioral techniques and of child behavioral change from the training setting to another setting. Although this has been sporadic when it was not systematically programmed for (Cordisco, Strain, & Depew, 1988; Dadds, Sanders, & James, 1987), parents have generalized well when training included techniques such as written prompts to use in the generalization settings (Powers, Singer, Stevens, & Sowers, 1992). M. R. Reese and Serna (1986) proposed that individualized education plans should be adapted to parent training programs, covering individual family needs, generalization of parenting skills across settings, and reinforcement of trained skills in the natural environment.

One approach developed by Sanders and Dadds (1982, 1987) to promote generalization is *planned activities training* (PAT). PAT is more informal, focusing on naturally occurring events in the home and emphasizing antecedent behaviors. Guidelines are provided for what to do when engaging in a wide range of activities, such as traveling in the car, shopping, or eating at restaurants. Several studies with parents of children with developmental disabilities have indicated that PAT facilitates setting generalization (Harrold, Lutzker, Campbell, & Touchette, 1992; Sanders & Plant, 1989). Finally, although there is some evidence for child response generalization, with gains demonstrated in nontargeted behaviors (Baker, 1989; Ducharme & Popynick, 1993), child behaviors typically have not been assessed broadly enough to determine whether response generalization occurred.

There has been little study in parent training for developmental disabilities of what Griest and Forehand (1982) called *family generalization*—changes in parents' personal and marital adjustment or extrafamilial interactions when the focus of treatment is on parent–child behavior. Parents who teach their children more effectively may experience positive changes (e.g., in their stress levels, attitudes about the child's capabilities, and sense of competence in the parenting role). Perhaps family members will communicate with each other and with the school more effectively, and perhaps siblings will benefit indirectly. Some special educators, however, have posited generalized negative effects. They caution that asking parents to carry out specific program activities may impose additional stress on the family (Gallagher, Beckman, & Cross, 1983) or that parents in the role of teacher often feel uncomfortable and may become frustrated with the child's progress (Allen & Hudd, 1987). Perhaps the parent–child relationship could be disturbed or the perceived burden of raising a child with disabilities could be increased by training (H. A. Benson & Turnbull, 1986). Family members relate to each other emotionally as well as didactically, and intervention that leads to too intensive concentration on the latter may inadvertently seem to diminish the importance or value of the former.

Although these are important concerns, the limited empirical evidence indicates positive family generalization after parent training for child conduct problems (Anastopoulos, Shelton, DuPaul, & Guevremont, 1993; Pisterman et al., 1992; Webster-Stratton, 1990) and for developmental disabilities (N. E. Hawkins et al., 1993; R. L. Koegel, Schriebman, Johnson, O'Neill, & Dunlap, 1984; Nixon & Singer, 1993; Powers et al., 1992). In one individual clinic and home-based program, parents of children with autism reported greater time teaching, less time in caretaking, and more family recreation relative to an untrained control group (R. L. Koegel et al., 1984). A study of family generalization following group parent training focused on adjustment variables that previous researchers had found were affected by a disability in the family: depression, stress, and satisfaction with the family (Baker et al., 1991). On all three dimensions, there was a significant improvement in adjustment following training.

A recent emphasis is to broaden the goals and content of parent training beyond teaching the target child, in an attempt to affect family members' individual and collective functioning. Program goals include, for example, improving parents' positive self-regard, problem solving, self-control, interpersonal communication, achievement of personal goals or extent of self-blame (Gammon & Rose, 1991; N. E. Hawkins et al., 1993; Nixon & Singer, 1993). Some of these are potential mediators of effective child management, whereas others may be important ends in and of themselves.

Practitioners must be careful, however, to distinguish between sensitivity to family system variables and re-creating the family pathologizing that, in the past, led professionals to recommend therapy when parents simply asked for guidance. If programs for parents embrace broadened goals, therapists need to continue study of the distresses or needs of families with a child with MR. For example, if a program is designed to focus on enhancing positive self-regard, it seems important first to ascertain whether the particular target families have less positive self-regard than others. Even establishing group differences is still not sufficient for recommending services for any given family (A. P. Turnbull & Turnbull, 1986). Moreover, it is important that professionals acknowledge and build on family strengths. Although a child with MR heightens family stress, there also are positive benefits to some families that have seldom been noted by professionals (Summers, Behr, & Turnbull, 1989; A. P. Turnbull et al., 1993).

Conclusion

In summary, it is essential that program evaluations continue as parent training is adapted to meet changing priorities and changes in the service system. MR is, in part, a social construct, and as such, this field is particularly apt to be influenced by changing social, philosophical, and institutional pressures. Professionals with an empirical orientation are often taken aback at how the practices promoted at any given time may be more the result of what policy makers think should be done than those indicated by systematic study. This leaves the field particularly vulnerable to overlooking validated practices while advocating for unproved ones. It is essential that, as the view of families and family needs evolves, intervention programs continue to build on what has been learned and that they are held up to the highest standards of empirical validation.

23

Sexuality and Sexual Development

Denise Valenti-Hein and Jason R. Dura

Wide discussion of sexual expression for people with mental retardation (MR) is a relatively recent occurrence. Even more recent is abandonment of the notion that sexual expression by people with MR should be classed as "problem behavior." In 1988, sex education was federally mandated for all people with MR residing in public residential facilities. In 1991, the American Association on Mental Retardation formed a special interest group on social and sexual issues. Numerous programs and materials are now available for people with MR that help to channel normal sexual drive into adaptive and functional sexual expression. Increased efforts are being made to provide people with MR with the information they need and the opportunities they desire to establish meaningful social and sexual lives.

Psychologists have traditionally served in a behavioral programming capacity regarding sexuality. The task was usually to eliminate maladaptive, disrupting, or offending behavior rather than to cultivate appropriate sexuality. This approach can be seen as one that ignores the needs of the client who is using sexual acting out as an inappropriate means toward an appropriate end. Recently, psychologists have developed and administered programs that support the client by providing accurate information and promoting the rights of sexual expression. This approach also may be a disservice because clients frequently returned to caretakers and environments that did not support their newly acquired behaviors. For this reason, we feel that a systems approach is the most appropriate means to address the sexuality of people with MR. This systems approach takes into account both the client and the social environment in which he or she lives.

We begin this chapter by discussing support of people with MR via appropriate assessment and treatment approaches. Next, we examine how caretakers can be incorporated into the process in order to work with rather than against the goal of supporting sexuality. Finally, we discuss how psychologists can support the systems and communities in which the client interacts by helping to write policies and advocate for the needs of this population.

Supporting the Individual Client

Sexuality and Clients With MR

Studies regarding the biological bases of sexuality suggest that individuals functioning in the mild-to-moderate range of MR show secondary sexual development similar to that of their intellectually average peers (Deisher, 1973). Those in the lower ranges of functioning develop these characteristics as well, but at a slower pace. Similarly, research from a health clinic has shown 50% of adolescent girls with mild MR and 30% of adolescent girls with moderate MR had been sexually active (Chamberlain, Rauth, Passer, McGrath, & Burket, 1984).

Research regarding nonbiological aspects of sexual development is less available; however, it is clear that people with MR are sexual beings and regard themselves as such (Heshusius, 1982). They actively seek out sexual education and opportunities for sexual expression, yet they vary widely in their attitudes regarding dating, marriage, intercourse, pregnancy, masturbation, and homosexuality (Edmonson, McCombs, & Wish, 1979). Knowledge about each of these topics also varies considerably. For example, although Edmonson et al. (1979) found individuals in their sample to be reasonably well informed, they also found specific weakness in knowledge regarding birth control and sexually transmitted disease.

What clients do know about sexuality is paramount to their ability to make informed decisions about their own sexual expression, and their ability to consent is at the core of many current debates regarding sexuality in this population. Consent defines whether a relationship is abusive. It is a topic central to understanding the expression of sexuality in people with MR and one that is central to providing intervention services for problems related to sexuality.

Assessing Sexuality: The Ability to Consent

Most clinicians would agree that if they do not apply the legal standard of guardianship to determine ability to consent to sexuality, they need to specify explicit rules to determine consensual sex. We discuss two sets of rules that have been proposed. One was developed to determine consent for both verbal and nonverbal individuals. The other is an adaptation of the assessment of informed consent for treatment developed by Planned Parenthood.

A liberal approach has been suggested by Kaeser (1991). This approach stipulates that if clients are engaging in behavior that does not endanger themselves or others and does not appear to be coercive (i.e., involving the use of force or threat of force), then it is consensual. This approach bases nonconsent on danger alone and does not consider the amount of knowledge or ability to judge actions or the consequences of actions. As such, it suggests that a client can consent without any factual basis for his or her response. This rule reduces consent to the absence of coercion and, thus, many have found it unacceptable.

A better way to determine informed consent, referred to as the BRAIDED model, was developed by Dollar and Billie (1983) to meet federal, state, and Planned Parenthood's requirements regarding consent to treatment. This approach stipulates that clients are able to consent if they can articulate and demonstrate decision making. Although initially used to determine consent to treatment (e.g., the administration of birth control), the main aspects of the model are adapted easily to decisions about consensual sexual behavior. The aspects that are crucial to the process of consent are identified by the acronym BRAIDED. If clients can list the benefits, risks, and alternative forms of sexuality, if they can make inquiries about the topic, arrive at a decision, and understand the explanations, and if the decision can be documented, they are presumed to be competent to engage in the form of sexual behavior under discussion.

One ambitious study to investigate the ability to consent was conducted by Morris and Niederbuhl (1992). They evaluated all clients on a residential ward using the Socio-Sexual Knowledge and Attitudes Test (Wish, McCombs, & Edmonson, 1980), along with a team staffing approach. They found that the majority of clients with mild MR could consent to sexual activity. When they could not, it was because of cognitive deficits associated with secondary psychiatric diagnoses. Individuals with moderate MR were usually unable to consent. Those with lower than moderate cognitive functioning were found to be unable to consent. Similarly, Morris, Niederbuhl, and Mahr (1993), using a structured interview method, replicated the finding of inability to provide informed consent for individuals with MR levels below the mild range. The method for determining informed consent, as described by Morris et al. (1993), produced an interrater kappa coefficient of .79. As opportunities for sexual expression for people with disabilities expand, a similar expansion in information about reliable methods of defining consent and determining ability to provide consent is needed.

Assessing Sexuality: Sexual Abuse

Being able to assess consent is crucial because many states define sexual abuse in this population by whether consent has occurred. Even when a client has not consented or has been unable to consent, the diagnostic skills of a clinician are still required to assess sexual abuse. Recent cases (e.g., *New Jersey v. Schwerzer, Schwerzer, Grober & Archer*, 1993) have drawn attention to the difficulty in obtaining reliable reports and the even greater difficulty in prosecuting these cases. Competency to be a witness to their own crime is frequently questioned (Valenti-Hein & Schwartz, 1993). Problems in report consistency, tainting of cases by inappropriate or leading questions, difficulty in communication, the disproportionate balance of power, and stress from the investigation process all complicate the investigations. This is further compounded by different societies' myths about people with MR that serve to devalue crimes committed against them. "They won't know what happened anyway" or "Mentally retarded people aren't sexually attractive so why would someone do something like that?" are examples of discounting myths (S. Cole, 1988).

In an effort to deal with some of these many issues, Valenti-Hein and Schwartz (1994) developed a protocol that uses multiple media and developmentally appropriate language to elicit more consistent reports of sexual activity that may indicate abuse. The Sexual Abuse Interview for the Developmentally Disabled (SAIDD) is designed to build rapport while determining developmental language levels. As with intellectually average children, adults with MR have differing abilities to understand and communicate information about concepts such as identification of people, places, or times. Thus, ability levels are first obtained by asking about nonthreatening events. Once the types of questions that a client can answer have been determined, the client is queried about the alleged incident in a manner consistent with these abilities. Because the exact questions are read to the client, there is little chance of asking questions in a leading or inappropriate manner. In addition to determining information for prosecution purposes, the SAIDD also can be used to determine treatment and training needs.

Although there is no empirical evidence regarding the SAIDD interview procedure, preliminary research with the protocol with 50 individuals with mild-to-moderate cognitive functioning suggests that the majority of clients demonstrate an ability to report consistently on people, places, and times. Moreover, the ability to describe events parallels the client's level of cognitive disability established by intelligence testing.

Sexuality Training and Treatment

Sexuality intervention in individuals with MR should proceed from relatively innocuous and simple approaches to progressively stronger interventions.[1] The first step, giving permission to determine how sexuality can be expressed, occurs as soon as the client is allowed to discuss sexuality in an open format. Without first agreeing that sexual expression is allowed at a facility, other interventions will have limited value. In most cases, however, the person with MR also will need information. Typically, this is provided by a sexuality educator using his or her own techniques or a commercially available training program.

Although several training programs in sexuality currently exist for individuals with MR, few are supported by research data on effectiveness. Those that have been studied, such as Valenti-Hein and Mueser's (1990) Dating Skills Program and Foxx and McMorrow's (1983) Stacking the Deck, provide relatively simple, short-term training. Two studies regarding the effectiveness of the Dating Skills Program (Mueser, Valenti-Hein, & Yarnold, 1987; Valenti-Hein, Yarnold, & Mueser, 1994) indicated that clients

[1]This section essentially follows the PLISSIT model. (PLISSIT is an acronym for permission giving, limited information, specific skills, and intensive therapy.)

who participated in the Dating Skills Program improved on several Likert rating scales based on client participation in six social problem-solving role plays relevant to dating. In particular, Dating Skills Program clients were rated as more physically attractive after participation in these groups and were rated more attractive than clients in control groups or in other treatment programs such as the use of relaxation to reduce social anxiety. In addition, clients in the Dating Skills Program demonstrated significantly more interactions with the opposite sex during break periods. Foxx and McMorrow (1983) found that clients who were trained using the Stacking the Deck procedure, which employed social and sexual skills, were able to increase appropriate responses to the problem questions over time. Moreover, they were able to generalize these responses to an interaction with a confederate outside of the training sessions. Many individuals may benefit from such programs, but there are others who will need more intensive work.

More intensive approaches may include the training of specific skills. It also may require therapy to deal with sexual offenders and abuse victims. Several methods have been developed for teaching specific skills, such as instructing how to masturbate (Dura & Nunemaker, 1993) or how to provide sexual pleasure to a partner and how to fantasize (Garwick, Jurkowski, & Valenti-Hein, 1993). Therapy techniques to deal with inappropriate sexual behavior also have been pioneered (Griffiths, Hingsburger, & Christian, 1985). Many of these techniques are controversial (e.g., the use of Depo-Provera), and others (e.g., the use of aversives) have their own areas of debate when used with those who have MR (Jacobson, 1993). These approaches deserve further study.

Whether a standardized program is chosen or one decides to develop an individualized program, there are some general guidelines to selection and practice. First and foremost, sexuality training must be adapted to the client's ability, but available to everyone. Individuals with profound MR can learn names for sexual body parts so that they have a receptive, if not expressive, understanding. Similarly, everyone can learn the importance of privacy by closing the door to bathrooms when they are in use. Sexuality training must contain information about positive, as well as negative, aspects of sexuality. Most important, sexuality training must specifically train ability to weigh alternatives, make choices, and put these choices into practice. Without this, therapists are not teaching sexuality, but morality. To be effective, sexuality training must be consistently supported across all members of a team. Similarly, sexuality training must be supported by the milieu to avoid encouraging behavior that violates group norms.

Supporting Caregivers

Regardless of the client's level of MR or living arrangement, response to his or her sexual feelings and behavior can be paramount. Of interest is the finding by Edmonson et al. (1979) that most clients hold negative attitudes regarding sexual expression. This is perhaps attributable to predominantly negative themes offered in sex education (Garwick et al., 1993), or it may be due to implicit messages transmitted by instructors conducting sex education. Caregivers are faced with responding to the client's sexual expression, and this response will have important consequences to the client's view of himself or herself and sexuality.

Parents

In community settings, sexual expression is most often influenced by parents. A smattering of research on parents' attitudes regarding sexual expression by their offspring who have MR similarly suggests several common concerns. Parents frequently worry that others will take advantage of their offspring sexually, that training will condone sexuality, that their offspring will be unable to parent, and that they will have genetically inferior children. Meetings with parents regarding sexual expression of their offspring prior to sexuality training have been conducted using individual and group approaches (Dura & Nunemaker, 1993; Pendler & Hingsburger, 1991). In both cases, the goal is to provide a forum for discussing concerns, along with content and rationale for training.

Intervention is often sought by parents in response to ongoing sexual behavior. When this is the case, the concern that sex education may cause sexual behavior is moot. Intervention then is discussed with regard to channeling preexisting sexual desires into safe and acceptable outlets. Barnes (1984) provided a brief, well-written account of her experiences as a mother dealing with her developmentally delayed daughter's sexuality, and this article can be a valuable resource when given to parents faced with their own offspring's sexuality.

It is important to recognize that many of the concerns that parents have are highly meaningful to them. For therapeutic reasons, it is necessary that parents become allies in this process. They must not be dealt with by minimization of their concerns or by merely teaching the "right way" to view sexuality in their offspring with MR. This will only create alienation. One way to create allies among parents is to ask them to list what they would like to have learned before dating. The list is usually enlightening and will indicate the nature of information and values the parents received while growing up. This list is then used to create a whole-person concept of sexuality. For example, education about menstruation can be viewed broadly as a hygiene issue. Wanting to know how to afford dates can be viewed as money management. Not feeling jealous about a girlfriend who is dating someone else can be seen as anger management. How to say no to a boyfriend can be viewed as assertiveness training. Few parents object to teaching concepts regarding sexuality when they are incorporated into more general training issues. When sexuality is viewed as a personal identity issue that surpasses specific body parts and activities, it becomes a matter of accepting the person.[2]

---

[2]This exercise is also useful in helping parents to empathize with their offsprings' confusion. For example, one mother was asked to imagine how she would feel if she were not told about menstruation before its onset. She was immediately able to see that her adolescent son's distress about having "wet the bed" was in part the result of not discussing the normal occurrence of wet dreams in male puberty.

Direct-Care Staff

In residential settings, direct-care staff are responsible for assisting individuals with MR in satisfying their needs and desires. Unfortunately, many professionals involved in sexual education advocate for the sexual expression of people with MR with little regard for the feelings and beliefs of direct-care staff who must assist the clients (Sumarah, Maksym, & Goudges, 1988). Research has consistently indicated that direct-care staff often have repressive attitudes with regard to the sexual expression of people with MR (Chapman & Pitceathly, 1985; Mulhern, 1975; E. J. Saunders, 1979; Trudel & Desjardins, 1992). Reiterations of dicta that supporting sexual expression contributes to personal growth and life satisfaction and is a job responsibility are neither effective nor well received.

Some professionals in the field of sexuality create programs with different levels of staff comfort in mind. Dura and Nunemaker (1993), in their book on masturbation training for men with MR, offered staff two levels of prompting that may be used in response to public masturbation. First, they suggested that staff who are uncomfortable with sexual issues prompt the client back to a private area and then direct him to a masturbation kit that is designed to cue the client through masturbation and clean up. Staff who are more comfortable with issues of sexuality are directed to verbally prompt the client back to a private area, to suggest that he undress, and to prompt him as to the availability of the masturbation kit. The kit provides a helpful resource to relieve staff of the uncomfortable situation of detailed verbal prompting. Dura and Nunemaker have reported this to be an effective methodology.

In addition to programming that incorporates sensitivity to staff needs, staff training must be an ongoing activity. Within the field of developmental disabilities, this training offers a significant opportunity to achieve fundamental changes in staff attitudes about sexual expression for people with MR. Evidence suggests that direct care staff attitudes can change in response to training (Brantlinger, 1983; Sumarah et al., 1988). Frequent exposure to accurate information regarding sexuality and disability can help change staff attitudes in many ways. First, it allows staff to understand their own beliefs and, thus, personal limitations in being able to help clients develop their own sexuality. It also serves to desensitize and educate staff, putting them at ease with a traditionally taboo topic about which all people hold some inaccurate information. Finally, it informs staff that administrators (not just sex educators) believe that these concepts are important for their clients to learn.

Supporting Systems

Rights Regarding Sexual Expression

Another way to communicate administrative opinions is via statements regarding the right to sexual expression. Given the discrepancy in opinions and approaches regarding the sexuality of people with MR, the important question to ask is, Who should determine the rights to sexuality of those with MR? Traditionally, this decision has been made by caretakers. In more recent history, advocacy groups have formulated policy agendas that include promoting sexuality as a basic human right. An excellent example of this can be seen in the work of the Illinois Association for Retarded Citizens, an advocacy group that developed a statement of human rights 6 years ago and has advocated the adoption of these rights in the policies of service providers.

The rights they listed include the following:

1. The right to dignity and respect as a total human being, which includes recognition as a sexual being.
2. The right to a positive self-image.
3. The right to be allowed natural contacts with members of the opposite sex.
4. The right to be given necessary sexual information at every age level in a manner that can be understood.
5. The right to be relieved of threats, guilt, and misinformation.
6. The right to be protected from sexual exploitation.
7. The right to be involved in an honest, sensitive, and realistic way in decisions affecting him or her.
8. The right to his or her feelings, be they anger, sexual, or other.
9. The right to appropriate expression of thoughts, feelings, and behavior.
10. The right to live within real limitations and to his or her maximum potential.
11. The right to make mistakes. These are valuable learning experiences.

Although the goal has been to affect policy and, therefore, the lives of people with MR, these effects are far from being realized. A recent survey of Illinois service providers on policies regarding sexual abuse suggested that few agencies provided formal guidance on the right to be protected from sexual exploitation, which is perhaps the least controversial area of sexual rights (Valenti-Hein, 1993). When issues regarding sexual expression arise, even less guidance is provided in policies. Because psychologists typically serve on human rights committees, they have a unique opportunity to impact on systems by their involvement in the writing of policies.

Development of Policy and Procedures

The procedure whereby a model policy can be developed by a committee within each community agency often includes the participation of staff psychologists. The development of a policy is an educational event that, albeit time-consuming and at times painful, is a worthwhile endeavor. It provides for the development of a core group of individuals who are familiar with the specifics of sexual education and often includes the cooperative development of training materials and the delineation of training responsibilities.

As defined here, policy and procedures are two separate, but connected, components. The policy is a brief general statement of philosophy regarding sexual expression. Procedures are a detailed outline of issues and actions whereby the global policy statement is implemented.

In studying the origins of policy statements, Dura (1993) found that most reiterate citizens' rights in the arena of sexual expression. The writers commonly spoke of promoting the individual as a complete person with sexual expression recognized as an important component of life. Frequently, policies include a statement of particular rights, including rights to sexual expression, privacy, information regarding sexuality, self-direction, and choice of marital status, gender preference, and procreation.

Multiple formats also are possible in the detailing of procedures. These include use of narratives, flowcharts, numbered points, and inclusion of forms. A comprehensive procedures section should address a wide variety of topics related to sex education, sexual preference, hygiene, sexual expression, protection from sexual abuse, socialization, and what constitutes inappropriate sexual behavior. Policies should include references to both staff and client behavior.

For each item, a definition of the topic being discussed and specification of staff response are needed. Both immediate responses (i.e., answering questions regarding sexuality in a forthright manner) and longer term responses (i.e., referring the individual for consideration for sexual education training) should be outlined. If the responsibilities of the staff vary regarding the incident (i.e., direct care staff report the situation to the program manager who then reports to the habilitation team), each role should be clearly defined.

As with sex education, how policies and procedures are written convey something about the sentiments of the writers regarding the topic. What is omitted becomes as important as what is included. Do policies about sexuality vary with age or level of client ability? Is sexuality listed among the statements on human rights, or is it listed among issues related to discipline? An articulate and accepted policy statement is the first crucial step toward advocacy for the client as a unique individual.

Advocacy

The building of an ethos that supports sexuality includes creating an atmosphere that promotes appropriate expression while destigmatizing people with disabilities. Even when policies are implemented, staff are trained, and clients are informed, there needs to be an appropriate setting for behavior to occur.

Creating an atmosphere that promotes appropriate sexuality requires only a few modest changes in the milieu. The provision of personal space is a priority. Some agencies provide private rooms, but many others find that it is more economical to have one or two privacy rooms that can be used by all clients on an individual basis. Opportunities for socialization also are needed. These can be in the form of dances or other social activities that encourage interaction. Other changes also can serve to enhance the environment to encourage appropriate outlets for sexuality (Valenti-Hein, 1991).

Destigmatization involves exposing the community at large to new ways of viewing individuals with MR. A good example of how images can be effective in altering attitudes can be seen in the work of Gorman-Smith (1991). By exposing first-year university students to one of two movies (a behavior modification film of people with severe MR and severe behavioral problems or a "60 Minutes" report about a married couple with MR living in the community), she was able to alter perceptions significantly. Participants who saw the behavior modification movie were less likely to see people with MR as competent. Those who saw the community living movie were more likely to view people with MR as capable individuals. Thus, images that challenge the stereotypical views of individuals with MR can contribute to attitude changes consistent with greater support of the human rights of people with MR.

Conclusion

In terms of alleviating inappropriate constraints on sexual expression, psychologists are now faced with a complex task that involves intervention on the individual level, the caregiver level, and the community level. Although this task may seem overwhelming, it is far less taxing than to continue to pit client, staff, parents, and communities against each other in deciding on what is best for the client. Psychologists, by virtue of their relationship to everyone involved, as well as by their knowledge of development and human behavior, can provide the focal point for discussions that can create the necessary milieu for promotion of appropriate sexuality.

The information in this chapter is intended to provide a starting point for work across many areas of need. Those who wish to pursue this field are encouraged to gain knowledge and clinical skills. A list of certified sex therapy supervisors can be obtained through the Association of Sex Educators, Counselors and Therapists. Information on specific topics related to sexuality and individuals with disabilities can be obtained through the Sex Educators Information Council of the United States.

24

The Mentally Retarded Offender

George S. Baroff

In this chapter, I describe clinical psychological activities on behalf of people with mental retardation (MR) who become involved with the criminal justice system from the perspective of a forensic psychologist and expert witness in serious criminal cases (Baroff, 1990, 1991; Baroff & Freedman, 1988). The topics addressed are (a) the prevalence of criminal behavior in retarded individuals; (b) attributes of the adult retarded offender population with regard to types of crimes and personal characteristics, with only a brief reference to the juvenile segment; and (c) vulnerabilities of the retarded defendant to the criminal justice system in relation to various "competencies" (i.e., to confess, stand trial, plead guilty, and when imprisoned).

Readers interested in this topic are also referred to the report of the President's Committee on Mental Retardation, in the monograph titled *The Criminal Justice System and Mental Retardation* (Conley, Luckasson, & Bouthilet, 1992). Of particular value to this chapter were the chapters of the monograph devoted to epidemiological aspects (Noble & Conley, 1992), forensic services (Petrella, 1992), and correctional programs (J. N. Hall, 1992).

Prevalence of Criminal Behavior in Adults and Juveniles With MR

Adults. In the absence of prevalence data at the time of arrest, estimates of the frequency of criminal behavior have largely reflected incarceration rates in state prison populations. A national survey of both state and federal correctional settings, using an IQ of 69 as the upper limit, indicated a 9.5% prevalence rate for MR (B. S. Brown & Courtless, 1971). This was actually the weighted average of rates varying from 2.6% in mountain states to 24.3% in southeastern ones. A later national study (Denkowski & Denkowski, 1985) showed considerably lower rates—6.2% and 2%—with the rates varying as a function of the kinds of intelligence tests used, group or individual. The higher rate was found with group tests and the lower with individually administered ones. Within-state studies using the Wechsler Adult Intelligence Scale–Revised (WAIS-R) found rates varying from 1% in Florida (Spruill & May, 1988), 5% in Georgia

(Irion, 1988), and 7% in Texas (Texas Department of Mental Health and Mental Retardation [TDMHMR], 1973). Such a wide variation indicates differences between the states in how their criminal justice systems deal with retarded offenders. In any case, the data indicate that the use of group intelligence tests (e.g., the BETA II, a test commonly used for classification purposes by correctional systems) tends to exaggerate about threefold the retardation rate derived from a WAIS-R evaluation. With an average WAIS-R prevalence rate of 2%, the proportion of the incarcerated adult population with MR virtually mirrors their numbers in the general population, an observation also made by MacEachron (1979). It should be noted that none of these surveys incorporated "adaptive behavior" in the diagnosis, with the classification of retardation being made solely on the basis of IQ.

Another way of looking at "prevalence," and one that is especially pertinent to this chapter, relates to the frequency of a diagnosis of MR in defendants seen for pretrial forensic examination. Referred by defense attorneys, prosecutors, or judges and usually for determination of competency to stand trial or criminal responsibility (culpability), frequencies from six states varied from 3% in Ohio to 7% in Virginia, with an average rate of 6% (Petrella, 1992). A somewhat higher prevalence rate is to be expected in a "forensic" population because it includes defendants whose cognitive difficulties are sufficiently obvious to catch the attention of attorneys. Nevertheless, a substantial segment of defendants, ultimately found to be mildly retarded, will not have been referred for forensic assessment either prior to trial or after conviction and incarceration.

Juveniles. Usually referring to youth under 18 years of age, a national survey of juvenile correctional facilities, so-called "training schools," indicated a near 10% prevalence rate (9.5%), with the great majority, 8%, being classified in school terminology as "educable" and 2% as "trainable" (Morgan, 1979). The prominence of those with mild MR (educable), as compared with those with more severe intellectual impairment, also is true of the adult population with MR.

Attributes of the Adult Retarded Offender

Types of offenses. Relative to the general prison population, the retarded inmate is more likely to have committed a crime against a person (B. S. Brown & Courtless, 1971; Sundram, 1989). A recent study of the North Carolina state correctional system showed that in a retarded inmate population of 470 (out of a total population of 15,004, a 3.1% state prevalence), slightly more than one half (52.3%) were convicted of crimes against people, whereas slightly less than half of the nonretarded majority were so convicted (46.6%). The broad distribution of crimes in these categories in the retarded and nonretarded population differed significantly (see Table 1), and closer examination suggests some interesting trends. Inspection of Table 1 shows that nearly one third of retarded inmates

Table 1. North Carolina State Prison Population as of March 31, 1991: Types of Crimes by IQ Ranges (Retarded and Nonretarded)

	IQs	
Offense	IQ to 69 (%)	IQ 70+ (%)
Crimes against persons		
Murder 1	4.9	3.3
Murder 2	11.1	8.1
Rape	14.7	8.8
Assault	5.3	5.0
Manslaughter	1.7	2.0
Sex	2.3	2.3
Kidnapping	1.7	1.8
Robbery	10.6	15.3
Total	52.3	46.6
Crimes against property		
Breaking and entering	14.3	15.2
Larceny	6.0	7.6
Auto theft	0.9	0.9
Burning	3.4	1.3
Burglary	7.2	4.3
Total	31.8	29.3
Crimes against public order		
Drugs (selling and nonselling)	10.6	16.3
Fraud	0.0	1.6
Forgery	0.4	2.2
Trespassing	0.4	0.1
Driving while impaired	1.9	1.3
Traffic	0.4	0.5
Worthless checks	0.2	0.1
Total	13.9	22.1

Note. The grand total is less than 100% because of a fourth category, "Other," which constituted only 2%. χ^2 (3, N = 15,004) = 10.4, $p < .015$.

(30.7%) were imprisoned for the more serious crimes against persons (first- and second-degree murder and rape), in contrast to a one-fifth rate (20.2%) in the nonretarded population. In no sense should these differences be interpreted as evidence of a greater proclivity for violence in people with MR; rather they reflect, in part, the fact that nonretarded inmates are imprisoned for a wider range of crimes. Table 1 also shows more similar rates for property crimes (31.8% in retarded and 29.3% in nonretarded inmates), but a much higher proportion of crimes against public order in the nonretarded segment (22.1% vs. 13.9%). Of course, prison statistics relate only to more serious offenses; only a study at the time of arrest and prior to disposition could illuminate this picture, and no such recent data appear to exist (Petrella, 1992).

Personal characteristics. The retarded adult inmate population is predominantly male (at least 85%; Irion, 1988; Rockowitz, 1986); disproportionately non-White (Black and Hispanic; Sundram, 1989; TDMHMR, 1973; H. V. Wood, 1976); mildly retarded, with IQs typically in the 60–70 range (B. S. Brown & Courtless, 1971; Irion, 1988; Steelman, 1987), although individuals with IQs in the higher level moderate range also are found (my first evaluation was of a man with an IQ of 41 on the Stanford-Binet L-M); and older than their nonretarded counterparts (e.g., 35 vs. 30 in Georgia [Irion, 1988] and 27 vs. 25 in Texas [TDMHMR, 1973]). The age difference is attributed to a tendency to serve longer sentences because of a higher frequency of infractions in prison and greater difficulty in securing parole (Noble & Conley, 1992).

Vulnerabilities of Retarded Defendants to the Criminal Justice System

Why Get Involved?

For the practitioner, forensic work on behalf of defendants who may be retarded offers an opportunity to help keep the criminal justice system fair. Like defense lawyers, who certainly do not condone the offenses with which their clients are charged, psychologists' activities on behalf of defendants are a means of ensuring that the accused's rights are protected. In the adversarial criminal justice system, it is not the responsibility of attorneys and their "expert witnesses," whether for the prosecution or for the defense, to judge the guilt of the accused; that role is left to a jury. The defense attempts to present the defendant's case in a manner most favorable to the defendant's interests, while the prosecution seeks an outcome that it views as in society's best interest. It is left to the jury to sort out conflicting arguments and reach a "just" verdict. To the degree that the intellectually impaired defendant, or any defendant, has access to resources that can assist him or her in ways guaranteed by the Constitution, the system of justice is supported. It is within this context that psychologists perform their functions on behalf of individuals charged with the most heinous crimes. Psychological services to these individuals and their lawyers—evaluation, consultation, and testimony—all translate into support for the criminal justice system.

Specific Threats to Fair Treatment

There are a number of issues that threaten fair treatment, and these have been addressed by Conley et al. (1992). They pertain to (a) establishing MR if it is present; (b) determining the defendant's competency to confess, stand trial, or plead guilty; (c) assessing the degree of criminal responsibility (culpability) and its relationship to an appropriate punishment if the defendant is convicted; and (d) ensuring reasonable protection and access to habilitative services if the defendant is imprisoned.

The issue of "criminal responsibility" is of special interest. So-called "insanity" defenses have commonly involved two elements: a failure to appreciate the wrongfulness of one's act (the traditional M'Naghten rule) or an inability to conform one's behavior to the requirements of the law (the irresistible impulse rule). The irresistible impulse defense has been particularly controversial, and its elimination has been recommended by both the American Bar Association and the American Psychiatric Association (Fitch, 1992). These organizations recommend a cognitive test that speaks to "appreciation" rather than "knowledge" of wrongfulness. It proposes that criminal responsibility should not be limited solely to knowledge that the act was "wrong" or illegal, but should include consideration of the ability to understand the significance of the act. It is here that examination of the retarded defendant's "moral" understanding becomes crucial and can form the basis for arguing for a lesser level of culpability, in effect, a "diminished capacity" or a "partial responsibility." Indeed, this is the rationale for offering MR as a "mitigating circumstance" in considering the punishment of the individual convicted of first-degree murder and facing a possible death penalty.

Establishing That the Defendant Meets Criteria for a Diagnosis of MR

In contrast to general clinical practice, where the diagnosis of MR is made by the psychologist or psychiatrist, in the courtroom, the acceptance of the defendant as "retarded" is made by the judge. In capital cases in the states that have excluded the death penalty for defendants who are retarded (as of 1994, Alaska, Georgia, Kentucky, Maryland, New Mexico, and Tennessee), this is, of course, crucial. Even where the death penalty continues to exist for all defendants, retarded or not, the presence of MR can be offered as a "mitigating" factor in the sentencing phase of a first-degree murder trial. In capital cases in which there has been a conviction, there is a second trial in which the jury is asked to determine the punishment. If MR has been established, the defense can offer it as grounds for a lesser sentence.

Establishing MR involves obtaining a developmental history whenever possible (a school history is absolutely essential); evaluating current adaptive functioning, apart from the offense with which the defendant is charged; and measuring IQ. Of these procedures, only conclusions drawn from intelligence tests are likely to be contentious. There is often a history of one or more tests prior to the current evaluation. These commonly reflect different IQ measures, possibly based on group tests as well as individual ones. Scores will vary both between and within tests, and the challenge is to draw conclusions from a psychometric history that can include IQs both above and below 70 (or 69). Reconciling of scores that could lead to a different diagnosis represents the greatest technical challenge to the psychologist and requires an understanding of all of the tests employed, their strengths and weaknesses, and their reliability and validity.

Even a history of only Wechsler tests can create problems in interpreting the defendant's intelligence level because of differences between the tests in their level of difficulty (Flynn, 1985; Spitz, 1986). For individuals with mild or moderate degrees of mental retardation, WAIS and WAIS-R measures tend to yield higher IQs than the Wechsler Intelligence Scale for Children–Revised (WISC-R), as does the WISC in relation to its successor. Moreover, WISC-R and WAIS-R quotients typically exceed those obtained on the Stanford-Binet L-M.

The psychologist is driven to explain how the defendant could have tested in the below-70 range at one time and above it, typically in the 70–79 range, at another. This entails clarifying for the court the nature of intelligence tests, what they measure, and the meaning of IQ. Moreover, the lack of sensitivity at the extremes of the WAIS-R (the lowest obtainable IQ is 45) makes it less useful for the defendant who scores in the below-60 range. The Stanford-Binet L-M may be used to supplement it, in part, because its "absurdity" items can convey clearly, to a potentially skeptical audience, the quality of the defendant's thinking. The "mental age" score of the Stanford-Binet L-M also provides a measure that permits comparing the defendant's intellectual level to that of a normally developing child or youth. This is a very useful way of communicating findings regarding the defendant's problem-solving abilities. If the defendant's problem solving is at something like the 10-year-old level, for example, this way of characterizing him offers much more information than simply describing him in terms of an IQ of 60.

The psychologist should also be prepared to describe what MR means in terms of the defendant's thinking: the capacity to reason (illustrated in "absurdity" items), to consider consequences, to make judgments, to learn, and to profit from experience. In this regard, special attention is given to verbal tests, such as the Verbal Scale of the WAIS-R, with particular focus on the Comprehension subtest. Attention should also be paid to the degree of the defendant's "suggestibility," a cognitive property of particular importance when the defendant was not acting alone.

Competency Vulnerabilities: Ability To Confess, Stand Trial, and Plead Guilty

Competency to confess. Most murder cases are solved by confession and it was the *Miranda* decision, which set the standard by which the acceptance or admissibility of a confession is to be judged (*Miranda v. Arizona*, 1966). A confession can be used as evidence only if it was voluntary, knowing, and intelligent. Assuming that it was not patently coerced, explaining its "knowing" element involves determining whether, before giving a confession, the defendants understand that they have a right to silence and the right to an attorney before being questioned; that an attorney will be appointed for them if they cannot afford one; and that even if they choose to answer the questions without an attorney present, they can stop at any time and request one.

The "intelligent" element involves relating those rights to the risks entailed in answering questions without an attorney present. That is, do the defendants understand that waiving their rights in favor of answering questions can place them in jeopardy because their answers can be used against them in court? Defendants must understand the risk of not remaining silent if they are to exercise an intelligent waiver of their right against self-incrimination.

The *Miranda* rights warning statement is typically administered by a police officer who simply reads each of these elements to a now-arrested defendant and asks him, after each has been presented, whether it is understood. In my experience, all retarded defendants uniformly answer "yes" to each of them. This is true even when later exploration reveals that the defendant had little or no idea of what his rights were. It is clear that when asked if we understand something, especially by an authority figure, we are likely to answer in the affirmative irrespective of our understanding in order to avoid giving the appearance of ignorance, another example of "the sin of pride." The challenge to the psychologist is to determine whether the "yes" answer really meant understanding, and this demands asking the defendant what each of the rights means, as expressed in his or her own words. A model *Miranda* statement has been developed for the examination of juveniles (Grisso, 1981) but, for testing comprehension, the clinician should use the same rights statement that was actually read to the defendant.

Another component of the *Miranda* examination consists of assessing the level of difficulty of the language used in the rights read to the defendant. Using Fry's (1977) system for evaluating the complexity of written material, the sentences within which the rights are presented are scored with reference to average sentence length and average word length (in syllables) per 100 words. These two variables combine to indicate the grade-level complexity of the material. Commonly, it is at a seventh-grade level of reading and "listening" difficulty; this is primarily based on average sentence length. (Comprehension of material that is either heard or read is comparable up to sixth grade; thereafter, reading becomes more efficient [Sticht & James, 1984].) It is this grade level and its mental age equivalent against which the defendant's abilities will be compared.

Because the average seventh grader is functioning at about the 13-year mental age level, a failure to comprehend the rights, in part or in whole, can be attributed, vocabulary aside, to the difference between the defendant's mental age and that necessary to an understanding of what he or she heard. It is in this context that Binet L-M mental ages become very useful. A Stanford-Binet IQ of 60, for example, will, in an adult, represent a mental age of 10 years. Thus, one can assert that 10-year-olds are usually operating at a fourth-grade level and that fourth graders are not expected to function intellectually like seventh graders.

It is not necessarily that with explanation the defendant could not have understood his or her rights, but that in the manner in which they were presented, without explanation and simple acceptance of "yes" as indicating comprehension, the defendant does not now understand them and did not at the time of original questioning. If the rights are now understood, often as a result of "education" by fellow inmates, the task is much more difficult because this requires determining whether they were understood at the time of arrest. Here, one needs to explore how the defendant came to acquire the understanding that he or she now has. This issue was made explicit by the appellate court of Illinois, which found that

> the fact that the Defendant was repeatedly read his rights [also not uncommon] and reportedly responded that he understood is of little consequence for, here the Defendant did not possess the intellectual or verbal skills to comprehend a *mere rote reading of his rights* [italics added]. Clearly none of the interrogating police officers made any attempt to *clarify or explain* [italics added] the Miranda warnings apart from reading Defendant his rights from a pre-printed form. (*People v. Redmon*, 1984, p. 1315)

With reference to the standard reply of yes to the police officer's question, "Do you understand?" the clinician can reveal how misleading the yes response may be by noting what occurs in classes at the university. At the end of each class, the instructor asks if there are any questions; typically, there never are. If this really meant full comprehension, there would be no need to give examinations!

Competency to stand trial. Perhaps the most common application of forensic psychology is to assess competency to stand trial. This involves determining whether the defendant understands with what he or she is charged and its seriousness or consequences if convicted; whether the defendant understands what a trial is and the respective roles of the principals; and whether the defendant can assist his or her attorney. Competency questions more often arise around "sanity" issues, but they also apply in retardation. A scale has been developed specifically for the evaluation of competency in retarded defendants, the Competence Assessment for Standing Trial for Defendants with Mental Retardation (Everington & Luckasson, 1992). Through an orally administered multiple-choice procedure, the defendant's understanding is explored in basic legal concepts, skills to assist defense, and understanding case events. It offers some numerical guidelines for making a competency determination, but it is intended to be used only as part of such an evaluation rather than as its sole basis. Generally, the question of trial competency tends to be reserved for either people with IQs in the below-60 range or those with a serious personality disorder in addition to retardation. Defendants with IQs in the 60–70 range are usually considered to be competent to stand trial.

Competency to plead guilty. Conceivably, the most challenging of the "competencies," the issue here is to decide whether to plead guilty, usually to a lesser charge, and thereby avoid the risk of a trial and its possible outcome. This requires a consideration of what might be rather than what is and the weighing of one course of action against another. Although the defendant's attorney will encourage a choice that is seen as in the defendant's best interest, the defendant must ultimately make the decision. Because a "plea" requires an acknowledgment of guilt, there may be strong resistance to it in an individual who has difficulty in recognizing what might be "the lesser of two evils." The psychologist will not ordinarily have a role with respect to this competency except when his or her knowledge of MR may contribute to recommendations to the attorney about how these options are presented to the defendant.

Criminal Responsibility (Culpability) and Appropriate Sanctions

Although relatively few retarded offenders will be unaware of the illegality or "wrongfulness" of their acts (e.g., Fitch, 1992), there is still the question of whether the defendant who is retarded should be held to the same standard of responsibility as those who are not. This issue was discussed earlier in connection with threats to fair treatment. The thrust of current judicial recommendations is that appreciation of the significance of the act also should be considered along with simple awareness that it is wrong.

In 1989, the Supreme Court overturned the death sentence of a young man with MR on the grounds that the sentencing jury had not been given the opportunity to consider his retardation in choosing an appropriate punishment (*Penry v. Lynaugh*, 1989). In the Court's opinion, given by Justice Sandra O'Connor, Penry's retardation, at least mild if not moderate in degree (IQs of 50–63), was relevant to his level of "personal blameworthiness." His intellectual impairment was seen as leaving him less able than nonretarded people to control his impulses and to consider the consequences of his actions (i.e., resulting in "diminished capacity"). With this knowledge, jurors could decide that he was less morally blameworthy and impose a lesser sentence.

The forensic consultant also may argue for a reduced degree of culpability, a diminished level of responsibility, on the grounds of the aforementioned lesser appreciation of why the offense was wrong. Routine inquiry of why it is wrong to rob or to kill typically evokes little understanding of why these laws exist. Such fundamental moral awareness as is conveyed by the "Golden Rule" is generally lacking in defendants with intellectual impairments, as is appreciation of the relationship of laws to general social harmony. Whether this moral lag is limited to the intellectually immature defendant is unclear; what is clear is that there is a lesser capacity to acquire this understanding in offenders with MR than in nonretarded offenders. MR creates a different "educability quotient." A sentence should not only fit the crime, but also it should be appropriate to an understanding of why one is being punished. To do less is truly to inflict "cruel and inhuman" punishment.

The Imprisoned Retarded Offender

If prison is viewed as a dangerous place for the nonretarded inmate, imagine the threat posed to the individual whose cognitive limitations render him or her vulnerable to the wishes of brighter and more exploitative inmates. One defendant, while awaiting trial, had been kept in a cell that was somewhat removed from that of the general jail population because a correctional officer saw him as a likely victim. The nature of this vulnerability is graphically portrayed in a judicial ruling:

> The [state of] has failed to meet its constitutional obligation to provide minimally adequate conditions of incarceration for mentally retarded inmates. Their special habilitative needs are practically unrecognized . . . , and they are subjected to a living environment which they cannot understand and in which they cannot succeed. Moreover, prison officials have done little to protect these mentally handicapped inmates from the type of abuse and physical harm which they suffer at the hands of other prisoners. Their conduct is judged by the same standards applicable to prisoners of average mental ability, and they are frequently punished for actions the import of which they do not comprehend. (*Ruiz v. Estelle*, 1980, p. 134; cited in J. N. Hall, 1992)

Because retarded inmates are underrepresented in prison rehabilitation programs (Coffey, 1989), with less than 10% receiving any special services (Wolford, 1987), and because they often serve longer sentences due to the earlier mentioned more frequent infractions and greater difficulty in securing parole (Noble & Conley, 1992), several states have developed special programs. These vary from (a) a special unit that provides housing and services for men and day services for women within a minimum security facility (South Carolina); to (b) the option of being housed in a separate unit in a maximum security prison (Georgia); to (c) assignment to a special facility specific to this population (Texas). In each, programs are offered that emphasize educational, vocational, and social skills and involve treatment teams that include psychological personnel.

Conclusion

This chapter has provided clinical psychologists with an orientation to a potential role in serving adults with MR who become involved with the criminal justice system. Through such activities, there is the likelihood of fairer treatment for the retarded individual and a strengthening of the criminal justice system for all. The clinical psychologist who is knowledgeable about MR performs evaluative, consultative, and educational functions with regard to these defendants. Knowledge gained through assessment is shared with attorneys who also expect the psychologist to help them organize it and, possibly, present it in court. In this respect, the psychologist assumes a vital consultative, as well as diagnostic, role. Finally, it is in the courtroom that the psychologist as expert witness performs an educational function in conveying to the judge and jury the nature of MR, including its distinction from mental illness, and the implications of MR for the defendant. It is within the context of a general understanding of MR and its behavioral effects by the judge and jury that the defendant's history and current psychological findings can be most clearly communicated and understood.

25

Psychopharmacology

Mark H. Lewis, Michael G. Aman,
Kenneth D. Gadow, Stephen R. Schroeder,
and Travis Thompson

In this chapter, we address issues related to the effective use of psychotropic medication in individuals with mental retardation (MR), including assessment of behavioral change and adverse effects. In addition, we provide a brief overview of the efficacy of medications used to treat behavioral disorders in individuals with MR and highlight the need for controlled studies.

The effective use of psychopharmacological treatments for people with MR has been hindered by a variety of factors. These include the lack of a necessary empirical research base, the relative lack of involvement of psychiatry in MR, difficulties in making psychiatric diagnoses, and ideological and disciplinary differences.

Excessive and inappropriate historical use of psychotropic drugs has fueled resistance to pharmacological treatment for behavioral disorders. The use of psychotropic medication is often seen as adherence to a "medical model" and inconsistent with conditioning and learning-based models of treatment. Because psychotropic drug use has historically meant neuroleptic use, many workers perceive that psychotropic drugs suppress behavior generally and are associated with serious side effects. New advances in psychopharmacology, however, are making more selective drugs available that are much better tolerated because they have fewer adverse effects. Unfortunately, many of the newer classes of compounds have not been studied with the requisite methodological rigor in people with MR.

There also is the assumption that etiology and treatment need be isomorphic. Etiology–treatment isomorphism assumes that if a behavior is found to be modulated by environmental factors, behavioral interventions are warranted and that most will be effective. Conversely, if no environmental mediation can be ascertained, then a biological etiology or mediation is invoked, and pharmacological intervention is thought to be the treatment of choice. In animal studies, however, drugs have dramatically altered conditioned or learned behavior, and environmental manipulations have had a substantial impact on the expression of behavior induced by pharmacological or other biological manipulations. Theories of etiology and treatment outcomes tend to be circular and delay advances in the field. Moreover, they persist in the face of growing evidence that illustrates the dynamic interaction between experience and biology.

Treatment Acceptability (Continuum of Restrictiveness and Risk–Benefit)

The acceptability of psychotropic drug treatment involves the extent to which people with MR and their care providers will tolerate the risks associated with psychopharmacological treatments in return for the potential or anticipated benefits. Risk–benefit assessment must take into account the physical status of the individual, age, and careful documentation of potential long- and short-term complications. In addition, the acceptability of psychotropic drug treatment often rests on the failure of other interventions. In any event, judgments about risk–benefit or intrusiveness should, if possible, be made by the individual with MR, the guardian, an interdisciplinary team, and the physician. The judgment process should include a review of the quality and intensity of previous attempts to treat the behavior problem and promote alternative behaviors, and of psychosocial and environmental conditions that may be contributing to the behavior problem. If such conditions can be identified, appropriate environmental changes should be implemented and evaluated (e.g., a functional analysis of the behavior or behaviors targeted for treatment should be conducted). Finally, the pharmacological intervention should be part of a comprehensive individual habilitation plan. Potentially adverse consequences of failure to use psychotropic medication must not be overlooked. The harmful effects of the behavior sometimes outweigh the potential harmful effects of the treatment. The rapidity with which drug interventions can be initiated and expected to yield positive results versus behavioral interventions also must be considered.

Diagnosis and the Medical Model

Effective medical treatments typically follow successful diagnosis of an underlying disorder. Although diagnosis may often convey information about pathophysiology and etiology, this is typically not the case in the mental health arena. Diagnosis of psychiatric disorders in people with MR using criteria from the fourth edition of the *Diagnostic and Statistical Manual of Mental Disorders* (*DSM–IV*; American Psychiatric Association, 1994) is a particularly challenging task. Diagnosis of major mental illnesses requires verbal and abstract reasoning ability on the individual's part in order to determine accurately cognitive and affective state. Thus, the reliability of classification or diagnostic schemes often suffer as the level of intellectual functioning decreases.

The frequency and presentation of psychiatric disorders are different in individuals with severe intellectual impairment. It is difficult to determine what behaviors are associated with MR and what behaviors represent specific forms of psychopathology (M. H. Lewis & MacLean, 1982; see also chapter 10 in this book). Nevertheless, it is now clear that people with MR are at a significantly greater risk for psychiatric disorders than are nonretarded individuals (M. H. Lewis & MacLean, 1982; Singh, Guernsey, & Ellis, 1992). Prevalence studies suggest that psychiatric disorders may occur among people with MR at four to five times the rate observed in the general population (M. H. Lewis & MacLean, 1982). It is also clear that the full spectrum of psychiatric disorders, including depression and anxiety disorders, can be observed in people with MR (Sovner & Hurley, 1983). Moreover, specific biomedical conditions (e.g., fragile X) associated with MR carry a substantial risk of certain behavioral or psychiatric disorders (e.g., Bregman, Leckman, & Ort, 1988).

Drug treatment can be targeted at desirable changes in specific behaviors rather than treatment of an underlying disorder for which a differential diagnosis can be applied. It also may be useful to focus on dimensions (e.g., aggression, self-injury, stereotypy, compulsions) that may cut across various diagnostic categories (Van Praag et al., 1990). For people with more severe MR, adopting an empirically derived taxonomy of efficacious drug treatments and specific dimensions of behavior may be more useful than selecting a psychotropic drug based on *DSM–IV* diagnoses.

Integration of Pharmacological and Behavioral Treatments

R. L. Sprague and Baxley (1978) and Schroeder, Lewis, and Lipton (1983), respectively, have suggested that the relative effects of drug treatment compared with other treatments and of the combined effects of drug treatment with other treatments be considered a methodological necessity. Little progress has been made toward achieving these goals.

The use of psychotropic medication is often thought to facilitate the effectiveness of environmental interventions or behavioral treatments. M. Campbell et al. (1978) demonstrated that treatment of children with autism using haloperidol increased the effectiveness of a language-based behavior therapy program. Various regulatory agencies now mandate that an individual receiving psychotropic medication also must be receiving active behavioral services. Unfortunately, there is little in the literature to support an additive or synergistic effect of pharmacological and behavioral treatments. Drugs may reduce levels of disordered behavior, increasing social relatedness and responsiveness to habilitative programming. In some cases, however, there may be sound neurobiological reasons for assuming that such treatments may be antagonistic. For example, a behavioral intervention that relies on use of stimuli or events that are positively reinforcing may be compromised by contemporaneous treatment with an antipsychotic drug (Hollis & St. Omer, 1972). Such drugs, because of their antagonist actions at dopamine receptors, may interrupt the neural circuits that are key to reward processes (Evenden, 1988; Wise, 1982). Drugs (e.g., neuroleptics) also may hinder cognitive functioning, induce side effects that can interfere with habilitative efforts, result in decreases in arousal and motivation, and inhibit prosocial behavior.

Other Issues in Psychopharmacological Treatment

Polypharmacy

Historically, psychopharmacological treatment of people with MR included inappropriately high doses of drugs and nonrational use of multiple psychotropic agents. As a result, polypharmacy has been considered by many workers in MR as something to be avoided; this is generally the case with two psychotropic drugs that have similar mechanisms of action. The concurrent use of two or more psychotropic drugs from different classes or with different mechanisms of action can have a rational basis and may prove to be effective. There are a number of examples in the treatment of psychiatric disorders in which concurrent medications have been shown to increase efficacy, but not compromise safety. However, the rationale for concurrent prescription should be clear and considerable care should be taken to monitor drug interactions.

Minimal Effective Dose and Drug-Free Periods

A formal minimal effective dose procedure is often recommended for people with MR who are receiving psychoactive drugs. Although generally this is a sound practice, certain drugs such as lithium must be maintained within a specified blood level range (0.5–0.9 mEq/L) in order to be effective or to avoid toxicity. It is generally recommended that systematic dosage reductions be carried out to achieve the minimal dosage necessary. It is also recommended, if not mandated, that the dosage should be reduced annually and subsequently discontinued for some time period. Such a practice has the obvious benefit of determining whether the individual is in continued need of pharmacotherapy for the specific behavioral disorder. A caveat to such a practice, however, is that in current thinking in psychiatry, discontinuation of drug therapy will increase the probability of relapse in some disorders (e.g., major depression); multiple episodes of the disorder are associated with increased number of depressive episodes and decreased intervals between episodes. Thus, some psychiatric disorders may require lifelong therapy, much as one might treat other medical disorders (e.g., some forms of diabetes).

Multimodal Assessment and Diagnostic Issues for Psychopharmacological Treatment

Decisions about psychotropic drug treatment should rely on the assessment of functioning in a number of behavioral domains using a variety of assessment techniques. Assessment is typically a major responsibility of psychologists working in interdisciplinary service settings, but, as we show later, the entire relevant picture is likely to cut across several disciplines. Determination of the presence of a psychiatric disorder (e.g., psychosis) or neurological disease (e.g., Rett syndrome) is critical, as is an analysis of the social and physical environment and its role in the genesis or maintenance of the maladaptive behavior. A family and clinical history, including previous pharmacological treatments, also will be important to establish.

Psychiatric Issues

Given the now well documented vulnerability of people with MR to psychiatric disorders, it is important in making decisions about the use of psychotropic drugs to screen for psychopathology. Several instruments are available for assessing psychopathology in people with MR. For example, the Reiss Screen for Maladaptive Behavior (Reiss, 1988) is a rating scale that is completed by informants who are well acquainted with the individual (e.g., caregivers, teachers). The items are designed to reflect symptoms of disorders from the revised third edition of the *DSM* (*DSM–III–R*). Multiple criteria are used in completing the ratings, including frequency, intensity, context, and degree of suffering. The test yields scores on seven scales. In addition, there are six maladaptive behavior items. The screen has been validated against psychiatric diagnoses and appears to correctly identify dually diagnosed individuals. Another instrument that may be useful is the Psychopathology Instrument for Mentally Retarded Adults (Senatore, Matson, & Kazdin, 1985).

Given the difficulties associated with the assessment and diagnosis of psychiatric disorders in people with MR, the use of biological markers to aid in predicting clinical responses to drug therapy may be useful. For example, elevated plasma concentrations of the dopamine metabolite homovanillic acid (HVA) appear to predict efficacious clinical responses to neuroleptics in patients with schizophrenia (Davidson et al., 1987). A blunted cortisol response to the synthetic glucocorticoid dexamethasone or a blunted prolactin response to the 5-hydroxytryptamine (5-HT) agonist fenfluramine may indicate the utility of antidepressant treatment (Shapira, Reiss, Kaiser, Kindler, & Lerer, 1989). There has been little attempt to use such strategies in MR, however.

Neurological Issues

In general, psychotropic drugs may have differential effects in individuals suffering from various forms of brain insult. Correct identification of an existing neurological disorder may have an important influence on treatment. Initiating or continuing neuroleptic treatment would certainly be contraindicated in an individual correctly diagnosed as suffering from pseudoakathisia or tardive dyskinesia. Identification of specific neurological disorders may clearly indicate choices of treatment. For example, an individual with MR suffering from Gilles de la Tourette's syndrome or another tic disorder may be effectively treated with haloperidol (A. K. Shapiro, Shapiro, & Eisenkraft, 1983).

Behavioral–Environmental Issues

Inadequate physical or social environments may account for a significant portion of the behavioral problems displayed by people with MR. Numerous animal studies have documented the unfavorable effects of restricted environmental conditions on the behavior and physiology of a wide range of species (Berkson, 1967; M. H. Lewis & Baumeister, 1982). In such cases, pharmacological intervention should be eschewed in favor of attempts to improve the amount and quality of habilitative services. Individual assessments should include behavioral analyses designed to identify functional roles played by the maladaptive behavior (e.g., avoidance of demands). If such functions can be identified, then appropriate behavioral manipulations can be carried out.

Monitoring and Assessing Drug Treatment Effects

Clinical Hypothesis Testing

Given the limited data available to practitioners, the psychopharmacological treatment of people with MR should be conducted in the context of clinical hypothesis testing. Psychoactive drugs should be prescribed on the basis of clear hypotheses about expected drug effects relevant to a psychiatric diagnosis or specific behavior disorders. Systematic behavioral data should be collected to document outcomes, including unexpected positive and adverse effects. For example, an efficient, yet comprehensive, graphic system for assessing drug effects for clinical purposes has been recently developed in a residential treatment facility (Spirrison & Grosskopf, 1991). Standardized evaluation tools should be used to document outcome and can include rating scales or checklists, as well as direct behavioral observations. The effects of systematically varying dosage should also be documented using these tools. Documenting drug effects on behavior observed in multiple environments and in response to provocative antecedents can be particularly helpful. It also is critical to archive such results so that unsuccessful or unnecessary treatments for an individual client can be reduced or eliminated.

Extratarget Symptom Measures

Documentation of the effects of psychotropic drug treatment should also include measures of "social validity." These can include decisions by treatment teams and guardians to maintain the drug regimen or other documentation of consumer satisfaction with the treatment. Collateral effects of the treatment on other domains of functioning also should be documented. This can include assessment of any changes in learning, attention, or memory that appear to be drug related. Assessment of social relatedness and changes in other problem behaviors not specifically targeted for drug treatment can be particularly helpful. Positive changes in mood (e.g., less irritability), activity, sleep, and appetite should be documented, as well as adverse effects on these functions.

Dosing Regimens and Drug Blood Levels

An important aspect of evaluating the efficacy (and adverse effects) of psychopharmacological treatment is the issue of optimal prescribed dosage. There also must be appropriate concentrations of drug available to target proteins in the brain, estimated by measuring drug blood levels (M. H. Lewis & Mailman, 1988). Systematic examination of the relationship of dose to target symptoms in people with MR has been largely confined to studies with stimulants (Gadow, 1992) and, to a lesser extent, with neuroleptics (Aman, in press). It should not be expected that drug dosages used to treat psychiatric disorders in people without MR will be the same dosages that will be effective in treating specific behavioral disorders. Thus, careful titration studies need to be done assessing dose–response relationships. For some drugs (e.g., lithium, nortriptyline), blood levels have proved to be predictive of clinical response, whereas for other drugs, a systematic relationship has not been established (M. H. Lewis & Mailman, 1988).

Evaluation Instruments

Rating instruments have been a mainstay of work in psychopharmacology, both in and outside the field of MR (Aman, 1993). Rating scales have a number of notable advantages and disadvantages. Among the advantages are the following. First, because most rating instruments can be completed in a brief period of time, they are relatively inexpensive to use. Second, raters can aggregate behavior over time and across settings, which enables infrequently occurring types of behavior to be rated meaningfully. Third, rating scales tend to be problem oriented and, presuming the right tool is selected, they are, therefore, of high relevance to consumers and practitioners. Fourth, many rating scales include normative data, which facilitate deciding whether a problem warrants treatment and whether the treatment is producing meaningful change.

There also are several problems associated with rating scales. The high subjectivity of these scales can lead to inaccurate portrayals of behavior. "Halo" effects occur, in which some raters tend to rate all of a client's traits in the direction of the rater's overall impression. One may overcome both of these problems by enlisting several raters and discerning differences across informants. However, marked differences do not necessarily signify error, because the interactions between two raters and a given client may differ tremendously (Achenbach, McConaughy, & Howell, 1987). A third difficulty with rating tools is that there is a tendency for extreme scores to moderate over time, without the introduction of any treatment (Milich, Roberts, Loney, & Caputo, 1980; Werry & Sprague, 1974). Because this usually occurs most noticeably between first and second ratings, the easiest remedy is simply to collect a second rating before instituting any change and using the second rating as a baseline against which to judge treatment effects (Aman, 1993). A final consideration relates to the type of problem being rated. Third-party informants are usually accurate and reliable in assessing externalizing problems, such as attention deficit hyperactivity disorder and hostility. However, such informants appear to be much less reliable and sensitive in noting internalizing problems, such as morbid anxiety and depression (Aman, 1993, 1994a; Barkley, 1988). Whenever possible, the client should be included as a "rater" when internalizing problems are the targets of treatment.

A discussion of specific rating scales follows. Comprehensive reviews of scales can be found in Aman (1991a, 1991b, 1993, 1994a), Barkley (1988), S. Reiss (1994), and Sturmey, Reed, and Corbett (1991). Here, rating instruments are classified as informant rated or self-rated and by their purpose (Aman, 1994a).

General Purpose Informant Scales

Included here are scales that have broad application and can often be used across a range of psychotropic drugs and types of presenting problems.

Aberrant Behavior Checklist (ABC). The ABC is one of the few instruments specifically developed to assess drug effects in people with MR. The ABC was developed by factor analysis, and its 58 items resolve into five subscales designated: Irritability, Agitation, Crying; Lethargy/Social Withdrawal; Stereotypic Behavior; Hyperactivity/Noncompliance; and Inappropriate Speech (Aman, Singh, Stewart, & Field, 1985a). The ABC has well-studied psychometric characteristics, and these are generally robust (Aman, Singh, Stewart, & Field, 1985b; Aman, Singh, & Turbott, 1987). The ABC has been used in numerous drug studies, both in institutions and in the community, and it has been shown to be medication sensitive in the large majority of these (Aman, 1994a, 1994b). Recently, the ABC has been revised slightly for community use (and for a broader range of functional levels), and a new version, the ABC-Community, has been developed and marketed (Aman, Burrow, & Wolford, 1994; Aman & Singh, 1994). The original version is now sold as the ABC-Residential. At this stage, the ABC has been the most widely used and probably the most sensitive rating tool in the drug literature in MR (Aman, 1994b).

Maladaptive Behavior Scale (MABS). The MABS is a one-page rating form in which a given behavior is rated in a row × column matrix (Thompson, 1988). The frequency of the behavior is rated from *did not occur* through *occurrence more than 12 times*, and intensity of the behavior is rated from *does not interfere with training* through to *injury to a person or property damage*. The unit of time over which the client is rated is an 8-hr work shift. The actual category of behavior to be rated is determined by the client's clinical team, making the MABS extremely versatile. To our knowledge, there is no published research on the psychometric characteristics of the MABS.

Developmental Behaviour Checklist (DBC). The DBC was originally called the Developmentally Delayed Child Behaviour Checklist and was structured after the well-known Child Behavior Checklist (Achenbach, 1991). The DBC has six subscales: Disruptive Behavior, Self-Absorbed Behavior, Language Disturbance, Anxiety, Autistic Relating, and Antisocial Behavior (Einfeld & Tonge, 1992). The DBC is available in a Primary Caregiver version (96 items) and a Teacher version (94 items), and items are scored from 0 (*not true as far as you know*) to 2 (*often true or very true*). It was developed for children and adolescents with moderate and severe MR living in the community or in residential settings. This instrument seems to have acceptable psychometric characteristics. However, there appears to be no drug research with the DBC, so its sensitivity to medication effects is largely unknown.

Emotional Problems Scale: Behavior Rating Scales. The Behavior Rating Scales were developed for rating adolescents and adults (14 years and older) with borderline IQ and mild MR (Strohmer & Prout, 1991). It has 135 items that are scored on 12 subscales. These in turn can be scored on an Externalizing and an Internalizing factor. Unfortunately, the Behavior Rating Scales were developed solely for completion by care workers, so there are no norms for parent ratings. Most psychometric data on this instrument appear to be adequate, although test–retest data appear to be lacking (Aman, 1991a). The Behavior Rating Scales appear to have potential for drug assessment.

Emotional Disorders Rating Scale–DD (EDRS-DD). The EDRS-DD was developed to assess disorders of mood and affect in children and adolescents with mild and moderate MR (Feinstein, Kaminer, & Barrett, 1988; Feinstein, Kaminer, Barrett, & Tylenda, 1988). Although designed to evaluate "emotional disorders," the EDRS-DD also includes subscales relating to externalizing problems. The EDRS-DD has 59 items, which are scored along eight subscales. The six emotional disorders scales are derived from the *DSM–III*. Each item is rated on a frequency scale ranging from *never* (0) to *often* (3) and on a severity scale ranging from *no problem* (0) to *severe* (3). The EDRS-DD was developed for completion by child-care workers, although it could be used by parents or teachers. The psychometric characteristics of this instrument have been found to be highly variable, with good interrater reliability and poor internal consistency and test–retest reliability (Aman, 1991a). To our knowledge, there has been no use of the EDRS-DD as a drug assessment tool.

Special Purpose Informant Instruments

Only measures for drug assessment with some of the more common problems and psychiatric conditions are discussed here. See Aman (1993) and Corcoran and Fischer (1987) for more extensive reviews.

Attention Deficit Hyperactivity Disorder (ADHD). This is one of the most common presenting complaints in children of average IQ, and it is also common in children and adolescents with MR. Conners' Teacher Rating Scale and Conners' Parent Rating Scale (Conners, 1990) have been widely used to assess ADHD and drug effects in average-ability youngsters. Recently, these scales also have been used successfully to assess treatment effects in children with mild and moderate MR and with ADHD (Handen, Breaux, Gosling, Ploof, & Feldman, 1990; Handen et al., 1992). It is unclear whether the Conners scales are suitable for rating children and adolescents with severe or profound MR.

Another instrument that should be considered for assessing ADHD is the Attention Checklist (Das & Melnyk, 1989). The Attention Checklist contains 12 items related to attention and impulsivity, although it has no items tapping physical overactivity. Checklist scores are highly correlated with scores on Conners' Teacher Rating Scale (Das & Melnyk, 1989). Limited work with this scale suggests that it has fairly robust psychometric characteristics, but it is untried in drug studies (Aman, 1994a).

Autism. The Real Life Rating Scale for Autism (Freeman, Ritvo, Yokota, & Ritvo, 1986) is an informant scale containing 47 items scoring on five subscales. Item assignment appears to be based on clinical grounds. This scale has been used in at least eight studies of fenfluramine and one or more subscales were sensitive in six investigations (Aman & Kern, 1989). The psychometric characteristics of the scale appear to be largely unstudied (Aman, 1994a).

The Children's Psychiatric Rating Scale (National Institute of Mental Health, 1985b) is a 63-item instrument that has frequently been featured in the Bellevue Hospital Nursery drug studies. The first 28 items pertain to observable behaviors that can be rated without cooperation from the child, whereas the remaining items depend on the child's report of occurrence during interview. This scale has 15 subscales, many of which resemble *DSM–III–R* categories. M. Campbell's group at Bellevue Hospital has progressively concentrated on 14 items taken from the first part of the scale. These items contribute to four factors relevant to autism: (a) Autism, (b) Anger/Uncooperativeness, (c) Hyperactivity, and (d) Speech Deviance (Overall & Campbell, 1988). These four factors have been moderately sensitive to medication effects (M. Campbell & Palij, 1985).

Conners' (1990) 10-item Abbreviated Symptom Questionnaire has been used frequently in autism research because of the prominence of ADHD symptomatology in this disorder (M. Campbell & Palij, 1985). With the subscales Social Withdrawal, Stereotypic Behavior, and Hyperactivity, the ABC has also been used for this purpose (Aman, 1994b).

Aggression. Aggressive and destructive behavior are among the most common reasons for pharmacotherapy in MR. The Behavior Problems Inventory is a 29-item scale with three subscales: Self Injury, Stereotypic Behavior, and Aggression (Rojahn, 1992). The instrument also allows for write-ins on each subscale. The Behavior Problems Inventory was originally developed for epidemiological research on self-injury and stereotypy (Rojahn, 1986), but lately it has been used mostly to assess aggression. Problem behaviors are scored on a 7-point frequency scale, ranging from *never* to *hourly*. The Behavior Problems Inventory is untested in drug research.

General Purpose Self-Rating Scales

There are only two instruments that are sufficiently advanced in their development to warrant mention. Neither has been assessed in medication studies.

Emotional Problem Scales: Self Report Inventory. The Self Report Inventory (Prout & Strohmer, 1991) is a companion to an informant scale (the Behavior Rating Scales; Strohmer & Prout, 1991) discussed earlier. It is made up of 162 items on six subscales: Anxiety, Depression, Impulse Control, Thought/Behavior Disorder, Low Self Esteem, and Lie scale. The Self Report Inventory was devised for completion by adolescents and adults with borderline IQs or mild MR. Like the informant scale, this one was designed to fit into preconceived clinical categories that were later tested by more empirical methods. Selected subscales of the inventory could be used for repeated drug assessments.

Another instrument, the Adolescent Behavior Checklist (Demb, Brier, Huron, & Tomer, 1994), with 86 items, is more than half as long as the Self Report Inventory. Its items are based on *DSM–III–R* symptomatology and are scored on eight subscales, including a Lie scale. It was designed for adolescents aged 12–21 years with borderline intelligence or mild MR. The checklist remains untested in formal drug studies.

Special Purpose Self-Rating Scales

Whenever management of an internalizing problem is the objective of treatment, it is a good idea to seek feedback from the client regarding the effect of that treatment. Assessment of these areas is still in its early stages. Instruments of possible interest include the Zung Self-Rating Anxiety Scale, adapted for adults with mild and moderate MR (Lindsay & Michie, 1988); the Fear Survey for Children With and Without Mental

Retardation (Ramirez & Kratchowill, 1990), a modification of an earlier children's fear survey; and the Self-Report Depression Questionnaire, a screening tool developed for use with adolescents and adults with relatively mild handicaps (W. M. Reynolds, 1989). Practitioners are urged to consult other reviews for more details (Aman, 1991a, 1994a; Corcoran & Fischer, 1987; Sturmey et al., 1991).

Monitoring and Assessing Adverse Drug Effects

Zametkin and Yamada (1993) offered several general drug assessment principles: (a) Expect side effects and look for them; (b) because many youngsters and clients with impairments do not complain, actively monitor them; (c) when appropriate, use caregivers as informants; (d) educate the client about possible side effects in developmentally appropriate language; (e) use a system to elucidate side effects; and (f) conduct a screen, as a baseline, before starting medication. Here, two types of tools for monitoring side effects are discussed: those for detecting early side effects and those for detecting tardive dyskinesia or akasthisia.

Instruments for Monitoring Short- and Medium-Term Side Effects

Perhaps the best known tool for detecting adverse effects is the Dosage and Treatment Emergent Symptom Scale (DOTES; National Institute of Mental Health, 1985c). The DOTES was developed by the National Institute of Mental Health to evaluate central nervous system and behavioral side effects. Each item is rated for severity (*not present* [1] to *severe* [4]), for relation to the medication taken (no relation through definite link), and for any action taken (seven possibilities, such as *treatment suspended*). The DOTES entails a systematic review of several behavioral and physical symptoms as well as biochemical and electrocardiographic work. Various sections or items can be dropped if they are deemed to be unrelated to the medication being evaluated.

Kalachnik and Nord (1985) developed the Monitoring of Side Effects System (MOSES) for use by personnel, especially nurses, working in residential settings. The MOSES presumes raters to have relatively little knowledge of body systems and pharmacological effects. It is organized by body area, and its instructions effectively require the rater to measure any change that coincides with drug treatment. The rater's function is to raise the alarm when side effects occur. The pattern of changes must be interpreted by a qualified physician. The MOSES provides a standardized tool for transmitting symptoms from care providers to physicians. It is not, of course, a replacement for regular, direct physician assessments.

Another standardized tool developed for children up to the age of 15 years is the Subjective Treatment Emergent Symptoms Scale (National Institute of Mental Health, 1985e), a 32-item scale to document physical, emotional, and cognitive complaints. These items can be elicited from the child, the parent, or other caregiver.

Several authors have developed special lists of symptoms for specific treatments. For example, Handen, Feldman, Gosling, Breaux, and McAuliffe (1991) used such a list to monitor methylphenidate (Ritalin) and found an apparent high rate of side effects in children with MR and ADHD. Handen and Aman (1994) developed a tool called the Side Effects Profile for Exceptional Children, which contains a listing of side effects associated with psychostimulant drugs. Such tailored lists are useful in that they are brief, but idiosyncratic side effects may not be detected. Kalachnik and Nord (1985) provided lists of side effects associated with each of the major psychoactive drug groups.

Zametkin and Yamada (1993) also discussed the use of neurological examinations for soft signs as a possible tool for monitoring drug effects. The Physical and Neurological Examination for Soft Signs (National Institute of Mental Health, 1985d) is one such tool.

Instruments for Assessing Tardive Dyskinesia

Tardive dyskinesia is a long-lasting or permanent movement disorder caused by chronic exposure to neuroleptic drugs. Many people with MR are treated for long periods of time with neuroleptics, so it is important that such clients be assessed prior to treatment and at regular intervals. If symptoms of dyskinesia are detected, attempts should be made to reduce the dosage or (preferably) discontinue the medication. A number of standardized tools have been developed to monitor tardive dyskinesia, including the Abnormal Involuntary Movement Scale (AIMS; National Institute of Mental Health, 1985a), the Tardive Dyskinesia Rating Scale (G. M. Simpson, Lee, Zoubok, & Gardos, 1979), the Withdrawal Emergent Symptom Checklist (Polizos, Engelhardt, Hoffman, & Waizer, 1973), and the Dyskinesia Identification System: Condensed Users System (DISCUS; Kalachnik & Sprague, 1993). We discuss only two of these instruments: the AIMS and the DISCUS.

The AIMS (National Institute of Mental Health, 1985a) is likely the most commonly used instrument for screening for tardive dyskinesia, probably because of its brevity. It has 12 items that rate the severity of dysfunction in the face, lips, jaw, tongue, upper and lower extremities, and trunk; items are rated on a 5-point scale. Separate items are available for rating global severity of dyskinesia, incapacitation, client awareness, and dental status.

The DISCUS (R. L. Sprague & Kalachnik, 1991) was developed for use with individuals who have MR. There are extensive norms available for this population, and psychometric data suggest that it is a reliable and valid tool (Kalachnik & Sprague, 1993; R. L. Sprague, White, Ullmann, & Kalachnik, 1984). With 15 items, the DISCUS is slightly longer than the AIMS, but the examination can be brief (usually in 10–14 min). The developers of the DISCUS have successfully taught workers in different disciplines (e.g., nurses, doctors, psychologists, pharmacists) to reliably use the instrument (Kalachnik & Sprague, 1994); a training videotape is available (Kalachnik, Sprague, & Kalles, 1991). Given the wealth of data, the DISCUS appears to be the optimal instrument for monitoring individuals with MR.

Instruments for Assessing Akathisia

Akathisia is a disorder that is typically, but not exclusively, associated with antipsychotic drug exposure. There are no clear criteria for diagnosis or consensus definition. Although severity rating scales are available (Sachdev, 1994), the diagnosis often relies on clinical judgment. The diagnosis of akathisia rests on an assessment of both cognitive and affective features (e.g., restlessness, tension) as well as motor features (e.g., repetitive limb movements, repeated shifting of body position, pacing). Because subjective symptoms typically will be unavailable when assessing individuals with more severe forms of MR, the diagnosis of pseudoakathisia can be made. Difficulty in assessing akathisia includes the multiple types of this disorder (Sachdev, 1994), which involve the temporal parameters associated with drug use.

Efficacy of Psychotropic Medications

Excellent reviews on psychopharmacology in MR are available (e.g., Aman & Singh, 1988; Baumeister, Todd, & Sevin, 1993). In this section, we provide a short overview, summarizing previous findings while emphasizing important recent developments.

Antipsychotics

The mainstay of pharmacotherapy has been antipsychotic drugs. It is estimated that almost half of the people with MR in residential facilities and more than 20% in the community are receiving antipsychotic drugs (B. K. Hill, Balow, & Bruininks, 1985; Intagliata & Rinck, 1985). Emphasis has been on strategies for reducing psychotropic drug use, and recent studies (Hancock, Weber, Kaza, & Her, 1991) have demonstrated significant reductions with little reported increase in problem behaviors. Reduction to "minimal effective dose" is now a goal of many agencies. However, Baumeister et al. (1993) reviewed the prevalence data that demonstrate relatively little change in the use of neuroleptics in spite of poor evidence of their efficacy.

Researchers have either examined the effects of neuroleptic withdrawal or used prospective designs, usually following a washout period (Schroeder, 1988). In the research literature, the efficacy of neuroleptics has been examined for stereotypy, aggression, self-injurious behavior, and hyperactivity. The one behavioral disorder for which antipsychotic drugs appear to be effective is stereotypy (Aman, in press).

Studies that support the utility of antipsychotic drugs have reported relatively modest treatment effects (e.g., Aman, White, & Field, 1984), and as Chadsey-Rusch and Sprague (1989) reported, individuals perceived to engage in stereotyped behavior tended to be kept on such medication despite a lack of compelling evidence of efficacy. Moreover, this class of drugs may increase the risk of long-term neurological side effects such as tardive dyskinesia and may have detrimental effects on learning and performance. A minority of studies have demonstrated either a lack of efficacy for antipsychotic drugs or an exacerbation of stereotyped behavior associated with such treatment (e.g., M. H. Lewis et al., 1986). Thus, the conclusion that antipsychotic drugs are effective in treating stereotyped behavior of people with MR may not be fully warranted.

Antidepressants

Antidepressant drugs such as tricyclic antidepressants, monoamine oxidase inhibitors, selective serotonin uptake inhibitors, and 5-HT_{1A} agonists also have been used to treat specific behavior problems in children, including ADHD, enuresis and encopresis, school phobia, night terrors, and sleep walking. Antidepressants are infrequently administered to people with MR (Baumeister et al., 1993), indicating, perhaps, a failure to diagnose depression in this population. Interest in antidepressants has increased recently because of the greater emphasis on recognizing symptoms of affective disorder and biological hypotheses concerning the role of serotonin in several behavioral disorders. Although a report (Howland, 1992) of an open trial of fluoxetine suggested significant improvement (20–40 mg over a 5- to 8-week period) in depression, Aman, White, Vaithianathan, and Teehan (1986) reported behavioral deterioration in people with profound MR who were treated with imipramine for depressive symptoms or acting-out behaviors.

Serotonin uptake inhibitors. Considerable interest has been shown recently in the use of serotonin uptake inhibitors in the treatment of ritualistic, stereotyped, or compulsive behaviors in people with autism and MR (M. H. Lewis, 1993). In general, studies support the efficacy of clomipramine (H. J. Garber, McGonigle, Slomka, & Monteverde, 1992; Gordon, Rapoport, Hamburger, State, & Mannheim, 1992; M. H. Lewis, Bodfish, Powell, & Golden, 1995; McDougle et al., 1992) and fluoxetine (E. H. J. Cook, Rowlett, Jaselskis, & Leventhal, 1992; Markowitz, 1992) in suppressing these behaviors, including self-injurious behavior. In addition, serotonin uptake inhibitors appear to result in increased sociability and decreased aggression (Bodfish & Madison, 1993; McDougle et al., 1992). There are indications that a significant period of treatment may be required (e.g., 12 weeks) before appreciable change occurs (McDougle et al., 1992), but the lack of well controlled studies and concomitant medication use mitigate the validity of these conclusions.

5-HT_{1A} agonists. Several compounds (e.g., buspirone) that display a high affinity for the 5-HT_{1A} receptor have been shown in animal studies to display antiaggressive effects and have been used clinically for anxiety and depression. There is mixed preliminary evidence for their efficacy in the treatment of anxiety-related aggressive behavior in people with MR (Kohen, 1992; Ratey, Sovner, Mikkelsen, & Chmielinski, 1989; Ratey, Sovner, Parks, & Rogentine, 1991; Verhoeven et al., 1992).

Anxiolytic and Sedative–Hypnotic Agents

The most frequently prescribed class of anxiolytic or antianxiety agents are the benzodiazepines, which include drugs such as diazepam (Valium) and chlordiazepoxide (Librium). Although such drugs, along with sedative–hypnotic agents, have been used to treat agitation, hyperactivity, and aggression, their efficacy has not been systematically studied in those with MR.

Mood-Stabilizing Agents

Anticonvulsants. Anticonvulsants (e.g., carbamazepine, valproic acid) have proved to be useful mood-stabilizing agents, particularly for rapidly cycling patients or patients showing symptoms of mixed mania. Moreover, these drugs appear to be better tolerated than lithium. Anticonvulsants may prove to be useful agents to treat a variety of behavioral problems (e.g., irritability, aggression, hyperactivity) that may reflect an underlying mood disorder. Although several reports suggest their efficacy in MR, there appears to be only one methodologically adequate study (A. H. Reid, Naylor, & Kay, 1981). In this study, carbamazepine was prescribed primarily for hyperactivity. Although no adverse medication effects were reported, carbamazepine did not appear to be clinically efficacious.

Lithium. A number of case reports suggest the efficacy of lithium in treating aggression and self-injurious behavior (Luchins & Dojka, 1989), as well as hyperactivity. D. A. Smith and Perry (1992) summarized the literature describing nonneuroleptic treatments of agitation in people with MR, autism, organic brain syndrome, and dementia. Their review of prospective evaluations of lithium for aggressive behavior in individuals with MR indicated an 83% improvement rate in open studies; 68% in double-blind, placebo-controlled studies; and, based on one study, a 30% placebo response rate. The authors pointed out that these studies suffered from the potential artifact of coadministration of antipsychotics and anticonvulsants, both of which have mood-stabilizing effects. As expected from the psychiatric literature, serum concentrations of 0.5–1.0 mEq/L were associated with good clinical outcome, whereas higher concentrations were associated with toxicity.

The adverse effects of lithium (e.g., polyuria, thirst, gastrointestinal distress), which typically are seen at blood levels greater than 1.0 mEq/L, are well documented and may, in people with MR, also result in cognitive changes (Elliot, 1986). Pary (1991) outlined criteria for an adequate trial of lithium in MR, including treatment rationale, contraindications, treatment goals, diagnostic and monitoring procedures (e.g., renal and thyroid tests), treatment parameters (e.g., duration of treatment, lithium concentrations), trial-ending conditions, and a discontinuation plan.

Stimulants

Stimulants were once uncommonly prescribed in MR, but their use in children with MR and ADHD has increased. Studies of stimulant medication in MR are generally well designed and usually support the efficacy of these drugs in the treatment of ADHD in children and adolescents with mild and moderate MR (Gadow, 1992). Whereas methylphenidate may be effective in higher functioning individuals, it does not appear to be efficacious in lower functioning people. There also is some indication that the indirect-acting serotonin agonist fenfluramine may be useful in treating ADHD, although concerns about its safety have been raised (Aman & Kern, 1989).

Opiate Antagonists

A possible mediating role for opioid peptides in autistic and self-injurious behavior has been postulated by a number of investigators (Thompson, Hackenburg, Cerutti, Baker, & Axtell, 1994). Indirect tests of this model have involved assessing the efficacy of the opiate antagonists naloxone or naltrexone. The longer elimination half-life of the latter drug makes it the drug of choice for clinical trials. The available data suggest that naltrexone is efficacious for some individuals, perhaps 50% according to a recent review (Baumeister et al., 1993), but not for others with self-injurious behavior. The factors related to a positive response to naltrexone have not yet been established. Naltrexone may also positively influence social affiliative behaviors and increase social relatedness. This latter hypothesis is based on observations made on animals and suggests that opioids mediate social affective responses in humans.

Beta-Blockers

The efficacy of beta-blockers in treating aggressive and disruptive behavior can be estimated from an 81% response rate in open trials and a 67% rate in controlled trials of individuals with MR, autism, organic brain syndrome, and dementia (D. A. Smith & Perry, 1992). Data on placebo responses are not available. Propranolol use was associated with clinically significant bradycardia or hypotension, an outcome not associated with pindolol. Unfortunately, the only methodologically sound study on MR investigated only a single participant (Baumeister et al., 1993).

Fenfluramine

Aman and Kern (1989) reviewed the efficacy of fenfluramine in the treatment of developmental disabilities. These studies were almost exclusively conducted with children with autism, and it appears that fenfluramine may result in improvements in social behavior, stereotypies, excessive motor behavior, and attention span. General cognitive ability did not appear to be affected. One study with 28 nonautistic children with MR and ADHD indicated that fenfluramine produced significant improvements in ratings of conduct problems, hyperactivity, and irritability (Aman, Kern, McGhee, & Arnold, 1993). There has been considerable debate concerning the possible neurotoxic effects of fenfluramine. Animal studies have shown fenfluramine-induced neuropathological changes and serotonin depletion. The implications of these studies for continued clinical testing of this drug are debatable.

Clonidine

The alpha-2 agonist clonidine has been used to treat Tourette's syndrome patients as well as individuals with autism. Clonidine may reduce hyperarousal behaviors such as stereotyped behavior, hyperactivity, and hypervigilance (Fankhauser, Karumanchi, German, Yates, & Karumanchi, 1992). These outcomes support the hypothesis of noradrenergic mediation of hyperarousal behaviors. To our knowledge, there have been no controlled trials of clonidine in MR.

Conclusion

The appropriate use of medication in people with MR and developmental disabilities requires a sophisticated and data-based approach. This is especially true in light of the difficulty many clients have in articulating subjective experiences and the presence of adverse effects. The risks of treatment must be weighed against the costs of not using treatment, and consideration should be given to integration with behavioral forms of management. Clinicians responsible for medication changes should consider the routine use of relevant assessment tools. The research on psychotropic medications thus far has often been of limited quality, and investigators have only begun to select participants for specific behavioral, psychiatric, or other characteristics relevant to a given drug's action. Nevertheless, the evidence suggests that there are types of symptoms and disorders that seem to respond (sometimes only modestly) to each of the major pharmacological groups.

26

Applied Behavioral Interventions

Nirbhay N. Singh, J. Grayson Osborne, and Nancy H. Huguenin

The application of behavioral procedures has improved the quality of life of people with mental retardation (MR) in ways that range from the teaching of basic living skills to the elimination of responses that may result in death. Although behavioral procedures have traditionally been applied to change specific responses, a current focus is on comprehensive lifestyle changes that improve all aspects of the individual's daily life (Evans & Meyer, 1987; Lovaas & Smith, 1989). In this chapter, we address the required components of applied behavioral interventions that include a model for clinical decision making that is necessary to program lifestyle changes in people with MR. We provide an overview rather than a comprehensive review of current practice (reviews of selected behavior analysis treatment applications in MR can be found in numerous texts, such as Matson, 1981b; Matson & Mulick, 1991a, 1991b; Van Houten & Axelrod, 1993).

Developing an Applied Behavioral Intervention Program

To assist individuals to make lifestyle changes, applied behavioral interventions focus on the development and strengthening of prosocial behavior and the reduction of problematic or antisocial behavior. The initial step in the development of an applied behavioral intervention program is to identify the goal of the program and to operationally define target and collateral responses in terms of their frequency, duration, intensity (severity), and context of occurrence. Responses are defined objectively, clearly, and completely (R. P. Hawkins & Dobes, 1975) so that they can be reliably observed and recorded.

Selecting a Measurement Technique

One of several techniques can be used to measure the occurrence of target and collateral responses. In applied behavior analysis, measurement procedures are either continuous (i.e., each response is recorded) or discontinuous (i.e., a sampling of responses is recorded; Johnston & Pennypacker, 1993; also see chapter 14 in this book). When measured continuously, responses are counted across some span of time (i.e., response frequency), particularly if they are discrete and each occurrence is relatively constant (e.g., a head slap). When responses are more continuous (e.g., social interaction, play, stereotypy), they are assessed in terms of their onset and offset in time (i.e., response duration). Responses also are recorded in terms of discrete categories, such as correct–incorrect or appropriate–inappropriate, and in terms of response latency, which is the time between a stimulus event (e.g., a prompt) and the onset of the response.

When measured discontinuously, responses are typically observed in blocks of time (e.g., 1 hr), with each block divided into short intervals (e.g., 10 s), and the occurrence or nonoccurrence of the response is recorded in each interval (called *interval recording*). Although popular, interval recording can either under- or overestimate actual response frequency (Johnston & Pennypacker, 1993). Thus, selection of an observation strategy is informed and depends on the nature of the target and collateral responses and on the purposes of the applied behavioral intervention program.

Functional Analysis

Once a method for the assessment of the target and collateral responses has been chosen and preliminary data collected, it is important to determine the functions that these responses serve for the individual. A *functional analysis* is a method designed to determine the relationship between a response and its antecedents and consequences. Several methods are used to discover these relationships, including interviews with people who know the individual well (O'Neill, Horner, Albin, Storey, & Sprague, 1990), direct observations of the individual in settings in which the response occurs (O'Neill et al., 1990), and manipulation of the putative antecedents and consequences of the responses (Iwata, Dorsey, Slifer, Bauman, & Richman, 1982). Although rating scales such as the Motivation Assessment Scale (Durand & Crimmins, 1988) have been devised for this purpose, they have not proved reliable, valid, or otherwise psychometrically robust (Singh et al., 1993; Zarcone, Rodgers, Iwata, Rourke, & Dorsey, 1991). Instructions for conducting functional analyses are provided by Iwata, Vollmer, and Zarcone (1990); Iwata, Vollmer, Zarcone, and Rodgers (1993); and Mace, Lalli, Lalli, and Shea (1993).

A thorough functional analysis provides the basis for the selection of the most appropriate treatment for the target response. One of the advantages of undertaking a functional analysis is that it can indicate whether the response is initiated or maintained by specific antecedent conditions in the individual's environment (e.g., presence of staff, interaction with peers, lack of stimulation), by its consequences (e.g., avoidance or escape from an unpleasant task, staff attention), or by both. When the analysis shows that the response is maintained by specific antecedent conditions, the focus of treatment is on environmental change. When the analysis shows that the response is maintained by particular consequences, the analysis implicates techniques that involve the manipulation of those same consequences. As of this writing, functional analysis has been used primarily to search for the causes of problematic, antisocial responses.

Selecting a Treatment Procedure: A Clinical Decision-Making Model

The Association for Behavior Analysis (ABA) Task Force (Van Houten et al., 1988) on the right to effective behavioral treatment stipulated that each individual has the right to the least restrictive effective treatment and to treatment that produces safe and meaningful behavior change. In line with this recommendation, a number of clinical decision-making models have been advanced to select treatment procedures that reduce problem behaviors (e.g., Donnellan, Mirenda, Mesaros, & Fassbender, 1984; Evans & Meyer, 1985). (Notably, none of these models has as its primary focus the development of prosocial behavior.) We present a brief description of the Axelrod, Spreat, Berry, and Moyer (1993) model because it fulfills the mandate of the ABA Task Force and includes procedures for complying with accreditation standards and state and federal regulations. The Axelrod et al. (1993) model includes the following components:

1. *Determine whether an important performance discrepancy exists.* The need for an applied behavioral intervention is determined by assessing whether there is a discrepancy between the actual and expected performance of the individual and whether the discrepancy is socially significant in terms of the person's overall quality of life.

2. *Conduct a functional analysis.* As noted earlier, a functional analysis includes the determination of the functions that the target and collateral responses serve for the individual and also helps to focus treatment procedures.

3. *Conduct a historical analysis of the person, behavior, and procedure.* This involves gathering information on the individual's behavioral, medical, and programmatic history, as well as on procedures successfully used to modify the same behavior in other individuals. Furthermore, a literature search is undertaken to determine the primary and secondary effects of various treatment procedures that have been used with the target response, their implementation requirements, and their social acceptability. Together with the data from the functional analysis, this information focuses the choice of a treatment procedure for the individual that will be most effective, safe, and durable.

4. *Choose the least restrictive effective treatment.* The ABA Task Force mandated that individuals receive the least restrictive effective treatment. That is, if two treatments are (theoretically) equally effective, the less restrictive treatment option is the treatment of choice. This model does not advocate the selection of procedures from a hierarchy of treatments based on restrictiveness because nonrestrictive procedures that are high on this hierarchy may be ineffective for the target behavior of the individ-

ual. What it does advocate is that the least restrictive effective treatment be used from the outset, even though the procedure may be more restrictive than others on the hierarchy that are ineffective. Thus, the entire spectrum of behavioral procedures, less and more restrictive, forms the pool from which the least restrictive effective treatment is chosen, based on a functional analysis of the target behavior of the individual.

5. *Conduct a risk–benefit analysis.* In compliance with judicial rulings (e.g., *Youngberg v. Romeo*, 1982) and accreditation standards, it is the change agent's responsibility to "select the treatment that achieves the most reasonable balance between likely benefits and potential risks" (Axelrod et al., 1993, p. 191). A number of risk–benefit analysis models have been proposed for this purpose (e.g., Meinhold & Mulick, 1992; Mulick, 1989; Spreat, 1982a), all of which include the following elements: (a) probability of treatment success, (b) total treatment time, (c) amount of distress or discomfort associated with the procedure, and (d) distress or discomfort caused by the behavior during treatment (Axelrod et al., 1993; Meinhold & Mulick, 1992). Although the evaluation of this component of the model is subjective, it is essential that a risk–benefit analysis be undertaken to fulfill regulatory requirements, as well as to heighten the sensitivity of change agents to the potential risks involved in the use of any treatment procedure.

6. *Complete a safeguards checklist.* The basic issue involved here is the protection of the individual's rights during the process of treatment (i.e., historical assessment, functional analysis, treatment selection, implementation, and evaluation). Axelrod et al. (1993, pp. 194–195) provided a checklist that operationalizes the activities that must be completed prior to behavioral intervention.

7. *Obtain the necessary authorizations.* The final step in this model requires the change agent to obtain the necessary authorizations mandated by state and federal regulations. Although state regulations vary, most require that the treatment program be developed by an interdisciplinary team. Furthermore, if potential risks are involved in the treatment process, additional review and approval from a peer review committee and a human rights committee are necessary. Finally, written consent is obtained from the individual (or legal guardian) before the proposed treatment program is instituted.

This model is based on current standards of behavioral practice and meets most statutory and regulatory requirements. If a behavioral treatment is paired with a psychopharmacological regimen, then it is essential that state and federal guidelines for drug treatment be incorporated in the safeguards and authorizations (Singh, Guernsey, & Ellis, 1992).

Design of the Applied Behavioral Intervention

An applied behavioral intervention program necessarily has a minimum of four phases, with measurement continuing until a stable picture of responding develops in each. In the first, or *baseline* phase, the occurrence of the target and collateral responses is recorded, without application of the intervention procedures. The second phase consists of the application of the intervention procedures. Additional phases are added subsequently to promote stimulus and response generalization (see the next section) and to determine the longevity (usually a minimum of several months) of the results (called the *follow-up* phase).

Techniques for Increasing Behaviors

In the following section, we discuss techniques in applied behavioral intervention programs that are used to develop and strengthen prosocial responses.

Positive Reinforcement

Positive reinforcement is an extremely effective procedure for increasing prosocial responses. A positive reinforcer is an event that increases the probability of occurrence of the response that directly precedes it. Positive reinforcers can be either primary (i.e., unconditioned) or secondary (i.e., conditioned). Primary reinforcers, such as food, water, and sex, are biologically given, whereas secondary reinforcers, such as toys and money, acquire their reinforcing value by becoming predictors of positive reinforcement. No event is always a positive reinforcer for all individuals, and the reinforcing value of potential reinforcers is determined empirically.

A particular relationship between responses also constitutes positive reinforcement. For example, if an individual responds at a low rate, this rate can be increased if a high-rate response is made contingent on the low-rate response. Thus, the high-rate response is a reinforcer for the low-rate response. In general terms, a high-probability response can act as a reinforcer for a low-probability response (Premack, 1965). Why this is so is not entirely clear, although one hypothesis is that when the higher probability response is made contingent on the lower probability response, the individual is deprived of engagement in the higher probability response. Thus, the individual engages in the lower probability response to reduce the deprivation (Timberlake & Allison, 1974).

Positive reinforcers used in programs for individuals with MR include edible, social, and activity reinforcers. As strong reinforcers, edibles are particularly useful in teaching new skills. In practice, to reduce the effects of satiation, a variety of edibles is used. Furthermore, praise is consistently paired with edibles so that after repeated pairings, praise alone acquires (conditioned) reinforcing properties and promotes normalization.

Shaping

One shortcoming of positive reinforcement is that the change agent must wait for the target response to occur before it can be reinforced. The change agent might desire to reinforce play skills in a child with MR, for example, but may never have the opportunity to do so because the child never touches a toy. A solution is to use shaping, a procedure that commences with the reinforcement of responses similar to, but different from, the target response. To accomplish shaping, the change agent (a) selects a strong positive reinforcer, (b) specifies the target response, (c) lists responses more and more similar to the target response, (d) reinforces the first response on the list, (e) discontinues reinforcement for that response after it has increased in frequency until a response closer to the desired response occurs, (f) reinforces this next response, (g) continues the cycle of (e) and (f) until the target response occurs, and (h) reinforces only the target response. Through this process of differential reinforcement, the individual's behavior is gradually shaped until the target response is created.

Stimulus Control Procedures

Once a new response has been acquired, an individual must produce it in the appropriate environmental context and in the presence of naturally occurring stimuli. Stimulus control is evident when the probability of occurrence of a response is determined by the presence or absence of a stimulus. A child's toothbrushing is under appropriate stimulus control if the child brushes his or her teeth after rather than before meals. Stimulus control can be achieved by differential reinforcement, which consists of reinforcing the target response only in the presence of a specific stimulus and withholding reinforcement if the response occurs in its absence.

Differential reinforcement is not an ideal teaching procedure for people with MR because it permits errors (i.e., responses under the control of nonprogrammed features of the environment). Errors prevent the individual's behavior from coming under the control of the relevant stimuli. Once errors occur in people with MR, they are difficult to eliminate and can generate misbehaviors, some of which can be severe. Fortunately, there are procedures that help stimulus control develop with few or no errors. Stimulus fading and stimulus shaping are two such procedures.

Stimulus fading. This is an errorless stimulus control procedure that has been used to teach a wide variety of skills to people with MR (Harchik, Harchik, Luce, & Sherman, 1990). In this procedure, a stimulus prompt —one that is known to produce the target response—is added to the training stimulus, when at the beginning of the training sequence the training stimulus does not produce the target response. Next, the added stimulus prompt is gradually removed until, in the final stages of the procedure, the training stimulus alone evokes the target response. Throughout the prompting sequence, the target response is reinforced as the added stimulus prompt is gradually decreased in magnitude.

Stimulus shaping. This is another errorless stimulus control procedure that has been used with people with MR (Karsh, Repp, & Lenz, 1990;

Repp, Karsh, & Lenz, 1990). Stimulus shaping differs from stimulus fading in that an added stimulus to prompt the correct response is not used. Rather, correct responses are produced with this procedure by exaggerating the distinctive features of the training stimuli. As the sequence progresses, exaggeration of these features is gradually reduced until terminal levels of the training stimuli are achieved. Thus, stimulus shaping uses criterion-related prompts, in contrast to stimulus fading, in which non-criterion-related prompts are used. Stimulus shaping is more effective than stimulus fading in the minimization of errors and in the establishment of stimulus control (e.g., Karsh et al., 1990; Repp et al., 1990; Schreibman, 1975).

Overselection. One explanation for the sometime failure of stimulus fading procedures to achieve errorless stimulus control with people with MR relates to overselective attention. When compound training stimuli are presented, people with MR and autism often attend to a more restricted portion of the stimulus compound than nondisabled individuals (Lovaas & Schreibman, 1971). Furthermore, the degree of stimulus overselectivity correlates negatively with intelligence level (Rincover & Ducharme, 1987). Stimulus fading procedures using an added non-criterion-related prompt can, therefore, fail because many people with MR appear to experience difficulty attending simultaneously to more than one stimulus feature. As a result, they do not transfer stimulus control from the added stimulus prompt to the training stimuli (Doran & Holland, 1979). This finding may explain the failure of non-criterion-related prompting procedures and the greater effectiveness of criterion-related prompts for these individuals.

An alternative explanation for the superiority of stimulus shaping procedures, which use criterion-related prompts, might reveal the influence of reinforcement histories. Stimulus shaping procedures, by emphasizing critical features of training cues, ensure that prior reinforcement contingencies bring the student's behavior under control of the relevant stimulus dimension before the training stimuli are provided. By establishing a prior reinforcement history for the stimulus prompt, which is compatible with the reinforcement contingencies of the training stimuli, errorless stimulus control is achieved. This does not occur in non-criterion-related prompting techniques, which, instead, establish prior reinforcement contingencies that bring the individual's behavior under control of stimulus dimensions irrelevant to the training stimuli. Such training is particularly disruptive for people with severe and profound MR, who often persist in responding to the irrelevant features of a task compared with their nondisabled counterparts.

Techniques for Decreasing Behaviors

Some behavioral intervention programs for people with MR involve the reduction of the frequency of self-stimulatory, self-injurious, and antisocial behaviors, all of which interfere with their continued development. Individuals with MR have a moral right to be free from behavior that interferes with this development (Van Houten et al., 1988).

Technique Selection

Ideally, behavior change techniques should be nonrestrictive and equally efficacious. None are. These facts necessitate the informed selection of technique. With severe behavior problems, the change agent's intent is to select a decelerative technique that achieves the maximum decrease in unwanted responses, in the shortest time possible, and that creates the least restriction for the individual. To accomplish this, the change agent must have knowledge of the target individual, technique efficacy, secondary effects of the technique, social and legal implications of its use, and practical considerations, such as the level of staff competence (Lennox & Miltenberger, 1990). However, controversy exists with respect to technique effectiveness, particularly when there are perceived undesirable secondary effects, and technique restrictiveness, particularly when the latter implies loss of freedom and dignity for the target individual or when the target individual is powerless (Repp & Singh, 1990). As a result, within a least restrictive treatment model, the use of behavior change techniques is decided on multiple grounds—only one of which is treatment effectiveness—and at several levels in order to protect the individual (see the section on the clinical decision-making model).

In practice, there is a direct correlation between the number of reviews and consents and the perceived restrictiveness of the technique. Moreover, it is necessary to show that less restrictive techniques (which might work) have been validly applied, yet failed. Finally, should consent be granted, limitations (such as time of application, and kind and intensity of aversive stimulation) are imposed.

We next outline decelerative behavior change procedures roughly in order of perceived restrictiveness and, therefore, in current frequency of use.

Differential Reinforcement Procedures

There are at least four variations of differential reinforcement procedures: (a) differential reinforcement of other behavior (DRO), (b) differential reinforcement of alternative behavior (DRA), (c) differential reinforcement of incompatible behavior (DRI), and (d) differential reinforcement of low rates (DRL). These techniques involve reinforcement for wanted behavior, either unspecified (DRO) or specified (DRA, DRI, and DRL), dependent on the absence (via extinction; see the next section) for periods of time of the unwanted behavior. They have been applied to a wide spectrum of problem behaviors with some success (Vollmer & Iwata, 1992). The effectiveness of these techniques is based on the joint validity of the extinction component and the reinforcers for the individual, both of which follow from a successful functional analysis. These differential reinforcement procedures are typically used in the absence of review procedures because they are not perceived to be highly restrictive.

With functional communication training, the individual is conditioned to emit a desirable response (often a sign) that produces the same reinforcer formerly produced by an aberrant response while the aberrant response is placed on extinction (Durand & Carr, 1991). Thus, the procedure is essentially a DRA or DRI, in which the alternative or incompatible response is a "communicative" one. Contingencies for the desirable and undesirable responses both appear to be necessary to the success of the procedure; hence, its classification as decelerative. The social nature of the alternative response may "trap" natural reinforcers and encourage generalization and maintenance. One potential drawback of functional communication training is that individuals may escape task demands (albeit with a high-frequency desirable response) to such an extent that their further development is delayed until the high-frequency response itself is brought under stimulus control. This procedure is also used in the absence of formal review for the same reason as the differential reinforcement procedures.

Extinction

Extinction is defined as the cessation of reinforcement for a response class and, functionally, the subsequent decrease of the response class to its baseline frequency (G. L. Martin & Osborne, 1993). If the baseline frequency of the response class is greater than zero, extinction does not result in a zero frequency of the response class. Extinction is commonly a sufficient condition for a number of secondary effects, including (a) a temporary increase in the dimensional measures of the extinguished response class (i.e., extinction burst); (b) emotional responses; (c) the increase in frequency of another response from the same response class; (d) aggression or property destruction; and (e) spontaneous recovery, a brief resumption of the response class at higher frequencies, when the student is again placed in the treatment environment at a later time.

Notwithstanding its status as a separate decelerative technique, extinction is an inseparable part of any reinforcement procedure. Because reinforcement is specific to a particular class of responses in any instance, responses not in the defined class are not reinforced. Therefore, they undergo extinction and contribute indirectly to the increase in frequency of responses in the reinforced class. Extinction is both a logical and functional part of all of the foregoing techniques. Successful extinction depends on the change agent's complete knowledge of and control over reinforcers for the response class, ability to preclude escape by the target individual, and patience because the duration of extinction is related to the reinforcement history of the response class. Extinction is less frequently used formally and as a stand-alone technique because of the difficulty of carrying it out successfully.

Punishment I (Positive)

Response-contingent aversive stimulation. These techniques involve the application of an aversive stimulus contingent on unwanted behavior. They include, but are not limited to, visual screening, water misting, aversive tastes, brief physical restraint, and faradic shock (Cataldo, 1989). These techniques typically are perceived to be highly restrictive, but they also are perceived to be highly effective because response suppression is often immediate and enduring (Linscheid, Iwata, Ricketts, & Williams, 1990). However, their uniqueness appears to make them easily discriminated, and generalization to other environments may be difficult. Furthermore, their use is controversial. These procedures require the most complete review; as a result, although they often have positive secondary effects (Lovaas & Simmons, 1969; Meinhold & Mulick, 1992), they are now more often used as a last resort such as when behavior is life threatening and intractable to other procedures.

Overcorrection. This is a treatment package that contains both reductive and accelerative procedures (Foxx & Bechtel, 1983). The reductive procedure typically involves (initially) the manual guidance of a reluctant target individual to motorically engage in either the restoration of some despoiled environment (or individual)—termed *restitutional overcorrection*—or the repeated practice of a response topographically or functionally incompatible with the undesired response—termed *positive practice overcorrection.* The accelerative procedures involve the increase in the frequency of the restorative or incompatible responses, which, through repeated practice, become more likely. Some of the drawbacks of the technique include (a) the potential necessity of physically guiding a reluctant individual through the procedure, (b) inadvertent (i.e., possibly reinforcing or physically damaging) contact with the individual while conducting the procedure, and (c) labor- and time-intensive features that necessitate high staff commitment level. Notwithstanding the foregoing, this may be the best researched reductive technique of all (Foxx & Bechtel, 1983; MacKenzie-Keating & McDonald, 1990), and when carried out appropriately, it is highly effective. Its components (i.e., guided movement training, positive practice) are probably used more now in the absence of the entire procedure than in its presence. In our experience, the components of this technique are used separately, informally, and without permission by institutional staff as standard behavior management procedures. Use of the entire package requires a complete review.

Punishment II (Negative)

This type of punishment involves the contingent withdrawal of reinforcement in terms of either an amount (response cost) or a period of time (time-out).

Response cost. Although it is effective with minor problem behaviors, response cost has only rarely been applied to the severe behavior problems (e.g., self-injury, aggression) that concern us here, so it is not further discussed.

Time-out (TO) from positive reinforcement. In the first of two variations of TO, the individual is removed from an assumedly reinforcing environment and is placed for a short period of time in an environment assumedly absent of reinforcement (*exclusionary TO*). In the second, the positively reinforcing environment is removed from the individual (*nonexclusionary TO*; see Schroeder, Mulick, & Schroeder, 1979, for additional variations). Differential reinforcement densities in each environment are critical to successful intervention, as is control over surreptitious reinforcement (e.g., staff attention while using the technique). Egress from the TO environment is usually contingent on the absence of the unwanted response and other emotional responses (i.e., DRO). This latter contingency is usually necessary for success but can prolong the time in TO. Exclusionary TO is strictly monitored to prevent self-injury by the individual and to prevent staff abuse, as staff may be negatively reinforced by the absence of the target individual. Application of exclusionary TO is problematic when the individual is large or reluctant, when isolation is not secure, and when complete observation is not possible. Withdrawal of the individual from the reinforcing environment can initially elicit emotional responses. Furthermore, short periods in TO appear to be as effective as longer periods in controlling unwanted behavior (McGuffin, 1991). TO may work in part because it serves to interrupt ongoing, unwanted responses. In our experience, this is a technique that is used frequently by institutional staff on an informal basis without consent.

Stimulus and Response Generalization

Generalization of treatment effects is an important goal of applied behavioral interventions. *Stimulus generalization* is evident whenever target behaviors occur in nontraining conditions in which the complete treatment program has never been introduced. *Response generalization* is evident when unreinforced responses from the target class occur either in training or nontraining conditions. Identifying manipulations that result in both kinds of generalization for people with MR is especially critical for their development. We present a brief summary of methods for producing both stimulus and response generalization and maintenance of treatment gains (for more complete discussions, see Horner, Dunlap, & Koegel, 1988; Huguenin, Weidenman, & Mulick, 1991).

Stimulus Generalization

Programming common cues. Stimulus generalization occurs when an individual's target responses are brought under the control of specified antecedent stimuli that are common to nontraining settings. Achieving high levels of stimulus control for designated stimuli in the training setting and then using the same or similar stimuli in other environments is a highly successful approach to stimulus generalization.

Training sufficient exemplars. Presenting more than one stimulus condition is another technique for achieving generalization among people with MR (Day & Horner, 1986; Matson, 1990). Stokes, Baer, and Jackson (1974) used prompting and shaping to teach a social greeting response to 4 children with MR. A multiple baseline design across participants showed that if only one experimenter taught the greeting response, generalization to persons outside training did not occur. With 3 of the 4 participants, however, training in the greeting response by two trainers resulted in generalization to more than 20 individuals who had not participated in the original training. Thus, a minimum of two exemplars appears to be necessary to produce some stimulus generalization. Training in the presence of different exemplars results in stimulus generalization because the irrelevant features of these new exemplars vary, and the controlling features of the new exemplars remain constant (Kirby & Bickel, 1988).

Response Generalization

Less has been done formally with the development of response generalization. Currently, there is a single focus: train sufficient response exemplars. Some important classes of responses (e.g., social skills) are constituted by a large number of response instances. After initial training with a narrowly defined response class, stimulus prompts to get a variety of other responses from the broader response class to occur can be routinely programmed and the new responses reinforced. Eventually, a class of functionally equivalent responses results.

Behavior Maintenance

The final requirement of any applied behavioral intervention is that the behavior change is maintained. This is accomplished by programming (a) formal contingencies on an intermittent basis (e.g., intermittent reinforcement), (b) natural contingencies to take effect, (c) permanent structural changes in the environment, and (d) the transference of control to the individual (an excellent form of empowerment).

Conclusion

Behavioral methods provide highly effective interventions to increase positive behaviors and decrease problem behaviors in people with MR. The technology of applied behavioral intervention has advanced enormously over the past 25 years, and well-validated methods for the behavioral assessment and treatment of pro- and antisocial behaviors are available to the behavior change agent. In this chapter, we have presented an overview of the requirements for the use of some of these methods, as well as a clinical decision-making model for the design and implementation of applied behavioral intervention programs.

27

Behavior Therapies: A Multimodal Diagnostic and Intervention Model

William I. Gardner, Janice L. Graeber, and Christine L. Cole

Within the past two decades, the behavior therapies and their applications to psychological problems presented by people with mental retardation (MR) have undergone notable advances (W. I. Gardner, 1988; W. I. Gardner & Graeber, 1994). These advances involve (a) an increased emphasis on interventions based on hypothesized instigating and maintaining factors (E. G. Carr, 1977; E. G. Carr & Durand, 1985a, 1985b); (b) the expansion of the unimodal (operant) behavioral model to include other psychological, biological, and socioenvironmental contributions to aberrant behavior (J. S. Bailey & Pyles, 1989; W. I. Gardner & Cole, 1984); (c) development of multimodal models that systematically guide the diagnostic–intervention formulation process to ensure appropriate staging and integration of behavioral interventions with those addressing biomedical and socioenvironmental influences (W. I. Gardner & Sovner, 1994); and (d) adoption of a skill deficit perspective with a concurrent habilitative intervention focus of teaching social and coping competency skills to replace aberrant responding (Foxx, Zukotynski, & Williams, 1994; Matson & Stephens, 1978). A collateral of the latter trend has been an increased emphasis on teaching self-management skills and providing choices as self-controlled alternatives to external management procedures (W. I. Gardner & Cole, 1989; Harchik, Sherman, Sheldon, & Bannerman, 1993).

In this chapter, we describe a contemporary multimodal behavioral diagnostic and intervention model that reflects these trends. Following this, illustrations of various behavior therapy procedures in the treatment of severe emotional and behavioral symptoms are provided. This material should be treated as a companion to the more basic chapters in this book on behavior analysis and interventions. Primary sources providing more comprehensive descriptions and critical evaluations of behavior therapy approaches include Cipani (1989), W. I. Gardner and Cole (1993), W. I. Gardner and Sovner (1994), Matson and Barrett (1993), Repp and Singh (1990), Thompson and Gray (1994), and Van Houten and Axelrod (1993).

The behavior therapies represent a constellation of clinical procedures derived from learning and related theoretical models of human functioning. Terms such as applied behavior analysis, behavior management, behavior modification, behavior therapy, behavioral treatment, cognitive–behavioral therapy, contingency management, emotional retraining, reinforcement therapy, and social skills training are used by various writers to refer either to specific groups of procedures or as generic labels to encompass the entire range of behavior analysis and change procedures and their major conceptual foundations. The major assumption underlying behavior therapy procedures is that behavioral and emotional difficulties reflect the effects of faulty or deficient learning experiences. The behavior therapies are used to offset the effects of these experiences through (a) removing or reducing current instigating and maintaining influences and (b) teaching more effective functional coping alternatives, including their motivational components.

To accomplish these objectives, the behavior therapist selects specific therapeutic procedures from an array of available strategies. This selection is guided by a diagnostic understanding of the personal characteristics of each specific client as these relate to instigating and maintaining influences producing specific psychological symptoms. As illustrations, on the basis of client-specific diagnostic formulations of instigating and maintaining conditions, a therapist may choose (a) systematic desensitization and related stimulus exposure procedures (a respondent-based learning paradigm) to eliminate clinically significant fears and obsessive–compulsive behaviors for some clients (Erfanian & Miltenberger, 1990; Hiss & Kozak, 1991); (b) a skills training program (an operant-based learning paradigm) to teach alternative functional communication skills to replace self-injurious and aggressive symptoms for a second client (Bird, Dores, Moniz, & Robinson, 1989; Durand, 1990); (c) a social skills program (a social learning paradigm) to teach prosocial interpersonal skills as alternatives to aggressive and other disruptive responding of adults with a dual diagnosis of psychosis and MR (Foxx, McMorrow, & Schloss, 1983; Matson & Stephens, 1978); or (d) a self-management program (a cognitive–behavioral learning paradigm) to teach coping alternatives to multiple behavioral and emotional symptoms for clients with chronic and severe behavior disorders (B. A. Benson, 1992; C. L. Cole, Gardner, & Karan, 1985; W. I. Gardner, Cole, Berry, & Nowinski, 1983; R. M. Reese, Sherman, & Sheldon, 1984).

Multimodal Functional Approach

Historically, behavioral and emotional symptoms presented by those with MR have been viewed from either a biomedical or a behavioral perspective, with the frequent result that behaviorally responsive symptoms or disorders were "medicalized" and biomedically responsive symptoms or disorders were "behavioralized." These practices resulted in the overuse of psychotropic medications and the misuse of behavioral procedures to suppress symptoms in the absence of a diagnostic understanding of the specific and frequently multiple factors influencing symptom presentation (W. I. Gardner, 1988; Spreat & Behar, 1994). Dissatisfaction with these isolated approaches, coupled with the need for a model to reflect the multiple and complex factors that may contribute to the instigation and maintenance of aberrant behaviors and emotions, has resulted in an integrative multimodal alternative to diagnosis and treatment selection. This *multimodal functional diagnostic and intervention model*, depicted in Figure 1, reflects a biopsychosocial view of human behavior, emphasizing that behavioral and emotional difficulties represent the effects of psychological and biomedical characteristics of a person as he or she interacts with physical and psychosocial environments (W. I. Gardner & Cole, 1993; W. I. Gardner & Sovner, 1994; Sovner & Hurley, 1992).

To illustrate the interaction of these influences, biologically based psychiatric conditions such as schizophrenia or a bipolar disorder may result in changes in cognitive functions, mood and affective states, emotional regulation, and psychomotor behaviors. These changing psychological and physical characteristics may result in new behavioral or emotional difficulties or may influence the occurrence or increased severity of problems that predated the current psychiatric episode (Lowry & Sovner, 1991a). These symptoms, in turn, create more than usual changes in the manner in which the social environment responds to and interacts with the person and his or her problem behaviors. These experiences with the social environment may, in a reciprocal manner, reinforce the problem behaviors or intensify the emotional arousal and affect the person's perceptions of the social feedback. A therapeutic program must be sensitive to these reciprocal interrelationships and provide attention to each set of influences (W. I. Gardner & Sovner, 1994).

A closely related concept of the multimodal functional approach is the interactive nature making up the psychological elements of this triad. Although the person's behavioral symptoms such as aggression or self-injurious acts frequently are those that create most concern, the functional approach recognizes the interactive effects of behaviors, emotions, and cognitions. A person's behavior (e.g., physical aggression) influences his or her feelings (e.g., anger, anxiety) and cognitions (e.g., "He deserved that"), just as the person's feelings or cognitions may influence each other as well as the behavior (W. I. Gardner & Moffatt, 1990).

Therapeutic intervention may be directed at changing any one or each of these interactive psychological components. For example, if it is assumed that a person's aggression is influenced by anger arousal, behavior therapy may focus on teaching the person to control or reduce his or her anger and, as a result, reduce the likelihood of aggressive behavior (B. A. Benson, 1986, 1992). In other instances, a person may engage in repetitive thoughts that a coworker is dangerous and attempting to harm him or her. As a result of this perceptual set, the person may act aggressively if provoked by the coworker. Reducing or eliminating the ruminative thinking through the use of behavior therapy or medication should reduce the aggressive acts (C. L. Cole & Gardner, 1990; W. I. Gardner, Clees, & Cole, 1983). Finally, a person's aggressive behaviors may be followed immediately by self-delivery of negative consequences. These experiences may

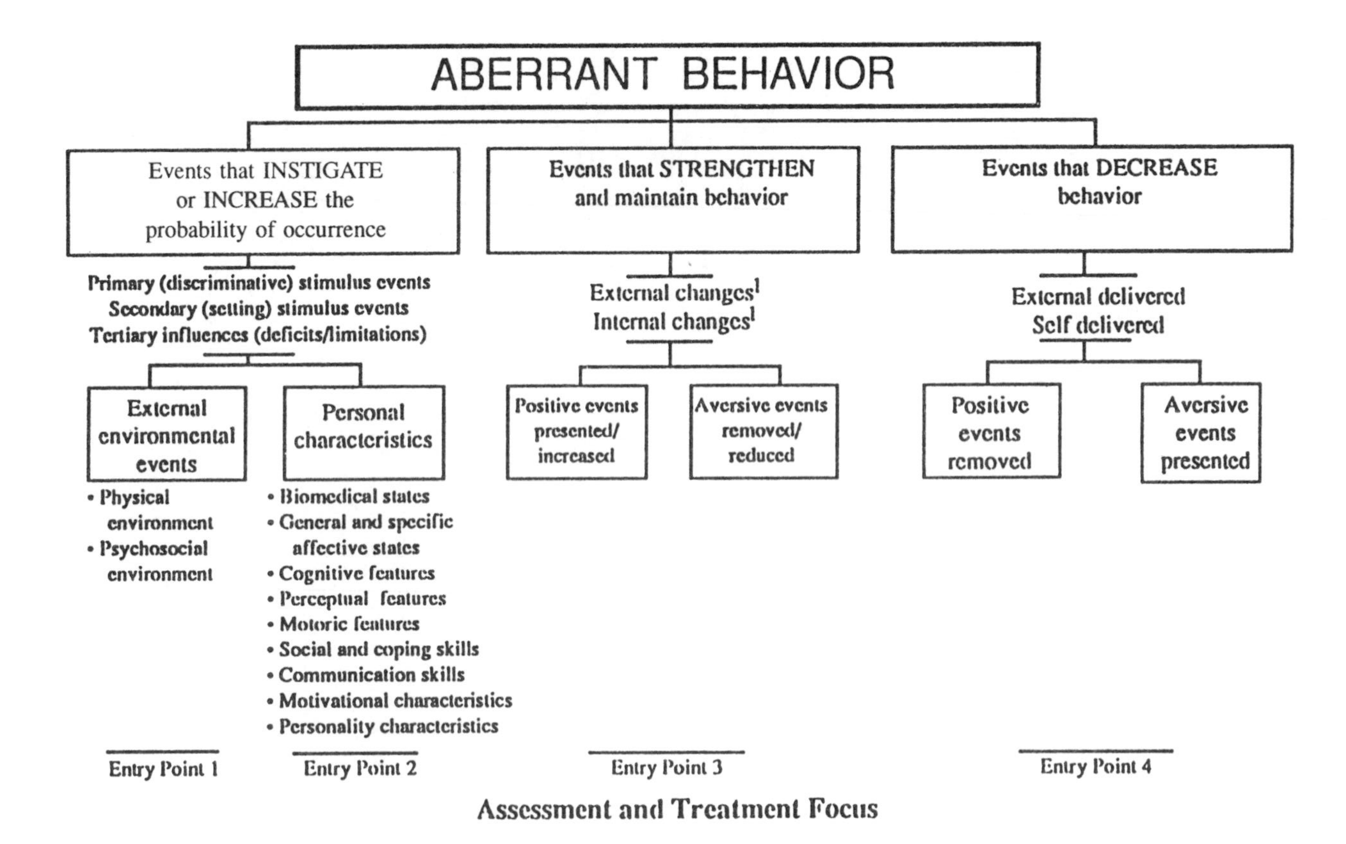

Figure 1. Multimodal functional diagnostic and intervention model.

result in inhibition of the aggression, changes in the person's cognitions (e.g., "I won't hit him because I'll lose my bonus"), and a reduction in the level of anger (C. L. Cole et al., 1985). In summary, regardless of the specific type or focus of intervention, each component of a person's psychological triad (behaviors, emotions, and cognitions) may be influenced. In view of this perspective, psychological interventions—or medical interventions when addressing biomedically related influences—may address any one or a combination of these interactive influences (Lowry & Sovner, 1991b; Sovner & Hurley, 1992).

The initial step in devising an intervention program consists of developing a set of interrelated diagnostic and treatment formulations reflecting biomedical, psychological, and social influences. Such formulations are necessary because aberrant behaviors are best viewed as a "final common pathway" reflecting an individual's adaptation to environmental demands and physical discomfort as well as to disturbances in neurochemical and physiological function (W. I. Gardner & Sovner, 1994; Nezu & Nezu, 1994). To guide selection of person-specific interventions, a set of diagnostic formulations evolve from the following three-step process.

Step 1

The initial diagnostic task as depicted in entry point 1 and entry point 2 of Figure 1 is that of identifying the current external (e.g., specific task demands, reduced social support following death of mother, crowded and noisy conditions, negative feedback) and physical, sensory, affective, and cognitive internal (e.g., seizure activity, paranoid ideation, fatigue, anxiety, premenstrual pain, anger, episodic periods of organically based heightened arousal) stimulus conditions of a biomedical, psychological, or socioenvironmental nature that contribute directly to the instigation of the aberrant symptoms (B. A. Benson, 1990; B. A. Benson, Rice, & Miranti, 1986; Dosen & Gielen, 1993; Fahs, 1989; W. I. Gardner, Clees, et al., 1983; Gedye, 1989; Kastner, Friedman, O'Brien, & Pond, 1990; Sovner & Pary, 1993). These conditions may reflect either a primary (discriminative) or secondary (setting) instigating function (W. I. Gardner, Cole, Davidson, & Karan, 1986; W. I. Gardner & Sovner, 1994; Kennedy & Itkonen, 1993; Schroeder, 1990).

Primary instigating influences are the necessary conditions that must be present for symptoms to occur. Because the same symptom may be controlled by more than a single condition, assessment identifies each separate condition and its relative instigative influences. *Secondary instigators* are the conditions whose presence increases or decreases the likelihood of symptom occurrence when the person is exposed to a primary instigator. For example, if experiencing auditory hallucinations (secondary instigator), a person may become verbally abusive when directed to engage in a low-preference activity (primary instigator). If the same staff provides the same directive (primary instigator) on another occasion when the person is in a positive mood state and lucid (secondary instigator), cooperative behavior may occur (Haynes, Spain, & Oliveira, 1993; Schroeder, 1990).

Step 2

After the target symptoms are placed in a context of instigating conditions, hypotheses are developed regarding the purposes or functions of the targets (e.g., terminate aversive demands, modulate pain, decrease unpleasant internal arousal, ensure sensory or social feedback; E. G. Carr, Robinson, & Palumbo, 1990; Iwata, Vollmer, Zarcone, & Rodgers, 1993; Lowry & Sovner, 1991b; Mace, Lalli, Lalli, & Shea, 1993). Entry point 3 of Figure 1 depicts this assessment focus.

Step 3

The final step in the diagnostic formulation process involves description of other relevant personal features of a psychological (e.g., anger management, communication, or coping skill deficits) and biomedical (e.g., sensory, neurological, or biochemical impairments or abnormalities) nature, along with socioenvironmental and ecological features (e.g., limited opportunity for social interaction, minimal social support systems, restrictions in type and frequency of structured program activities) that, by their absence or low strength or aberrant nature, may contribute indirectly to symptom occurrence (E. G. Carr et al., 1990).

Additional client characteristics that may contribute to aberrant responding, as depicted in entry point 1 and entry point 2 of Figure 1, include trait or personality variables and motivational characteristics. A person with profound MR, an example of the former, may have a generalized low threshold of tolerating changes and thus be prone to aggressive outbursts when there are frequent unplanned disruptions in his or her daily routine (W. I. Gardner, 1988). Motivational characteristics include the variety and relative influence of events that serve as positive reinforcers (e.g., adult approval, exercise of control over others) and the variety and relative effects of aversive events controlling negative emotional reactions that activate avoidance and escape behaviors (J. S. Bailey & Pyles, 1989; E. G. Carr & Durand, 1985a, 1985b; Rolinder & Van Houten, 1993). A restriction in the range and schedule of available positive events and an overabundance of aversive events render the person more vulnerable to conditions influencing aberrant responding (Matson & Sevin, 1994). Although not directly involved in symptom occurrence, these vulnerability-related personal and environmental features are viewed as tertiary influences because these increase the likelihood that the person will engage in maladaptive behaviors under specific primary and secondary instigating stimulus conditions (E. G. Carr & Durand, 1985a, 1985b; Durand, 1990; W. I. Gardner & Cole, 1989).

These diagnostic hypotheses about primary and secondary instigating conditions, the functionality of the target symptoms, and tertiary vulnerability factors form the basis for formulation of diagnostically based interventions addressing each of the presumed contributing influences. Major program efforts are focused on (a) removing or minimizing biomedical and psychosocial factors hypothesized to contribute to the instigation and maintenance of the target symptoms; (b) teaching prosocial coping skills as well as increasing the personal motivation to use these newly acquired skills as adaptive functional replacements for the target symptoms; and (c) reducing or eliminating impoverished socioenvironmental conditions, biomedical abnormalities, and tertiary psychological characteristics that increase the person's vulnerability to aberrant responding (W. I. Gardner & Sovner, 1994; Nezu & Nezu, 1994; Nezu, Nezu, & Gill-Weiss, 1992; Sovner & Hurley, 1986).

Behavior Therapy Applications

Descriptions of use of various behavior therapy procedures are provided in the remaining sections. These interventions, when diagnostically indicated, should be coordinated closely with interventions of a biomedical and socioenvironmental nature. As suggested earlier, a major objective of behaviorally based therapy programs is that of increasing the person's coping skill competencies. To guide the focus of interventions, a coping skills training model (see Figure 2) is used to organize the presentation of specific groups of behavior therapy procedures.

Coping Skill Deficits

As depicted in Figure 2, the therapist, on the basis of information obtained from multimodal diagnostics, determines whether the person has a functionally equivalent behavior in his or her repertoire that could be used in the stimulus context in which the aberrant symptoms occur. If assessment reveals a skill deficit, that is, the absence of a replacement coping behavior (a tertiary or vulnerability condition), the focus of behavior therapy intervention becomes one of teaching this coping alternative. The behavior therapy literature is rich in successful applications of this strategy (E. G. Carr et al., 1994; Durand, 1990; Reichle & Wacker, 1993). For example, Durand and Kishi (1987) taught young adults with severe and profound MR and dual sensory impairments either to sign or present a token as a means of communicating their requests for staff attention or access to favorite objects. Functional diagnostics produced the hypothesis that the persons' self-injurious behaviors (SIBs) served these communicative functions prior to therapy. After training in functional alternatives to cope with states of deprivation, significant reductions in SIBs were observed when these communicative alternatives produced the valued consequences.

Durand and Carr (1991) taught functional communication skills to children with developmental disabilities as coping alternatives. A substantial reduction in challenging behaviors was obtained. Furthermore, these new coping skills transferred across new tasks, environments, and teachers and were maintained on long-term follow-up. Bird et al. (1989) determined, through functional assessment, that severe aggression and

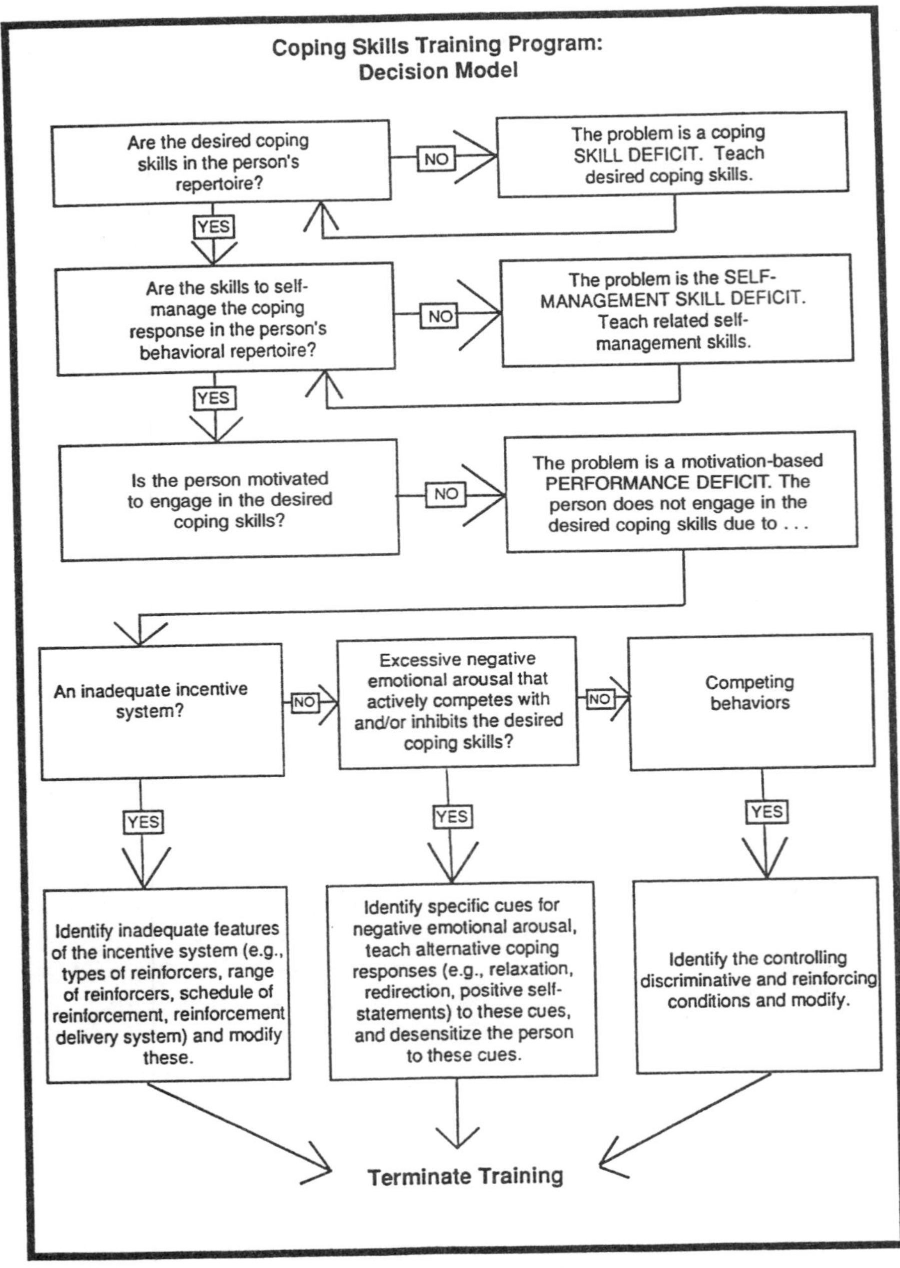

Figure 2. Coping skills training model.

SIBs of an adult were escape motivated (from demand situations) as well as reinforcement motivated (by desire for tangible reinforcers). A therapy program that taught alternative coping replacement behaviors for use under both motivational conditions resulted in significant reductions in problem behavior. These new coping skills were maintained across a number of different conditions. Matson and Zeiss (1978), and Matson and Stephens (1978), providing behavior therapy to adults presenting a range of psychiatric diagnoses, used a skills training program to decrease the chronic explosive behaviors and to increase social and interpersonal alternatives to these aberrant reactions. The skills training program, consisting of instructions, modeling, role playing, feedback, and in vivo role playing, resulted in increased prosocial interpersonal skill and a reduction in the aberrant behaviors. Foxx et al. (1983) described a successful structured program for teaching a variety of social skills to people presenting challenging behaviors.

Self-Management Skill Deficits

Because one of the major objectives of behavior therapy programs is to increase the person's independent use of coping skills, the next behavior therapy focus, as depicted in Figure 2, is that of teaching self-management skills. The self-management of coping skills represents an alternative to the external management present in most biomedical and behavioral interventions. This focus is consistent with current legal guidelines for least restrictive treatment and reflects a basic ethical commitment to providing the most normalizing treatment available.

Although the majority of the self-management literature describes applications to a range of social (Marchetti & Campbell, 1990), vocational (J. E. Martin, Marshall, & Maxson, 1993), daily living (Lovett & Haring, 1989), and academic (E. S. Shapiro & Cole, 1994) behaviors, there is a growing literature reporting successful applications to treatment of clinically significant aberrant behaviors (W. I. Gardner & Cole, 1989; L. K. Koegel, Koegel, & Parks, 1992). Self-management training typically is combined with other behavior therapy procedures in treating severe conduct difficulties. A skill deficit rationale underlies these applications, with the assumption being that self-management skills would serve to instigate coping alternatives to the impulsive, aberrant reactions under varying conditions of provocation (W. I. Gardner & Cole, 1989).

Harvey, Karan, Bhargava, and Morehouse (1978) used various self-managed and externally managed procedures to eliminate violent outbursts in an adult with moderate MR. More recently, W. I. Gardner, Clees, et al. (1983) and W. I. Gardner, Cole, et al. (1983) used a multicomponent self-management package to reduce high-rate conduct problems in adults with moderate MR. Using an expanded version of this treatment package, C. L. Cole et al. (1985) demonstrated the therapeutic value of self-management with adults with mild and moderate MR whose chronic and severe conduct difficulties prevented their participation in community vocational rehabilitation programs. The treatment package included the self-management skills of self-monitoring, self-evaluation, and self-consequence of their own appropriate and inappropriate work-related behaviors. The adults were taught to self-instruct prosocial behaviors that served as alternatives to aggression under conditions of provocation. In addition to a significant reduction of verbal and physical aggression, other behaviors not specifically treated showed positive effects. Maintenance of treatment gains was demonstrated. R. L. Koegel and Koegel (1990) and L. K. Koegel, Koegel, and Parks (1992) provided multiple illustrations of successful reduction of severely disruptive behaviors such as self-injury and self-stimulatory activities following teaching self-management skills to people with severe disabilities. Finally, Grace, Cowart, and Matson (1988) demonstrated the value of teaching self-management skills in the reduction of severe self-injury in a person with Lesch–Nyhan syndrome.

Performance Deficits

If multimodal diagnostics reveals that alternative functional behaviors are in the person's repertoire but are not being used, a performance rather than a skill deficit becomes the focus of therapy. As depicted in Figure 2, this performance difficulty may reflect inadequate type, range, schedule, and mode of delivery of reinforcing conditions (B. F. Williams, Williams, & McLaughlin, 1989) or excessive emotional arousal that actively competes with or inhibits desired coping skills (B. A. Benson, 1990), or it may reflect the fact that other behaviors mask the coping behaviors because of greater control by existing instigating and maintaining conditions (R. L. Koegel & Koegel, 1990; Mackintosh, 1977).

Performance deficits: inadequate incentives. E. G. Carr, Newsom, and Binkoff (1980) and E. G. Carr and Newsom (1985) provided illustrations of this procedure by introducing strongly preferred reinforcers for prosocial behaviors. After an initial demonstration that children with developmental disabilities engaged in low-rate compliance and high-rate tantrum behaviors when instructional demands were presented in a classroom setting, the teacher provided strongly preferred reinforcers for each correct response (i.e., complying with teacher directives). Tantrums were reduced to a negligible level under the demand-plus-reinforcer condition, and compliance improved significantly. The compliance behavior was present in the children's repertoires, but it occurred only when adequate incentives were provided.

Performance deficits: competing emotional arousal. As depicted in Figure 1, interventions may be designed to modify or remove the stimulus conditions that precede the occurrence of aberrant responding. This may involve removing or modifying unconditioned or conditioned stimulus events that control emotional (respondent) behavior (Matson & Sevin, 1994; Ollendick, Oswald, & Ollendick, 1993). This respondent-conditioning paradigm has been used to account for escape and avoidance behavior when a person is confronted with specific stimulus conditions. On exposure to these stimulus conditions, a number of fear and anxiety responses accompany and provide motivation for escape or avoidance behaviors. In these instances, varied systematic desensitization procedures, combined with participant modeling, have been used to reduce the fear-provoking qualities of specific stimulus conditions (B. A. Benson, 1990; McNally, 1991; Ollendick et al., 1993). As fear-arousing features of stimulus conditions are reduced, motivation for the aberrant escape and avoidance behavior decreases. For example, reducing the fear-evoking qualities of a dentist and the dental office and equipment decreases or eliminates a child's escape–avoidance behaviors of screaming, struggling, and refusal to permit the dentist to conduct a dental examination. Descriptions of these stimulus change procedures based predominantly on the respondent-conditioning model are followed in the final section by illustrations of other procedures to alter the primary discriminative stimulus conditions instigating aberrant behaviors.

Rivenq (1974) used a modified systematic desensitization procedure to eliminate trichophobia in a 13-year-old boy with a dual diagnosis of mild MR and schizophrenia. The boy's fear of body hair was reported to be so intense that he said he wanted to have a feminine body. He turned his head away whenever he was exposed to the therapists' hairy arms and hands. Graduated exposure to the fear-provoking stimulus through a series of pictures depicting increasingly hairy men, combined with a counterconditioning procedure of providing candies and French pastries as each picture was exposed, resulted in the elimination of the phobia. Freeman, Roy, and Hemmick (1976) described the elimination of a fear of physical examination in a 7-year-old boy with mild MR through a systematic desensitization procedure. The child had a retinal disorder that required frequent examinations by physicians. His fear became so intense that the biannual ophthalmologic examinations had to be conducted while he was under general anesthesia. An 11-step hierarchy of the ophthalmologic examination experience was developed, beginning with the boy entering the examination room and ending with having his eyes examined with an ophthalmoscope. During the 11th session, the boy remained cooperative as the physician completed the entire examination. In addition, the positive behavioral effects generalized to unfamiliar physicians and to another type of physical examination.

Mansdorf (1976) used a modified systematic desensitization procedure to successfully reduce an extreme fear of riding in cars in a 35-year-old woman with moderate MR. A 19-item graduated exposure hierarchy depicting the client's car-riding phobia was constructed. The usual procedure of pairing a state of relaxation with successive steps in the hierarchy was replaced by token reinforcement following the completion of each step. Only 9 of 19 items, ranging from "Talking to therapist in office about cars" through "Talking to therapist with car door open and both inside," were completed before the behavioral objective of "Taking ride to workshop" was attained. A 10-month follow-up revealed that the client continued to use automobile transportation to attend community programs.

Erfanian and Miltenberger (1990) used contact desensitization for the treatment of an intense fear of dogs in two individuals with MR. Both clients' extreme fear of dogs interfered with their adjustment to the community. On seeing a dog, the clients would become agitated until the dog was out of sight. If forced to approach the dog or if the dog approached them, both clients would run away. On several occasions, on unexpectedly seeing a dog, both clients had risked their lives by running across the street without looking for traffic. Both clients dramatically decreased avoidance of the dog after treatment, approaching within 1 ft (25.48 cm) of the dog while showing no signs of distress. Furthermore, during the treatment and later testing sessions, clients were able to pet the dog on its back on request. Anecdotal reports from staff indicated that after treatment, neither client showed any further avoidance behavior on seeing a dog in public.

Runyan, Stevens, and Reeves (1985) described the successful use of contact desensitization in 3 adults with severe to profound levels of MR who refused to ride escalators. Treatment was conducted at main hall escalators and within various stores of a local shopping mall generally during evening hours when the stores were closed. This procedure of contact desensitization with social approval reduced avoidance behavior toward escalators in all 3 adults. During a shopping trip 1 month after treatment, each client used both up- and down-escalators.

Matson (1981a) successfully eliminated the excessive fear of participating in community-based activities of 24 adults with MR using a participant modeling technique of teaching relevant social skills. As a final illustration, Love, Matson, and West (1990) successfully used participant modeling for the treatment of phobias in 2 children with autism. The phobias involved refusal to go outside unaccompanied by a parent with the door closed behind them and avoidance behaviors at the sight and sound of a running bathroom shower. Treatment, conducted at home, occurred three times weekly during 1-hr meetings, with approximately three treatment sessions per meeting. Sessions ranged from 5 to 10 min. The children's mothers served as therapists, modeling graduated exposure and providing reinforcement contingent on approaching the feared situations. Following intervention, the children functioned effectively in previously fearful situations without vocalization or appearance of fear. Five-month and 1-year follow-up assessments with 1 child showed maintenance of treatment effects.

Performance deficits: competing behaviors. As noted, in some instances a person may have appropriate behaviors in his or her response repertoire, but these do not occur because of the presence of stimulus conditions for competing aberrant behaviors or the absence of stimulus conditions controlling appropriate behaviors. In these cases, a therapy program designed to modify the nature and strength of these stimulus conditions would be provided. As illustrations, Madden, Russo, and Cataldo (1980) provided three different settings to children who had been hospitalized for lead poisoning caused by pica (i.e., an abnormal desire to eat substances not normally eaten, such as chalk or ashes): an enriched individual play environment, a group play environment, and an impoverished individual play environment. Numerous and varied educational activities and toys, combined with opportunities for social interaction, were present in the individual and group play environments. The impoverished environment, by contrast, contained an observer who did not interact with the child, no toys, and five common household items. The rates of pica were three to five times greater in the impoverished environment than in the enriched settings, with the aberrant behavior decreasing under stimulus conditions that instigated play and social alternatives.

Favell, McGimsey, and Schnell (1982) noted that the SIBs of eye-poking, hand-mouthing, and pica of a group of young adults with profound MR occurred primarily when they were alone and bored. These antecedent stimulus conditions associated with the aberrant behaviors were altered by providing toys that set the occasion for an appropriate alternative to the SIBs. Under these enriched conditions, these adults had opportunities to engage in toy play that provided sensory reinforcement similar to that associated with SIBs. Following demonstration of the value of this environmental alteration in producing alternative play behaviors and a substantial reduction of SIBs, an added treatment component of external reinforcement of more appropriate conventional toy play resulted in a further reduction. In each case, the self-stimulation produced by the toys involved the same sensory modality as that associated with the SIBs (i.e., clients who eye-poked used toys to produce visual self-stimulation, those who engaged in hand-mouthing and pica began chewing the toys). These results emphasize the value of matching the sensory activities provided by the intervention program with the sensory stimulation provided by the aberrant behaviors.

Sigafoos and Kerr (1994) reported similar reductions in behaviors such as aggression, SIBs, property destruction, and stereotypy of adults with severe disabilities under increased conditions of opportunity to engage in age-appropriate leisure activities. Prosocial behaviors served to replace the inappropriate responding.

Lancioni, Smeets, Ceccarani, Capodaglio, and Campanari (1984), under the assumption that the antecedent activating stimulus conditions of severe tantrum behaviors of adults with multiple impairments consisted of sensory deprivation, provided daily periods of gross motor activities designed to provide varying sensory input. By providing an alternative means of obtaining sensory stimulation through a variety of gross motor activities, the tantrums decreased in frequency and duration.

Engelmann and Colvin (1983) described a strategy of minimizing the effects of stimulus conditions controlling aberrant behaviors that involved the delivery of three to five requests immediately prior to presenting a difficult task or situation in an educational setting. Singer, Singer, and Horner (1987) used this procedure with elementary school-age students with moderate and severe disabilities to increase compliance in returning to work from recess and to decrease aggression. Three to five easy requests preceded instruction to return to work. Story and Horner (1988) further suggested that these requests should

> (a) require responses that take no more than a few seconds to complete, (b) be responses that the learner has a history of performing with a

> high probability of accuracy and speed, (c) be followed by praise, (d) be delivered in rapid succession, and (e) be delivered immediately prior to the presentation of the difficult task or situation.

With this approach, success and praise were experienced immediately prior to the presentation of the task with aversive qualities. Finally, Mace et al. (1988) and Mace and Belfiore (1990) used this procedure of manipulating antecedent stimulus conditions to increase compliance and decrease aggression and escape-motivated stereotypic behavior in adults with severe MR. Using the concept of behavioral momentum (Nevin, Mandell, & Atak, 1983) to guide this behavior management procedure, a series of three to four high-probability commands were followed by a low probability of compliance directive. These immediately preceding experiences provided the "momentum" of compliance that increased the probability of compliance after presentation of the previously determined low-probability directive.

A novel strategy for modifying stimulus conditions that control aberrant behaviors that actively compete with prosocial behaviors is that of providing choices (Bambara, Koger, Katzer, & Davenport, 1995; C. L. Cole, Davenport, Bambara, & Ager, 1995; Dyer, Dunlap, & Winterling, 1990; Harchik et al., 1993). It is reasoned that providing choice opportunities allows the person to express preferences, make personal decisions, and experience control over aspects of the environment. This strategy reduces conflicts and removes events that serve to instigate aberrant escape behaviors. Several studies have demonstrated that, when allowed to choose their academic activities, students with disabilities exhibit fewer aberrant behaviors than when no choice is provided (Bambara et al., 1995; Dyer et al., 1990; R. L. Koegel, Dyer, & Bell, 1987). Bambara et al. found a reduction in severe problem behaviors in an adult with developmental disabilities after being provided choices in his residential setting. Dyer et al. demonstrated that children with autism exhibited fewer problem behaviors involving self-injury and aggression when provided the opportunity for choices of tasks, materials, and reinforcers. Finally, children with autism demonstrated less social avoidance (e.g., looking and moving away) when engaged in activities they preferred (R. L. Koegel et al., 1987). In summary, these and similar studies demonstrate that choice may reduce the aversiveness of situations that instigate aberrant behaviors and serve to increase participation, improve performance, and reduce problem behaviors.

Conclusion

Consistent with contemporary best professional practice, behavior therapy interventions for aberrant behaviors presented by people with MR should be diagnostically based and coordinated with biomedical and socioenvironmental interventions. A multimodal functional diagnostic and treatment model is offered to guide this practice. Because the major objective of behavior therapy is to enhance the person's competencies and independence in coping with conditions that control aberrant behavior, behavior therapy procedures are selected to teach new coping skills when deficits are detected or to ensure that prosocial coping skills currently in the person's repertoire gain dominance over aberrant ones.

28

Counseling and Psychotherapy

Anne DesNoyers Hurley, Al Pfadt, Dan Tomasulo, and William I. Gardner

Although service providers have increasingly recognized that individuals with mental retardation (MR) may be afflicted with a wide range of psychiatric and adjustment disorders, as are individuals in the normal range of intelligence, counseling and psychotherapy are often neglected as treatment modalities because it is assumed that MR precludes effective participation in the therapeutic process. Such beliefs are unfounded, as demonstrated by numerous case reports and writings that reflect the effectiveness of individual psychotherapy and group psychotherapy (Fletcher, 1993; Hurley, 1989; Leland & Smith, 1965; Nezu, Nezu, & Gill-Weiss, 1992; Pfadt, 1991; Sarason, 1953; Szymanski, 1980; Szymanski & Rosefsky, 1980; Tomasulo, 1992). Few controlled studies have been performed, but results of those that have generally have been positive (Albini & Dinitz, 1965; B. A. Benson, Rice, & Miranti, 1986; Gorlow, Butler, Einig, & Smith, 1963; Matson, 1981b, 1982; Obler & Terwillinger, 1970; Peck, 1977; Rosen & Rosen, 1969; Silvestri, 1977; Stone & Coughlin, 1973).

A number of erroneous assumptions and biases have limited the availability of counseling and psychotherapy for people with MR. Mental health practitioners have assumed that most individuals with MR are unable to generate verbal mediators that serve as cues in regulating overt, nonverbal behavior. Second, a similar deficiency has been postulated in the ability to develop "insight" or recognize causes and consequences of behavior. Third, the emotional disorders displayed by people with MR are thought to be a function of brain dysfunction and therefore are not amenable to remediation by psychotherapy. Finally, problems have been conceptualized according to simplistic dichotomies that recognize either mental illness or behavior disorders and that advocate either pharmacological or behavior treatments.

Individuals with MR can participate effectively in counseling and psychotherapy, but the approaches used by the clinicians must be adapted for each individual's cognitive level. In this chapter, we review practical issues in the implementation and evaluation of psychotherapeutic interventions for individuals with MR who have behavior disorders or psychiatric impairments. In this review, we use a broad definition of counseling and psychotherapy, which includes a wide variety of procedures or specialized techniques designed to treat mental disorders or problems of everyday adjustment. Although the approaches vary widely from psychodynamic methods to behavioral therapy techniques, there is a surprising consensus regarding the adaptions needed, as these are described in turn.

Modification of Techniques

In treating any patient, the clinician is obliged to assess the person's cognitive level of functioning and affective state, as well as competence in life skills and social supports, in order to develop and implement an appropriate treatment plan. The initial evaluation session is devoted to this assessment, as well as establishing a working diagnosis that incorporates the functional impairments to be addressed. The treatment approaches subsequently used must be appropriate to the client's cognitive and developmental levels.

When treating people with MR, the clinician must be attuned to the cognitive level and adjust the treatment techniques for that person. Among individuals with MR, the level and type of cognitive abilities vary greatly. For example, individuals with mild MR may have verbal skills ranging from highly functional to concrete and repetitive. The mental health clinician may refer to previous psychological and educational assessments to gain a clear idea of how best to work with each individual. An understanding of the cognitive resources of each individual must guide treatment and dictate appropriate modifications.

Simplification

Because of the concrete nature of cognitive abilities among people with MR, many techniques must be simplified. Cautela and Groden (1978), for example, revised relaxation training procedures significantly but did not change the essential method. Systematic desensitization has been used successfully by restructuring material and making it more concrete and repetitive (Guralnick, 1973; H. J. Jackson, 1983; H. J. Jackson & Hooper, 1981; H. J. Jackson & King, 1982; Mansdorf, 1976; Mansdorf & Ben-David, 1986; Matson, 1981b; Obler & Terwillinger, 1970; Peck, 1977; Silvestri, 1977; Waranch, Iwata, Wohl, & Nidiffer, 1981; Wilson & Jackson, 1980). Many therapists also have augmented verbal discussion by adding visualization techniques, role playing, and rehearsal (Deutsch, 1985; Tomasulo, 1992).

Material presented in sessions also can be simplified by taking a psychoeducational approach. Hurley and Sovner (1991) suggested that, rather than deepening appreciation of positive self-qualities through abstract discussion, the therapist should assist the client in gaining positive self-esteem by helping him or her develop a simple list of positive characteristics, such as having nice hair or being a good dancer. Material generally can be simplified by breaking it into small chunks, by using examples, or by experiencing success on a project that was the work of a counseling session.

Language

Compared with individuals of normal intelligence, the person with MR will, by definition, communicate on a concrete level. Assessments can indicate the extent of language usage, work knowledge, verbal reasoning skills, and ability to use and understand grammatical structures. Clinicians, who are used to conversing on a professional level, often use language that is too complex for individuals with MR. By contrast, people with MR are used to not understanding much of what many people communicate to them, and they are not prone to interrupt and ask for clarification or indicate in any manner that the conversation is too complex.

In sessions, it is important that concrete communication be used to build rapport and trust. The therapist must be vigilant in self-monitoring communication. Clinicians may use initial sessions to develop a working "therapeutic" vocabulary that will be used in treatment (Ludwig & Hingsburger, 1987; Scanlon, 1978). In this way, there will be a mutual understanding with which to proceed to the therapeutic work.

Activities

Many therapeutic techniques involve supervising, instructing, or guiding the client in an activity, ranging from behavioral techniques such as systematic desensitization to play therapy. Activities must be appropriately matched to adaptive skills, visual–perceptual and visual–motor skills, and nonverbal reasoning skills. For example, the standard progression of sessions during systematic desensitization can be made shorter, and more in vivo sessions might be added for individuals with MR, allowing for more hands-on practice and learning opportunities (H. J. Jackson, 1983; H. J. Jackson & Hooper, 1981; H. J. Jackson & King, 1982; Leland & Smith, 1965; Peck, 1977; Waranch et al., 1981).

In vivo methods with motoric and tactile activities are valuable for individuals with moderate-to-profound MR. For individuals with higher levels of functioning, activities still serve as another learning modality through which the learning of psychotherapy is enhanced and repeated.

Homework assignments enhance progress in meeting treatment goals outside the psychotherapy session and also serve as an activity-based component to enhance learning. Compliance with treatment regimens such as homework is a problem in all patient populations, and the person with MR should not be presumed to be necessarily poor in this area. Motivation of the individual and appropriateness of the assignment will determine success, as will ability to follow instructions and complete the task. Caregivers may assist in homework assignments, which is a great advantage because it can generalize the benefits of psychotherapy to the natural environment. Indeed, caregivers are increasingly regarded as cotherapists in many psychotherapeutic approaches current in MR, as is reflected in chapters 19 and 22 in this book and numerous other sources (e.g., S. L. Harris, 1983; Lovaas, 1987).

Developmental Level

Developmental level must be assessed carefully in choosing the particular therapeutic approach. A diversity of opinion has existed about the ethics of using techniques that are based on child psychology with adults who have MR. Sternlicht (1965, 1966, 1977), for example, asserted that the use of nonverbal techniques is essential for all people with developmental disabilities (e.g., using balloons, mirrors, and noisemakers). Play therapy and art therapy, as used with children, has been suggested by many clinicians (Baum, 1990; Chess, 1962; Hellendoorn, 1990; Jakab, 1978; Leland & Smith, 1965; F. Page, 1986). The clinician must, however, carefully use techniques that are based on developmental approaches and conduct the treatment in a normalized age-appropriate manner. For example, art therapy can be an adult therapeutic tool or children's tool, depending on the content, presentation, and manner in which it is offered to the person. Clinicians also have used developmental theory to structure psychotherapy and have obtained beneficial results (Dosen, 1990).

Use of Directive Style

Individuals with MR respond best to structured environments and structured learning situations. Impairments in the ability to organize, plan, and analyze complex sources of data require that information be organized, simplified, and presented in a concrete context. A directive style provides the structure that is often necessary when treating individuals with MR.

Structuring Sessions

A directive style begins by structuring each therapeutic session (Fletcher, 1984; Hurley, 1989; Hurley & Hurley, 1985, 1987). The client should understand the purpose of therapy and the reason that it is being sought if requested by caregivers. When treating individuals of normal intelligence, the therapist often will be tactful and indirect. When treating individuals with MR, the therapist may have to be quite direct in order to be understood. For example, on the first visit, the therapist must clarify problems (e.g., "the staff of the vocational center said that you have been hitting other workers"). Directness and clarity frame the problem and the source of information, and potentially build trust because of such honesty. Therapists must be sensitive to the effect of such directions, however, for it also may result in a defensive reaction and mistrust. The work to be done must be clarified, stating the time of visits, number of visits, and what will be entailed and expected for clients who can understand such verbal information. For clients with significant cognitive limitations, the structure of the therapy can be communicated through adherence to a standard protocol using repetitive routines and predictability.

Use of directive techniques does not preclude responsive listening, supportive approaches, or psychodynamic therapy. These treatments all can be conducted with adaptations to cognitive level (Abel, 1953; Caton, 1988; Prouty, 1976; Sarason, 1953; Symington, 1981).

Active and Interactive Techniques

Active techniques stimulate more sensory and affective modes of learning than the verbal modality alone, and they have been successful in treating people with developmental disabilities. In pretherapy (Prouty, 1976; Prouty & Kubiak, 1988), the therapist uses innovative procedures, such as reflecting the person's body language, to build a therapeutic relationship. Psychodrama action techniques have been found to be highly effective for people with MR (Tomasulo, 1992). In contrast to a purely verbal discussion, these methods provide individuals with the chance to practice new social skills and express their feelings in a variety of verbal and behavioral modalities. Action techniques also provide the opportunity to experience another person's perspective, resulting in a new understanding of the people in their lives (Steinberg & Garcia, 1989).

Flexible Methods

Therapists who treat individuals with MR must be flexible in the structure of the counseling or psychotherapy and in adherence to any particular therapeutic approach. The therapist must be flexible enough to revise and modify his or her preferred approach when little progress is made, when regression is noted, or when multiple therapeutic needs are evident. Adhering to a psychodrama modality regardless of response, for example, would be a mistake. Timing of appointments and length of visit may need to be adjusted, as well as the basic use of technique. Lindsay, Howells, and Pitcaithly (1993), for example, described modifications of cognitive therapy of depression for people with MR that included a structured form for monitoring negative thoughts and rating the intensity. Counselors and therapists may integrate a variety of approaches with a basic orientation, for example, using behavioral techniques and supportive counseling together.

Caregiver Involvement

Most individuals with MR have full- or part-time caregivers involved with them, including personnel from educational, vocational, residential, protective, or state agencies. These staff are an invaluable resource to assist the therapist. Therapeutic work can be accelerated by embedding treatment into the person's daily environments (Hurley, 1989; Sarason, 1953). Clinicians have suggested that the therapeutic use of caregivers to assist in treatment parallels therapeutic approaches to children, including the initial referral that is typically generated by a caregiver rather than self-referral by the client (Menolascino, Gilson, & Levitas, 1986; Szymanski, 1980; Szymanski & Kiernan, 1980; Szymanski & Rosefsky, 1980).

Caregivers can be particularly useful when the client has cognitive limitations that preclude the use of verbal mediation methods. Mansdorf and Ben-David (1986), for example, assisted a boy with moderate delay with grief after a severely emotional reaction following the death of his brother. The family assisted by verbalizing and rehearsing appropriate behaviors and praised the youngster for performing therapeutic tasks.

When involving caregivers, the therapist establishes firm boundaries on the process, guards confidentiality, and provides positive feedback to caregivers. Individuals with MR are often surprised that such confidential conditions exist and should be advised clearly of this fact if they are able to understand such information. Any information conveyed to caregivers should be positive and openly conveyed in the presence of the client. The therapist also must be careful in assessing the caregiver's capacity to be therapeutic because the therapist's own personal problems may limit his or her ability to positively help the client. Furthermore, if the caregivers are providing services in a system that is suffering from understaffing and other management problems, caregiver interventions may be inadequate or nonproductive (Nezu et al., 1992). Thus, it is important to carefully assess the caregivers' environment prior to engaging them in the therapeutic process.

Transference and Countertransference

Psychotherapists have noted that individuals with MR display transference reactions that are more rapid, pronounced, and primitive than those seen in the general population (Bernstein, 1985; Levitas & Gilson, 1987; Szymanski, 1980). Such reactions are not pathological, but represent the effects of the developmental level on ego, cognition, and social skills. Strong transference reactions, in fact, may make psychotherapy particularly effective with this population. Because of the strong reactions possible, therapists must be prepared to often review the limits of therapy. Clarifying the psychotherapeutic relationship in clear, concrete terms will help the person maintain a working relationship. Otherwise, the client may quickly see the therapist as a "friend" or possible romantic partner because individuals with developmental disabilities do not verbalize well and clues to the transference may not be apparent or obvious.

Countertransference issues have been compared to those seen in children. Rescue fantasies, overprotection, and ridicule of the parents are common pitfalls (Bernstein, 1985; Jakab, 1978; Szymanski, 1980). Often, therapists may be so taken with the disability that they fail to see independence. Szymanski aptly asserted that seeing clients with developmental delays as "children" can lead to becoming the "parent." Therapists must guard against becoming an "advocate" rather than a therapist. Behavior during individualized service plan and education plan meetings must be carefully monitored, and the therapist must resist speaking for the person (Levitas & Gilson, 1989). Godschalx (1983) emphasized the need for ongoing peer supervision for counselors and therapists seeing clients with MR.

Disability and Rehabilitation Approaches

Mental retardation is a disability. Disabling conditions challenge personal growth and development as well as independence in adulthood. These conditions need not be debilitating; many individuals with MR lead full and productive lives.

Unfortunately, individuals with disabilities suffer greatly in society as members of a devalued group (Wolfensberger, 1972, 1983; Wright, 1983). Stigmatization, social rejection, and many failure experiences leave their mark on each individual. Furthermore, because of the nature of the disability, such individuals cannot independently ascertain why others are responding negatively. Szymanski and Rosefsky (1980) stated that, on finding out that they are just "slow" in certain developmental areas, many individuals with MR react with relief. S. Reiss and Benson (1984) also noted that, if attuned, therapists will find that disability issues inevitably arise during the course of counseling and psychotherapy. It is also with counselors and psychotherapists that many individuals with MR have their first opportunity for discussion of their condition, with full acceptance and unconditional positive regard of a professional.

In addition to using clear explanations of the disability, the therapist must adhere to a strong rehabilitation counseling approach. The basic strategy is two-fold: Acknowledge and understand the disability while helping the person appreciate his or her abilities. Practical treatment goals emphasize enhancing strengths and positive attributes. Thus, although one cannot read, one may be able to cook well or dance well, have friends, or take public transportation. The individual with MR can benefit from reframing of abilities within counseling and psychotherapy, as well as encouragement to further develop his or her areas of strength.

Conclusion

Research has suggested that individuals with MR have responded positively to a variety of individual and group psychotherapeutic interventions. The literature, which consists of several well-controlled studies, and many case reports and theoretical pieces, describes generally positive accounts of treatment outcome. Clinicians have treated a wide variety of disorders, including anxiety disorders, depression and adjustment disorders, as well as social and interpersonal difficulties. Individuals with MR have been reported to participate in treatment enthusiastically and cooperatively.

Because of the cognitive and developmental disabilities of individuals with MR, however, it is necessary to adapt standard techniques in a variety of ways. There is, in fact, strong consensus about the types of modifications that are needed. Strategies involve simplifying language, altering the therapeutic process itself, and structuring the form that psychotherapy takes. Clinicians must be more directive and use active and interactive techniques to aid learning. In addition, there is general agreement that, in most cases, the personal, social, and habilitative specialist network of the client should be actively involved in the treatment process, when appropriate. Addressing the disability itself is a major treatment objective that builds self-acceptance.

A strong body of research is needed to address the central outcome questions in psychotherapy with individuals who have MR (i.e., which procedures are effective for particular individuals and under which specific conditions; Hurley, 1989; Nezu & Nezu, 1994; Pfadt, 1991). Large, controlled studies are needed to specify the type of treatment and its utility with particular disorders. Adaptation of standard psychotherapeutic treatments or innovative approaches can be examined, ideally in multicenter studies. Research also must clarify the individual characteristics that best match particular approaches. With these research needs and procedural modifications in mind, psychotherapists should feel encouraged to treat individuals with MR. However, guidelines and protocols need to be established through systematic study.

Part IV

Service Delivery

Introduction

The clinical practice of psychology in the field of mental retardation (MR) often occurs in the context of comprehensive service organizations as diverse as general hospitals and specialized clinics, and in community service agencies that vary markedly in their resources and capabilities. There has been long-standing and continuing concern about whether community services are effectively serving people with MR. This was especially true in the early years of deinstitutionalization among nascent organizations, and it has arisen more recently in the context of complex and inconsistently coordinated community services networks. The most pressing concerns are for people with MR who have broad or pronounced requirements for health, health-related, and behavioral services. The chapters in this section address concerns related to these issues, with a focus on organizational impacts and improvements, the provision of psychological services in an interdisciplinary context, and the alteration of accustomed structures and processes of community service to produce more efficient, flexible, and responsive delivery of community support.

Organizational factors play a critical role in influencing clinicians' activities as well as opportunities for people with MR. The current diverse nature of the networks of community services in Western cultures present incentives for the perpetuation of both habilitative and counterhabilitative practices. In many cases, counterhabilitative incentives and activities stem from the perpetuation of administrative and managerial practices that are founded in, or are reactions to, the legacy of institutional care that dominated MR services for the better part of this century. Consequently, interventions by clinicians at the organizational level to identify counterhabilitative practices and align access to and use of resources with the requirements of people with MR can lead to extensive and generalized benefits in the quality of life and the quality of services for large numbers of people.

29

Management and Organizational Issues in the Delivery of Psychological Services for People With Mental Retardation

Todd R. Risley and Dennis H. Reid

Psychological services represent one of the most pervasive types of support necessary to assist people with mental retardation (MR) in experiencing a satisfying quality of life. As well reflected in other chapters in this book, developing effective psychological treatment requires a comprehensive understanding of human development, including developmental, social, and psychoeducational aspects. The provision of psychological services for people with MR also requires special attention to a wide array of treatment implementation considerations. In particular, treatment services, such as those directed at reducing severe problem behaviors, often must encompass all waking hours of individuals (i.e., in contrast to many types of psychological services for nonretarded people provided in circumscribed therapy sessions). Relatedly, treatment must be provided in large part by the routine caregivers of people with MR, be they teachers, parents, group home staff, or institutional personnel.

To ensure that psychological treatment is indeed provided effectively throughout the day by routine caregivers in settings serving people with MR, psychologists frequently must work to arrange organizational and management systems that allow treatment services to occur (Schroeder et al., 1982). Without organizational and management support, it is highly unlikely that psychological treatment services will be provided in a manner that benefits many people with MR (Liberman, 1983). In this chapter we discuss issues related to establishing organizational and management support necessary for psychological treatment to be implemented effectively within agencies serving people with MR. We also present guidelines for psychologists for working within, and consulting with, such agencies in terms of (a) what is meant by organizational and management support and (b) procedures for establishing the necessary support.

Before discussing organizational and management factors related to the provision of psychological services, we emphasize that there are two basic premises on which this chapter is based (see the APA Guidelines on

Effective Behavioral Treatment for Persons With Mental Retardation and Developmental Disabilities in Appendix A for elaboration). The first premise is that the focus of all psychological treatment is always the needs of an individual client. Individual client needs must determine the types of psychological services to be provided as well as the types of organizational and management support necessary to ensure those services are provided effectively. The second premise is that obtaining and maintaining the necessary organizational and management support for a client's psychological services is also a psychologist's professional responsibility.

The first premise has been well acknowledged (Favell, Favell, Riddle, & Risley, 1984). The second premise is not nearly so well acknowledged or accepted (Baumeister & Hillsinger, 1984). Our experience suggests that many psychologists, partly because of their training and related professional expectations, limit their role to assessing client needs and prescribing subsequent psychological treatment. Although psychologists may view establishing organizational and management support for psychological treatment as important, they also view the responsibility for establishing such support as falling under somebody else's jurisdiction. Unfortunately, the latter view often sets the occasion for ineffective psychological treatment and even the absence of any true semblance of treatment. We elaborate on this contention in the following sections.

Fundamental Elements of the Psychologist's Job

Clarification and Tracking of Client Treatment Goals

In light of the basic premise that the central focus of all psychological treatment is an individual client's needs, it logically follows that psychological treatment begins with an assessment of an individual's needs, as well as his or her likes and dislikes, with subsequent determination of treatment goals. However, in contrast to typical psychological practice with nonretarded individuals, the determination of psychological treatment goals is not the sole responsibility of the psychologist. Rather, it is the joint responsibility of the client's interdisciplinary treatment team. The interdisciplinary team process is standard operating procedure in essentially all MR and related service agencies. Psychological treatment goals must be formalized as part of an overall team-determined client treatment plan, exemplified most notably in individualized education plans in school settings and individualized habilitation plans in residential settings. For interdisciplinary teams to reach agreement on psychological treatment goals as part of a client's overall treatment plan, a key component of the psychologist's job is to explain psychological treatment goals in terms readily understood by all team members, whether they are professional clinicians in other disciplines, paraprofessional clinician and teacher assistants, residential and vocational direct service staff, client family members, or the clients themselves.

Clear explanation of psychological treatment goals is necessary not only for allowing team member understanding and support of the goals just discussed, but also for reliable tracking of client progress in attaining respective goals. In this regard, the progress of many people with MR in achieving treatment goals is often slow, encompassing weeks and months of treatment duration. Progress frequently occurs in small steps, as does treatment regression, such that without adequate tracking of client performance the small steps (or lack thereof) are likely to go unnoticed and appropriate treatment alteration or refinement to ensure progress cannot be accomplished in a timely manner.

Treatment Prescription

Once client treatment goals have been identified and articulated in clearly understandable terms, the treatment itself must be developed. This is the component of a psychologist's job for which the psychologist usually has received the bulk of his or her professional training. However, sometimes lacking in that training is how to specify precisely what constitutes the psychological treatment. Because most, if not all, of the treatment typically must be carried out by direct caregivers of the client, as noted earlier, it is essential that the treatment be clearly specified for the caregivers. Such specification should include not only *what* should occur (i.e., the treatment procedures), but also *where* and *when* treatment should occur and *who* should provide treatment during the course of the routine day. One excellent means of providing sufficient procedural specification in terms of what should occur is the use of performance checklists. As described by Risley and Favell (1979), performance checklists provide essential procedural information in a brief but descriptive step-by-step format. Checklists also facilitate treatment delivery (see the next section) in terms of enhancing the training of staff in how to implement treatment procedures, as well as the subsequent monitoring of staff provision of treatment (Lattimore, Stephens, Favell, & Risley, 1984).

Ensuring Treatment Delivery

Ensuring that treatment is delivered in the manner it is prescribed relates directly to a basic premise noted previously: Psychologists must obtain organizational and management support for psychological treatment delivery. This component of psychological treatment for people with MR frequently receives insufficient attention by psychologists. Even in situations in which psychologists seriously attend to obtaining organizational and management support, their efforts often are unsuccessful, which results in considerable professional frustration (Fisher, 1983). Much of the frustration relates to the organizational structure and dynamics of human service agencies, in that psychologists typically have no supervisory authority over the caregivers who must carry out the psychological treatment procedures with agency clients. Nevertheless, in most cases, if psychological treatment is to be effective, the necessary organizational and management support must be obtained. The following are guidelines for psychologists to obtain the support, as well as a more detailed description of what is meant by the term *support*.

Analyzing and altering the treatment environment. Before steps can be taken to obtain organizational and management support, the specific nature of the support within a particular agency must be determined. Hence, the agency environment in which treatment is to be provided should be assessed. The first assessment step should focus on the therapeutic qualities of the environment or lack thereof. Therapeutic parameters of environments are varied, ranging, for example, from quantity and quality of interactions between clients and caregivers in congregate care settings (Christian & Romanczyk, 1986) to provision of meaningful learning opportunities in educational and vocational settings (D. H. Reid et al., 1985).

It is beyond the scope of this chapter to describe the entire range of quality indicators of therapeutic environments. However, determining the therapeutic nature of environments involves skills many psychologists possess as a function of their training and experience. By contrast, determining appropriate corrective actions in agencies where therapeutic environments do not exist, such that effective treatment can occur, requires skills that are much less prevalent among psychologists. The latter skills entail conducting an ecological analysis of a client's social and physical environment (J. S. Bailey & Pyles, 1989). One of the most important variables to assess in such an analysis is whether there are enough staff members to conduct the necessary treatment procedures during the client's day. Relatedly, whether the available staff have sufficient time to implement the prescribed treatment procedures proficiently must be determined. If lack of sufficient staff and time appear to be obstacles to treatment delivery, then the specific staff ratios and duties that impede effective implementation of psychological treatment procedures must be identified. Subsequently, strategies for removing the treatment obstacles can be considered, such as reassignment of staff within the agency, reassignment of duties across staff, streamlining certain duties to reduce the time involvement of staff, and elimination of certain duties in lieu of assignment of duties related to psychological treatment delivery.

Implementing strategies to ensure that a therapeutic environment exists and that psychological treatment realistically can be delivered by staff almost invariably requires actions by staff supervisors and agency executives (Harchik, Sherman, Sheldon, & Strouse, 1992). Consequently, it is paramount that a psychologist involve someone in the treatment delivery process who is in a position of authority to make changes in staff allocation and assignments. One important step in that involvement process is to articulate clearly the existing obstacles to treatment delivery, as well as to describe in practical terms how those obstacles hinder or preclude treatment.

Table 1. Primary Steps for Training Staff to Implement Psychological Treatment Procedures

Step	Training activity
1	Develop a checklist-type set of instructions for implementing the treatment procedures.
2	Provide checklist instructions for staff to read.
3	Verbally describe the checklist's content.
4	Demonstrate the procedures on the checklist.
5	Observe staff practice the procedures on the checklist.
6	Provide diagnostic and positive feedback regarding staff performance of the procedures on the checklist.
7	Repeat Steps 3–6 until staff demonstrate proficiency in performing the checklist procedures.

Training treatment providers. If routine caregivers are to be responsible for implementing psychological treatment procedures, then the caregivers must, of course, be skilled in treatment implementation. Ensuring that caregivers have the necessary procedural skills usually entails a formal training process. Training caregivers to implement psychological treatment procedures historically has involved a psychologist conducting a group in-service session with staff and reviewing the treatment procedures, perhaps along with distribution of a written copy of the procedures. Such a training procedure can be effective, but usually is not (Favell et al., 1984). An alternative and more effective approach for training caregivers in designated treatment skills has been developed through a considerable amount of applied research (D. H. Reid, Parsons, & Green, 1989, chapter 3). A summary of the key steps of an effective training program based on the research to date is provided in Table 1. Although modifications in the training model presented in Table 1 can be made, depending on idiosyncratic features associated with a given treatment program and setting, one important training component should never be altered. Specifically, it should never be assumed that treatment providers have been sufficiently trained until each person is observed to conduct the treatment procedures proficiently, preferably within the person's routine work situation with the client.

Although the specific technology of caregiver training has been well discussed, the logistics of successfully implementing the technology have not been. Several guidelines are offered for consideration. First, attention should be directed to who will conduct the training. The caregiver trainer must have good familiarity with the psychological treatment procedures, as well as the technology for training caregivers. Frequently, the psychologist is responsible for training caregivers, although it can be very useful to involve the immediate supervisor (e.g., school principal, group home manager, work site supervisors) in the training of the direct service personnel. Second, sufficient trainer and trainee time must be allocated for the training. Third, at least some of the training, and certainly the last components of the training model, must be conducted on the job as caregivers interact with a particular client as part of the routine work situation (e.g., in the classroom setting, work environment, client home). Fourth, consideration should be given to the entry skills of the trainees who will be trained to conduct the client treatment. It may be, for example, that realistically some caregivers do not have the physical capability to carry out some aspects of the prescribed treatment proficiently and safely. In such cases, the psychologist must ensure that the supervisor of the caregivers is aware of the inability of certain individuals to conduct treatment, as well as the corresponding need to make readjustments in staff allocation and job assignments.

Monitoring and supporting treatment delivery. Once support personnel have been trained in the necessary procedures and begin client treatment, the next component of the psychologist's job is to establish monitoring and support systems for the caregivers' day-to-day treatment delivery. This is not to suggest that the psychologist himself or herself should be solely responsible for monitoring caregiver performance and providing support on a daily basis. In many cases, particularly for psychologists who provide community-based consulting services, the psychologist does not have enough time to provide adequate monitoring and support. Nevertheless, it is the psychologist's responsibility to participate at least partially in this aspect of treatment delivery. It also is the psychologist's job to make sure that an appropriate monitoring system is established. The psychologist must likewise ensure that personnel who are intricately involved in the agency's day-to-day services are explicitly assigned the responsibility of monitoring staff performance and providing support for treatment provision. The latter personnel typically should include the immediate supervisor of the direct service staff and may also include other individuals, such as the treatment team leader and more senior supervisory people (D. H. Reid, Parsons, & Schepis, 1990).

The monitoring of caregiver treatment delivery often is considered a separate set of responsibilities from providing support for treatment provision. On closer examination, though, the two aspects of psychological treatment delivery cannot be separated. Respective agency personnel cannot functionally provide adequate support unless they routinely observe treatment implementation to determine when and what type of support is required. Relatedly, the act of systematic monitoring itself can function as a form of support. Overt monitoring by the psychologist, supervisor, and so forth, can demonstrate to the staff the importance of proficient treatment delivery (Parsons, Schepis, Reid, McCarn, & Green, 1987). If the monitoring is followed by performance feedback—which is the way monitoring of psychological treatment implementation generally should be conducted—the proficiency of the treatment services can be strengthened and, if necessary, corrected (D. H. Reid et al., 1989, chapter 4). To fulfill the latter two functions, it is paramount that the feedback accompanying the monitoring of staff performance be diagnostic and positive in nature. The diagnostic component of feedback relates to identifying specifically for staff how their implementation does or does not comport to the psychologist's prescribed treatment protocol. By using a checklist of treatment procedures, the diagnostic quality of the feedback can be greatly enhanced.

The second necessary component of feedback, the positive feature, can serve as motivational support for caregiver performance. There are numerous ways of providing feedback to caregivers in a manner that positively reinforces their proficient implementation of treatment procedures. The most common and readily available form of positive feedback, though, is verbal acknowledgment of proficient performance (D. H. Reid et al., 1989, chapter 4). Whatever type of feedback is provided, the person providing the feedback must have the skills to present the feedback in a diagnostic and positive manner.

In addition to providing motivational support for staff implementation of psychological treatment, frequent monitoring can provide support by removing obstacles staff face in delivering treatment. Regardless of how well psychological treatment plans are developed and prescribed, because treatment is delivered in the client's routine environment on a daily basis, obstacles to treatment delivery often arise (Stacy, Doleys, & Bruno, 1983). Such obstacles may relate to unexpected reactions of the client to treatment, which result in caregivers being uncertain about how to respond to the client's behavior; temporary shortages in staff due to resignations, sickness, and so on, which impede existing staff's ability to implement treatment; cancellation of educational programs or temporary lack of remunerative work activities; and admission of new clients to an agency that compete with staff's time for treatment delivery. Through regular monitoring, these and related obstacles can be detected quickly and even predicted beforehand, such that the psychologist and other treatment monitors can negotiate with appropriate agency personnel to take corrective actions in a timely manner.

Providing professional oversight. A highly recommended procedure for any psychologist working in MR is to include a serious component of professional oversight for the psychologist's prescribed treatment services (Christian & Romanczyk, 1986). In short, it is unwise for a psychologist to work in professional isolation. The types of psychological treatment procedures available for application with people who have MR continue to evolve over time. In particular, advances in psychological assessment and treatment appear in the professional literature almost continuously, and those advances need to affect the practicing psychologist's services if people with MR are to benefit from the advances. Incorporating regular professional oversight of psychological services provided within an agency is one means of helping to ensure a psychologist's treatment services are professionally current and that agency clients receive the best treatment available.

Professional oversight commonly entails having a psychologist external to an agency's routine service provision periodically review the psychological component of services and offer suggestions for improvement when appropriate (Christian & Romanczyk, 1986). Such a review can be conducted by one designated professional several times during the year.

Alternatively or concurrently, different treatment professionals can periodically be employed on a short-term consultant basis to provide an independent perspective on the adequacy of an agency's psychological services.

Treatment evaluation and refinement. The final basic component of a psychologist's job is to ensure periodic evaluation, and subsequent alteration and refinement as necessary, of the entire psychological treatment for a given client. Actually, several of the job components previously discussed relate integrally to this final component. However, a crucial step in the evaluation and refinement component not yet noted is the identification of a specific individual within the client's agency to have the clearly designated responsibility (and authority) of ensuring that recommended changes in treatment delivery actually occur. Unless such a responsibility is specifically and overtly assigned to a given individual, it is likely many of the necessary recommendations for treatment success (e.g., stemming from the routine treatment monitoring or external professional oversight) will never be satisfactorily implemented to the client's benefit.

Conclusion: The Advocacy Role of the Psychologist

Management and organizational support is essential if psychological treatment is to be effective. A primary component of the psychologist's job is to obtain such support. Despite a psychologist's best efforts to obtain organizational and management support, there are some service settings in which the support will not exist (Favell, 1990). The lack of necessary support may be due, for example, to insufficient motivation to change aspects of service delivery on the part of significant people in the agency's organizational structure. In situations in which agency support is not obtained despite serious efforts by the psychologist, the role of the psychologist then becomes one of a client advocate: The psychologist is professionally responsible to inform agency executives that the psychological treatment prescribed for that client cannot be provided in the agency as it exists and to advocate for changes in service delivery. Advocating for necessary changes should involve at a minimum the following steps. First, the psychologist should clearly identify in writing for responsible agency representatives what constitutes the obstacles to effective treatment delivery. Second, the psychologist should provide in writing possible remedial actions. However, whereas the description of existing obstacles should be specific, in some cases suggestions for remediation can be more general, such that agency executives can determine for themselves precisely what corrective steps should be taken. The third advocacy step is for the psychologist to meet with appropriate agency officials to discuss openly, as an advocate for client treatment, the treatment obstacles and possible resolutions. If the preceding steps are successful, then the necessary changes in service delivery can be made and the process discussed in this chapter can continue. If the steps do not result in appropriate changes in service delivery, then it is incumbent on the psychologist to specify openly that in the service system as it exists, the psychological treatment needs of a particular client are unlikely to be met.

30

Interdisciplinary Collaboration in the Practice of Mental Retardation

Dennis D. Drotar and Lynne A. Sturm

Psychologists who provide service to children, adolescents, and adults with mental retardation (MR) do so in collaboration with a wide range of other professional disciplines (e.g., educators, nurses, nutritionists, occupational and physical therapists, physicians, social workers, speech–language pathologists, and vocational counselors). Interdisciplinary cooperation is especially important in service delivery for several reasons. MR includes complex conditions that require the services of many professional disciplines to best manage the wide range of problems that present at different points in the life span (Scheiner, 1992). Optimal delivery of services and effective partnerships with families of people with MR also require highly coordinated efforts among different professionals. Moreover, as service settings expand, interdisciplinary collaboration will assume increasing importance (Matson & Mulick, 1991b). For psychologists to make highly effective contributions to the lives of people with MR and their families, they must develop and maintain informed awareness of the contributions of other professions, incorporate these perspectives in their work, know when and how to involve others, and how best to coordinate their work with that of other professionals (Cullinane & Crocker, 1992).

However, there is often a discrepancy between the promise and practice of collaboration in clinical practice, as is the case in practice related to MR and developmental disabilities (Drotar, 1993). Professionals do not necessarily collaborate, even when it may be in the best interest of clients and their families to do so, and they often have difficulties communicating with one another. Such tensions are understandable given the many obstacles inherent in collaborative efforts. Most professionals who work with people with MR, including psychologists, are trained within their own disciplines. Many have had relatively little opportunity to acquire and practice the complex set of skills needed for successful collaboration (e.g., communication, patience, and knowledge of professional contributions). Moreover, problems in the coordination of care delivery systems, profession-specific administrative and organizational structure of settings, and patterns of reimbursement provide considerable disincentives for collaborative activity. Roles and responsibilities related to interdisciplinary collaboration are not clearly addressed in standards of professional practice.

Moreover, research concerning collaboration has been limited. To address this need, we describe issues in interdisciplinary collaboration that pertain to practice in the field of MR.

Historical Overview

The creation of university-affiliated facilities (UAFs) in 1963 via Pub. L. 88-164, the Mental Retardation and Community Health Centers Construction Act (B. D. Tucker & Goldstein, 1992), was an important prototype for interdisciplinary team collaboration in the field of developmental disabilities (Magrab & Schmidt, 1980). These university-based programs had as their goal practical clinical training and interdisciplinary diagnosis, care, and treatment of people with MR of all ages. Psychologists were, and continue to be, among the many professionals (e.g., educators, nurses, nutritionists, physicians, occupational and physical therapists, and speech–language pathologists) receiving clinical training at UAFs. Although each of these professional groups was expected to use discipline-specific knowledge in programs for persons with developmental disabilities, interdisciplinary collaboration was strongly emphasized. UAF-trained personnel were expected to understand the roles and contributions of other disciplines and to work effectively in interdisciplinary group decision making.

Federal laws established to define and authorize legal rights and services for children and adolescents with MR or developmental disabilities include the Education for All Handicapped Children Act of 1977, Pub. L. 94-142 (Jacobs & Walker, 1978; B. D. Tucker & Goldstein, 1992). In Pub. L. 94-142, the team process was used to identify eligibility and service priorities for children aged 3–21 years with special needs in schools. Pub. L. 99-457, enacted in 1986, specifically requires a multidisciplinary approach to the evaluation and treatment of young children with developmental delays or risk for such problems (Education of the Handicapped Amendments of 1986; B. D. Tucker & Goldstein, 1992). The multidisciplinary composition of each team is to be tailored to the unique characteristics of the child and his or her family. Furthermore, parents have been designated as team members, and family-identified needs and concerns about the child have replaced the more traditional definition of desired goals and outcomes by professionals. Thus, the interdisciplinary family service plan is intended to be family generated, rather than designed by professionals (P. A. Campbell, 1990), and the degree of family involvement on this team is generally much greater than is the case with older clients. Thus, there are now greater demands on psychologists to collaborate with other professionals and parents, both in assessment and intervention planning, than typically has been the case with either school-based individualized educational plans or individual habilitation plans for adult clients. These recent developments in interdisciplinary service models necessitate that psychologists become more skillful at interdisciplinary collaboration.

Functions and Value of Collaboration

In this context, the most important outcomes of interdisciplinary collaboration relate to the clinical care of people with MR and their families and ultimately to improved outcomes such as quality of life and functional adaptation for service recipients. Several features of interdisciplinary collaboration enhance delivery of services to people with MR and their families. By contributing advice that is based on their unique professional experiences concerning assessment or management of clinical problems, a team of professionals potentially can formulate a more comprehensive and thorough plan for services than could occur by working in isolation.

The second major issue in collaborative team management in clinical practice concerning MR involves improved coordination of care. It is ordinarily difficult to organize the efforts of diverse professional disciplines, especially if they are in different settings. Uncoordinated professional efforts can be stressful to people with developmental disabilities and their families, who must reconcile different professional languages and recommendations and carry out multiple recommendations for services. By contrast, the goal of effective collaborative management is production of a coordinated, prioritized set of program recommendations that addresses short-term and long-term management goals and is negotiated with people with MR and their families (Cullinane & Crocker, 1992).

Finally, collaborative clinical management may have important advantages to professionals beyond what can be achieved in solo or parallel service efforts. These include mutual support, shared learning experiences, and awareness of the circumstances, resources, and problems of people with developmental impairments (Cullinane & Crocker, 1992). At this time, however, research or evaluation studies do not demonstrate the extent to which collaborative teams do achieve superior coordination of therapies and training, produce more comprehensive plans of services, or support greater effectiveness of team members.

It is important to recognize that the nature and quality of interdisciplinary collaboration in MR practice varies dramatically as a function of the setting, characteristics of participants and resources, and the care philosophy of specific programs. However, the core dimensions of interdisciplinary team functioning include the level of communication, trust, mutual reliance, and recognition of different professional competencies that develops among team members (Magrab & Schmidt, 1980). Successful collaborators are generally clear, open communicators who can effectively use information from their colleagues and set aside professional biases in favor of collaborative decision making (Magrab & Schmidt, 1980). Potential important influences on the quality of successful interdisciplinary collaboration include (a) participants' beliefs and expectations (e.g., that collaboration is necessary and effective); (b) participants' knowledge, skills, and prior experiences in collaborative activities with particular professional disciplines and specific populations; and (c) situational incentives versus constraints (e.g., time pressures, reimbursement patterns; Drotar, 1993).

Psychologists who provide services to people with MR are often called on to consult with professionals from many disciplines who provide services in the client's residence and work or training setting. Consultation can occur on a one-to-one or small-group basis. The following case example illustrates the role of the psychologist in interpreting both cognitive and socioemotional functioning of people with MR to service providers:

A physician who provided medical services to a group home facility contacted the psychologist at a university teaching hospital. She referred a young adult with severe physical disabilities, borderline intellectual functioning, and a dependent personality disorder, with intermittent periods of intense depression. Over the course of outpatient therapy, the psychologist met with group home staff to discuss milieu approaches to the patient's interpersonal difficulties and depressive episodes and to help them understand how her cognitive deficits interacted with her personality functioning. Staff–client relationship issues also were a major focus of consultation. The staff interpreted the client's lack of organization and failure to attend planned activities as a reflection of "manipulative" behavior. However, assessment using neuropsychological measures revealed an uneven profile of skills and significant deficits in attention and memory that would be expected to interfere with her ability to respond to staff expectations. Test findings were also instrumental in adjusting vocational education goals to be more compatible with the nature of her cognitive deficits. The psychologist also facilitated a psychiatric consultation concerning pharmacological approaches to the patient's irritability and depression.

Tensions in Interdisciplinary Consultation

Despite the potential advantages of collaborative team management as opposed to discipline-specific management in clinical practice concerning MR, it is often difficult to effectively implement a collaborative practice model. One reason relates to the inherent tensions involved in interdisciplinary collaboration. To anticipate tensions that can develop between professionals and develop strategies to lessen them, it is useful to consider specific stresses that can arise in practice related to MR.

Differences in Roles and Models of Practice

Shonkoff and Meisels (1990) observed that planning and delivering early intervention services to children with developmental disabilities and their families poses a serious challenge to traditional disciplinary boundaries. This blurring of discipline-specific knowledge and skills can intensify tension between the psychologist and other professionals, especially if interprofessional relationships are already strained by limited fiscal resources and competition for reimbursement. Profession-specific differences in training result in much different models of practice concerning MR, as well as differences in the language that is used to describe people with MR, views about research, and program evaluation in this field.

Professionals are trained primarily (sometimes exclusively) by members of their own discipline and adopt the values, ethical standards, and implicit clinical practices and viewpoints that characterize their particular profession. Different professions set different priorities for clinical assessment and intervention, especially with respect to the particular aspects of the individual's functioning they regard as most important. Professionals also differ in the types of relationships they form with clients and families, and in their experience and attitudes toward research and program evaluation. At the least, such differences make it difficult for professionals to understand one another's approach to practice. Moreoever, to the extent that an individual considers his or her profession as having primary claim to the "only" and "right" clinical viewpoint, interprofessional conflicts can become serious and even irreconcilable.

Models of Relationships With Clients and Families

Professionals who work with individuals with MR may have different expectations and standards concerning the type of professional relationships they form with people with MR. Psychologists are bound by ethical standards to refrain from nonprofessional relationships, as defined by the American Psychological Association (1992), with clients or patients and their families. Conversely, boundaries of personal disclosure and relationships between other professionals and their clients may be demarcated differently. Such differences can lead to tensions between professionals who are involved with the same families. Cirillo and Sorrentino (1986) noted that "the rehabilitation worker's technical role often places him or her on a level analogous to that of a 'grandparent' " (p. 291). With families of child clients, psychologists in particular may have difficulty understanding and accepting the actions of professionals who develop and maintain relationships with clients with developmental disabilities and their family members that extend beyond the work situation. However, other professionals generally regard their relationships with their clients as personally meaningful and necessary and may view the psychologist who questions their practice as cold or unduly rigid.

Differences in Language and Concepts Pertaining to MR

Professionals from different disciplines vary in their comfort with the specific language that is used to describe people with MR, their problems, and competencies. For example, professionals in educational systems may use the term *developmental handicap* or *mild-to-severe deficit*, whereas physicians may refer to *developmental delay* or *MR* to describe the same problem. Professionals' use of various diagnostic labels and attitudes toward labeling relate to differences in training and philosophies of treatment.

For example, physicians are trained to arrive at a diagnosis in order to recommend a treatment plan. Other professionals may be more comfortable with an approach to assessment that emphasizes a functional description of strengths and deficits and normalization of functioning. Variations in language also may involve assumptions about the nature of the individual's problem, such as in the following example:

Mike was a 4½-year-old boy with MR whose professional parents had obtained a wide array of developmental therapies for him throughout the preschool years. On referral from the child's pediatrician, the psychologist evaluated the child and obtained information from all the therapists who had worked with him. The available data documented a consistent rate of slower than expected development. When the psychologist communicated the diagnosis of mild MR, the occupational therapist and speech–language pathologist were distressed by the term *mental retardation* and argued against its application to their client, citing progress in skills made during the preschool period and their expectation and hope that the child's development would catch up to that of his peers. To alleviate this conflict, it helped to discuss the meaning of the MR diagnosis with each professional and clarify the source of their disagreement. The occupational therapist and speech–language pathologist felt that the psychologist's use of the diagnosis of MR meant that the child would not improve in response to intervention, which was not the case. The differences in the professionals' approach to the use of the MR diagnosis were also discussed with the child's parents.

Differences in the Relationship of Research to Practice

An important role for psychologists in the field of developmental disabilities has involved research concerning the causes of the condition, prevention, and education and treatment approaches (Matson & Mulick, 1991b). Collaboration between psychologists and those in other disciplines in evaluating the efficacy of new treatment approaches for people with MR could potentially expand the knowledge base of professional practice. However, in some instances, research and evaluation may threaten professionals' assumptions of the efficacy of their diagnostic and intervention procedures. For this reason, psychologists' efforts to evaluate therapeutic practices identified with particular professional disciplines, such as facilitated communication techniques (Wheeler, Jacobson, Paglieri, & Schwartz, 1993) or sensory integration therapy (Arendt, MacLean, & Baumeister, 1988), may contribute to interprofessional tensions. For example, findings from controlled studies may cast doubt on assumptions founded on case studies or demonstrate ineffectiveness or markedly circumscribed effectiveness of therapies.

Many of these interprofessional tensions are deeply rooted in training and years of practice and will not yield easily to reconciliation. For this reason, professionals need to recognize their inherent difficulties in their work relationships with those in other disciplines, clarify their perspectives (rather than assume that they will always be understood), recognize the sensitivities of other professionals, and openly discuss and negotiate any problems that arise. The leaders of collaborative teams also should consider ways of addressing potential collaborative problems through communication and problem-solving strategies. In situations in which professionals emphasize much different areas of need or produce conflicting recommendations, the team leader should facilitate conflict resolution and a decision concerning treatment priorities on the basis of evidence for treatment efficacy, family preference, and availability of services. Awareness of the available empirical data on the efficacy of treatments typically recommended by various professionals is particularly important in effectively weighing treatment alternatives for people with MR and their families (G. W. Brown, 1987).

Recommendations for Training

Magrab and Schmidt (1980) observed the need to encourage a receptivity to collaboration as early in the training of professionals as possible. They noted, however, that most professionals receive training about interdisciplinary process on the job in team meetings. Recommendations for earlier and more consistent interdisciplinary training certainly applies to the preparation of psychologists. For example, a discussion of three formats for interdisciplinary training in the early intervention field (Rooney, Fullagar, & Gallagher, 1993) targeted personnel training and orientation as the time for fostering an interdisciplinary attitude. Rooney et al. recommended that courses be team taught to model interdisciplinary collaboration and that continuing education efforts be planned and implemented within an interdisciplinary consortium.

Psychologists typically do not receive formal training in interdisciplinary collaboration or team process. For this reason, supervised observation and training in the specific skills required in collaborative encounters are important (Drotar, 1993). Ideally, such training should include exposure to models of team-based service delivery and interdisciplinary collaboration, supervision, and practice in collaborating with parents and professionals to design service plans (N. K. Klein & Campbell, 1991), as well as participation on interdisciplinary teams in a range of settings.

The importance of interdisciplinary collaboration to practice related to MR warrants continuing education beyond formal internship and postdoctoral training. Useful approaches include workshops that focus on effective strategies to recognize and resolve typical collaborative problems and the development of collaborative research, clinical, or teaching programs in MR. In addition, ongoing opportunities for professionals to share their experiences and frustrations concerning collaboration and obtain feedback and support from colleagues need to be developed (Drotar, 1993).

Implications and Future Directions

What future directions in interdisciplinary collaboration can one anticipate? Psychologists have been accustomed to a central role in the diagnosis and management of MR. However, the American Association on Mental Retardation (1992) guidelines now emphasize the multidisciplinary team process in decision making about individuals who have MR. Additional procedures (e.g., interviews with caregivers, observations, review of medical records) are now expected to supplement standardized tests of intellectual functioning, which are typically contributed by psychologists. The team is then expected to use clinical judgment and information obtained from multiple sources and settings in order to validate or invalidate the test results. However, this is not a satisfactory procedure for several critical reasons. There are no explicit guidelines on how teams should achieve consensus. There also is no research indicating that a team process will result in determinations that are as reliable and valid as those resulting from well established standardized measures of intellectual and adaptive functioning.

Moreover, the American Association on Mental Retardation's guidelines do not specify which personnel should conduct the diagnostic process, but imply that the team will determine the level of needed supports in four dimensions: intellectual functioning and adaptive skills; psychological and emotional factors; physical, health, and etiological considerations; and environmental issues. This approach is likely to lead to confusion in professional roles and responsibilities.

This emphasis on team process has been echoed by the standards of the Accreditation Council on Services for People with Developmental Disabilities (1990). Its manual presents a model of interdisciplinary services delivery that heightens the need for interdisciplinary collaboration. Psychologists are expected to collaborate within a multidisciplinary team, using team consensus, to develop an initial comprehensive evaluation of clients. Behavioral goals and objectives are then expected to reflect team consensus on behavioral tasks and skills to be learned by the individual in the coming year.

Thus far, interdisciplinary collaboration concerning clinical practice in MR has eluded empirical scrutiny. However, research would have a valuable function in helping to focus attention on collaboration and in developing methods to operationalize various aspects of collaborative activities, process, and outcomes. Several types of research would be especially useful. For example, researchers need empirical descriptions of professionals' models of beliefs, expectations, and decision making concerning clinical practice in MR. Wolraich, Siperstein, and Reed's (1992) recent review indicated that physicians were less optimistic in their expectations concerning the future attainments of people with MR, as were educators. Such pessimism may unintentionally contribute to pediatricians' underreferral of children with MR for psychological and early intervention services (Goodman & Cecil, 1987).

It also will be important to consider the relationship of different types of collaborative teams and models to clinically relevant outcomes such as the satisfaction of professionals and consumers of services and adaptive outcomes of people with MR. The strongest inferences will be made from tests of interventions designed to enhance the frequency or quality of collaborative management of clinical problems in MR and to facilitate specific skills (e.g., problem identification, clear communication) expected to improve interdisciplinary cooperation.

31

Wraparound Services

John D. Burchard, Margaret Atkins, and
Sara N. Burchard

In this chapter, we describe and illustrate a process for serving people with emotional and behavioral problems that is referred to as *wraparound services.* Although wraparound services have been used with people experiencing all levels of emotional and behavioral problems, the approach was developed as a community-based alternative to residential treatment (Burchard, Burchard, Sewell, & VanDenBerg, 1993; Burchard & Clarke, 1990; Burchard & Schaefer, 1992; Clarke, Burchard, Schaefer, & Welkowitz, 1992; VanDenBerg, 1993). After describing the principles that are involved in the administration of wraparound services, we present a case to illustrate the use of this approach with a child who was given a dual diagnosis of mental retardation and severe emotional disturbance.

The development of wraparound services has been recent. In a landmark study conducted by the Children's Defense Fund in 1982, it was estimated that two thirds of the children who were experiencing severe emotional and behavioral problems were not receiving adequate services (Knitzer, 1982). Whether the children were identified through the schools (e.g., classified with serious emotional disturbance in accordance with the Education of the Handicapped Act of 1975) or the mental health system (e.g., diagnosed as mentally disabled in accordance with criteria set forth in the third edition of the *Diagnostic and Statistical Manual of Mental Disorders* [*DSM–III*]; American Psychiatric Association, 1980), the response of the service delivery system tended to be (a) no services available; (b) referral to outpatient therapy or counseling; or (c) placement with similar children in a segregated classroom, segregated school, a residential treatment center, or a psychiatric hospital. In general, for children whose services were perceived as inadequate, the services were crisis driven, categorical, overly restrictive, poorly coordinated, and unable to meet the expressed needs of the child or family. The personal distress and destruction that can result from such inadequate services has been well documented in a detailed description of three cases (Gutkind, 1993).

The wraparound process is a response to these shortcomings in the service delivery system. In general, the process involves "wrapping" services around the child and family that are tailored to meet their needs and continuing to work with the child and family until services are no longer needed. Wraparound services include an interagency partnership among providers and family members, with the establishment of community-based service plans that focus on the needs and strengths of both the child and family. This is contrary to the more traditional, categorical system of care that tends to fit the child and family into an array of preexisting programs and services. These programs usually have acceptance and discharge criteria, offer similar interventions to all of their clients, are time limited, and are not well coordinated with each other.

In many locations, wraparound services have become the treatment of choice for children with severe emotional and behavioral problems. Recent data suggest that 75%–90% of these children improve over time, and their rate of improvement is greater than they would have achieved through residential treatment (Bruns, Burchard, & Yoe, 1995).

Because wraparound services involve a process rather than a specific set of procedures, the services will vary from one location to another. The procedures, however, are based on a number of principles, as follows:

1. Child and Family Focus. The child and family are the focus of the service plan. Goals and objectives are based on what children and parents perceive as their needs and strengths, not just what the "professionals" think. There is a strong emphasis on family involvement in all aspects of the planning and delivery of services.
2. Core Services Team. Each family has a team of people who work with them to provide support and assistance in planning, implementing, and monitoring services. The team should be made up of strong advocates selected by the child and parents, as well as key service providers. For example, a team might include the youth (if appropriate), a friend of the youth, the parents, the parents' advocate, a teacher, a school aide, a respite worker, a case manager, and a therapist. Each participant brings his or her own unique perspective to the team, and together they can make the best decisions for the youth and family.
3. Unconditional Care. Unconditional care is one of the most important components of wraparound services. The core services team, including the family and all of the agencies involved in providing services, must agree to be unconditional in their support of the family and child. This means that no matter how difficult the situation becomes, the team will stand by the family and will be willing to make changes in the plan in order to accommodate the child's and family's evolving needs. For many children and families, this is the first time they can feel supported in every facet of their lives.
4. Individualized Service Plan. Every family's plan is unique to the strengths and needs of that particular child and family. Service availability is not based on the programmatic structure that exists within the agency that is providing the services. That is, services that are provided to the family are noncategorical. If

only categorical services exist and they are deemed inappropriate, then more meaningful services will be created.

5. Strength Based. The individual plans are based on the individual's and family's strengths rather than on their "problems." The idea is to build on the family's positive attributes and, by doing so, lessen the occurrence of some of their problems. People feel better when the primary focus is on their strengths rather than on the things that make them and others unhappy.
6. Community Based. Services are provided to the child and family in their community, preferably in their home. If living at home is not an option for the child, then another community setting is created to meet the child's needs. If restrictive residential services are used, the placement is focused on short-term stabilization in accordance with a crisis plan.
7. Culturally Competent. The planning for the child and family is consistent with the cultural norms that are relevant to the child and family. If team members and providers are from a different culture, they will receive adequate training in the delivery of services that are appropriate to the culture of the child and family.
8. Interagency Collaboration. Essential agencies that have a responsibility to provide services to the child and family (e.g., education, mental health, mental retardation, social services, juvenile services) are represented on the core services team and participate in the allocation of resources. To facilitate this collaboration at the individual case level, an interagency committee of administrators and parents problem solves bureaucratic barriers and ensures pooled funding for services specified by each team.
9. Flexible Funding. The agencies that are providing the dollars to fund the services, no matter how unusual the request for financing may be, must make the funding as flexible as possible so that the team can purchase the services or items that the child and family need. Although the examples are endless, they include services and items not usually provided through the traditional service delivery system (e.g., fixing a car to facilitate transportation, providing a phone to enhance communication, purchasing a washing machine to alleviate the stress of having to take a child with autism to a laundromat, or buying concert tickets as part of an incentive system).

   Clearly, there are funding limits with any case involving wraparound services. Therefore, it is the job of the core services team to allocate resources in a manner that is consistent with a prioritized list of needs. In some cases, transportation, appliances, or recreation may be more critical than the traditional, categorical services that agencies are more prepared to provide (e.g., therapy, medications, and psychological evaluations).
10. Crisis Plan. The core services team should have a written, detailed crisis plan that specifies the most likely crises that might

occur and the services that will be administered should they happen. It is critical that the service response is timely and that the plan clearly indicates who does what and when. It also is important that the agency or person responsible for paying for the services be identified in advance.

Given these 10 principles, the wraparound process begins with the formation of the core services team and the development of the individualized service plan. In constructing the service plan, the team addresses the child and family needs in each of the following eight life domain areas: (a) residential (a place to live); (b) family or surrogate family; (c) social (friends and contact with other people); (d) educational and vocational; (e) medical; (f) psychological and emotional; (g) legal (especially for children with juvenile justice needs); and (h) safety (the need to be safe). Other specific life domain areas such as cultural or ethnic needs, gender needs, and community needs receive the necessary attention on an individual basis. To provide a better understanding of the wraparound process, we describe the case of a boy for whom wraparound services were administered.

The Case of Peter

Peter was a 9-year-old boy with a dual diagnosis who manifested the characteristics of both mild mental retardation and severe emotional disturbance. He lived in a large metropolitan area, where he had been receiving wraparound services for the past 18 months. A multiaxial timeline was produced to illustrate the significant behaviors and events that occurred during Peter's lifetime. The timeline is shown in Figure 1, with all material to the left of the dotted line representing baseline or preexisting conditions prior to wraparound services. From top to bottom, the five timelines reflect (a) the onset and continuation of Peter's major problem behaviors; (b) major events in Peter's life that could have been related to his behavior problems; (c) community-based services (of which there were none in baseline); (d) educational services; and (e) residential services. In general, the boxes on each timeline designate when services started and stopped, and the height of the boxes approximates the restrictiveness of the service. For other examples of the use of the multiaxial timeline, see Burchard et al. (1993) and Burchard et al. (1995).

Although the records of Peter's early years were incomplete, there was considerable evidence that he experienced a highly unstable, chaotic, and traumatic childhood. His father died 1 month before he was born, and his mother was illiterate and homeless. The records mentioned considerable neglect (e.g., unsafe housing, poor nutrition, lead poisoning), as well as periodic physical abuse prior to age 4 years and 7 months, when the child protection agency placed him in a diagnostic center. His primary behavior problems at that time included hyperactivity, tantrums, property damage, and language delay. In the assessment, he was described as "a foul-

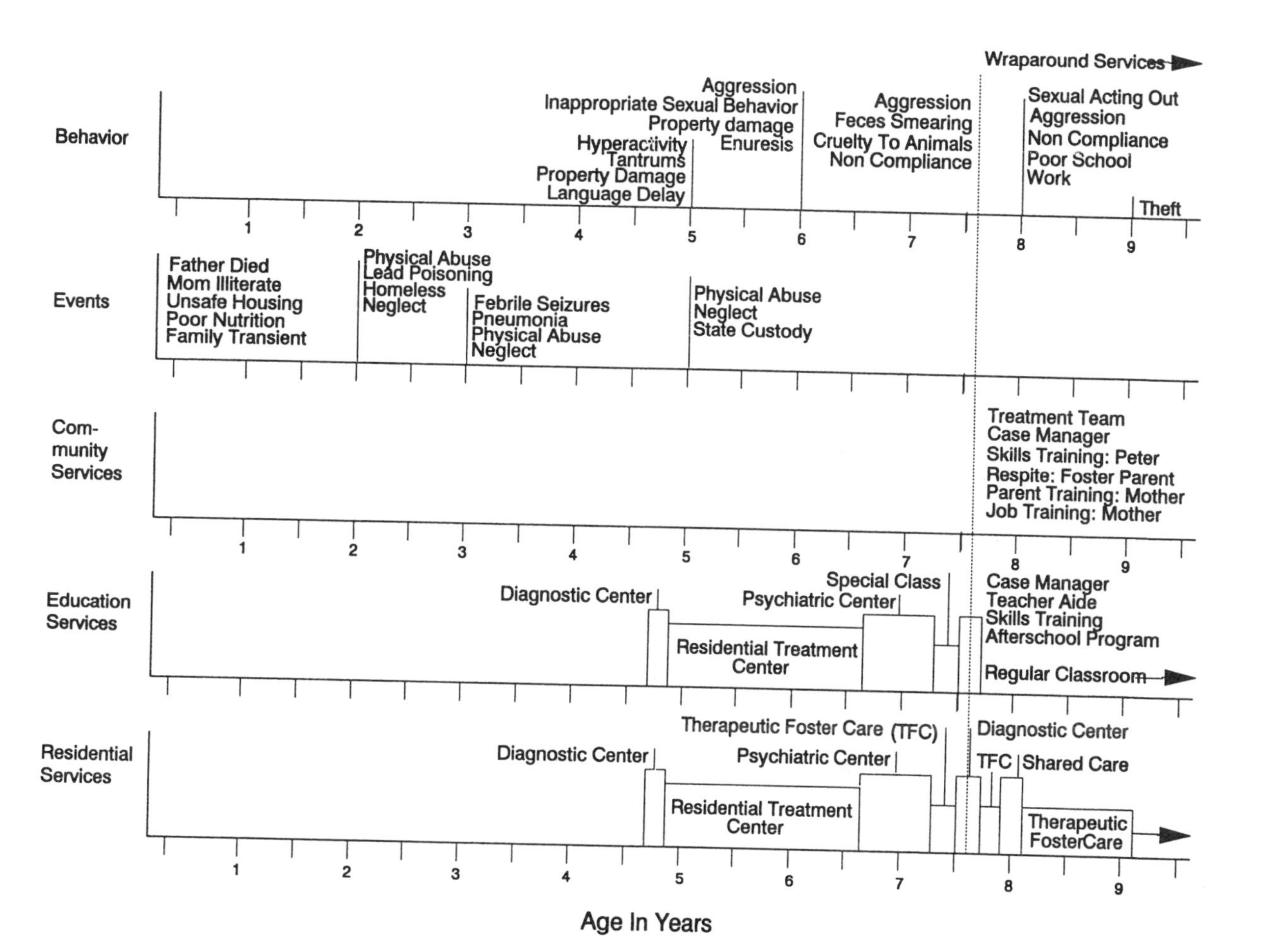

Figure 1. Multiaxial Timeline: Peter.

mouthed boy who would exhaust two adults on an everyday basis. A residential treatment center is recommended for at least 1 year."

Between the ages 5 and 7 years, Peter resided at a fairly large residential treatment center, where little progress was achieved. The records indicated that his school performance was poor and that his behavior problems escalated to include physical aggression and sexual acting out. Toward the end of his second year in residential treatment, Peter's aggressive behavior escalated to the point where he was placed in a residential psychiatric center for more intensive assessment and treatment.

After making progress in the psychiatric center, Peter was transferred to a therapeutic foster home. Peter continued to progress during the first 6 weeks of foster care, but his aggression (which included a severe beating of the family dog) resulted in his return to the diagnostic center.

Shortly after his readmission to the diagnostic center, a referral was made for Peter to receive wraparound services. At that time, a psychiatric evaluation revealed the following formal multiaxial diagnosis (from the fourth edition of the *DSM* (American Psychiatric Association, 1994):

Axis I:	Post Traumatic Stress Disorder (p. 247)
	Dissociative Disorder, NOS [not otherwise specified] (p. 277)
	Oppositional Defiant Disorder (p. 56)
	R/O [Rule Out] Psychotic Disorder, NOS (p. 211)
Axis II:	Specific Developmental Disorder, NOS (p. 49)
Axis III:	HX [history] of lead poisoning (p. 18)
	HX of seizure disorder
Axis IV:	Psychosocial stressors (p. 11)
	Severity: 4 and 5, acute and enduring
Axis V:	Current GAF [Global Assessment of Functioning Scale] (p. 12): 10
	Past Year GAF: Unknown.

A private, nonprofit agency that specializes in the delivery of wraparound services was placed under contract to serve Peter and his family. The wraparound services that were provided by the agency were facilitated by an interagency committee that ensured interagency collaboration and pooled funding. The core services team included a case manager, the mother, a friend of the mother, a foster mother, a teacher, and a therapist. The providers and advocates on the team agreed that they would stick with Peter and his mother no matter how challenging his behavior became.

A strengths and needs assessment was then conducted across each of the eight life domains. The team identified some of Peter's strengths as his affection toward his mother, his sense of humor, his ability to be likeable and friendly on most occasions, and his interest in music. Peter's mother's strengths included her affection for Peter, her interest in becoming a better parent, and her interest in becoming more independent.

The highlights of Peter's needs were a structured behavior management program within a foster care setting, a chance to spend more time with his mother, enrollment in a regular classroom at school with a full-time aide, more friends, school tutoring, anger and aggression control training, social skills training, a more precise assessment of the effects of medication, access to rock music and games, and access to fast food restaurants. Peter's mother's major needs included parent training, driver's education, and job training.

Although it is beyond the scope of this chapter to describe the complete array of services that were provided for Peter and his family, the primary ones that were in place when Peter entered wraparound services included the following:

1. A case manager who "brokered" services for the team (Santarcangelo, Birkett, & McGrath, 1995). This person's primary responsibility was the implementation of the services specified in the written service plan. In addition, the case manager provided all team members with ongoing support and assistance in problem solving and was available during any crisis that might occur.
2. Therapeutic foster care with an experienced family that included a foster mother, who was a full-time parent, a foster father who had a full-time job as a mechanic, and a 12-year-old foster brother who was enrolled in the sixth grade in the local public school.
3. An experienced respite family that cared for Peter for one weekend each month.
4. A regular class placement in the local public school with a full-time teacher's aide who was trained in behavior management techniques. The aide was responsible for coordinating a comprehensive behavior modification program (with the help of an outside consultant) that focused on academic and prosocial behaviors in both the home and school (Davies & Rogers, 1985; Lochman & Curry, 1986). In addition, the aide provided Peter with one-on-one training in self-regulation skills (Nezu & Nezu, 1991), anger control skills (Lochman, Lampron, Gemmer, & Harris, 1987), and problem-solving skills (L. K. Koegel, Koegel, & Parks, 1990).
5. An afterschool program that had adequate activities and supervision to meet Peter's needs.
6. Parent training and family therapy sessions with Peter's mother and Peter that focused on issues related to her inability to care for Peter at home (Forehand & King, 1977).
7. Employment training for Peter's mother.
8. A crisis plan in which immediate assistance was provided if Peter's aggressive behavior was beyond the control of his mother, his foster parents, or the school. At any given time, a person trained in the management of aggression was accessible by beeper.

As is typical with many wraparound programs for very challenging children, it was not long before the core services team had to make significant service adjustments to meet Peter's changing needs. Although he was making good progress in school, and the respite and the visitations with his mother were going well, improvement was more qualified in the foster home. The foster parents reported a slight increase in his overall level of compliance; however, they were unable to cope with an increase in the frequency and severity of Peter's aggressive outbursts toward his foster sibling. Even though the person on-call responded to the beeper in a timely fashion, the foster parents felt that the situation had become too dangerous to continue. Therefore, as the timeline indicates, after 2 months, the core services team placed Peter in a staffed apartment where he could receive a greater intensity of supervision and training to control his aggression.

This type of placement, which was basically a temporary group home for one person, was used with several youths in the Alaska Youth Initiative (Burchard et al., 1993). Also referred to as "shared care," the placement involved trained staff who provided Peter with more intensive training in behavior management (e.g., prosocial skills, anger control, self-regulation of aggression, and contingency management). The training program also involved graduated exposure to increasing social situations that replicated a family setting that included other children.

After 6 weeks of relatively steady improvement, the core services team began to move Peter gradually into the home of one of the staff who worked in the shared-care program. All members of the team (including Peter) agreed that it was not in Peter's best interest to return to the first foster home, even though the foster parents indicated a willingness to give it another try.

At this point, Peter continues to make progress in his second foster placement, although the core services team has had to make minor service changes to cope with periodic setbacks in his adjustment. He is a long way from being able to live with his mother without the need for any services, but he is moving in that direction. How close Peter can come to that objective remains to be seen.

Conclusion

Wraparound services exemplify a different philosophy and approach to serving children and families. In the traditional service delivery system, parents are not equal partners in the decision-making process, professional services are not implemented and terminated by team consensus, agencies do not pool their resources together to provide whatever services are necessary to meet highly individualized needs, and most interagency decision makers and providers do not transcend failed placements unless they are legally mandated to do so. Clearly, the wraparound process is a different way of doing business.

Because of the strong emphasis on interagency collaboration, the wraparound process is especially well suited for people with a dual diagnosis of mental retardation and some form of severe emotional disturbance. Wraparound services were developed as an alternative to residential treatment for the most challenging children in the service delivery system. By design, the services focused on those children and families that were being served by multiple service agencies. As a result, many of the children who were the first to receive wraparound services had a diagnosis of mild mental retardation.

With respect to the effectiveness of wraparound services, the evidence is very encouraging, but far from conclusive. Comprehensive case studies and follow-up studies involving some of the most challenging youth in the system report relatively stable, community-based adjustment in 80%–90% of the cases a year after entry into wraparound services (Bruns et al., 1995; Burchard et al., 1993; see also the *Journal of Child and Family Studies* [March, 1996], which focuses exclusively on wraparound services). This is especially encouraging, given the high recidivism rates for children who are placed in mental health residential treatment centers (E. C. Brown & Greenbaum, 1994). On the other hand, the controlled comparison studies that can yield more definitive outcomes have yet to be conducted. At this stage of development, the wraparound approach represents a promising service that should be pursued clinically, as well as through further research.

32

Professional Advocacy and Legal Issues

Richard J. Landau

Thirty years ago, there would have been little substance to a chapter dealing with the rights of people with mental retardation (MR). What could have been written largely would have dealt with the procedures developed over the centuries for systematically depriving people with this disability of their legal rights under the pretense of due process. People with MR were typically presumed to be legally incompetent and unable to provide meaningful input into decisions dealing with their daily lives. Long-term institutionalization was the most widely accepted form of "treatment" (*Halderman v. Pennhurst,* 1978). Compulsory sterilization statutes were common (Murdock, 1974). In this chapter, we focus on the evolution of the basic legal rights of people with MR. As such, detailed analyses on the right to treatment, litigation on appropriate placement, decision making with respect to body integrity, and related issues such as advocacy outside the legal context are beyond the scope of this chapter (see Beyer, 1991, and Fiedler & Antonak, 1991, for more information on these topics).

By 1990, the legal status of all people with disabilities, including people with MR, had radically changed. In that year, Congress enacted the Americans With Disabilities Act (ADA), describing its purpose as

> (1) to provide a clear and comprehensive national mandate for the elimination of discrimination against individuals with disabilities;
> (2) to provide clear, strong, consistent enforceable standards addressing discrimination against individuals with disabilities;
> (3) to ensure that the Federal Government plays a central role in enforcing the standards established in this Act on behalf of individuals with disabilities; and
> (4) to invoke the sweep of congressional authority, including the power to enforce the Fourteenth Amendment and to regulate commerce, in order to address the major areas of discrimination faced day-to-day by people with disabilities (Americans With Disabilities Act [ADA], 1990, 42 U.S.C. § 12101)

The fact remains, however, that in giving meaning to statutory enactments such as the ADA, people with MR will continue to present professionals advocating on their behalf with a myriad of special problems unique to this group. Although this area of the law stubbornly resists summary treatment because of differing federal and state precedents, evolving case law, and diverse applications of psychiatric disability case law in MR (see Perlin, Gould, & Dorfman, 1995), in this chapter we provide a brief overview of the legal issues confronting clinicians who choose to advocate on behalf of people with MR.

Competency and Informed Consent

Effective advocacy on behalf of people with disabilities requires that advocates advance positions on issues that are consistent with the special needs and interests of their clients. When a client's cognitive and emotional development has clearly reached a level where the advocate is comfortable with the client's ability to make life choices, and the choice is a relatively benign one, the issues confronting the advocate will be little different from those encountered by advocates on behalf of people with disabilities generally. Choices such as what room of a residence the client wishes to occupy or whether to walk or take the bus to work will rarely involve issues of competency and informed consent. When, however, the choice confronting the client has potentially permanent consequences or exposes the client to the risk of injury, issues of individual competency, and how to deal with these issues, become very important. These issues must be addressed before the advocate takes any steps toward vindicating the perceived rights of the client.

Guardianship

In coming to grips with the special advocacy problems presented by people with MR, advocates must first recognize the importance of the doctrine of *parens patriae* in the history of legal reasoning concerning the rights of people with disabilities. The term *parens patriae* (literally, "parent of the country") refers to the role of government as the guardian of people with disabilities. When a court has determined that an individual lacks the cognitive ability to understand the consequences of making personal decisions in his or her own self-interest, the *parens patriae* powers of the state permit the court to appoint a competent person to serve as legal guardian with the authority to make decisions on behalf of the person with a disability.

The precise legal standard applied by the court depends on the state in which the client resides. Michigan's statute, which is typical, authorizes the appointment of a guardian when it is established by clear and convincing evidence that an individual has a developmental disability and is "totally without capacity to care for himself or herself" (Michigan Mental Health Code, 1974, § 618, Michigan Compiled Laws Annotated § 330.1618). More limited guardianships also may be secured that permit the ward to retain certain of his or her legal and civil rights (Michigan Mental Health Code, 1974).

Determinations of a client's competence thus cannot be predicated solely on a clinical assessment. If the client is under 18 years of age, the client's parent will typically have decision-making power regardless of the child's level of functioning. If a decision confronting an adult client has potentially irreversible consequences, or even if the decision involves the expenditure of significant financial resources, the advocate is best advised to ask the client or his or her caregivers whether the person has a court-appointed guardian. If a guardian has not been appointed and the advocate has any doubt as to the client's competence, guardianship proceedings should be commenced in the state court vested with authority to make such appointments. If a guardian has been appointed, the advocate should bear in mind that the guardian must be consulted in making determinations regarding what is or is not in the client's best interests. Indeed, in the case of a client who is under 18 or a client with a court-appointed guardian, for most clinically significant decisions the parent or guardian stands in the shoes of the person with a disability. An advocate who seeks to override the wishes of a client's parent or guardian is best advised to seek judicial approval before doing so.

Informed Consent

A variety of special legal interests related to the issue of competency become implicated when decisions on behalf of the person with MR involve life-sustaining medical treatment or experimentation. In recent years, the courts have increasingly come to recognize that even the appointment of a legal guardian may be insufficient to protect the legal interests of people with MR when the decisions confronting the guardian implicate the person's constitutional "liberty interests." These interests include the right of an individual to be "free from nonconsensual invasion of his [or her] bodily integrity" (*Superintendent of Belchertown v. Saikewicz,* 1977). Different states have adopted different procedures when such rights are implicated. In some states, the authority to make such decisions is vested in institutional ethics committees (e.g., *In re Quinlan,* 1976), whereas in others prior judicial approval may be necessary (e.g., *Superintendent of Belchertown v. Saikewicz,* 1977).

Psychologists must bear in mind that prior consultation with a neutral decision maker other than a guardian also may be required if the psychologist is considering the use of certain behavioral interventions. In some states, the use of restrictive behavioral procedures, such as aversive conditioning, contingent restraint, or food deprivation, requires the prior judicial appointment of a guardian who has the specific authority to make such decisions on behalf of the client (e.g., Massachusetts Regulations for Behavior Modification Treatment Programs, 1987). Clinicians should be careful, however, to avoid permitting such additional legal requirements to bias them against the use of such procedures.

As we discuss more fully later, state and federal law may in certain instances require that clinicians consider the use of procedures, however restrictive, that permit their clients to attain their maximum potential. If, for example, the short-term use of an aversive conditioning program has the potential to decrease or eliminate the long-term use of physical restraints or debilitating psychotropic medication, the clinician may be obligated to at least consider the use of such interventions (Landau, 1993). In such situations, the clinician should consult legal counsel to determine how to proceed.

Clinical research also implicates the doctrine of informed consent. Whenever a clinician or researcher contemplates the participation of a person with MR in a clinical research program, it is imperative that the express written informed consent to the person's participation in the study be secured from the individual and, as appropriate, his or her court-appointed guardian. Most hospitals and universities have their own in-house institutional review committees or boards created for the purpose of reviewing research protocols and their associated informed consent forms. Typically, these committees are expressly mandated by or modeled after regulations governing human experimentation promulgated by state or federal agencies, such as the Department of Education (e.g., United States Department of Education Regulations, 1991). Informed consent forms used in research settings must specifically disclose the known risks associated with the research, as well as the purposes of the study and the anticipated benefits.

Nondiscrimination on the Basis of Disability

The most rapidly evolving area of disabilities law is that which protects individuals from discrimination on the basis of disability. The landmark federal legislation in this area includes Section 504 of the Rehabilitation Act of 1973 (hereafter referred to as simply Section 504), the Individuals With Disabilities Education Act (IDEA) of 1990 and related regulations (1992), as well as the ADA. Although state laws frequently provide similar, and occasionally even more extensive, protections against discrimination on the basis of disability, these federal statutes apply generally throughout the country, and clinicians and advocates should have at least some knowledge about the scope of their requirements.

Section 504 and the ADA

The only substantive difference between Section 504 and the ADA is the type of institution regulated by each statute. Section 504 applies to recipients of federal financial assistance. Typical recipients include most universities, hospitals, and public elementary and secondary schools, as well as providers who receive Medicaid funding for services. The scope of the ADA is much broader. The ADA applies to state and local government agencies, regardless of whether they receive federal financial assistance, as well as any private entity that operates a "public accommodation." A public accommodation is defined so broadly under the ADA (including, e.g., stores, professional offices, service establishments, and "places of" education, recreation, and public gathering) that it becomes difficult to envision businesses or organizations that would not fall within the act (e.g., *Sandison v. Michigan High School Athletic Association,* 1994).

Both statutes generally prohibit subject entities from discriminating against people with disabilities in the areas of employment practices and transportation services. In addition, Section 504 and the ADA prohibit subject entities from denying people with disabilities goods, services, facilities, privileges, advantages, or accommodations that are available to nondisabled people. Moreover, subject entities must adjust their work requirements and eligibility standards to accommodate the needs of people with disabilities.

Although the ADA is fairly new, and there has been little in the way of case law that interprets its scope, its plain terms make it an extraordinarily comprehensive nondiscrimination statute. As a remedial statute, the language of the ADA is to be construed broadly by the courts (*Kinney v. Yerusalem,* 1993). Any person with disabilities who has a claim under the ADA may file a civil lawsuit in federal court seeking an order compelling action on the part of the subject entity or to recover damages. If the person with the disability prevails, both Section 504 and the ADA permit the recovery of the person's attorney's fees and costs incurred in filing and prosecuting the lawsuit.

One of the principal obstacles to taking action under either Section 504 or the ADA is unlikely to present any problem for people with MR. Both statutes apply only to qualified individuals with disabilities. To be "qualified," the person's disability must limit one or more of the major life activities (ADA Regulations, 1993). Because the definition of "major life activities" encompasses caring for oneself, learning, and working, a diagnosis of MR is virtually certain to entitle the person with this disability to the protections afforded under these statutes.

The issue that is more likely to confront people with MR and their advocates is the extent to which, for example, an employer must accommodate MR in the workplace. Both Section 504 and the ADA require only "reasonable" accommodation. Work adjustments, such as changes in job requirements and modifications of examinations and training procedures, are not required if they would present an "undue hardship" to the employer (i.e., the accommodation would cause the employer's business significant difficulty or expense). Given the broad remedial purposes of these statutes, as well as the subjective definitions of limitations such as "undue hardship," however, employers will need to be extremely careful about making any a priori assumptions about the employment positions unavailable to people with MR purely because of their cognitive limitations. Thus, the scope of employment opportunities that the ADA has opened up for people with MR has only just begun to be explored.

The IDEA

The IDEA is an old statute with a new name. It was enacted by Congress in 1975 as Pub. L. 94-142, and, until 1990, it was commonly known as the Education for All Handicapped People Act. In 1990, it was revised and renamed the Individuals With Disabilities Education Act (IDEA). Unlike Section 504 and the ADA, the IDEA does not simply prohibit discrimination against people with disabilities; it affirmatively commands state and local school authorities to provide a "free appropriate public education" to all children with disabilities. Each and every student with a disability must be evaluated by the school districts in which they reside in order to determine whether the student is eligible to receive publicly funded special education and related services. If the student is eligible, an individualized education plan (IEP) must be developed, specifying the special education and related services to which the student is entitled. In a very real sense, the IEP becomes a contract for services between the parent and the school district. The IEP places significant limits on a school's discretion to cut services to the student (*Honig v. Doe,* 1988).

People with MR typically will have little difficulty qualifying for services under the IDEA. MR is defined as "significantly subaverage general intellectual functioning existing concurrently with deficits in adaptive behavior and manifested during the developmental period that adversely affects a child's educational performance" (IDEA Regulations, 1992, 34 C.F.R. § 300.7).

Although the IDEA is an extremely powerful tool for vindicating the rights of school-age people with disabilities, some limitations on its scope should be kept in mind. For example, the IDEA mandates only the level of special education services that are reasonably calculated to enable the child to receive educational benefits (*Board of Education v. Rowley,* 1982). It is well established, however, that individual states can, if they so choose, raise the level of services to which students are entitled above this federally mandated "floor" (*Thomas v. Board of Education,* 1990). In Michigan, for example, the standard is the level of services necessary to enable the student to attain his or her "maximum potential" (*Barwacz v. Department of Education,* 1987).

The level of services mandated under individual state statutes has broad implications for the advocate seeking to secure particular services for a student with MR. Services that might be required in a state with a "maximum potential" standard may be characterized as unnecessary in a state that complies only with the more lenient federal standard (*Doe v. Board of Education,* 1993). No matter what the standard, however, no student, including students with little cognitive ability, can be deprived of educational and rehabilitative opportunities under the guise that he or she does not stand to benefit from such services (*Timothy W. v. Rochester New Hampshire School District,* 1989).

Another standard that has particular resonance for people with MR is the IDEA's requirement that students with disabilities be educated in the "least restrictive environment" (IDEA Regulations, 1992). The IDEA establishes a continuum of placement options, with placement in a regular public school classroom being the least restrictive option for any child with a disability. Under this framework, confinement in state-run institutions would be the most restrictive environment in which a person with MR may be placed. The IDEA mandates that, as between two placement options, both of which provide the student with a free appropriate public education, the least restrictive placement is preferred.

The tension between the "free appropriate public education" requirement and the "least restrictive environment" standard is perhaps best illustrated by the ongoing debate over "mainstreaming" or "inclusive education." In the past two decades of experience under the IDEA, a variety of programs for these individuals have been developed that seek to deliver services in settings physically and administratively segregated from regular education classrooms (*Daniel R. v. Board of Education,* 1989). In recent years, considerable debate has arisen among parents, clinicians, and educators regarding whether this segregation of people with MR is in their best educational interests and in the spirit of the IDEA's least restrictive environment standard. Some parents, as well as some school districts, have insisted that segregated educational programs for students with MR should be phased out and that these students should be placed in regular education classrooms with support from ancillary staff consistent with their special needs (Giangreco, Edelman, Cloninger, & Dennis, 1992).

Clinicians and advocates confronted with issues regarding the placement of students with MR should be cautious about any dogmatic assertion as to what placement is or is not in a particular student's best interests. One central characteristic of the IDEA is that the focus of the educational planning process must always be on the individual student. Broad assertions concerning the general "best interests" of an entire class of students with disabilities can never take precedence over the particular needs of individual students (Landau, 1993).

Abuse and Neglect

Given the unique history of the treatment of people with MR in the United States, considerable attention has been devoted to the development of legal safeguards that can effectively protect against the abuse and neglect of this vulnerable population. Perhaps the most visible manifestation of society's increased concern for protecting against some of the more egregious instances of abuse and neglect to which people with MR may be exposed is the widespread adoption of protective state laws. Many states have passed statutes that mandate that caregivers, teachers, and other professionals who frequently interact with people with MR report instances of abuse and neglect to designated state agencies. Failure to do so can leave the individual or agency open to criminal penalties and liability for damages (e.g., the Michigan Mental Health Code, 1974).

Even in states without protective state or local laws, the courts are increasingly recognizing that vulnerable populations, such as people with

MR, have a constitutional right to be free from abuse and neglect when their care is entrusted to state or local governments. The United States Supreme Court has held that people with MR who are placed in state-run institutions must be provided with the necessary habilitative services that will permit them to maintain the skills they possessed when they entered the institution (*Youngberg v. Romeo,* 1982). Moreover, people with MR confined in state-run institutions also have a constitutional right to safe living conditions and to be free from unnecessary body restraint (*Jackson by Jackson v. Fort Stanton Hospital and Training School,* 1992). By enacting the Developmental Disabilities Act of 1984, Congress sought to ensure that these rights would be protected by mandating that states create local protection and advocacy agencies to assist in the enforcement of these legal and human rights.

There are, of course, limits to a state's responsibility for failing to safeguard the rights of people with disabilities. For example, depending on the degree of a state's involvement in the circumstances of an individual's placement in a particular program, the state may be able to avoid liability for harm that befalls an individual while in that program (e.g., *DeShaney v. Winnebago County,* 1989). It is becoming increasingly well established, however, that individuals who are vulnerable in some way, with little choice regarding their placement in a particular program, are entitled to be free from abuse from their caregivers (e.g., *Waechter v. School District No. 14-030,* 1991).

Conclusion

Over the past three decades, the area of disabilities law has blossomed and grown to the point where it has become a fairly daunting legal specialty. The area of special education law alone has become complex enough that many lawyers in general practice are intimidated. Thirty years ago, familiarity with the laws applicable to people with MR would have required only a general knowledge of the law of guardianship and civil commitment; today, however, knowledge of these areas is simply the jumping off point into a web of sometimes vague and occasionally conflicting state and federal laws. The range of professionals called on to apply these laws also has expanded. This role now extends beyond judges and lawyers and encompasses individuals employed by school districts, various state and federal agencies, as well as a broad array of advocacy and professional groups.

It should go without saying that each of these groups views the laws concerning people with MR from their own unique, and not infrequently, conflicting perspectives. The advocate should bear in mind that, contrary to the rhetoric that each particular group may be inclined to use, the law will rarely provide a clear and definite answer to the question of what is or is not in the best interests of a particular person with MR. All the law can do is provide the advocate with the factors to be weighed, and the procedures to be used, in resolving the inevitable differences of opinion that will confront those responsible for the welfare of people with MR.

Part V

Conclusion

33

Concluding Comments

James A. Mulick

A manual such as this is necessary when two conditions are met: when there is enough of a scientific foundation for the range of routine practices in the field and when society is rapidly changing. In psychology, study and research for roughly a century has yielded deep understanding of the definition, measurement, and developmental course of individual differences. The prevailing view in psychology about how to define mental retardation (MR) in research and professional practice is presented in this manual, and standards are set forth concerning the application of the definition in terms of widely used measures of cognitive and behavioral functioning. As most practitioners know, but sometimes forget to specify in everyday discourse, measurement is not done in a vacuum, but always proceeds because of some need or purpose. Most often, either narrowly or broadly, depending on the area of application to groups or individuals, measures are taken to permit prediction. Predictions, however, are most often highly probabilistic in this field. This should neither come as a surprise nor lead to dismay. Limitations in information gathering and incomplete knowledge of external conditions mean that predictions made about any living, adapting system are necessarily probabilistic. Nevertheless, the conclusion can be stated with good confidence that reliably measured human differences lead to fairly well defined adaptive and practically meaningful outcomes in modern society. Furthermore, advances in psychological measurement have yielded a better understanding of the conditional aspect of both our measures and the outcomes they predict. In many ways, despite the very definition of MR affirmed in this book in terms of certain practical limitations of individuals, the process of formulating and applying the definition yields insight that, in turn, generates an ethos of optimism on behalf of the people so classified and described. This is because as the conditional nature of both measurement and prediction are better understood, in many specific instances the possibilities for prevention and treatment are often suggested as well.

Social change, technological change, and even political change all increase pressure on scientific and professional practitioners to prove themselves and to document their continuing contributions. In general, a manual is an assessment of major historical influences on a field, a selective account of the most salient activities of its practitioners, and a guide for others entering the field or seeking to extend its current limitations. If we have succeeded in capturing the current conditions and limitations, the psychology of MR will benefit and advance. A few words about the types of advances that can be expected are in order.

Assessment will continue to be refined and integrated with treatment. Psychophysiological and biochemical measures will augment functional performance measures, and imaging technology will help delineate conditions that lead to developmental problems. Measures of social, behavioral, and cognitive processes will be refined so that treatment and education can be tailored to better meet individual needs. Assessment in early childhood will be an active area of research and development. The general classification of MR probably will be augmented even more by descriptions of neurobiological and behavioral syndromes or typologies describing causes of developmental disability or functional impairment. A similar trend will be evident in work at the other end of the life cycle, although the measurement work will more heavily emphasize preservation of function, social participation, personal satisfaction, and quality of life. Behavioral measures of performance will be in demand to measure the sensory abilities of people with MR, to document the effects of medical and pharmacological treatment, and to assess the effects of educational, social, and regulatory policy changes. These developments, in turn, will stimulate prevention and treatment efforts.

Where will treatment advances be focused? Behavioral treatments will continue to emphasize efficiency and effectiveness, and we will learn how to better adapt the details of treatment to the treatment settings. As the integration of people with MR continues, there will be continued emphasis on the individualization of education and support. Many of these treatments will start early in life, in the services available to pregnant mothers and young children and their families. Because human development is both social and biological, treatment will be interdisciplinary and include the health, nutrition, and family environment of people with MR. Families will be increasingly recognized as part of the team. Beyond this, treatment will incorporate new information and communication technologies so that better support can be offered. Intimate human contact can be expected to represent a major modality and objective of future services and supports. In psychology, adaptations to counseling and psychotherapy services will be made in response to the increased demand for these services by people with MR and their caregivers. There will be a mainstreaming trend in the referral of problems related to MR for professional services. Professional psychologists will seek to expand their practices in areas that were once considered the exclusive domain of disability specialists. Professional training will change under pressure from both legislative mandates for equal access to services for people with disabilities and the emphasis on general practice that will characterize managed care environments. This pressure will require wider understanding in the practitioner community of what has been learned about MR and other disabilities. Specialists in MR will still exist, but their role will move increasingly toward consultation and innovation as the delivery of care is restructured.

This book is a first pass at furthering the general understanding in professional psychology of the existing knowledge and practice base of MR and developmental disabilities. The editors, reviewers, and contributors were united by their interests and their dedication to communicating high standards of empirical evaluation. They also were united by shared compassion for people with disabilities and their families and for the many people who depend on the guidance of reliable knowledge to further their service efforts. Psychologists will continue to be challenged to state their areas of expertise forcefully and to be called on to document the effectiveness of their treatments. Psychologists also can expect the field to continue to expand as a growing psychological specialty in coming decades, just as it has done in the past.

If this book represents a sort of conversation with ourselves as scientists and professionals, there remains an aspect of practice and communication that has not been addressed: the public representation of psychologists and the general dissemination of psychological knowledge to ensure the continued health of the field. Readers and contributors both share responsibility for a dialogue with society. What psychologists do is compelling, but their work easily can be distorted or misunderstood. Recent history suggests that advocacy for the individual with MR can be too detached from the science of MR. No policy about a human problem can be called progressive if it is based on false premises. No person has ever been helped by reasoning from an a priori belief system that ignores crucial details about the individual or society. Psychological scientists owe the public fair compensation for supporting their work, and this would best be provided by sharing the knowledge gained from research. Practitioners owe potential clients and society a chance to hear the story of the many successful solutions to human problems their practice makes possible. The advances in the care, treatment, and study of MR are among the most successful of the stories psychologists have to offer. Joint and collaborative advances in the biomedical and behavioral sciences have contributed to both the longevity and the quality of life for people with MR, and the degree to which this is true exceeds the expectations of informed authorities and the general public of just a few decades ago. Psychologists are in the best position to tell the story of their work because they will shape its application and future.

Appendix A

Guidelines on Effective Behavioral Treatment for Persons With Mental Retardation and Developmental Disabilities: A Resolution by APA Division 33

Whereas concerns have been voiced by many persons about the use of behavioral procedures, principally those that are restrictive,

And whereas Division 33 shares concerns that persons with disabilities should receive the highest quality treatment services available,

And whereas the members of Division 33 include applied behavior analysts continually engaged in research and practice with persons with disabilities, the Division has adopted the following guidelines as policy:

This policy pertains to the development, implementation, and monitoring of applied behavior analytic procedures with persons with mental retardation and other developmental disabilities. The following is a statement of foundations and principles.

Foundations

Applied behavior analytic services encompass all applications of operational procedures and techniques derived from manipulations of controlling stimuli or manipulations of motivational conditions, positive reinforcement, negative reinforcement, positive punishment, and negative punishment principles as defined within the body of research-based knowledge known as operant learning theory.

Applied behavior analytic services are provided in accordance with the American Psychological Association's most current edition of the Standards for Providers of Psychological Services and, as additionally applicable, the most current relevant Specialty Guidelines.

No provision of these principles shall be interpreted as limiting applied research or publication of research findings using behavior analytic procedures that have been approved by a relevant human subjects review board, and that meet ethical standards for research with human subjects as described in other APA policies and publications.

Principles

The composition and application of applied behavior analytic procedures provided by a practitioner or service unit shall be responsive to the needs of the persons and of the settings served.

The needs of the persons served shall take precedence over the organizational needs or ideological position of the settings in which services are delivered.

The protection of legal and civil rights of persons served, as determined in prevailing statutes, standards, and policies applicable in the particular service setting, shall be of primary concern.

Applied behavior analytic treatment procedures will be employed for the purposes of increasing the self-control of persons, and for the purpose of assisting them in achieving enhanced participation in life activities and their fullest human potential.

When the client does not evidence pathological behavior (deemed undesirable by referral agents and clients or duly appointed guardians according to law), but does evidence substantial adaptive deficits, there is an assumed need for the psychologist to participate in the development and implementation of positive programming services designed to increase self-care, social, and other skill performances.

Highly restrictive procedures (which may entail interventions often referred to as aversive) shall not be instituted without the combined use of procedures that reinforce incompatible, alternate, or other behavior. Highly restrictive procedures shall not be employed until there has been sufficient determination that the use of less restrictive procedures was or would be ineffective or harm would come to the client because of gradual change in the client's particular problematic behavior.

Highly restrictive or aversive procedures are applied only in instances in which there is an immediate physical danger to self or others, or there may be permanent sensory or other physical impairment, or the client may be prevented from receiving necessary medical, surgical, or emergency medical services, or the frequency or intensity of the problematic behavior prevents adequate participation in normal activities appropriate for the individual's circumstances and personal goals.

Highly restrictive procedures shall be discontinued when the individual's response to less restrictive procedures indicates that treatment benefits can be maintained through these less restrictive procedures. Evaluation of the individual's response to less restrictive procedures shall be ongoing and documented.

Multiple high restriction procedures shall only be employed in instances in which more limited applications of restrictive components have been ineffective, and reinforcing contingencies are instituted for incompatible, alternate, or other behavior.

Procedures selected for application and implementation of an intervention shall meet the following criteria, all of which must be satisfied:

1. Determination on the basis of the professional and scientific liter-

ature of the probability that a specific technique will be appropriate for this particular behavior and individual.

Peer-reviewed intervention studies shall constitute the primary source of information for the rendering of the determination of the appropriateness of a treatment technique. It is recognized that all behavioral treatments must be tailored to the individual and the natural environment; hence, alterations in procedures from those in published reports of studies will be necessary. Nevertheless, there are several factors that may enhance the salience of particular studies to the design of interventions for specific individuals.

These factors include (a) presentation of objective information to account for all components of the intervention as applied, (b) demonstration of experimental control of the target behavior, (c) similarities in age of target individuals, and in related learning histories, (d) ability to determine whether the disability characteristics of target subjects are similar to those of the potential client (e.g., presence of multiple handicapping conditions, specific neurological factors, medical contraindications), and (e) ability to apply the intervention approximately as designed due to the ability to obtain the necessary ancillary personnel and/or agreement of qualified personnel or consultants to develop or implement a comparable, but individualized, intervention.

2. Determination on the basis of behavioral assessment of the probability that a specific technique will be appropriate for this particular behavior and individual.

Behavior assessment may encompass baseline data gathering, functional analysis, application of attention or activity control conditions, activity re-scheduling, assessment of pre-existing reinforcing values of various classes of stimulation and activity, review of previous accounts of attempts at treatment, and other procedures that are currently demonstrated to be accurate procedures to assess behavior.

3. Determination on the basis of peer and human rights review procedures and guardian approval of the appropriateness of the specific techniques for the particular behavior and individual. Participation of the client will be secured in accordance with the Standards for Providers of Psychological Services.

Procedures for which approval shall be sought shall be those which have met the criteria 1 and 2 above, and constitute the least restrictive procedure considered likely to be effective.

4. Determination on the basis of continued monitoring of whether the intervention should be continued, modified, discontinued, or supplanted by a different intervention. Such determination shall be rendered on a periodic basis as determined appropriate by the practitioner or required by programmatic policies or consent obtained or agreements during the course of due process.

5. Determination of the success of a treatment procedure shall be rendered with regard to an array of criteria.

Criteria against which the success of a treatment procedure shall be assessed include (a) degree and rapidity of behavioral change, (b) generalization, (c) maintenance, (d) the character and magnitude of side effects, positive or negative (if any), (e) consumer (client, family or advocate) satisfaction and lifestyle outcomes, and (f) local public acceptability of treatment and maintenance procedures and degree of behavior change.

No provision of these principles should be interpreted as proscribing the use of any applied behavior analytic procedure which is indicated as appropriate according to the foregoing criteria. The responsibility for the design, implementation, and evaluation of an applied behavior analytic procedure is solely that of the supervising practitioner, subject to the initial and subsequent approval of the legal guardian and duly constituted review boards.

Appendix B

Resolution on Facilitated Communication by the American Psychological Association

Adopted in Council, August 14, 1994, Los Angeles, CA

Facilitated communication (FC) has been widely adopted throughout North America in special/vocational education services for individuals with developmental disabilities who are nonverbal. A basic premise of facilitated communication is that people with autism and moderate and profound mental retardation have "*undisclosed literacy*" consistent with *normal intellectual functioning*. Peer reviewed, scientifically based studies have found that the typed language output (represented through computers, letter boards, etc.) attributed to the clients was directed or systematically determined by the paraprofessional/professional therapists who provided facilitated assistance (Bligh & Kupperman, 1993; Cabay, 1994; Crewe et al., in press; Eberlin, McConnachie, Ibel, & Volpe, 1993; Hudson, Melita, & Arnold, 1993; Klewe, 1993; Moore, Donovan, & Hudson, 1993; Moore, Donovan, Hudson, Dykstra, & Lawrence, 1993; Regal, Rooney, & Wandas, 1994; Shane & Kearns, 1994; Siegel, in press; Simon, Toll, & Whitehair, 1994; Szempruch & Jacobson, 1993; Vasquez, 1994; Wheeler, Jacobson, Paglieri, & Schwartz, 1993). Furthermore, it has not been scientifically demonstrated that the therapists are aware of their controlling influence.

Consequently, specific activities contribute immediate threats to the individual civil and human rights of the person with autism or severe mental retardation. These include use of facilitated communication as a basis for a) actions related to nonverbal accusations of abuse and mistreatment (by family members or other caregivers); b) actions related to nonverbal communications of personal preferences, self-reports about health, test and classroom performance, and family relations; c) client response in psychological assessment using standardized assessment procedures; and d) client–therapist communication in counseling or psychotherapy, taking therapeutic actions, or making differential treatment decisions. Instances are widely noted where use of facilitated communication in otherwise unsubstantiated allegations of abuse has led to psychological distress, alienation, or financial hardship of family members and caregivers. The experimental and unproved status of the technique does not preclude continued research on the utility of facilitated communication and related scientific issues. Judicious clinical practice involving use of facilitated communication should be preceded by the use of fully informed consent procedures, including communication of both potential risks and likelihood of benefit.

Facilitated communication is a process by which a facilitator supports the hand or arm of a communicatively impaired individual while using a keyboard or typing device. It has been claimed that this process enables persons with autism or mental retardation to communicate. Studies have repeatedly demonstrated that facilitated communication is not a scientifically valid technique for individuals with autism or mental retardation. In particular, information obtained via facilitated communication should not be used to confirm or deny allegations of abuse or to make diagnostic or treatment decisions.

THEREFORE, BE IT RESOLVED that APA adopts the position that facilitated communication is a controversial and unproved communication procedure with no scientifically demonstrated support for its efficacy.

References

Bligh, S., & Kupperman, P. (1993). Evaluation procedure for determining the source of the communication in facilitated communication accepted in a court case. *Journal of Autism and Developmental Disorders, 23,* 553–557.

Cabay, M. (1994). A controlled evaluation of facilitated communication with four autistic children. *Journal of Autism and Developmental Disorders, 24,* 517–527.

Crewe, W. D., Sanders, E. C., Hensley, L. G., Johnson, Y. M., Bonaventura, S., & Rhodes, R. D. (in press). An evaluation of facilitated communication in a group of nonverbal individuals with mental retardation. *Journal of Autism and Developmental Disorders.*

Eberlin, M., McConnachie, G., Ibel, S., & Volpe, L. (1993). Facilitated communication: A failure to replicate the phenomenon. *Journal of Autism and Developmental Disorders, 23,* 507–530.

Hudson, A., Melita, B., & Arnold, N. (1993). Brief report: A case study assessing the validity of facilitated communication. *Journal of Autism and Developmental Disorders, 23,* 165–173.

Klewe, L. (1993). An empirical evaluation of spelling boards as a means of communication for the multihandicapped. *Journal of Autism and Developmental Disorders, 23,* 559–566.

Moore, S., Donovan, B., & Hudson, A. (1993). Facilitator-suggested conversational evaluation of facilitated communication. *Journal of Autism and Developmental Disorders, 23,* 541–551.

Moore, S., Donovan, B., Hudson, A., Dykstra, J., & Lawrence, J. (1993). Evaluation of facilitated communication: Eight case studies. *Journal of Autism and Developmental Disorders, 23,* 531–539.

Regal, R. A., Rooney, J. R., & Wandas, T. (1994). Facilitated communication: An experimental evaluation. *Journal of Autism and Developmental Disorders, 24,* 345–355.

Shane, H. C., & Kearns, K. (1994). An examination of the role of the facilitator in "facilitated communication." *American Journal of Speech–Language Pathology, 3,* 48–54.

Siegel, B. (in press). Assessing allegations of sexual molestation made through facilitated communication. *Journal of Autism and Developmental Disorders.*

Simon, E. W., Toll, D. M., & Whitehair, P. M. (1994). A naturalistic approach to the validation of facilitated communication. *Journal of Autism and Developmental Disorders, 24,* 647–657.

Szempruch, J., & Jacobson, J. W. (1993). Evaluating the facilitated communications of people with developmental disabilities. *Research in Developmental Disabilities, 14,* 253–264.

Vasquez, C. (1994). A multi-task controlled evaluation of facilitated communication. *Journal of Autism and Developmental Disorders, 24,* 369–379.

Wheeler, D. L., Jacobson, J. W., Paglieri, R. A., & Schwartz, A. A. (1993). An experimental assessment of facilitated communication. *Mental Retardation, 31,* 49–60.

References

Abel, E. L., & Sokol, R. J. (1991). A revised estimate of the economic impact of fetal alcohol syndrome [Monograph]. *Recent Developments in Alcoholism, 9,* 117–126.

Abel, T. M. (1953). Resistances and difficulties in psychotherapy of mental retardates. *Journal of Clinical Psychology, 9,* 152–156.

Abikoff, H., & Klein, R. G. (1992). Attention-deficit hyperactivity and conduct disorder: Comorbidity and implications for treatment. *Journal of Consulting and Clinical Psychology, 60,* 881–892.

Abramowicz, H. K., & Richardson, S. A. (1975). Epidemiology of severe mental retardation in children: Community studies. *American Journal of Mental Deficiency, 80,* 18–39.

Accreditation Council on Services for People with Developmental Disabilities. (1990). *Standards and interpretive guidelines for services for people with developmental disabilities.* Landover, MD: Author.

Achenbach, T. M. (1991a). *The Child Behavior Checklist.* Burlington: Department of Psychiatry, University of Vermont.

Achenbach, T. M. (1991b). *Manual for the CBCL/4-18 and profile.* Burlington: Department of Psychiatry, University of Vermont.

Achenbach, T. M., & Edelbrock, C. S. (1978). The classification of child psychopathology: A review and analysis of empirical efforts. *Psychological Bulletin, 85,* 1275–1301.

Achenbach, T. M., McConaughy, S. H., & Howell, C. T. (1987). Child/adolescent behavioral and emotional problems: Implications of cross-informant correlations for situational specificity. *Psychological Bulletin, 101,* 213–232.

Adams, G. L. (1985). Using empirical item sequencing in developing the comprehensive test of adaptive behavior. *Education, 106,* 197–201.

Adesso, V. J., & Lipson, J. W. (1981). Group training of parents as therapists for their children. *Behavior Therapy, 12,* 625–633.

Adult Performance Level Project (APL). (1975). *Adult functional competency.* Austin: University of Texas Office of Continuing Education.

Agran, M., & Moore, S. C. (1994). *How to teach self-instruction of job skills.* Washington, DC: American Association on Mental Retardation Innovations Series.

Albin, R. W., & Horner, R. H. (1988). Generalization with precision. In R. H. Horner, R. L. Koegel, & G. Dunlap (Eds.), *Generalization and maintenance: Life-style changes in applied settings* (pp. 99–120). Baltimore: Brookes.

Albini, J. L., & Dinitz, S. (1965). Psychotherapy with disturbed and defective children: An evaluation of changes in behavior and attitudes. *American Journal of Mental Deficiency, 69,* 560–567.

Albion, F. M., & Salzberg, C. L. (1982). The effects of self-instructions on the role of correct addition problems with mentally retarded children. *Education and Treatment of Children, 5,* 121–131.

Alexander, D. (1991, February). *A national strategy for addressing conditions that negatively affect mother and children.* Paper presented at the National Summit on the National Effort to Prevent Mental Retardation and Related Disabilities, Washington, DC.

Allen, D. A., & Hudd, S. S. (1987). Are we professionalizing parents? Weighing the benefits and pitfalls. *Mental Retardation, 25,* 133–139.

Alley, G. R., & Deshler, D. D. (1979). *Teaching the learning disabled adolescent: Strategies and methods.* Denver, CO: Love Publishing.

Altman, D. I., Perlman, J. M., Volpe, J. J., & Powers, W. J. (1993). Cerebral oxygen metabolism in newborns. *Pediatrics, 92,* 99–104.

Altman, D. I., & Volpe, J. J. (1991). Positron emission tomography in newborn infants. *Clinics in Perinatology, 18,* 549–562.

Aman, M. G. (1991a). *Assessing psychopathology and behavior problems in persons with mental retardation: A review of available instruments* (DHHS Publication No. ADM 91-1712). Rockville, MD: U.S. Department of Health and Human Services.

Aman, M. G. (1991b). Review and evaluation of instruments for assessing emotional and behavioural disorders. *Australia and New Zealand Journal of Developmental Disabilities, 17,* 127–145.

Aman, M. G. (1993). Monitoring and measuring drug effects—Behavioral, emotional, and cognitive effects. In J. S. Werry & M. G. Aman (Eds.), *Practitioner's guide to psychoactive drugs in children and adolescents* (pp. 99–159). New York: Plenum Press.

Aman, M. G. (1994a). Instruments for assessing treatment effects in developmentally disabled populations. *Assessment in Rehabilitation and Exceptionality, 1,* 1–20.

Aman, M. G. (1994b). *Annotated bibliography on the Aberrant Behavior Checklist (ABC).* Palmerston North, New Zealand: Department of Psychology, Massey University.

Aman, M. G. (in press). Recent studies in psychopharmacology in mental retardation. In N. N. Bray (Ed.), *International review of research in mental retardation.* San Diego, CA: Academic Press.

Aman, M. G., Burrow, W. H., & Wolford, P. L. (1994). The Aberrant Behavior Checklist—Community: Factor validity and effect of subject variables for adults in group homes. *American Journal of Mental Retardation, 100,* 283–292.

Aman, M. G., & Kern, R. A. (1989). Review of fenfluramine in the treatment of the developmental disabilities. *Journal of the American Academy of Child and Adolescent Psychiatry, 28,* 549–565.

Aman, M. G., Kern, R. A., McGhee, D. E., & Arnold, L. E. (1993). Fenfluramine and methylphenidate in children with mental retardation and ADHD: Clinical and side effects. *Journal of the American Academy of Child and Adolescent Psychiatry, 32,* 851–859.

Aman, M. G., & Singh, N. N. (Eds.). (1988). *Psychopharmacology of the developmental disabilities.* New York: Springer-Verlag.

Aman, M. G., & Singh, N. N. (1994). *Supplement to Aberrant Behavior Checklist manual.* East Aurora, NY: Slosson Educational Publications.

Aman, M. G., Singh, N. N., Stewart, A. W., & Field, C. J. (1985a). The Aberrant Behavior Checklist: A behavior rating scale for the assessment of treatment effects. *American Journal of Mental Deficiency, 89,* 485–491.

Aman, M. G., Singh, N. N., Stewart, A. W., & Field, C. J. (1985b). Psychometric characteristics of the Aberrant Behavior Checklist. *American Journal of Mental Deficiency, 89,* 492–502.

Aman, M. G., Singh, N. N., & Turbott, S. H. (1987). Reliability of the Aberrant Behavior Checklist and the effect of variations in instructions. *American Journal of Mental Deficiency, 92,* 237–240.

Aman, M. G., White, A. J., & Field, C. (1984). Chlorpromazine effects on stereotypic and conditioned behaviour of severely retarded patients: A pilot study. *Journal of Mental Deficiency Research, 28,* 253–260.

Aman, M. G., White, A. J., Vaithianathan, D., & Teehan, C. (1986). Preliminary study of imipramine in profoundly retarded residents. *Journal of Autism and Developmental Disorders, 16,* 263–273.

Ambuel, B., & Rappaport, J. (1992). Developmental trends in adolescents' psychological and legal competence to consent to abortion. *Law & Human Behavior, 16,* 129–154.

American Association on Mental Retardation. (1992). *Mental retardation: Definition, classification, and systems of supports* (9th ed.). Washington, DC: Author.

American Psychiatric Association. (1980). *Diagnostic and statistical manual of mental disorders* (3rd ed.). Washington, DC: Author.

American Psychiatric Association. (1987). *Diagnostic and statistical manual of mental disorders* (3rd ed. rev.). Washington, DC: Author.

American Psychiatric Association. (1994). *Diagnostic and statistical manual of mental disorders* (4th ed.). Washington, DC: Author.

American Psychological Association (1985). *Standards for educational and psychological testing.* Washington, DC: Author.

American Psychological Association. (1992). Ethical principles of psychologists and code of conduct. *American Psychologist, 47,* 1597–1611.

Americans With Disabilities Act, 42 U.S.C. §§ 12101–12213 (1990).

Americans With Disabilities Act Regulations, 28 C.F.R. § 35.104 (1993).

Ammerman, R. T., VanHasselt, V. B., & Hersen, M. (1991). Parent–child problem-solving interactions in families of visually impaired youth. *Journal of Pediatric Psychology, 16,* 87–101.

Anaesthesia Advisory Committee to the Chief Coroner of Ontario. (1987). Intraoperative death during caesarian section in a patient with sickle-cell trait. *Canadian Journal of Anaesthesia, 34,* 67–70.

Anastasi, A. (1986). Intelligence as a quality of behavior. In R. J. Sternberg & D. K. Detterman (Eds.), *What is intelligence? Contemporary viewpoints on its nature and definition* (pp. 19–22). Norwood, NJ: Ablex.

Anastopoulos, A. D., Shelton, T. L., DuPaul, G. J., & Guevremont, D. C. (1993). Parent training for attention-deficit hyperactivity disorder: Its impact on parent functioning. *Journal of Abnormal Child Psychology, 21,* 581–596.

Anderson, P. P., & Fenichel, E. S. (1989). *Serving culturally diverse families of infants and toddlers with disabilities.* Washington, DC: National Center for Clinical Infant Programs.

Anderson, S. R. (1989). Autism. In B. L. Baker (Ed.), *Parent training and developmental disabilities* (pp. 137–153). Washington, DC: American Association on Mental Retardation.

Anderson-Inman, L., Paine, S. C., & Deutchman, L. (1984). Neatness counts: Effects of direct instruction and self-monitoring on the transfer of neat-paper skills to nontraining settings. *Analysis and Intervention in Developmental Disabilities, 4,* 137–155.

Andrews, F. M., & Withey, S. B. (1976). *Social indicators of well-being.* New York: Plenum Press.

Arendt, B. E., MacLean, W. E., & Baumeister, A. A. (1988). Critique of sensory integration therapy and its application to mental retardation. *American Journal of Mental Retardation, 92,* 401–411.

Aschkenasy, A. (1957). On the pathogenesis of anemias and leukopenias induced by dietary protein deficiency. *American Journal of Clinical Nutrition, 5,* 14–25.

Ashley, C. T., Jr., Wilkinson, K. D., Reines, D., & Warren, S. T. (1993). FMR-1 protein: Conserved RNP family domains and selective RNA binding. *Science, 262,* 563–565.

Ashman, A. (1978). *The relationship between planning and simultaneous and successive synthesis.* Unpublished doctoral dissertation, University of Alberta, Edmonton, Alberta, Canada.

Ashman, A. F. (1982). Cognitive processes and perceived language performance of retarded persons. *Journal of Mental Deficiency Research, 26,* 131–141.

Ashman, A. (1985). Problem solving and planning: Two sides of the same coin. In A. Ashman & R. Laura (Eds.), *The education and training of the mentally retarded* (pp. 169–214). New York: Nichols.

Atkinson, L. (1990). Intellectual and adaptive functioning: Some tables for interpreting the Vineland in combination with intelligence tests. *American Journal of Mental Retardation, 95,* 198–203.

Atkinson, L., & Cyr, J. J. (1988). Low IQ samples and WAIS–R factor structure. *American Journal of Mental Retardation, 93,* 278–282.

Ault, M. J., Gast, D. L., & Wolery, M. (1988). Comparison of progressive and constant time delay procedures in teaching community-sign word reading. *American Journal of Mental Retardation, 93,* 44–56.

Axelrod, S., Spreat, S., Berry, B., & Moyer, L. (1993). A decision-making model for selecting the optimal treatment procedure. In R. Van Houten & S. Axelrod (Eds.), *Behavior analysis and treatment* (pp. 183–202). New York: Plenum Press.

Azrin, N. H., & Foxx, R. M. (1971). A rapid method of toilet training the institutionalized retarded. *Journal of Applied Behavior Analysis, 4,* 89–99.

Azzopardi, D., Wyatt, J. S., Cady, E. B., Delpry, D. T., Baudin, J., Stewart, A. L., Hope, P. L., Hamilton, P. A., & Reynolds, E. O. (1989). Prognosis of newborn infants with hypoxic–ischemic brain injury assessed by phosphorous magnetic resonance spectroscopy. *Pediatric Research, 25,* 445–451.

Baer, D. M., Wolf, M. M., & Risley, T. R. (1968). Some current dimensions of applied behavior analysis. *Journal of Applied Behavior Analysis, 1,* 91–97.

Bailey, D. B., Blasco, P. M., & Simeonsson, R. J. (1992). Needs expressed by mothers and fathers of young children with disabilities. *American Journal of Mental Retardation, 97,* 1–10.

Bailey, J. S., & Pyles, D. A. (1989). Behavioral diagnostics. In E. Cipani (Ed.), *The treatment of severe behavior disorders: Behavior analysis approaches* (pp. 85–107). Washington, DC: American Association of Mental Retardation.

Baker, B. L. (1984). Intervention in families with young severely handicapped children. In J. B. Blacher (Ed.), *Severely handicapped young children and their families: Research in review* (pp. 319–375). San Diego, CA: Academic Press.

Baker, B. L. (1989). *Parent training and developmental disabilities*. Washington, DC: American Association on Mental Retardation.

Baker, B. L., & Brightman, A. J. (1989). *Steps to independence: A skills training guide for parents and teachers of children with special needs* (2nd ed.). Baltimore: Brookes.

Baker, B. L., Heifetz, L. J., & Murphy, D. (1980). Behavioral training for parents of retarded children: One-year follow-up. *American Journal of Mental Deficiency, 85*, 31–38.

Baker, B. L., Landen, S. J., & Kashima, K. J. (1991). Effects of parent training on families of children with mental retardation: Increased burden or generalized benefit? *American Journal of Mental Retardation, 96*, 127–136.

Baldwin, J. M. (1894). *The development of the child and the race*. New York: Macmillan.

Balla, D., & Zigler, E. (1979). Personal development in retarded persons. In N. R. Ellis (Ed.), *Handbook of mental deficiency: Psychological theory and research* (2nd ed., pp. 143–168), Hillsdale, NJ: Erlbaum.

Bambara, L. M., Koger, F., Katzer, T., & Davenport, T. (1995). Reducing problem behaviors through choice and control: An experimental case study. *Journal of the Association for Persons With Severe Handicaps, 20,* 185–195.

Barkley, R. A. (1987). *Defiant children: A clinician's manual for parent training.* New York: Guilford Press.

Barkley, R. A. (1988). Child behavior rating scales and checklists. In M. Rutter, A. H. Tuma, & I. Lann (Eds.), *Assessment and diagnosis in child psychopathology* (pp. 113–155). New York: Guilford Press.

Barna, S., Bidder, R. T., Gray, O. P., Clements, J., & Gardner, S. (1980). The progress of developmentally delayed pre-school children in a home-training scheme. *Child: Care, Health and Development, 6,* 157–164.

Barnes, K. (1984, December). Sex education: Let's not pretend. *The Exceptional Parent,* 43–44.

Baroff, G. S. (1986). *Mental retardation: Nature, cause, and management* (2nd ed.). New York: Hemisphere.

Baroff, G. S. (1990). Establishing mental retardation in capital defendants. *American Journal of Forensic Psychology, 8*(2), 35–44.

Baroff, G. S. (1991). Establishing mental retardation in capital cases: A potential matter of life and death. *Mental Retardation, 29,* 343–349.

Baroff, G. S., & Freedman, S. C. (1988, April). Mental retardation and *Miranda*. *The Champion*, 6–9.

Baron-Cohen, S. (1989). The autistic child's theory of mind: A case of specific developmental delay. *Journal of Child Psychology and Psychiatry, 30,* 285–297.

Baron-Cohen, S., Tager-Flusberg, H., & Cohen, D. J. (Eds.). (1993). *Understanding other minds: Perspectives from* Autism. London: Oxford University Press.

Barwacz v. Department of Education, 674 F. Supp. 1296 (W.D. Mich. 1987).

Bates, P. (1980). The effectiveness of interpersonal skills training on the social skill acquisition of moderately and mildly retarded adults. *Journal of Applied Behavior Analysis, 13*, 237–248.

Baum, N. T. (1990). Therapy for people with dual diagnosis: Treating the behaviors or the whole person? In A. Dosen, A. van Gennep, & G. J. Zwanikken (Eds.), *Treatment of mental illness and behavioral disorder in the mentally retarded* (pp. 143–155). Leiden, the Netherlands: Logon Publications.

Baumeister, A. A. (1991). Cocaine exposed infants: A complex problem awaiting coherent policy. *The Child, Youth, and Family Services Quarterly, 14,* 8–9.

Baumeister, A. A., Dokecki, P. R., & Kupstas, F. (1988). *New morbidity.* Washington, DC: U.S. Department of Health and Human Services, Office of Human Development Services, President's Committee on Mental Retardation.

Baumeister, A. A., & Hillsinger, L. B. (1984). Role of psychologists in public institutions for the mentally retarded revisited. *Professional Psychology: Research and Practice, 15,* 134–141.

Baumeister, A. A., Kupstas, F., & Klindworth, L. M. (1991). The new morbidity: A national plan of action. In T. Thompson & S. Hupp (Eds.), *Saving children at risk* (pp. 143–177). Newbury Park, CA: Sage.

Baumeister, A. A., Kupstas, F. D., & Woodley-Zanthos, P. (1993). *The new morbidity: Recommendations for action and an updated guide to state planning for the prevention of mental retardation and related conditions associated with socioeconomic conditions.* Washington, DC: President's Committee on Mental Retardation.

Baumeister, A. A., Todd, M. E., & Sevin, J. A. (1993). Efficacy and specificity of pharmacological therapies for behavioral disorders in persons with mental retardation. *Clinical Neuropharmacology, 16,* 271–294.

Baumgart, D., Brown, L., Pumpian, I., Nisbet, J., Ford, A., Sweet, M., Messina, R., & Schroeder, J. (1982). The principle of partial participation and individual adaptation in educational programs for severely handicapped students. *Journal of the Association for Persons With Severe Handicaps, 7,* 17–27.

Bayley, N. (1969). *Bayley Scales of Infant Development.* New York: Psychological Corporation.

Bean, A. G., & Roszkowski, M. J. (1982). Item-domain relationships in the Adaptive Behavior Scale (ABS). *Applied Research in Mental Retardation, 3,* 359–367.

Beavers, J. S., Hampson, R. B., Hulgus, Y. F., & Beavers, W. R. (1986). Coping in families with a retarded child. *Family Process, 25,* 365–378.

Bech, P. (1992). Quality of life measurement in the medical setting. *International Journal of Methods in Psychiatric Research, 2,* 139–144.

Begab, M., & Richardson, S. (1975). *The mentally retarded and society.* Baltimore: University Park Press.

Behr, S. K., & Murphy, D. (1993). Research progress and promise: The role of perceptions in cognitive adaptation to disability. In A. P. Turnbull, J. M. Patterson, S. K. Behr, D. L. Murphy, J. G. Marquis, & M. J. Blue-Banning (Eds.), *Cognitive coping, families, and disability* (pp. 151–164). Baltimore: Brookes.

Bellugi, U., Wang, P. P., & Jernigan, T. L. (1994). Williams syndrome: An unusual neuropsychological profile. In S. H. Broman & J. Grafman (Eds.), *Atypical cognitive deficits in developmental disorders: Implications for brain function* (pp. 23–56). Hillsdale, NJ: Erlbaum.

Bennett, M. (Ed.). (1993). *The development of social cognition.* New York: Guilford Press.

Bensberg, G. J., & Irons, T. (1986). A comparison of the AAMD adaptive behavior scale and the Vineland adaptive behavior scale within a sample of persons classified as moderately and severely mentally retarded. *Education and Training of the Mentally Retarded, 21,* 220–228.

Benson, B. A. (1986). Anger management training. *Psychiatric Aspects of Mental Retardation Reviews, 5,* 51–55.

Benson, B. A. (1990). Anxiety disorders and depression. In J. L. Matson (Ed.), *Handbook of behavior modification with the mentally retarded* (2nd ed., pp. 391–420). New York: Plenum Press.

Benson, B. A. (1992). *Teaching anger management to persons with mental retardation.* Worthington, OH: International Diagnostic Systems.

Benson, B. A., Rice, C. J., & Miranti, S. V. (1986). Effects of anger management training with mentally retarded adults in group treatment. *Journal of Counseling and Clinical Psychology, 54,* 728–729.

Benson, H. A., & Turnbull, A. P. (1986). Approaching families from an individualized perspective. In R. H. Horner, L. H. Meyer, & H. D. B. Fredericks (Eds.), *Education of learners with severe handicaps: Exemplary service strategies* (pp. 127–157). Baltimore: Brookes.

Benton, A. L. (1970). Neuropsychological aspects of mental retardation. *Journal of Special Education, 4,* 3–11.

Benton, A. L. (1974). Clinical neuropsychology of childhood: An overview. In R. M. Reitan & L. A. Davison (Eds.), *Clinical neuropsychology: Current status and applications.* Washington, DC: Winston.

Berge, P., Russo, P., & Utermohlen, V. (1991). Risk factors for in utero transmission of cytomegalovirus infection. *American Journal of Epidemiology, 134,* 781.

Berkson, G. (1967). Abnormal stereotyped motor acts. In J. Zubin & H. F. Hunt (Eds.), *Comparative psychopathology: Animal and human* (pp. 76–94). New York: Grune & Stratton.

Berkson, G. (1973). Behavior. *Mental Retardation and Developmental Disabilities: An Annual Review, 5,* 55–71.

Berkson, G. (1978). Social ecology and ethology of mental retardation. In G. P. Sackett (Ed.), *Observing behavior* (pp. 403–409). Baltimore: University Park Press.

Berkson, G., & Landesman-Dwyer, S. (1977). Behavioral research on severe and profound mental retardation (1955–1974). *American Journal of Mental Deficiency, 81,* 428–454.

Berkson, G., & Romer, D. (1980). Social ecology of supervised communal facilities for mentally disabled adults: I. Introduction. *American Journal of Mental Deficiency, 85,* 219–228.

Bernard, J. A. (1991). *Cultural competence training handbook.* Ventura County, CA: Ventura County Mental Health Care Agency.

Bernheimer, L. P., & Keogh, B. K. (1988). Stability of cognitive performance in children with developmental delays. *American Journal of Mental Retardation, 92,* 539–542.

Bernstein, N. (1985). Psychotherapy and the retarded adolescent. *Adolescent Psychiatry, 12,* 406–413.

Beyer, H. A. (1991). Litigation involving people with mental retardation. In J. L. Matson & J. A. Mulick (Eds.), *Handbook of mental retardation* (2nd ed., pp. 74–93). Elmsford, NY: Pergamon Press.

Biglan, A. (1989). A contextual approach to the clinical treatment of parental distress. In G. H. S. Singer & L. K. Irvin (Eds.), *Support for caregiving families: Enabling positive adaptation to disability* (pp. 299–312). Baltimore: Brookes.

Bijou, S. W. (1963). Theory and research in mental (developmental) retardation. *Psychological Record, 13,* 95–110.

Bijou, S. W. (1966). A functional analysis of retarded development. *International Review of Research in Mental Retardation, 1,* 19.

Biklen, D. (1993). *Communication unbound.* New York: Teachers College Press.

Biklen, D., & Duchan, J. F. (1994). "I am intelligent": The social construction of mental retardation. *JASH, 19,* 173–184.

Binet, A., & Simon, T. H. (1905). Sur le nécessité d'établir un diagnostic scientifique des états inférieurs de l'intelligence [The necessity of establishing the scientific diagnosis of inferior states of intelligence]. *L'Anñee Psychologique, 11,* 163–190.

Binet, A., & Simon, T. H. (1905/1976). The necessity of establishing the scientific diagnosis of inferior states of intelligence. In M. Rosen, G. Clark, & M. Kivitz (Eds.), *History of mental retardation: Collected papers* (Vol. 1, pp. 329–354). Baltimore: University Park Press.

Birch, H., Richardson, S., Baird, D., Horobin, G., & Illsley, R. (1970). *Mental subnormality in the community: A clinical and epidemiological study.* Baltimore: Williams & Wilkins.

Bird, F., Dores, P. A., Moniz, D., & Robinson, J. (1989). Reducing severe aggressive and self-injurious behaviors with functional communication training. *American Journal of Mental Retardation, 94,* 37–48.

Birnbrauer, J. S., & Leach, D. (1993). The Murdoch early intervention program after two years. *Behaviour Change, 10,* 63–74.

Birrin, J., Kinney, D. K., Schaie, K. W., & Woodruff D. S. (1981). *Developmental psychology.* Boston: Houghton Mifflin.

Blacher, J. (1984). A dynamic perspective on the impact of a severely handicapped child on the family. In J. Blacher (Ed.), *Severely handicapped young children and their families: Research in review* (pp. 3–50). Baltimore: Brookes.

Blackledge, M. J., Rajogopalan, B., Oberhaensli, R. D., Bolas, N. M., Styles, P., & Radda, G.K. (1987). Quantitative studies of human cardiac metabolism by 31P rotating-frame NMR. *Proceedings of the National Academy of Sciences USA, 84*, 4283–4287.

Blackman, J. A., Healy, A., & Ruppert, E. S. (1992). Participation by pediatricians in early identification: Impetus from Public Law 99–457. *Pediatrics, 89*, 98–102.

Blair, C., Ramey, C. T., & Hardin, J. M. (1995). Early intervention for low birthweight, premature infants: Participation and intellectual development. *American Journal of Mental Retardation, 99*, 542–554.

Blick, D. W., & Test, D. W. (1987). Effects of self-recording on high-school students' on-task behavior. *Learning Disabilities Quarterly, 10*, 203–213.

Bligh, S., & Kupperman, P. (1993). Evaluation procedure for determining the source of the communication in facilitated communication accepted in a court case. *Journal of Autism and Developmental Disorders, 23*, 553–557.

Bloch, F., Hansen, W. W., & Packard, M. E. (1946). Nuclear induction. *Physical Review, 69*, 127.

Bloom, A. S., Allard, A. M., Zelko, F. A. J., Brill, W. J., Topinka, C. W., & Pfohl, W. (1988). Differential of the K-ABC for lower functioning preschool children versus those of higher ability. *American Journal of Mental Retardation, 93*, 273–277.

Board of Education v. Rowley, 102 S. Ct. 3034 (1982).

Bock, W. H., & Weatherman, R. F. (1977). *Minnesota Developmental Planning System Behavior Scale—Revised.* Minneapolis: University of Minnesota.

Bodfish, J. W., & Madison, J. T. (1993). Diagnosis and fluoxetine treatment of compulsive behavior disorder of adults with mental retardation. *American Journal of Mental Retardation, 98*, 360–367.

Bogolepov, N. N. (1983). *Ultrastructure of the brain in hypoxia.* Moscow: Mir.

Bollen, K. A. (1989). *Structural equations with latent variables*. New York: Wiley.

Bonwich, L., & Reid, J. C. (1991). Medical rehabilitation: Issues in assessment of functional change. *Evaluation Practice, 12*, 205–215.

Borgatta, E. F., & Bohrnstedt, G. W. (1981). Level of measurement: Once over again. In G. W. Bohrnstedt & E. F. Borgatta (Eds.), *Social measurement: Current issues* (pp. 23–37). Beverly Hills, CA: Sage.

Borkowski, J. G., & Vanhagan, C. K. (1984). Transfer of learning strategies: Contrast of self-instructional and traditional training formats with EMR children. *American Journal of Mental Deficiency, 38*, 369–379.

Bornstein, M. H., & Sigman, M. D. (1986). Continuity in mental development from infancy. *Child Development, 57*, 251–274.

Bornstein, P. H., Bach, P. J., McFall, M. E., Friman, P. C., & Lyons, P. D. (1980). Application of a social skills training program in the modification of interpersonal skills deficits among retarded adults: A clinical replication. *Journal of Applied Behavior Analysis, 13*, 171–176.

Borthwick-Duffy, S. A. (1986). *Quality of life of mentally retarded people: Development of a model.* Unpublished doctoral dissertation, University of California, School of Education, Riverside.

Borthwick-Duffy, S. A. (1992). Quality of life and quality of care in mental retardation. In L. Rowitz (Ed.), *Mental retardation in the year 2000* (pp. 52–66). New York: Springer-Verlag.

Borthwick-Duffy, S. A., & Eyman, R. K. (1990). Who are the dually diagnosed? *American Journal of Mental Retardation, 94*, 586–595.

Bosselman, B., & Kraines, S. H. (1937). Mental changes including aphasia in a patient with sickle cell anemia. *American Journal of Psychiatry, 94*, 709–712.

Brabeck, M. M. (1983). Critical thinking skills and reflective judgment development: Redefining the aims of higher education. *Journal of Applied Developmental Psychology, 4*, 23–34.

Bradley, R. H., Caldwell, B. M., & Elardo, R. (1977). Home environment, social status, and mental test performance. *Journal of Educational Psychology, 69*, 697–701.

Bradley, R. H., Caldwell, B. M., Rock, S. L., Barnard, K. E., Gray, C., Hammon, M. A.,

Mitchell, S., Siegel, L., Ramey, C. T., Gottfried, A. W., & Johnson, D. L. (1989). Home environment and cognitive development in the first 3 years of life: A collaborative study involving six sites and three ethnic groups in North America. *Developmental Psychology, 25,* 217–235.

Bradley, R. H., Rock, S. L., Caldwell, B. M., & Brisby, J. A. (1989). Uses of the HOME inventory for families with handicapped children. *American Journal of Mental Retardation, 94,* 313–330.

Bradley, V. J., Knoll, J., & Agosta, J. M. (1992). *Emerging issues in family support.* Washington, DC: American Association on Mental Retardation.

Brady, M. P., & McEvoy, M. A. (1989). Social skills training as an integration strategy. In R. Gaylord-Ross (Ed.), *Integration strategies for students with handicaps* (pp. 213–232). Baltimore: Brookes.

Braginsky, D. D., & Braginsky, B. M. (1971). *Hansels and Gretels: Studies of children in institutions for the mentally retarded.* New York: Holt, Rinehart & Winston.

Brantlinger, E. (1983). Measuring variation and change in attitudes of residential care staff toward the sexuality of mentally retarded persons. *Mental Retardation, 21,* 17–22.

Brassell, W. R. (1977). Intervention with handicapped infants: Correlates of progress. *Mental Retardation, 15,* 18–22.

Brazy, J. E. (1991). Near infrared spectroscopy. *Clinics in Perinatology, 18,* 519–534.

Bregman, J. D., & Hodapp, R. M. (1991). Current developments in the understanding of mental retardation: Part I. Biological and phenomenological perspectives. *Journal of the American Academy of Child and Adolescent Psychiatry, 30,* 707–719.

Bregman, J. D., Leckman, J. F., & Ort, S. I. (1988). Fragile X syndrome: Genetic predispositions to psychopathology. *Journal of Autism and Developmental Disorders, 18,* 343–354.

Breiner, J., & Beck, S. (1984). Parents as change agents in the management of their developmentally delayed children's noncompliant behaviors: A critical review. *Applied Research in Mental Retardation, 5,* 259–278.

Breslau, N., & Davis, G. C. (1986). Chronic stress and major depression. *Archives of General Psychiatry, 43,* 309–314.

Brightman, R. P., Baker, B. L., Clark, D. B., & Ambrose, S. A. (1982). Effectiveness of alternative parent training formats. *Journal of Behavior Therapy and Experimental Psychiatry, 13,* 113–117.

Bristol, M. (1987). Mothers of children with autism or communication disorders: Successful adaptation and the double ABCX model. *Journal of Autism and Developmental Disorders, 17,* 469–486.

Bristol, M., Gallagher, J. J., & Schopler, E. (1988). Mothers and fathers of young developmentally disabled and nondisabled boys: Adaptation and spousal support. *Developmental Psychology, 23,* 441–451.

Britton, W. H., & Eaves, R. C. (1986). Relationship between the Vineland Adaptive Behavior Scales—Classroom version and the Vineland Social Maturity Scales. *American Journal of Mental Deficiency, 91,* 105–107.

Broca, P. (1861). Perta de parole, remollissement chronique et destruction partielle du lobe antérieur gauche du cerveau [Loss of speech, chronic reduction and partial destruction of the left frontal lobe of the brain]. *Bulletin de la Sociéte Anthropoligique, 2,* 87–97.

Bronfenbrenner, U. (1977). Toward an experimental ecology of human development. *American Psychologist, 32,* 513–531.

Bronfenbrenner, U. (1979). *The ecology of human development.* Cambridge, MA: Harvard University Press.

Bronfenbrenner, U. (1989). Ecological systems theory. In R. Vasta (Ed.), *Six theories of child development* (pp. 185–245). Greenwich, CT: JAI Press.

Browder, D. M., Morris, M. W., & Snell, M. G. (1981). The use of time delay to teach manual signs to a severely retarded student. *Education and Training of the Mentally Retarded, 16,* 252–258.

Browder, D. M., Snell, M. E., & Wildonger, B. A. (1988). Simulation and community-based instruction of vending machines with time delay. *Education and Training in Mental Retardation, 23,* 175–185.

Brown, B. S., & Courtless, T. (1971). *The mentally retarded offender*. Washington, DC: President's Commission on Law Enforcement and Administration of Justice.

Brown, E. C., & Greenbaum, P. E. (1994, March). *Reinstitutionalization after discharge from residential mental health facilities: An example of competing-risks survival analyses.* Paper presented at the Seventh Annual Florida Mental Health Institute Research Conference, Tampa, FL.

Brown, G. W. (1987). Controversial therapy. In M. I. Gottlieb & J. E. Williams (Eds.), *Textbook of developmental pediatrics* (pp. 431–452). New York: Plenum Press.

Brown, J. D. (1993). Coping with stress: The beneficial role of positive illusions. In A. P. Turnbull, J. M. Patterson, S. K. Behr, D. L. Murphy, J. G. Marquis, & M. J. Blue-Banning (Eds.), *Cognitive coping, families, and disability* (pp. 123–133). Baltimore: Brookes.

Brown, L. B., Branston, M. B., Hamre-Nietupski, S., Pumpian, I., Certo, N., & Gruenewald, L. (1979). A strategy for developing chronological-age–appropriate and functional curricular content for severely handicapped adolescents and young adults. *Journal of Special Education, 13*, 81–90.

Brown, M. C., Hanley, A. T., Nemeth, C., Epple, W., Bird, W., & Bontempo, A. (1988). *The Developmental Disabilities Profile: Final report—The design, development and testing of the core instrument*. Albany, NY: New York State Office of Mental Retardation and Developmental Disabilities, Program Research Unit.

Brown, R. I. (Ed.). (1988). *Quality of life for handicapped people*. New York: Croom Helm.

Brown, R., Holvoet, J., Guess, D., & Mulligan, J. (1980). The individualized curriculum sequencing model: III. Small group instruction. *Journal of the Association for Persons with Severe Handicaps, 5*, 352–367.

Brown, S. C. (1993). Revitalizing "handicap" for disability research. *Journal of Disability Policy Research, 4*(2), 57–76.

Brown v. Board of Education of Topeka, Kansas, 347 U.S. 483 (1954).

Bruininks, R. H., Hill, B. K., Weatherman, R. F., & Woodcock, R. W. (1986). *Inventory for Client and Agency Planning*. Chicago: Riverside.

Bruininks, R. H., & McGrew, K. (1987). *Exploring the structure of adaptive behavior* (Report No. 87-1). Minneapolis: University of Minnesota, Department of Educational Psychology.

Bruininks, R., McGrew, K., & Maruyama, G. (1988). Structure of adaptive behavior in samples with and without mental retardation. *American Journal of Mental Retardation, 93*, 265–272.

Bruininks, R. H., Thurlow, M., & Gilman, C. J. (1987). Adaptive behavior and mental retardation. *Journal of Special Education, 21,* 69–88.

Bruininks, R. H., Woodcock, R. W., Hill, B. K., & Weatherman, R. F. (1985). *Development and standardization of the Scales of Independent Behavior.* Allen, TX: DLM Teaching Resources.

Bruininks, R., Woodcock, R., Weatherman, R., & Hill, B. (1984). *Scales of Independent Behavior: Woodcock-Johnson Psychoeducational Battery. Part 4*. Allen, TX: DLM Teaching Resources.

Brunner, R. L., Brown, E. H., & Berry, H. K. (1987). Phenylketonuria revisited: Treatment of adults with behavioral manifestations. *Journal of Inherited Metabolic Disease, 10,* 171–173.

Bruns, E. J., Burchard, J. D., & Yoe, J. T. (1995). Evaluating the Vermont system of care: Outcomes associated with community-based wraparound services. *Journal of Child and Family Studies, 4,* 321–339.

Bryan, T. (1991). Assessment of social cognition: Review of research in learning disabilities. In H. L. Swanson (Ed.), *Handbook on the assessment of learning disabilities: Theory, research, and practice* (pp. 285–311). Austin, TX: Pro-Ed.

Burack, J. A., Hodapp, R. M., & Zigler, E. (1988). Issues in the classification of mental retardation: Differentiating among organic etiologies. *Journal of Child Psychology and Psychiatry, 29*, 765–779.

Burchard, J. D., Burchard, S. N., Sewell, R., & VanDenBerg, J. (1993). *One kid at a time: The case study evaluation and implementation of the Alaska Youth Initiative demonstration project.* Washington, DC: Georgetown University Press.

Burchard, J. D., & Clarke, R. T. (1990). The role of individualized care in a service delivery system for children and adolescents with severely maladjusted behavior. *Journal of Mental Health Administration, 17,* 48–60.

Burchard, J. D., Hinden, B., Carro, M., Schaefer, M., Bruns, E., & Pandina, N. (1995). Using case-level data to monitor a case management system. In B. J. Friesen & J. Poertner (Eds.), *From case management to service coordination for children with emotional, behavioral, or mental disorders* (pp. 169–188). Baltimore: Brookes.

Burchard, J. D., & Schaefer, M. C. (1992). Improving accountability in a service delivery system in children's mental health. *Clinical Psychology Review, 12,* 867–882.

Burgio, L. D., Whitman, T. L., & Johnson, M. R. (1980). A self-instructional package for increasing attending behavior in educable mentally retarded children. *Journal of Applied Behavior Analysis, 13,* 443–459.

Butterfield, E. C. (1983). To cure cognitive deficits of mentally retarded persons. In F. J. Menolascino, R. Newman, & J. A. Stark (Eds.), *Curative aspects of mental retardation: Biomedical and behavioral advances* (pp. 203–221). Baltimore: Brookes.

Byrne, P., Welch, R., Johnson, M. A., Darrah, J., & Piper, M. (1990). Serial magnetic resonance imaging in neonatal hypoxic–ischemic encephalopathy. *Journal of Pediatrics, 117,* 694–700.

Cabay, M. (1994). A controlled evaluation of facilitated communication with four autistic children. *Journal of Autism and Developmental Disorders, 24,* 517–527.

California State Department of Developmental Services. (1978). *Client development evaluation report.* Sacramento, CA: Author.

Callias, M. (1987). Teaching parents, teachers and nurses. In W. Yule & J. Carr (Eds.), *Behavior modification for people with mental handicaps* (2nd ed., pp. 211–244). London: Croom Helm.

Campbell, A. (1981). *The sense of well-being in America: Recent patterns and trends.* New York: McGraw-Hill.

Campbell, F. A., & Ramey, C. T. (1993, March). Cognitive and school outcomes for high risk students at middle adolescence: Positive effects of early intervention. In C. T. Ramey (Chair), *Efficacy of early intervention for poverty children: Results of three longitudinal studies.* Symposium presented at the Society for Research in Child Development, New Orleans, LA.

Campbell, M., Anderson, L. T., Meier, M., Cohen, I. L., Small, A. M., Samit, C., & Sachar, E. J. (1978). A comparison of haloperidol and behavior therapy and their interaction in autistic children. *Journal of the American Academy of Child Psychiatry, 17,* 640–655.

Campbell, M., & Palij, M. (1985). Behavioral and cognitive measures used in psychopharmacological studies of infantile autism. *Psychopharmacology Bulletin, 21,* 1047–1052.

Campbell, P. A. (1990). *The individualized family service plan: A guide for families and early intervention professionals.* Tallmadge, OH: Family Learning Center.

Campbell, V., Smith, R., & Wool, R. (1982). Adaptive behavior scale differences in scores of mentally retarded individuals referred for institutionalization and those never referred. *American Journal of Mental Deficiency, 86,* 425–428.

Campione, J. C., Brown, A. L., & Ferrara, R. A. (1982). Mental retardation and intelligence. In R. Sternberg (Ed.), *Handbook of human intelligence* (pp. 392–491). Cambridge, England: Cambridge University Press.

Canfield, R. L., & Ceci, S. J. (1992). Integrating learning into a theory of intellectual development. In R. J. Sternberg & C. A. Berg (Eds.), *Intellectual development* (pp. 278–300). Cambridge, England: Cambridge University Press.

Cantor, N., & Kihlstrom, J. F. (1987). *Personality and social intelligence.* Englewood Cliffs, NJ: Prentice Hall.

Cantrell, J. K. (1982). Assessing adaptive behavior: Current practices. *Education and Training of the Mentally Retarded, 17,* 147–149.

Carnine, D., Silbert, J., & Kameenui, E. (1990). *Direct instruction reading* (2nd ed.). Columbus, OH: Merrill.

Carr, E. G. (1977). The motivation of self-injurious behavior: A review of some hypotheses. *Psychological Bulletin, 84,* 800–816.

Carr, E. G. (1994). Emerging themes in the functional analysis of problem behavior. *Journal of Applied Behavior Analysis, 27,* 393–400.

Carr, E. G., & Durand, V. M. (1985a). Reducing behavior problems through functional communication training. *Journal of Applied Behavior Analysis, 18,* 111–126.

Carr, E. G., & Durand, V. M. (1985b). The social–communicative basis of severe behavior problems in children. In S. Reiss & R. P. Bootzin (Eds.), *Theoretical issues in behavior therapy* (pp. 219–254). San Diego, CA: Academic Press.

Carr, E. G., Levin, L., McConnachie, G., Carlson, J. I., Kemp, D. C., & Smith, C. E. (1994). *Communication-based intervention for problem behavior.* Baltimore: Brookes.

Carr, E. G., & Newsom, C. D. (1985). Demand-related tantrums: Conceptualization and treatment. *Behavior Modification, 9,* 403–426.

Carr, E. G., Newsom, C. D., & Binkoff, J. A. (1980). Escape as a factor in the aggressive behavior of two retarded children. *Journal of Applied Behavior Analysis, 13,* 101–117.

Carr, E. G., Robinson, S., & Palumbo, L. W. (1990). The wrong issue: Aversive versus nonaversive treatment. The right issue: Functional versus nonfunctional treatment. In A. C. Repp & N. N. Singh (Eds.), *Perspectives on the use of nonaversive and aversive interventions for persons with developmental disabilities* (pp. 361–379). Sycamore, IL: Sycamore Publishing.

Carr, J. (1980). *Helping your handicapped child: A step-by-step guide to everyday problems.* New York: Penguin Books.

Carroll, J. B. (1986). What is intelligence? In R. J. Sternberg & D. K. Detterman (Eds.), *What is intelligence? Contemporary viewpoints on its nature and definition* (pp. 51–54). Norwood, NJ: Ablex.

Carroll, J. B. (1989). Factor analysis since Spearman: Where do we stand? What do we know? In R. Kanfer, P. L. Ackerman, & R. Cudeck (Eds.), *Abilities, motivation, and methodology: The Minnesota Symposium on Learning and Individual Differences* (pp. 43–67). Hillsdale, NJ: Erlbaum.

Carroll, J. B. (1993). *Human cognitive abilities: A survey of factor-analytic studies.* Cambridge, England: Cambridge University Press.

Carroll, J. B., & Horn, J. L. (1981). The scientific basis of ability testing. *American Psychologist, 10,* 1012–1020.

Carsrud, A. L., Carsrud, K. B., Dodd, B. G., Thompson, M., & Gray, W. K. (1981). Predicting vocational aptitude of mentally retarded persons: A comparison of assessment systems. *American Journal of Mental Deficiency, 86,* 275–280.

Carter, B., & McGoldrick, M. (1988). Overview: The changing family life cycle: A framework for family therapy. In B. Carter & M. McGoldrick (Eds.), *The changing family life cycle* (2nd ed., pp. 3–28). New York: Gardner.

Carter, B., & McGoldrick, M. (1989). *The changing family life cycle: A framework for family therapy* (2nd ed.). Boston: Allyn & Bacon.

Case, R. (1985). *Intellectual development: Birth to adulthood.* San Diego, CA: Academic Press.

Caspersson, N., & Zech, L. (Eds.). (1972). *Chromosome identification: Nobel symposia on medicine and natural sciences.* San Diego, CA: Academic Press.

Casto, G., & Lewis, A. (1984). Parent involvement in infant and preschool programs. *Journal of the Division of Early Childhood, 9,* 49–56.

Casto, G., & White, K. R. (1993). Longitudinal studies of alternative types of early intervention: Rationale and design. *Early Education and Development, 4,* 224–237.

Cataldo, M. F. (1989, September). *The effects of punishment and other behavior reducing procedures on the destructive behaviors of persons with developmental disabilities.* Unpublished manuscript, National Institutes of Health, Bethesda, MD.

Caton, J. (l988). Symbolic interaction therapy: A treatment intervention for the mentally retarded adult. *Psychiatric Aspects of Mental Retardation Reviews, 7,* 7–12.

Cattell, R. B. (1949). *The Culture Free Intelligence Test.* Champaign, IL: Institute for Personality and Ability Testing.

Cattell, R. B. (1963). Theory of crystallized intelligence: A critical experiment. *Journal of Educational Psychology, 54,* 1–22.

Cattell, R. B. (1966). The scree test for the number of factors. *Multivariate Behavioral Research, 1,* 245–276.

Cattell, R. B. (1971). *Abilities: Their structure, growth, and action.* Boston: Houghton Mifflin.

Cautela, J., & Groden, J. (1978). *Relaxation: A comprehensive manual for adults, children, and children with special needs*. Champaign, IL: Research Press.

Cavaletti, G., Moroni, R., Garavaglia, P., & Tredici, G. (1987). Brain damage after high altitude climbs without oxygen. *Lancet, 10,* 101.

Cawley, J., Miller, J., & Carr, S. (1989). Arithmetic. In J. R. Patten, E. A. Polloway, & L. R. Argent (Eds.), *Best practices in mild mental disabilities* (pp. 89–107). Reston, VA: Council for Exceptional Children.

Ceci, S. J. (1990). *On intelligence . . . more or less: A bio-ecological treatise on intellectual development.* Englewood Cliffs, NJ: Prentice Hall.

Ceci, S. J., & Liker, J. (1986). A day at the races: A study of IQ, expertise, and cognitive complexity. *Journal of Experimental Psychology: General, 115,* 255–266.

Centers for Disease Control. (1992). Recommendations for the use of folic acid to reduce the number of cases of spina bifida and other neural tube defects. *Morbidity and Mortality Weekly Report, 14,* 1–7.

Centers for Disease Control. (1993a). Absence of reported measles—United States, November, 1993. *Morbidity and Mortality Weekly Report, 42,* 925–926.

Centers for Disease Control. (1993b). Recommendations and reports: 1993 sexually transmitted diseases treatment guidelines. *Morbidity and Mortality Weekly Report, 42,* 1–102.

Centers for Disease Control. (1994a). Vaccines for children's program, 1994. *Morbidity and Mortality Weekly Report, 43,* 705.

Centers for Disease Control. (1994b). Blood lead levels—United States, 1988–1991. *Morbidity and Mortality Weekly Report, 43,* 545–548.

Centers for Disease Control. (1995a). State-specific pregnancy and birth rates among teenagers—United States, 1991–1992. *Morbidity and Mortality Weekly Report, 44,* 677–684.

Centers for Disease Control. (1995b). Sociodemographic and behavioral characteristics associated with alcohol consumption during pregnancy—United States. *Morbidity and Mortality Weekly Report, 44,* 261–264.

Centers for Disease Control. (1995c). CDC surveillance summaries. *Morbidity and Mortality Weekly Report, 44,* SS-1.

Chadsey-Rusch, J. (1987). *The sense of well-being in America: Recent patterns and trends.* New York: McGraw-Hill.

Chadsey-Rusch, J. (1992). Toward defining and measuring social skills in employment settings. *American Journal of Mental Retardation, 96,* 405–418.

Chadsey-Rusch, J., & Sprague, R. L. (1989). Maladaptive behaviors associated with neuroleptic drug maintenance. *American Journal of Mental Retardation, 93,* 607–617.

Chamberlain, A., Rauth, J., Passer, A., McGrath, M., & Burket, R. (1984). Issues in fertility control for mentally retarded female adolescents: I. Sexual activity, sexual abuse and contraception. *Pediatrics, 73,* 445–450.

Chapman, J. W., & Pitceathly, A. S. (1985). Sexuality and mentally handicapped people: Issues of sex education, marriage, parenthood, and care staff attitudes. *Australia and New Zealand Journal of Developmental Disabilities, 10,* 227–235.

Charny, A. M. (1961). *Pathophysiology of hypoxic states.* Moscow: Mir.

Chess, S. (1962). Psychiatric treatment of the mentally retarded child with behavior problems. *American Journal of Orthopsychiatry, 32,* 863–869.

Chiron, R., & Gerken, K. (1983). The effects of a self-monitoring technique on the locus of control orientation of educable mentally retarded children. *School Psychology Review, 12,* 87–92.

Chisholm, J. S. (1989). Biology, culture and the development of temperament: A Navajo example. In J. K. Nugent, B. M. Lester, & T. B. Brazelton (Eds.), *The cultural context of infancy: Biology, culture, and infant development* (Vol. 1, pp. 341–364). Norwood, NJ: Ablex.

Chisholm, J. S., & Heath, G. D. (1987). Evolution and pregnancy: A biosocial view of prenatal influences. In C. Super (Ed.), *The role of culture in developmental disorder* (pp. 42–93). San Diego, CA: Academic Press.

Christensen, A., Johnson, S. M., Phillips, S., & Glasgow, R. E. (1980). Cost effectiveness in behavioral family therapy. *Behavior Therapy, 11,* 208–226.

Christian, W. P., & Malone, D. R. (1973). Relationships among three measures used in screening mentally retarded for placement in special education. *Psychological Republic, 33,* 415–418.

Christian, W. P., & Romanczyk, R. G. (1986). Evaluation. In F. J. Fuoco & W. P. Christian (Eds.), *Behavior analysis and therapy in residential programs* (pp. 145–193). New York: Van Nostrand Reinhold.

Ciancetti, C., Sannio-Fancello, G., Fratta, A., Manconi, F., Orano, A., Pischedda, M. P., Pruna, D., Spinicci, G., Archidiacono, N., & Filipi, G. (1991). Neuropsychological, psychiatric, and physical manifestations in 149 members from 18 fragile X families. *American Journal of Medical Genetics, 40,* 234–243.

Cicchetti, D. V., & Sparrow, S. S. (1981). Developing criteria for establishing interrater reliability of specific items: Applications to assessments of adaptive behavior. *American Journal of Mental Deficiency, 86,* 127–137.

Cicchetti, D. V., Sparrow, S. S., & Rourke, B. P. (1991). Adaptive behavior profiles of psychologically disturbed and developmentally disabled children. In J. L. Matson & J. A. Mulick (Eds.), *Handbook of mental retardation* (pp. 222–237). Elmsford, NY: Pergamon Press.

Cipani, E. (Ed.). (1989). *The treatment of severe behavior disorders.* Washington, DC: American Association on Mental Retardation.

Cipani, E., & Morrow, R. D. (1991). Educational assessment. In J. L. Matson & J. A. Mulick (Eds.), *Handbook of mental retardation* (pp. 260–275). Elmsford, NY: Pergamon Press.

Cirillo, S., & Sorrentino, A. M. (1986). Handicap and rehabilitation: Two types of information upsetting family organization. *Family Process, 24,* 283–292.

Clark, D. B., & Baker, B. L. (1983). Predicting outcome in parent training. *Journal of Consulting and Clinical Psychology, 51,* 309–311.

Clarke, A. M., & Clarke, A. D. B. (1974). Criteria and classification of subnormality. In A. M. Clarke & A. D. B. Clarke (Eds.), *Mental deficiency: The changing outlook* (3rd ed., pp. 13–30). New York: Free Press.

Clarke, R. T., Burchard, J. D., Schaefer, M., & Welkowitz, J. W. (1992). Wrapping community-based mental health services around children with a severe behavioral disorder: An evaluation of project wraparound. *Journal of Child and Family Studies, 1,* 241–261.

Clausen, J. A. (1972). Quo vadis, AAMD? *Journal of Special Education, 6,* 51–60.

Clayton-Smith, J., & Pembrey, M. E. (1992). Angelman syndrome. *Journal of Medical Genetics, 29,* 412–415.

Cliff, N. (1988). The eigenvalues-greater-than-one rule and the reliability of components. *Psychological Bulletin, 103,* 276–279.

Coffey, O. D. (1989). *Programming for mentally retarded and learning disabled inmates: A guide for correctional administrators* (p. IX). Washington, DC: U.S. Department of Justice, National Institute of Corrections.

Cohen, H. G. (1988). Measurement of adaptive behavior: Origins, trends, issues. *Child & Youth Services, 10,* 37–81.

Cohen, J. (1960). A coefficient of agreement for nominal scales. *Educational and Psychological Measurement, 20,* 37–46.

Cohen, S., Agosta, J., Cohen, J., & Warren, R. (1989). Supporting families of children with severe disabilities. *Journal of the Association of Persons With Severe Handicaps, 14,* 155–162.

Coie, J. D., Watt, N., Markman, H., West, S., Hawkins, D., Asarnow, J., Ramey, S. L., Shure, M., & Long, B. (1991). *The science of prevention: A conceptual framework and some directions for a national research program.* Bethesda, MD: National Institute of Mental Health.

Cole, C. L., Davenport, T. L., Bambara, L. M., & Ager, C. L. (1995). *Assessing the effects of choice and preference on the task performance of students with disabilities.* Manuscript submitted for publication.

Cole, C. L., & Gardner, W. I. (1990). Effects of staff- and self-assessment procedures on disruptive behavior in a vocational setting: A case study. *Vocational Evaluation and Work Adjustment Bulletin, 23,* 41–46.

Cole, C. L., Gardner, W. I., & Karan, O. C. (1985). Self-management training of mentally retarded adults presenting severe conduct difficulties. *Applied Research in Mental Retardation, 6*, 337–347.

Cole, K. N., Dale, P. S., Mills, P. E., & Jenkins, J. R. (1993). Interaction between early intervention curricula and student characteristics. *Exceptional Children, 16*, 17–28.

Cole, M. (1992). Culture in development. In M. H. Bornstein & M. E. Lamb (Eds.), *Developmental psychology: An advanced text* (3rd ed., pp. 731–790). Hillsdale, NJ: Erlbaum.

Cole, S. (1988). Facing the challenges of sexual abuse in persons with disabilities. *Sexuality and Disability, 7*, 71–88.

Collison, G. O. (1974). Concept formation in a second language: A study of Ghanaian school children. *Harvard Educational Review, 44*, 441–457.

Columbo, J., & Fagen, J. W. (Eds.). (1990). *Individual differences in infancy: Reliability, stability, and prediction.* Hillsdale, NJ: Erlbaum.

Comrey, A. L., & Lee, H. B. (1992). *A first course in factor analysis* (2nd ed.). Hillsdale, NJ: Erlbaum.

Cone, J. D. (1987). Intervention planning using adaptive behavior instruments. *Journal of Special Education, 21*, 127–148.

Conley, R. W., Luckasson, R., & Bouthilet, G. N. (Eds.). (1992). *The criminal justice system and mental retardation.* Baltimore: Brookes.

Conners, C. K. (1990). *Manual for Conners' Rating Scales: Conners Teacher Rating Scales and Conners Parent Rating Scales.* North Tonawanda, NY: Multihealth Systems.

Connor, E. M., Sperling, R. S., Gelber, R., Kiselev, P., Scott, G., O'Sullivan, M. J., VanDyke, R., Bey, M., Shearer, W., Jacobson, R. L., Jimenez, E., O'Neill, E., Bazin, B., Delfraissy, J. F., Culnane, M., Coombs, R., Elkins, M., Moye, J., Stratton, P., & Balsley, J. (1994). Reduction of maternal-infant transmission of human immunodeficiency virus type 1 with zidovudine treatment. *New England Journal of Medicine, 331*, 1173–1180.

Conroy & Feinstein Associates. (1986). *Choice Making Scale.* Philadelphia: Author.

Conroy, J., Efthimiou, J., & Lemanowicz, J. (1982). A matched comparison in the developmental growth of institutionalized and deinstitutionalized mentally retarded clients. *American Journal of Mental Deficiency, 86*, 581–587.

Cook, E. H. J., Rowlett, R., Jaselskis, C., & Leventhal, B. L. (1992). Fluoxetine treatment of children and adults with autistic disorder and mental retardation. *Journal of the American Academy of Child and Adolescent Psychiatry, 31*, 739–745.

Cook, T. D., & Campbell, D. T. (1979). *Quasi-experimentation: Design and analysis issues for field settings.* New York: Holt, Rinehart & Winston.

Cooper, J. L., Heron, T. E., & Heward, W. L. (1987). *Applied behavior analysis.* Columbus, OH: Charles E. Merrill.

Copher, J. I. (1988). *Integration into the life of the community of residents of small community residential facilities for individuals with mental retardation.* Unpublished doctoral dissertation, University of Illinois at Urbana-Champaign.

Coplin, J. W., & Houts, A. C. (1991). Father involvement in parent training for oppositional child behavior: Progress or stagnation? *Child and Family Behavior Therapy, 13*, 29–51.

Corcoran, K., & Fischer, J. (1987). *Measures for clinical practice. A sourcebook.* New York: Free Press.

Cordisco, L. K., Strain, P. S., & Depew, N. (1988). Assessment for generalization of parenting skills in home settings. *Journal of the Association for Persons With Severe Handicaps, 13*, 202–210.

Cormick, W., Olson, L. G., Hensley, M. J., & Saunders, N. A. (1986). Nocturnal hypoxaemia and quality of sleep in patients with chronic obstructive lung disease. *Thorax, 41*, 846–854.

Cornwall, A. (1990). Social validation of psychoeducational reports. *Journal of Learning Disabilities, 23*, 413–416.

Correa, V. I., Paulson, C. L., & Salzberg, C. L. (1984). Training and generalization of reach-grasp behavior in blind, retarded young children. *Journal of Applied Behavior Analysis, 17*, 57–69.

Coulter, D. L. (1992). An ecology of prevention for the future. *Mental Retardation, 6*, 363–369.

Courchesne, E., Townsend, J. P., Akshoomoff, N. A., Yeung-Courchesne, R., Press, G. A.,

Murakami, J. W., Lincoln, A. J., James, H. E., Saitoh, O., Egaas, B., Haas, R. H., & Schriebman, L. (1994). A new finding: Impairment in shifting attention in autistic and cerebellar patients. In S. H. Broman & J. Grafman (Eds.), *Atypical cognitive deficits in developmental disorders: Implications for brain function* (pp. 101–138). Hillsdale, NJ: Erlbaum.

Cowan, C. P., & Cowan, P. A. (1988). Who does what when partners become parents: Implications for men, women, and marriage. In R. Palkovitz & M. Susman (Eds.), *Transitions to parenthood* (pp. 105–131). New York: Haworth Press.

Crewe, W. D., Sanders, E. C., Hensley, L. G., Johnson, Y. M., Bonaventura, S., & Rhodes, R. D. (in press). An evaluation of facilitated communication in a group of nonverbal individuals with mental retardation. *Journal of Autism and Developmental Disorders.*

Crnic, K. A., Friedrich, W. N., & Greenberg, M. T. (1983). Adaptation of families with mentally retarded children: A model of stress, coping, and family ecology. *American Journal of Mental Deficiency, 88,* 125–138.

Crocker, A. C. (1992). Symposium: Prevention of mental retardation and disabilities. Introduction: Where is the prevention movement? *Mental Retardation, 30,* iii–v.

Cronbach, L. J. (1970). *Essentials of psychological testing* (3rd ed.). New York: Harper & Row.

Cronbach, L. J. (1975). Beyond the two disciplines of scientific psychology. *American Psychologist, 30,* 116–127.

Cross, T. L., Bazron, B. J., Dennis, K. W., & Isaacs, M. R. (1989). *Towards a culturally competent system of care* (monograph). Washington, DC: CASSP Technical Assistance Center.

Crowe, S. F., & Hay, D. A. (1990). Neuropsychological dimensions of the fragile X syndrome: Support for a non-dominant hemisphere dysfunction hypothesis. *Neuropsychologia, 28,* 9–15.

Cullinane, M. M., & Crocker, A. C. (1992). Service coordination. In M. D. Levine, W. B. Carey, & A. C. Crocker (Eds.), *Developmental behavioral pediatrics* (2nd ed., pp. 737–739). Philadelphia: W. B. Saunders.

Cummins, R. A. (1991). The Comprehensive Quality of Life Scale—Intellectual Disability: An instrument under development. *Australia and New Zealand Journal of Developmental Disabilities, 17,* 259–264.

Cummins, R. A. (1992). *The comprehensive quality-of-life scale: Intellectual disability* (3rd ed.). Melbourne, Australia: Psychology Research Centre, Deakin University.

Cunningham, C. E., Bremner, R., & Secord-Gilbert, M. (1993). Increasing the availability, accessibility, and cost efficacy of services for families of ADHD children: A school-based systems-oriented parenting course. *Canadian Journal of School Psychology, 9,* 1–15.

Cunningham, T. R., & Tharp, R. G. (1981). The influence of settings on accuracy and reliability of behavioral observation. *Behavioral Assessment, 3,* 67–78.

Cutting, G. R., & Antonarakis, S. E. (1992). Prenatal diagnosis and carrier detection by DNA analysis. *Pediatrics in Review, 13,* 138–143.

Czeizel, A. E., & Dudás, I. (1992). Prevention of the first occurrence of neural-tube defects by periconceptual vitamin supplementation. *New England Journal of Medicine, 327,* 1832–1835.

Dadds, M. R., Sanders, M. R., & James, J. E. (1987). The generalization of treatment effects in parent training with multidistressed parents. *Behavioural Psychotherapy, 15,* 289–313.

Damon, W. (1983). *Social and personality development.* New York: Norton.

Dangel, R. F., & Polster, R. A. (1984). *Parent training.* New York: Guilford Press.

Daniel R. v. Board of Education, 874 F.2d 1036 (5th Cir. 1989).

Das, J. P. (1973). Structure of cognitive abilities: Evidence for simultaneous and successive processing. *Journal of Educational Psychology, 65,* 103–108.

Das, J. P. (1984a). Aspects of planning. In J. R. Kirby (Ed.), *Cognitive strategies and educational performance* (pp. 13–31, 35–50). San Diego, CA: Academic Press.

Das, J. P. (1984b). Cognitive deficits in mental retardation: A process approach. In P. H. Brooks, R. Sperber, & C. McCauley (Eds.), *Learning and cognition in the mentally retarded* (pp. 115–128). Hillsdale, NJ: Erlbaum.

Das, J. P. (1992). Beyond a unidimensional scale of merit. *Intelligence, 16,* 137–149.

Das, J. P., & Bower, A. C. (1971). Orienting responses of mentally retarded and normal children. *British Journal of Psychology, 62,* 89–96.

Das, J. P., & Dash, U. N. (1983). Hierarchical factor solution of coding and planning processes: Any new insights? *Intelligence, 7,* 27–37.

Das, J. P., Kirby, J. R., & Jarman, R. F. (1979). *Simultaneous and successive cognitive processes.* San Diego, CA: Academic Press.

Das, J. P., & Melnyk, L. (1989). Attention Checklist: A rating scale for mildly mentally handicapped adolescents. *Psychological Reports, 64,* 1267–1274.

Das, J. P., & Mishra, R. K. (1995). Assessment of cognitive decline associated with aging: A comparison of individuals with Down syndrome and other etiologies. *Research in Developmental Disabilities, 16,* 11–25.

Das, J. P. , Mishra, R. K., Davison, M., & Naglieri, J. A. (in press). Measurement of dementia in individuals with mental retardation: Comparison based on PPVT and Dementia Rating Scale. *The Clinical Neuropsychologist.*

Das, J. P., Naglieri, J. A., & Kirby, J. R. (1994). *Assessment of cognitive processes: The PASS theory of intelligence.* Needham Heights, MA: Allyn & Bacon.

Davidson, M., Giordani, A. B., Mohs, R. C., Horvath, T. B., Davis, B. M., Powchik, P., & Davis, K. L. (1987). Short-term haloperidol administration acutely elevates human plasma homovanillic acid concentration. *Archives of General Psychiatry, 44,* 189.

Davies, R. R., & Rogers, E. S. (1985). Social skills training with persons who are mentally retarded. *Mental Retardation, 23,* 186–196.

Day, H. M., & Horner, R. H. (1986). Response variation and the generalization of a dressing skill: Comparison of single instance and general case instruction. *Applied Research in Mental Retardation, 7,* 189–202.

De Boulle, K., Verkerk, A. J., Reyniers, E., Vits, L., Hendricks, J., Van Roy, B., Van den Bos, F., de Graaf, E., Oostra, B. A., & Willems, P. J. (1993). A point mutation in the FMR-1 gene associated with fragile X mental retardation. *Nature Genetics, 3,* 31–35.

Decker, T. W., & Polloway, E. A. (1989). Written language. In J. R. Patton, E. A. Polloway, & L. R. Argent (Eds.), *Best practices in mild mental disabilities* (pp. 89–107). Reston, VA: Council for Exceptional Children.

Deisher, R. W. (1971). Sexual behavior of retarded in institutions. In F. F. de la Cruz & G. D. La Veck (Eds.), *Human sexuality and the mentally retarded* (pp. 145–152). New York: Brunner/Mazel.

Delong, G. R. (1978). A neurological interpretation of infantila autism. In M. Rutter & E. Schopler (Eds.), *Autism: A reappraisal of concepts and treatment* (pp. 207–218). New York: Plenum Press.

Delquadri, J., Greenwood, C., Whorton, D., Carta, J., & Hall, R. (1986). Classwide peer tutoring. *Exceptional Children, 52,* 535–542.

Demb, H. B. (1995). The role of comorbidity in the differential diagnosis of young children with deviant behavior. *Developmental and Behavioral Pediatrics, 16* (3, June Suppl.), S3–S6.

Demb, H. B., Brier, N., Huron, R., & Tomer, E. (1994). The Adolescent Behavior Checklist: Normative data and sensitivity and specificity of a screening tool for diagnosable psychiatric disorders in adolescents with mental retardation and other developmental disabilities. *Research in Developmental Disabilities, 15,* 151–165.

Demerath, R. R. (1988). *Psychobiological stresses associated with sickle cell disease: The effects on human development and behavior.* Unpublished doctoral dissertation, The Ohio State University, Columbus.

Deming, E. W. (1982). *Quality, productivity, and competitive position.* Cambridge, MA: MIT Press.

Deming, E. W. (1986). *Out of the crisis.* Cambridge, MA: MIT Press.

Denays, R., Van Pachterbeke, T., Tondeur, M., Spehl, M., Toppet, J., Ham, H., Piepsz, H., Rubinstein, M., Noel, P., & Haumont, D. (1989). Brain single-photon emission computed tomography in neonates. *Journal of Nuclear Medicine, 30,* 1337–1383.

Denkowski, G. C., & Denkowski, K. M. (1985). The mentally retarded offender in the state prison system: Identification, prevalance, adjustment, and rehabilitation. *Criminal Justice Behavior, 12,* 55–70.

Dennis, R. E., Williams, W., Giangreco, M. F., & Cloninger, C. J. (1993). Quality of life as context for planning and evaluation of services for people with disabilities. *Exceptional Children, 59*, 499–512.

DeShaney v. Winnebago County, 109 S. Ct. 998 (1989).

Deshler, D. D., & Schumaker, J. B. (1986). Learning strategies: An instructional alternative for low-achieving adolescents. *Exceptional Children, 52*, 583–589.

Detterman, D. K. (1987). Theoretical notions of intelligence and mental retardation. *American Journal of Mental Deficiency, 92*, 2–11.

Detterman, D. K., & Daniel, M. H. (1989). Correlations of mental tests with each other and with cognitive variables are highest for low IQ groups. *Intelligence, 13*, 349–359.

Detterman, D. K., Mayer, J. D., Caruso, D. R., Legree, P. J., Conners, F. A., & Taylor, R. (1992). Assessment of basic cognitive abilities in relation to cognitive deficits. *American Journal of Mental Retardation, 97*, 251–286.

Deutsch, H. (1985). Grief counseling with the mentally retarded client. *Psychiatric Aspects of Mental Retardation Reviews, 4*, 17–20.

Developmental Disabilities Act of 1977, Pub. L. No. 95–602.

Developmental Disabilities Act of 1984, 42 U.S.C. §§ 6001–6083.

Devys, D., Lutz, Y., Rouyer, N., Bellocq, J. R., & Mandel, J. L. (1993). The FMR-1 protein is cytoplasmic, most abundant in neurons and appears normal in carriers of a fragile X permutation. *Nature Genetics, 4*, 335–340.

Diamond, A. (1985). Development of the ability to use recall to guide action, as indicated by infants' performance on AB̄. *Child Development, 56*, 868–883.

Diamond, A., & Doar, B. (1989). The performance of human infants on a measure of frontal cortex function: The delayed response task. *Developmental Psychobiology, 22*, 271–294.

Diamond, A., & Goldman-Rakic, P. S. (1989). Comparison of human infants and rhesus monkeys on Piaget's A not B task: Evidence for dependence on dorsolateral prefrontal cortex. *Experimental Brain Research, 74*, 24–40.

Diamond, A., Hurwitz, W., Lee, E. Y., Grover, W., & Minarcik, C. (in press). Cognitive deficits on frontal cortex tasks in children with early treated PKU: Results of two years of longitudinal study.

Diamond, G. W., & Cohen, H. J. (1987, December). AIDS and developmental disabilities. In *Prevention update from the National Coalition on Prevention of Mental Retardation*. Silver Spring, MD: American Association of University Affiliated Programs for Persons with Developmental Disabilities.

Diener, E. (1984). Subjective well-being. *Psychological Bulletin, 95*, 542–575.

Dishion, T. J. (1990). The family ecology of boys' peer relations in middle childhood. *Child Development, 61*, 874–892.

Dishion, T. J., & Patterson, G. R. (1992). Age effects in parent training outcome. *Behavior Therapy, 23*, 719–729.

Doe v. Board of Education, 9 F.3d 455 (6th Cir. 1993).

Dokecki, P. R., Baumeister, A. A., & Kupstas, F. D. (1989). Biomedical and social aspects of pediatric AIDS. *Journal of Early Intervention, 13*, 99–113.

Doll, E. A. (1936). President's address: Current thoughts on mental deficiency. *Journal of Psycho-Asthenics, 18*, 40–41.

Dollar, M. B., & Billie, J. (1983). *Informed consent for family planning*. Atlanta, GA: Regional Training Center for Family Planning.

Donnellan, A. M., Mirenda, P. L., Mesaros, R. A., & Fassbender, L. L. (1984). Analyzing the communicative functions of aberrant behavior. *Journal of the Association for Persons with Severe Handicaps, 9*, 201–212.

Doran, J., & Holland, J. G. (1979). Control by stimulus features during fading. *Journal of the Experimental Analysis of Behavior*, 31, 177–187.

Dosen, A. (1990). Developmental–dynamic relationship therapy. In A. Dosen, A. Van Gennep, & G. Zwanikken (Eds.), *Treatment of mental illness and behavioral disorders in the mentally retarded* (pp. 37–44). Leiden, the Netherlands: Logon Publications.

Dosen, A., & Gielen, J. J. M. (1993). Depression in persons with mental retardation. In R. M. Fletcher & A. Dosen (Eds.), *Mental health aspects of mental retardation* (pp. 70–97). Lexington, MA: Lexington Books.

Doyle, L. W., Nahmias, C., Firnau, G., Kenyon, D. B., Garnett, E. S., & Sinclair, J. C. (1983).

Regional cerebral glucose metabolism of newborn infants measured by positron emission tomography. *Developmental Medicine and Child Neurology, 25,* 143–151.

Drotar, D. (1993). Influences on collaborative activities among psychologists and pediatricians: Implications for practice, training and research. *Journal of Pediatric Psychology, 18,* 159–172.

Dubowitz, L. M. S., & Bydder, G. M. (1990). Magnetic resonance imaging of the brain in neonates. *Seminars in Perinatology, 14,* 212–223.

Ducharme, J. M., & Popynick, M. (1993). Errorless compliance to parental requests: Treatment effects and generalization. *Behavior Therapy, 24,* 209–226.

Dumas, J. E. (1984). Child, adult-interactional, and socioeconomic setting events as predictors of parent training outcome. *Education and Treatment of Children, 7,* 351–364.

Dunlap, W. R., & Iceman, D. J. (1985). The development and validation of a set of instruments to assess the independent living skills of the handicapped. *Educational and Psychological Measurement, 45,* 925–929.

Dunst, C. J., Trivette, C. M., & Deal, A. G. (1988). *Enabling and empowering families: Principles and guidelines for practice.* Cambridge, MA: Brookline Books.

Dunst, C. J., Trivette, C. M., Hamby, D. M., & Pollock, B. (1990). Family systems correlates of the behavior of young children with handicaps. *Journal of Early Intervention, 14,* 204–218.

Dunst, C. J., Trivette, C. M., Starnes, A. L., Hamby, D. W., & Gordon, N. J. (1993). *Building and evaluating family support initiatives: A national study of programs for persons with developmental disabilities.* Baltimore: Brookes.

Dura, J. (1993, June). *Sex education and policy issues.* Paper presented at the annual conference of the American Association on Mental Retardation, Washington, DC.

Dura, J., & Nunemaker, H. (1993). *Masturbation instruction for men who have developmental disabilities.* Bowling Green, OH: Practical Programming Group.

Durand, V. M. (1990). *Severe behavior problems: A functional communication training approach.* New York: Guilford Press.

Durand, V. M., & Carr, E. G. (1987). Social influences on "self-stimulatory" behavior: Analysis and treatment application. *Journal of Applied Behavior Analysis, 20,* 119–132.

Durand, V. M., & Carr, E. G. (1991). Functional communication training to reduce challenging behaviors: Maintenance and application in new settings. *Journal of Applied Behavior Analysis, 24,* 251–264.

Durand, V. M., & Crimmins, D. B. (1988). Identifying the variables maintaining self-injurious behavior. *Journal of Autism and Developmental Disorders, 18,* 99–117.

Durand, V. M., & Kishi, G. (1987). Reducing severe behavior problems among persons with dual sensory impairments: An evaluation of a technical assistance model. *Journal of the Association for Persons with Severe Handicaps, 12,* 2–10.

Durkin, M. S., Schupf, N., Stein, Z. A., & Susser, M. W. (1994). Epidemiology of mental retardation. In M. Levene & R. Lilford (Eds.), *Fetal and neonatal neurology and neurosurgery* (2nd ed., pp. 693–710). London: Churchill Livingstone.

Dworkin, P. H. (1989). British and American recommendations for developmental monitoring: The role of surveillance. *Pediatrics, 84,* 1000–1010.

Dyer, K., Dunlap, G., & Winterling, V. (1990). Effects of choice making on the serious problem behaviors of students with severe handicaps. *Journal of Applied Behavior Analysis, 23,* 515–524.

Dykens, E. M., Hodapp, R. M., & Leckman, J. F. (1994). *Behavior and development in fragile X syndrome.* Newbury Park, CA: Sage.

Dykens, E., & Leckman, J. (1990). Developmental issues in fragile-X syndrome. In R. M. Hodapp, J. A. Burack, & E. Zigler (Eds.), *Issues in the developmental approach to mental retardation* (pp. 226–242). Cambridge, England: Cambridge University Press.

Eaton, L. F., & Menolascino, F. J. (1982). Psychiatric disorders in the mentally retarded: Types, problems, and challenges. *American Journal of Psychiatry, 139,* 1297–1303.

Eberlin, M., McConnachie, G., Ibel, S., & Volpe, L. (1993). Facilitated communication: A failure to replicate the phenomenon. *Journal of Autism and Developmental Disorders, 23,* 507–530.

Edgerton, R. B. (1967). *The cloak of competence: Stigma in the lives of the mentally retarded.* Berkeley: University of California Press.

Edgerton, R. B. (1968). Anthropology and mental retardation: A plea for the comparative study of incompetence. In H. Prehm, L. Hammerlynck, & J. Crosson (Eds.), *Behavioral research in mental retardation* (Rehabilitation Research in Mental Retardation and Training Monograph No. 1). Eugene: Rehabilitation Research in Mental Retardation and Training Center, University of Oregon.

Edgerton, R. B. (1970). Mental retardation in non-Western societies: Towards a cross-cultural perspective on incompetence. In H. C. Haywood (Ed.), *Socio-cultural aspects of mental retardation* (pp. 523–559). New York: Appleton-Century-Crofts.

Edgerton, R. B. (1984). (Ed.). *Lives in process: Mildly retarded adults in a large city.* Washington, DC: American Association on Mental Deficiency.

Edgerton, R. B. (1988). Community adaptation of persons with mental retardation. In J. F. Kavanagh (Ed.), *Understanding mental retardation: Research accomplishments and new frontiers* (pp. 311–318). Baltimore: Brookes.

Edgerton, R. B., & Bercovici, S. M. (1976). The cloak of competence: Years later. *American Journal of Mental Deficiency, 80,* 485–497.

Edmonson, B., McCombs, K., & Wish, J. (1979). What retarded adults believe about sex. *American Journal of Mental Deficiency, 84,* 11–18.

Education for All Handicapped Children Act of 1975, Pub. L. No. 94-142.

Education for All Handicapped Act. 42 *Federal Register,* 42478 (1977).

Education of the Handicapped Amendments of 1986. *Federal Register,* November 18, 1987, 1145–1177.

Egel, A. L., & Powers, M. D. (1989). Behavioral parent training: A view of the past and suggestions for the future. In E. Cipani (Ed.), *The treatment of severe behavior disorders: Behavior analysis approaches* (pp. 153–173). Washington, DC: American Association on Mental Retardation.

Ehrmann, L. C., Aeschleman, S. R., & Svanum, S. (1995). Parental reports of community activity patterns: A comparison between young children with disabilities and their nondisabled peers. *Research in Developmental Disabilities, 16,* 331–343.

Eimas, P. D., Siqueland, E. R., Jusczyk, P., & Vigorito, J. (1971). Speech perception in infants. *Science, 171,* 303–306.

Einfeld, S. L., & Tonge, B. J. (1992). *Manual for the Developmental Behaviour Checklist (DBC).* Randwich, New South Wales, Australia: Prince of Wales Hospital, Department of Child and Adolescent Psychiatry.

Elliot, R. L. (1986). Lithium treatment and cognitive changes in two mentally retarded patients. *Journal of Nervous and Mental Disease, 174,* 689–692.

Emerson, E. B. (1985). Evaluating the impact of deinstitutionalization on the lives of mentally retarded people. *American Journal of Mental Deficiency, 90,* 227–288.

Engelmann, S., & Carnine, D. (1982). *Theory of instruction: Principles and applications.* New York: Irvington.

Engelmann, S., & Colvin, D. (1983). *Generalized compliance training: A direct instruction program for managing severe behavior problems.* Baltimore: Brookes.

Epstein, M. H., Polloway, E. A., Patton, J. R., & Foley, R. (1989). Mild retardation: Student characteristics and services. *Education and Training in Mental Retardation, 24,* 7–16.

Erfanian, N., & Miltenberger, R. G. (1990). Brief report: Contact desensitization in the treatment of dog phobias in persons who have mental retardation. *Behavioral Residential Treatment, 5,* 55–60.

Ernst, J., Bornstein, P. H., & Weltzein, R. T. (1984). Initial considerations in subjective evaluation research: Does knowledge of treatment affect performance ratings? *Behavioral Assessment, 6,* 121–127.

Escalona, S. K. (1982). Babies at double hazard: Early development of infants at biologic and social risk. *Pediatrics, 70,* 670–676.

Etzel, B. C., & LeBlanc, J. M. (1979). The simplest treatment alternative: The law of parsimony applied to choosing appropriate instructional control and errorless-learning procedures for the difficult-to-teach child. *Journal of Autism and Developmental Disorders, 9,* 361–382.

Evans, I., & Meyer, L. H. (1985). *An educative approach to behavior problems: A practical decision model for intervention with severely handicapped learners.* Baltimore: Brookes.

Evans, I., & Meyer, L. H. (1987). Moving to educational validity: A reply to Test, Spooner, and Cooke. *Journal of the Association for Persons with Severe Handicaps,* 12, 103–106.

Evans, I. M., Okifuji, A., Engler, L., Bromley, K., & Tishelman, A. (1993). Home–school communication in the treatment of childhood behavior problems. *Child and Family Behavior Therapy, 15,* 37–59.

Evenden, J. L. (1988). Issues in behavioral pharmacology: Implications for developmental disorders. In M. G. Aman & N. N. Singh (Eds.), *Psychopharmacology of the developmental disabilities* (pp. 216–238). New York: Springer-Verlag.

Everington, C. T., & Luckasson, R. (1992). *Competency Assessment for Standing Trial (CAST-MR).* Orlando Park, IL: International Diagnostic Systems.

Eyde, L. D., Robertson, G. J., Krug, S. E., Moreland, K. L., Robertson, A. G., Shewan, C. M., Harrison, P. L., Porch, B. E., Hammer, A. L., & Primoff, E. S. (1993). *Responsible test use: Case studies for assessing human behavior.* Washington, DC: American Psychological Association.

Eyman, R. K., Grossman, H. J., Chaney, R. H., & Call, T. L. (1990). The life expectancy of profoundly handicapped persons with mental retardation. *New England Journal of Medicine, 323,* 584–589.

Eyman, R. K., & Widaman, K. F. (1987). Life-span development of institutionalized and community-based mentally retarded persons, revisited. *American Journal of Mental Deficiency, 91,* 559–569.

Fahs, J. J. (1989). Anxiety disorders. In American Psychiatric Association (Ed.), *Treatment of psychiatric disorders* (Vol. 1, pp. 14–19). Washington, DC: American Psychiatric Association.

Fankhauser, M. P., Karumanchi, V. C., German, M. L., Yates, A., & Karumanchi, S. D. (1992). A double blind, placebo-controlled study of the efficacy of transdermal clonidine in autism. *Journal of Clinical Psychiatry, 53,* 77–82.

Fantz, R. L. (1964). Visual experience in infants: Decreased attention to familiar patterns relative to novel ones. *Science, 146,* 668–670.

Farber, B. (1959). Effects of a severely retarded child on family integration. *Monographs of the Society for Research in Child Development, 24* (Whole No. 71).

Farber, B. (1960). Family organization and crisis: Maintenance of integration in families with a severely retarded child. *Monographs of the Society for Research in Child Development, 25* (1, Serial No. 75).

Farran, D., Metzger, J., & Sparling, J. (1986). Immediate and continuing adaptations in parents of handicapped children: A model and an illustration. In J. J. Gallagher & P. M. Vietze (Eds.), *Families of handicapped persons: Research, programs, and policy issues* (pp. 143–163). Baltimore: Brookes.

Farrell, A. D., Curran, J. P., Zwick, W. R., & Monti, P. M. (1983). Generalizability and discriminant validity of anxiety and social skills ratings in two populations. *Behavioral Assessment, 6,* 1–14.

Favell, J. E. (1990). Issues in the use of nonaversive and aversive interventions. In S. L. Harris & J. S. Handleman (Eds.), *Aversive and nonaversive interventions: Controlling life-threatening behavior by the developmentally disabled* (pp. 36–56). New York: Springer.

Favell, J. E., Favell, J. E., & McGimsey, J. F. (1978). Relative effectiveness and efficiency of group vs. individual training of severely retarded persons. *American Journal of Mental Deficiency, 83,* 104–109.

Favell, J. E., Favell, J. E., Riddle, J. I., & Risley, T. R. (1984). Promoting change in mental retardation facilities: Getting services from the paper to the people. In W. P. Christian, G. T. Hannah, & T. J. Glahn (Eds.), *Programming effective human services: Strategies for institutional change and client transition* (pp. 15–37). New York: Plenum Press.

Favell, J. E., & McGimsey, J. F. (1993). Defining an acceptable treatment environment. In R. Van Houten & S. Axelrod (Eds.), *Behavior analysis and treatment* (pp. 25–45). New York: Plenum Press.

Favell, J. E., McGimsey, J. F., & Schnell, R. M. (1982). Treatment of self-injury by providing alternate sensory activities. *Analysis and Intervention in Developmental Disabilities, 2,* 83–104.

Featherstone, H. (1980). *A difference in the family: Life with the disabled child.* New York: Basic Books.

Feinstein, C. A. (1985). *Life safety code instrument.* Philadelphia: Conroy & Feinstein Associates.

Feinstein, C., Kaminer, Y., & Barrett, R. (1988). *The Emotional Disorders Rating Scale: Developmental Disabilities.* Unpublished scale, Emma Pendleton Bradley Hospital, East Providence, RI.

Feinstein, C., Kaminer, Y., Barrett, R. P., & Tylenda, B. (1988). The assessment of mood and affect in developmentally disabled children and adolescents: The Emotional Disorders Rating Form. *Research in Developmental Disabilities, 9,* 109–122.

Felce, D., deKock, U., Thomas, M., & Saxby, H. (1986). Changes in adaptive behaviour of severely and profoundly mentally handicapped adults in different residential settings. *British Journal of Psychology, 77,* 489–501.

Ferguson, D. L., & Baumgart, D. (1991). Partial participation revisited. *Journal of the Association for Persons with Severe Handicaps, 16,* 218–227.

Ferretti, R. P., & Cavalier, A. R. (1991). Constancy in the problem solving of persons with mental retardation. *International Review of Research in Mental Retardation, 17,* 153–192.

Feuerstein, R. (1977). A theoretical basis for cognitive human modifiability during adolescence. In P. Mittler (Ed.), *Research to practice in mental retardation* (Vol. 2, pp. 105–116). Baltimore: University Park Press.

Feuerstein, R., Klein, P. S., & Tannenbaum, A. J. (Eds.). (1991). *Mediated learning experience: Theoretical, psychosocial and learning implications.* London: Freund.

Fiedler, C. R., & Antonak, R. F. (1991). Advocacy. In J. L. Matson & J. A. Mulick (Eds.), *Handbook of mental retardation* (2nd ed., pp. 23–32). Elmsford, NY: Pergamon Press.

Filsinger, E. E., & Lewis, R. A. (1981). *Assessing marriage: New behavioral approaches.* Beverly Hills, CA: Sage.

Firestone, P., Kelly, M. J., & Fike, S. (1980). Are fathers necessary in parent training groups? *Journal of Clinical Child Psychology, 9,* 44–47.

Fischer, K. W. (1980). A theory of cognitive development: The control and construction of hierarchies of skills. *Psychological Review, 87,* 477–531.

Fischer, K. W., & Farrar, M. J. (1987). Generalizations about generalization: How a theory of skill development explains both generality and specificity. *International Journal of Psychology, 22,* 643–677.

Fisher, D. (1983). The going gets tough when we descend from the ivory tower. *Analysis and Intervention in Developmental Disabilities, 3,* 249–255.

Fitch, W. L. (1992). Mental retardation and criminal responsibility. In R. W. Conley, R. Luckasson, & G. N. Bouthilet (Eds.), *The criminal justice system and mental retardation* (pp. 121–136). Baltimore: Brookes.

Flanagan, J. C. (1978). A research approach to improving our quality of life. *American Psychologist, 33,* 138–147.

Flanagan, J. C. (1982). Measurement of quality of life: Current state of the art. *Archives of Physical Medicine and Rehabilitation, 63,* 56–59.

Flavell, J. H. (1963). *The developmental psychology of Jean Piaget.* Princeton, NJ: Van Nostrand Reinhold.

Fleiss, J. L., & Cohen, J. (1973). The equivalence of weighted kappa and the intraclass correlation as measures of reliability. *Education and Psychological Measurement, 33,* 613–619.

Fletcher, R. J. (1984). Group therapy with mentally retarded persons with emotional disorders. *Psychiatric Aspects of Mental Retardation Reviews, 3,* 21–24.

Fletcher, R. J. (1993). Individual psychotherapy for persons with mental retardation. In R. J. Fletcher & A. Dosen (Eds.), *Mental health aspects of mental retardation: Progress in assessment and treatment* (pp. 327–349). Lexington, MA: Lexington Books.

Flick, G. L., & Duncan, C. (1973). Perceptual–motor dysfunction in children with sickle cell trait. *Perceptual and Motor Skills, 36,* 234.

Floyd, F. J. (1989). Segmenting interactions: Coding units for assessing marital and family behaviors. *Behavioral Assessment, 11,* 13–29.

Floyd, F. J., & Phillippe, K. A. (1993). Parental interactions with children with and without mental retardation: Behavior management, coerciveness, and positive exchange. *American Journal of Mental Retardation, 97,* 673–684.

Floyd, F. J., & Saitzyk, A. R. (1992). Social class and parenting children with mild and moderate mental retardation. *Journal of Pediatric Psychology, 17,* 607–631.

Floyd, F. J., Weinand, J. W., & Cimmarusti, R. A. (1989). Clinical family assessment: Applying structured measurement procedures in treatment settings. *Journal of Marital and Family Therapy, 15,* 271–288.

Floyd, F. J., & Zmich, D. E. (1991). Marriage and the parenting partnership: Perceptions and interactions of parents with mentally retarded and typically developing children. *Child Development, 62,* 1434–1448.

Flynn, J. R. (1985). Wechsler intelligence tests: Do we really have a criterion of mental retardation? *American Journal of Mental Deficiency, 90,* 236–244.

Flynn, R. J., & Heal, L. W. (1981). Short form of Pass #3. *Evaluation Review, 5,* 357–376.

Fodor, J. (1983). *The modularity of mind.* Cambridge, MA: MIT Press.

Folkman, S., & Lazarus, R. S. (1980). An analysis of coping in a middle-aged community sample. *Journal of Health and Social Behavior, 21,* 219–239.

Folstein, M. F., Folstein, S. E., & McHugh, P. R. (1975). "Mini-mental state": A practical method for grading the cognitive state of patients for the clinician. *Journal of Psychiatric Research, 12,* 189–198.

Ford, A., Schnorr, R., Meyer, L., Davern, L., Black, M. S., & Dempsey, M. S. (1989). *The Syracuse community-referenced curriculum guide for students with moderate and severe disabilities.* Baltimore: Brookes.

Forehand, R., & Atkeson, B. M. (1977). Generality of treatment effects with parents as therapists: A review of assessment and implementation procedures. *Behavior Therapy, 8,* 575–593.

Forehand, R., & Baumeister, A. A. (1976). Deceleration of aberrant behavior among retarded individuals. In M. Hersen, R. M. Eisler, & P. M. Miller (Eds.), *Progress in behavior modification* (Vol. 2, pp. 238–278). San Diego, CA: Academic Press.

Forehand, R., & King, H. E. (1977). Noncompliant children: Effects of parent training on behavior and attitude change. *Behavior Modification. 1,* 93–108.

Forehand, R., & McMahon, B. (1981). *Helping the non-compliant child: A clinician's guide to parent training.* New York: Guilford Press.

Forman, E. A., & Minick, M. (Eds.). (1993). *Contexts for learning: Sociocultural dynamics in children's development.* New York: Oxford University Press.

Fortier, L. M., & Wanlass, R. L. (1984). Family crisis following the diagnosis of a handicapped child. *Family Relations, 33,* 13–24.

Foster, M., Berger, M., & McLean, M. (1981). Rethinking a good idea: A reassessment of parent involvement. *Topics in Early Childhood Special Education, 1,* 55–56.

Foster, R., & Nihira, K. (1969). Adaptive behavior as a measure of psychiatric impairment. *American Journal of Mental Deficiency, 73,* 401–404.

Foster, S. L., Prinz, R. J., & O'Leary, K. D. (1983). Impact of problem solving communication training and generalization procedures on family conflict. *Child and Family Behavior Therapy, 5,* 1–23.

Foster-Gaitskell, D., & Pratt, C. (1989). Comparison of parent and teacher ratings of adaptive behavior of children with mental retardation. *American Journal of Mental Retardation, 94,* 177–181.

Fox, H. (Ed.). (1978). *Pathology of the placenta.* Philadelphia: W. B. Saunders.

Foxx, R. M. (1981). *Effective behavioral programming: Graduated guidance and backward chaining.* Champaign, IL: Research Press.

Foxx, R. M. (1982a). *Decreasing the behaviors of severely retarded and autistic persons.* Champaign, IL: Research Press.

Foxx, R. M. (1982b). *Increasing the behaviors of severely retarded and autistic persons.* Champaign, IL: Research Press.

Foxx, R. M. (1990). "Harry": A ten year follow-up of the successful treatment of a self-injurious man. *Research in Developmental Disabilities, 11,* 67–76.

Foxx, R. M., & Bechtel, D. R. (1983). Overcorrection: A review and analysis. In S. Axelrod & J. Apsche (Eds.), *The effects of punishment on human behavior* (pp. 133–220). San Diego, CA: Academic Press.

Foxx, R. M., Bittle, R. G., & Faw, G. D. (1989). A maintenance strategy for discontinuing aversive procedures: A 52-month follow-up of the treatment of aggression. *American Journal of Mental Retardation, 94,* 27–36.

Foxx, R. M., & Faw, G. D. (1990). Long-term follow-up of echolalia and question answering. *Journal of Applied Behavior Analysis, 23,* 387–396.

Foxx, R. M., Kyle, M. S., Faw, G. D., & Bittle, R. G. (1989). Cues-pause-point training and simultaneous communication to teach the use of signed labeling repertoires. *American Journal of Mental Retardation, 93,* 305–311.

Foxx, R. M., & Livesay, J. (1984). Maintenance of response suppression following overcorrection: A ten year retrospective examination of eight cases. *Analysis and Intervention in Developmental Disabilities, 4,* 65–79.

Foxx, R. M., & McMorrow, M. J. (1983). *Stacking the deck.* Champaign, IL: Research Press.

Foxx, R. M., McMorrow, M. J., & Schloss, C. N. (1983). Stacking the deck: Teaching social skills to retarded adults with a modified table game. *Journal of Applied Behavior Analysis, 16,* 157–170.

Foxx, R. M., McMorrow, M. J., Storey, K., & Rogers, B. M. (1984). Teaching social/sexual skills to mentally retarded adults. *American Journal of Mental Deficiency, 89,* 9–15.

Foxx, R. M., Zukotynski, G., & Williams, D. E. (1994). Measurement and evaluation of treatment outcomes with extremely dangerous behavior. In T. Thompson & D. Gray (Eds.), *Treatment of destructive behavior in developmental disabilities* (Vol. 2, pp. 261–273). Newbury Park, CA: Sage.

Frank, H., & Fiedler, E. R. (1969). A multifactor behavioral approach to the genetic-etiological diagnosis of mental retardation. *Multivariate Behavioral Research, 4*(2), 131–145.

Frank, S. J., Olmsted, C. L., Wagner, A. E., Laub, C. C., Freeark, K., Breitzer, G. M., & Peters, J. M. (1991). Child illness, the parenting alliance and parenting stress. *Journal of Pediatric Psychology, 16,* 361–371.

Frattali, C. M. (1993). Perspectives on functional assessment: Its use for policy making. *Disability and Rehabilitation, 15*(1), 1–9.

Freeman, B. J., Ritvo, E. R., Yokota, A., & Ritvo, A. (1986). A scale for rating symptoms of patients with the syndrome of autism in real life settings. *Journal of the American Academy of Child Psychiatry, 25,* 130–136.

Freeman, B. J., Roy, R. R., & Hemmick, S. (1976). Extinction of a phobia of physical examination in a seven-year-old mentally retarded boy: A case study. *Behavior Research and Therapy, 14,* 63–64.

Freeman, B. J., & Schroth, P. C. (1984). The development of the Behavioral Observation System (BOS) for autism. *Behavioral Assessment, 6,* 177–187.

Frey, K., Greenberg, M., & Fewell, R. (1989). Stress and coping among parents of handicapped children: A multidimensional approach. *American Journal of Mental Retardation, 94,* 240–249.

Friedrich, W. N. (1979). Predictors of the coping behavior of mothers of handicapped children. *Journal of Consulting and Clinical Psychology, 47,* 1140–1141.

Fry, E. B. (1977). Fry's Readability Graph: Clarifications, validity, and extension to level 17. *Journal of Reading, 21,* 242–252.

Frye, D., & Moore, C. (Eds.). (1991). *Children's theories of mind: Mental states and social understanding.* Hillsdale, NJ: Erlbaum.

Fryers, T. (1987). Epidemiological issues in mental retardation. *Journal of Mental Deficiency Research, 31,* 365–384.

Fryns, J. P. (1987). Chromosomal anomalies and autosomal syndromes. *Birth Defects Original Article Series, 23,* 7–32.

Fuchs, D., & Fuchs, L. S. (1994). Inclusive schools movement and the radicalization of special education reform. *Exceptional Children, 66,* 294–309.

Furman, W., & Buhrmester, D. (1985). Children's perceptions of the qualities of sibling relationships. *Child Development, 56,* 448–461.

Futterman, A. D., & Arndt, S. (1983). The construct and predictive validity of adaptive behavior. *American Journal of Mental Deficiency, 87,* 546–550.

Gadow, K. D. (1992). Pediatric psychopharmacotherapy: A review of recent research. *Journal of Child Psychology and Psychiatry, 33,* 153–195.

Gallagher, J. J. (1994). Teaching and learning: New models. *Annual Review of Psychology, 45,* 171–195.

Gallagher, J. J., Beckman, P., & Cross, A. H. (1983). Families of handicapped children: Sources of stress and its amelioration. *Exceptional Children, 50,* 10–19.

Gallimore, R., Weisner, T. S., Bernheimer, L. P., Guthrie, D., & Nihira, K. (1993). Family responses to young children with developmental delays: Accommodation activity in ecological and cultural context. *American Journal of Mental Retardation, 98,* 185–206.

Gamble, W. C., & McHale, S. M. (1989). Coping with stress in sibling relationships: A comparison of children with disabled and nondisabled siblings. *Journal of Applied Developmental Psychology, 10,* 353–373.

Gammon, E. A., & Rose, S. D. (1991). The Coping Skills Training Program for parents of children with developmental disabilities: An experimental evaluation. *Research on Social Work Practice, 1,* 244–256.

Garber, H. J., McGonigle, J. J., Slomka, G. T., & Monteverde, E. (1992). Clomipramine treatment of stereotypic behaviors and self-injury in patients with developmental disabilities. *Journal of the American Academy of Child and Adolescent Psychiatry, 31,* 1157–1160.

Garber, H. L. (1988). *The Milwaukee Project: Preventing mental retardation in children at risk.* Washington, DC: American Association on Mental Retardation.

Garcia, J. (1981). The logic and limits of mental aptitude testing. *American Psychologist, 36,* 1172–1180.

Gardner, H. (1983). *Frames of mind: The theory of multiple intelligences.* New York: Basic Books.

Gardner, W. I. (1988). Behavior therapies: Past, present, and future. In J. Stark, F. Menolascino, M. Albarelli, & V. Gray (Eds.), *Mental retardation and mental health: Classification, diagnosis, treatment, services* (pp. 161–172). New York: Springer-Verlag.

Gardner, W. I., Clees, T. J., & Cole, C. L. (1983). Self-management of disruptive verbal ruminations by a mentally retarded adult. *Applied Research in Mental Retardation, 4,* 41–58.

Gardner, W. I., & Cole, C. L. (1984). Aggression and related conduct difficulties in the mentally retarded: A multicomponent behavior model. In S. E. Breuning, J. L. Matson, & R. P. Barrett (Eds.), *Advances in mental retardation and developmental disabilities: A research annual* (Vol. 2, pp. 41–84). Greenwich, CT: JAI Press.

Gardner, W. I., & Cole, C. L. (1986). Aggression and related conduct difficulties. In J. L. Matson (Ed.), *Handbook of behavior modification with the mentally retarded* (pp. 225–254). New York: Plenum Press.

Gardner, W. I., & Cole, C. L. (1989). Self-management approaches. In E. Cipaini (Ed.), *The treatment of severe behavior disorders: Behavior analysis approaches* (pp. 19–35). Washington, DC: American Association on Mental Retardation.

Gardner, W. I., & Cole, C. L. (1993). Aggression and related conduct disorders: Definition, assessment, treatment. In J. L. Matson & R. P. Barrett (Eds.), *Psychopathology in the mentally retarded* (2nd ed., pp. 213–252). Boston: Allyn & Bacon.

Gardner, W. I., Cole, C. L., Berry, D. L., & Nowinski, J. M. (1983). Reduction of disruptive behaviors in mentally retarded adults: A self-management approach. *Behavior Modification, 7,* 76–96.

Gardner, W. I., Cole, C. L., Davidson, D. P., & Karan, O. C. (1986). Reducing aggression in individuals with developmental disabilities: An expanded stimulus control assessment and intervention model. *Education and Training of the Mentally Retarded, 21,* 3–12.

Gardner, W. I., & Graeber, J. L. (1994). Use of behavioral therapies to enhance personal competency: A multimodal diagnostic and intervention model. In N. Bouras (Ed.), *Mental retardation and mental health: The way ahead* (pp. 205–223). Cambridge, England: Cambridge University Press.

Gardner, W. I., & Moffatt, C. W. (1990). Aggressive behaviour: Definition, assessment, treatment. *International Review of Psychiatry, 2,* 91–100.

Gardner, W. I., & Sovner, R. (1994). *Self-injurious behavior.* Willow Street, PA: Vida Publishing.

Garwick, G., Jurkowski, E., & Valenti-Hein, D. (1993, May). *Full normalization: Goal based romance, sensuality and friendship skill-building for people with developmental disa-*

bilities. Paper presented at the annual conference of the American Association on Mental Retardation, Washington, DC.

Gazaway, R. (1969). *The longest mile.* New York: Doubleday.

Gedeon, A. K., Baker, E., Robinson, H., Partington, M. W., Gross, B., Manca, H., Korn, B., Poustka, A., Yu, S., Sutherland, G. R., et al. (1992). Fragile X syndrome without CCG amplification has an FMR1 deletion. *Nature Genetics, 1,* 341–344.

Gedye, A. (1989). Episodic rage and aggression attributed to frontal lobe seizure. *Journal of Mental Deficiency Research, 33,* 369–379.

Gelb, S. A. (1987). Social deviance and the "discovery" of the moron. *Disability, Handicap and Society, 2,* 247–258.

Gergen, K. J. (1994). Exploring the post modern: Perils or potentials? *American Psychologist, 49,* 412–417.

Gersten, R. (1985). Direct instruction with special education students: A review of evaluation research. *Journal of Special Education, 19,* 41–58.

Gettinger, M., & Kratochwill, T. R. (1987). Behavioral assessment. In C. L. Frame & J. L. Matson (Eds.), *Handbook of assessment in childhood psychopathology* (pp. 131–132). New York: Plenum Press.

Gettinger, M., & White, M. A. (1979). Which is the stronger correlate of school learning? Time to learn or measured intelligence? *Journal of Educational Psychology, 71,* 405–412.

Giangreco, M. F., Edelman, S., Cloninger, C., & Dennis, R. (1992). My child has a classmate with severe disabilities: What parents of nondisabled children think of full inclusion. *Developmental Disabilities Bulletin, 20*(2), 1–12.

Gibson, T. J., Rice, P. M., Thompson, J. D., & Heringa, J. (1993). Protein sequence motifs: KH domains within the FMR-1 sequence suggests that fragile X syndrome stems from a defect in RNA metabolism. *Trends in Biochemical Science, 18,* 331–333.

Gilbert, G. J. (1987). Turtle headaces and Parkinson's disease. *Headache, November,* 588–589.

Gilbert, T. F. (1978). *Human competence.* New York: McGraw-Hill.

Gladwin, T. (1959). Methodologies applicable to the study of learning deficits. *American Journal of Mental Deficiency, 64,* 311–315.

Glascoe, F. P., & Dworkin, P. H. (1993). Obstacles to effective developmental surveillance: Errors in clinical reasoning. *Developmental and Behavioral Pediatrics, 14,* 344–349.

Glendenning, N. J., Adams, G. L., & Sternberg, L. (1983). Comparison of prompt sequences. *American Journal of Mental Deficiency, 88,* 321–325.

Glidden, L. M. (1986). Families who adopt mentally retarded children: Who, why, and what happens. In J. J. Gallagher & P. M. Vietze (Eds.), *Families of handicapped persons: Research, programs, and policy issues* (pp. 115–128). Baltimore: Brookes.

Glidden, L. M. (1993). What we do not know about families with children who have developmental disabilities: Questionnaire on resources and stress as a case study. *American Journal of Mental Retardation, 97,* 481–495.

Glidden, L. M., Kiphart, M. J., Willoughby, J. C., & Bush, B. A. (1993). Family functioning when rearing children with developmental disabilities. In A. P. Turnbull, J. M. Patterson, S. K. Behr, D. L. Murphy, J. G. Marquis, & M. J. Blue-Banning (Eds.), *Cognitive coping, families, and disability* (pp. 183–194). Baltimore: Brookes.

Goddard, H. H. (1914). *Feeble-mindedness: Its causes and consequences.* New York: Macmillan.

Godschalx, S. M. (1983). Mark: Psychotherapy with a developmentally disabled adult. *Image: The Journal of Nursing Scholarship, 5,* 12–15.

Goffman, E. (1961). *Asylums: Essays on the moral situation of mental patients and other inmates.* Garden City, NY: Doubleday.

Gold, M. W. (1980). *Did I say that?* Champaign, IL: Research Press.

Goldman, J. J. (1987). Differential WAIS/WAIS–R IQ discrepancies among institutionalized mentally retarded persons. *American Journal of Mental Deficiency, 91,* 633–635.

Goode, D. A. (1988). *Proceedings of the national conference on quality of life for persons with disabilities.* Valhalla, NY: The Mental Retardation Institute.

Goode, D. A. (Ed.). (1994). *Quality of life for persons with disabilities.* Cambridge, MA: Brookline Books.

Goodman, J. F., & Cecil, H. S. (1987). Referral practices and attitudes of pediatricians toward young mentally retarded children. *Journal of Developmental and Behavioral Pediatrics, 8,* 97–105.

Goodnow, J. J. (1986). A social view of intelligence. In R. J. Sternberg & D. K. Detterman (Eds.), *What is intelligence? Contemporary viewpoints on its nature and definition* (pp. 85–90). Norwood, NJ: Ablex.

Goplerud, J. M., & Delivoria-Papadopoulos, M. (1993). Nuclear magnetic resonance imaging and spectroscopy following asphyxia. *Clinics in Perinatology, 20,* 345–367.

Gordon, C. T., Rapoport, J. L., Hamburger, S. D., State, R. C., & Mannheim, G. B. (1992). Differential response of seven subjects with autistic disorder to clomipramine and desipramine. *American Journal of Psychiatry, 149,* 363–366.

Gore, R. M., Weinberg, P. E., Anandappa, E., Shkolnick, A., & White, H. (1981). Intracranial complications of pediatric hematologic disorders: Computed tomographic assessment. *Investigative Radiology, 16,* 175–180.

Gorlow, L., Butler, A., Einig, K. K. G., & Smith, J. A. (1963). An appraisal of self-attitudes and behavior following group psychotherapy with retarded young adults. *American Journal of Mental Deficiency, 67,* 893–898.

Gorman-Smith, D. (1991). *Image generalization: A further analysis of the concept.* Unpublished doctoral dissertation, Department of Psychology, University of Illinois.

Gorsuch, R. L. (1983). *Factor analysis* (2nd ed.). Hillsdale, NJ: Erlbaum.

Gowen, J. W., Johnson-Martin, N., Goldman, B. D., & Appelbaum, M. (1989). Feelings of depression and parenting competence of mothers of handicapped and nonhandicapped infants: A longitudinal study. *American Journal of Mental Retardation, 94,* 259–271.

Grace, N., Cowart, C., & Matson, J. L. (1988). Reinforcement and self-management in Lesch–Nyhan syndrome. *Journal of the Multihandicapped Person, 1,* 53–59.

Granger, C. V., Cotter, A. C., Hamilton, B. B., & Fiedler, R. C. (1993). The Functional Independence Measure (FIM) and the Sickness Impact Profile (SIP). *Archives of Physical Medicine and Rehabilitation, 74,* 133–138.

Gray, S. W., Ramsey, B. K., & Klaus, R. A. (1982). *From 3 to 20: The early training project.* Baltimore: University Park Press.

Graziano, A. M., & Diament, D. M. (1992). Parent behavioral training: An examination of the paradigm. *Behavior Modification, 16,* 3–38.

Green, C. W., Reid, D. H., White, L. K., Halford, R. C., Brittain, D. P., & Gardner, S. M. (1988). Identifying reinforcers for persons with profound handicaps: Staff opinion versus systematic assessment of preferences. *Journal of Applied Behavior Analysis, 21,* 32–43.

Green, G. (1994). The quality of the evidence. In H. Shane (Ed.), *Facilitated communication: The clinical and social phenomenon* (pp. 157–225). San Diego, CA: Singular Press.

Green, G., Mackay, H. A., McIlvane, W. J., Saunders, R. R., & Sraci, S. (1990). Perspectives on relational learning in mental retardation. *American Journal of Mental Retardation, 95,* 249–259.

Greenfield, P. M., & Cocking, R. R. (1994). Preface. In P. M. Greenfield (Ed.), *Cross-cultural roots of minority child development* (pp. ix–xix) Hillsdale, NJ: Erlbaum.

Greenspan, S. (1979). Social intelligence in the retarded. In N. R. Ellis (Ed.), *Handbook of mental deficiency: Psychological theory and research* (2nd ed., pp. 483–531). Hillsdale, NJ: Erlbaum.

Greenspan, S. (1981). Social competence and handicapped individuals: Implications of a proposed model. *Advances in Special Education, 3,* 41–82.

Greenspan, S. (1994). Review of 1992 AAMR manual. *American Journal of Mental Retardation, 98,* 544–549.

Greenspan, S., & Delaney, K. (1983). Personal competence of institutionalized adult males with and without Down syndrome. *American Journal of Mental Deficiency, 88,* 218–220.

Greenspan, S., & Granfield, J. M. (1992). Reconsidering the construct of mental retardation: Implications of a model of social competence. *American Journal of Mental Retardation, 96,* 442–453.

Greenspan, S., & Love, P. (in press). Social intelligence and developmental disorder: Mental retardation, autism and learning disabilities. In W. MacLean (Ed.), *Handbook of mental deficiency* (3rd ed.). Hillsdale, NJ: Erlbaum.

Greenspan, S., & McGrew, K. (1993). *Response to Mathias and Nettelbeck*. Unpublished manuscript, University of Connecticut at Storrs.

Greenspan, S., & Shoultz, B. (1981). Why mentally retarded adults lose their jobs: Social competence as a factor in work adjustment. *Applied Research in Mental Retardation, 2,* 23–38.

Greenspan, S., Shoultz, B., & Weir, M. M. (1981). Social judgment and work success of mentally retarded adults. *Applied Research in Mental Retardation, 2,* 335–346.

Gresham, F. M., & Elliott, S. N. (1987). The relationship between adaptive behavior and social skills: Issues in definition and assessment. *Journal of Special Education, 21,* 167–181.

Gresham, F. M., & Elliot, S. N. (1990). *Social Skills Questionnaire*. Circle Pines, MN: American Guidance Service.

Gresham, F. M., Elliot, S. N., & Black, F. L. (1987). Teacher-rated social skills of mainstreamed mildly handicapped and nonhandicapped children. *School Psychology Review, 16,* 78–88.

Gresham, F. M., & Reschly, D. J. (1987). Dimensions of social competence: Method factors in the assessment of adaptive behavior, social skills, and peer acceptance. *Journal of School Psychology, 25,* 367–381.

Griest, D. L., & Forehand, R. (1982). How can I get any parent training done with all these other problems going on? The role of family variables in child behavior therapy. *Child and Family Behavior Therapy, 4,* 73–80.

Griest, D. L., Forehand, R., Rogers, T., Breiner, J. L., Furey, W., & Williams, C. A. (1982). Effects of parent enhancement therapy on the treatment outcome and generalization of a parent training program. *Behaviour Research and Therapy, 20,* 429–436.

Griffiths, D., Hingsburger, D., & Christian, R. (1985). Treating developmentally handicapped sexual offenders: The York Behavior Management Services treatment program. *Psychiatric Aspects of Mental Retardation Reviews, 4,* 49–52.

Grigsby, J. P., Kemper, M. B., Hagerman, R. J., & Myers, R. J. (1990). Neuropsychological dysfunction among affected heterozygous fragile X females. *American Journal of Medical Genetics, 35,* 28–35.

Grisso, T. (1981). *Juveniles' waiver of rights*. New York: Plenum Press.

Grossman, H. J. (Ed.). (1973). *Manual on terminology and classification in mental retardation*. Washington, DC: American Association on Mental Deficiency.

Grossman, H. J. (Ed.). (1977). *Manual on terminology and classification in mental retardation*. Washington, DC: American Association on Mental Deficiency.

Grossman, H. J. (Ed.). (1983). *Classification in mental retardation*. Washington, DC: American Association on Mental Deficiency.

Grotevant, H. D., & Carlson, C. I. (1989). *Family assessment: A guide to methods and measures*. New York: Guilford Press.

Grotta, J. C., Manner, C., Pettigrew, L. C., & Yatsym, F. M. (1986). Red blood cell disorders and stroke. *Stroke, 17,* 811–817.

Gruenberg, E. M. (1964). Epidemiology. In H. A. Stevens & R. F. Heber (Eds.), *Mental retardation: A review of research* (pp. 259–306). Chicago: University of Chicago Press.

Grunewald, K. (1979). Mentally retarded children and young people in Sweden. *Acta Pediatrica Scandinavica, 75*(Suppl. 275), 75–84.

Gualtieri, C. T. (1987). Fetal antigenicity and maternal immunoreactivity: Factors in mental retardation. In S. R. Schroeder (Ed.), *Toxic substances and mental retardation: Neurobehavioral toxicology and teratology* (pp. 33–69). Washington, DC: American Association on Mental Deficiency.

Guarnaccia, V. K. (1976). Factor structure and correlates of adaptive behavior in noninstitutionalized retarded adults. *American Journal of Mental Deficiency, 80,* 179–203.

Guerin, B. (1992). Behavior analysis and the social construction of knowledge. *American Psychologist, 47,* 1423–1432.

Guilford, J. P. (1967). *The nature of human intelligence*. New York: McGraw-Hill.

Guralnick, M. J. (1973). Behavior therapy with an acrophobic mentally retarded young adult. *Journal of Behavior Therapy and Experimental Psychiatry, 4,* 263–265.

Guralnick, M. J. (1975). Effects of distinctive-feature training and instructional technique on letter and form discrimination. *American Journal of Mental Deficiency, 80*, 202–207.

Gustafsson, J. E. (1984). A unifying model for the structure of intellectual abilities. *Intelligence, 8*, 179–203.

Guthrie, R., & Edwards, J. (1990). Prevention of mental retardation and developmental disabilities: An overview. In S. M. Pueschel & J. A Mulick (Eds.), *Prevention of developmental disabilities* (pp. 11–23). Baltimore: Brookes.

Gutkind, L. (1993). *Stuck in time: The tragedy of childhood mental illness*. New York: Henry Holt.

Halderman v. Pennhurst State School and Hospital, 446 F. Supp. 1295 (E.D. Pa. 1978).

Hall, J. N. (1992). Correctional services for inmates with mental retardation: Challenge or catastrophe? In R. W. Conley, R. Luckasson, & G. N. Bouthilet (Eds.), *The criminal justice system and mental retardation* (pp. 176–190). Baltimore: Brookes.

Hall, J. W., & Tinzmann, M. B. (1989). Sources of improved recall during the school years. *Bulletin of the Psychonomic Society, 27*, 315–316.

Halpern, A. S. (1993). Quality of life as a conceptual framework for evaluating transition outcomes. *Exceptional Children, 59*, 486–498.

Halpern, A. S., Lehmann, J. P., Irvin, L. K., & Heiry, T. J. (1982). *Contemporary assessment for mentally retarded adolescents and adults*. Baltimore: University Park Press.

Hamilton, P. A., Hope, P. L., Cady, E. B., Delpry, D. T., Wyatt, J. S., & Reynolds, E. O. (1986). Impaired energy metabolism in brain of newborn infants with increased cerebral echodensities. *Lancet, 1*, 1242–1246.

Hampson, R. B., Hulgus, Y. F., Beavers, W. R., & Beavers, J. (1988). The assessment of competence in families with a retarded child. *Journal of Family Psychology, 2*, 32–53.

Hampson, R., Judge, K., & Renshaw, J. (1984). *Environmental checklist*. Canterbury, Kent, UK: Cornwallis Building, The University.

Hancock, R. D., Weber, S. L., Kaza, R., & Her, K. S. (1991). Changes in psychotropic drug use in long-term residents of an ICF/MR facility. *American Journal of Mental Retardation, 96*, 137–141.

Handen, B. L., & Aman, M. G. (1994). *Side Effects Profile for Exceptional Children (SEPEC)*. Pittsburgh, PA: Western Psychiatric Institute and Clinic.

Handen, B. L., Breaux, A. M., Gosling, A., Ploof, D. L., & Feldman, H. (1990). Efficacy of methylphenidate among mentally retarded children with attention deficit hyperactivity disorder. *Pediatrics, 86*, 922–930.

Handen, B. L., Breaux, A. M., Janosky, J., McAuliffe, S., Feldman, H., & Gosling, A. (1992). Effects and non-effects of methylphenidate in children with mental retardation and ADHD. *Journal of the American Academy of Child and Adolescent Psychiatry, 31*, 455–461.

Handen, B. L., Feldman, H., Gosling, A., Breaux, A. M., & McAuliffe, S. (1991). Adverse side effects of Ritalin among mentally retarded children with ADHD. *Journal of the American Academy of Child and Adolescent Psychiatry, 30*, 241–245.

Hanson, M. H. (1987). *Teaching the infant with Down syndrome: A guide for parents and professionals*. Austin, TX: Pro-Ed.

Harchik, A. E., Harchik, A. J., Luce, S. C., & Sherman, J. A. (1990). Teaching autistic and severely handicapped children to recruit praise: Acquisition and generalization. *Research in Developmental Disabilities, 11*, 77–95.

Harchik, A. E., Sherman, J. A., Sheldon, J. B., & Bannerman, D. J. (1993). Choice and control: New opportunities for people with developmental disabilities. *Annals of Clinical Psychiatry, 5*, 151–162.

Harchik, A. E., Sherman, J. A., Sheldon, J. B., & Strouse, M. C. (1992). Ongoing consultation as a method of improving performance of staff members in a group home. *Journal of Applied Behavior Analysis, 25*, 599–610.

Harel, S., & Anastasiow, N. J. (1985). *The at risk infant: Psycho/social/medical aspects*. Baltimore: Brookes.

Hargis, K., & Blechman, E. Q. (1979). Social class and training of parents as behavior change agents. *Child Behavior Therapy, 1*, 69–74.

Haring, T. G. (1993). Research basis of instructional procedures to promote social interaction and integration. In R. A. Gable & S. F. Warren (Eds.), *Strategies for teaching students with mild to severe mental retardation* (pp. 129–164). Baltimore: Brookes.

Harris, D. (1992). A cultural model for assessing growth and development. *Journal of Multicultural Counseling and Development, 20,* 158–167.

Harris, S. L. (1983). *Families of the developmentally disabled: A guide to behavioral intervention.* Elmsford, NY: Pergamon Press.

Harris, S. L. (1986). Parents as teachers: A four to seven year follow up of parents of children with autism. *Child and Family Behavior Therapy, 8,* 39–47.

Harris, S. L., Alessandri, M., & Gill, M. J. (1991). Training parents of developmentally disabled children. In J. L. Matson & J. A. Mulick (Eds.), *Handbook of mental retardation* (2nd ed., pp. 373–381). Elmsford, NY: Pergamon Press.

Harrison, P. L. (1987). Research with adaptive behavior scales. *Journal of Special Education, 21,* 37–68.

Harrison, P. L., Kaufman, A. S., Kaufman, N. L., Bruininks, R. H., Ilmer, S., Rynders, J., Sparrow, S. S., & Cicchetti, D. A. (1990). *Early Screening Profiles.* Circle Pines, MN: American Guidance Service.

Harrold, M., Lutzker, J. R., Campbell, R. V., & Touchette, P. E. (1992). Improving parent–child interactions for families of children with developmental disabilities. *Journal of Behavior Therapy and Experimental Psychiatry, 23,* 89–100.

Harter, S. (1977). The effects of social reinforcement and task difficulty on the pleasure derived by normal and retarded children from cognitive challenge and mastery. *Journal of Experimental Child Psychology, 24,* 476–494.

Harter, S. (1978). Effectance motivation reconsidered. *Human Development, 21,* 34–64.

Harter, S. (1982). The perceived competence scale for children. *Child Development, 53,* 87–97.

Haruda, F., Friedman, J. H., Ganti, S. R., Hoffman, N., & Chutorian, A. M. (1981). Rapid resolution of organic mental syndrome in sickle cell anemia in response to exchange transfusion. *Neurology, 31,* 1015–1016.

Harvey, J. R., Karan, O. C., Bhargava, D., & Morehouse, N. (1978). Relaxation training and cognitive behavioral procedures to reduce violent temper outbursts in a moderately retarded woman. *Journal of Behavior Therapy and Experimental Psychiatry, 9,* 347–351.

Hauser-Cram, P., Pierson, D. E., Walker, D. K., & Tivnan, R. (1991). *Early education in the public schools.* San Francisco: Jossey-Bass.

Hawkins, G. D., & Cooper, D. H. (1990). Adaptive behavior measures in mental retardation research: Subject description in AJMD/AJMR articles (1979–1987). *American Journal of Mental Retardation, 94,* 654–660.

Hawkins, N., & Powers, L. (1990). *Stress management training: A manual for practitioners.* Eugene: Oregon Research Institute.

Hawkins, N. E., Singer, G. H. S., & Nixon, C. D. (1993). Short-term behavioral counseling for families of persons with disabilities. In G. H. S. Singer & L. E. Powers (Eds.), *Families, disability, and empowerment: Active coping skills and strategies for family interventions* (pp. 317–342). Baltimore: Brookes.

Hawkins, R. P., & Dobes, R. W. (1975). Behavioral definitions in applied behavior analysis: Explicit or implicit. In B. C. Etzel, J. M. LeBlanc, & D. M. Baer (Eds.), *New developments in behavioral research: Theory, methods, and applications* (pp. 167–188). Hillsdale, NJ: Erlbaum.

Haxby, J. V. (1989). Neuropsychological evaluation of adults with Down's syndrome: Patterns of selective impairment in non-demented old adults. *Journal of Mental Deficiency Research, 33,* 193–210.

Haxby, J. V., & Schapiro, M. B. (1992). Longitudinal study of neuropsychological function in older adults with Down syndrome. In C. Epstein & L. Nadel (Eds.), *Alzheimer's disease in Down syndrome* (pp. 35–50). New York: Wiley.

Hayden, A. H., & Haring, N. G. (1976). Early intervention for high risk infants and young children: Programs for Down's syndrome children. In T. D. Tjossem (Ed.), *Intervention strategies for high risk infants and young children* (pp. 573–607). Baltimore: University Park Press.

Hayes, S. C. (1987). A contextual approach to therapeutic change. In N. Jacobson (Ed.),

Psychotherapists in clinical practice: Cognitive and behavioral perspectives (pp. 327–387). New York: Guilford Press.

Haynes, S. N., Spain, E. H., & Oliveira, J. (1993). Identifying causal relationships in clinical assessment. *Psychological Assessment, 5*, 281–291.

Haywood, H. C., & Switzky, H. N. (1986). Intrinsic motivation and behavioral effectiveness in retarded persons. *International Review of Research in Mental Retardation, 14,* 1–46.

Haywood, H. C., & Wachs, T. D. (1981). Intelligence, cognition, and individual differences. In M. J. Begab, H. C. Haywood, & H. Garber (Eds.), *Psychosocial influences in retarded performance: Issues and theories in development* (pp. 95–126). Baltimore: University Park Press.

Hazel, J. S., Schumaker, J. B., Sherman, J. A., & Sheldon-Wildgen, J. (1981). *ASSET: A social skills program for adolescents*. Champaign, IL: Research Press.

Heal, L. (1985). Methodology for community integration research. In R. H. Bruininks & K. C. Lakin (Eds.), *Living and learning in the least restrictive environment* (pp. 199–224). Baltimore: Brookes.

Heal, L. W., & Chadsey-Rusch, J. (1985). The lifestyle satisfaction scale (LSS): Assessing individuals' satisfaction with residence, community setting, and associated services. *Applied Research in Mental Retardation, 6,* 475–490.

Heal, L., & Fujiura, G. (1984). Methodological considerations in research on residential alternatives for developmentally disabled persons. *International Review of Research in Mental Retardation, 12,* 205–244.

Heal, L. W., Harner, C., Amado, A. R. N., & Chadsey-Rusch, J. (1993). *The Lifestyle Satisfaction Scale*. Columbus, OH: International Diagnostics System.

Heal, L. W., & Sigelman, C. K. (1990). Methodological issues in measuring the quality of life of individuals with mental retardation. In R. L. Schalock (Ed.), *Quality of life: Perspective and issues* (pp. 161–176). Washington, DC: American Association on Mental Retardation.

Heath, C. P., & Obrzut, J. E. (1984). Comparison of three measures of adaptive behavior. *American Journal of Mental Deficiency, 89*, 205–208.

Heath, C. P., & Obrzut, J. E. (1986). Adaptive behavior: Concurrent validity. *Journal of Psychoeducational Assessment, 4*, 53–59.

Hebb, D. O. (1949). *The organization of behavior: A neuropsychological theory.* New York: Wiley.

Heber, R. (1961). *A manual on terminology and classification in mental retardation* (Rev. ed.). Washington, DC: American Association on Mental Deficiency.

Heimberg, R. G., Mueller, G. P., Holt, D. A., & Liebowitz, M. R. (1992). Assessment of anxiety in social interaction and being observed by others: The Social Interaction Anxiety Scale and the Social Phobia Scale. *Behavior Therapy, 23*, 53–74.

Hellendoorn, J. (1990). Indications and goals for play therapy with the mentally retarded. In A. Dosen, A. van Gennep, & G. J. Zwanikken (Eds.), *Treatment of mental illness and behavioral disorder in the mentally retarded* (pp. 179–188). Leiden, the Netherlands: Logon Publications.

Hendrickson, J. M., & Frank, A. R. (1993). Engagement and performance feedback: Enhancing the classroom achievements of students with mild mental disabilities. In R. A. Gable & S. F. Warren (Eds.), *Strategies for teaching students with mild to severe disabilities* (pp. 11–47). Baltimore: Brookes.

Henshel, A. (1972). *The forgotten ones.* Austin: University of Texas Press.

Hersen, M., & Bellack, A. S. (1976). Social skills training for chronic psychiatric patients: Rationale, research findings and future directions. *Comprehensive Psychiatry, 17,* 559–580.

Herson, M., & Barlow, D. H. (1976). Single case experimental designs: Strategies for studying behavior change. Elmsford, NY: Pergamon Press.

Heshusius, L. (1982). Sexuality, intimacy, and persons we label mentally retarded: What they think—What we think. *Mental Retardation, 20,* 164–168.

Heward, W., Courson, F., & Narayan, J. (1989). Using choral responding to increase active student response. *Teaching Exceptional Children, 21,* 72–75.

Heyns, B. L. (1978). *Summer learning and the effects of schooling*. San Diego, CA: Academic Press.

Hill, B. K., Balow, E. A., & Bruininks, R. H. (1985). A national study of prescribed drugs in institutions and community residential facilities for mentally retarded people. *Psychopharmacology Bulletin, 21,* 279–284.

Hill, B. K., & Bruininks, R. H. (1984). Maladaptive behavior of mentally retarded individuals in residential facilities. *American Journal of Mental Deficiency, 88,* 380–387.

Hill, D. A., & Leary, M. R. (1994). *Moving on: A literature review and comparative study of symptoms of autism and movement disturbance.* Toronto, Ontario, Canada: Geneva Centre.

Hill, T. C., Holman, B. L., Lovett, R., O'Leary, D. H., Front, D., Magistretti, P., Zimmerman, R. E., Moore, S., Clouse, M. E., Wu, J. L., Lin, T. H., & Baldwin, R. M. (1982). Initial experience with SPECT (single-photon computerized tomography) of the brain using *N*-iso-propyl-(I-123)-*p*-iodoamphetamine: Concise communication. *Journal of Nuclear Medicine, 23,* 191–195.

Hill, T. C., Magistretti, P. L., Holman, B. L., Lee, R. G., O'Leary, D. H., Uren, R. F., Royal, H., Mayman, C. I., Kolodney, G. M., & Cluse, M. E. (1984). Assessment of regional cerebral blood flow (rCBF) in stroke using SPECT and *N*-iso-propyl-(I-123)-*p*-iodoamphetamine (IMP). *Stroke, 15,* 40–45.

Hingsburger, D. (1987). Sex counseling with the developmentally handicapped: The assessment and management of seven critical problems. *Psychiatric Aspects of Mental Retardation Reviews, 6,* 41–46.

Hinton, V. J., Dobkin, C. S., Halperin, J. M., Jenkins, E. C., Brown, W. T., Ding, X. H., Cohen, I. L., Rousseau, F., & Miezeyeski, C. M. (1992). Mode of inheritance influences behavioral expression of molecular control of cognitive deficits in female carriers of the fragile X syndrome. *American Journal of Medical Genetics, 43,* 87–95.

Hiss, H., & Kozak, M. J. (1991). Exposure treatment of obsessive–compulsive disorders in the mentally retarded. *The Behavior Therapist, 14,* 163–167.

Hodapp, R. M., Leckman, J. F., Dykens, E. M., Sparrow, S. S, Zelinsky, D. C., & Ort, S. I. (1992). K-ABC profiles in children with fragile X syndrome, Down syndrome, and nonspecific mental retardation. *American Journal of Mental Deficiency, 97,* 39–46.

Hodapp, R. M., & Zigler, E. (1986). Reply to Barnett's comments on the definition and classification of mental retardation. *American Journal of Mental Deficiency, 91,* 117–119.

Hollis, J. H., & St. Omer, V. V. (1972). Direct measurement of psychopharmacologic response: Effects of chlorpromazine on motor behavior of retarded children. *American Journal of Mental Deficiency, 76,* 397–407.

Holman, B. L., & Tumeh, S. S. (1990). Single-photon emission computed tomography (SPECT): Applications and potential. *Journal of the American Medical Association, 263,* 561–564.

Holroyd, J. (1974). The Questionnaire on Resources and Stress: An instrument to measure family response to a handicapped family member. *Journal of Community Psychology, 2,* 92–94.

Honig v. Doe, 108 S. Ct. 592 (1988).

Hooper, S. R., Boyd, T. A., Hynd, G. W., & Rubin, J. (1993). Definitional issues and neurobiological foundations of selected severe neurodevelopmental disorders. *Archives of Clinical Neuropsychology, 8,* 279–307.

Hope, P. L., Costello, A. M., Cady, E. B., Delpry, D. T., Tofts, P. S., Chu, A., Hamilton, P.A., Reynolds, E. O., & Wilkie, D. R. (1984). Cerebral energy metabolism studied with phosphorous NMR spectroscopy in normal and birth-asphyxiated infants. *Lancet, 2,* 366–370.

Hope, P. L., & Moorcraft, J. M. (1991). Magnetic resonance spectroscopy. *Clinics in Perinatology, 18,* 535–548.

Horn, E., & Fuchs, D. (1987). Using adaptive behavior in assessment and intervention: An overview. *Journal of Special Education, 21,* 11–26.

Horn, J. L. (1986). Intellectual ability concepts. In R. L. Sternberg (Ed.), *Advances in the psychology of human intelligence* (Vol. 3, pp. 35–77). Hillsdale, NJ: Erlbaum.

Horn, J. L. (1988). Thinking about human abilities. In J. R. Nesselroade & R. B. Cattell

(Eds.), *Handbook of multivariate experimental psychology* (2nd ed., pp. 645–685). New York: Plenum Press.

Horn, J. L., & Cattell, R. B. (1966). Refinement and test of the theory of fluid and crystallized intelligence. *Journal of Educational Psychology, 51*, 253–270.

Horn, J. L., & Hofer, S. M. (1992). Major abilities and development in the adult period. In R. J. Sternberg & C. A. Berg (Eds.), *Intellectual development* (pp. 44–99). Cambridge, England: Cambridge University Press.

Horn, S. D., & Horn, R. A. (1986). Reliability and validity of the Severity of Illness Index. *Medical Care, 24*, 159–178.

Horner, R. H., Dunlap, G., & Koegel, R. L. (1988). *Generalization and maintenance.* Baltimore: Brookes.

Horner, R. H., Jones, D., & Williams, J. A. (1985). A functional approach to teaching generalized street crossing. *Journal of the Association for Persons with Severe Handicaps, 10*, 71–78.

Horner, R. H., Sprague, J., & Wilcox, F. (1982). Constructing general case programs for community activities. In B. Wilcox & G. T. Bellamy (Eds.), *Design of high school programs for severely handicapped students* (pp. 61–98). Baltimore: Brookes.

Howland, R. H. (1992). Fluoxetine treatment of depression in mentally retarded adults. *Journal of Nervous and Mental Disease, 180*, 202–205.

Hudson, A., Melita, B., & Arnold, N. (1993). Brief report: A case study assessing the validity of facilitated communication. *Journal of Autism and Developmental Disorders, 23*, 165–173.

Hudson, A. M. (1982). Training parents of developmentally handicapped children: A component analysis. *Behavior Therapy, 13*, 325–333.

Hug, N., Barclay, A., Collins, H., & Lamp, R. (1978). Validity and factor structure of the preschool attainment record in Head Start children. *Journal of Psychology, 99*, 71–74.

Hughes, C., Harmer, M. L., Killian, D. J., & Niarhos, F. (1995). The effects of multiple-exemplar self-instructional training on high school students' generalized conversational interactions. *Journal of Applied Behavior Analysis, 28*, 201–218.

Hughes, C., Hwang, B., Kim, J., Eisenman, L. T., & Killian, D. J. (1995). Quality of life in applied research: A review and analysis of empirical measures. *American Journal of Mental Retardation, 99*, 623–641.

Hughes, J. G., Diggs, L. W., & Gillespie, C. E. (1940). The involvement of the nervous system in sickle-cell anemia. *Journal of Pediatrics, 17*, 166–184.

Huguenin, N. H., Weidenman, L. E., & Mulick, J. A. (1991). Programmed instruction. In J. L. Matson & J. A. Mulick (Eds.), *Handbook of mental retardation* (2nd ed., pp. 451–467). Elmsford, NY: Pergamon Press.

Hull, J. T., Keats, J. G., & Thompson, J. (1984). Community residential facilities for the mentally ill and the mentally retarded: Environmental quality and adaptive functioning. *Canadian Journal of Community Mental Health, 3*, 5–14.

Hunt, E. (1987). Science, technology, and intelligence. In R. R. Ronning, J. A. Glover, J. C. Conoley, & J. C. Witt (Eds.), *The influence of cognitive psychology on testing* (pp. 13–41). Hillsdale, NJ: Erlbaum.

Hunt, E. B. (1974). Quote the raven? Nevermore! In L. Gregg (Ed.), *Knowledge and cognition.* Potomac, MD: Erlbaum

Hunt, J. M. (1961). *Intelligence and experience*. New York: Ronald Press.

Hurley, A. D. (1989). Individual psychotherapy with mentally retarded individuals: A review and call for research. *Research in Developmental Disabilities, 10*, 261–275.

Hurley, A. D., & Hurley, F. J. (1985). Counseling and psychotherapy with mentally retarded clients: I. The initial interview. *Psychiatric Aspects of Mental Retardation Reviews, 5*, 22–26.

Hurley, A. D., & Hurley, F. J. (1987). Counseling and psychotherapy with mentally retarded clients: II. Establishing a relationship. *Psychiatric Aspects of Mental Retardation Reviews, 6*, 15–20.

Hurley, A. D., & Sovner, R. (1991). Cognitive behavioral therapy for depression in individuals with developmental disabilities. *The Habilitative Mental Healthcare Newsletter, 10*, 41–47.

Hurt, J., & Naglieri, J. A. (1992). Performance of delinquent and nondelinquent males on planning, attention, simultaneous, and successive cognitive processing tasks. *Journal of Clinical Psychology, 48,* 120–128.

Iams, J. D., Johnson, F. F., & Creasy, R. K. (1988). Prevention of preterm birth. *Clinical Obstetrics and Gynecology, 31,* 599–614.

Iivanainen, M., Launes, J., Pinko, H., Nikkinen, P., & Lindroth, L. (1990). Single-photon emission computed tomography of brain perfusion: Analysis of 60 pediatric cases. *Developmental Medicine and Child Neurology, 32,* 63–68.

Ilmer, S., Bruininks, R. H., & Hill, B. K. (1988). Discriminant analysis of intellectual ability groups with measures of adaptive behavior. *Journal of School Psychology, 26,* 293–296.

In re Quinlan, 70 N.J. 10, 355 A.2d 647 (1976).

Individuals With Disabilities Education Act of 1985, Pub. L. No. 99-457.

Individuals With Disabilities Education Act of 1990, Pub. L. No. 101-476, 104 Stat. 1103 (1990) [codified as amended at 20 U.S.C. §§ 1400–1485 (Supp. 2)].

Individuals With Disabilities Education Act Regulations, 34 C.F.R. §§ 300.7, 300.52 (1992).

Infant Health and Development Program. (1990). Enhancing the outcomes of low-birth-weight, premature infants: A multisite, randomized trial. *Journal of the American Medical Association, 263,* 3035–3042.

Inhelder, B. (1968). *The diagnosis of reasoning in the mentally retarded.* New York: Chandler.

Insel, P. M., & Moos, R. H. (1974). Psychological environments: Expanding the scope of human ecology. *American Psychologist, 29,* 179–188.

Intagliata, J., & Rinck, C. (1985). Psychoactive drug use in public and community residential facilities for mentally retarded persons. *Psychopharmacology Bulletin, 21,* 268–278.

Irion, J. (1988). *Mentally retarded inmates in Georgia's prison system.* Atlanta: Georgia Department of Corrections.

Isaacs, M. R. (1986). *Developing mental health programs for minority youth and their families.* Washington, DC: Georgetown University Child Development Center (CASSP Technical Assistance Center).

Isaacs, M. R., & Benjamin, M. P. (1991). *Towards a culturally competent system of care: Programs which utilize culturally competent principles.* Washington, DC: Georgetown University Child Development Center.

Ittenbach, R. F., Spiegel, A. N., McGrew, K. S., & Bruininks, R. H. (1992). Confirmatory factor analysis of early childhood ability measures within a model of personal competence. *Journal of School Psychology, 30,* 307–323.

Iwata, B. A., Dorsey, M. F., Slifer, K. J., Bauman, K. F., & Richman, G. S. (1982). Toward a functional analysis of self-injury. *Analysis and Intervention in Developmental Disabilities, 2,* 3–20.

Iwata, B. A., Pace, G. M., Cowdrey, G. E., & Miltonbeger, R. G. (1994). What makes extinction work: An analysis of procedural form and function. *Journal of Applied Behavior Analysis, 27,* 131–144.

Iwata, B. A., Pace, G. M., Dorsey, M. F., Zarcone, J. R., Vollmer, T. R., Smith, R. G., Rodgers, T. A., Lerman, D. C., Shore, B. A., Mazaleski, J. L., Goh, H., Cowdrey, G. E., Kalisher, M. J., McCosh, K. C., & Willis, K. D. (1994). The functions of self-injurious behavior: An experimental-epidemiological analysis. *Journal of Applied Behavior Analysis, 27,* 215–240.

Iwata, B. A., Vollmer, T. R., & Zarcone, J. R. (1990). The experimental (functional) analysis of behavior disorders: Methodology, applications, and limitations. In A. C. Repp & N. N. Singh (Eds.), *Perspectives on the use of non-aversive and aversive interventions for persons with developmental disabilities* (pp. 301–330). Sycamore, IL: Sycamore.

Iwata, B. A., Vollmer, T. R., Zarcone, J. R., & Rodgers, T. A. (1993). Treatment classification and selection based on behavioral function. In R. Van Houten & S. Axelrod (Eds.), *Behavior analysis and treatment* (pp. 101–125). New York: Plenum Press.

Jackson by Jackson v. Fort Stanton Hospital and Training School, 964 F.2d 980 (10th Cir. 1992).

Jackson, D. J., & Borgatta, E. F. (1981). Introduction: Measurement in sociological research. In D. J. Jackson & E. F. Borgatta (Eds.), *Factor analysis and measurement in sociological research: A multi-dimensional perspective* (pp. 3–7). Beverly Hills, CA: Sage.

Jackson, H. J. (1983). Current trends in the treatment of phobias in autistic and mentally retarded persons. *Australia and New Zealand Journal of Developmental Disabilities, 9,* 191–208.

Jackson, H. J., & Hooper, J. P. (1981). Some issues arising from the desensitization of a dog phobia in a mildly retarded female: Or should we take the bite out of the bark? *Australian Journal of Developmental Disabilities, 7,* 9–16.

Jackson, H. J., & King, N. J. (1982). The therapeutic management of an autistic child's phobia using laughter as the anxiety inhibitor. *Behavioral Psychotherapy, 10,* 364–369.

Jacob, H. (1984). *Using published data: Errors and remedies.* Beverly Hills, CA: Sage.

Jacob, T., & Tennenbaum, D. L. (1988). *Family assessment: Rationale, methods, and future directions.* New York: Plenum Press.

Jacobs, F. H., & Walker, D. W. (1978). Pediatricians and the Education for All Handicapped Children Act of 1975 (Public Law 94-142). *Pediatrics, 61,* 135–139.

Jacobson, J. W. (1982). Problem behavior and psychiatric impairment in a developmentally disabled population: I. Behavior frequency. *Applied Research in Mental Retardation, 3,* 121–139.

Jacobson, J. W. (1990). Assessing the prevalence of psychiatric disorders in a developmentally disabled population. In E. Dibble & D. B. Gray (Eds.), *Assessment of behavior problems in persons with mental retardation living in the community* (DHHS Publication No. ADM 90-1642). Rockville, MD: U.S. Department of Health and Human Services.

Jacobson, J. W. (1993, May). *Facilitated communication: Empirical data and considerations for practice.* Paper presented at the annual conference of the American Association on Mental Retardation, Washington, DC.

Jacobson, J. W., & Janicki, M. P. (1983). Observed prevalence of multiple developmental disabilities. *Mental Retardation, 21,* 87–94.

Jacobson, J. W., & Janicki, M. P. (1987). Needs for professional and generic services within a developmental disabilities service system. In J. A. Mulick & R. F. Anotonak (Eds.), *Transitions in mental retardation* (Vol. 2, pp. 23–45). Norwood, NJ: Ablex.

Jacobson, J. W., & Mulick, J. A. (1995). The misapprehension of merit and ability: The bell curve, egalitarianism, and early intervention. *Psychology in Mental Retardation and Developmental Disabilities, 20*(3), 11–17.

Jacobson, J. W., & Schwartz, A. A. (1991). Evaluating living situations of people with developmental disabilities. In J. L. Matson & J. A. Mulick (Eds.), *Handbook of mental retardation* (2nd ed., pp. 35–62). New York: Plenum Press.

Jacobson, N. S., & Revenstorf, D. (1988). Statistics for assessing the clinical significance of psychotherapy techniques: Issues, problems, and new developments. *Behavioral Assessment, 10,* 133–145.

Jakab, I. (1978). Basal ganglia calcification and psychosis in mongolism. *European Neurology, 17,* 300–314.

Jamieson, J. (1993). *Adults with mental handicap: Their quality of life.* Vancouver: British Columbia Ministry of Social Services.

Janicki, M. P., & Jacobson, J. W. (1982). The character of developmental disabilities in New York State: Preliminary observations. *International Journal of Rehabilitation Research, 5,* 191–202.

Janicki, M. P., & Jacobson, J. W. (1986). Generational trends in sensory, physical, and behavioral abilities among older mentally retarded persons. *American Journal of Mental Deficiency, 90,* 490–500.

Janoff-Bulman, R. (1992). *Shattered assumptions: Toward a new psychology of trauma.* New York: Free Press.

Jenkinson, J. C. (1993). Who shall decide? The relevance of theory and research to decision-making by people with intellectual disability. *Disability, Handicap, and Society, 8,* 361–375.

Johnson, B. F., & Cuvo, A. J. (1981). Teaching mentally retarded adults to cook. *Behavior Modification, 5,* 187–202.

Johnston, J. M., & Pennypacker, H. S. (1993). *Strategies and tactics of behavioral research* (2nd ed.). Hillsdale, NJ: Erlbaum.

Joint Commission on Accreditation of Hospitals. (1994). *Accreditation manual for hospitals.* Chicago, IL: Author.

Jones, D. P. H. (1994). Autism, facilitated communication, and allegations of child abuse and neglect. *Child Abuse and Neglect, 19,* 491–493.

Jones, K. L. (Ed.). (1988). *Smith's recognizable patterns of human malformation* (4th ed.). Philadelphia: W. B. Saunders

Jöreskog, K. G., & Sörbom, D. (1989). *LISREL 7: A guide to the program and applications* (2nd ed.). Chicago: SPSS.

Jöreskog, K. G., & Sörbom, D. (1993). *LISREL 8: Structural equation modeling with the SIMPLIS command language.* Chicago: Scientific Software.

Kaeser, F. (1991). *Understanding and managing the sexual needs and expressions of people with profound and severe developmental disabilities.* Columbus: The Ohio State University.

Kagan, L. (1991). Moving from here to there: Rethinking continuity in transitions in early care and education. In B. Spodek & O. Saracho (Eds.), *The yearbook in early childhood education* (Vol. 2, pp. 132–151). New York: New York Teachers College.

Kahn, J. V. (1983). Sensorimotor period and adaptive behavior development of severely and profoundly mentally retarded children. *American Journal of Mental Deficiency, 88,* 69–75.

Kahn, J. V. (1992). Predicting adaptive behavior of severely and profoundly mentally retarded children with early cognitive measures. *Journal of Intellectual Disability Research, 36,* 101–114.

Kail, R. (1992). General slowing of information-processing by persons with mental retardation. *American Journal of Mental Retardation, 97,* 333–341.

Kalachnik, J. E., & Nord, G. B. (1985). *Psychotropic medication monitoring.* St. Paul: Minnesota Department of Human Services.

Kalachnik, J. E., & Sprague, R. L. (1993). The Dyskinesia Identification System: Condensed User Scale (DISCUS): Reliability, validity, and a total score cut-off for mentally ill and mentally retarded populations. *Journal of Clinical Psychology, 49,* 177–189.

Kalachnik, J. E., & Sprague, R. L. (1994). How well do physicians, pharmacists, and psychologists assess tardive dyskinesia movements? *Annals of Pharmacotherapy, 28,* 185–190.

Kalachnik, J. E., Sprague, R. L., & Kalles, R. (1991). *Tardive dyskinesia monitoring and the Dyskinesia Identification System: Condensed User Scale (DISCUS).* East Hanover, NJ: Sandoz.

Kameenui, E. J., & Simmons, D. C. (1990). *Designing instructional strategies: The prevention of academic learning problems.* Columbus, OH: Merrill.

Kamphaus, R. W. (1987). Conceptual and psychometric issues in the assessment of adaptive behavior. *Journal of Special Education, 21,* 27–35.

Kark, J. A., Posey, D. M., Schumacher, H. R., & Ruehle, C. J. (1987). Sickle-cell trait as a risk factor for sudden death in physical training. *New England Journal of Medicine, 317,* 781–787.

Karsh, K. G., & Repp, A. C. (1992). The task demonstration model: A concurrent model for teaching groups of students with severe disabilities. *Exceptional Children, 59,* 54–67.

Karsh, K. G., Repp, A. C., & Lenz, M. W. (1990). A comparison of the task demonstration model and the standard prompting hierarchy in teaching word identification to persons with moderate retardation. *Research in Developmental Disabilities, 11,* 395–410.

Kastner, T., Friedman, D. L., O'Brien, D. R., & Pond, W. S. (1990). Health care and mental illness in persons with mental retardation. *The Habilitative Mental Healthcare Newsletter, 9,* 17–24.

Katz, K. S. (1989). Strategies for infant assessment: Implications of P. L. 99–457. *Topics in Early Childhood Special Education, 9,* 99–109.

Katz-Garris, L., Hadley, T. J., Garris, R. P., & Barnhill, B. (1980). A factor analytic study of the Adaptive Behavior Scale. *Psychological Reports, 47,* 807–814.

Kaufman, A. S., & Kaufman, N. L. (1983). *Kaufman Assessment Battery for Children.* Circle Pines, MN: American Guidance Service.

Kavanaugh, K. (1988). Infants weighing less than 500 grams at birth: Providing parental support. *Journal of Perinatal and Neonatal Nursing, 2,* 58–66.

Kazdin, A. E. (1977). Assessing the clinical or applied importance of behavior change through social validation. *Behavior Modification, 1,* 427–451.

Keith, K. D. (1990). Quality of life: Issues in community integration. In R. L. Schalock (Ed.), *Quality of life: Perspectives and issues* (pp. 93–100). Washington, DC., American Association on Mental Retardation.

Keltner, B., & Ramey, S. L. (1992). The family. *Current Opinion in Psychiatry, 5,* 638–644.

Keltner, B., & Ramey, S. L. (1993). Family issues. *Current Opinion in Psychiatry, 6,* 629–634.

Kendler, H. H. (1993). Psychology and the ethics of public policy. *American Psychologist, 48,* 1046–1053.

Kennedy, C. H., & Itkonen, T. (1993). Effects of setting events on the problem behavior of students with severe disabilities. *Journal of Applied Behavior Analysis, 26,* 321–328.

Kiely, M. (1987). The prevalence of mental retardation. *Epidemiologic Reviews, 9,* 194–218.

King, R. D., Raynes, R. V., & Tizard, J. (1971). *Patterns of residential care: Sociological studies in institutions for handicapped children.* London: Routledge & Kegan Paul.

Kinney v. Yerusalem, 812 F. Supp. 547 (E.D. Pa. 1993).

Kirby, J. R., & Das, J. P. (1978). Skills underlying Coloured Progressive Matrices. *Alberta Journal of Educational Research, 24,* 94–99.

Kirby, J. R., & Lawson, M. J. (1983). Effects of strategy training on progressive matrices performance. *Contemporary Educational Psychology, 8,* 127–139.

Kirby, K. C., & Bickel, W. K. (1988). Toward an explicit analysis of generalization: A stimulus control interpretation. *The Behavior Analyst, 11,* 115–129.

Kitchener, K. S., Lynch, C. L., Fischer, K. W., & Wood, P. K. (1993). Developmental range of reflective judgment: The effect of contextual support and practice on developmental stage. *Developmental Psychology, 29,* 893–906.

Klausmeier, H. J., & Ripple, R. E. (1971). *Learning and human abilities: Educational psychology* (3rd ed.). New York: Harper & Row.

Klein, N. K., & Campbell, P. (1991). Preparing personnel to serve at risk infants and disabled infants, toddlers, and preschoolers. In S. J. Meisels & J. P. Shonkoff (Eds.), *Handbook of early childhood intervention* (pp. 679–699). Cambridge, England: Cambridge University Press.

Klein, S. D. (1993). The challenge of communicating with parents. *Developmental and Behavioral Pediatrics, 14,* 184–191.

Kleinberg, J., & Galligan, B. (1983). Effects of deinstitutionalization on adaptive behavior of mentally retarded adults. *American Journal of Mental Deficiency, 88,* 21–27.

Klewe, L. (1993). An empirical evaluation of spelling boards as a means of communication for the multihandicapped. *Journal of Autism and Developmental Disorders, 23,* 559–566.

Klindworth, L. M., Dokecki, P. R., Kupstas, F. D., & Baumeister, A. A. (1989). AIDS and developmental disabilities in children: Education and policy issues. *AIDS Education and Prevention, 1,* 291–302.

Knitzer, J. (1982). *Unclaimed children: The failure of public responsibility to children and adolescents in need of mental health services.* Washington, DC: Children's Defense Fund.

Kobe, F. H., Mulick, J. A., Rash, T. A., & Martin, J. (1994). Nonambulatory persons with profound mental retardation: Physical, developmental and behavioral characteristics. *Research in Developmental Disabilities, 15,* 413–423.

Koch, R., Azen, C., Friedman, E. G., & Williamson, M. L. (1984). Paired comparisons between early treated PKU children and their matched sibling controls on intelligence and school achievement test results at eight years of age. *Journal of Inherited Metabolic Disease, 7,* 86–90.

Koegel, L. K., Koegel, R. L., & Parks, D. R. (1990). *How to teach self-management to people with severe disabilities: A training manual.* Washington, DC: U.S. Department of Education, Office of Educational Research and Improvement, Educational Resources Information Center.

Koegel, L. K., Koegel, R. L., & Parks, D. R. (1992). *How to teach self-management to people with severe disabilities.* Santa Barbara: University of California.

Koegel, R. L., Dyer, D., & Bell, L. K. (1987). The influence of child-preferred activities on autistic children's social behavior. *Journal of Applied Behavior Analysis, 20,* 243–252.

Koegel, R. L., & Koegel, L. K. (1990). Extended reduction in stereotypic behavior through self-management in multiple community settings. *Journal of Applied Behavior Analysis, 23*, 119–127.

Koegel, R. L., & Rincover, A. (1977). Research on the difference between generalization and maintenance in extra-therapy settings. *Journal of Applied Behavior Analysis, 10*, 1–12.

Koegel, R. L., Schreibman, L., Johnson, J., O'Neill, R. E., & Dunlap, G. (1984). Collateral effects of parent training of families with autistic children. In R. F. Dangel & R. A. Polster (Eds.), *Parent training: Foundations of research and practice* (pp. 358–378). New York: Guilford Press.

Kohen, D. (1992). Eltoprazine for aggression in mental handicap. *Lancet, 341*, 628–629.

Kolb, B. Y., & Whishaw, I. Q. (1990). *Fundamentals of human neuropsychology*. New York: Freeman.

Konarski, E. A., Favell, J. E., & Favell, J. E. (1993). *Manual for the assessment and treatment of the behavior disorders of people with mental retardation*. Morganton, NC: Western Carolina Center Foundation.

Konstantareas, M. M., & Homatidis, S. (1989). Assessing child symptom severity and stress in parents of autistic children. *Journal of Child Psychology and Psychiatry, 30*, 459–470.

Korinek, L., & Polloway, E. A. (1993). Social skills: Review and implications for instruction for students with mild mental retardation. In F. A. Gable & S. F. Warren (Eds.), *Strategies for teaching students with mild to severe mental retardation* (pp. 71–97). Baltimore: Brookes.

Kovitz, K. E. (1976). Comparing group and individual methods for training parents in child management techniques. In E. J. Mash, L. D. Hamerlynhk, & L. C. Handy (Eds.), *Behavior modification approaches to parenting* (pp. 124–138). New York: Brunner/Mazel.

Krauss, M. W., & Jacobs, F. (1990). Family assessment: Purposes and techniques. In S. J. Meisels & J. P. Shonkoff (Eds.), *Handbook of early childhood intervention* (pp. 303–325). Cambridge, England: Cambridge University Press.

Krauss, M. W., & Seltzer, M. M. (1993). Coping strategies among older mothers of adults with retardation: A life-span developmental perspective. In A. P. Turnbull, J. M. Patterson, S. K. Behr, D. L. Murphy, J. G. Marquis, & M. J. Blue-Banning (Eds.), *Cognitive coping, families, and disability* (pp. 173–182). Baltimore: Brookes.

Krauss, M. W., Simeonsson, R. J., & Ramey, S. L. (Eds.). (1989). Research on families [Special issue]. *American Journal of Mental Retardation, 94*, 195–346.

Krupski, A. (1977). The role of attention in the reaction time performance of mentally retarded adolescents. *American Journal of Mental Deficiency, 82*, 79–83.

Kuenzel, M. W. (1939). Social status of foster families engaged in community care and training of mentally deficient children. *American Journal of Mental Deficiency, 44*, 244–253.

La Plante, M. D. (1989). Disability in basic life activities across the lifespan. *Disability Services Report I.* San Francisco: University of California, Institute for Health and Aging.

Lachman, R., Lachman, J., & Butterfield, E. (1979). *Cognitive psychology and information processing: An introduction*. Hillsdale, NJ: Erlbaum.

Lamb, M. E. (1985). The changing role of fathers. In M. E. Lamb (Ed.), *The father's role: Applied perspectives* (pp. 3–28). New York: Wiley.

Lambert, N. M. (1979). Contributions of school classification, sex, and ethnic status to adaptive behavior measurement. *Journal of School Psychology, 17*, 3–16.

Lambert, N. (1986). Evidence on age and ethnic status bias in factor scores and the comparison score for the AAMD Adaptive Behavior Scale—School Edition. *Journal of School Psychology, 24*, 143–153.

Lambert, N., & Hartsough, C. S. (1981). Development of a simplified diagnostic scoring method for the school version of the Adaptive Behavior Scale. *American Journal of Mental Deficiency, 86*, 138–147.

Lambert, N. M., & Nicoll, R. C. (1976). Dimensions of adaptive behavior of retarded and nonretarded public school children. *American Journal of Mental Deficiency, 81*, 135–146.

Lancioni, G. E. (1983). Using pictorial representations as communication means with low-functioning children. *Journal of Autism and Developmental Disorders, 13,* 87–105.

Lancioni, G. E., & Smeets, P. M. (1986). Procedures and parameters of errorless discrimination training with developmentally impaired individuals. *International Review of Research in Mental Retardation, 14,* 135–161.

Lancioni, G. E., Smeets, P. M., Ceccarani, P. S., Capodaglio, L., & Campanari, G. (1984). Effects of gross motor activities on the severe self-injurious tantrums of multihandicapped individuals. *Applied Research in Mental Retardation, 5,* 471–482.

Lancy, D. F., & Strathern, A. J. (1981). Making two's: Pairing as an alternative to the taxonomic mode or representation. *American Anthropologist, 83,* 773–795.

Landau, R. J. (1993). Legislation and regulation in the age of the "new" aversives. *Child and Adolescent Mental Health Care, 3,* 19–29.

Landesman, S. (1986). Toward a taxonomy of home environments. *International Review of Research in Mental Retardation, 14,* 259–289.

Landesman, S. (1987). The changing structure and function of institutions: A search for optimal group care environments. In S. Landesman & P. Vietze (Eds.), *Living environments and mental retardation* (pp. 79–126). Washington, DC: American Association on Mental Retardation.

Landesman, S., Jaccard, J., & Gunderson, V. (1991). The family environment: The combined influence of family behavior, goals, strategies, resources, and individual experiences. In M. Lewis & S. Feinman (Eds.), *Social influences and socialization in infancy* (pp. 63–96). New York: Plenum Press.

Landesman, S., & Ramey, C. (1989). Developmental psychology and mental retardation: Integrating scientific principles with treatment practices. *American Psychologist, 44,* 409–415.

Landesman, S., & Vietze, P. (Eds.). (1987). *Living environments and mental retardation.* Washington, DC: American Association on Mental Retardation.

Landesman-Dwyer, S. (1981). Living in the community. *American Journal of Mental Deficiency, 86,* 223–234.

Landesman-Dwyer, S., & Butterfield, E. C. (1983). Mental retardation: Developmental issues in cognitive and social adaptation. In M. Lewis (Ed.), *Origins of intelligence: Infancy and early childhood* (2nd ed., pp. 299–322). New York: Plenum Press.

Landry, S. H., Garner, P. W., Pirie, D., & Swank, P. R. (1994). Effects of social context and mothers' requesting strategies on Down's syndrome children's social responsiveness. *Developmental Psychology, 30,* 293–302.

Laosa, L. M., & Sigel, I. E. (Eds.). (1982). *Families as learning environments for children.* New York: Plenum Press.

Laptook, A. R. (1990). Magnetic resonance: Safety considerations and future directions. *Seminars in Perinatology, 14,* 189–192.

LaQuey, A. (1981). *Adult Performance Level Adaptation and Modification Project.* Austin, TX: Educational Service Center, Region 13.

Lashley, K. S. (1929). *Brain mechanisms in intelligence.* Chicago: University of Chicago Press.

Lattimore, J., Stephens, T. E., Favell, J. E., & Risley, T. R. (1984). Increasing direct care staff compliance to individualized physical therapy body positioning prescriptions: Prescriptive checklists. *Mental Retardation, 22,* 79–84.

Lawson, M. J., & Kirby, J. R. (1981). Training in information processing algorithms. *British Journal of Educational Psychology, 51,* 321–335.

Lazarus, R. S., & Folkman, S. (1984). *Stress, appraisal, and coping.* New York: Springer.

Ledbetter, D. H., Zachary, J. M., Simpson, J. L., Golbus, M. S., Pergament, E., Jackson, L., Mahoney, R. J., Desnick, R. J., Schulman, J., Copeland, K. L., Verlinsky, Y., Yang-feng, T., Schonberg, S. A., Babus, A., Tharapel, A., Dorfmann, H. A., Lubs, G. G., Rhoads, G. G., Fowler, S. E., & de la Cruz, F. (1992). Cytogenetic results from the U.S. collaborative study of CVS. *Prenatal Diagnosis, 12,* 317–345.

Lee, R. G., Hill, T. C., Holman, B. L., & Clouse, M. E. (1982). *N*-iso-propyl-(I-123)-*p*-iodoamphetamine brain scans with single-photon emission tomography: Discordance with transmission computed tomography. *Radiology, 145,* 795–799.

Lee, T. F. (1991). *The Human Genome Project: Cracking the genetic code of life.* New York: Plenum Press.

Leffert, J. S., & Siperstein, G. (1994). *Social competence and mental retardation: Assessment of social cognitive processes and their relationship to social behavior.* Unpublished manuscript, University of Massachussetts, Boston.

Leland, H. (1991). Adaptive behavior scales. In J. L. Matson & J. A. Mulick (Eds.), *Handbook of mental retardation* (pp. 211–221). Elmsford, NY: Pergamon Press.

Leland, H. (1992, May). *Adaptive behavior or adaptive skills? Dimensions in coping development.* Paper presented at the annual meeting of the American Association on Mental Retardation.

Leland, H., & Smith, E. D. (1965). *Play therapy with mentally subnormal children.* New York: Grune & Stratton.

Lennox, D. B., & Miltenberger, R. G. (1990). On the conceptualization of treatment acceptability. *Education and Training in Mental Retardation, 25,* 211–224.

Leon, J. A., & Pepe, H. J. (1983). Self-instructional training: Cognitive behavior modification for remediating arithmetic deficits. *Exceptional Children, 50,* 54–60.

Leva, R. A. (1976). Relationship among the self-directive, responsibility, and socialization domains of the Adaptive Behavior Scale. *American Journal of Mental Deficiency, 81,* 297–298.

Levine, S., & Elzey, F. F. (1968). Factor analysis of the San Francisco Vocational Competency Scale. *American Journal of Mental Deficiency, 73,* 509–513.

Levitas, A., & Gilson, S. (1987). Transference, countertransference, and resistance. *National Association for the Dually Diagnosed Newsletter, 1,* 2–7.

Levitas, A., & Gilson, S. (1989). Psychodynamic psychotherapy with mildly and moderately retarded patients. In R. Fletcher & F. J. Menolascino (Eds.), *Mental retardation and mental illness: Assessment, treatment, and service for the dually diagnosed* (pp. 71–109). Lexington, MA: Lexington Books.

Lewis, A. J. (1976). *Mechanisms of neurological disease.* Boston: Little, Brown.

Lewis, M. H. (1993). Recent advances in pharmacotherapy. *Current Opinion in Psychiatry, 6,* 659–664.

Lewis, M. H., & Baumeister, A. A. (1982). Stereotyped mannerisms in mentally retarded persons: Animal models and theoretical analyses. *International Review of Research in Mental Retardation, 11,* 123–161.

Lewis, M. H., Bodfish, J. W., Powell, S. B., & Golden, R. N. (1995). Clomipramine treatment for stereotypy and related repetitive movement disorders associated with mental retardation. *American Journal of Mental Retardation, 100,* 299–312.

Lewis, M. H., & MacLean, W. E., Jr. (1982). Issues in treating emotional disorders of the mentally retarded. In J. L. Matson & R. P. Barrett (Eds.), *Psychopathology of the mentally retarded* (pp. 1–36). New York: Grune & Stratton.

Lewis, M. H., & Mailman, R. B. (1988). Psychotropic drug blood levels: Measurement and relation to behavioral outcome in mentally retarded persons. In M. Aman & N. Singh (Eds.), *Psychopharmacology of the developmental disabilities* (pp. 58–81). New York: Springer-Verlag.

Lewis, M. H., Steer, R. A., Favell, J., McGimsey, J., Clontz, L., Trivette, C., Jodry, W., Schroeder, S., Kanoy, R., & Mailman, R. B. (1986). Thioridazine metabolism and effects on stereotyped behavior in mentally retarded patients. *Psychopharmacology Bulletin, 22,* 1040–1044.

Lezak, M. (1995). *Neuropsychological assessment* (3rd ed.). New York: Oxford University Press.

Liberman, R. P. (1983). Guest editor's preface. *Analysis and Intervention in Developmental Disabilities, 3,* iii–iv.

Libet, J., & Lewinsohn, P. (1973). The concept of social skills with special reference to the behavior of depressed persons. *Journal of Consulting and Clinical Psychology, 40,* 304–312.

Lilienfeld, A. M., & Pasamanick, B. (1956). The association of maternal and fetal factors with the development of mental deficiency: II. Relationship to maternal age, birth order, previous reproductive loss and degree of mental deficiency. *American Journal of Mental Deficiency, 60,* 557–569.

Lindsay, W. R., Howells, L., & Pitcaithly, D. (1993). Cognitive therapy for depression with individuals with intellectual disabilities. *British Journal of Medical Psychology, 66,* 135–141.

Lindsay, W. R., & Michie, A. M. (1988). Adaptation of the Zung Self-Rating Anxiety Scale for people with a mental handicap. *Journal of Mental Deficiency Research, 32,* 485–490.

Linehan, M. M. (1980). Content validity: Its relevance to behavioral assessment. *Behavioral Assessment, 2,* 147–160.

Linscheid, T. R., Haertel, F., & Cooley, N. (1993). Are aversive procedures durable: A five year follow-up of three cases treated with contingent electric shock. *Child and Adolescent Mental Health Care, 3,* 1–10.

Linscheid, T. R., Iwata, B. A., Ricketts, R. W., & Williams, D. E. (1990). Clinical evaluation of the self-injurious behavior inhibiting system (SIBIS). *Journal of Applied Behavior Analysis, 23,* 53–78.

Linscheid, T. R., Rasnake, L. K., Tarnowski, K. J., & Mulick, J. A. (1989). Behavioral assessment. In J. Luiselli (Ed.), *Behavioral medicine and developmental disabilities* (pp. 21–44). New York: Springer-Verlag.

Lloyd, J. W., Singh, N. N., & Repp, A. C. (Eds.). (1991). *The regular education initiative: Alternative perspectives on concepts, issues, and models.* Sycamore, IL: Sycamore Publishing.

Lloyd, J. W., Talbott, E., Tankersley, M., & Trent, S. C. (1993). Using cognitive-behavioral techniques to improve classroom performance of student with mild mental retardation. In R. A. Gable & S. F. Warren (Eds.), *Strategies for teaching students with mild to severe mental retardation* (pp. 99–116). Baltimore: Brookes.

Lochman, J. E., & Curry, J. F. (1986). Effects of social problem-solving training and self-instruction training with aggressive boys. *Journal of Clinical Child Psychology, 15,* 159–164.

Lochman, J. E., Lampron, L. B., Gemmer, T. C., & Harris, S. R. (1987). Anger coping intervention with aggressive children: A guide to implementation in school settings. *Innovations in clinical practice: A source book, 6,* 339–356.

Loehlin, J. C. (1992). *Latent variable models: An introduction to factor, path, and structural analysis* (2nd ed.). Hillsdale, NJ: Erlbaum.

Lovaas, O. I. (1987). Behavioral treatment and normal educational and intellectual functioning in young autistic children. *Journal of Clinical and Consulting Psychology, 55,* 3–9.

Lovaas, O. I., Ackerman, A. B., Alexander, D., Firestone, P., Perkins, J., & Young, D. (1980). *Teaching developmentally disabled children: The me book.* Austin, TX: Pro-Ed.

Lovaas, O. I., & Schreibman, L. (1971). Stimulus overselectivity of autistic children in a two stimulus situation. *Behavior Research and Therapy, 9,* 305–310.

Lovaas, O. I., & Simmons, J. Q. (1969). Manipulation of self-destruction in three retarded children. *Journal of Applied Behavior Analysis, 2,* 143–157.

Lovaas, O. I., & Smith, T. (1989). A comprehensive behavioral theory of autistic children: Paradigm for research and treatment. *Journal of Behavior Therapy and Experimental Psychiatry, 20,* 17–29.

Love, S. R., Matson, J. L., & West, D. (1990). Mothers as effective therapists for autistic children's phobias. *Journal of Applied Behavior Analysis, 23,* 379–385.

Loveland, K. A., & Kelley, M. L. (1988). Development of adaptive behavior in adolescents and young adults with autism and Down syndrome. *American Journal of Mental Retardation, 93,* 84–92.

Loveland, K. A., & Kelley, M. L. (1991). Development of adaptive behavior in preschoolers with autism or Down syndrome. *American Journal of Mental Retardation, 96,* 13–20.

Lovett, D. L., & Haring, K. A. (1989). The effects of self-management training on the daily living of adults with mental retardation. *Education and Training in Mental Retardation, 24,* 306–323.

Lowe, M. R., & Cautela, J. R. (1978). A self-report measure of social skills. *Behavior Modification, 9,* 535–544.

Lowry, M. A., & Sovner, R. (1991a). Severe behavior problems associated with rapid cycling bipolar disorder in two adults with profound mental retardation. *Journal of Intellectual Disability Research, 36*, 269–281.

Lowry, M. A., & Sovner, R. (1991b). The functional significance of problem behavior: A key to effective treatment. *The Habilitative Mental Healthcare Newsletter, 10*, 119–123.

Lubs, H. A. (1969). A marker X chromosome. *American Journal of Human Genetics, 21*, 231.

Luchins, D. J., & Dojka, D. (1989). Lithium and propranolol in aggression and self-injurious behavior in the mentally retarded. *Psychopharmacology Bulletin, 25*, 372–375.

Luckasson, R., Coulter, D. L., Polloway, E. A., Reiss, S., Schalock, R. L., Snell, M. E., Spitalnik, D. M., & Stark, J. A. (1992). *Mental retardation: Definition, classification, and system of supports* (9th ed.). Washington, DC: American Association on Mental Retardation.

Ludwig, A., & Hingsburger, D. (1987). Preparation for counseling and psychotherapy: Teaching about feelings. *Psychiatric Aspects of Mental Retardation Reviews, 8*, 2–7.

Luiselli, J. K. (Ed.). (1989). *Behavioral medicine and developmental disabilities*. New York: Springer-Verlag.

Luria, A. R. (1966). *Human brain and psychological processes*. New York: Harper & Row.

Luria, A. R. (1973). *The working brain: An introduction to neuropsychology*. New York: Basic Books.

Luria, A. R. (1980). *Higher cortical functions in man*. New York: Basic Books.

Lynch, E. W., & Hanson, M. J. (1992). *Developing cross-cultural competence*. Baltimore: Brookes.

MacDonald, L., & Barton, L. E. (1986). Measuring severity of behavior: A revision of part II of the Adaptive Behavior Scale. *American Journal of Mental Deficiency, 90*, 418–424.

Mace, F. C., & Belfiore, P. (1990). Behavioral momentum in the treatment of escape-motivated stereotypy. *Journal of Applied Behavior Analysis, 23*, 507–514.

Mace, F. C., Hock, M. L., Lalli, J. S., West, B. J., Belfiore, P., & Brown, D. K. (1988). Behavioral momentum in the treatment of noncompliance. *Journal of Applied Behavior Analysis, 21*, 123–141.

Mace, F. C., & Lalli, J. S. (1991). Linking descriptive and experimental analyses in the treatment of bizarre speech. *Journal of Applied Behavior Analysis, 24*, 553–562.

Mace, F. C., Lalli, J. S., Lalli, E. P., & Shea, M. C. (1993). Functional analysis and treatment of aberrant behavior. In R. Van Houten & S. Axelrod (Eds.), *Behavior analysis and treatment* (pp. 75–99). New York: Plenum Press.

Mace, F. C., Page, T. J., Ivancic, M. T., & O'Brien, S. (1986). Analysis of environmental determinants of aggression and disruption on mentally retarded children. *Applied Research in Mental Retardation, 7*, 203–221.

MacEachron, A. E. (1979). Mentally retarded offenders: Prevalence and characteristics. *American Journal of Mental Deficiency, 84*, 165–176.

MacKenzie-Keating, S. E., & McDonald, L. (1990). Overcorrection: Reviewed, revisited and revised. *The Behavior Analyst*, 13, 39–48.

MacKinnon-Lewis, C., Volling, B. L., Lamb, M. E., Dechman, K., Rabiner, D., & Curtner, M. E. (1994). A cross-contextual analysis of boys' social competence: From family to school. *Developmental Psychology, 30*, 325–333.

Mackintosh, N. J. (1977). Stimulus control attentional factors. In W. K. Honig & J. E. R. Staddon (Eds.), *Handbook of operant behavior* (pp. 481–513). Englewood Cliffs, NJ: Prentice Hall.

MacMillan, D. L. (1982). *Mental retardation in school and society* (2nd ed.). Boston: Little, Brown.

MacMillan, D. L. (1988). Issues in mild mental retardation. *Education and Training in Mental Retardation, 23*, 273–284.

MacMillan, D. L. (1993). Development of operational definitions in mental retardation: Similarities and differences with the field of learning disabilities. In G. R. Lyon, D. B. Gray, J. F. Kavanaugh, & N. A. Krasnegor (Eds.), *Better understanding learning disabilities: New views from research and their implications for education and public policies* (pp. 117–152). Baltimore: Brookes.

MacMillan, D. L., Gresham, F. M., & Siperstein, G. N. (1993). Conceptual and psychometric concerns about the 1992 AAMR definition of mental retardation. *American Journal of Mental Retardation, 98*, 325–335.

MacMillan, D. L., Gresham, F. M., & Siperstein, G. N. (1995). Heightened concerns over the 1992 AAMR definition: Advocacy versus precision. *American Journal of Mental Retardation, 100*, 87–97.

MacMillan, D. L., Meyers, C. E., & Morrison, G. M. (1980). System-identification of mildly mentally retarded children: Implications for interpreting and conducting research. *American Journal of Mental Deficiency, 85*, 108–115.

Madden, J., Levenstein, P., & Levenstein, S. (1976). Longitudinal IQ outcomes of the Mother-Child Home Program. *Child Development, 46*, 1015–1025.

Madden, N. A., Russo, D. C., & Cataldo, M. F. (1980). Environmental influences on mouthing in children with lead intoxication. *Journal of Pediatric Psychology, 5*, 207–216.

Magnusson, D. (Ed.). (1981). *Toward a psychology of situations: An interactional perspective*. Hillsdale, NJ: Erlbaum.

Magrab, P. R., & Schmidt, L. M. (1980). Interdisciplinary collaboration: A prelude to coordinated services delivery. In J. O. Elder & P. R. Magrab (Eds.), *Coordinating services to handicapped children: A handbook for interagency collaboration* (pp. 13–24). Baltimore: Brookes.

Malone, D. R., & Christian, W. P. (1975). Adaptive Behavior Scale as a screening measure for special education placement. *American Journal of Mental Deficiency, 79*, 367–371.

Mandlebaum, L. H. (1989). Reading. In J. R. Patten, E. A. Polloway, & L. R. Argent (Eds.), *Best practices in mild mental disabilities* (pp. 89–107). Reston, VA: Council for Exceptional Children.

Mansdorf, I. J. (1976). Eliminating fear in a mentally retarded adult by behavioral hierarchies and operant techniques. *Journal of Behavior Therapy and Experimental Psychiatry, 7*, 189–190.

Mansdorf, I. J., & Ben-David, N. (1986). Operant and cognitive intervention to restore effective functioning following a death in a family. *Behavior Therapy and Experimental Psychiatry, 17*, 193–196.

Marcell, M. M., & Cohen, S. (1992). Hearing abilities of Down syndrome and other mentally handicapped adolescents. *Research in Developmental Disabilities, 13*, 533–551.

Marchetti, A. G., & Campbell, V. A. (1990). Social skills. In J. L. Matson (Ed.), *Handbook of behavior modification with the mentally retarded* (2nd ed., pp. 333–350). New York: Plenum Press.

Markowitz, P. I. (1992). Effect of fluoxetine on self-injurious behavior in the developmentally disabled: A preliminary study. *Journal of Clinical Psychopharmacology, 12*, 27–31.

Marradi, A. (1981). Factor analysis as an aid in the formation and refinement of empirically useful concepts. In D. J. Jackson & E. F. Borgatta (Eds.), *Factor analysis and measurement in sociological research: A multi-dimensional perspective* (pp. 11–49). Beverly Hills, CA: Sage.

Marsh, D. T. (1992). *Families and mental retardation: New directions in professional practice.* New York: Praeger.

Marshall, K. J., Lussie, R., & Stradley, M. (1989). Social studies. In J. R. Patten, E. A. Polloway, & L. R. Argent (Eds.), *Best practices in mild mental disabilities* (pp. 89–107). Reston, VA: Council for Exceptional Children.

Marshburn, E. C., & Aman, M. G. (1992). Factor validity and norms for the Aberrant Behavior Checklist in a community sample of children with mental retardation. *Journal of Autism and Developmental Disorders, 22*, 357–373.

Martin, G. L., & Osborne, J. G. (1993). *Psychology, adjustment, and everyday living* (2nd ed.). Englewood Cliffs, NJ: Prentice Hall.

Martin, J. E. (1988). Providing training in community and domestic skills. In L. W. Heal, J. I. Haney, & A. R. N. Amado (Eds.), *Integration of developmentally disabled individuals into the community* (2nd ed., pp. 169–191). Baltimore: Brookes.

Martin, J. E., Marshall, L. H., & Maxson, L. L. (1993). Transition policy: Infusing self-determination and self-advocacy into transition programs. *Career Development for Exceptional Individuals, 16*, 53–61.

Martin, J. P. (1977). Brief family intervention: Effectiveness and the importance of including the father. *Journal of Consulting and Clinical Psychology, 45*, 1002–1010.

Martin, S. L., Ramey, C. T., & Ramey, S. L. (1990). The prevention of intellectual impairment in children of impoverished families: Findings of a randomized trial of educational day-care. *American Journal of Public Health, 80,* 844–847.

Maslow, A. H. (1954). *Motivation and personality.* New York: Harper & Row.

Mason, J. (1989). *The Cultural Competence Self-Assessment Questionnaire.* Portland, OR: Portland Research and Training Center for Children and Youth With Serious Emotional Handicaps and Their Families.

Massachusetts Regulations for Behavior Modification Treatment Programs, 104 C.M.R. § 20.15 (1987).

Mathews, R. M., Whang, P. L., & Fawcett, S. B. (1980). Development and validation of an occupational skills assessment instrument. *Behavioral Assessment, 2,* 71–85.

Mathias, J. L., & Nettelbeck, T. (1992). Construct and criterion validity of Greenspan's model of adaptive intelligence. *Research in Developmental Disabilities, 13,* 113–129.

Matson, J. L. (1981a). A controlled outcome study of phobias in mentally retarded adults. *Behavior Research and Therapy, 19,* 101–107.

Matson, J. L. (1981b). *Handbook of behavior modification with the mentally retarded.* New York: Plenum Press.

Matson, J. L. (1982). Treatment of the behavioral characteristics of depression in the mentally retarded. *Behavior Therapy, 13,* 209–218.

Matson, J. L. (Ed.). (1990). *Handbook of behavior modification with the mentally retarded* (2nd ed.). New York: Plenum Press.

Matson, J. L. (1994). *Matson Evaluation of Social Skills for Individuals with Severe Retardation: MESSIER* (professional manual). Baton Rouge, LA: Scientific International Publications.

Matson, J. L., & Barrett, R. P. (Eds.). (1993). *Psychopathology in the mentally retarded.* Boston: Allyn & Bacon.

Matson, J. L., Gardner, W. I., Coe, D. A., & Sovner, R. (1990). *Diagnostic Assessment for the Severe Handicapped (DASH) Scale* (user manual). Unpublished manuscript, Louisiana State University.

Matson, J. L., Helsel, W. J., Bellack, A. S., & Senatore, V. (1983). Development of a rating scale to assess social skills deficits in mentally retarded adults. *Applied Research in Mental Retardation, 4,* 399–407.

Matson, J. L., Kazdin, A. E., & Senatore, V. (1985). Psychometric properties of the Psychopathology Instrument for Mentally Retarded Adults. *Applied Research in Mental Retardation, 5,* 81–89.

Matson, J. L., & Mulick, J. A. (Eds.). (1991a). *Handbook of mental retardation* (2nd ed.). Elmsford, NY: Pergamon Press.

Matson, J. L., & Mulick, J. A. (1991b). Introduction: A continuum of service and research. In J. L. Matson & J. A. Mulick (Eds.), *Handbook of mental retardation* (2nd ed., pp. xi–xv). Elmsford, NY: Pergamon Press.

Matson, J. L., & Ollendick, T. H. (1988). *Enhancing children's social skills: Assessment and treatment.* New York: Plenum Press.

Matson, J. L., Rotatori, A. F., & Helsel, W. J. (1983). Development of a rating scale to measure social skills in children: The Matson Evaluation of Social Skills in Youths (MESSY). *Behaviour Research and Therapy, 21,* 335–340.

Matson, J. L., & Sevin, J. A. (1994). Theories of dual diagnosis in mental retardation. *Journal of Consulting and Clinical Psychology, 62,* 6–16.

Matson, J. L., & Stephens, R. M. (1978). Increasing appropriate behavior of explosive chronic psychiatric patients with a social skills training package. *Behavior Modification, 2,* 61–76.

Matson, J. L., & Zeiss, R. A. (1978). Group training of social skills in chronically explosive severely disturbed psychiatric patients. *Behavioral Engineering, 5,* 41–50.

Matthews, C. G. (1974). Applications of neuropsychological test methods in mentally retarded subjects. In R. M. Reitan & L. A. Davison (Eds.), *Clinical neuropsychology: Current status and applications.* Washington, DC: Winston.

Maurice, P., & Trudel, G. (1982). Self-injurious behavior prevalence and relationships to environmental events. In J. H. Hollis & C. E. Meyers (Eds.), *Life-threatening behavior: Analysis and interventions.* Washington, DC: American Association on Mental Deficiency.

Mayfield, K. L., Forman, S. G., & Nagle, R. J. (1984). Reliability of the AAMD Adaptive Behavior Scale—Public School Version. *Journal of School Psychology, 22,* 53–61.

Mazzocco, M. M. M., Hagerman, R. J., Cronister-Silverman, A., & Pennington, B. F. (1992). Specific frontal lobe deficits among women with the fragile X gene. *Journal of the American Academy of Child Adolescent Psychiatry, 31,* 1141–1148.

McBride, B. A. (1991a). Parent education and support programs for fathers: Outcome effects on paternal involvement. *Early Child Development and Care, 67,* 73–85.

McBride, B. A. (1991b). Parental support programs and paternal stress: An exploratory study. *Early Childhood Research Quarterly, 6,* 137–149.

McCall, R. B., & Carriger, M. S. (1993). A meta-analysis of infant habituation and recognition memory performance as predictors of later IQ. *Child Development, 64,* 57–79.

McCallum, R. S., Helm, H. W., & Sanderson, C. E. (1986). Local norming and validation of an adaptive behavior screening instrument. *Educational and Psychological Measurement, 46,* 709–718.

McCarver, R. R., & Campbell, V. A. (1987). Future developments in the concept and application of adaptive behavior. *Journal of Special Education, 21,* 197–207.

McConachie, H. (1986). *Parents and young mentally handicapped children: A review of research issues.* London: Croom Helm.

McCubbin, H. I., & Patterson, J. M. (1983). The family stress process: The double ABCX model of adjustment and adaptation. *Marriage and Family Review, 6,* 7–37.

McDougle, C. J., Price, L. H., Volkmar, F. R., Goodman, W. K., Ward-O'Brien, D., Nielsen, J., Bregman, J., & Cohen, D. J. (1992). Clomipramine in autism: Preliminary evidence of efficacy. *Journal of the American Academy of Child and Adolescent Psychiatry, 31,* 746–750.

McEachin, J. J., Smith, T., & Lovaas, O. I. (1993). Long-term outcome for children with autism who received early intensive behavioral treatment. *American Journal of Mental Retardation, 97,* 359–372.

McEvoy, M. A., Shores, R. E., Wehlby, J. H., Johnson, S. M., & Fox, J. J. (1990). Special education teachers' implementation of procedures to promote social interaction among children in integrated settings. *Education and Training in Mental Retardation, 25,* 267–276.

McGrew, K., & Bruininks, R. (1989). The factor structure of adaptive behavior. *School Psychology Review, 18,* 64–81.

McGrew, K. S., & Bruininks, R. H. (1990). Defining adaptive and maladaptive behavior within a model of personal competence. *School Psychology Review, 19,* 53–73.

McGrew, K. S., Bruininks, R. H., & Johnson, D. R. (in press). A confirmatory factor analysis investigation of Greenspan's model of personal competence. *American Journal of Mental Retardation.*

McGrew, K. S., Ittenbach, R. F., Bruininks, R. H., & Hill, B. K. (1991). Factor structure of maladaptive behaviors across the lifespan of persons with mental retardation. *Research in Developmental Disabilities, 12,* 181–199.

McGuffin, P. W. (1991). The effect of timeout duration on frequency of aggression in hospitalized children with conduct disorders. *Behavioral Residential Treatment,* 6, 279–288.

McHale, S. M., & Pawletko, T. M. (1992). Differential treatment of siblings in two family contexts. *Child Development, 63,* 68–81.

McIver, J. P., & Carmines, E. G. (1981). *Unidimensional scaling.* Beverly Hills, CA: Sage.

McKean, C. M. (1972). The effects of high phenylalanine concentrations on serotonin and catecholamine metabolism in the human brain. *Brain Research, 47,* 469–476.

McKusick, V. A. (1992). *Mendelian inheritance in man: Catalogs of autosomal dominant, autosomal recessive and X-linked phenotypes.* Baltimore: Johns Hopkins University Press.

McKusick, V. A., Francomano, C. A., & Antonarakis, S. E. (1993). *Mendelian inheritance in man: Catalogs of autosomal dominant, autosomal recessive, and X-linked phenotypes* (11th ed.). Baltimore: Johns Hopkins University Press.

McKusick, V. A., Francomano, C. A., Antonarakis, S. E., & Pearson, P. L. (1994). *Mendelian inheritance in man: A catalog of human genes and genetic disorders* (11th ed.). Baltimore: Johns Hopkins University Press.

McLain, R. E., Silverstein, A. B., Hubbell, M., Brownless, L., Sutter, P., & Mayeda, T. (1979).

The residential management survey. Pomona, CA: Riverside Research Group at Lanterman Developmental Center.

McLaren, J., & Bryson, S. E. (1987). Review of recent epidemiological studies of mental retardation: Prevalence, associated disorders, and etiology. *American Journal of Mental Retardation, 92,* 243–254.

McMahon, R. J., Forehand, R., & Griest, D. L. (1981). Effects of knowledge of social learning principles on enhancing treatment outcome and generalization in a parent training program. *Journal of Consulting and Clinical Psychology, 49,* 526–532.

McMahon, R. J., Forehand, R., Griest, D. L., & Wells, K. C. (1981). Who drops out of treatment during parent behavior training? *Behavioral Counseling Quarterly, 1,* 79–85.

McNally, R. J. (1991). Anxiety and phobias. In J. L. Matson & J. A. Mulick (Eds.), *Handbook of mental retardation* (2nd ed., pp. 413–423). Elmsford, NY: Pergamon Press.

McNeil, E. B. (1969). *Human socialization.* Monterey, CA: Brooks-Cole.

McQueen, P. C., Spence, M. W., Winsor, E. J. T., Garner, J. B., & Pereira, L. H. (1986). Causal origins of major mental handicap in the Canadian Maritime Provinces. *Developmental Medicine and Child Neurology, 28,* 697–707.

Meichenbaum, D. (1977). *Cognitive-behavior modification.* New York: Plenum Press.

Meinhold, P. M., & Mulick, J. A. (1992). Social policy and science in the treatment of severe behavior disorders: Defining and securing a healthy relationship. *Clinical Psychology Review, 12,* 585–603.

Menolascino, F. J., Gilson, S. F., & Levitas, A. (1986). Issues in the treatment of mentally retarded patients in the community mental health system. *Community Mental Health Journal, 22,* 314–327.

Menolascino, F. J., & Stark, J. A. (1984). (Eds.). *Handbook of mental illness in the mentally retarded.* New York: Plenum Press.

Mercer, J. R. (1973a). *Labelling the mentally retarded child: Clinical and social systems perspectives on mental retardation.* Berkeley: University of California Press.

Mercer, J. R. (1973b). The Pluralistic Assessment Project: Sociocultural effects in clinical assessment. *School Psychology Digest, 2,* 10–18.

Mercer, J. R. (1974a). A policy statement on assessment procedures and the rights of children. *Harvard Educational Review, 44,* 125–140.

Mercer, J. R. (1974b). Latent functions of intelligence testing in the public schools. In L. Miller (Ed.), *The testing of black students* (pp. 77–94). Englewood Cliffs, NJ: Prentice Hall.

Mercer, J. R. (1979). In defense of racially and culturally non-discriminatory assessment. *School Psychology Digest, 8,* 89–215.

Mercer, J. R. (1992). The impact of changing paradigms of disability on mental retardation in the year 2000. In L. Rowitz (Ed.), *Mental retardation in the year 2000* (pp. 15–38). New York: Springer-Verlag.

Mercer, J. R, Gomez-Palacio, M., & Padillo, E. (1986). The development of practical intelligence in cross-cultural perspective. In R. J. Sternberg & R. K. Wagner (Eds.), *Practical intelligence: Nature and origins of competence in the everyday world* (pp. 307–337). Cambridge, England: Cambridge University Press.

Meyer, D. J. (1985). Fathers of children with mental handicaps. In M. E. Lamb (Ed.), *The father's role: Applied perspectives* (pp. 227–254). New York: Wiley.

Meyers, C., Nihira, K., & Zetlin, A. (1979). The measurement of adaptive behavior. In N. R. Ellis (Ed.), *Handbook of mental deficiency: Psychological theory and research* (2nd ed., pp. 431–481). Hillsdale, NJ: Erlbaum.

Michigan Mental Health Code, Mich. Comp. Laws Ann. §§ 330.1618, 330.1620, 330.1723 (1974).

Middleton, H. A., Keene, R. G., & Brown, G. W. (1990). Convergent and discriminant validities of the Scales of Independent Behavior and the Revised Vineland Adaptive Behavior Scales. *American Journal of Mental Retardation, 94,* 669–673.

Milich, R., Roberts, M. A., Loney, J., & Caputo, J. (1980). Differentiating practice effects and statistical regression on the Conners Hyperkinesis Index. *Journal of Abnormal Child Psychology, 8,* 549–552.

Milledge, J. S. (1985). Acute mountain sickness: Pulmonary and cerebral oedema of high altitude. *Intensive Care Medicine, 11,* 110–114.

Miller, G., Galanter, E., & Pribram, K. (1960). *Plans and the structure of behavior.* New York: Holt.

Mills v. Board of Education of the District of Columbia, 348 F. Supp. 866 (D. D. C. 1972).

Millsap, P. A., Thackrey, M. T., & Cook, V. J. (1987). Dimensional structure of the Adaptive Behavior Inventory for Children (ABIC): Analyses and implications. *Journal of Psychoeducational Assessment, 5,* 61–66.

Milner, B. (1970). Memory and the medial temporal regions of the brain. In K. H. Pribram & D. E. Broadbent (Eds.), *Biology of memory* (pp. 29–50). San Diego, CA: Academic Press.

Milunsky, A., Ulrickas, M., Rothman, K. J., Willet, W., Jick, S. S., & Jick, H. (1992). Maternal heat exposure and neural tube defects. *Journal of the American Medical Association, 268,* 882–885.

Mink, I. T., Blacher, J., & Nihira, K. (1988). Taxonomy of family life styles: III. Replication with families with severely mentally retarded children. *American Journal of Mental Retardation, 93,* 250–264.

Mink, I. T., Meyers, C. E., & Nihira, K. (1984). Taxonomy of family life styles: II. Homes with slow-learning children. *American Journal of Mental Deficiency, 89,* 111–123.

Mink, I. T., & Nihira, K. (1987). Direction of effects: Family life styles and behavior of TMR children. *American Journal of Mental Deficiency, 92,* 57–64.

Mink, I. T., Nihira, K., & Meyers, C. E. (1983). Taxonomy of family life styles: I. Homes with TMR children. *American Journal of Mental Deficiency, 87,* 484–497.

Miranda v. Arizona, 384 U.S. 436 (1966).

Mischel, W. (1977). The interaction of person and situation. In D. Magnusson & N. S. Endler (Eds.), *Personality at the crossroads: Current issues in interactional psychology* (pp. 333–352). Hillsdale, NJ: Erlbaum.

Mittler, P. (1984). Quality of life and services for people with disabilities. *Bulletin of the British Psychological Society, 37,* 218–225.

Mittler P., & Serpell, R. (1985). Services: An international perspective. In A. M. Clarke, A. D. B. Clarke, & J. M. Berg (Eds.), *Mental deficiency: The changing outlook* (4th ed., pp. 715–787). London: Methuen.

Molony, H., & Taplin, J. E. (1990). The deinstitutionalization of people with a developmental disability under the Richmond Program: I. Changes in adaptive behavior. *Australia and New Zealand Journal of Developmental Disabilities, 16,* 149–159.

Monroe, J. E. (1988). Generalization and maintenance in therapeutic systems: Analysis and proposal for change. *Professional Psychology: Research and Practice, 19,* 449–453.

Montanelli, R. G., Jr., & Humphreys, L. G. (1976). Latent roots of random data correlation matrices with squared multiple correlations on the diagonal: A Monte Carlo study. *Psychometrika, 41,* 341–348.

Montee, B. B., Miltenberger, R. G., & Wittrock, D. (1995). An experimental analysis of facilitated communication. *Journal of Applied Behavior Analysis, 28,* 189–200.

Monti, P., Abrams, D., Binkoff, J., & Zuick, W. (1986). Social skills training and substance abuse. In C. Hollin & P. Tower (Eds.), *Handbook of social skills* (Vol. 2, pp. 111–142). Elmsford, NY: Pergamon Press.

Moorcraft, J., Bolas, N. M., Hope, P. L., Ives, N. K., Rajagopalan, B., Sutton, P., & Radda, G. K. (1989). Patterns of abnormal cerebral energy metabolism following birth asphyxia. *Pediatric Research, 26,* 510A.

Moore, S., Donovan, B., & Hudson, A. (1993). Facilitator-suggested conversational evaluation of facilitated communication. *Journal of Autism and Developmental Disorders, 23,* 541–551.

Moore, S., Donovan, B., Hudson, A., Dykstra, J., & Lawrence, J. (1993). Evaluation of facilitated communication: Eight case studies. *Journal of Autism and Developmental Disorders, 23,* 531–539.

Moos, R. H. (1973). Conceptualizations of human environments. *American Psychologist, 28,* 652–665.

Moos, R. H. (1974). *Family Environment Scale—Form* R. Palo Alto, CA: Consulting Psychologists Press.

Moos, R. H. (1975). *Evaluating correctional and community settings.* New York: Wiley.

Moos, R. H., & Moos, B. S. (1986). *Family Environment Scale manual* (2nd ed.). Palo Alto, CA: Consulting Psychologists Press.

Morgan, D. J. (1979). Prevalence and types of handicapping conditions found in juvenile correctional institutions: A national survey. *Journal of Special Education, 13,* 283–295.

Morgenstern, M., & Klass, E. (1991). Standard intelligence tests and related assessment techniques. In J. L. Matson & J. A. Mulick (Eds.), *Handbook of mental retardation* (2nd ed., pp. 195–210). Elmsford, NY: Pergamon Press.

Morley, R. E. (1989). Vocational education: A source of promise. In G. A. Robinson, J. R. Patton, E. A. Polloway, & L. R. Argent (Eds.), *Best practices in mild mental disabilities* (pp. 375–394). Reston, VA: Council for Exceptional Children.

Morreau, L. E., & Bruininks, R. H. (1989). *Checklist of Adaptive Living Skills.* Chicago: Riverside.

Morris, C. D., & Niederbuhl, J. M. (1992, December). *Sexual knowledge of dually diagnosed persons and the capability to consent to sexual contact.* Paper presented at the conference of the National Association on Dual Diagnosis, Toronto, Ontario, Canada.

Morris, C. D., Niederbuhl, J. M., & Mahr, J. M. (1993). Determining the capability of individuals with mental retardation to give informed consent. *American Journal of Mental Retardation, 98,* 263–272.

Moser, H. W., Ramey, C. T., & Leonard, C. O. (1983). Mental retardation. In A. E. H. Emery & D. L. Rimoin (Eds.), *The principles and practices of medical genetics* (Vol. 1, pp. 467–478). London: Churchill Livingstone.

Moses, K. L. (1983). The impact of initial diagnosis: Mobilizing family resources. In J. A. Mulick & S. M. Pueschel (Eds.), *Parent-professional partnerships in developmental disability services* (pp. 11–41). Cambridge, MA: Ware Press.

Mosk, M. D., & Butcher, B. (1984). Prompting and stimulus shaping procedures for teaching visual motor skills to retarded children. *Journal of Applied Behavior Analysis, 17,* 23–34.

Moss, S., & Hogg, J. (1990). Factorial and hierarchical cluster analysis of the adaptive behavior scales: I & II. In a population of older people (50 years +) with severe intellectual impairment (mental handicap). *Australia and New Zealand Journal of Developmental Disabilities, 16,* 381–392.

Mountain, R. D. (1987). High-altitude medical problems. *Clinical Orthopedics, 216,* 50–54.

Mulhern, T. J. (1975). Survey of reported sexual behavior and policies characterizing residential facilities for retarded citizens. *American Journal of Mental Deficiency, 79,* 670–673.

Mueser, K. T., Valenti-Hein, D. C., & Yarnold, P. (1987). Teaching dating skills to mentally retarded adults: Relaxation vs. social skills training. *Behavior Modification, 11,* 200–208.

Mulick, J. (1989, April). *Restrictive behavioral interventions and their alternatives.* Paper presented at the Young Adult Institute Symposium on Ensuring Quality of Life from Infancy through Adulthood, New York.

Mulick, J. A., & Meinhold, P. M. (1992). Analyzing the impact of regulations on residential ecology. *Mental Retardation, 30,* 151–161.

Mulick, J. A., & Meinhold, P. M. (1994). Developmental disorders and broad effects of the environment on learning and treatment effectiveness. In E. Schopler & G. R. Mesibov (Eds.), *Behavioral issues in autism: Current issues in autism* (pp. 99–128). New York: Plenum Press.

Munk, D. D., & Repp, A. C. (1994). Behavioral assessment of feeding problems of individuals with severe disabilities. *Journal of Applied Behavior Analysis, 24,* 241–250.

Murdock, C. (1974). Sterilization of the retarded: A problem or a solution? *California Law Review, 62,* 917–924.

Murphy, J. M., & Leighton, A. H. (Eds.). (1965). *Approaches to cross-cultural psychiatry.* Ithaca, NY: Cornell University Press.

Naglieri, J. A. (1985a). Assessment of mentally retarded children with the Kaufman Assessment Battery for Children. *American Journal of Mental Deficiency, 89,* 367–371.

Naglieri, J. A. (1985b). *Matrix Analogies Test—Expanded Form.* San Antonio, TX: Psychological Corporation.

Naglieri, J. A. (1985c). Use of the WISC–R and K-ABC with learning disabled, borderline mentally retarded, and normal children. *Psychology in the Schools, 22,* 133–141.

Naglieri, J. A. (1989). A cognitive processing theory for the measurement of intelligence. *Educational Psychologist, 24,* 185–206.

Naglieri, J. A., & Das, J. P. (1990). Planning, attention, simultaneous, and successive (PASS) cognitive processes as a model for intelligence. *Journal of Psychoeducational Assessment, 8,* 303–337.

Naglieri, J. A., Das, J. P., & Jarman, R. F. (1990). Planning, attention, simultaneous, and successive cognitive processes as a model for assessment. *School Psychology Review, 19,* 423–442.

Naglieri, J. A., Das, J. P., Stevens, J. J., & Ledbetter, M. F. (1991). Confirmatory factor analysis of planning, attention, simultaneous, and successive cognitive processing tasks. *Journal of School Psychology, 29,* 1–17.

Naglieri, J. A., Prewett, P., & Bardos, A. N. (1989). An exploratory study of planning, attention, simultaneous and successive cognitive processes. *Journal of School Psychology, 27,* 347–364.

Naglieri, J. A., & Reardon, S. M. (1993). Traditional IQ is irrelevant to learning disabilities—Intelligence is not. *Journal of Learning Disabilities, 26,* 127–133.

National Institute of Mental Health. (1985a). Abnormal Involuntary Movement Scale (AIMS). *Psychopharmacology Bulletin, 21,* 1077–1080.

National Institute of Mental Health. (1985b). Children's Psychiatric Rating Scale. *Psychopharmacology Bulletin, 21,* 765–770.

National Institute of Mental Health. (1985c). Dosage and Treatment Emergent Symptom Scale (DOTES). *Psychopharmacology Bulletin, 21,* 1067–1068.

National Institute of Mental Health. (1985d). Physical and Neurological Examination for Soft Signs. *Psychopharmacology Bulletin, 21,* 791–800.

National Institute of Mental Health. (1985e). Subjective Treatment Emergent Symptoms Scale (STESS). *Psychopharmacology Bulletin, 21,* 1073–1075.

Neef, N. A., Lensbower, J., Hackersmith, I., DePalma, V., & Gray, K. (1990). In vivo versus simulation training: An interactional analysis of range and type of training examples. *Journal of Applied Behavior Analysis, 23,* 447–458.

Neel, A. F. (1977). Social and biological factors in child development. *Psychological Reports, 40,* 1143–1146.

Nelson, C. M. (1988). Social skills training for handicapped students. *Teaching Exceptional Children, 20,* 19–23.

Nelson, R. O., Lipinski, D. P., & Boykin, R. A. (1978). The effects of self-recorders, training and the obtrusiveness of the self-recording device on the accuracy and reactivity of self-monitoring. *Behavior Therapy, 9,* 200–208.

Nevin, J. A., Mandell, C., & Atak, J. R. (1983). The analysis of behavioral momentum. *Journal of Experimental Analysis of Behavior, 39,* 49–59.

New Jersey v. Schwerzer, Schwerzer, Grober & Archer. (1993). Indictment File No. 4165-9-91.

Newton, J. S., Stoner, S. K., Bellamy, G. T., Boles, S. M., Horner, R. H., LeBaron, N., Moskowitz, D., Romer, L., Romer, M., & Schlesinger, D. (1988). *Valued outcomes information system (VOIS) operations manual.* Eugene: Center of Human Development, University of Oregon.

Newton, J. T., & Sturmey, P. (1991). The Motivation Assessment Scale: Inter-rater reliability and internal consistency in British sample. *Journal of Mental Deficiency Research, 35,* 472–474.

Nezu, C. M., & Nezu, A. M. (1991). Assertiveness and problem-solving training for mentally retarded persons with a dual diagnosis. *Research in Developmental Disabilities, 12,* 371–386.

Nezu, C. M., & Nezu, A. M. (1994). Outpatient psychotherapy for adults with mental retardation and concomitant psychopathology: Research and clinical imperatives. *Journal of Consulting and Clinical Psychology, 62,* 34–42.

Nezu, C. M., Nezu, A. M., & Gill-Weiss, M. J. (1992). *Psychopathology in persons with mental retardation: Clinical guidelines for assessment and treatment.* Champaign, IL: Research Press.

Nihira, K. (1969a). Factorial dimensions of adaptive behavior in adult retardates. *American Journal of Mental Deficiency, 73,* 868–878.

Nihira, K. (1969b). Factorial dimensions of adaptive behavior in mentally retarded children and adolescents. *American Journal of Mental Deficiency, 74,* 130–141.

Nihira, K. (1976). Dimensions of adaptive behavior in institutionalized mentally retarded children and adults: Developmental perspective. *American Journal of Mental Deficiency, 81,* 215–226.

Nihira, K. (1978). Factorial descriptions of the AAMD Adaptive Behavior Scale. In W. A. Coulter & H. W. Morrow (Eds.), *Adaptive behavior: Concepts and measurements* (pp. 45–57). New York: Grune & Stratton.

Nihira, K., Foster, R., Shellhaas, M., & Leland, H. (1969). *AAMD Adaptive Behavior Scale.* Washington, DC: American Association on Mental Deficiency.

Nihira, K., Foster, R., Shellhaas, M., & Leland, H. (1975). *AAMD Adaptive Behavior Scale* (Rev). Washington, DC: American Association on Mental Deficiency.

Nihira, K., Mink, I. T., & Meyers, C. E. (1985). Home environment and development of slow-learning adolescents: Reciprocal relations. *Developmental Psychology, 21,* 784–794.

Nihira, K., Webster, R., Tomiyasu, Y., & Oshio, C. (1988). Child-environment relationships: A cross-cultural study of educable mentally retarded children and their families. *Journal of Autism and Developmental Disorders, 18,* 327–341.

Nihira, K., Weisner, T. S., & Bernheimer, L. P. (1994). Ecocultural assessment in families of children with developmental delays: Construct and concurrent validities. *American Journal of Mental Retardation, 98,* 551–566.

Nixon, C. (1992). *A cognitive behavioral intervention for self blame and guilt in parents of children with disabilities: A treatment manual.* Unpublished manuscript, Oregon Research Institute, Eugene, OR.

Nixon, C. D., & Singer, G. H. S. (1993). Group cognitive-behavioral treatment for excessive parental self-blame and guilt. *American Journal of Mental Retardation, 97,* 665–672.

Noble, J. H., Jr., & Conley, R. W. (1992). Toward an epidemiology of relevant attributes. In R. W. Conley, R. Luckasson, & G. N. Bouthilet (Eds.), *The criminal justice system and mental retardation* (pp. 17–53). Baltimore: Brookes.

Nora, J. J., & Fraser, F. C. (1994). *Medical genetics: Principles and practice* (2nd ed.). Philadelphia: Lea & Febiger.

Northrup, J., Wacker, D., Sasso, G., Steege, M., Cigrand, K., Cook, J., & DeRaas, A. (1991). A brief functional analysis of aggressive and alternative behavior in an outclinic setting. *Journal of Applied Behavior Analysis, 24,* 509–522.

Obler, M., & Terwillinger, R. F. (1970). Pilot study on the effectiveness of systematic desensitization with neurologically impaired children with phobic disorders. *Journal of Consulting and Clinical Psychology, 34,* 314–318.

Obrzut, A., Obrzut, J., & Shaw, D. (1987). Construct validity of the Kaufman Assessment Battery for Children with learning disabled and mentally retarded. *Psychology in the Schools, 21,* 417–424.

O'Dell, S., Tarler-Benlolo, L. A., & Flynn, J. M. (1979). An instrument to measure knowledge of behavioral principles as applied to children. *Journal of Behavior Therapy and Experimental Psychiatry, 10,* 29–34.

Ogbu, J. U. (1985). A cultural ecology of competence among inner-city Blacks. In M. B. Spencer, G. K. Brookins, & W. R. Allen (Eds.), *Beginnings: The social and affective development of black children* (pp. 45–66). Hillsdale, NJ: Erlbaum.

Ogbu, J. U. (1992). Understanding cultural diversity. *Educational Researcher, 21,* 5–14.

Olds, D. L., Henderson, C. R., Tatelbaum, R., & Chamberlain, R. (1986). Improving the delivery of prenatal care and outcomes of pregnancy: A randomized trial of nurse home visitation. *Pediatrics, 77,* 16–28.

Oliver, P. (1983). Effect of teaching different tasks in group vs. individual training formats with severely handicapped individuals. *Journal of the Association for Persons with Severe Handicaps, 8,* 79–91.

Ollendick, T. H., Oswald, D. P., & Ollendick, D. G. (1993). Anxiety disorders in mentally retarded persons. In J. L. Matson & R. P. Barrett (Eds.), *Psychopathology in the mentally retarded* (2nd ed., pp. 41–86). Boston: Allyn & Bacon.

Olney, R. S., Khoury, M. J., Alo, C. J., Costa, P., Edmonds, L. D., Flood, T. J., Harris, J. A.,

Howe, H. L., Moore, C. A., Olsen, C. L., Panny, S. R., & Shaw, G. M. (1995). Increased risk for transverse digital deficiency after chorionic villus sampling: Results of the United States Multistate Case-Control Study, 1988–1992. *Teratology, 51,* 20–29.

Olshansky, S. (1962). Chronic sorrow: A response to having a mentally defective child. *Social Casework, 43,* 190–193.

Olson, D. H., Portner, J., & Lavee, Y. (1985). *FACES III manual.* Available from D. H. Olson, Family Social Science, University of Minnesota, 290 McNeal Hall, St. Paul, MN 55108.

Olweus, D. (1979). Stability of aggressive reaction patterns in males: A review. *Psychological Bulletin, 86,* 852–875.

O'Neill, R. E., Horner, R. H., Albin, R. W., Storey, K., & Sprague, J. R. (1990). *Functional analysis: A practical assessment guide.* Sycamore, IL: Sycamore.

Orlandi, M. A. (Ed.). (1992). *Cultural competence for evaluators.* Rockville, MD: Office of Substance Abuse Prevention.

Ornitz, E. M. (1985). Neurophysiology of infantile autism. *Journal of the American Academy of Child Psychiatry, 24,* 251–262.

Osterlind, S. J. (1983). *Test item bias.* Beverly Hills, CA: Sage.

Overall, J. E., & Campbell, M. (1988). Behavioral assessment of psychopathology in children: Infantile autism. *Journal of Clinical Psychology, 44,* 708–716.

Owens, E. P., & Bowling, D. H. (1970). Internal consistency and factor structure of the Preschool Attainment Record. *American Journal of Mental Deficiency, 75,* 170–171.

Owens, W. A. (1953). Age and mental abilities: A longitudinal study. *Genetic Psychology Monographs, 48,* 3–54.

Ozonoff, S., Pennington, B. S., & Rogers, S. J. (1990). Are there emotion perception deficits in young autistic children? *Journal of Child Psychology and Psychiatry, 31,* 343–361.

Ozonoff, S., Pennington, B. S., & Rogers, S. J. (1991). Executive function deficits in high-functioning autistic individuals: Relationship to theory of mind. *Journal of Child Psychology and Psychiatry, 32,* 1081–1105.

Page, E. B. (1980). Tests and decisions for the handicapped: A guide to evaluation under the new laws [Monograph]. *Journal of Special Education, 14,* 423–484.

Page, F. (1986). The therapeutic use of puppetry with mentally handicapped people. *Occupational Therapy, 18,* 122–125.

Page, T. J., & Iwata, B. A. (1986). Interobserver agreement: History, theory, and current methods. In A. D. Poling & R. W. Fuqua (Eds.), *Research methods in applied behavior analysis: Issues and advances* (pp. 99–166). New York: Plenum Press.

Pahl, J., & Quine, L. (1987). Families with mentally handicapped children. In J. Orford (Ed.), *Treating the disorder, treating the family* (pp. 39–61). Baltimore: Johns Hopkins University Press.

Pansofer, E. L., & Bates, P. (1985). The impact of the acquisition of successive training exemplars on generalization. *Journal of the Association for Persons with Severe Handicaps, 10,* 95–104.

Parent, W. (1992). Quality of life and consumer choice. In P. Wehman (Ed.), *ADA mandate for social change* (pp. 19–41). Baltimore: Brookes.

Parke, R. D. (1979). Interactional designs. In R. B. Cairns (Ed.), *The analysis of social interactions: Methods, issues, and illustrations* (pp. 15–35). New York: Wiley.

Parker, R. M. (1990). Power, control, and validity in research. *Journal of Learning Disabilities, 23,* 613–620.

Parmenter, T. R. (1992). Quality of life for people with developmental disabilities. *International Review of Research in Mental Retardation, 18,* 247–287.

Parsons, M. B., Schepis, M. M., Reid, D. H., McCarn, J. E., & Green, C. W. (1987). Expanding the impact of behavioral staff management: A large-scale, long-term application in schools serving severely handicapped students. *Journal of Applied Behavior Analysis, 20,* 139–150.

Pary, R. J. (1991). Towards defining adequate lithium trials for individuals with mental retardation and mental illness. *American Journal of Mental Retardation, 95,* 681–691.

Patrick, J. L., & Reschly, D. J. (1982). Relationship of state educational criteria and demographic variables to school-system prevalence of mental retardation. *American Journal of Mental Deficiency, 86,* 351–360.

Patterson, C. J., Vaden, N. A., & Kupersmidt, J. B. (1991). Family background, recent life events, and peer rejection during childhood. *Journal of Social and Personal Relationships, 8*, 347–361.

Patterson, G. R. (1977). *Families: Applications of social learning to family life* (Rev. ed.). Champaign, IL: Research Press.

Patterson, G. R. (1982). *Coercive family process*. Eugene, OR: Castalia.

Patterson, G. R., & Gullion, M. E. (1976). *Living with children: New methods for parents and teachers* (Rev. ed.). Champaign, IL: Research Press.

Patton, J. R., Beirne-Smith, M., & Payne, J. S. (1990). *Mental retardation* (3rd ed.). New York: Merrill.

Patton, J. R., Cronin, M. E., Polloway, E. A., Hutchinson, D., & Robinson, G. A. (1989). Curriculum consideration: A life skills orientation. In G. A. Robinson, J. R. Patton, E. A. Polloway, & L. R. Argent (Eds.), *Best practices in mild mental disabilities* (pp. 23–38). Reston, VA: Council for Exceptional Children.

Pawlarczyk, D., & Schumacher, K. (1983). Concurrent validity of the Behavior Development Survey. *American Journal of Mental Deficiency, 87*, 619–627.

Peck, C. L. (1977). Desensitization for the treatment of fear in the high level adult retardate. *Behavior Research and Therapy, 15*, 137–148.

Peden, C. J., Cowan, F. M., Bryant, D. J., Sargentoni, J., Cox, I. J., Menon, D. K., Gadion, D. G., Bell, J. D., & Dubowitz, L. M. (1990). Proton MR spectroscopy in the brain of infants. *Journal of Computer Assisted Tomography, 14*, 886–894.

Pendler, B., & Hingsburger, D. (1991). Sexuality: Dealing with parents. *Sexuality and Disability, 9*, 123–130.

Penry v. Lynaugh, 109 S. Ct. 2934 (1989).

People v. Redmon, 468 N.E.2d 1310 (1984).

Perlin, M. L., Gould, K. K., Dorfman, D. A. (1995). Therapeutic jurisprudence and the civil rights of institutionalized disabled persons: Hopeless oxymoron or path to redemption? *Psychology, Public Policy, and Law, 1*, 80–119.

Perry, A., & Factor, D. C. (1989). Psychometric validity and clinical usefulness of the Vineland Adaptive Behavior Scales and the AAMD Adaptive Behavior Scale for an autistic sample. *Journal of Autism and Developmental Disorders, 19*, 41–55.

Pervin, L. A., & Lewis, M. (Eds.). (1978). *Perspectives in interactional psychology*. New York: Plenum Press.

Petrella, R. C. (1992). Defendants with mental retardation in the forensic services system. In R. W. Conley, R. Luckasson, & G. N. Bouthilet (Eds.), *The criminal justice system and mental retardation* (pp. 79–96). Baltimore: Brookes.

Petronko, M. R., Harris, S. L., & Kormann, R. J. (1994). Community-based behavioral training approaches for people with mental retardation and mental illness. *Journal of Consulting and Clinical Psychology, 62*, 49–54.

Pfadt, A. (1991). Group psychotherapy with mentally retarded adults: Issues related to design, implementations, and evaluation. *Research in Developmental Disabilities, 12*, 261–286.

Phillips, L. R., Morrison, E. F., & Chao, Y. M. (1990). The QUALCARE Scale: Developing an instrument to measure the quality of home care. *International Journal of Nursing Studies, 27*, 61–75.

Piaget, J. (1950). *The psychology of intelligence*. New York: Harcourt, Brace.

Pieretti, M., Zhang, F., Fu, Y-H., Warren, S. T., Oostra, B. A., Caskey, C. T., & Nelson, D. L. (1991). Absence of expression of the FMR-1 gene in fragile X syndrome. *Cell, 66*, 817–822.

Pisterman, S., McGrath, P., Firestone, P., Goodman, J., Webster, I., Mallory, R., & Goffin, B. (1992). The effects of parent training on parenting stress and sense of competence. *Canadian Journal of Behavioral Science, 24*, 41–58.

Platt, L. O., Kamphaus, R. W., Cole, R. W., & Smith, C. L. (1991). Relationship between adaptive behavior and intelligence: Additional evidence. *Psychological Reports, 68*, 139–145.

Plomin, R., & McClearn, G. E. (1993). *Nature, nurture, and psychology*. Washington, DC: American Psychological Association.

Polizos, P., Engelhardt, D. M., Hoffman, S. P., & Waizer, J. (1973). Neurological consequences of psychotropic drug withdrawal in schizophrenic children. *Journal of Autism and Childhood Schizophrenia, 3,* 247–253.

Polloway, E. A., Patton, J. R., Epstein, M. H., & Smith, T. G. C. (1989). Comprehensive curriculum for students with mild handicaps. *Focus on Exceptional Children, 21,* 1–11.

Polloway, E. A., & Smith, J. D. (1983). Changes in mild mental retardation: Population, programs, and perspectives. *Exceptional Children, 50,* 149–159.

Popoff-Walker, L. E. (1982). IQ, SES, adaptive behavior, and performance on a learning potential measure. *Journal of School Psychology, 20,* 222–231.

Powars, D., & Imbus, C. (1980). Cerebral vascular accidents in sickle cell anemia. *Texas Reports on Biology and Medicine, 40,* 293–301.

Powell, C., & Grantham-McGregor, S. (1989). Home visiting of varying frequency and child development. *Pediatrics, 84,* 157–164.

Powers, L. E. (1993). Disability and grief: From tragedy to challenge. In G. Singer & L. Powers (Eds.), *Families, disability, and empowerment: Active coping skills and strategies for family interventions* (pp. 119–150). Baltimore: Brookes.

Powers, L. E., Singer, G. H., Stevens, T., & Sowers, J. A. (1992). Behavioral parent training in home and community generalization settings. *Education and Training in Mental Retardation, 27,* 13–27.

Pratt, M. W., Luszez, M. A., & Brown, M. E. (1979). *Group home management schedule.* Halifax, Nova Scotia: Department of Psychology, Mount St. Vincent University.

Premack, D. (1965). Reinforcement theory. In D. Levine (Ed.), *Nebraska Symposium on Motivation* (pp. 123–180). Lincoln: University of Nebraska.

President's Committee on Mental Retardation. (1970). *The six-hour retarded child.* Washington, DC: U.S. Government Printing Office.

Price, R. H., Cowen, E. L., Lorion, R. P., & Ramos-McKay, J. (Eds.). (1988). *Fourteen ounces of prevention: A casebook for practitioners.* Washington, DC: American Psychological Association.

Prieto-Bayard, M., & Baker, B. L. (1986). Parent training for Spanish speaking families with a retarded child. *Journal of Community Psychology, 14,* 134–143.

Prigatano, G. P., Parsons, O., Wright, E., Levin, D. C., & Hawayluk, G. (1983). Neuropsychological test performance in mildly hypoxemic patients with chronic obstructive pulmonary disease. *Journal of Consulting and Clinical Psychology, 51,* 108–116.

Prigatano, G. P., Wright, E. C., & Levin, D. (1984). Quality of life and its predictors in patients with mild hypoxemia and chronic obstructive pulmonary disease. *Archives of Internal Medicine, 144,* 1613–1619.

Prout, H. T., & Strohmer, D. C. (1991). *Emotional Problem Scales: Self Report Inventory.* Schenectady, NY: Genium Publishing.

Prouty, G. (1976). Pre-therapy: A method of treating pre-expressive psychotic and retarded patients. *Psychotherapy: Theory, Research, and Practice, 13,* 290–294.

Prouty, G., & Kubiak, M. A. (1988). Pre-therapy with mentally retarded/psychotic clients. *Psychiatric Aspects of Mental Retardation Reviews, 7,* 61–66.

Prudhoe Unit. (1987). *Continuous audit of residential environment standards.* Northumberland, UK: Prudhoe Hospital.

Pueschel, S. M. (1984). *The young child with Down syndrome.* New York: Human Sciences Press.

Pueschel, S. M., Gallagher, P. L., Zartler, A. S., & Pezzullo, J. C. (1987). Cognitive and learning processes in children with Down syndrome. *Research in Developmental Disabilities, 8,* 21–27.

Pueschel, S. M., Scola, P. S., Weidenman, L. E., & Bernier, L. C. (1995). *The special child: A source book for parents and children with developmental disabilities* (2nd ed.). Baltimore: Paul H. Brooks.

Purcell, E. M., Torrey, H. C., & Pound, R. V. (1946). Resonance absorption by nuclear moments in solid. *Physical Review, 69,* 37–38.

Quine, L., & Pahl, J. (1986). First diagnosis of severe mental handicap: Characteristics of unsatisfactory encounters between doctors and patients. *Social Science and Medicine, 22,* 53–62.

Raggio, D. J., & Massingale, T. W. (1990). Comparability of the Vineland Social Maturity

Scales and the Vineland Adaptive Behavior Scale survey form with infants evaluated for developmental delay. *Perceptual and Motor Skills, 71,* 415–418.

Raichle, M. E. (1983). Positron emission tomography. *Annual Review of Neuroscience, 6,* 249–267.

Ramey, C. T., Bryant, D. M., Campbell, F. A., Sparling, J. J., & Wasik, B. H. (1988). Early intervention for high-risk children: The Carolina Early Intervention Program. In R. H. Price, E. L. Cowen, R. P. Lorion, & J. Ramos-McCay (Eds.), *Fourteen ounces of prevention: A casebook for practitioners* (pp. 32–43). Washington, DC: American Psychological Association.

Ramey, C. T., Bryant, D. M., Wasik, B. H., Sparling, J. J., Fendt, K. H., & LaVange, L. M. (1992). The Infant Health and Development Program for low birthweight, premature infants: Program elements, family participation, and child intelligence. *Pediatrics, 89,* 454–465.

Ramey, C. T., & Campbell, F. A. (1992). Poverty, early childhood education, and academic competence: The Abecedarian experiment. In A. Houston (Ed.), *Children in poverty.* Cambridge, England: Cambridge University Press.

Ramey, C. T., & MacPhee, D. (1985). Developmental retardation: A systems theory perspective on risk and preventive intervention. In D. C. Farran & J. D. McKinney (Eds.), *Risk in intellectual and psychosocial development* (pp. 61–81). New York: Academic Press.

Ramey, C. T., MacPhee, D., & Yeates, K. O. (1982). Preventing developmental retardation: A general systems model. In J. M. Joffee & L. A. Bond (Eds.), *Facilitating infant and early childhood development* (pp. 343–401). Hanover, NH: University Press of New England.

Ramey, C. T., & Ramey, S. L. (1992a). *At risk does not mean doomed.* National Health/Education Consortium, Occasional Paper #4, Washington, DC.

Ramey, C. T., & Ramey, S. L. (1992b). Effective early intervention. *Mental Retardation, 6,* 337–345.

Ramey, C. T., Yeates, K. O., & Short, E. J. (1984). The plasticity of intellectual development: Insights from prevention intervention. *Child Development, 55,* 1913–1925.

Ramey, S. L. (1991). The family. *Current Opinion in Psychiatry, 4,* 678–682.

Ramey, S. L., Krauss, M. W., & Simeonsson, R. J. (1989). Research on families: Current assessment and future opportunities. *American Journal of Mental Retardation, 94,* ii–vi.

Ramey, S. L., & Ramey, C. T. (1992). Early educational intervention with disadvantaged children—To what effect? *Applied & Preventive Psychology, 1,* 131–140.

Ramirez, S. Z., & Kratchowill, T. R. (1990). Development of the Fear Survey for Children With and Without Mental Retardation. *Behavioral Asssessment, 12,* 457–470.

Ratey, J. J., Sovner, R., Mikkelsen, E., & Chmielinski, H. E. (1989). Buspirone therapy for maladaptive behavior and anxiety in developmentally disabled persons. *Journal of Clinical Psychiatry, 50,* 382–384.

Ratey, J. J., Sovner, R., Parks, A., & Rogentine, K. (1991). Buspirone treatment of aggression and anxiety in mentally retarded patients: A multiple baseline placebo lead-in study. *Journal of Clinical Psychiatry, 52,* 159–162.

Rautman, A. (1949). Society's first responsibility to the mentally retarded. *American Journal of Mental Deficiency, 54,* 155–162.

Raven, J. C. (1956). *Coloured Progressive Matrices: Sets A, Ab, B.* London: H. K. Lewis.

Raynes, N. V. (1988). *Assessment of community residental settings.* Manchester, England: University of Manchester.

Raynes, N. V., Pratt, M. W., & Roses, S. (1979). *Index of community involvement form I.* Manchester, England: University of Manchester.

Raynes, N. V., Sumpton, R. C., & Pettipher, C. (1986). *Index of adult autonomy.* Manchester, England: University of Manchester.

Reardon, S. M., & Naglieri, J. A. (1992). PASS cognitive processing characteristics of normal and ADHD males. *Journal of School Psychology, 30,* 151–163.

Reese, M. R., & Serna, L. (1986). Planning for generalization and maintenance in parent training: Parents need I.E.P.s too. *Mental Retardation, 24,* 87–92.

Reese, R. M., Sherman, J. A., & Sheldon, J. (1984). Reducing agitated-disruptive behavior of mentally retarded residents of community group homes: The roles of self-recording and peer prompted self-recording. *Analysis and Intervention in Developmental Disabilities, 4*, 91–108.

Regal, R. A., Rooney, J. R., & Wandas, T. (1994). Faciliated communication: An experimental evaluation. *Journal of Autism and Developmental Disorders, 24,* 345–355.

Rehabilitation Act of 1973, 29 U.S.C. § 794 (1973).

Reich, W., & Welner, Z. (1988). *Diagnostic Interview for Children and Adolescents, DICA-R-C, DSM-III-R Version, Revised Version of DICA for Children Ages 6–12.* Unpublished manuscript, Washington University, St. Louis, MO.

Reichle, J., & Wacker, D. P. (1993). *Communicative alternative to challenging behavior*. Baltimore: Brookes.

Reichle, J., York, J., & Sigafoos, J. (1991). *Implementing augmentative and alternative communication: Strategies for learners with severe disabilities.* Baltimore: Brookes.

Reid, A. H., Naylor, G. J., & Kay, D. S. G. (1981). A double-blind, placebo-controlled, crossover trial of carbamazepine in overactive, severely mentally handicapped patients. *Psychological Medicine, 11,* 109–113.

Reid, D. H., Parsons, M. B., & Green, C. W. (1989). *Staff management in human services: Behavioral research and application.* Springfield IL: Charles C Thomas.

Reid, D. H., Parsons, M. B., McCarn, J. E., Green, C. W., Phillips, J. F., & Schepis, M. M. (1985). Providing more appropriate education for severely handicapped persons: Increasing and validating functional classroom tasks. *Journal of Applied Behavior Analysis, 18,* 289–301.

Reid, D. H., Parsons, M. B., & Schepis, M. M. (1990). Management practices that affect the relative utility of aversive and nonaversive procedures. In S. L. Harris & J. S. Handleman (Eds.), *Aversive and nonaversive interventions: Controlling life-threatening behavior by the developmentally disabled* (pp. 144–162). New York: Springer.

Reiss, A. L., Freund, L., Abrams, M. T., Boehm, C., & Kazazian, H. (1993). Neurobehavioral effects of the fragile X permutation in adult women: A controlled study. *American Journal of Human Genetics, 52,* 884–894.

Reiss, S. (1985). The mentally retarded, emotionally disturbed adult. In M. Sigman (Ed.), *Children with dual diagnosis: Mental retardation and mental illness.* New York: Grune & Stratton.

Reiss, S. (1988). *Reiss Screen for Maladaptive Behavior.* Worthington, OH: International Diagnostic Systems.

Reiss, S. (1990). Prevalence of dual diagnosis in community-based day programs in the Chicago metropolitan area. *American Journal of Mental Retardation, 94,* 578–585.

Reiss, S. (1994). *Handbook of challenging behavior: Mental health aspects of mental retardation.* Worthington, OH: International Diagnostic Systems.

Reiss, S., & Benson, B. A. (1984). Awareness of negative social conditions among mentally retarded, emotionally disturbed outpatients. *American Journal of Psychiatry, 141,* 88–90.

Reiss, S., Levitan, G. W., & Szyszko, J. (1982). Emotional disturbance and mental retardation: Diagnostic overshadowing. *American Journal of Mental Deficiency, 86,* 567–574.

Repp, A. C. (1983). *Teaching the mentally retarded.* Englewood Cliffs, NJ: Prentice Hall.

Repp, A. C., & Karsh, K. G. (1991). The task demonstration model: A program for teaching persons with severe handicaps. In R. Remington (Ed.), *Severe mental retardation and applied behavior analysis* (pp. 263–283). New York: Wiley.

Repp, A. C., Karsh, K. G., & Lenz, M. (1990). A comparison of two teaching procedures on acquisition and generalization of severely handicapped persons. *Journal of Applied Behavior Analysis, 23,* 43–52.

Repp, A. C., & Singh, N. N. (Eds.). (1990). *Perspectives on the use of nonaversive and aversive interventions for persons with developmental disabilities.* Sycamore, IL: Sycamore.

Reschly, D. J. (1981a). Evaluation of the effects of SOMPA measures on classification of students as mildly mentally retarded. *American Journal of Mental Deficiency, 86,* 16–20.

Reschly, D. J. (1981b). Psychological testing in educational classification and assessment. *American Psychologist, 36,* 1094–1102.

Reschly, D. J. (1985). Best practices: Adaptive behavior. In A. Thomas & J. Grimes (Eds.),

Best practices in school psychology (pp. 353–368). Washington, DC: National Association of School Psychology.

Reschly, D. J. (1988). Assessment issues, placement litigation, and the future of mild mental retardation classification and programming. *Education and Training in Mental Retardation, 23,* 285–301.

Reschly, D. J., & Jipson, F. J. (1976). Ethnicity, geographic locale, age, sex, and urban-rural residence as variables in the prevalence of mild mental retardation. *American Journal of Mental Deficiency, 81,* 154–161.

Reschly, D. J., & Ward, S. M. (1991). Use of adaptive behavior measures and overrepresentation of Black students in programs for students with mild mental retardation. *American Journal on Mental Retardation, 96,* 257–268.

Resnick, L. B., & Klopfer, L. (Eds.). (1989). *Toward the thinking curriculum: Current cognitive research.* Alexandria, VA: Association for Supervision and Curriculum Development.

Reynolds, C. R., & Clark, J. H. (1985). Profile analysis of standardized intelligence test performance of very low functioning individuals. *Journal of School Psychology, 23,* 277–283.

Reynolds, M. C. (1991). Classification and labeling. In J. W. Lloyd, N. N. Singh, & A. C. Repp (Eds.), *The regular education initiative: Alternative perspectives on concepts, issues, and models* (pp. 29–41). Sycamore, IL: Sycamore.

Reynolds, W. M. (1981). Measurement of personal competence of mentally retarded individuals. *American Journal of Mental Deficiency, 85,* 368–376.

Reynolds, W. M. (1989). *Self-Report Depression Questionnaire (SRDQ) administration booklet.* Odessa, FL: Psychological Assessment Resources.

Reynolds, W. M., & Baker, J. A. (1988). Assessment of depression in persons with mental retardation. *American Journal of Mental Retardation, 93,* 93–103.

Richardson, S. A. (1989). Issues in the definition of mental retardation and the representativeness of studies. *Research in Developmental Disabilities, 10,* 285–294.

Richardson, S. A., Koller, H., & Katz, M. (1986). Comments on Baird and Sadovnick's "Mental retardation in over half-a-million consecutive livebirths: An epidemiological study." *American Journal of Mental Deficiency, 90,* 449–450.

Richman, J. S., Sonderby, T., & Kahn, J. V. (1980). Prerequisite vs. in vivo acquisition of self-feeding skills. *Behavior Research and Therapy, 18,* 327–332.

Richmond, B. O., & Blagg, D. E. (1985). Adaptive behavior, social adjustment, and academic achievement of regular and special education students. *The Exceptional Child, 32,* 93–98.

Rider, M. E., & Mason, J. L. (1990). *Issues in culturally competent service delivery: An annotated bibliography.* Portland, OR: Research and Training Center of Family Support and Children's Mental Health.

Rimmerman, A. (1989). Provision of respite care for children with developmental disabilities: Changes in maternal coping and stress over time. *Mental Retardation, 27,* 99–103.

Rinck, C. (1987). *Annotated descriptions of Adaptive Behavior Scales.* Kansas City: University of Missouri, Institute for Human Development.

Rinck, C., & Brown, C. (1987, October). *Interpretive guidelines to the AAMD Adaptive Behavior Scale.* Kansas City: University of Missouri, Institute for Human Development.

Rinck, C., Calkins, C. F., Neff, F. W., Griggs, P., & Brown, C. (1987). *Refining Missouri's assessment of persons with developmental disabilities.* Kansas City: University of Missouri, Institute for Human Development.

Rincover, A., & Ducharme, J. M. (1987). Variables influencing stimulus overselectivity and 24 "tunnel vision" in developmentally delayed children. *American Journal of Mental Deficiency, 91,* 422–430.

Rinn, R. C., Vernon, J. C., & Wise, M. J. (1975). Training parents of behaviorally-disordered children in groups: A three years' program evaluation. *Behavior Therapy, 6,* 378–387.

Risley, T. R., & Favell, J. E. (1979). Constructing a living environment in an institution. In L. A. Hamerlynck (Ed.), *Behavioral systems for the developmentally disabled: II. Institutional, clinic, and community environments* (pp. 3–24). New York: Brunner/Mazel.

Rivenq, B. (1974). Behavioral therapy of phobias: A case with gynecomastia and mental retardation. *Mental Retardation, 12,* 44–45.

Rivers, W. H. R. (1926). *Psychology and ethnology*. New York: Harcourt Brace.

Roberts, R. (1989). *Developing culturally competent programs for children with special needs.* Washington, DC: Georgetown University Development Center.

Robinson, N. M. (1978). Mild mental retardation: Does it exist in the People's Republic of China? *Mental Retardation, 16,* 295–299.

Robinson, N. M., & Robinson, H. B. (1976). *The mentally retarded child: A psychological approach* (2nd ed.). New York: McGraw-Hill.

Rockowitz, R. J. (1986). *Developmentally disabled offender project: Final report* (Grant #90-DD0046). Rochester, NY: Developmentally Disabled Offender Project.

Rodrigue, J. R., Morgan, S. B., & Geffken, G. R. (1991). A comparative evaluation of adaptive behavior in children and adolescents with autism, Down syndrome, and normal development. *Journal of Autism and Developmental Disorders, 21,* 187–196.

Roff, M., Sell, B., & Golden, M. M. (1972). *Social adjustment and personality development in children.* Minneapolis: University of Minnesota Press.

Rogers, R. C., & Simensen, R. J. (1987). Fragile X syndrome: A common etiology of mental retardation. *American Journal of Mental Deficiency, 91,* 445–449.

Rogers, T. R., Forehand, R., Griest, D. L., Wells, K. C., & McMahon, R. J. (1981). Socioeconomic status: Effects on parent and child behaviors and treatment outcomes of parent training. *Journal of Clinical Child Psychology, 10,* 98–101.

Rogoff, B. (1990). *Apprenticeship in thinking: Cognitive development in social contexts.* New York: Oxford University Press.

Rogoff, B., & Morelli, G. (1989). Perspectives on children's development from cultural psychology. *American Psychologist, 44,* 343–348.

Rojahn, J. (1986). Self-injurious and stereotypic behavior of non-institutionalized mentally retarded people: Prevalence and classification. *American Journal of Mental Deficiency, 91,* 268–276.

Rojahn, J. (1992). *Behavior Problem Inventory: A prospectus.* Unpublished manuscript, Nisonger Center–UAP, Ohio State University, Columbus, OH.

Rojahn, J. (1994). Epidemiology and topographic taxonomy of self-injurious behavior. In T. Thompson (Ed.), *Destructive behavior in developmental disabilities: Diagnosis, measurement, and evaluating treatment outcome* (pp. 49–67). Newbury Park, CA: Sage.

Rojahn, J., Borthwick-Duffy, S. A., & Jacobson, J. W. (1993). The association between psychiatric diagnoses and severe behavior problems in mental retardation. *Annals of Clinical Psychiatry, 5,* 163–170.

Rojahn, J., Polster, L. M., Mulick, J. A., & Wisniewski, J. J. (1989). Reliability of the Behavior Problems Inventory. *Journal of the Multihandicapped Person, 2,* 283–293.

Rojahn, J., & Schroeder, S. R. (1991). Behavioral assessment. In J. L. Matson & J. A. Mulick (Eds.), *Handbook of mental retardation* (2nd ed., pp. 240–259). Elmsford, NY: Pergamon Press.

Rolinder, A., & Van Houten, R. (1993). The interpersonal treatment model: Teaching appropriate social inhibitions through the development of personal stimulus control by the systematic introduction of antecedent stimuli. In R. Van Houten & S. Axelrod (Eds.), *Behavior analysis and treatment* (pp. 127–168). New York: Plenum Press.

Ronka, C. S., & Barnett, D. (1986). A comparison of adaptive behavior ratings: Revised Vineland and AAMD ABS-SE. *Special Services in the Schools, 2,* 87–96.

Rooney, R., Fullagar, P., & Gallagher, J. (1993). *Distinctive personnel preparation models for Part H: Three case studies.* Chapel Hill: Carolina Policy Studies Program, University of North Carolina at Chapel Hill.

Rosen, H. G., & Rosen, S. (1969). Group therapy as an instrument to develop a concept of self-worth in the adolescent and young adult mentally retarded. *Mental Retardation, 7,* 52–55.

Rosenberg, I. H. (1992). Folic acid and neural tube defects—Time for action? *New England Journal of Medicine, 327,* 1875–1876.

Rosenberg, P. S. (1995). Scope of the AIDS epidemic in the United States. *Science, 270,* 1372–1375.

Ross, L. E., & Ross, S. M. (1984). Oculomotor functioning and the learning and cognitive processes of the intellectually handicapped. In P. H. Brooks, R. Sperber, & C. McCauley (Eds.), *Learning and cognition in the mentally retarded* (pp. 217–236). Hillsdale, NJ: Erlbaum.

Roszkowski, M. J., & Bean, A. G. (1981). Abbreviated procedure for obtaining sum scores on the Adaptive Behavior Scale. *Exceptional Children, 48,* 265–267.

Roszkowski, M. J., & Spreat, S. (1981). A comparison of the psychometric and clinical methods of determining level of mental retardation. *Applied Research in Mental Retardation, 2,* 359–366.

Roszkowski, M. J., Spreat, S., & Isett, R. (1983). Mentally retarded persons' adaptive behavior status and direct-care technicians' perceptions of their global impairment levels. *Journal of Psychiatric Treatment and Evaluation, 5,* 19–23.

Rovet, J., Ehrlich, R. M., & Sorbara, D. L. (1989). Effect of thyroid hormone level on temperament in infants with congenital hypothyroidism detected by screening of neonates. *Journal of Pediatrics, 114,* 63–68.

Rovet, J. F. (1990). The cognitive and neuropsychological characteristics of females with Turner syndrome. In B. Bock & B. G. Bender (Eds.), *Sex chromosome abnormalities and behavior: Psychological studies* (pp. 38–77). Boulder, CO: Westview Press.

Rowan, K. E. (1994). Why rules for risk communication are not enough: A problem-solving approach to risk communication. *Risk Analysis, 14,* 365–374.

Rueda, R. S., & Martinez, I. (1992). Fiesta educativa: One community's approach to parent training in developmental disabilities for Latino families. *Journal of the Association for Persons with Severe Handicaps, 17,* 95–103.

Runyan, M. C., Stevens, D. H., & Reeves, R. (1985). Reduction of avoidance behavior of institutionalized mentally retarded adults through contact desensitization. *American Journal of Mental Deficiency, 90,* 222–225.

Rusch, F. R., Chadsey-Rusch, J., & Lagomarcino, T. (1987). Preparing students for employment. In M. E. Snell (Ed.), *Systematic instruction for persons with severe handicaps* (3rd ed., pp. 471–490). Columbus, OH: Merrill.

Rusch, F. R., Destefano, L., Chadsey-Rusch, J., Phelps, L. A., & Syzmanski, E. (1992). *Transition from school to adult life: Models, linkages, and policy.* Sycamore, IL: Sycamore Publishing.

Rusch, F. R., Schutz, R. P., & Agran, M. (1982). Validating entry-level survival skills for service occupations: Implications for curriculum development. *Journal of the Association for the Severely Handicapped, 7,* 32–41.

Rusch, F. R., Syzmanski, E., & Chadsey-Rusch, J. (1992). The emerging field of transition services. In F. R. Rusch, L. Destefano, J. Chadsey-Rusch, L. A. Phelps, & E. Syzmanski (Eds.), *Transition from school to adult life: Models, linkages, and policy* (pp. 1–15). Sycamore, IL: Sycamore Publishing.

Russell, A. T. (1988). The association between mental retardation and psychiatric disorder: Epidemiological issues. In J. A. Stark, F. J. Menolascino, M. H. Albarelli, & V. C. Gray (Eds.), *Mental retardation and mental health: Classification, diagnosis, treatment, services.* New York: Springer-Verlag.

Russell, A. T., & Forness, S. R. (1985). Behavioral disturbance in mentally retarded children in TMR and EMR classrooms. *American Journal of Mental Deficiency, 89,* 338–344.

Russell, J. A., & Ward, W. (1982). Environmental psychology. *Annual Review of Psychology, 33,* 651–688.

Ruth, V., Virkola, K., Petau, R., & Raivio, K. O. (1988). Early high-dose phenobarbital treatment for prevention of hypoxic-ischemic brain damage in very low birth weight infants. *Journal of Pediatrics, 112,* 81–86.

Rutter, M., Tizard, J., Yule, W., Graham, P., & Whitmore, K. (1976). Isle of Wight studies, 1964–1974. *Psychological Medicine, 6,* 313–332.

Ryff, C. D., & Seltzer, M. M. (1995). Family relations and individual development in adulthood and aging. In R. Blieszner & V. Bedford (Eds.), *Handbook on aging and the family* (pp. 95–113). Westport, CT: Greenwood Press.

Sachdev, P. (1994). Research diagnostic criteria for drug-induced akathisia: Conceptualization, rationale, and proposal. *Psychopharmacology, 14,* 181–186.

Sadler, O. W., Seyden, T., Howe, B., & Kaminsky, T. (1976). An evaluation of "Groups for

Parents": A standardized format encompassing both behavior modification and humanistic methods. *Journal of Community Psychology, 4,* 157–163.

Sagan, C. (1993, March 7). What's really going on? *Parade Magazine*, pp. 4–7.

Saitzyk, A. R., & Floyd, F. J. (1992, August). *Conjugal social support between parents of children with mental retardation.* Paper presented at the meeting of the International Association for the Scientific Study of Mental Deficiency, Queensland, Australia.

Salagaras, S., & Nettelbeck, T. (1983). Adaptive behavior of mentally retarded adolescents attending school. *American Journal of Mental Deficiency, 88,* 57–68.

Salagaras, S., & Nettelbeck, T. (1984). Adaptive behavior of mentally retarded adults in work-preparation settings. *American Journal of Mental Deficiency, 88,* 437–441.

Salisbury, C. L., & Intagliata, J. (Eds.). (1986). *Respite care: Support for persons with developmental disabilities and their families.* Baltimore: Brookes.

Salthouse, T. A. (1988). Initiating the formalization of theories of cognitive aging. *Psychology and Aging, 3,* 3–16.

Salzinger, K., Feldman, R. S., & Portnoy, S. (1970). Training parents of brain injured children in the use of operant conditioning procedures. *Behavior Therapy, 1,* 4–32.

Sameroff, A. J., Seifer, R., Baldwin, A., & Baldwin, C. (1993). Stability of intelligence from preschool to adolescence: The influence of social and family risk factors. *Child Development, 64,* 80–97.

Sameroff, A. J., Seifer, R., Barocas, B., Zax, M., & Greenspan, S. (1987). IQ scores of 4-year-old children: Social-environmental risk factors. *Pediatrics, 79,* 343–350.

Sampson, E. E. (1993). Identity politics: Challenges to psychology's understanding. *American Psychologist, 48,* 1219–1230.

Sander, C. H. (1985). The surgical pathologist examines the placenta. *Pathology Annual, 20,* 235–288.

Sanders, M. R., & Dadds, M. R. (1982). The effects of planned activities and child management procedures on parent training: An analysis of setting generality. *Behavior Therapy, 13,* 452–461.

Sanders, M. R., & Dadds, M. R. (1987). *Planned activities training.* Queensland, Australia: University of Queensland, Department of Psychology.

Sanders, M. R., & Plant, K. (1989). Programming for generalization to high and low risk parenting situations in families with oppositional developmentally disabled preschoolers. *Behavior Modification, 13,* 283–305.

Sandford, D. A., Elzinga, R. H., & Grainger, W. (1987). Evaluation of residential behavioral program for behaviorally disturbed, mentally retarded young adults. *American Journal of Mental Deficiency, 91,* 431–434.

Sandison v. Michigan High School Athletic Association, No. 94–73231 (United States District Court for the Eastern District of Michigan, Sept. 13, 1994).

Sandler, A., & Coren, A. (1981). Integrated instruction at home and school: Parents' perspective. *Education and Training of the Mentally Retarded, 16,* 183–187.

Santarcangelo, S., Birkett, N., & McGrath, J. (1995). Therapeutic case management: Vermont's system for individualized care. In B. J. Friesen & J. Poertner (Eds.), *From case management to service coordination for children with emotional, behavioral, or mental disorders* (pp. 301–316). Baltimore: Brookes.

Santelli, B., Turnbull, A., Lerner, E., & Marquis, J. (1993). Parent to parent programs: A unique form of mutual support for families of persons with disabilities. In G. Singer & L. Powers (Eds.), *Families, disability, and empowerment: Active coping skills and strategies for family interventions* (pp. 27–58). Baltimore: Brookes.

Sarason, S. B. (1953). *Psychological problems in mental deficiency.* New York: Harper.

Sarason, S. B., & Doris, J. (1969). *Psychological problems in mental deficiency* (4th ed.). New York: Harper & Row.

Sasso, G. M., Reimers, T. M., Cooper, L. J., Wacker, D., Berg, W., Steege, M., Kelly, L., & Allaire, A. (1992). Use of descriptive and experimental analyses to identify the functional properties of aberrant behavior in school settings. *Journal of Applied Behavior Analysis, 25,* 809–821.

Sattler, J. M. (1988). *Assessment of children* (3rd ed.). Available from Jerome M. Sattler, Publisher, PO Box 151677, San Diego, CA 92115.

Saunders, E. J. (1979). Staff members' attitudes toward the sexual behavior of mentally retarded residents. *American Journal of Mental Deficiency, 84,* 206–208.

Saunders, R. R., Saunders, M. D., & Hull, D. D. (1991). *CAPPS: A comprehensive assessment and program planning system.* Parsons, KS: Parsons Research Center.

Saunders, R. R., & Spradlin, J. E. (1991). A supported routines approach to active treatment for enhancing independence, competence, and self-worth. *Behavioral Residential Treatment, 6,* 11–37.

Scanlon, P. L. (1978). Social work with the mentally retarded client. *Social Casework, 59,* 161–166.

Scarr, S. (1981). Testing for children: Assessment and the many determinants of intellectual competence. *American Psychologist, 36,* 1159–1166.

Scarr, S. (1985). Constructing psychology: Making facts and fables for our times. *American Psychologist, 40,* 449–512.

Scarr, S., & Carter-Saltzman, L. (1982). Genetics and intelligence. In R. J. Sternberg (Ed.), *Handbook of intelligence* (pp. 792–900). Cambridge, England: Cambridge University Press.

Scarr, S., & McCartney, K. (1988). Far from home: An experimental evaluation of the mother–child home program in Bermuda. *Child Development, 59,* 531–543.

Schachter, M. (1983). Neuropsychology and exceptional children. In C. J. Golden & P. J. Vicente (Eds.), *Foundations of clinical neuropsychology* (pp. 369–400). New York: Plenum Press.

Schaefer, G. B., & Bodensteiner, J. B. (1992). Evaluation of the child with idiopathic mental retardation. *Pediatric Clinics of North America, 39,* 929–943.

Schalock, R. L. (1990). *Quality of life: Perspective and issues.* Washington, DC: American Association on Mental Retardation.

Schalock, R. L. (1994). Quality of life, quality enhancement, and quality assurance: Implications for program planning and evaluation in the field of mental retardation and developmental disabilities. *Evaluation and Program Planning, 17,* 121–131.

Schalock, R. L., & Heal, L. W. (1988). Research in quality of life: Current status and policy recommendations. In D. Goode (Ed.), *Proceedings from quality of life for persons with disabilities.* Valhalla, NY: Mental Retardation Institute University Affiliated Facility.

Schalock, R. L., & Jensen, C. M. (1986). Assessing the goodness-of fit between persons and their environments. *Journal of the Association for Persons with Severe Handicaps, 11,* 103–109.

Schalock, R. L., Keith, K. D., & Hoffman, K. (1990). *1990 quality of life questionnaire standardization manual.* Hastings, NE: Mid-Nebraska Mental Retardation Services.

Schalock, R. L., Keith, K. D., Hoffman, K., & Karan, O. C. (1989). Quality of life: Its measurement and use in human services programs. *Mental Retardation, 27,* 25–31.

Schapiro, M. B., Haxby, J. V., & Grady, C. L. (1992). Nature of mental retardation and dementia in Down syndrome: Study with PET, CT, and neuropsychology. *Neurobiology of Aging, 13,* 723–734.

Scheiner, A. P. (1992). Referral processes. In M. D. Levine, W. B. Carey, & A. C. Crocker (Eds.), *Developmental behavioral pediatrics* (2nd ed., pp. 765–768). Philadelphia: W. B. Saunders.

Schlottmann, R. S., & Anderson, V. H. (1982). Developmental changes of institutionalized mentally retarded children: A semilongitudinal study. *American Journal of Mental Deficiency, 87,* 277–281.

Schmidt, F. L., & Hunter, J. E. (1981). Employment testing. *American Psychologist, 36,* 1128–1137.

Schopler, E. (1994). Neurobiologic correlates in the classification and study of autism. In S. H. Broman & J. Grafman (Eds.), *Atypical cognitive deficits in developmental disorders: Implications for brain function* (pp. 57–66). Hillsdale, NJ: Erlbaum.

Schreibman, L. (1975). Effects of within-stimulus and extra-stimulus prompting on discrimination learning in autistic children. *Journal of Applied Behavior Analysis, 8,* 91–112.

Schreibman, L., & Charlop, M. H. (1981). S+(plus) versus S−(minus) fading in prompting procedures with autistic children. *Journal of Experimental Child Psychology, 31,* 508–520.

Schroeder, S. R. (Ed.). (1987). *Toxic substances and mental retardation: Neurobehavioral toxicology and teratology.* Washington, DC: American Association on Mental Deficiency.

Schroeder, S. R. (1988). Neuroleptic medications for persons with developmental disabilities. In M. G. Aman & N. N. Singh (Eds.), *Psychopharmacology of the developmental disabilities* (pp. 82–100). New York: Springer-Verlag.

Schroeder, S. R. (Ed.). (1990). *Ecobehavioral analysis and developmental disabilities: The twenty-first century.* New York: Springer-Verlag.

Schroeder, S. R., Kanoy, R. C., Mulick, J. A., Rojahn, J., Thios, S. J., Stephens, M., & Hawk, B. (1982). Environmental antecedents which affect management and maintenance of programs for self-injurious behavior. In J. H. Hollis & C. E. Meyers (Eds.), *Life-threatening behavior: Analysis and intervention* (pp. 105–159) [AAMD Monograph No. 5]. Washington, DC: American Association on Mental Deficiency.

Schroeder, S. R., Lewis, M. H., & Lipton, M. A. (1983). Interactions of drugs with behavior management among learning and behaviorally disordered children. In K. D. Gadow & I. Bialer (Eds.), *Advances in learning and behavioral disabilities* (Vol. 2, pp. 179–225). Greenwich, CT: JAI Press.

Schroeder, S. R., & MacLean, W. (1987). If it isn't one thing, it's another: Experimental analysis of covariation in behavior management data of severe behavior disturbances. In S. Landesman & P. Vietze (Eds.), *Living environments and mental retardation* (pp. 315–337). Washington, DC: American Association on Mental Retardation.

Schroeder, S. R., Mulick, J., & Schroeder, C. (1979). Management of severe behavior problems of the retarded. In N. Ellis (Ed.), *Handbook of mental deficiency* (2nd ed., pp. 341–366). Hillsdale, NJ: Erlbaum.

Schroeder, S. R., Rojahn, J., & Mulick, J. A. (1978). Ecobehavioral organization of developmental day care for the chronically self-injurious. *Journal of Pediatric Psychology, 3,* 81–88.

Schweinhart, L. J., & Weikart, D. P. (1981). Effects of the Perry Preschool Program on youth through age 15. *Journal of the Division of Early Childhood, 4,* 29–39.

Scola, P. S. (1991). Infections. In J. L. Matson & J. A. Mulick (Eds.), *Handbook of mental retardation* (pp. 151–157). Elmsford, NY: Pergamon Press.

Scott, K. G., Swales, T. P., & Danhour, K. R. (1990). Critical issues in the assessment of child psychopathology: An overview of the current state of the art. In E. Dibble & D. B. Gray (Eds.), *Assessment of behavior problems in persons with mental retardation living in the community* (pp. 1–17). Rockville, MD: National Institute of Mental Health.

Scott, L. S., Mastenbrook, J. L., Fisher, A. T., & Gridley, G. C. (1982). Adaptive behavior inventory for children: The need for local norms. *Journal of School Psychology, 20,* 39–44.

Scribner, S. (1984). Studying working intelligence. In B. Rogoff & J. Lave (Eds.), *Everyday cognition: Its development in social context* (pp. 9–40). Cambridge, MA: Harvard University Press.

Sedlack, R. A., Doyle, M., & Schloss, D. (1982). Video games: A training and generalization demonstration with severely retarded adolescents. *Education and Training of the Mentally Retarded, 17,* 332–336.

Seligman, M. E. P. (1975). *Helplessness: On depression, development and death.* New York: Freeman.

Seligman, M., & Darling, R. B. (1989). *Ordinary families, special children: A systems approach to childhood disabilities.* New York: Guilford Press.

Seltzer, G. B. (1983). Systems of classification. In J. L. Matson & J. A. Mulick (Eds.), *Handbook of mental retardation* (pp. 143–156). Elmsford, NY: Pergamon Press.

Seltzer, M. M. (1992, March). *Depression in aging mothers of adults with mental retardation.* Paper presented at the Gatlinburg Conference on Research and Theory in Mental Retardation and Developmental Disabilities, Gatlinburg, TN.

Seltzer, M. M., & Krauss, M. W. (1989). Aging parents with mentally retarded children: Family risk factors and sources of support. *American Journal of Mental Retardation, 94,* 303–312.

Seltzer, M. M., & Ryff, C. (1994). Parenting across the life-span: The normative and non-normative cases. In D. L. Featherman, R. M. Lerner, & M. Perlmutter (Eds.), *Life-span development and behavior* (pp. 1–40). Hillsdale, NJ: Erlbaum.

Seltzer, M. M., & Seltzer, G. B. (1976). *The Community Adjustment Scale*. Madison: University of Wisconsin Waisman Center.

Seltzer, M. M., & Seltzer, G. B. (1991). Classification and social status. In J. L. Matson & J. A. Mulick (Eds.), *Handbook of mental retardation* (2nd ed., pp. 166–180). Elmsford, NY: Pergamon Press.

Senatore, V., Matson, J. L., & Kazdin, A. E. (1985). An inventory to assess psychopathology of mentally retarded adults. *American Journal of Mental Deficiency, 89*, 459–466.

Serna, L. A., & Patton, J. R. (1989). Science. In J. R. Patten, E. A. Polloway, & L. R. Argent (Eds.), *Best practices in mild mental disabilities* (pp. 89–107). Reston, VA: Council for Exceptional Children.

Serpell, R. (1990). Audience, culture, and psychological explanation: A reformulation of the emic–etic problem in cross-cultural psychology. *The Quarterly Newsletter of the Laboratory of Comparative Human Cognition, 12*, 99–132.

Serpell, R., Mariga, L., & Harvey, K. (1993). Mental retardation in African countries: Conceptualization, services, and research. In N. W. Bray (Ed.), *International review of research in mental retardation* (pp. 1–39). San Diego, CA: Academic Press.

Sexton, D., Thompson, B., Perez, J., & Rheams, T. (1990). Maternal versus professional estimates of developmental status for young children with handicaps: An ecological approach. *Topics in Early Childhood Special Education, 10*, 80–95.

Shackelford, J. (1992, October). State jurisdiction eligibility definitions for Part H. *NEC*TAS Notes*, pp. 1–13.

Shafer, M. S., Ingle, K. J., & Hill, J. (1986). Acquisition, generalization, and maintenance of automated banking skills. *Educational and Training of the Mentally Retarded, 21*, 265–272.

Shane, H. C., & Kearns, K. (1994). An examination of the role of the facilitator in "faciliated communication." *American Journal of Speech–Language Pathology, 3*, 48–54.

Shank, M. S., & Turnbull, A. K. (1993). Cooperative family problem solving: An intervention for single parent families of children with disabilities. In G. H. S. Singer & L. Powers (Eds.), *Families, disability, and empowerment: Active coping skills and strategies for family interventions* (pp. 231–254). Baltimore: Brookes.

Shankaran, S., Kottamasu, S. R., & Kuhns, L. (1993). Brain sonography, computed tomography, and single-photon emission computed tomography in term neonates with perinatal asphysia. *Clinics in Perinatology, 20*, 379–394.

Shapira, B., Reiss, A., Kaiser, N., Kindler, S., & Lerer, B. (1989). Effect of imipramine treatment on the prolactin response to fenfluramine and placebo challenge in depressed patients. *Journal of Affective Disorders, 16*, 1–4.

Shapiro, A. K., Shapiro, E., & Eisenkraft, G. J. (1983). Treatment of Gilles de la Tourette syndrome with pimozide. *American Journal of Psychiatry, 140*, 1183–1186.

Shapiro, E. S., & Cole, C. L. (1994). *Behavior change in the classroom: Self-management interventions*. New York: Guilford Press.

Sharp, M. C., Strauss, R. P., & Lorch, S. C. (1992). Communicating medical bad news: Parents' experiences and preferences. *Journal of Pediatrics, 121*, 539–546.

Shearer, D. E., & Loftin, C. R. (1984). The Portage Project: Teaching parents to teach their preschool children in the home. In R. F. Dangel & R. A. Polster (Eds.), *Parent training: Foundations of research and practice* (pp. 93–126). New York: Guilford Press.

Shearer, M., & Shearer, D. (1972). The Portage Project: A model for early childhood education. *Exceptional Children, 36*, 172–178.

Shechtman, A. (1970). Age patterns in children's psychiatric symptoms. *Child Development, 41*, 683–693.

Shonkoff, J. P., Hauser-Cram, P., Krauss, M. W., & Upshur, C. C. (1992). Development of infants with disabilities and their families. *Monographs of the Society for Research in Child Development, 57*(Serial No. 230).

Shonkoff, J. P., & Meisels, S. J. (1990). Early childhood intervention: The evolution of a concept. In S. J. Meisels & J. P. Shonkoff (Eds.), *Handbook of early childhood intervention* (pp. 3–32). Cambridge, England: Cambridge University Press.

Short, R. J., Simeonsson, R. J., & Huntington, G. S. (1990). Early intervention: Implications of Public Law 99-457 for professional child psychology. *Professional Psychology: Research and Practice, 21*, 88–93.

Shucard, D. W., Shucard, J. L., Clopper, R. R., & Schachter, M. (1992). Electrophysiological and neuropsychological indices of cognitive processing deficits in Turner syndrome. *Developmental Neuropsychology, 8,* 299–323.

Siegel, B. (in press). Assessing allegations of sexual molestation made through facilitated communication. *Journal of Autism and Developmental Disorders.*

Sigafoos, J. (1995). Testing for spontaneous use of requests after sign language training with two severely handicapped adults. *Behavioral Interventions, 10,* 1–16.

Sigafoos, J., & Kerr, M. (1994). Provision of leisure activities for the reduction of challenging behavior. *Behavioral Interventions, 9,* 43–54.

Sigafoos, J., & York, J. (1991). Using ecological inventories to promote functional communication. In J. Reichle, J. York, & J. Sigafoos (Eds.), *Implementing augmentative and alternative communication: Strategies for learners with severe disabilities* (pp. 61–70). Baltimore: Brookes.

Sigel, I. E., & Laosa, L. M. (Eds.). (1983). *Changing families.* New York: Plenum Press.

Sigman, M. (1994). What are the core deficits in autism? In S. H. Broman & J. Grafman (Eds.), *Atypical cognitive deficits in developmental disorders: Implications for brain function* (pp. 139–158). Hillsdale, NJ: Erlbaum.

Silverman, W. A. (1993). Doing more good than harm. In K. S. Warren & F. Mosteller (Eds.), *Doing more harm than good: The evaluation of health care interventions* (pp. 5–11). New York: New York Academy of Sciences.

Silverman, W. P., Silver, E. J., Lubin, R. A., & Sersen, E. A. (1983). Structure of the Minnesota Developmental Programming System Behavioral Scales, Alternate Form C. *American Journal of Mental Deficiency, 88,* 170–176.

Silverstein, A. B., Lozano, G. D., & White, J. F. (1989). A cluster analysis of institutionalized mentally retarded individuals. *American Journal of Mental Retardation, 94,* 1–5.

Silverstein, B., Wothke, W., & Slabaugh, R. D. (1988). Toward parsimony with comprehensiveness: Management applications of MDPS factor scores. *Mental Retardation, 26,* 145–153.

Silvestri, R. (1977). Implosive therapy treatment of emotionally disturbed retardates. *Journal of Consulting and Clinical Psychology, 45,* 14–22.

Simensen, R. J., & Fisch, G. S. (1993). Fragile X syndrome. *Psychology in Mental Retardation and Developmental Disabilities, 19,* 3–5.

Simeonsson, R. J. (1978). Social competence. *Mental Retardation and Developmental Disabilities, 10,* 130–171.

Simeonsson, R. J., Bailey, D. B., Smith, T., & Buysse, V. (in press). Young children with disabilities: Functional assessment by teachers. *Journal of Developmental and Physical Disabilities.*

Simon, E., & Rosen, M. (1993, August). *Quality of life: A cognitive definition.* Paper presented at the annual convention of the American Psychological Association, Toronto, Ontario, CA.

Simon, E. W., Toll, D. M., & Whitehair, P. M. (1994). A naturalistic approach to the validation of facilitated communication. *Journal of Autism and Developmental Disorders, 24,* 647–657.

Simons, K. (1986a). *The relative schedule.* Sheffield, UK: Department of Sociological Studies, University of Sheffield.

Simons, K. (1986b). *The resident interview.* Sheffield, UK: Department of Sociological Studies, University of Sheffield.

Simpson, G. M., Lee, J. H., Zoubok, B., & Gardos, G. (1979). A rating scale for tardive dyskinesia. *Psychopharmacology, 64,* 171–179.

Simpson, R. L. (1988). Needs of parents and families whose children have learning and behavior problems. *Behavioral Disorders, 14,* 40–47.

Simpson, R. L., & Fiedler, C. R. (1989). Parent participation in individualized educational program (IEP) conferences: A case for individualization. In M. J. Fine (Ed.), *The second handbook on parent education: Contemporary perspectives* (pp. 145–171). San Diego, CA: Academic Press.

Singer, G. H. S. (1993). When changing your mind is hard to do: Reflections on cognitive behavior change in parents of children with disability. In A. P. Turnbull, J. M. Patterson, S. K. Behr, D. L. Murphy, J. G. Marquis, & M. J. Blue-Banning (Eds.), *Cognitive coping, families, and disability* (pp. 195–206). Baltimore: Brookes.

Singer, G., & Irvin, L. (1990). Supporting families of persons with severe disabilities: Emerging findings, practices, and questions. In L. H. Meyer, C. A. Peck, & L. Brown (Eds.), *Critical issues in the lives of people with severe disabilities* (pp. 271–312). Baltimore: Brookes.

Singer, G. H. S., Irvin, L., & Hawkins, N. E. (1988). Stress management training for parents of severely handicapped children. *Mental Retardation, 26,* 269–277.

Singer, G. H. S., Irvin, L. K., Irvine, B., Hawkins, N. E., Hegreness, J., & Jackson, R. (1993). Helping families adapt positively: Overcoming demoralization through community supports. In G. H. S. Singer & L. Powers (Eds.), *Families, disability, and empowerment: Active coping skills and strategies for family interventions* (pp. 67–83). Baltimore: Brookes.

Singer, G. H. S., & Nixon, C. (1996). A report on the concerns of parents of children with acquired brain injury. In G. H. S. Singer, A. Glang, & J. M. Williams (Eds.), *Children with acquired brain injury and their families.* Baltimore: Brookes.

Singer, G. H. S., & Powers, L. (Eds.). (1993a). *Families, disability, and empowerment: Active coping skills and strategies for family interventions.* Baltimore: Brookes.

Singer, G. H. S, & Powers, L. (1993b). Supporting resilience in families of children with disabilities. In G. H. S. Singer & L. Powers (Eds.), *Families, disability, and empowerment: Active coping skills and strategies for family interventions* (pp. 1–26). Baltimore: Brookes.

Singer, G. H., Singer, J., & Horner, R. H. (1987). Using pretask requests to increase the probability of compliance for students with severe disabilities. *Journal of the Association for Persons with Severe Handicaps, 12,* 287–291.

Singh, N. N., Donatelli, L. S., Best, A., Williams, D. E., Barrera, F. J., Lenz, M. W., Landrum, T. J., Ellis, C. R., & Moe, T. L. (1993). Factor structure of the Motivation Assessment Scale. *Journal of Intellectual Disability Research, 37,* 65–74.

Singh, N. N., Guernsey, T. F., & Ellis, C. R. (1992). Drug therapy for persons with developmental disabilities: Legislation and litigation. *Clinical Psychology Review, 12,* 665–679.

Slate, N. M. (1983). Nonbiased assessment of adaptive behavior: Comparison of three instruments. *Exceptional Children, 50,* 67–70.

Slater, M., & Wikler, L. (1984). Normalized family resources for families with a developmentally disabled child. *Social Work, 31,* 385–390.

Slifer, K. J., Ivancic, M. T., Parrish, J. M., Page, T. J., & Burgio, L. (1986). Assessment and treatment of multiple behavior problems exhibited by a profoundly retarded adolescent. *Journal of Behavior Therapy and Experimental Psychiatry, 17,* 203–213.

Smeets, P. M., Lancioni, G. E., & Hoogeveen, F. R. (1984a). Effects of different stimulus manipulations on the acquisition of word recognition in trainable mentally retarded children. *Journal of Mental Deficiency Research, 28,* 109–122.

Smeets, P. M., Lancioni, G. E., & Hoogeveen, F. R. (1984b). Using stimulus shaping and fading to establish stimulus control in normal and retarded children. *Journal of Mental Deficiency Research, 28,* 207–218.

Smith, D. A., & Perry, P. J. (1992). Nonneuroleptic treatment of disruptive behavior in organic mental syndromes. *Annals of Pharmacotherapy, 26,* 1400–1408.

Smith, J. D. (1985). *Minds made feeble: The myth and legacy of the Kallikaks.* Rockville, MD: Aspen.

Snart, F., O'Grady, M., & Das, J. P. (1982). Cognitive processing in subgroups of moderately retarded children. *American Journal of Mental Deficiency, 86,* 465–472.

Snell, M. E., & Zirpoli, T. J. (1987). Intervention strategies. In M. E. Snell (Ed.), *Systematic instruction of persons with severe handicaps* (3rd ed., pp. 110–149). Columbus, OH: Merrill.

Snow, C. E., & Pan, B. A. (1993). Ways of analyzing the spontaneous speech of children with mental retardation: The value of cross-domain analyses. In N. W. Bray (Ed.), *International review of research in mental retardation* (pp. 163–192). San Diego, CA: Academic Press.

Song, A., Jones, S., Lippert, J., Metzgen, K., Miller, J., & Borreca, C. (1984). Wisconsin

Behavior Rating Scale: Measure of adaptive behavior for the developmental levels of 0 to 3 years. *American Journal of Mental Deficiency, 88*, 401–410.

Sostek, A. M., Vietze, P., Zaslow, M., Kreiss, L., van der Waals, F., & Rubinstein, D. (1981). Social context in caregiver–infant interaction: A film study of Fais and the United States. In T. Field, A. M. Sostek, P. Vietze, & P. H. Leiderman (Eds.), *Culture and early interactions* (pp. 21–40). Hillsdale, NJ: Erlbaum.

Sovner, R., & Hurley, A. (1983). Do the mentally retarded suffer from affective illness? *Archives of General Psychiatry, 40*, 61–67.

Sovner, R., & Hurley, A. (1986). Managing aggressive behavior: A psychiatric approach. *Psychiatric Aspects of Mental Retardation, 5*, 16–21.

Sovner, R., & Hurley, A. D. (1992). The diagnostic treatment formulation for psychotropic drug therapy. *The Habilitative Mental Healthcare Newsletter, 11*, 81–86.

Sovner, R., & Pary, R. J. (1993). Affective disorders in developmentally disabled persons. In J. L. Matson & R. P. Barrett (Eds.), *Psychopathology in the mentally retarded* (pp. 87–147). Boston: Allyn & Bacon.

Soyster, H. D., & Ehly, S. W. (1986). Parent-rated adaptive behavior and in-school ratings of students referred for EMR evaluation. *American Journal of Mental Deficiency, 90*, 460–463.

Soyster, H. D., & Ehly, S. W. (1987). Relation between parent-rated adaptive behavior and school ratings of students referred for evaluation as educable mentally retarded. *Psychological Reports, 60*, 271–277.

Spanier, G. B. (1976). Measuring dyadic adjustment: New scales for assessing the quality of marriage and similar dyads. *Journal of Marriage and the Family, 44*, 731–738.

Sparrow, S. S., Balla, D. A., & Cicchetti, D. V. (1984). *Vineland Adaptive Behavior Scales*. Circle Pines, MN: American Guidance Service.

Sparrow, S. S., & Cicchetti, D. V. (1978). Behavior rating inventory for moderately, severely, and profoundly retarded persons. *American Journal of Mental Deficiency, 82*, 365–374.

Sparrow, S. S., & Cicchetti, D. V. (1984). The Behavior Inventory for Rating Development (BIRD): Assessments of reliability and factorial validity. *Applied Research in Mental Retardation, 5*, 219–231.

Sparrow, S. S., & Cicchetti, D. V. (1987). Adaptive behavior and the psychologically disturbed child. *Journal of Special Education, 21*, 89–100.

Spearman, C. E. (1904). General intelligence objectively determined and measured. *American Journal of Psychology, 15*, 201–293.

Spearman, C. (1927). *The abilities of man*. London: Macmillan.

Spense, S. H., & Liddle, B. (1990). Self-report measures of social competence for children: An evaluation of the Matson Evaluation of Social Skills for Youngsters and the List of Social Situation Problems. *Behavioral Assessment, 12*, 317–336.

Spirrison, C. L., & Grosskopf, L. G. (1991). Psychotropic medication efficacy graphs: An application of applied behavior analysis. *Mental Retardation, 29*, 139–147.

Spitz, H. H. (1986). Disparities in mentally retarded persons' IQs derived from different intelligence tests. *American Journal of Mental Deficiency, 90*, 588–591.

Spitz, H. H. (1988). Inverse relationship between the WISC–R/WAIS–R score disparity and IQ level in the lower range of intelligence. *American Journal of Mental Retardation, 92*, 376–378.

Spitzer, R. L., Williams, J. B. W., Gibbon, M., & First, M. B. (1990). *User's guide for the Structured Clinical Interview for DSM–III–R*. Washington, DC: American Psychiatric Press.

Spradlin, J. E., & Girardeau, F. L. (1966). The behavior of moderately and severely retarded persons. *International Review of Research in Mental Retardation, 1*, 257–298.

Sprague, J. R., & Horner, R. H. (1984). The effects of single instance, multiple instance, and general case training on generalized vending machine use by moderately and severely handicapped students. *Journal of Applied Behavior Analysis, 17*, 273–278.

Sprague, R. L., & Baxley, G. B. (1978). Drugs for behavior management with comments of some legal aspects. *Mental Retardation and Developmental Disabilities, 10*, 92–129.

Sprague, R. L., & Kalachnik, J. E. (1991). Reliability, validity, and a total score cutoff for the Dyskinesia Identification System: Condensed User Scale (DISCUS) with mentally ill and mentally retarded populations. *Psychopharmacology Bulletin, 27*, 51–58.

Sprague, R. L., White, D., Ullmann, R., & Kalachnik, J. E. (1984). Methods for selecting items in a tardive dyskinesia rating scale. *Psychopharmacology Bulletin, 20*, 339–345.
Spreat, S. (1982a). *Weighing treatment alternatives: Which is less restrictive?* (Woodhaven Center E & R Tech. Rep. 82-11-1). Philadelphia: Temple University Press.
Spreat, S. (1982b). The AAMD Adaptive Behavior Scale: A psychometric review. *Journal of School Psychology, 20*, 45–56.
Spreat, S. (1982c). An empirical analysis of item weighting on the Adaptive Behavior Scale. *American Journal of Mental Deficiency, 87*, 159–163.
Spreat, S., & Behar, D. (1994). Trends in the residential (inpatient) treatment of individuals with a dual diagnosis. *Journal of Consulting and Clinical Psychology, 62*, 43–48.
Spruill, J., & May, J. (1988). The mentally retarded offender: Prevalence rates based on individual versus group intelligence tests. *Criminal Justice and Behavior, 15*, 484–491.
Stack, J. G. (1984). Interrater reliabilities of the Adaptive Behavior Scale with environmental effects controlled. *American Journal of Mental Deficiency, 88*, 396–400.
Stacy, D., Doleys, D. M., & Bruno, J. (1983). Implementing behavioral programs in the community. In J. L. Matson & F. Andrasik (Eds.), *Treatment issues and innovations in mental retardation* (pp. 37–60). New York: Plenum Press.
Stark, J. A., Menolascino, F. J., Albarelli, M. H., & Gray, V. C. (1988). *Mental retardation and mental health: Classification, diagnosis, treatment, services*. New York: Springer-Verlag.
Starr, E. (1994). Facilitated communication: A response by child protection. *Child Abuse and Neglect, 18*, 515–527.
Steelman, D. (1987). *The mentally impaired in New York's prisons: Problems and solutions*. New York: Correctional Association of New York.
Stein, Z., & Susser, M. (1975). Public health and mental retardation: New power and new problems. In M. Begab & S. Richardson (Eds.), *The mentally retarded and society: A social science perspective* (pp. 53–73). Baltimore: University Park Press.
Stein, Z. A., & Susser, M. W. (1984). The epidemiology of mental retardation. In N. R. Butler & B. D. Connor (Eds.), *Stress and disability in childhood* (pp. 21–46). Bristol, England: Wright.
Steinberg, T., & Garcia, A. (1989). *Sociodrama: Who's in your shoes?* New York: Praeger.
Stern, W. (1914). *The psychological methods of testing intelligence*. Baltimore: Warwick & York.
Sternberg, R. J. (1984). Macrocomponents and microcomponents of intelligence: Some proposed loci of mental retardation. In P. H. Brooks, R. Sperber, & C. McCauley (Eds.), *Learning and cognition in the mentally retarded* (pp. 89–114). Hillsdale, NJ: Erlbaum.
Sternberg, R. J. (1985). *Beyond IQ: A triarchic theory of human intelligence*. Cambridge, England: Cambridge University Press.
Sternberg, R. J., & Detterman, D. K. (Ed.). (1986). *What is intelligence? Contemporary viewpoints on its nature and definition*. Norwood, NJ: Ablex.
Sternberg, R. J., & Wagner, R. K. (1986). *Practical intelligence: Nature and origins of competence in the everyday world*. Cambridge, England: Cambridge University Press.
Sternlicht, M. (1965). Psychotherapeutic techniques useful with the mentally retarded: A review and critique. *Psychiatric Quarterly, 39*, 84–90.
Sternlicht, M. (1966). Psychotherapeutic procedures with the retarded. *International Review of Research in Mental Retardation, 2*, 119–124.
Sternlicht, M. (1977). Issues in counseling and psychotherapy with mentally retarded individuals. In I. Bialer & M. Sternlicht (Eds.), *The psychology of mental retardation: Issues and approaches* (pp. 453–490). New York: Psychological Dimensions.
Sticht, T. G., & James, J. H. (1984). Listening and reading. In P. D. Pearson (Ed.), *Handbook of reading research* (Vol. 1, pp. 293–317). New York: Longman.
Stokes, T. F., & Baer, D. M. (1977). An implicit technology of generalization. *Journal of Applied Behavior Analysis, 10*, 349–367.
Stokes, T. F., Baer, D. M., & Jackson, R. L. (1974). Programming the generalization of a greeting response in four retarded children. *Journal* of *Applied Behavior Analysis, 7*, 599–610.
Stokes, T. F., & Osnes, P. G. (1988). The developing applied technology of generalization and

maintenance. In R. H. Horner, R. L. Koegel, & G. Dunlap (Eds.), *Generalization and maintenance: Life-style changes in applied settings* (pp. 5–20). Baltimore: Brookes.

Stokols, D. (1981). Group X place transactions: Some neglected issues in psychological research on settings. In D. Magnusson (Ed.), *Toward a psychology of situations* (pp. 393–415). Hillsdale, NJ: Erlbaum,

Stokols, D. (1982). Environmental psychology: A coming of age. In A. Kraut (Ed.), *G. Stanley Hall Lecture Series* (Vol. 2, pp. 155–205). Washington, DC: American Psychological Association.

Stone, D., & Coughlin, P. M. (1973). Four process variables in counseling with mentally retarded patients. *American Journal of Mental Deficiency, 77,* 408–414.

Stoneman, Z., & Brody, G. H. (1993). Sibling relations in the family context. In Z. Stoneman & P. W. Berman (Eds.), *The effects of mental retardation, disability, and illness on sibling relationships: Research issues and challenges* (pp. 3–30). Baltimore: Brookes.

Story, K., & Horner, R. H. (1988). Pretask requests help manage behavior problems. *Direct Instruction News, 7,* 1–3.

Stowitschek, J., Stowitschek, C., Hendrickson, J., & Day, R. (1984). *Handbook of direct teaching tactics for exceptional children.* Gaithersburg, MD: Aspen.

Strohmer, D. C., & Prout, H. T. (1989). *Strohmer-Prout Behavior Rating Scale.* Schenectady, NY: Genium Publishing.

Strohmer, D. C., & Prout, H. T. (1991). *Emotional Problems Scales: Behavior rating scales.* Schenectady, NY: Genium Publishing.

Sturmey, P., & Bertman, L. J. (1994). Validity of the Reiss Screen for Maladaptive Behavior. *American Journal of Mental Retardation, 99,* 201–206.

Sturmey, P., Reed, J., & Corbett, J. (1991). Psychometric assessment of psychiatric disorders in people with learning difficulties (mental handicap): A review of measures. *Psychological Medicine, 21,* 143–155.

Suen, H. K. (1988). Agreement, reliability, accuracy and validity: Toward a clarification. *Behavioral Assessment, 10,* 343–366.

Suen, H. K., Ary, D., & Ary, R. M. (1986). A note on the relationship among eight indices of interobserver agreement. *Behavioral Assessment, 8,* 301–303.

Sugai, G., & Rowe, P. (1984). The effect of self-recording on out-of-seat behavior of an EMR student. *Education and Training of the Mentally Retarded, 19,* 23–28.

Sullivan, L. W. (1987). The risks of sickle cell trait. *New England Journal of Medicine, 317,* 830–831.

Sulsky, L. M., & Streiner, D. D. (1991). Design, analysis, and measurement issues in mental retardation research: An integrated approach. In J. L. Matson & J. A. Mulick (Eds.), *Handbook of mental retardation* (pp. 541–551). Elmsford, NY: Pergamon Press.

Sumarah, J., Maksym, D., & Goudges, J. (1988). The effects of a staff training program on attitudes and knowledge of staff toward the sexuality of persons with intellectual handicaps. *Canadian Journal of Rehabilitation, 1,* 169–175.

Summers, J. A., Behr, S. K., & Turnbull, A. P. (1989). Positive adaptation and coping strengths of families who have children with disabilities. In G. H. S. Singer & L. K. Irvin (Eds.), *Support for caregiving families: Enabling positive adaptation to disability* (pp. 27–40). Baltimore: Brookes.

Sundberg, N. D., Snowden, L. R., & Reynolds, W. M. (1978). Toward assessment of personal competence and incompetence in life situations. *Annual Review of Psychology, 29,* 179–221.

Sundram, C. (1989). *Developmentally disabled offenders in New York State prisons: An interim report.* Albany: New York State Commission on Quality of Care for the Mentally Disabled.

Super, C. (1987). *The role of culture in developmental disorder.* San Diego, CA: Academic Press.

Super, C. M. (1980). Cognitive development: Looking across at growing up. *New Directions for Child Development: Anthropological Perspectives on Child Development, 8,* 59–69.

Superintendent of Belchertown State School v. Saikewicz, 373 Mass. 728, 370 N.E.2d 417 (1977).

Susser, M. W. (1968). *Community psychiatry.* New York: Random House.

Susser, M. W. (1990). *1990 Psychological bulletin—World Health Organization.* Geneva,

Switzerland: World Health Organization, International Classification of Impairments, Disabilities and Handicaps.

Susser, M. W., & Stein, Z. A. (1992). Mental retardation. *Public Health and Preventive Medicine, 13,* 963–972.

Sutherland, G. R. (1977). Fragile sites on human chromosomes: Demonstration of their dependence on the type of cell culture medium. *Science, 197,* 265.

Switzky, H. N. (in press). Individual differences in personality and motivational systems in persons with mental retardation. In W. E. MacLean, Jr. (Ed.), *Handbook of mental deficiency, psychological theory and research* (3rd ed.). Hillsdale, NJ: Erlbaum.

Switzky, H. N., & Haywood, H. C. (1991). Self-reinforcement schedules in persons with mild mental retardation: Effects of motivational orientation and instructional demands. *Journal of Mental Deficiency Research, 35,* 221–230.

Switzky, H. N., Haywood, H. C., & Rotatori, A. F. (1982). Who are the severely and profoundly mentally retarded? *Education and Training of the Mentally Retarded, 17,* 268–272.

Switzky, H. N., & Heal, L. (1990). Research issues and methods in special education. In R. Gaylord-Ross (Ed.), *Issues and research in special education* (pp. 1–81). New York: Teachers College Press.

Switzky, H. N., & Utley, C. A. (1991). Sociocultural perspectives on the classification of persons with mental retardation. *American Association on Mental Retardation Psychology Division Newsletter, 1,* 1–4.

Symington, N. (1981). The psychotherapy of a subnormal patient. *British Journal of Medical Psychology, 54,* 187–199.

Szasz, T. S. (1961). *The myth of mental illness: Foundations of the theory of personal conduct.* New York: Dell Publishing.

Szempruch, J., & Jacobson, J. W. (1993). Evaluating the facilitated communications of people with developmental disabilities. *Research in Developmental Disabilities, 14,* 253–264.

Szymanski, L. S. (1980). Individual psychotherapy with retarded persons. In L. S. Szymanski & P. E. Tanguay (Eds.), *Emotional disorders of mentally retarded persons: Assessment, treatment, and consultation* (pp. 131–148). Baltimore: University Park Press.

Szymanski, L. S., & Kiernan, W. E. (1980). Multiple family group therapy with developmentally disabled adolescents and young adults. *International Journal of Group Psychotherapy, 33,* 521–534.

Szymanski, L. S., & Rosefsky, Q. B. (1980). Group psychotherapy with retarded persons. In L. S. Szymanski & P. E. Tanguay (Eds.), *Emotional disorders of mentally retarded persons: Assessment, treatment, and consultation* (pp. 173–194). Baltimore: University Park Press.

Tarjan, G. (1970). Some thoughts on sociocultural retardation. In H. C. Haywood (Ed.), *Social-cultural aspects of mental retardation* (pp. 745–758). New York: Appleton-Century-Crofts.

Tawney, J. W., Knapp, D. S., O'Reilly, C. D., & Pratt, S. S. (1979). *Programmed environments curriculum: A curriculum handbook for teaching basic skills to severely handicapped persons.* Columbus, OH: Merrill.

Taylor, B. A., & Harris, S. L. (1995). Teaching children with autism to seek information: Acquisition of novel information and generalization of responding. *Journal of Applied Behavior Analysis, 28,* 3–14.

Taylor, E. H., & Cadet, J. L. (1989). Social intelligence: A neurological system? *Psychological Reports, 64,* 423–444.

Taylor, S. J., Knoll, J. A., Lehr, S., & Walker, P. M. (1989). Families for all children: Value-based services for children with disabilities and their families. In G. H. S. Singer & L. K. Irvin (Eds.), *Support for caregiving families: Enabling positive adaptation to disability* (pp. 41–53). Baltimore: Brookes.

Telzrow, C. F. (1993). Commentary on comparative evaluation of early intervention alternatives. *Early Education and Development, 4,* 350–365.

Terman, L. M. (1916). *The measurement of intelligence.* Boston: Houghton Mifflin.

Terman, L. M. (1925). *Mental and physical traits of a thousand gifted children.* Stanford, CA: Stanford University Press.

Terrasi, S., & Airasian, P. W. (1989). The relationship between adaptive behavior and intelligence for special needs students. *Psychology in the Schools, 26,* 202–208.

Texas Department of Mental Health and Mental Retardation. (1973). Project CAMIO [Correctional Administration and the Mentally Incompetent Offender] (Vols. 4, 5). In *The mentally retarded in an adult correctional institution.* Austin, TX: Author.

Thackrey, M. (1991). A principal components analysis of the Comprehensive Test of Adaptive Behavior. *American Journal of Mental Retardation, 96,* 213–215.

Thomas v. Board of Education, 918 F.2d 618 (6th Cir. 1990).

Thompson, T. (1988). *Maladaptive Behavior Scale (MABS).* Unpublished scale, Vanderbilt University, Nashville, TN.

Thompson, T., & Gabrowski, J. (1972). *Behavior modification of the mentally retarded.* New York: Oxford University Press.

Thompson, T., & Gray, D. (Eds.). (1994). *Treatment of destructive behavior in developmental disabilities* (Vol. 2). Newbury Park, CA: Sage.

Thompson, T., Hackenburg, T., Cerutti, D., Baker, D., & Axtell, S. (1994). Opioid antagonist effects on self-injury in adults with mental retardation: Response form and location as determinants of medication effects. *American Journal of Mental Retardation, 99,* 85–102.

Thompson, T., Robinson, J., Graff, M., & Ingemey, R. (1990). Home-like architectural features of residential environments. *American Journal of Mental Retardation, 95,* 328–341.

Thorndike, E. L. (1920). Intelligence and its uses. *Harper's Magazine, 140,* 227–235.

Thorndike, R. (1936). Factor analysis of social and abstract intelligence. *Journal of Educational Psychology, 27,* 231–233.

Thorndike, R. L., Hagen, E. P., & Sattler, J. M. (1980). *Stanford-Binet Intelligence Scale: Fourth Edition.* Chicago: Riverside.

Thorp, P. S., Levin, S. D., Garnett, E. S., Nahmias, C., Firnau, G., Toi, A., Upton, A. R., Nobbs, P. T., & Sinclair, J. C. (1988). Patterns of cerebral glucose metabolism using ^{18}FDG and positron emission tomography in the neurologic investigation of the full term infant. *Neuropediatrics, 19,* 146–153.

Thunedborg, K., Allerup, P., Bech, P., & Joyce, C. R. B. (1993). Development of the repertory grid for measurement of individual quality of life in clinical trials. *International Journal of Methods in Psychiatric Research, 3,* 45–56.

Thurstone, L. L. (1931). Multiple factor analysis. *Psychological Review, 38,* 406–427.

Thurstone, L. L. (1938). Primary mental abilities. *Psychometric Monographs* (No. 1).

Thurstone, L. L., & Thurstone, T. G. (1941). Factorial studies of intelligence. *Psychometric Monographs* (No. 2).

Timberlake, W., & Allison, J. (1974). Response deprivation: An empirical approach to instrumental performance. *Psychological Review, 81,* 146–164.

Timothy W. v. Rochester New Hampshire School District, 875 F.2d 954 (1st Cir. 1989).

Tomasulo, D. (1992). *Group counseling for people with mild to moderate mental retardation/developmental disabilities: An interactive-behavioral model.* New York: Young Adult Institute.

Tombokan-Runtukahu, J., & Nitko, A. J. (1992). Translation, cultural adjustment, and validation of a measure of adaptive behavior. *Research in Developmental Disabilities, 13,* 481–501.

Touchette, P. E., MacDonald, R. F., & Langer, S. N. (1985). A scatter plot for identifying stimulus control of problem behavior. *Journal of Applied Behavior Analysis, 18,* 343–351.

Tredgold, A. F. (1922). *Mental deficiency.* New York: Wood.

Tredgold, R. F., & Soddy, K. (1963). *Tredgold's textbook of mental deficiency (subnormality).* (10th ed.). Baltimore: Williams & Wilkins.

Trent, J. W. (1994). *Inventing the feeble mind: A history of mental retardation in the United States.* Berkeley: University of California Press.

Trent, J. W. (1995). Suffering fools. *The Sciences, 35*(4), 18–22.

Trivedi, P. K. (1988). *Community mental retardation policies: Satisfaction as a component.* Unpublished dissertation, University of Texas, Arlington.

Trudel, G., & Desjardins, G. (1992). Staff reaction toward the sexual behaviors of people living in institutional settings. *Sexuality and Disability, 10,* 173–187.

Tucker, B. D., & Goldstein, B. A. (1992). *Legal rights of persons with disabilities: An analysis of law.* Horsham, PA: LRP Publications.

Tucker, D. K., & Berry, G. W. (1980). Teaching severely multihandicapped students to put on their own hearing aids. *Journal of Applied Behavior Analysis, 13,* 65–75.

Turnbull, A. P. (1983). Parental participation in the IEP process. In J. A. Mulick & S. M. Pueschel (Eds.), *Parent-professional partnerships in developmental disability services* (pp. 107–122). Cambridge, MA: Ware Press.

Turnbull, A. P., Patterson, J. M., Behr, S. K., Murphy, D. L., Marquis, J. G., & Blue-Banning, M. J. (Eds.). (1993). *Cognitive coping, families, and disability.* Baltimore: Brookes.

Turnbull, A. P., Summers, J., & Brotherson, M. (1986). Family life cycle: Theoretical and empirical implications and future directions for families with mentally retarded members. In J. J. Gallagher & P. M. Vietze (Eds.), *Families of handicapped persons: Research, programs, and policy issues* (pp. 45–65). Baltimore: Brookes.

Turnbull, A. P., & Turnbull, H. R. (1986). *Families, professionals, and exceptionality: A special partnership.* Columbus, OH: Merrill.

Turnbull, A. P., & Turnbull, H. R. (1990). *Families, professionals, and exceptionality: A special partnership* (2nd ed.). Columbus, OH: Merrill.

Ullman, L. P., & Krasner, L. (1975). *A psychological approach to abnormal behavior* (2nd ed.). Englewood Cliffs, NJ: Prentice Hall.

United States Department of Education Regulations, 34 C.F.R. Part 97 (1991).

Valenti-Hein, D. (1991, November). *Teaching social-sexual skills for adults with mental retardation.* Paper presented at the annual conference of the National Association on Dual Diagnosis, Washington, DC.

Valenti-Hein, D. (1993, June). *Sexual abuse: Agency policy, detection, and response to allegations.* Paper presented at the annual conference of the American Association on Mental Retardation, Washington, DC.

Valenti-Hein, D. C., & Mueser, K. T. (1990). *The dating skills program: Teaching social/sexual skills to adults with mental retardation.* Worthington, OH: International Diagnostic Systems.

Valenti-Hein, D., & Schwartz, L. (1993). Witness competency in people with mental retardation: Implications for the prosecution of sexual abuse. *Sexuality and Disability, 11,* 287–294.

Valenti-Hein, D., & Schwartz, L. (1994). *The sexual abuse interview for the developmentally disabled.* Los Angeles: James Stanfield.

Valenti-Hein, D. C., Yarnold, P., & Mueser, K. T. (1994). Evaluation of the Dating Skills Program for improving heterosocial interactions in people with mental retardation. *Behavior Modification, 18,* 32–46.

Valk, J., & van der Knapp, M. S. (1989). *Magnetic resonance of myelin, myelinization, and myelin disorders.* Berlin, Germany: Springer-Verlag.

Vallecorsa, A. L., & Tittle, C. K. (1985). AAMD Adaptive Behavior Scale—School Edition. *Journal of Counseling and Development, 63,* 532–534.

Van Houten, R., & Axelrod, S. (Eds.). (1993). *Behavior analysis and treatment.* New York: Plenum Press.

Van Houten, R., Axelrod, S., Bailey, J. S., Favell, J. E., Foxx, R. M., Iwata, B. A., & Lovaas, O. I. (1988). The right to effective behavioral treatment. *The Behavior Analyst, 11,* 111–114.

Van Praag, H. M., Asnis, G. M., Kahn, R. S., Brown, S. L., Korn, M., Harkavy-Friedman, J. M., & Wetzler, S. (1990). Monoamines and abnormal behavior: A multi-aminergic perspective. *British Journal of Psychiatry, 157,* 723–734.

VanDenBerg, J. (1993). Integration of individualized services into the system of care for children and adolescents with emotional disabilities. *Administration and Policy in Mental Health, 20,* 247–257.

VanDenPol, R. A., Iwata, B. A., Ivancic, M. T., Page, T. J., Neef, N. A., & Whitely, P. F. (1981). Teaching the handicapped to eat in public places: Acquisition, generalization, and maintenance of restaurant skills. *Journal of Applied Behavior Analysis, 14,* 61–69.

Vandergriff, D. V., Hester, J. R., & Mandra, D. A. (1987). Composite ratings on the AAMD Adaptive Behavior Scale. *American Journal of Mental Deficiency, 92,* 203–206.

Vasquez, C. (1994). A multi-task controlled evaluation of facilitated communication. *Journal of Autism and Developmental Disorders, 24,* 369–379.

Verhoeven, W. M. A., Tuinier, S., Sijben, N. A. S., Van Den Berg, Y. W. H. M., De Witte-Van Der Schoot, E. P. P. M., Pepplinkhuizen, L., & Van Nieuwenhuizen, O. (1992). Eltoprazine in mentally retarded self-injuring patients. *Lancet, 340,* 1037–1038.

Verkerk, A. J., Pieretti, M., Sutcliffe, J. S., Fu, Y. H., Kuhl, D. P., Pizzuti, A., Reiner, O., Richards, S., Victoria, M. F., Zhang, F. P., et al. (1991). Identification of a gene (FMR-1) containing CGG repeat coincident with a breakpoint cluster region exhibiting length variation in fragile X syndrome. *Cell, 65,* 905–914.

Vernon, P. E. (1956). *The measurement of abilities.* London: University of London Press.

Ville, I., Ravaud, J. F., Marchal, F., Paicheler, H., & Fardeau, M. (1992). Social identity and the international classification of handicaps: An evaluation of the consequences of facioscapulohumeral muscular dystrophy. *Disability and Rehabilitation, 14*(4), 168–175.

Virmani, R., Robinowitz, M., & McAllister, H. A. (1985). Exercise and the heart: A review of cardiac pathology associated with physical activity. *Pathology Annual, 20,* 431–462.

Volkmar, F. R., Sparrow, S. S., Goudreau, D., Cicchetti, D. V., Paul, R., & Cohen, D. J. (1987). Social deficits in autism: An operational approach using the Vineland Adaptive Behavior Scales. *Journal of the American Academy of Child and Adolescent Psychiatry, 26,* 156–161.

Vollmer, T. R., & Iwata, B. A. (1992). Differential reinforcement as a treatment for behavior disorders: Procedural and functional variations. *Research in Developmental Disabilities, 13,* 393–417.

Volpe, J. J., Herscovitch, P., & Perlman, J. M. (1985). Positron emission tomography in the asphyxiated newborn: Parasagittal impairment of cerebral blood flow. *Annals of Neurology, 17,* 287–296.

Volpe, J. J., Herscovitch, P., Perlman, J. M., & Raichle, M. E. (1983). Positron emission tomography in the newborn: Extensive impairment of regional cerebral blood flow with intraventricular hemorrhage and hemorrhageic intracerebral involvement. *Pediatrics, 72,* 589–601.

Vygotsky, L. S. (1962). *Thought and language.* Cambridge, MA: MIT Press. (Original work published 1934)

Vygotsky, L.S. (1978). *Mind in society: The development of higher psychological processes.* Cambridge, MA: Harvard University Press.

Vyse, S. A., & Mulick, J. A. (1990). A correlational approach to ecobehavioral assessment. In S. R. Schroeder (Ed.), *Ecobehavioral analysis and developmental diabilities* (pp. 64–81). New York: Springer-Verlag.

Wacker, D. P., Steege, M. W., Northrup, J., Sasso, G., Berg, W., Reimers, T., Cooper, L., Cigrand, K., & Donn, L. (1990). A component analysis of functional communication training across three topographies of severe behavior problems. *Journal of Applied Behavior Analysis, 23,* 417–429.

Wade, D. T., & Collin, C. (1988). The Barthel ADL Index: A standard of measure of physical disability. *International Disability Studies, 10,* 64–67.

Waechter v. School District No. 14–030, 773 F. Supp. 1005 (W.D. Mich. 1991).

Walker, L. S., Ortiz-Valdes, J. A., & Newbrough, J. R. (1989). The role of maternal employment and depression in the psychological adjustment of chronically ill, mentally retarded, and well children. *Journal of Pediatric Psychology, 14,* 357–370.

Walsh, P. N., & McConkey, R. (1989). Dimensions of social competence in a population of adults with mental handicap. *Mental Handicap Research, 2,* 119–128.

Wang, P. P., Doherty, S., Hasselink, J., & Bellugi, U. (1992). Callosal morphology concurs with neurobehavioral and neuropathological findings in two neurodevelopmental syndromes. *Archives of Neurology, 49,* 407–411.

Waranch, H. R., Iwata, B. A., Wohl, M. K., & Nidiffer, F. D. (1981). Treatment of a retarded adult's mannequin phobia through in vivo desensitization and shaping approach responses. *Journal of Behavior Therapy and Experimental Psychiatry, 12,* 359–362.

Warkany, J., Lemire, R. J., Cohen, M. M., Jr. (Eds.). (1981). Introduction. In *Mental retar-*

dation and congenital malformations of the central nervous system (p. 3). Chicago: Yearbook.

Warshaw, M. G., Lavori, P. W., & Leon, A. (1992). Analyzing patient responses by domain using global statistics: Applications to quality of life data. *International Journal of Methods in Psychiatric Research, 2,* 225–231.

Wasik, B. H., Ramey, C. T., Bryant, D. M., & Sparling, J. J. (1990). A longitudinal study of two early intervention strategies: Project CARE. *Child Development, 61,* 1682–1692.

Webster-Stratton, C. (1990). Enhancing the effectiveness of self-administered videotape parent training for families with conduct-problem children. *Journal of Abnormal Child Psychology, 18,* 479–492.

Webster-Stratton, C., & Hammond, M. (1990). Predictors of treatment outcome in parent training for families with conduct problem children. *Behavior Therapy, 21,* 319–337.

Wechsler, D. (1939). *The measurement of adult intelligence.* Baltimore: Williams & Wilkins.

Wechsler, D. (1974). *Wechsler Intelligence Scale for Children—Revised.* New York: Psychological Corporation.

Wechsler, D. (1991). *Wechsler Intelligence Scale for Children* (3rd ed.). San Antonio, TX: Psychological Corporation.

Welfel, E. R. (1982). How students make judgments: Do educational level and academic major make a difference? *Journal of College Student Personnel, 23,* 490–497.

Welfel, E. R., & Davison, M. L. (1986). The development of reflective judgment during the college years: A 4-year longitudinal study. *Journal of College Student Personnel, 27,* 209–216.

Wellman, H. M. (1990). *The child's theory of mind.* Cambridge, MA: MIT Press.

Welsh, M. C., Pennington, B. F., Rouse, B., & McCabe, E. R. B. (1990). Neuropsychology of early treated phenylketoneuria: Specific executive function deficits. *Child Development, 61,* 1697–1713.

Werner, H. (1957). *Comparative psychology of mental development* (3rd ed.). New York: International Universities Press.

Werry, J. S., & Sprague, R. L. (1974). Methylphenidate in children: Effect of dosage. *Australia and New Zealand Journal of Psychiatry, 8,* 9–19.

West, J. B. (1986). Do climbs to extreme altitude cause brain damage? *Lancet, 16,* 387–388.

Westling, D. L., Ferrell, K., & Swenson, K. (1982). Intraclassroom comparison of two arrangements for teaching profoundly mentally retarded children. *American Journal of Mental Deficiency, 86,* 601–608.

Weyhing, M. C. (1983). Parental reactions to handicapped children and familial adjustments to routines of care. In J. A. Mulick & S. M. Pueschel (Eds.), *Parent-professional partnerships in developmental disability services* (pp. 125–138). Cambridge, MA: Ware Press.

Wheeler, D. L., Jacobson, J. W., Paglieri, R. A., & Schwartz, A. A. (1993). An experimental assessment of facilitated communication. *Mental Retardation, 31,* 49–60.

White, B. J. (1994). The Turner syndrome: Origin, cytogenetic variants, and factors affecting the phenotype. In S. H. Broman & J. Grafman (Eds.), *Atypical cognitive deficits in developmental disorders: Implications for brain function* (pp. 183–196). Hillsdale, NJ: Erlbaum.

White, K. R. (1993). Using research to improve the cost-effectiveness of early intervention programs. *Early Education and Development, 4,* 346–357.

White, K. R., & Boyce, G. C. (Eds.). (1993). Comparative evaluations of early intervention alternatives [Special Issue]. *Early Education and Development, 4,* 795–805.

White, R. W. (1959). Motivation reconsidered: The concept of competence. *Psychological Review, 66,* 297–333.

White, W. A. T. (1988). A meta-analysis of the effects of direct instruction in special education. *Education and Treatment of Children, 11,* 364–374.

Whitehurst, G. J., & Crone, D. A. (1994). Social constructivism, positivism, and facilitated communication. *JASH, 19,* 191–195.

Whiting, B., & Edwards, C. (1988). *Children of different worlds: The formation of social behavior.* Cambridge, MA: Harvard University Press.

Whiting, H. P. A., & Wade, M. G. (1986). (Eds.). *Themes in motor development.* Dordrecht, the Netherlands: Martinus-Nijhoff.

Whitman, T. L. (1990). Self-regulation and mental retardation. *American Journal of Mental Retardation, 94*, 347–362

Whitman, T., & Johnston, M. B. (1983). Teaching addition and subtraction with regrouping to educable mentally retarded children: A group self-instructional training program. *Behavior Therapy, 14*, 127–143.

Widaman, K. F. (1985). Hierarchically nested covariance structure models for multitrait–multimethod data. *Applied Psychological Measurement, 9*, 1–26.

Widaman, K. F. (1990). Bias in pattern loadings represented by common factor analysis and component analysis. *Multivariate Behavioral Research, 25*, 89–95.

Widaman, K. F. (1991). Properly characterizing clusters of families with mentally retarded children: A comment on Mink, Blacher, and Nihira (1988). *American Journal of Mental Retardation, 96*, 217–220.

Widaman, K. F. (1993). Common factor analysis versus principal component analysis: Differential bias in representing model parameters? *Multivariate Behavioral Research, 28*, 263–311.

Widaman, K. F., Borthwick-Duffy, S. A., & Little, T. D. (1991). The structure and development of adaptive behaviors. *International Review of Research in Mental Retardation, 17*, 1–54.

Widaman, K. F., Gibbs, K. W., & Geary, D. C. (1987). Structure of adaptive behavior: I. Replication across fourteen samples of nonprofoundly mentally retarded people. *American Journal of Mental Deficiency, 91*, 348–360.

Widaman, K. F., Reise, S. P., & Clatfelter, D. L. (1994, March). *Assessing the measurement structure of adaptive behavior: Factor analytic versus item response theory approaches.* Paper presented at the Gatlinburg Conference on Research and Theory in Mental Retardation and Developmental Disabilities, Gatlinburg, TN.

Widaman, K. F., Stacy, A. W., & Borthwick-Duffy, S. A. (1993). Construct validity of dimensions of adaptive behavior: A multitrait–multimethod evaluation. *American Journal of Mental Retardation, 98*, 219–234.

Wikler, L. (1981). Chronic stresses of families of mentally retarded children. *Family Relations, 30*, 281–288.

Willer, B., & Intagliata, J. (1980, June). *Symposium on evaluating quality of life as an outcome of human services programs.* Buffalo: State University of New York at Buffalo Medical Center.

Williams, B. F., Williams, R. L., & McLaughlin, T. F. (1989). The use of token economies with individuals who have developmental disabilities. In E. Cipani (Ed.), *The treatment of severe behavior disorders: Behavior analysis approaches* (pp. 3–18). Washington, DC: American Association on Mental Retardation.

Williams, R. L. (1972). *The Black Intelligence Test of Cultural Homogeneitey-100: A culture specific test* (ERIC Document 070799). Bethesda, MD: ERIC Documentation Reproduction Service, LEASCO Information Products.

Williams, R. L. (1974). The problem of match and mismatch in testing Black children. In L. Miller (Ed.), *The testing of Black students* (pp. 17–30). Englewood Cliffs, NJ: Prentice Hall.

Wilson, B., & Jackson, H. J. (1980). An in vivo approach to the desensitization of a retarded child's toilet phobia. *Australian Journal of Developmental Disabilities, 6*, 137–141.

Wilson, B. J., & English, R. A. (1975). Reading order and recall: A developmental look. *Psychological Reports, 36*, 127–130.

Windle, C. (1962). Prognosis of mental subnormals. *American Journal of Mental Deficiency* (monograph supplement), *66*, 1–180.

Wing, L., Holmes, N., & Shah, A. (1985). *Relative opinions schedule.* DeCrespigny Park, England: MRC Social Psychiatry Unit, Institute of Psychiatry.

Wise, R. A. (1982). Neuroleptics and operant behavior: The anhedonia hypothesis. *Behavioural and Brain Sciences, 5*, 39–87.

Wish, J., McCombs, K., & Edmonson, B. (1980). *The socio-sexual knowledge and attitudes test.* Chicago: Stoelting.

Wisniewski, H. M., & Rabe, A. (1986). Discrepancy between Alzheimer-type neuropathology and dementia in persons with Down syndrome. In H. M. Wisniewski & D. A. Snider

(Eds.), *Mental retardation: Research, education, and technology transfer* (pp. 247–260). New York: New York Academy of Sciences.

Wisniewski, H. M., & Snider, D. A. (Eds.). (1986). *Mental retardation: Research, education, and technology transfer.* New York: New York Academy of Sciences.

Wisniewski, K. E., Wisniewski, H. M., & Yen, G. Y. (1985). Occurrence of neuropathological changes and dementia of Alzheimer's disease in Down's syndrome. *Annals of Neurology, 17,* 278–282.

Wolery, M., & Gast, D. L. (1984). Effective and efficient procedures for the transfer of stimulus control. *Topics in Early Childhood Special Education, 4,* 52–77.

Wolf, M. M. (1976, August). *Social validity: The case for subjective measurement or how applied behavior analysis is finding its heart.* Paper presented at the annual meeting of the American Psychological Association, Washington, DC.

Wolfe, V. F., & Cuvo, A. J. (1978). Effects of within-stimulus and extra-stimulus prompting on letter discrimination by mentally retarded persons. *American Journal of Mental Deficiency, 83,* 297–303.

Wolfensberger, W. (Ed.). (1972). *The principle of normalization in human services.* Downsview, Ontario, Canada: National Institute on Mental Retardation.

Wolfensberger, W. (1983). Social role valorization: A proposed new term for the principle of normalization. *Mental Retardation, 21,* 234–239.

Wolfensberger, W. (1992). *A brief introduction to social role valorization as a high-order concept for structuring human services* (2nd rev. ed.). Syracuse, NY: Training Institute for Human Service Planning, Leadership, and Change Agentry, Syracuse University.

Wolfensberger, W., & Thomas, S. (1983). *PASSING (Program analysis of service systems' implementation of normalization goals): Normalization criteria and ratings manual* (2nd ed.). Toronto, Ontario, Canada: National Institute on Mental Retardation.

Wolford, B. I. (1987). Correctional education: Training and education opportunities for delinquent and criminal offenders. In C. M. Nelson, R. B. Rutherford, Jr., & B. I. Wolford (Eds.), *Special education in the criminal justice system* (pp. 53–82). Columbus, OH: Merrill.

Wolraich, M. L., Siperstein, G. N., & Reed, D. (1992). Prognostications of physicians about mentally retarded individuals. *Advances in Developmental & Behavioral Pediatrics, 10,* 109–130.

Wonderlic, E. F., & Hovland, C. I. (1939). The Personnel Test: A restandardization of the Otis S-A test for business and industrial use. *Journal of Applied Psychology, 23,* 685–702.

Wood, H. V. (1976). The retarded person in the criminal justice system. In *Proceedings of the One Hundred and Sixth Annual Congress of the American Correctional Association* (pp. 142–146). College Park, MD: American Correctional Association.

Wood, P. H. N., & Badley, E. M. (1978). An epidemiological appraisal of disablement. In A. E. Benett (Ed.), *Recent advances in community medicine* (pp. 149–173). London: Churchill Livingstone.

Woodcock, R. W., & Johnson, M. B. (1989). *Woodcock-Johnson Psycho-Educational Battery—Revised.* Chicago: Riverside.

Woolfolk, R. L. (1992). Hermeneutics, social constructionism and other items of intellectual fashion: Intimations for clinical science. *Behavior Therapy, 23,* 213–223.

Woolfolk, R. L., & Richardson, F. C. (1984). Behavior therapy and the ideology of modernity. *American Psychologist, 39,* 777–786.

World Health Organization. (1980a). *International classification of diseases* (9th ed.). Geneva, Switzerland: Author.

World Health Organization. (1980b). *International classification of impairments, disabilities and handicaps.* Geneva, Switzerland: Author.

World Health Organization. (1995). *International classification of diseases: Clinical modifications* (9th ed.). Geneva, Switzerland: Author.

Wozniack, R. H., & Fischer, K. (Eds.). (1973). *Development in contact: Acting and thinking in specific environments.* Hillsdale, NJ: Erlbaum.

Wright, B. A. (1983). *Physical disability: A psychosocial approach.* New York: Harper & Row.

Wright, L., Schaefer, A. B., & Solomons, G. (Eds.). (1979). *Encyclopedia of pediatric psychology* (pp. 581–591). Baltimore: University Park Press.

Yerkes, R. M. (Ed.). (1921). *Psychological examining in the U.S. Army*. Washington, DC: National Academy of Sciences.

Young, E. C., & Kramer, B. M. (1991). Characteristics of age-related language decline in adults with Down syndrome. *Mental Retardation, 29,* 75–79.

Youngberg v. Romeo, 102 S. Ct. (1982).

Younkin, D., Medoff-Cooper, B., Guillet, R., Sinwell, T., Chance, B., & Delivoria-Papadopoulos, M. (1988). In vivo ^{31}P nuclear magnetic resonance measurement of chronic changes in cerebral metabolites following neonatal intraventricular hemorrhage. *Pediatrics, 82,* 331–336.

Zametkin, A. J., & Yamada, E. M. (1993). Monitoring and measuring drug effects: I. Physical effects. In J. S. Werry & M. G. Aman (Eds.), *Practitioner's guide to psychoactive drugs for children and adolescents* (pp. 99–159). New York: Plenum Press Medical Books.

Zane, T., Walls, R. T., & Thvedt, J. E. (1981). Prompting and fading guidance procedures: Their effects on chaining and whole task teaching strategies. *Education and Training of the Mentally Retarded, 16,* 125–135.

Zarcone, J. R., Rodgers, T. A., Iwata, B. A., Rourke, D., & Dorsey, M. F. (1991). Reliability analysis of the Motivation Assessment Scale: A failure to replicate. *Research in Developmental Disabilities, 12,* 349–360.

Zaslow, M., & Rogoff, B. (1981). The cross-cultural study of early interaction: Implications from research on culture and cognition. In T. Field, A. M. Sostek, P. Vietze, & P. H. Leiderman (Eds.), *Culture and early interactions* (pp. 237–256). Hillsdale, NJ: Erlbaum.

Zautra, A., & Goodhart, D. (1979). Quality of life indicators: A review of the literature. *Community Mental Health Review, 4,* 2–10.

Zautra, A. J., & Reich, J. W. (1983). Life events and perceptions of life quality: Developments in a two-factor approach. *Journal of Community Psychology, 11,* 121–132.

Zawlocki, R. J., & Walls, R. T. (1983). Fading of the S+, the S−, both, or neither. *American Journal of Mental Deficiency, 87,* 462–464.

Zeaman, D., & House, B. J. (1963). The role of attention in retarded discrimination learning. In N. R. Ellis (Ed.), *Handbook of mental deficiency* (pp. 159–223). New York: McGraw-Hill.

Zetlin, A., & Murtaugh, M. (1990). Whatever happened to those with borderline IQs? *American Journal of Mental Retardation, 94,* 463–469.

Zigler, E., Balla, D., & Butterfield, E. C. (1968). A longitudinal investigation of the relationship between preinstitutional social deprivation and social motivation in institutionalized retardates. *Journal of Personality and Social Psychology, 10,* 437–445.

Zigler, E., Balla, D., & Hodapp, R. (1984). On the definition and classification of mental retardation. *American Journal of Mental Deficiency, 89,* 215–230.

Zigler, E., & Hodapp, R. (1986). *Understanding mental retardation.* Cambridge, England: Cambridge University Press.

Zigler, E., & Seitz, V. (1982). Social policy and intelligence. In R. J. Sternberg (Ed.), *Handbook of human intelligence* (pp. 586–641). Cambridge, England: Cambridge University Press.

Zigman, W. B., Schupf, N., Lubin, R. A., & Silverman, W. P. (1987). Premature regression in adults with Down syndrome. *American Journal of Mental Deficiency, 92,* 161–168.

Zucker, S. H., & Polloway, E. A. (1987). Issues in identification and assessment in mental retardation. *Education and Training in Mental Retardation, 22,* 69–76.

Zwick, W. R., & Velicer, W. F. (1986). Comparison of five rules for determining the number of components to retain. *Psychological Bulletin, 99,* 432–442.

Author Index

Subject Index

About the Editors

John W. Jacobson received his BS in psychology from Union College, Schenectady, NY; his MS in general applied psychology, applied operant specialty, from the University of Bridgeport, CT; and his PhD in general applied psychology, developmental disabilities sequence, from the University of Vermont, Burlington. From 1972 to 1977 he worked as a psychology assistant in community developmental disabilities services, in an autism specialty educational center and a private practice, and as a university teaching assistant and instructor in behavior modification and self-management. After receiving his MS degree he worked as a staff neuropsychologist in the Neurology Service of the New Hampshire Hospital, Concord. Since 1978 he has been Associate Planner and applied researcher with the New York State Office of Mental Retardation and Developmental Disabilities, Albany. For the past decade he has also been affiliated with Independent Living in the Capital District, a community agency providing housing services for people with physical disabilities.

Dr. Jacobson has published extensively on the topics of developmental disabilities and population disability demographics, program evaluation, clinical servies management and development, psychiatric disability, adaptive development, and treatment efficacy. He is principal editor of *Community Living for People With Developmental and Psychiatric Disabilities* and a member of the editorial boards of the *American Journal on Mental Retardation*, the *Adult Residential Care Journal*, and *Behavioral Interventions*. He is a Fellow of the American Association on Mental Retardation (AAMR) and has served as a state, regional, and national officer of AAMR. He is the 1994 recipient of the Association for Behavior Analysis Award for Excellence in Public Service in Behavior Analysis. Dr. Jacobson is a Fellow of the American Psychological Association and is currently President of the Division of Mental Retardation and Developmental Disabilities (Division 33). His present work focuses on clinical and managerial issues in the delivery of supported housing and individual support services for people with developmental disabilities.

James A. Mulick received his BA degree in psychology from Rutgers College in New Brunswick, NJ, and then completed graduate studies at the University of Vermont, where he received his MA and PhD degrees in general psychology, specializing in learning and behavioral development. He completed a postdoctoral fellowship in clinical child psychology at the Child Development Institute, Division for Disorders of Development and Learning, at the University of North Carolina, Chapel Hill. He has held clinical supervisor positions at Murdoch Center, Butner, NC, the Eunice Kennedy Shriver Center for Mental Retardation in Waltham, MA, and the Child Development Center of Rhode Island Hospital in Providence. Dr. Mulick has taught and held graduate faculty appointments at Northeastern University, the University of Rhode Island, and the Brown University

Program in Medicine, and presently has joint appointments as Professor in the departments of Pediatrics and Psychology at The Ohio State University, Columbus.

Dr. Mulick has authored numerous publications in the areas of learning, developmental psychobiology, behavior analysis, mental retardation and developmental disabilities, policy analysis, and curriculum development for advanced and postdoctoral professional education. He is co-editor of the award-winning *Handbook of Mental Retardation*, *Parent–Professional Partnerships in Developmental Disability Services*, and *Prevention of Developmental Disabilities*, and Series Editor of the four-volume *Transitions in Mental Retardation* monograph series. He is a member of the editorial review boards of *Research in Developmental Disabilities*, *The Behavior Analyst*, *Behavioral Interventions*, and the *American Journal of Mental Retardation*. Dr. Mulick has served in elected and appointed leadership roles in several scientific and professional societies, is a Fellow of the American Psychological Association, the American Association for Applied and Preventive Psychology, and the American Psychological Society, and a Clinical Fellow of the Behavior Therapy and Research Society. He is past President of the Division of Mental Retardation and Developmental Disabilities (Division 33) of the American Psychological Association. Research interests include basic and applied behavior analysis, ecological methods in behavior analysis, early childhood and developmental psychopathology, mental retardation, psychopharmacology, and policy analysis relating to children and to persons with disabilities.